Monographs in Theoretical Computer Science
An EATCS Series

Editors: J. Hromkovič   M. Nielsen
Founding Editors: W. Brauer   G. Rozenberg   A. Salomaa

On behalf of the European Association
for Theoretical Computer Science (EATCS)

More information about this series at http://www.springer.com/series/776

Dines Bjørner

Domain Science and Engineering

A Foundation for Software Development

 Springer

Dines Bjørner
Technical University of Denmark
Holte, Denmark

ISSN 1431-2654   ISSN 2193-2069   (electronic)
Monographs in Theoretical Computer Science. An EATCS Series
ISBN 978-3-030-73486-2   ISBN 978-3-030-73484-8   (eBook)
https://doi.org/10.1007/978-3-030-73484-8

This Springer imprint is published by the registered company Springer Nature Switzerland AG
The registered company address is: Gewerbestrasse 11, 6330 Cham, Switzerland

Kari
Charlotte & WeiWei, Nikolaj & Bodil
Camilla, Marianne, Katrine, Caroline and Jakob

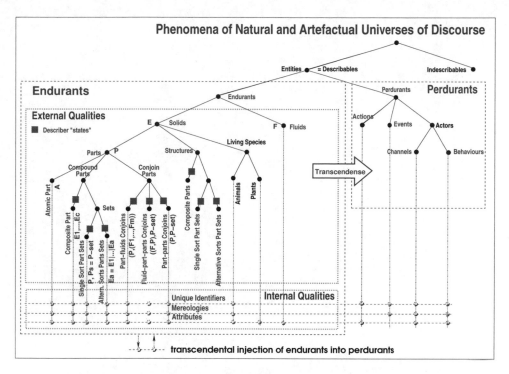

Ontology Graph 1: The Ontology for Chapters 4–7s Domain Analysis

• • •

Ontology Graph 2: A "Minimal" Ontology for Domain Analysis

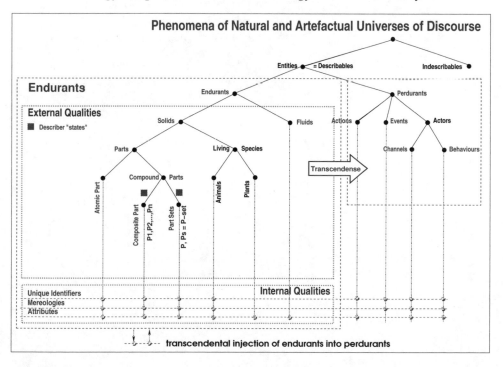

Preface

The Triptych Dogma

In order to *specify* **software**,
we must understand its requirements.
In order to *prescribe* **requirements**
we must understand the **domain**.
So we must **study, analyse** and **describe** domains.

Domains – What Are They ?

By a *domain* we shall understand a *rationally describable* segment of a *discrete dynamics* segment of a *human assisted reality*, i.e., of the world, its *solid or fluid entities*: *natural* ["God-given"] and *artefactual* ["man-made"], and its *living species entities*: *plants* and *animals* including, notably, *humans*. Examples of domains are: *rail, road, sea and air transport; water, oil and gas pipelines; industrial manufacturing; consumer, retail and wholesale markets; health care;* et cetera.

Aim and Objectives

- The **aim** of this monograph is to contribute to a methodology for analysing and describing domains.
- The **objectives** – in the sense of 'how is the aim achieved' – is reflected in the structure and contents and the didactic approach of this monograph. The main elements of my approach – along one concept-axis – can be itemized:

  ∞ There is the founding of our analysis & description approach in providing a base **philosophy**, cf. Chapter 1.
  ∞ There is the application of ideas of **taxonomy** [see Item 41 on page 8], as in Chapter 4, and **ontology** [see Item 25 on page 6], as in Chapter 5, to understand the possibly hierarchical structuring of domain phenomena respectively the understanding of properties of phenomena and relations between then.
  ∞ There is the notions **endurants** and **perdurants** – with endurants being the phenomena that can be observed, or conceived and described, as a "complete thing" at no matter which given snapshot of time [281, Vol. I, pg. 656], and perdurants being the phenomena for which only a fragment exists if we look at or touch them at any given snapshot in time [281, Vol. II, pg. 1552].
  ∞ There is the introduction of base elements of **calculi** for analysing and describing domains.
  ∞ And finally there is the notion of **transcendental deduction**, cf. Chapter 6, for "morphing" certain kinds of endurants into certain kinds of perdurants, Chapter 7.

  Along another conceptual-axis the below are further elements of my approach:

  ∞ We consider domain descriptions, requirements prescriptions and software design specifications to be **mathematical** quantities.
  ∞ And we consider them basically in the sense of **recursive function theory** [351, Hartley Rogers, 1952] and **type theory** [330, Benjamin Pierce, 1997].

∞ That is, we do not consider rather appealing diagrammatic description approaches such as for example `Petri nets` [343, 344, 345, 347, 348, Wolfgang Reisig][1].

An Emphasis

When we say *domain analysis & description* we mean that the result of such a domain analysis & description is to be a model that describes a usually infinite set of domain instances. Domains exhibit endurants and perdurants. A domain model is therefore something that defines the *nouns* (roughly speaking the endurants) and *verbs* (roughly speaking the verbs) – and their combination – of a *language* spoken in and used in writing by the practitioners of the domain. Not an instantiation of nouns, verbs and their combination, but all possible and sensible instantiations.

Doing Science Versus Using Science

We are not doing mathematics, we use it !

We must distinguish between doing mathematics and using mathematics. This monograph uses mathematics to investigate the universe of domain science & engineering. My books [42, 43, 44] teach their readers how to use simple mathematics to develop software, and, in this monograph, to specifically develop domain models.

I use philosophy to underpin my approach. I do not philosophize. My source, Kai Sørlander does and must. I cannot prevent domain modelers, e.g.., those who use the methodology of this monograph, from ("lightweight") philosophizing, but I do not teach them to do it.

Far too many computing science courses and scientists of computers/computing confuse these two things, **doing science** versus **using science**. It is as if their teachers would rather do mathematics than computing.

Relations to Philosophy

Rather unusual, this monograph contains what the author considers an important chapter, Chapter 2, on **Philosophy**. Not a survey of philosophy topics that might be relevant to the domain science & engineering researchers and scientists, but the promulgation of a rather specific angle under which to pursue domain science & engineering studies. It is very much inspired by the work of the Danish philosopher Kai Sørlander [366, 367, 368, 369, 1994–2016].

General

The claim of this monograph is twofold:

- that domain engineering is a **viable**,
- yes, we would claim, **necessary** initial phase of software development; and
- that domain science &[2] engineering is a **worthwhile** topic of research.

---

[1] In a recent technical report, [82], we present, following the method of this monograph, a domain description of an example drawn from a `Petri` net like, i.e., HERAKLIT, description of a *retailer* system [162].

[2] We use the ampersand '&' to emphasize that domain science & engineering is one topic, not two.

I mean this rather seriously:

- How can one think of implementing **software**,
- preferably satisfying some **requirements**,
- without demonstrating that one understands the **domain**?

So in this monograph I shall

- explain what domain engineering is,
- some of the science that goes with it, and
- how one can "derive" requirements prescriptions

  ∞ (for computing systems)
  ∞ from domain descriptions.

But **there is an altogether different reason**, also, for presenting these papers in monograph form:

- Software houses may not take up the challenge to develop software

  ∞ that satisfies customers' expectations, that is, reflects the domain such as these customers know it,
  ∞ and software that is correct with respect to requirements, with proofs of correctness often having to refer to the domain.

- But computing scientists are shown, in this monograph, that domain science & engineering is a field full of interesting problems to be researched.

Application Areas

Computers are man-made. They are artefacts. Physicists and engineers compute over domains of **physics** and **engineering designs**, and their computations range mostly over *phenomena of physics*. Manufacturing, logistics and transport firms as well as goods importers/exporters, wholesalers and retail firms use computers significantly. Their domain is mostly **operations research**. With **domain science & engineering** the domain (of possible software applications) is now definable in terms of what the method of this monograph is capable of handling. Briefly, but by far not exhaustively, that domain includes such which focus on man-made objects, i.e., on artefacts, and the interaction of humans with these. In that respect the domain science & engineering, when used for the purposes of software development, straddles the aforementioned application areas but now, we claim, with some firm direction.

Work in Progress

The state of this monograph reflects that it is *'work in progress'*. The first publications indicating what is presented here were [56, 60, Summer 2010]. Since then there has been a number of publications in peer-reviewed journals [73, 79, 77, 81, Years 2017–2019]. In the period of submission of the most recent of these [81, Spring 2018], and during the writing of this monograph, up to this very moment this *Preface* is being written, new research discoveries are made. The way that these new research ideas fit well within the framework, also in its detailed aspects, makes me think that the body of work presented here is stable and durable. I have therefore decided to release the monograph now in the hope that it might inspire others to continue the research.

The Monograph as a Textbook

Many universities appear to teach their science students, whether BSc or MSc, only such material for which there exists generally accepted and stable theories. I have over the years, since 1976, when I first joined a university staff — then as a full professor — mostly not adhered to this limitation, but taught, to BSc/MSc students, such material that yet had to reach the maturity of a *scientific theory*. So, go ahead, use this monograph in teaching!

Specific

This monograph is intended for the following mathematics-minded audiences:

- primarily researchers, lecturers and PhD students in the sciences of computers and computing – conventionally speaking: those who have few preconceived objections to the use of discrete mathematics;
- hopefully also their similarly oriented, curious and serious MSc students;
- and finally, recent, and not so recent, practicing software engineers and programmers – again open-minded with respect to new foundations for programming and formalisms.

At the end of most chapters' *'Problem Exercise'* sections, we suggest a number of anywhere from engineering to science challenges: project-oriented domain analysis & description class-project exercises as well as more individual research problems of more-or-less "standard" degree of difficulty to plain challenging studies. The class-project exercises amount to rather "full-scale" 4–6 student term projects.

Sources

This is a monograph of 11 chapters. Except for three (Chapters 1, 3 and 11), these chapters build on the following publications:

- **Chapter 2: Philosophy** [80]   11–18
- **Chapter 4: External Qualities** [81, Sects. 2–3][3]   47–106
- **Chapter 5: Internal Qualities** [81, Sect. 4]   107–153
- **Chapter 6: Transcendental Deduction** [81, Sects. 5–6] and [80]   155–157
- **Chapter 7: Perdurants** [81, Sect. 7]   159–204
- **Chapter 8: Domain Facets** [78, 55]   205–240
- **Chapter 9: Requirements** [69, 47]   243–298
- **Chapter 10: Demos, Simulators, Monitors and Controllers** [61]   301–311

Chapters 1–3 pave the way. They introduce the reader to a **vocabulary of concepts** specific to computing science; to some **fundamental ideas of philosophy** – a new for any treatise of our field; and to **prerequisite concepts of discrete mathematics**, of **space, time** and **matter**, and of **unique identification** and **mereology** – also new for any treatise of our field.

Chapters 4–7 **form the real core of this monograph.** It is here we develop what we shall, unashamedly, refer to as both a science and an engineering, i.e., a methodology for understanding the concept of *'domains'* such as we shall define it. These chapters study and

---

[3] [73] is a precursor for [81]

develop **calculi** for the **analysis** of domains and for their **description**. At **the same time as presenting this study** these chapters also **present a method** for actually developing *domain descriptions*. This duality, the beginnings of *a scientific, theoretical foundation* for *domain analyser & describer*, and the beginnings of *a method* for actual *engineering development*, may seem confusing if the twin aspects are not kept clear from one another. We have endeavoured to present the two aspects reasonably separated.

Chapters 8–10 are "bonus" chapters! They contain some quite original concepts: **domain facets** (Chapter 8) such as *intrinsics, support technology, rules & regulations, scripts, license languages, management & organisation* and *human behaviour*; **requirements engineering** (Chapter 9) concepts such as the distinction into *domain requirements, interfaces requirements* and *machine requirements, projection, instantiation, determination, extension* and *fitting*, and more – not quite the way conventional requirements engineering textbooks treat the field; and **demos, simulators, monitors** and **controllers** (Chapter 10) are all concepts that, we claim, can be interestingly understood in light of *domain descriptions* being developed into *requirements prescriptions* and these into *software designs* and *software*. These chapters may, for better or worse, not be of interest to some computer scientists, but should be of interest to software engineering practitioners and people who do study the more mundane aspects of software engineering.

Some Caveats

This monograph uses the **RAISE Specification Language, RSL** [190, 187] for its formal presentations and for its mixed mathematical notation and RSL informal explanations. We refer to Appendix **C** for a résumé of RSL. [188, 179, 183] provide short, concise introductions to the RAISE Method and to RSL. We refer to **https://raisetools.github.io/** for Web-based information about RAISE and the RAISE Tool Sets.

Equally relevant other specification languages could be **VDM SL** [92, 93, 164], **Z** [397], the **B Method** notation [2], **Alloy** [262], and others. Also algebraic approaches are possible, for example: **CafeOBJ** [168], **CASL** [135] or **Maude** [298, 133]. Lecturer and students, readers in general, perhaps more familiar with some of the above languages than with **RSL**, should be able to follow our presentations, but perform their exercise/term project work in the language of their choice.

This monograph is the first in which domain science & engineering is presented in a coherent form, ready for scientific study as well as for university classes. But it is far from a polished textbook: Not all "corners" of describable, manifest and artefactual domains are here given "all the necessary" *principles, techniques and [language] tools* necessary for "run-of-the-mill" software development. We have given sufficiently many university courses, over previous texts, and these have shown, we claim, that most students can be expected, under guidance of professionals experienced in formal specifications, to contribute meaningfully to professional domain analysis & description projects.

We have left out of this monograph potential chapters on for example: possible **Semantic Models** of the domain analysis & description calculi [65]. We invite the reader to study this reference as well as to contribute to domain science. Examples of the latter could, for example, entail: **A Study of Analysis & Description Calculi:** *on the order of analysis & description prompts; on the top-down analysis & description, as suitable, for artefactual domains versus bottom-down analyses & descriptions, as perhaps more suitable, for natural and living specific domains, including humans; a deeper understanding of* **Intentional Pull**, et cetera.

Acknowledgments

This is most likely the last book that I may be able to publish. Over the years I have co-edited, edited, co-authored or authored a number of published books. Some more noteworthy are: [92, 35, 96, 93, 36, 87, 21, 94, 42, 43, 44, 83, 48, 49, 50, 52, 53, 54].

Over all these years I have benefited in my research from a large number of wonderful people. I bear tribute, in approximate chronological order, to a few of these: (the late) Cai Kinberg, Gunnar Wedell, (the late) Jean Paul Jacob, Peter Johansen, Ivan Havel, Leif Saalbach Andersen, (the late) Gerald Weinberg, (the late) Lotfi Zadeh, (the late) E.F. Codd, (the late) John W. Backus, (the late) Peter Lucas, Cliff B. Jones, (the late) Hans Bekič, Kurt Walk, (the late) Christian Gram, Hans Bruun, (the late) Asger Kjerbye Nielsen, Hans Henrik Løvengreen, Andrzej Blikle, Dömölki Balint, Jozef Gruska, Erich Neuhold, (the late) Douglas T. Ross, Neil D. Jones, Ole N. Oest, (the late) Søren Prehn, Michael A. Jackson, Sir Tony Hoare, Hans Langmaack, (the late) Gilles Kahn, (the late) Kesav V. Nori, Larry E. Druffel, Enn S. Tyugu, Mathai Joseph, Olivier Danvy, Dominique Méry, Jorge R. Cuellar, Zhou Chao Chen, Kokichi Futatsugi, Kazuhiro Ogata, Chris George, Tetsuo Tamai, Klaus Havelund, Jin Song Dong, Arutyun Avetisyan, Marko Schütz-Schmuck, and Krzysztof M. Brzeziński.

I also wish to thank the many colleagues around the world who, in recent years, since my retirement, at age 70, in 2007, have let me try out the ideas of earlier versions of this monograph on their students in MSc/PhD courses: Egon Börger (Pisa), Dominique Méry (Nancy), Wolfgang J. Paul (Saarbrücken), Alan Bundy (Edinburgh), Tetsuo Tamai (Tokyo), Dömölki Balint (Budapest), Andreas Hamfeldt (Uppsala), Luıs Barbosa (Braga), Jin Song Dong (Singapore), Jens Knoop (Vienna), Magne Haveraaen (Bergen), Zhu Huibiao (Shanghai) and Chin Wei Ngan (Singapore).

I thank my Springer editor *Ronan Nugent* for his indefatigable, courageous and time-consuming work in getting this monograph published. Ronan's support is deeply appreciated. Thanks Ronan!

I finally wish to thank *Kai Sørlander* for his Philosophy [366, 367, 368, 369]. As you shall find out, Sørlander's Philosophy has inspired me tremendously. Ideas that were previously vague are now, to me, clear. I am sure that You will be likewise enlightened.

Dines Bjørner. August 30, 2021: 10:46 am
Fredsvej 11, DK-2840 Holte, Denmark

Contents

Part I
SETTING THE SCOPE

- The first three chapters: 1, 2 and 3, provide a personal, intellectual introduction to the field of software engineering.
- Behind this monograph and [42, 43, 44] there is, however, a view of the **Concepts** that I view as the basis for these books, hence "our field". They are covered in Chapter 1. They are briefly characterised. These characterisations can be found in ordinary dictionaries and on Wikipedia. It is their juxtaposition, here in this monograph, that, to me is significant and personal. They have formed and form a terminological foundation upon which I have built in the last almost half century.
- In Chapter 2 I summarize essential aspects of **Kai Sørlanders Philosophy**[4]. That Philosophy, such as I use it, is covered in four of his monographs: [366, 367, 368, 369]. It is thought that this introduction of a philosophical basis for the computer & computing sciences is novel!
- In Chapter 3 we bring three fundamental concepts: **Space, Time** and **Matter** together. They are all inherent in Kai Sørlander's Philosophy. I then explore aspects of **Identity** and **Mereology** – and refer to the published [79].
- Chapter 1 is basically "cozy armchair reading"!
- Chapter 2 requires a serious study!
- Chapter 3 less so.

---

[4] I spell that with a capital **P** in order to name a specific philosophy

Chapter 1
CONCEPTS

This monograph introduces a rather large number of new concepts. In a conventional software engineering setting, and, as in this case, in a technical/scientific monograph, an introductory chapter such as this is unusual. I present this chapter because of the large number of new concepts. In order for the reader to find the way around, that reader must be made aware of the background concepts that underlie my treatment of a **new** *branch of software engineering,* **the domain science and engineering.**

1.1 A General Vocabulary

1 **Abstraction:**

> Conception, my boy, fundamental brain-work,
> is what makes the difference in all art
>
> *D.G. Rossetti[5]: letter to H. Caine[6]*

Abstraction is a tool, used by the human mind, and to be applied in the process of describing (understanding) complex phenomena.

Abstraction is the most powerful such tool available to the human intellect.

Science proceeds by simplifying reality. The first step in simplification is abstraction. Abstraction (in the context of science) means leaving out of account all those empirical data which do not fit the particular, conceptual framework within which science at the moment happens to be working.

Abstraction (in the process of specification) arises from a conscious decision to advocate certain desired objects, situations and processes as being fundamental; by exposing, in a first, or higher, level of description, their similarities and — at that level — ignoring possible differences.

[From the opening paragraphs of [248, C.A.R. Hoare *Notes on Data Structuring*]][7]

2 **Calculation:** A calculation is a deliberate process that transforms one or more inputs into one or more results. The term is used in a variety of senses, from the very definite arithmetical calculation of using an algorithm, to the vague heuristics of calculating a strategy in a competition, or calculating the chance of a successful relationship between two people [`Wikipedia`].

3 **Computation:** A computation is any type of calculation that includes both arithmetical and non-arithmetical steps and which follows a well-defined model (e.g. an algorithm).

---

[5] Dante Gabrielli Rosetti, 1828–1882, English poet, illustrator, painter and translator.

[6] T. Hall Caine, 1853–1931, British novelist, dramatist, short story writer, poet and critic.

[7] We shall use another quote of Tony Hoare as the last proper text of this monograph, see Sect. **11.9** on page 319.

© The Author(s), under exclusive license to Springer Nature Switzerland AG 2021
D. Bjørner, *Domain Science and Engineering*, Monographs in Theoretical Computer Science. An EATCS Series,
https://doi.org/10.1007/978-3-030-73484-8_1

Mechanical or electronic devices (or, historically, people) that perform computations are known as computers. An especially well-known discipline of the study of computation is computer science [Wikipedia].

4 **Computer:** A computer is a collection of *hardware* and *software*, that is, is a machine that can be instructed to carry out sequences of arithmetic or logical operations automatically via computer programming [Wikipedia].

5 **Computer Science:** is the study and knowledge of the abstract phenomena that "occur" within computers [DB].
As such computer science includes *Theory of computation, automata theory, formal language theory, algorithmic complexity theory, probabilistic computation, quantum computation, cryptography, machine learning and computational biology.*

6 **Computing Science:** is the study and knowledge of how to construct "those things" that "occur" within computers [DB].
As such computing science embodies *algorithm and data structure design, functional-, logic-, imperative-* and *parallel programming; code testing, model checking* and *specification proofs.* Much of this can be pursued using *formal methods* (see Item 11).

7 **Domain Engineering:** is the engineering of *domain descriptions* based on the engineering of *domain analyses* [DB].
Chapters 4–8 covers domain engineering.
We shall later, in Chapter 11, summarise the "benefits" of domain engineering. Suffice it here to say that basing software development on domain analysis & description shall help secure that the eventually emerging software *meets customer expectations.*

8 **Domain Requirements:** are those requirements which can be expressed sôlely in terms of domain concepts.

9 **Engineering:** is the use of scientific principles to design and build machines, structures, and other items, including bridges, tunnels, roads, vehicles, and buildings [Wikipedia].
The engineer *walks the bridge between science and technology:* analysing man-made devices for their possible scientific properties and constructing technology based on scientific insight.
We refer to $[\![\iota 7,\pi 4]\!]$, $[\![\iota 29,\pi 6]\!]$, $[\![\iota 37,\pi 7]\!]$.

10 **Epistemology:** is the branch of philosophy concerned with the theory of knowledge – and is the study of the nature of knowledge, justification, and the rationality of belief [Wikipedia].

11 **Formal Method:** By a *formal method* we shall here understand a *method* whose techniques and tools can be understood mathematically.
For *formal domain, requirements* or *software engineering* methods *formality* means the following:

- There is a set, one or more, of **specification languages** – say for domain descriptions, requirements prescriptions, software specifications, and software coding, i.e., programming languages.[8]
- These are all to be formal, that is, to have a formal syntax, a formal semantics, and a formal, typically *Mathematical Logic* proof system.
- Some of the *techniques* and *tools* must be supported by a mathematical understanding.

---

[8] Most formal specification languages are textual, but graphical languages like Petri nets [348], Message Sequence Charts [260], Statecharts [210], Live Sequence Charts [211], etc., are also formal.

12 **Hardware:** The physical components of a computer: electronics, mechanics, optics, etc. [Wikipedia].

13 **Interface Requirements:** are those requirements which can be expressed in a combination of both domain and machine concepts. They are so because certain entities, whether endurants or perdurants, are *shared between the domain and the machine.*

14 **Language:** By *language* we shall, with [Wikipedia], mean a *structured system* of communication. Language, in a broader sense, is the method of communication that involves the use of – particularly human – languages. The 'structured system' that we refer to has come to be known as *Syntax, Semantics* and *Pragmatics.* We refer to $[\![\iota\,39,\pi\,7]\!]$[9], $[\![\iota\,33,\pi\,7]\!]$, and $[\![\iota\,27,\pi\,6]\!]$.

15 **Linguistics:** By *linguistics* we shall mean the scientific study of language.

16 **Machine:** By a *machine* we shall understand a combination of software and hardware.

17 **Machine Requirements:** are those requirements which can be expressed sôlely in terms of machine concepts.

18 **Mathematics:** By *mathematics* we shall here understand such human endeavours that make precise certain facets of language $[\![\iota\,14,\pi\,5]\!]$, whether natural or 'constructed' (as for mathematical notation), and out of those endeavours, i.e., mathematical constructions, also called theories, build further abstractions. We refer to Sects. **3.2–3.3.**

19 **Metaphysics:** is the branch of philosophy that examines the fundamental nature of reality, including the relationship between mind and matter, between substance and attribute, and between potentiality and actuality [282] [Wikipedia].
One may claim that this monograph is [also] about metaphysics.

20 **Mereology:** is the theory of parthood relations: of the relations of part to whole and the relations of part to part within a whole [380, 365, 122].
The concept of 'mereology' and its study is accredited to the Polish mathematician, philosopher and logician Stanisław Leśniewski (1886–1939).

21 **Method:** By a method we shall understand a *set of* **principles** for *selecting* and *applying* a *set of* **procedures** which deploy a *set of* **techniques** which *uses* a *set of* **tools** in order to *construct* an *artefact.*
We shall in this primer focus on a *method* for pursuing *domain analysis* and for constructing *domain descriptions.* Key chapters will summarise some methodological aspects of their content.

22 **Methodology:** is the comparative study and knowledge of methods [DB].
[The two terms: 'method' and 'methodology' are often confused, including used interchangeably.]

23 **Model:** A mathematical model is a description of a system using mathematical concepts and language. We shall include descriptions[10], prescriptions[11] and specifications[12] using formal languages in presenting models.

---

[9] By $[\![\iota\,39,\pi\,7]\!]$ we mean to refer to *i*tem 39 *π*age 7

[10] as for domains

[11] as for requirements

[12] as for software

24 **Modelling:** Modelling is the act of creating models, which include discrete mathematical structures (sets, Cartesians, lists, maps, etc.), and are logical theories represented as algebras. That is, any given RSL text denotes a set of models, and each model is an algebra, i.e., a set of named values and a set of named operations on these. Modelling is the engineering activity of establishing, analysing and using such structures and theories. Our models are established with the intention that they "model" "something else" other than just being the mathematical structure or theory itself. That "something else" is, in our case, some part of a reality[13], or of a construed such reality, or of requirements to the, or a reality[14], or of actual software[15].

25 **Ontology:** is the branch of metaphysics dealing with the nature of being; a set of concepts and categories in a subject area or domain that shows their properties and the relations between them [114, 115] [Wikipedia]. An ontology identifies and distinguishes concepts and their relationships; it describes content and relationships [Bob Bater]. Ontologies *specify*.
Chapter 5 focus on the ontology of domains.
The two terms, taxonomy and ontology relate. We refer to the term 'taxonomy', Item 41 on page 8.

26 **Philosophy:** is the study of general and fundamental questions about existence, knowledge, values, reason, mind, and language. Such questions are often posed as problems to be studied or resolved [Wikipedia].

27 **Pragmatics:** studies the ways in which context contributes to meaning.
Pragmatics encompasses speech act theory, conversational implicature, talk in interaction and other approaches to language behaviour in philosophy, sociology, linguistics and anthropology [318, 303] [Wikipedia].

28 **Requirements:** By a requirements we understand (cf., [256, IEEE Standard 610.12]): "*A condition or capability needed by a user to solve a problem or achieve an objective*".
In *software development* the requirements explain what properties the desired software should have, not how these properties might be attained. In our, the *triptych* approach, requirements are to be "derived" from domain descriptions.

29 **Requirements Engineering:** is the engineering of constructing requirements [DB].
The aim of requirements engineering is to **design the machine.** Chapter 9 covers requirements engineering.

30 **Requirements Prescription:** By a requirements prescription we mean a document which outlines the requirements that some software is expected to fulfill.

31 **Requirements Specification:** By a requirements specification we mean the same as a requirements prescription.

32 **Science:** is a systematic activity that builds and organizes knowledge in the form of testable explanations and predictions about the universe [Wikipedia].
Science is the intellectual and practical activity encompassing the systematic study of the structure and behaviour of the physical and natural world through observation and experiment.

---

[13] — as in domain modelling

[14] — as in requirements modelling

[15] — as in software design

33 **Semantics:** is the linguistic and philosophical study of meaning in language, programming languages, formal logics, and semiotics. It is concerned with the relationship between signifiers — like words, phrases, signs, and symbols — and what they stand for in reality, their denotation [119] [Wikipedia].

The languages that we shall be concerned with are, on one hand, the language[s] in which we describe domains [as here a variant of RSL, the RAISE Specification Language, extended, as we shall see in Chapters 4–7] and, on the other hand, the language that emerges as the result of our domain analysis & description: a domain specific language. There are basically three kinds of semantics, expressed somewhat simplistically:

- **Denotational Semantics** model-theoretically assigns a *meaning*, a *denotation*, to each *phrase structure*, i.e., *syntactic category*.
- **Axiomatic Semantics** or **Mathematical Logic Proof Systems** is an approach based on mathematical logic for proving the correctness of specifications.
- **Algebraic Semantics** is a form of axiomatic semantics based on algebraic laws for describing and reasoning about program semantics in a formal manner.

34 **Semiotics:** is the study and knowledge of sign process (semiosis), which is any form of activity, conduct, or any process that involves signs, including the production of meaning [Wikipedia].

A sign is anything that communicates a meaning, that is not the sign itself, to the interpreter of the sign. The meaning can be intentional – such as a word uttered with a specific meaning, or unintentional – such as a symptom being a sign of a particular medical condition. Signs can communicate through any of the senses, visual, auditory, tactile, olfactory, or gustatory [Wikipedia]. The study and knowledge of semiotics is often "broken down" into the studies, etc., of *syntax, semantics* and *pragmatics*.

35 **Software:** is the set of all the documents that have resulted from a completed *software development: domain analysis & description, requirements analysis & prescription, software: software code, software installation manuals, software maintenance manuals, software users guides, development project plans, budget, etc.*

36 **Software Design:** is the engineering of constructing software [DB].

Whereas software requirements engineering focus on the logical properties that desired software should attain, software design, besides focusing on achieving these properties *correctly*, also focus on the properties being achieved *efficiently*.

37 **Software Engineering:** to us, is then the combination of domain and requirements engineering with software design [DB].

This is my characterisation of software engineering. It is at the basis of this monograph as well as [42, 43, 44].

38 **Software Development:** is then the combination of the development of domain description, requirements prescription and software design [DB].

This is my characterisation of software engineering. It is at the basis of this monograph as well as [42, 43, 44].

39 **Syntax:** is the set of rules, principles, and processes that govern the structure of sentences (sentence structure) in a given language, usually including word order [Wikipedia].

We assume, as an absolute minimum of knowledge, that the reader of this monograph is well aware of the concepts of BNF (*Backus Normal Form*) Grammars and CFGs (*Context Free Grammars*).

40 **Syntax, Semantics and Pragmatics:** With the advent of computing and their attendant programming languages these concepts of semiotics has taken on a somewhat additional meaning. When, in computer & computing science and in software engineering, we speak of syntax, we mean a quite definite and (mathematically) precise thing. With the advent of our ability to mathematically precisely describe the semantics of programming languages, we similarly mean quite definite and (mathematically) precise things. For natural, i.e., human languages, this is not so. As for pragmatics there is this to say. Computers have not pragmatics. Humans have. When, in this monograph we bring the term 'pragmatics' into play we are referring not to the computer "being pragmatic", but to our pragmatics, as scientists, as engineers.

41 **Taxonomy:** is the practice and science of classification of things or concepts, including the principles that underlie such classification [Wikipedia].
A taxonomy formalizes the hierarchical relationships among concepts and specifies the term to be used to refer to each; it prescribes structure and terminology.
Taxonomies *classify*.
Chapter 4 focus on the taxonomy of domains.
The two terms, taxonomy and ontology relate. We refer to the term 'ontology', Item 25 on page 6.

42 **Technology:** is the sum of techniques, skills, methods, and processes used in the production of goods or services or in the accomplishment of objectives, such as scientific investigation [Wikipedia].
Technology can be the knowledge of techniques, processes, and the like, or it can be embedded in machines to allow for operation without detailed knowledge of their workings. Systems (e.g. machines) applying technology by taking an input, changing it according to the system's use, and then producing an outcome are referred to as technology systems or technological systems [Wikipedia].

43 **Triptych:** The *triptych [of software development]* centers on the three 'engineerings': domain, requirements and software [DB].
We refer to *The Triptych Dogma* of page V in the preface.

1.2 More on Method

We elaborate on issues arising from the concept of 'method'. These are brought here in some, hopefully meaningful, but not alphabetic order!

44 **Method:** By a method we shall understand a *set of* **principles** for *selecting* and *applying* a *set of* **procedures** which deploy a *set of* **techniques** which *uses a set of* **tools** in order to *construct* an *artefact*.

    a. **Principle:** By a *principle* we shall, loosely, understand *(i) elemental aspect of a craft or discipline, (ii) foundation, (iii) general law of nature, etc.* [www.etymonline.com].
We shall, at the end of several chapters[16] summarise the principles, techniques and tools covered by these chapters.

    c. **Procedure:** By a **procedure** we shall understand instructions or recipes, a set of commands that show how to achieve some result, such as to prepare or make something; a step-by-step instruction to achieve some result [Wikipedia].

    c. **Technique:** By a *technique* we shall, loosely, understand *(i) formal practical details in artistic, etc., expression, (ii) art, skill, craft in work* [www.etymonline.com].

---

[16] See Sects. **4.22.3** on page 99, **5.10.3** on page 149, **7.13.4** on page 198, **8.9.1** on page 236, **9.7.2** on page 292

d. **Tool:** By a *tool* we shall, loosely, understand *(i) instrument, implement used by a craftsman or laborer, weapon, (ii) that with which one prepares something, etc.* [www.etymonline.com].

a. Among **basic principles**, to be applied across all phases of software development, and hence in all phases of software engineering are those of:

i **Abstraction:** We refer to Item 1 on page 3.

ii **Conservative Extension:** An extension of a logical theory is conservative, i.e., conserves, if every theorem expressible in the original theory is also derivable within the original theory [en.wiktionary.org/wiki/conservative_extension].

iii **Divide and Conquer:** In computer science, divide and conquer is an algorithm design paradigm based on multi-branched recursion. A divide-and-conquer algorithm works by recursively breaking down a problem into two or more sub-problems of the same or related type, until these become simple enough to be solved directly [Wikipedia].
But this monograph is not about the exciting field of *algorithm design*.
Yet, the principle of *divide and conquer* is also very strongly at play here: In the top-down analysis of a *domain* into what can be *described* and what is *indescribable*, of *describable entities* into *endurants* and *perdurants*, of *endurants* into *solids* and *fluids*, of *solids* into *parts, structures* and *living species*, and so forth [cf. Fig. 4.1 on page 53].

iv **Intentional Pull:** The concept of intentional pull is a wider notion than that of invariant. Here we are not concerned with pre-/post-conditions on operations. Intentional pull is exerted between two or more phenomena of a domain when their relation can be asserted to **always** hold.

v **Invariants:** The concept of invariants in the context of computing science is most clearly illustrated in connection with the well-formedness of data structures. Invariants then express properties that must hold, i.e., as a **pre-condition**, before any application of an operation to those data structures and shall hold, i.e. as a **post-condition** after any application of an operation to those data structures.

vi **Narration & Formalisation:** To communicate what a domain "is", one must be able to narrate of what it consists. To understand a domain one must give a formal description of that domain. When we put an ampersand, &, between the two terms we mean to say that they form a whole: not one without the other, either way around! In our domain descriptions we enumerate narrative sentences and ascribe this enumeration to formal expressions.

vii **Nondeterminism:** Non-determinism is a fundamental concept in computer science. It appears in various contexts such as automata theory, algorithms and concurrent computation. ... The concept was developed from its inception by Rabin & Scott, Floyd and Dijkstra; as was the interplay between non-determinism and concurrency [Michal Armoni and Mordechai Ben-Ari].

viii **Operational Abstraction** abstract the way in which we express operations on usually representationally abstracted values. In conventional programming we refer to operational abstract as *procedure abstraction*.

ix **Refinement** is a verifiable transformation of an abstract (i.e., high-level) formal specification into a less abstract, we say more concrete (i.e., low-level) specification or an executable program. Step-wise refinement allows the refinement of a program, from a specification, to be done in stages [www.igi-global.com/dictionary].

x **Representational Abstraction** abstracts the representation of type values, say in the form of just plain **sorts**, or, when concrete **types**, then in, for example, the form of mathematical sets, or maps (i.e., discrete functions, usually from finite definition sets into likewise representationally abstracted ranges), or Cartesians (i.e., group-ings of likewise abstracted elements), etc. In conventional programming we refer to representational abstract as *data abstraction*.

45 **Syntax and Semantics:** When we write:

  let a:A **in** $\mathcal{B}$(a) **end**

We mean that the [free] a in the $\mathcal{B}$(a) clause is bound to the value a of type A in **let** a:A.

46 **Syntax Names:** To express that we refer to the syntactic name of a sort or type, A, we write:

  " A "

That is, **" ... "** is a special, meta-linguistic distributed-fix **quote [unquote]** operator. It is explained in Sect. **3.3.5.2** page 25.

1.3 Some More Personal Observations

47 **Informatics:** We understand informatics as a confluence of mathematics, of the com-puter and computing sciences, of the domain science & engineering as espoused in this monograph, of requirements engineering and software design.

48 **IT – Information Technology:** We understand information technology as the confluence of nanophysics, electronics, computers and communication (hardware), sensors, actuators, etc.

- **Two Universes:** Two diverse universes appear to emerge.

  ∞ **Information Technology** is, to this author, a ***universe of both material quality and quantity***. It is primarily materially characterised, such as I see it, by such terms as *bigger, smaller, faster, slower, costly, inexpensive,* and *environment "friendly"*.

  ∞ **Informatics** is, to this author, a ***universe of intellectual quality***. As such it is primarily characterised, such as I see it, by such terms as *better, more fit for purpose, appropriate, logically correct* and *meets user expectations*.

1.4 Informatics Thinking

A concept of *computational thinking* [389, Jeannette M. Wing, 2006] has recently gained currency. Instead of that concept we suggest a concept of *Informatics Thinking*. Basically informatics thinking espouses informatics. We thus delineate it as an amalgam of abilities

- (i) to *abstract*;
- (ii) to act *methodically* – that is, to define and apply *principles, techniques* and *tools*;
- (iii) to analyse describable phenomena into decomposed or composed such;
- (iv) to identify and handle, separately, issues of *semiotics* – that is, to clearly identify, separate and rigorously use *syntactics, semantics* and *pragmatics*;
- and (v) to both succinctly *narrate* and *mathematically formalise*, issues that eventually end up being the subject of computations.

The present monograph, as well as our three monographs of *Software Engineering* [42, 43, 44, 2006], facilitate and convey 'informatics thinking'.

Chapter 2
DOMAIN PHILOSOPHY

In this chapter we cover such notions of philosophy that we claim are fundamental to our understanding of domain science and engineering.

There is a fundamentally un-avoidable reason for this. What we are to analyse & describe are fragments of a real world. That is, basically of an informal world. A world for which we can never claim that a mathematical model is that world! The "clash" between informal and formal is why we need to bring in issues of philosophy.

We shall base some of our domain analysis decisions on Kai Sørlander's Philosophy [366, 367, 368, 369]. A main contribution of Kai Sørlander is, on the philosophical basis of the *possibility of truth* (in contrast to Kant's *possibility of self-awareness*), to *rationally* and *transcendentally deduce the absolutely necessary conditions for describing any world*. These conditions presume a *principle of contradiction* and lead to the *ability* to *reason* using *logical connectives* and to *handle asymmetry, symmetry* and *transitivity*. *Transcendental deductions* then lead to *space* and *time*, not as priory assumptions, as with Kant, but derived facts of any world. From this basis Kai Sørlander then, by further transcendental deductions, arrive at kinematics, dynamics and the bases for Newton's Laws.

We build on Sørlander's basis to argue that the **domain analysis & description** calculi are necessary and sufficient for the analysis & description of domains and that a number of relations between domain entities can be understood transcendentally and as "variants" of laws of physics, biology, etc.!

2.1 Some Preliminaries

Familiarity with some basic notions are in order.

2.1.1 What must be in any Domain Description

The question is: *"what, if anything, is of such necessity, that it could under no circumstances be otherwise?"* or *"which are the necessary characteristics of any possible world?"*. We take it that the necessary characteristics of any domain is equivalent with the conceptual, logical conditions for any possible description of that domain.

In this chapter and from Chapters 4–7, we shall see that the following *philosophy-motivated concepts*, many of them first explained in Chapters 4–7, are at the very basis of any domain: *entities*, i.e., phenomena that can be described, reasoned about, *time* and *space*, *endurants*, i.e., entities that can be observed in space, and *perdurants*, i.e., entities that can be observed over time, with perdurants "emerging" from endurants, by *transcendental deduction*, and the laws of Newton, and hence their derivatives.

D. Bjørner, *Domain Science and Engineering*, Monographs in Theoretical Computer Science. An EATCS Series,
https://doi.org/10.1007/978-3-030-73484-8_2

2.1.2 Some Issues of Philosophy

Sørlander puts forward the thesis of *the possibility of truth* and then, basing *transcendental deductions* on indisputable logical relations, arrives at the conceptual, logical conditions for any possible description of any domain.

The starting point, now, in a series of deductions, is that of logic and that we can *assert* a property, $\mathcal{P}$, and its negation $\neg\mathcal{P}$. *These two assertions cannot both be true,* that is, that $\mathcal{P} \wedge \neg\mathcal{P}$ cannot be true. So the *possibility of truth* is a universally valid condition. When we claim that, we also claim *the contradiction principle*. The *implicit meaning theory* is this: *"in assertions there are mutual dependencies between the meaning of designations and consistency relation between assertions".* When we claim that a philosophy-basis is that of the possibility of truth, then we assume that this basis include the contradiction principle and the implicit meaning theory. We shall also refer to the implicit meaning theory as the **inescapable meaning assignment**.

As an example of what "goes into" the *inescapable meaning assignment*, we bring, albeit from the world of computer science, that of the description of the **stack** data type (its endurants and operations).

Inescapable Meaning Assignment, Narrative

Example 1

49 Stacks, s:S, have elements, e:E;
50 the empty_S operation takes no arguments and yields a result stack;
51 the is_empty_S operation takes an argument stack and yields a Boolean value result.
52 the stack operation takes two arguments: an element and a stack and yields a result stack.
53 the unstack operation takes an non-empty argument stack and yields a stack result.
54 the top operation takes an non-empty argument stack and yields an element result.

The consistency relations:

55 an empty_S stack is_empty, and a stack with at least one element is not;
56 unstacking an argument stack, stack(e,s), results in the stack s; and
57 inquiring the top of a non-empty argument stack, stack(e,s), yields e.

Inescapable Meaning Assignment, Formalisation

Example 2
type
1. E, S
value
2. empty_S: **Unit** $\rightarrow$ S
3. is_empty_S: S $\rightarrow$ **Bool**
4. stack: E $\times$ S $\rightarrow$ S
5. unstack: S $\overset{\sim}{\rightarrow}$ S
6. top: S $\overset{\sim}{\rightarrow}$ E

The consistency relations:
7. is_empty(empty_S()) = **true**
7. is_empty(stack(e,s)) = **false**
8. unstack(stack(e,s)) = s
9. top(stack(e,s)) = e

2.1.3 Transcendence

> **Definition: 1 Transcendental:** By **transcendental** *we shall understand the philosophical notion: the a priori or intuitive basis of knowledge, independent of experience* ∎

> **Definition: 2 Transcendental Deduction:** By a **transcendental deduction** *we shall understand the philosophical notion: a transcendental 'conversion' of one kind of knowledge into a seemingly different kind of knowledge* ∎

Transcendental philosophy, with Kant and Sørlander, seeks to find the necessary conditions for experience, recognition and understanding. Transcendental deduction is then the "process", based on the principle of contradiction and the implicit meaning theory, by means of which – through successive concept definitions – one can deduce a system of base concepts which must be assumed in any possible description of the world. The subsequent developments of the logical connectives, modalities, existence, identity, difference, relations, numbers, space, time and causality, are all transcendental deductions.

We shall return to the notions of transcendence in Chapter 6.

2.2 Overview of the Sørlander Philosophy

In this section we shall give a very terse summary of main elements of Kai Sørlander's philosophy. We shall primarily base this overview on [369]. It is necessarily a terse summary. What we overview is developed in [369] over some 50 pages. Sørlander's books [366, 367, 368, 369], relevant to this overview, are all in Danish. Hence the need for this section.

2.2.1 Logical Connectives

The logical connectives can be justified purely on rational grounds. The connectives are: **negation**: ¬, **conjunction** and **disjunction**: ∧ and ∨, and **implication**: ⇒.

2.2.1.1 Negation: ¬:

The logical connective, **negation** (¬), is defined as follows: if assertion $\mathcal{P}$ holds then assertion ¬$\mathcal{P}$ does not hold. That is, the contradiction principle understood as a definition of the concept of negation.

2.2.1.2 Conjunction and Disjunction: ∧ and ∨

Assertion $\mathcal{P} \wedge Q$ holds, i.e., is true, if both $\mathcal{P}$ **and** Q holds.
Assertion $\mathcal{P} \vee Q$ holds, i.e., is true, if **either** $\mathcal{P}$ **or** Q **or both** $\mathcal{P}$ and Q holds.

2.2.1.3 Implication: $\Rightarrow$

Assertion $\mathcal{P} \Rightarrow Q$ holds, i.e., is true, if the first assertion, $\mathcal{P}$, holds, t, and the second assertion, Q, is not false, $\neg f$. $[(\mathcal{P},Q),\mathcal{P} \Rightarrow Q]$: $[(t,t),t]$, $[(t,f),f]$, $[(f,t),t]$, and $[(f,f),t]$. $\Rightarrow$ used in logic is also called *material implication*.

2.2.2 Towards a Philosophy-Basis for Physics and Biology

In a somewhat long series of deductions we shall, based on Sørlander's Philosophy, motivate the laws of Newton and more, not on the basis of empirical observations, but on the basis of transcendental deductions and rational reasoning.

2.2.2.1 Possibility and Necessity

Based on logical implication we can transcendentally define the two *modal operators:* **necessity** and **possibility**.

Definition: 3 Necessarily True Assertions: An assertion is **necessarily** true if its truth follows from the definition of the designations by means of which it is expressed ∎

Definition: 4 Possibly True Assertions: An assertion is **possibly** true if its negation is not necessary ∎

2.2.2.2 Empirical Assertions

There can be assertions whose truth value does **not only depend** on the definition of the designations by means of which they are expressed. Those are assertions whose truth value **depend also** on the assertions **referring** to something that exists independently of the designations by means of which they are expressed. We shall call such assertions *empirical*.

2.2.2.3 Existence of Entities

With Sørlander we shall now argue that **there exist many entities in any world:** [369, pp 145] "Entities, in a first step of reasoning, that can be referred to in empirical assertions, do not necessarily exist. It is, however, an empirical fact that they do exist; hence there is a logical necessity that they do not exist[17]. In a second step of reasoning, these entities must exist as a necessary condition for their actually being ascribed the predicates which they must necessarily befit in their capacity of of being entities referred to in empirical assertions."

---

[17] Here we need to emphasize that the above quote from Sørlander is one between the *type* and a *value* of that type. So the empirical assertions motivate that we speak of the type of an entity. Empirical facts then states that some specific value of that type need not exist. In fact, there is, most likely, an indefinite number of values of the asserted type that do not exist.

2.2.2.4 Identity, Difference and Relations

[369, pp 146] "An entity, referred to by A, is **identical** to an entity, referred to by B, if A cannot be ascribed a predicate in-commensurable with a predicate ascribed to B." That is, if A and B cannot be ascribed in-commensurable predicates. [369, pp 146] "Entities A and B are **different** if they can be ascribed in-commensurable predicates." [369, pp 147] "**Identity** and **difference** are thus transcendentally derived through these formal definitions and must therefore be presupposed in any description of any domain and must be expressible in any language." *Identity* and *difference* are **relations**. [369, pp 147] "As a consequence *identity* and *difference* imply relations. **Symmetry** and **asymmetry** are also relations: A identical to B is the same as B identical to A. And A different from B is the same as B different from A. Finally **transitivity** follows from A identical to B and B identical to C implies A identical to C."

2.2.2.5 Sets

We can, as a consequence of two or more different entities satisfying a same predicate, say $\mathcal{P}$, *define* the notion of the **set** of all those entities satisfying $\mathcal{P}$. And, as a consequence of two or more entities, $e_i, ..., e_j$, all being *distinct*, therefore implying in-commensurable predicates, $Q_i, ..., Q_j$, but still satisfying a common predicate, $\mathcal{P}$, we can claim that they all belong to a same set. The predicate $\mathcal{P}$ can be said to **type** that set. And so forth: following this line of reasoning we can introduce notions of cardinality of sets, finite and infinite sets, existential ($\exists$) and universal ($\forall$) quantifiers, etc.; and we can in this way transcendentally deduce the concept of (positive) numbers, their addition and multiplication; and that such are an indispensable aspect of any domain. We leave it then to mathematics to study number theory.

2.2.2.6 Space and Geometry

Definition: 5 Space: [369, pp 154] *"The two relations **asymmetric** and **symmetric**, by a transcendental deduction, can be given an interpretation: the relation (spatial) **direction** is asymmetric; and the relation (spatial) **distance** is symmetric. Direction and distance can be understood as spatial relations. From these relations are derived the relation in-between. **Hence** we must conclude that **primary entities exist in space**. Space is therefore an un-avoidable characteristic of any possible world"* ■

[369, pp 155] "Entities, to which reference can be made in simple, empirical assertions, must exist in space; they must be spatial, i.e., have a certain extension in all directions; they must therefore "fill up some space", have surface and form." From this, by further reasoning one can develop notions of points, line, surface, etc., i.e., Euclidean as well as non-Euclidean **geometry**. We refer to Sects. **3.4** on page 26 and **3.4.4** on page 27 for more on space.

2.2.2.7 States

We introduce a notion of **state**. [369, pp 158–159] "Entities may be ascribed predicates which it is not logically necessary that they are ascribed. How can that be possible? Only if we accept that entities may be ascribed predicates which are in-commensurable with predicates that they are actually ascribed." That is possible, we must conclude, if entities can **exist** in distinct **states**. We shall let this notion of state further undefined – till Sect. **4.19**.

2.2.2.8 Time and Causality

Definition: 6 Time: [369, pp 159] *"Two different states must necessarily be ascribed different incompatible predicates. But how can we ensure so ? Only if states stand in an asymmetric relation to one another. This state relation is also transitive. So that is an indispensable property of any world. By a transcendental deduction we say that* **primary entities exist in time**. *So every possible world must exist in time"* ∎

We refer to Sect. **3.5** on page 29 for more on time.

So space and time are not phenomena, i.e., are not entities. They are, by transcendental reasoning, aspects of any possible world, hence, of any description of any domain. In a concentrated series [369, 160-163] of logical reasoning and transcendental deductions, Sørlander, introduce the concepts of the empirical circumstances under which entities exist, implying *non-logical implication* between one-and-the-same entity at distinct times, leading to the notions of **causal effect** and **causal implication** – all deduced transcendentally. Whereas Kant's *causal implication* is transcendentally deduced as necessary for the *possibility of self-awareness*. Sørlander's *causal implication* does not assume *possibility of self-awareness*. The **principle of causality** is a necessary condition for assertions being about the same entity at different times.

2.2.2.9 Kinematics

[369, pp 164] "Entities are in both space and time; therefore it must be assumed that they can change their spatial properties; that is, are subject to **movement**. An entity which changes location is said to **move**. An entity which does not change location is said to be **at rest**." In this way [369] transcendentally introduces the notions of *velocity* and *acceleration*, hence *kinematics*.

2.2.2.10 Dynamics

[369, pp 166] "When combining the *causality principle* with *dynamics* we deduce that when an entity changes its state of movement then there must be a cause, and we call that cause a **force**." [369, pp 166] "The **change** of state of entity movement must be **proportional** to the applied *force*; an entity not subject to an external force will remain in its *state of movement*: This is **Newton's 1st Law.**"

[369, pp 166] "But to change an entity's state of movement, by some force, must imply that the entity exerts a certain **resistance** to that change; the entity must have a **mass**. Changes in an entity's state of movement besides being proportional to the external force, must be **inverse proportional** to its mass. This is **Newton's 2nd Law.**"

[369, pp 166-167] "The forces that act upon entities must have as source other entities: entities may **collide;** and when they collide **the forces** they exert on each other must be **the same but with opposite directions.** This is **Newton's 3rd Law.**"

[369, pp 167-168] "How can entities be the source of forces? How can they have a mass? Transcendentally it must follow from what we shall refer to as **gravitational pull**. Across all entities of mass, there is a mutual attraction, **Universal Gravitation.**" [369, pp 168-169] "Gravitation must, since it has its origin in the individual entities, propagate with a definite velocity; and that velocity must have a limit, a constant of nature, the **universal speed limit.**"

2.3 From Philosophy to Physics and Biology

Based on logical reasoning and transcendental deductions one can thus derive major aspects of that which must be (assumed to be) in any description of any world, i.e., domain. In our domain description ontology we shall let the notions of **solid endurants (parts)** and **fluid endurants** cover what we have covered so far: they are those entities which satisfy the laws of physics. In the next sections we shall make further use of Sørlander's Philosophy to logically and transcendentally justify the inevitability of **living species: plants** and **animals** including, notably, **humans**, in any description of any domain.

2.3.1 Purpose, Life and Evolution

[369, pp 174] "For language and meaning to be possible there must exist entities that are not constrained to just the laws of physics. This is possible if such entities are further subject to a **"purpose-causality"** directed at the future. These entities must strive to maintain their own existence." We shall call such entities **living species**. Living species must maintain and also further develop their form and do so by an exchange of materials with the surroundings, i.e., **metabolism**, with one kind of living species subject only to development, form and **metabolism**, while another kind additionally **move purposefully**, The first we call **plants**, the second **animals**. Animals, consistent with the principle of causality, must possess **sensory organs**, a **motion apparatus**, and **instincts, feelings, promptings** so that what has been sensed, may be responded to [through motion]. The **purpose-directness** of animals must be built into the animals. Biology shows that that is the case. The animal genomes appear to serve the **purpose-directness** of animals. [369, pp 178] "Biology shows that it is so; transcendental deduction that it must be so."

2.3.2 Awareness, Learning and Language

[369, pp 180] "Animals, to **learn** from **experience**, must be able to feel **inclination** and **disinclination**, and must be able to remember that it has acted in some way leading to either the feeling of inclination or disinclination. As a consequence, an animal, if when acting in response to sense impression, ι, experiences the positive feeling of inclination (desire), then it will respond likewise when again receiving sense impression ι, until it is no longer so inclined. If, in contrast, the animal feels the negative feeling of disinclination (dislike), upon sense impression ι, then it will avoid responding in this manner when receiving sense impression ι." [369, pp 181] "Awareness is built up from the sense impressions and feelings on the basis of, i.e., from what the individual animal has learned. Different animals can be expected to have different levels of consciousness; and different levels of consciousness assume different biological bases for learning. This is possible, biology tells us, because of there being a central nervous system with building blocks, the neurons, having an inner determination for learning and consciousness." [369, pp 181–182] "In the mutual interaction between animals of a higher order of consciousness these animals learn to use **signs** developing increasingly complex sign systems, eventually "arriving" at **languages**." It is thus we single out **humans**. [369, pp 183] "Any human language which can describe reality, must assume the full set of concepts that are prerequisites for any world description."

2.4 Philosophy, Science and the Arts

We quote extensively from [367, Kai Sørlander, 1997].
  [367, pp 178]   "Philosophy, science and the arts are products of the human mind."
  [367, pp 179]   "Philosophy, science and the arts each have their own goals."

- **Philosophers** seek to find the inescapable characteristics of any world.
- **Scientists** seek to determine how the world actually, really is, and our situation in that world.
- **Artists** seek to create objects for experience.

 We shall elaborate. [367, pp 180]   "Simplifying, but not without an element of truth, we can relate the three concepts by the **modalities:**"

- *philosophy is the* **necessary**,
- *science is the* **real**, and
- *art is the* **possible**.

... Here we have, then, a distinction between philosophy and science. ... From [366] we can conclude the following about the results of philosophy and science. These results must be consistent [with one another]. This is a necessary condition for their being *correct*. ... ...
The **real** must be a *concrete realisation* of the **necessary**.

Chapter 3
SPACE, TIME and MATTER

*From Kai Sørlander's Philosophy we can, by logical reasoning, infer **space** and **time** as facts. We do not have to presume them, as did Immanuel Kant. In this chapter we shall examine the concepts of space and time, as already introduced in the previous chapter, and introduce the concept of **matter** as more-or-less ex/implicitly referred to also in Kai Sørlander's Philosophy.*

In addition to the space, time and matter issues we also, ever so briefly, introduce the concepts of **logic, mathematics, identity,** and **mereology**.

3.1 Prologue

There are three main elements of this chapter. They are (i) An introduction to notions of **logic** and **mathematics**, Sects. **3.2–3.3**. (ii) The main elements on **space, time** and **matter**, Sects. **3.4–3.7**. They were already introduced in Chapter 2. In the first two of these we shall make use of notions of mathematical logic introduced earlier. (iii) Finally a cursory, i.e., an initial view of the notions of **identity** and **mereology** – also already introduced in that chapter, Chapter 2. Identity and mereology will be core *internal qualities* of endurants – and dealt with in Sects. **5.2** and **5.3**. Mereology will be further treated in Appendix **B**.

Space can be logically reasoned to exist. So can time. Matter is implicit in Kai Sørlander's Philosophy – in that the properties that can be expressed about entities include properties that, by transcendental deduction, entail matter: that which one can see and touch and those which can be [otherwise] "measured", that is, that exist in space and satisfy laws of nature.

3.2 Logic

Definition: 7 Logic: By **logic** we shall here mean: the kind of reasoning that was shown in Chapter 2. It was based on *the possibility of truth,* and hence on *the necessity of negation,* from which was derived the logic operators *conjunction* and *disjunction* and, subsequently, as a result of *the necessity of existence, identity* and *multiplicity* of entities, the *equality* operator.

In this monograph we are indeed very much concerned with the logic of domains.

© The Author(s), under exclusive license to Springer Nature Switzerland AG 2021
D. Bjørner, *Domain Science and Engineering*, Monographs in Theoretical Computer Science. An EATCS Series,
https://doi.org/10.1007/978-3-030-73484-8_3

Philosophical logic is the branch of study that concerns questions about reference, predication, identity, truth, quantification, existence, entailment, modality, and necessity. Philosophical logic is includes the application of formal logical techniques to philosophical problems.

3.3 Mathematics

Mathematics has no generally accepted definition[18].

By **mathematics** we shall here, *operationally*[19] mean the study and knowledge of algebra, calculus, combinatorics, geometry, graph theory, logic, whence **mathematical logic**, number theory, probability, set theory, statistics et cetera – alphabetically listed !

3.3.1 Mathematical Logic

Definition: 8 Mathematical Logic: By **mathematical logic** we shall here mean: the study and knowledge of set theory, propositions, predicates, first-order logic, definability, model theory, proof theory and recursion theory – more-or-less arbitrarily listed !

Some basic notions of mathematical logic are: **truth values: true, false, chaos**[20], **~true, ~false, true∧false, ~true∧false, ...: ground terms:** ~a, a∧b, a∨b, a⇒b, a=b, a≠b, a≡b (variables a, b, ... to range over truth values), **propositions: true, false, ~true, ~false, true∧false, ~true∧false, ...**, a, b, ..., a∧true, a∧b, ...; and **predicates: true, false, ~true, ~false, true∧false, ~true∧false, ...**, a, b, ..., a∧true, a∧b, ..., ∀x:X•true, ∀x:X•x∧..., ∃x:X•x∧ ...

Three cornerstones of mathematical logic are: *inference rules, axiom systems* and *proofs*.

Definition: 9 Inference Rules: An *inference rule* consists of a list of one or more *premises* (predicates) and a *conclusion* (also a logical term):

$$p_1, p_2, ..., p_n \vdash c.$$

This expression states that whenever in the course of some logical derivation the given premises, $(p_1, p_2, ..., p_n)$, have been obtained, the specified conclusion, c, can be taken for granted as well ∎

Definition: 10 Axioms and Axiom System: An *axiom* (or a *postulate*) is a statement that is taken to be true, to serve as a premise or starting point for further reasoning and arguments ∎

An *axiom system* is a set of one or more axioms ∎

---

[18] Mathematics is what mathematicians do !

[19] – that is, in terms of the names of fields of mathematics

[20] Yes, our notations, both the mathematical and RSL, have a three-valued logic where evaluation of a Boolean expression involving **chaos** leads to everything being undefined !

We illustrate some axiom systems. *Metric Space*, Axiom System 1 on page 28; J. van Benthem's *A Continuum Theory of Time*, Axiom System 2 on page 31; and Wayne D. Blizard's *A Theory of Time-Space*, Axiom System 3 on page 32. These are brought, not because we shall actually 'use' them, but to illustrate what axiom systems are.

Definition: 11 Proof: Proof, in logic, is an argument that establishes the validity of a proposition, p. The argument usually requires a sequence of proof steps, i, each, usually, refers to the steps in the argument that represents the premises, a proof rule, and the conclusion, c, which becomes a new step ∎

Some related concepts of mathematical logic in software engineering are: *interpretation, satisfiability, validity* and *model.*

Definition: 12 Interpretation: By an interpretation of a predicate we mean an assignment of a truth value to a predicate where the assignment may entail an assignment of values, in general, to the terms of the predicate ∎

Definition: 13 Satisfiability: By the satisfiability of a predicate we mean that the predicate is true for some interpretation ∎

Definition: 14 Validity: By the validity of a predicate we mean that the predicate is true for all interpretations ∎

Definition: 15 Model: By a model of a predicate (an axiom system) we mean an interpretation for which the predicate (of the axiom system) holds ∎

3.3.2 Sets

Sørlander argues that sets, that is, collections of zero, one or more endurants, are an inescapable consequence of any world. From the basic philosophy aspects of sets mathematicians can then develop further aspects.

Set theory is a branch of mathematical logic that studies sets, which informally are collections of objects. Although any type of object can be collected into a set, set theory is applied most often to objects that are relevant to mathematics [Wikipedia]. We shall make extensive use of the Zermelo-Fraenkel [165] version (1908, 1921) of set theory[21]. Set theory, as we now know it, was founded by Gottlob Frege [166, *"Begriffsschrift"*] (see also [376, van Heijenoort 1967, pp. 5–82]), and Georg Cantor [118, *Über unendliche, linear Punktmannichfaltigkeiten*].

---

[21] en.wikipedia.org/wiki/Zermelo-Fraenkel_set_theory

3.3.3 Types

Definition: 16 Type: By a *type* [as a noun] we shall mean a possibly infinite set of values[22] of some kind.

The 'kind' is what determines the type. The type of natural numbers, including the number 0, we give the name **Nat**; the integer type is named **Intg**; the type of real numbers is named **Real**. The type of truth values, Booleans, is named **Bool**.

When defining types, which we shall very often need to do, we shall make use of the RAISE Specification Language (RSL)'s type definition concept. We refer to Appendix Sect. **D.1** on page 369.

We shall often use the term 'type' in the specific sense of there being a model for values of the type in the form of either the basic, atomic types given above, or in the form of

- mathematical sets, A-**set**, A-**infset**[23],
- Cartesian products, $A \times B \times \cdots \times C$[24],
- sequences, A^*, A^{ω}[25],
- maps, $A \underset{m}{\rightarrow} B$[26], and
- functions, $A \rightarrow B$ or $A \overset{\sim}{\rightarrow} B$[27],

over basic or mathematical values, i.e., types A, B, C, etc.

We use the RSL type definition approach. T stands for types. S stands for sorts. Q stands for further undefined atomic values. Recursively defined map and function types are not allowed.

$$
\begin{aligned}
\text{T} ::= &\ \textbf{Bool} \mid \textbf{Nat} \mid \text{Intg} \mid \textbf{Real} \mid \text{Q} \mid \text{S} \\
&\mid \text{T-set} \mid \text{T-infset} && \text{[finite, respectively possibly infinite sets]} \\
&\mid \text{T} \times \text{T} \times ... \times \text{T} && \text{[Cartesians]} \\
&\mid \text{T}^* \mid \text{T}^{\omega} && \text{[finite, respectively possibly infinite lists]} \\
&\mid \text{T} \underset{m}{\rightarrow} \text{T} \mid \text{T} \underset{m}{\leftrightarrow} \text{T} && \text{[maps, respectively bijective maps]} \\
&\mid \text{T} \rightarrow \text{T} \mid \text{T} \overset{\sim}{\rightarrow} \text{T} && \text{[total, respectively partial functions]}
\end{aligned}
$$

Definition: 17 Sort: We shall use the term 'sort' to designate a possibly infinite set of values of some further undefined kind.

The term 'sort' is commonly used in algebraic semantics [355].

---

[22] We shall take a classical set-theoretic, i.e., Zermelo-Fraenkel [165], view of types and sort in this monograph.

[23] finite sets can be enumerated: $\{a_1, a_2, ..., a_n\}$. Operators are $\in, \cup, \cap, \subseteq, \subset, \notin$, **card**inality, etc.

[24] Cartesians are expressed as $(a, b, ..., c)$.

[25] finite sequences can be enumerated: $\langle a_1, a_2, ..., a_n \rangle$. Operators are **hd** (head), **tl** (tail), **length**, $\frown$, [i], **elems**, etc.

[26] finite maps can be enumerated: $[a_1 \mapsto b_1, a_2 \mapsto b_2, ..., a_n \mapsto b_n]$. Operators are: $\cdot$ ($m(a)$), **dom**ain, **rng** (range), etc.

[27] Functions are defined: $\lambda x \bullet \mathcal{E}(x)$, see Example 3 on the facing page.

3.3.4 Functions

Definition: 18 Function: By a function we shall understand 'something', which when *applied* to an *argument* value of some type, say A, yields a *result* value of some type, say B (where A and B may be the same type).

Definition: 19 Signature: By the signature of a function we mean a quadruple: (i) the, or a, name of the function, (ii) either the total function designator, $\rightarrow$, or the partial function designator, $\tilde{\rightarrow}$, (iii) the type of its argument value(s), and (iv) the type of its result value.

Let the name of (i, iii, iv) be f, A and B, respectively, then we present the signature of the total and the partial functions f as follows:

    value f: $A \rightarrow B$ **value** f: $A \tilde{\rightarrow} B$

Example 3 A Classical Function Definition A classical function is the *factorial* function. It can, for example, be defined as follows:

    value f: **Nat** $\rightarrow$ **Nat**, f(n) $\equiv$ **if** n $\equiv$ 0 **then** 1 **else** n×f(n−1) **end**

3.3.4.1 Total and Partial Functions

Definition: 20 Total Function: By a total function we mean a function which is defined for all arguments of its argument type.

Definition: 21 Partial Function: By a partial function we mean a function which is not defined for all the values of its argument type.

3.3.4.2 Predicate Functions

Definition: 22 Predicate: By a predicate we mean a function whose result type is Boolean, i.e., **Bool**.

Predicates are, by necessity, total functions.

• • •

We have listed a number of concepts of mathematical logic. Several of these have related to the possibility of proofs. But *alas !* In this monograph we shall use the notation of mathematical logic extensively. But not for proofs of properties neither of our descriptions nor of domains. We shall leave the ultimately desirable goal of formulating such properties: invariants and laws, and of their proofs to follow on the heals of this monograph. Before we can run we must learn to walk.

3.3.5 Mathematical Notation versus Formal Specification Languages

3.3.5.1 Mathematics as a Notation – in General

We shall primarily make use of mathematics as a precise notation in which to express ideas about and the prompt calculi — including some, usually not computable, functions. That is: we shall not use mathematics to develop a proper theory of domain analysis & description. For that we refer to [65, *Domain Analysis: Endurants – An Analysis & Description Process Model, 2014*]. We have indicated issues of axiom systems, and we shall illustrate three axiom systems in this chapter: an *Axiom System for Metric Spaces*, Sect. **3.4.5** on page 27; J. van Benthem's *A Continuum Theory of Time*, Sect. **3.5.4** on page 31; and Wayne D. Blizard's *A Theory of Time Space*, Sect. **3.5.5** on page 32.

3.3.5.2 Mathematics as a Notation – in Specific

In many of the more than 100 examples, cf. appendix Sect. **E.3** on page 395 [an index of all examples], those that illustrate formalisation of domains, we use RSL [187], the RAISE Specification Language [190]. But almost elsewhere in the text, in particular in Chapters 4–7, we use a mathematical notation. We comment here on that notation.

Mathematics "as our notation" reflects that the mathematics we rely upon is what is often referred to as *discrete mathematics* [370, 147, 331, 259, 258, 146, 324, 9]. By *discrete mathematics* we mean such mathematics, whose disciplines rests *set theory* and *mathematical logic*, entails important constructive mathematical structures as

- [i] **sets**, i.e., definite or indefinite collections of mathematical values, {a,b,...,c}, respectively {a,b,...} (where the ..., see below, indicates "and so forth, possibly "ad infinitum"");
- [ii] **Cartesians**, i.e., definite groupings, (a,b,...c), of mathematical values;
- [iii] **lists**, i.e., definite or indefinite sequences of mathematical values, ⟨a,b,...,c⟩, respectively ⟨a,b,...⟩;
- [iv] **maps**, e.g., m, i.e., explicitly enumerated functions, [a1↦b1, a2↦b2, ..., an↦bn], from finite definition sets, **dom** m = {a1,a2,...,an}, to finite range, or co-domain sets, **rng** m = {b1,b2,...,bn}, of mathematical values; and
- [v] **functions**, i.e., *lambda-definable* [132, 106, 17, 18, 19] function values: $\lambda x.\mathcal{E}(x)$ where x is an arbitrary free identifier and $\mathcal{E}(x)$ is an arbitrary expression in which x occurs, usually free – the expressions $\mathcal{E}(x)$ otherwise over the kind of values listed above and including respective operators.

The mathematical values include *ground* values of

- *Booleans*, **false, true, chaos : Bool**;
- *natural numbers*, 0, 1, 2, ... : **Nat**;
- *integers*, ..., -2 -1, 0, 1, 2, ... : **Intg**; and
- *reals*, ..., -3.14159265359..., -0.5, ..., 0 ..., 1, +2.71828182846..., ... : **Real**.

The mathematical values finally include such which are defined through a **type definition** system "inherited" from RSL. In general our mathematical notation includes many of the clause structures of RSL, structures also found in VDM SL [33, 163, 164], its predecessor, as well as in many programming languages since Algol 60 [269][28] We refer to Appendix Sect. **D** for details. Example clause structures are:

---

[28] Algol W [391], CPL [20], PL/1 [293], Algol 68 [32, 112, 23], Pascal [267, 392], Modula [393, 310], Oberon [394, 395, 396], Ada [34], CHILL [123, 113, 10], Java [196, 359], C # [244], etc.

- var := clause,
- if b then c else a end,
- case p of e1→c1, ..., en→cn end,
- (p1→c1, ..., pn→cn) or (p1→c1, ..., _→cn),
- for ∀ e:E · e ∈ set do c(e) end,
- while e do c end,
- do c while e end,
- c1; ...; cn and
- skip.

That is commensurate with the fact the the formal specification languages, VDM SL [92, 93, 164] and RSL [187], (whose development and initial use, this author has been and is actively involved in since their inception) deeply reflects a *discrete mathematics*.

⋆ The Dot-dot-dot Notation

It is very common, also in strict, "formalistic" mathematics papers to use an inductive form of dot notation: .... Our mathematics notation deploys that good practice. As an interesting paper we refer to [7, *Deductive Synthesis of Dot Expressions*].

⋆ The Quote Notation

Here comes an interesting "twist" to our mathematical notation. We refer to the use of **quotes** By **quoting** an expression, say the expression **if** b **then** c **else** a **end**, that is, by writing **❝ if** b **then** c **else** a **end ❞** we mean, not the valuation of the unquoted expression, but the text between the quotes; that is, we use the "bracketing" symbols **❝** ... **❞** to indicate what, ..., is quoted.

Our need for quoting is motivated as follows: The whole purpose of *domain analysis & description* is to be able to (i) logically analyse a domain and (ii) produce a textual description of that domain. It is with respect to the description procedures that there is a need for mathematically formally specify that a textual description be yielded. Hence the quotes.

So keep your mind straight when, in Chapters 4–7 we "switch" between mathematical notation's use of quotes with RSL-like expressions and "clean" RSL with no [need for] quotes.

Historically the use of quoting can be attributed to John McCarthy [294, 295, 296, 1960s][29] and is manifest in Lisp [297]. Lisp's use of quotes is explained and discussed by *Mc Bain* in milesmcbain.xyz/the-roots-of-quotation, in en.m.wikipedia.org/wiki/M-expression [Wikipedia], stackoverflow.com/questions/134887/when-to-use-or-quote--in-lisp and gnu.org/software/emacs/manual/html_node/elisp/Quoting.html.

3.3.5.3 An Interplay between Mathematical Notation and Specification Languages

Thus this monograph illustrates a common phenomenon: that research-in-progress, into computing science, sometimes, as here, starts with, as here, domain analysis & description ideas, proceeds with these, making use of mathematical notation, gradually introducing more formal specification language-like notation, while eventually, and thus, as here, implicitly, evolving what looks like a full, formal specification language. We have not found the need, here, to design such a proper *domain analyser & describer* language. Mathematical notation has no formal syntax and no formal semantics. So, for the time being, "RSL", and as we shall later introduce, RSL⁺, has no formal syntax and no formal semantics. We leave that to interested readers!

---

[29] John McCarthy: www-formal.stanford.edu/jmc/recursive.pdf
Paul Graham: www.paulgraham.com/rootsoflisp.html
Paul Graham: sep.yimg.com/ty/cdn/paulgraham/jmc.ps?t=1564708198&

3.4 Space

Mathematicians and physicists model space in, for example, the form of Hausdorff (or topo-logical) space[30]; or a metric space which is a set for which distances between all members of the set are defined; Those distances, taken together, are called a metric on the set; a metric on a space induces topological properties like open and closed sets, which lead to the study of more abstract topological spaces; or Euclidean space, due to *Euclid of Alexandria*.

3.4.1 Space Motivated Philosophically

Definition: 23 Indefinite Space: We motivate the concept of indefinite space as follows: [369, pp 154] "The two relations *asymmetric* and *symmetric*, by a transcendental deduction, can be given an interpretation: The relation (spatial) *direction* is asymmetric; and the relation (spatial) *distance* is symmetric. Direction and distance can be understood as spatial rela-tions. From these relations are derived the relation *in-between*. Hence we must conclude that *primary entities exist in space. Space* is therefore an unavoidable characteristic of any possible world" ∎

From the direction and distance relations one can derive *Euclidean Geometry*.

Definition: 24 Definite Space: By a *definite space* we shall understand a space with a definite metric ∎

There is but just one space. It is all around us, from the inner earth to the farthest galaxy. It is not manifest. We can not observe it as we observe a road or a human.

3.4.2 The Spatial Value

58 There is an abstract notion of (definite) $\mathbb{SPACE}$(s) of further unanalysable points; and
59 there is a notion of $\mathbb{POINT}$ in $\mathbb{SPACE}$.

type
58 $\mathbb{SPACE}$
59 $\mathbb{POINT}$

Space is not an attribute of endurants. Space is just there. So we do not define an observer, **observe_space**. For us, bound to model mostly artifactual worlds on this earth there is but one space. Although $\mathbb{SPACE}$, as a type, could be thought of as defining more than one space we shall consider these isomorphic!

---

[30] Armstrong, M. A. (1983) [1979]. Basic Topology. Undergraduate Texts in Mathematics. Springer. ISBN 0-387-90839-0.

3.4.3 Spatial Observers

60 A point observer, observe_POINT, is a function which applies to endurants, e, and yield a point, ℓ : POINT.

value
60   observe_POINT: E → POINT

3.4.4 Spatial Attributes

We suggest, besides POINTs, the following spatial attribute possibilities:

61 EXTENT as a dense set of POINTs;
62 Volume, of concrete type, for example, m^3, as the "volume" of an EXTENT such that
63 SURFACEs as dense sets of POINTs have no volume, but an
64 Area, of concrete type, for example, m^2, as the "area" of a dense set of POINTs;
65 LINE as dense set of POINTs with no volume and no area, but
66 Length, of concrete type, for example, m.

For these we have that

67 the *intersection*, ∩, of two EXTENTs is an EXTENT of possibly nil Volume,
68 the intersection, ∩, of two SURFACEs may be either a possibly nil SURFACE or a possibly nil LINE, or a combination of these.
69 the intersection, ∩, of two LINEs may be either a possibly nil LINE or a POINT.

Similarly we can define

70 the *union*, ∪, of two not-disjoint EXTENTs,
71 the *union*, ∪, of two not-disjoint SURFACEs,
72 the *union*, ∪, and of two not-disjoint LINEs.

and:

73 the *[in]equality*, ≠, =, of pairs of EXTENT, pairs of SURFACEs, and pairs of LINEs.

We invite the reader to first first express the signatures for these operations, then their preconditions, and finally, being courageous, appropriate fragments of axiom systems.

3.4.5 Mathematical Models of Space

Figure 3.1 on the next page diagrams some mathematical models of space. We shall hint[31] at just one of these spaces.

---

[31] Figure 3.1 on the following page is taken from https://en.wikipedia.org/wiki/Space_(mathematics).

3.4.5.1 Metric Spaces

──────────────────────────── **Metric Space** ────────────────────────────

Axiom System 1

A metric space is an ordered pair (M,d) where M is a set and d is a metric on M, i.e., a function:

$$d : M{\times}M \to \textbf{Real}$$

such that for any $x,y,z \in M$, the following holds:

$$d(x,y) = 0 \equiv x = y \quad \text{identity of indiscernibles} \tag{3.1}$$

$$d(x,y) = d(y,x) \quad \text{symmetry} \tag{3.2}$$

$$d(x,z) \le d(x,y) + d(y,z) \quad \text{sub-additivity or triangle inequality} \tag{3.3}$$

Given the above three axioms, we also have that $d(x,y) \ge 0$ for any $x,y \in M$. This is deduced as follows:

$$d(x,y) + d(y,x) \ge d(x,x) \quad \text{triangle inequality} \tag{3.4}$$

$$d(x,y) + d(y,x) \ge d(x,x) \quad \text{by symmetry} \tag{3.5}$$

$$2d(x,y) \ge 0 \quad \text{identity of indiscernibles} \tag{3.6}$$

$$d(x,y) \ge 0 \quad \text{non-negativity} \tag{3.7}$$

The function d is also called distance function or simply distance. Often, d is omitted and one just writes M for a metric space if it is clear from the context what metric is used.

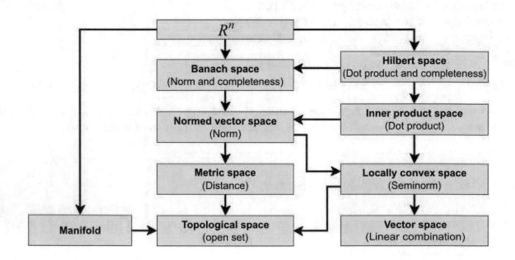

Fig. 3.1 Variety of Abstract Spaces. An arrow from space A to space B implies that A is also a kind of B.

3.5 Time

a moving image of eternity;
the number of the movement in respect of the before and the after;
the life of the soul in movement as it passes
from one stage of act or experience to another;
a present of things past: memory,
a present of things present: sight,
and a present of things future: expectations[32]

This thing all things devours:
Birds, beasts, trees, flowers;
Gnaws iron, bites steel,
Grinds hard stones to meal;
Slays king, ruins town,
And beats high mountain down.[33]

Concepts of time continue to fascinate philosophers and scientists
[374, 161, 299, 333, 334, 335, 336, 337, 338, 339, 350] and [167].

3.5.1 Time Motivated Philosophically

Definition: 25 Indefinite Time: *We motivate the abstract notion of time as follows.* [369, pp 159] "Two different states must necessarily be ascribed different incompatible predicates. But how can we ensure so? Only if states stand in an asymmetric relation to one another. This state relation is also transitive. So that is an indispensable property of any world. By a transcendental deduction we say that *primary entities exist in time. So every possible world must exist in time*" ∎

Definition: 26 Definite Time: By a ***definite time*** we shall understand an abstract representation of time such as for example year, month, day, hour, minute, second, et cetera ∎

Temporal Notions of Endurants

Example 4 *By temporal notions of endurants we mean time properties of endurants, usually modelled as attributes. Examples are: (i) the time stamped link traffic, cf. Item 192 on page 125 and (ii) the time stamped hub traffic, cf. Item 188 on page 124.*

---

[32] Quoted from [14, Cambridge Dictionary of Philosophy]
[33] J.R.R. Tolkien, The Hobbit

3.5.2 Time Values

We shall not be concerned with any representation of time. That is, we leave it to the domain analyser cum describer to choose an own representation [167]. Similarly we shall not be concerned with any representation of time intervals.[34]

74 So there is an abstract type T*ime*,
75 and an abstract type TI: T*ime*I*nterval*.
76 There is no T*ime* origin, but there is a "zero" TIme interval.
77 One can add (subtract) a time interval to (from) a time and obtain a time.
78 One can add and subtract two time intervals and obtain a time interval – with subtraction respecting that the subtrahend is smaller than or equal to the minuend.
79 One can subtract a time from another time obtaining a time interval respecting that the subtrahend is smaller than or equal to the minuend.
80 One can multiply a time interval with a real and obtain a time interval.
81 One can compare two times and two time intervals.

type
74 T
75 TI
value
76 **0**:TI
77 +,−: $T \times TI \to T$

78 +,−: $TI \times TI \xrightarrow{\sim} TI$
79 −: $T \times T \to TI$
80 ∗: $TI \times \textbf{Real} \to TI$
81 $<,\le,=,\ne,\ge,>$: $T \times T \to \textbf{Bool}$
81 $<,\le,=,\ne,\ge,>$: $TI \times TI \to \textbf{Bool}$
axiom
77 $\forall$ t:T · t+**0** = t

3.5.3 Temporal Observers

82 We define the signature of the meta-physical time observer.

type
82 T
value
82 **record_**TIME(): **Unit** $\to$ T

The time recorder applies to nothing and yields a time. **record_**TIME() can only occur in action, event and behavioural descriptions.

•••

Caveat: You may wish to skip the rest of this chapter's many sections, i.e., Sects. **3.5.4–3.5.10**, on time. That may come as a surprise to you. But in our domain modelling we shall refrain from modelling temporal aspects of domains! So why bring all this material? We bring ("all") this material so that you will know what you are missing! That is, what should also be considered in domain modelling. We therefore leave it to others[35] to redress this omission. Besides, most of the present work on applying temporal logics in our field has been to software design (requirements).

---

[34] – but point out, that although a definite time interval may be referred to by number of years, number of days (less than 365), number of hours (less than 24), number of minutes (less than 60) number of seconds (less than 60), et cetera, this is not a time, but a time interval.

[35] – that is: other researchers, lecturers, textbooks

• • •

Modern models of time, by mathematicians and physicists evolve around spacetime[36] We shall not be concerned with this notion of time.

Models of time related to computing differs from those of mathematicians and physicists in focusing on divergence and convergence, zero (Zenon) time and interleaving time [401] are relevant in studies of real-time, typically distributed computing systems. We shall also not be concerned with this notion of time.

3.5.4 J. van Benthem

The following is taken from Johan van Benthem [374]: Let P be a point structure (for example, a set). Think of time as a continuum; the following axioms characterise ordering ($<$, $=$, $>$) relations between (i.e., aspects of) time points. The axioms listed below are not thought of as an axiom system, that is, as a set of independent axioms all claimed to hold for the time concept, which we are encircling. Instead van Benthem offers the individual axioms as possible "blocks" from which we can then "build" our own time system — one that suits the application at hand, while also fitting our intuition. Time is transitive: If $p<p'$ and $p'<p''$ then $p<p''$. Time may not loop, that is, is not reflexive: $p \not< p$. Linear time can be defined: Either one time comes before, or is equal to, or comes after another time. Time can be left-linear, i.e., linear "to the left" of a given time. One could designate a time axis as beginning at some time, that is, having no predecessor times. And one can designate a time axis as ending at some time, that is, having no successor times. General, past and future successors (predecessors, respectively successors in daily talk) can be defined. Time can be dense: Given any two times one can always find a time between them. Discrete time can be defined.

─────────────────── **A Continuum Theory of Time** ───────────────────

Axiom System 2

[TRANS: Transitivity] $\forall$ p,p′,p″:P • p < p′ < p″ $\Rightarrow$ p < p″
[IRREF: Irreflexitivity] $\forall$ p:P • p $\not<$ p
[LIN: Linearity] $\forall$ p,p′:P • (p=p′ $\vee$ p<p′ $\vee$ p>p′)
[L–LIN: Left Linearity]
   $\forall$ p,p′,p″:P • (p′<p $\wedge$ p″<p) $\Rightarrow$ (p′<p″ $\vee$ p′=p″ $\vee$ p″<p′)
[BEG: Beginning] $\exists$ p:P • ~$\exists$ p′:P • p′<p
[END: Ending] $\exists$ p:P • ~$\exists$ p′:P • p<p′
[SUCC: Successor]
  [PAST: Predecessors] $\forall$ p:P,$\exists$ p′:P • p′<p
  [FUTURE: Successor] $\forall$ p:P,$\exists$ p′:P • p<p′
[DENS: Dense] $\forall$ p,p′:P (p<p′ $\Rightarrow$ $\exists$ p″:P • p<p″<p′)
[CDENS: Converse Dense] $\equiv$ [TRANS: Transitivity]
   $\forall$ p,p′:P ($\exists$ p″:P • p<p″<p′ $\Rightarrow$ p<p′)
[DISC: Discrete]
   $\forall$ p,p′:P • (p<p′ $\Rightarrow$ $\exists$ p″:P • (p<p″ $\wedge$ ~$\exists$ p‴:P • (p<p‴<p″))) $\wedge$
   $\forall$ p,p′:P • (p<p′ $\Rightarrow$ $\exists$ p″:P • (p″<p′ $\wedge$ ~$\exists$ p‴:P • (p″<p‴<p′)))

---

[36] The concept of **Spacetime** was first "announced" by Hermann Minkowski, 1907–08 – based on work by Henri Poincaré, 1905–06, https://en.wikisource.org/wiki/Translation: The_Fundamental_Equations_for_Electromagnetic_Processes_in_Moving_Bodies

A strict partial order, SPO, is a point structure satisfying TRANS and IRREF. TRANS, IRREF and SUCC imply infinite models. TRANS and SUCC may have finite, "looping time" models.

3.5.5 Wayne D. Blizard: A Theory of Time–Space

We shall present an axiom system [105, Wayne D. Blizard, 1980] which relate abstracted entities to spatial points and time. Let $A, B, \ldots$ stand for entitites, $p, q, \ldots$ for spatial points, and t, τ for times. 0 designates a first, a begin time. Let t' stand for the discrete time successor of time t. Let $N(p,q)$ express that p and q are spatial neighbours. Let = be an overloaded equality operator applicable, pairwise to entities, spatial locations and times, respectively. A_p^t expresses that entity A is at location p at time t. The axioms — where we omit (obvious) typings (of A, B, P, Q, and T): ' designates the time successsor function: t'.

A Theory of Time–Space

Axiom System 3

(I)	$\forall A \forall t \exists p : A_p^t$	
(II)	$(A_p^t \wedge A_q^t) \supset p = q$	
(III)	$(A_p^t \wedge B_p^t) \supset A = B$	
(IV)(?)	$(A_p^t \wedge A_p^{t'}) \supset t = t'$	
(V i)	$\forall p, q : N(p,q) \supset p \neq q$	Irreflexivity
(V ii)	$\forall p, q : N(p,q) = N(q,p)$	Symmetry
(V iii)	$\forall p \exists q, r : N(p,q) \wedge N(p,r) \wedge q \neq r$	No isolated locations
(VI i)	$\forall t : t \neq t'$	
(VI ii)	$\forall t : t' \neq 0$	
(VI iii)	$\forall t : t \neq 0 \supset \exists \tau : t = \tau'$	
(VI iv)	$\forall t, \tau : \tau' = t' \supset \tau = t$	
(VII)	$A_p^t \wedge A_q^{t'} \supset N(p,q)$	
(VIII)	$A_p^t \wedge B_q^t \wedge N(p,q) \supset \sim (A_q^{t'} \wedge B_p^{t'})$	

(II–IV,VII–VIII):   The axioms are universally 'closed'; that is: We have omitted the usual $\forall A, B, p, q, t$s.

(I):   For every entity, A, and every time, t, there is a location, p, at which A is located at time t.

(II):   An entity cannot be in two locations at the same time.

(III):   Two distinct entities cannot be at the same location at the same time.

(IV):   Entities always move: An entity cannot be at the same location at different times. *This is more like a conjecture: Could be questioned.*

(V):   These three axioms define N.

(V i):   Same as $\forall p :\sim N(p,p)$. "Being a neighbour of", is the same as "being distinct from".

(V ii):   If p is a neighbour of q, then q is a neighbour of p.

(V iii):   Every location has at least two distinct neighbours.

(VI):   The next four axioms determine the time successor function '.

(VI i):   A time is always distinct from its successor: time cannot rest. There are no time fix points.

(VI ii):   Any time successor is distinct from the begin time. Time 0 has no predecessor.

(VI iii):   Every non–begin time has an immediate predecessor.

(VI iv):   The time successor function ' is a one–to–one (i.e., a bijection) function.

(VII):   The *continuous path axiom:* If entity A is at location p at time t, and it is at location q in the immediate next time (t'), then p and q are neighbours.

(VIII):   No *"switching":* If entities A and B occupy neighbouring locations at time t them it is not possible for A and B to have switched locations at the next time (t').

Except for Axiom (IV) the system applies both to systems of entities that "sometimes" rests, i.e., do not move. These entities are spatial and occupy at least a point in space. If some entities "occupy more" space volume than others, then we interpret, in a suitable manner, the notion of the point space P (etc.). We do not show so here.

3.5.6 "Soft" and "Hard" Real-time

We loosely identify a spectrum of from "soft" to "hard" temporalities — through some informally worded texts. On that background we can introduce the term 'real-time'. And hence distinguish between 'soft' and 'hard' real-time issues. From an example of trying to formalise these in RSL, we then set the course for this chapter.

3.5.7 Soft Temporalities

You have often wished, we assume, that *"your salary never goes down, say between your ages of 25 to 65".*

How to express that?

Taking into account other factors, you may additionally wish that *"your salary goes up."*

How do we express that?

Taking also into account that your job is a seasonal one, we may need to refine the above into *"between un-employments your salary does not go down".*

How now to express that?

3.5.8 Hard Temporalities

The above quoted ("...") statements may not have convinced you about the importance of speaking precisely about time, whether narrating or formalising.

So let's try some other examples:

"The alarm clock must sound exactly at 6 am unless someone has turned it off sometime between 5am and 6 am the same morning."

"The gas valve must be open for exactly 20 seconds every 60 seconds."

"The sum total of time periods — during which the gas valve is open and there is no flame consuming the gas — must not exceed one twentieth of the time the gas valve is open."

"The time between pressing an elevator call button on any floor and the arrival of the cage and the opening of the cage door at that floor must not exceed a given time $t_{arrival}$".

The next sections will hint at ways and means of speaking of time.

3.5.9 Soft and Hard Real-time

The informally worded temporalities of "soft real-time" can be said to involve time in a very "soft" way:

No explicit times (eg., 15:45:00), deadlines (eg., *"27'th February 2004")*, or time intervals (eg., *"within 2 hours")*, were expressed.

The informally worded temporalities of "hard real-time", in contrast, can be said to involve time in a "hard" way: Explicit times were mentioned.

For pragmatic reasons, we refer to the former examples, the former "invocations" of 'temporality', as being representative of soft real-time, whereas we say that the latter invocations are typical of hard real-time.

Please do not confuse the issue of soft versus hard real-time: It is as much hard real-time if we say that something must happen two light years and five seconds from tomorrow at noon!

Soft Real-Time Models Expressed in "Ordinary" RSL Logic

Example 5 Let us assume a salary data base SDB which at any time records your salary. In the conventional way of modelling time in RSL we assume that SDB maps time into Salary:

type
    Time, Sal
    SDB = Time $\overrightarrow{m}$ Sal
value
    hi: (Sal×Sal)|(Time×Time) → **Bool**
    eq: (Sal×Sal)|(Time×Time) → **Bool**
    lo: (Sal×Sal)|(Time×Time) → **Bool**
axiom
    $\forall$ σ:SDB,t,t':Time • {t,t'}$\subseteq$**dom**$\sigma \wedge$hi(t',t)$\Rightarrow$~lo(σ(t'),σ(t))
    $\forall$ t,t':Time •
        (hi(t',t)$\equiv$~(eq(t',t)$\vee$lo(t',t))) $\wedge$
        (lo(t',t)$\equiv$~(eq(t',t)$\vee$hi(t',t))) $\wedge$
        (eq(t',t)$\equiv$~(lo(t',t)$\vee$hi(t',t))) ... /* same for Sal */

Hard Real-Time Models Expressed in "Ordinary" RSL Logic

Example 6 To express hard real-time using just RSL we must assume a demon, a process which represents the clock:

type
    $\mathbb{T}$ = **Real**
value
    time: **Unit** → $\mathbb{T}$
    time() **as** t
axiom
    time() $\neq$ time()

The axiom is informal: It states that no two invocations of the time function yields the same value. But this is not enough. We need to express that "immediately consecutive" invocations of the time function yields "adjacent" time points. $\mathbb{T}$ provides a linear model of real-time.
variable

```
    t1,t2 : 𝕋
axiom
    □ (t1 := time();
        t2 := time();
        t2 − t1 = /* infinitesimally small time interval: 𝕋𝕀*/ ∧
        t2 > t1 ∧ ~∃ t:𝕋· t1 < t < t2 )
```

𝕋𝕀 provides a linear model of intervals of real-time.[37] The □ operator is here the "standard" RSL modal operator over states: Let P be a predicate involving globally declared variables. Then □P asserts that P holds in any state (of these variables). But even this is not enough. Much more is needed.

3.5.10 Temporal Logics

"The term Temporal Logic has been broadly used to cover all approaches to the representation of temporal information within a logical framework, and also more narrowly to refer specifically to the modal-logic type of approach introduced around 1960 by Arthur Prior under the name of Tense Logic and subsequently developed further by logicians and computer scientists."[38]

"Applications of Temporal Logic include its use as a formalism for clarifying philosophical issues about time, as a framework within which to define the semantics of temporal expressions in natural language, as a language for encoding temporal knowledge in artificial intelligence, and as a tool for handling the temporal aspects of the execution of computer programs."

3.5.10.1 The Issues

The basic issue is simple: To be able to speak of temporal phenomena without having to explicitly mentioning time. That goes for vague, or "soft" notions of time: What we could call "soft real-time", that something happens at a time, or during a time interval, but with no "fixing" of absolute times nor time intervals. It also, of course, goes for precise, or "hard" notions of time: What we could call "hard real-time", that something happens at a very definitive point in time, or during a time interval of a very specific length, and thus with "fixing" of absolute times or time intervals.

3.5.10.2 A. N. Prior's Tense Logics

We present a philosophical linguistics motivated temporal logic. Following the Stanford Encyclopedia of Philosophy,[39] Arthur Prior [337, 338, 339] developed a *tense logic* along the lines presented below:

---

[37] Of course, we really do not need make a distinction between 𝕋 and 𝕋𝕀, The former tries to model a real-time since time immemorial, i.e., the creation of the universe. If we always work with a time axis from "that started recently", i.e., a relative one, then we can "collapse" 𝕋 and 𝕋𝕀 into just 𝕋.

[38] This and the next slanted quoted text paragraphs are taken from http://plato.stanford.edu/entries/-logic-temporal/.

[39] http://plato.stanford.edu/entries/prior/

- Pp: "It has at some time been the case that p held"
- Fp: "It will at some time be the case that p holds"
- Hp: "It has always been the case that p held"
- Gp: "It will always be the case that p holds"

P and F are known as the weak tense operators, while H and G are known as the strong tense operators. The two pairs are generally regarded as inter-definable by way of the equivalences:

$$P p \equiv \sim H(\sim p)$$
$$F p \equiv \sim G(\sim p)$$

On the basis of these intended meanings, Prior used the operators to build formulas expressing various philosophical theses about time, which might be taken as axioms of a formal system if so desired. Some examples of such formulas, with Prior's own glosses (from [338]), are:

Gp⇒Fp:
    What will always be, will be
G(p⇒q)⇒(Gp⇒Gq)
    If p will always imply q, then if p will always be the case, so will q
Fp⇒FFp
    If it will be the case that p, it will be – in between – that it will be
~Fp⇒F~Fp
    If it will never be that p then it will be that it will never be that p

A special temporal logic is the Minimal Tense Logic Kt. It is generated by the four axioms:

p⇒HFp
    What is, has always been going to be
p⇒GPp
    What is, will always have been
H(p⇒q)⇒(Hp⇒Hq)
    Whatever always follows from what always has been, always has been
G(p⇒q)⇒(Gp⇒Gq)
    Whatever always follows from what always will be, always will be

3.5.10.3 The Duration Calculus

The *duration calculus*, DC, is due to *Zhou Chao Chen, C.A.R. Hoare, Anders P. Ravn, Michael Reichhardt Hansen* and others. The definitive introductory work on DC is [404]. We present a terse summary.

⋆ A Function & Safety Example

We show a classical example.

(1) For a lift system to be adequate it must always be safe and function adequately. There are three functional requirements.

(2) For the lift system to be safe, then for any duration that the door on floor i is open, the lift must be also at that floor.

(3) The length of time between when someone pushes a button, inside a lift cage, to send it to floor i, and the arrival of that cage at floor i must be less than some time t_s.

(4) The length of time between when someone pushes a button, at floor i, to call it to that floor, and the arrival of a cage at that floor must be less than some time t_c.

(5) The length of time that a door is open when a cage is at floor i must be at least some time t_o.

(1) Req ≡
   □(SafetyReq ∧ FunctReq1 ∧ FunctReq2 ∧ FunctReq3)
(2) SafetyReq ≡
   ⌈door=i⌉ ⇒ ⌈floor=i⌉
(3) FunctReq1 ≡
   (⌈i ∈ send⌉ ; **true** ⇒ $\ell \leq t_s$) ∨ ($\ell \leq t_s$; ⌈door=i⌉ ; **true**)
(4) FunctReq2 ≡
   (⌈i ∈ call⌉ ; **true** ⇒ $\ell \leq t_c$) ∨ ($\ell \leq t_c$; ⌈door=i⌉ ; **true**)
(5) FunctReq3 ≡
   ⌈door≠i⌉ ; ⌈door=i⌉ ; ⌈door≠i⌉ ⇒ $\ell \geq t_o$

★ The Syntax

We only present an overview of the DC syntax. The presentation of this part follows that of Skakkebæk et al. [364] (1992).

◇ Simple Expressions:

We define simple, i.e., atomic expressions.

x,y,...,z:State_Variable
a,b,...,c:Static_Variable
ff,tt:Bool_Const
k,k',...,k'':Const

Static variables designate time-independent values. We assume some context which helps us determine the type of variables.

◇ State Expressions and Assertions:

We define state expressions and state assertions. A state assertion is a state expression of type **Bool**, and op is an operator symbol of arity n. We assume a context which helps us determine that an identifier is an op!

se:State_Expr ::= Const | Bool_Const | op(se$_1$,...,se$_n$)
P:State_Asrt ::= State_Expr

We assume a context which helps us determine that a state expression is of type **Bool**, i.e., is a state assertion.

◇ Durations and Duration Terms:

If P is a state assertion, then $\int P$ is a duration.
We define duration terms.

dt:Dur_Term ::= $\int$ P | **Real** | op(dt$_1$,...,dt$_n$) | ℓ

ℓ is an abbreviation for the duration term $\int tt$. op is an n operator symbol of type **Real.** We assume a context which helps us determine that an identifier is an op!

◇ Duration Formulas:

We define duration formulas. Let A be any n-ary predicate symbol over real-valued duration arguments. We assume a context which helps us determine that an identifier is an A!

d:Dur_Form ::= A(dt$_1$,...,dt$_n$)
            | **true** | **false** |
            | ~d$'$ | d$_1$∨d$_n$
            | d$_1$;d$_n$
            | d$_1$∧d$_n$
            | d$_1$⇒d$_n$
            | d$_1$∧d$_n$
            | ∀ a: d /∗ a is ∗/ Static_Variable

Delimiting parentheses can be inserted to clarify precedence.

◇ **Common Duration Formula Abbreviations:**

We make free use of the following common abbreviations:

⌈⌉ :	$\ell = 0$	:	point duration
⌈P⌉ :	$\int P = \ell \wedge \ell > 0$	:	almost everywhere P
◇d :	**true**;d;**true**	:	somewhere d
□d :	$\neg(\diamond\neg d)$	:	always d
$d_1 \rightarrow d_2$:	d_1;**true** $\Rightarrow d_1 \vee (d:1;d:2;$**true**$)$	:	d_2 follows d_1

Precedence Rules:

    First : ¬ □ ◇
    Second : ∨ ∧ ;
    Third : ⇒ →

⋆ **Discussion: From Domains to Designs**

We have covered core aspects of the Duration Calculus. The Duration Calculus offers a logic based on intervals and real-time. One can use the Duration Calculus to abstractly express constraints, i.e., requirements, on the duration of states. One can also use the Duration Calculus to abstractly express properties of the domain, i.e., of the application area for which software is sought. And one can finally hint at major design decisions also using the Duration Calculus.

Only in a very implicit sense can Duration Calculus expressions be said to specify sequential programs — such as we are normally prepared to implement in computing systems: in terms of sequential programs. A Duration Calculus expression, however, usually implies a sequential program, or a set of cooperating such. RSL specifications, the "closer" we get to software design, i.e., the more "concrete" such specifications become, rather specifically specify sequential programs. At least, it would be a good idea for the developer to make sure that this is so!

Now how can we combine the ability of the Duration Calculus to express quantitative properties of software (to be designed) and the actual specification of such software?

We turn to this question next. That is, we may seem to completely abandon thoughts and concepts of Duration Calculus, in favour of rather "down to earth" concepts of explicit timing in what could be considered a specification programming language, Timed RSL, TRSL.

3.6 Spatial and Temporal Modelling

It is not always that we are compelled to endow our domain descriptions with those of spatial and/or temporal properties. In our experimental domain descriptions, for example, [70, 99, 74, 72, 45, 58, 67, 39], we have either found no need to model space and/or time, or we model them explicitly, using slightly different types and observers than presented above.

We have brought this material on various temporal logics in order to strongly hint at their being used in domain modelling – so there is an interesting challenge!

3.7 Matter

Space, in the sense of $SPACE$, is "inhabited"! The inhabitants are the entities that Kai Sørlander's Philosophy refers to, Page 14. They possess properties about which we reason. We shall take the view that these entities are of $MATTER$. *Matter is anything that has mass and takes up space.*

The modelling of matters, sometimes referred to as $MATTER$, is done primarily by means of **attributes.** We refer to a future, extensive section, Sect. 5.4, on *Attributes*. But already here is a good place to discuss the 'matter' of matter! How does matter manifest itself to you, a human mortal, the *domain analyser & describer*? You, yourself, your body, is a manifestation of matter. The room, you are in, is matter. The things in it, each are matter. The outdoor environment, in which you walk, is matter. Is the air, you breathe, matter? Yes we say! Is the atmosphere[40] matter? Yes indeed. Really? Does atmosphere have mass? Yes, indeed!

There is a notion: *substance theory*[41]. We shall not discuss its possible rôle here.

3.8 Identity and Mereology

Identity, as a philosophical issue, has emerged from Kai Sørlander's Philosophy, Chapter 2. We shall make capital use of that concept in this monograph. Mereology, is a philosophy and logic issue. It was studied by Stanisław Leśniewski, a Polish philosopher/logician in the 1920s [284, 381, 365]. We shall likewise make capital use of that concept in this monograph. Section 3.8.2 next provides an informal discussion of the concept.

3.8.1 Identity

It is a fact, that is, an absolutely necessary condition for our description of any world, that its entities have unique identity. It is, however a problem in our *domain analyser & describer*, to secure such identity; so we must, wherever necessary present **axioms** expressing so. This will be done in Sect. 5.2. A further treatment of mereology, beyond the next section, is given in Appendix **B**.

3.8.2 Mereology: Philosophy and Logic

"Mereology (from the Greek $\mu\epsilon\rho o\varsigma$ 'part') is a theory of part-hood relations: of the relations of part to whole and the relations of part to part within a whole"[42].

---

[40] – the troposphere, stratosphere, ozone layer, mesosphere, thermosphere, ionosphere, exosphere, ...

[41] Substance theory, or substance-attribute theory, is an ontological theory about object-hood positing that a substance is distinct from its properties. A thing-in-itself is a property-bearer that must be distinguished from the properties it bears [Wikipedia].

[42] Achille Varzi: Mereology, http://plato.stanford.edu/entries/mereology/ 2009 and [122].

3.8.2.1 Mereology Understood Spatially

In this contribution we restrict 'parts' to be those that, firstly, are spatially distinguishable, then, secondly, while "being based" on such spatially distinguishable parts, are conceptually related. We use the term 'part' in a more general sense than in [73]. The relation: "being based", shall be made clear in this book. Accordingly two parts, p_x and p_y, (of a same "whole") are either "adjacent", or are "embedded within", one within the other, or are overlapping. as loosely indicated in Fig. 3.2. 'Adjacent' parts are direct parts of a same third part, p_z, i.e., p_x

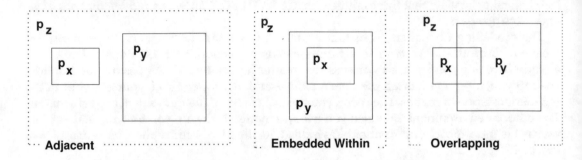

Fig. 3.2 Immediately 'Adjacent', 'Embedded Within' and Overlapping Parts

and p_y are "embedded within" p_z; or one (p_x) or the other (p_y) or both (p_x and p_y) are parts of a same third part, p'_z "embedded within" p_z; et cetera; as loosely indicated in Fig. 3.3, or one is "embedded within" the other — etc. as loosely indicated in Fig. 3.3.

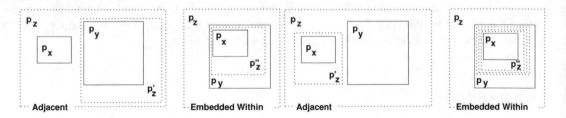

Fig. 3.3 Transitively 'Adjacent' and 'Embedded Within' Parts

How can physical parts "overlap"? Well, if we consider consider parts as possibly consisting of two or more sub-parts, as we indeed shall be doing, then Fig. 3.4 illustrates "overlap".

3.8.2.2 Our Informal Understanding of Mereology

Mereology, to us, is the study and knowledge about how physical and conceptual parts relate and what it means for a part to be related to another part: *being disjoint, being adjacent, being neighbours, being contained properly within, being properly overlapped with,* et cetera.

By physical parts we mean such spatial individuals which can be pointed to.

Examples: *a road net (consisting of street segments and street intersections); a street segment (between two intersections); a street intersection; a road (of sequentially neighbouring street segments of the same name); a vehicle; and a platoon (of sequentially neighbouring vehicles).*

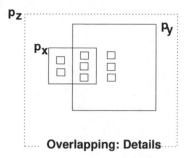

Fig. 3.4 Parts P_x consists of 5 parts, P_y of 6 parts – 3 are in common

By a conceptual part we mean an abstraction with no physical extent, which is either present or not.

Examples: *a bus timetable (not as a piece or booklet of paper, or as an electronic device, but) as an image in the minds of potential bus passengers; and routes of a pipeline, that is, neighbouring sequences of pipes, valves, pumps, forks and joins, for example referred to in discourse: "the gas flows through "such-and-such" a route".* The tricky thing here is that a route may be thought of as being both a concept or being a physical part — in which case one ought give them different names: a planned route and an actual road, for example.

The mereological notion of subpart, that is: *contained within* can be illustrated by **examples:** *the intersections and street segments are subparts of the road net; vehicles are subparts of a platoon; and pipes, valves, pumps, forks and joins are subparts of pipelines.*

The mereological notion of adjacency can be illustrated by **examples.** We consider *the various controls of an air traffic system, cf. Fig. B.1 on page 349, as well as its aircraft, as adjacent within the air traffic system; the pipes, valves, forks, joins and pumps of a pipeline, cf. Fig. B.6 on page 353, as adjacent within the pipeline system; two or more banks of a banking system, cf. Fig. B.3 on page 351, as being adjacent.*

The mereo-topological notion of neighbouring can be illustrated by **examples:** *Some adjacent pipes of a pipeline are neighbouring (connected) to other pipes or valves or pumps or forks or joins, et cetera; two immediately adjacent vehicles of a platoon are neighbouring.* The mereological notion of proper overlap can be illustrated by **examples** some of which are of a general kind: *two routes of a pipelines may overlap; and two conceptual bus timetables may overlap with some, but not all bus line entries being the same;* and some really reflect adjacency: *two adjacent pipe overlap in their connection, a wall between two rooms overlap each of these rooms — that is, the rooms overlap each other "in the wall".*

3.9 A Foundation

Mathematics is studied also with respect to its *philosophy*, from [353, Bertrand Russell: *Introduction to Philosophy of Mathematics*, 1919] via [246, Jaakko Hintikka, selected essays: *The Philosophy of Mathematics*, 1969] to [287, 288, Penelope Maddy: *Realism and Naturalism in Mathematics*, 1990–1997].

This, then, is the foundation upon which this monograph is built: the **Concepts**, as outlined in Chapter 1, the **Philosophy** of Kai Sørlander, as outlined in Chapter 2, and **Logic** and **Mathematics**, the closer inspection of the concepts SPACE, TIME and MATTER, and **Identity**, and **Mereology** of the present chapter.

Chapter 4–8 Overview

In the next four chapters *"we introduce a domain science & engineering"* of domain analysis & description. These four chapters treat "more-or-less" separable core topics of domain analysis & description. The treatment focuses on what we shall call the *intrinsics*, the essentials of domains.

- Chapter 4 introduces the concepts of *entities, endurants* and *perdurants* and unveils basic principles and techniques for the analysis & description of what we shall call *external endurant qualities*, those which we can experience by looking at them!
- Chapter 5 unveils basic principles and techniques for the analysis & description of what we shall call *internal endurant qualities*, like *identity, mereology* or those *attributes* which we can otherwise measure by physical instruments or which record *events*.
- Chapter 6 provides a bridge between the principles and techniques of Chapters 4–5 and Chapter 7 by further elaborating on the idea of transcendental deduction first introduced in Chapter 2.
- Chapter 7, finally, concludes the basic domain analysis & description principles and techniques by transcendentally relating *endurants*, the "still" *entities*, observable in *space*, to *perdurants*, the "discrete dynamic" *entities*, observable also in *time: actions, events* and *behaviours*.

Chapters 4–5 show you how to systematically develop descriptions of the structure and values of domains while Chapter 7 shows you how to follow that up with the development of core aspects of the behaviour of domains.

- Chapter 8 covers some principles and techniques of mostly non-intrinsical domain entities.

A Theory, not 'The' Theory

We write: *"we introduce **a** domain science & engineering ..."*. By this we mean: *"there may be other such domain science & engineerings"*! The science & engineering we refer to are the *domain analysis & description prompts*. We shall introduce these analysis & description prompts in the next four chapters. But there could be another composition than the one we offer. The present one has served well in guiding the domain analysis & description of many domains [84]. The notions of *conjoins*, for example, are based very much on a mixture of observations and pragmatism, and as such could be replaced! Anyway, the reader is guided, in the next 4 chapters, into this ontology and should, from there, be able to modify that ontology to suit the problem at hand.

On Learning a Theory and on Learning a Method

In this monograph we aim to develop a theory of domain analysis & description, and to develop a method of analysing & describing domains. The two things are not quite the same, but, obviously, related. It is important that the reader understands the next subsections. Because of the double aim it is possible that the reader misses the distinction, and hence to learn either!

First you learn about it! Then you learn to do it!

Towards a Theory of Domain Analysis & Description

Before one can practice a method *one must learn (i) its possible theoretical basis.*

In this monograph the text from which you should learn about a theoretical basis for domain analysis & description is interwoven with the text from which you should learn about the method, i.e. the practice of applying some of the theory. Being interwoven may mean that the reader forgets what it is that is being communicated.

The unfolding of the "story" of the possible theoretical basis is careful, "slow", almost pedantic. It is perhaps easy to get lost and forget *that other thing to be learned, (ii), the method.*

A Method for Domain Analysis & Description

_____ **Some Caveats** _____

We cannot, ever, describe a domain completely.

When we use informal language, that is, the narrative form to describe a domain, and if that domain is already [somewhat] known to the writer and/or reader of the description, the reader may ascribe semantics to these partially known terms.

That might be a serious mistake.

The meaning of the terms being defined in both the narrative and the formal domain description only transpires from a complete description.

Whichever properties can be reasoned from a complete domain description are then to be assumed properties of that domain.

If properties can be deduced from a complete domain description that are not intended properties of the domain, then the domain description is no good!

The method, to repeat, embodies principles, techniques and tools for the analysis & description of domains.

So how does one proceed in doing a domain model? First one decides what domain to analyse & describe. You start by focusing on what we shall call endurants. Then you analyse it as prescribed. At one point you are then ready to describe the root of the domain, as an atomic, or as a composite, or as a structure, or as a fluid. That description leads to the analysis of sub-endurants, usually several. In a single person project you therefore have to put some of these 'several' other endurants on hold, say put as a reminder on what we shall call a *notice board.* Then later, again and again, from the subsequent analysis & description of these other endurants emerges yet more endurants to be analysed & described. Et cetera.

The method involves an iterative process.

When professional, practicing *domain analyser & describers,* as is covered in Chapter 4, analyse & describe the external qualities of endurants they are fully aware of there being also internal qualities to analyse & describe, and also, subsequently, their transcendental deduction into *perdurants: channels, variables* and *behaviours.*

In Chapter 4, however, we pose exercise problems, at a stage where the problem solver has yet to learn, as in subsequent chapters, 5–7, about internal qualities — which ultimately decide on the sort of an endurant; thus the problem solvers are, to an extent, disadvantaged; hence may, after, for example, Chapter 5 (etc.), have to return to "improve" on a proposed problem solution. It cannot be otherwise.

Chapters 4–8 deal with some basic issues that cannot be treated only with recourse to mathematics. These basic issues are those of the "real world". The world that physicists have studied for millennia. And where their studies have increasingly necessitated philosophical discourses. Where physics is concerned with unraveling the complexities of the universe from the smallest to the largest scale. Likewise for the domains that we shall analyse & describe. Philosophy deals with foundational questions of the most general kind: what there is, what we know and how we came to know it, et cetera. Hence Chapter 2.

Chapter 4
DOMAINS – A Taxonomy: External Qualities

In this chapter we introduce the concepts of endurants and perdurants, the concept of external qualities[43] of endurants, and cover the analysis and description of external qualities of endurants.

We shall investigate the, as we shall call them, external qualities of domains. That is the possibly hierarchical composition of observable endurants. The outcome of this chapter is that the reader will be able to model the external qualities of domains. Not just for a particular domain instance, but a possibly infinite set of domain instances[44].

External qualities of endurants of a manifest domain are, in a simplifying sense, those we can see and touch. They, so to speak, take form.

4.1 Overview

This is a large chapter. It spans pages 47–106. To help the reader we present this overview. Some sections can be "armchair-read". They introduce overall concepts. These are Sects. **4.2**, **4.3**, **4.5**, and **4.14**. Section **4.21** presents background theory material. It can be skipped, but, when read, must be read carefully. Sections **4.6**–**4.13** form a first "half" of "serious-study" sections on the ontology of entities and the analysis of external qualities of endurants. Sections **4.16**–**4.20** form the second "half" of serious study sections on the description of external qualities of endurants.

4.2 Domains

> **Definition: 27 Domain:** By a **domain** we shall understand a **rationally describable** segment of a **discrete dynamics** segment of a **human assisted reality**, i.e., of the world, its **solid or fluid entities**: *natural* ["God-given"] and *artefactual* ["man-made"], and its *living species entities: plants* and *animals* including, notably, *humans*.
>
> These are *endurants* ("still"), as well as *perdurants* ("alive"). Emphasis is placed on *"human-assisted"*, that is, that there is *at least one (man-made) artefact* and, therefore, that *humans* are a primary cause for change of endurant *states* as well as perdurant *behaviours*
> ∎

This is a terse, but not a fully satisfactory characterisation. But it is the best we can come up with! Let us examine it in some detail.

---

[43] We refer to Definition 29 on page 51 [Sect. **4.4**] for an attempt to define the concept of external quality.

[44] By this we mean: You are not just analysing a specific domain, say the one manifested around the corner from where you are, but any instance, anywhere in the world, which satisfies what you have described.

© The Author(s), under exclusive license to Springer Nature Switzerland AG 2021
D. Bjørner, *Domain Science and Engineering*, Monographs in Theoretical Computer Science. An EATCS Series,
https://doi.org/10.1007/978-3-030-73484-8_4

- By a **rational description** we mean: a description which is logical, that is, a description over which one can reason; furthermore we shall in addition to this, by rational, mean a description which otherwise deploys additional mathematical concepts.
- By **discrete dynamics** we mean: a behaviour of the domain which, over time, varies, *but in discrete steps: endurant entities* may move or change form in space, values of *endurant mereologies* may vary, and/or values of *endurant attributes* may vary.

Control theory, the study of the control of continuously operating dynamical systems in engineered processes and machines, is one thing; *domain engineering* is "a different thing".

Control theory builds upon classical physics, and uses classical mathematics, partial differential equations, etc., to model phenomena of physics and therefrom engineered 'machines'.

Domain science & engineering, in some contrast, builds upon mathematical logic, and, to some extent, modern algebra, to model phenomena of mostly artefactual systems.

- By "a **reality**" we mean: that which we, as humans, with our senses, can see, hear, smell, taste and touch — as well as that for which we humans have devised apparatuses that measure: *mass* **(kg)**, *time interval* **(s)**, *temperature* **(K)**, *electric current* **(A)**, *amount of substance* **(mol)**, *luminous intensity* **(cd)**, *distance* **(m)**, et cetera.
- By "a **human assisted reality**" we mean: a world in which focus is on man-made endurants and human instigated actions, events and behaviours.

The other *technical terms* will be explained more formally in the rest of this chapter.

Definition: 28 Domain Description: By a *domain description* we shall understand a combination of **narration** and **formalisation** of a domain. A **formal specification** is a collection of *sort*, or *type* definitions, *function* and *behaviour* definitions, together with *axiom*s and *proof obligation*s constraining the definitions. A **specification narrative** is a natural language text which in terse statements introduces the names of (in this case, the domain), and, in cases, also the definitions, of sorts (types), functions, behaviours and axioms; not anthropomorphically, but by emphasizing their properties ∎

Domain descriptions are (to be) void of any reference to future, contemplated software, let alone IT systems, that may then[45] support entities of the domain. As such *domain models*[46] can be studied separately, for their own sake, for example as a basis for investigating possible domain theories, or can, subsequently, form the basis for requirements engineering with a view towards development of ('future') software, etc. *Our aim is to provide a method for the precise analysis and the formal description of domains.*

4.3 Universe of Discourse

By a **universe of discourse** we shall understand the same as the **domain of interest**, that is, the *domain* to be *analysed & described* ∎

---

[45] – but it may be that a domain being analysed & described depends crucially on IT and software – in which case that must somehow, "ever so abstractly", be described!

[46] We use the terms *'domain descriptions'* and *'domain models'* interchangeably.

Universes of Discourse

Example 7 [47] *We refer to a number of Internet accessible experimental reports*[48] *of descriptions of the following domains:*

- **railways** [38, 89, 41],
- **container shipping** [45],
- **stock exchange** [58],
- **oil pipelines** [63],
- **"The Market"** [39],
- **Web systems** [57],

- **weather information** [70],
- **credit card systems** [67],
- **document systems** [74],
- **urban planning** [99],
- **swarms of drones** [72],
- **container terminals** [76]

Method Step 1 Select Domain of Interest: A *principle* of the method is, as an initial step of the development of a *domain analyser & describer*, is to *select* the universe of discourse, to *ascribe* it a *sort name*, say UoD, and to *remember* that that universe, and, as a *technique*, be subject to analysis & description ∎

Domain Description Prompt 1 `name_and_sketch_universe_of_discourse:`

❝ Naming:
   type UoD
 Rough Sketch:
   informal text ... ❞

The rough-sketching of [what] a domain [is,] is not a trivial matter. It is not done by a committee! It usually requires repeated "trial sketches". To carry it out, i.e., the sketching, normally requires a combination of physical visits to domain examples, if possible; talking with domain professionals, at all levels; reading relevant literature. It also includes searching the Internet for information.

A Road Transport Domain: Basics

Example 8
Naming:
   type RTS
Rough Sketch: The road transport system that we have in mind consists of a road net and a set of vehicles such that the road net serves to convey vehicles. We consider the road net to consist of hubs, i.e., street intersections, or just street segment connection points, and links,

---

[47] In this monograph we bring several categories of numbered examples. There are the examples, let us call them the *text explanatory examples*; then there are two kinds of examples related to domains: the *informal domain examples* and *formal domain examples*. The latter exemplify the kind of domain analysis & descriptions this monograph studies and for which this monograph presents a method for their construction. We leave it to the reader to discern *which examples are what*!

[48] These are **draft** reports, more-or-less complete. The writing of these reports was finished when sufficient evidence, conforming or refuting one or another aspect of the ***domain analysis & description* method**.

i.e., street segments between adjacent hubs. We consider vehicles to additionally include departments of motor vehicles (DMVs), bus companies, each with zero, one or more buses, and vehicle associations, each with zero, one or more members who are owners of zero, one or more vehicles[49]   □

It may be a **"large" domain**, that is, consist of many, as we shall see, *endurants* and *perdurants,* of many *parts* and *fluids,* of many *humans* and *artefacts,* and of many *actors, actions, events* and *behaviours.*

Or it may be a **"small" domain**, that is, consist of a few such entities.

The choice of "boundaries", that is, of how much or little to include, and of how much or little to exclude is entirely the choice of the domain engineer cum scientist: the choice is crucial, and is not always obvious. The choice delineates an *interface*, that is, that which is within the boundary, i.e., is in the domain, and that which is without, i.e., outside the domain, i.e., is the **context of the domain**, that is, the **external domain interfaces**. Experience helps set reasonable boundaries.

There are two "situations": Either a **domain analysis & description** endeavour is pursued in order to prepare for a subsequent development of *requirements modeling,* in which case one tends to choose a **"narrow" domain**, that is, one that "fits", includes, but not much more, the domain of interest for the requirements. Or a **domain analysis & description** endeavour is pursued in order to research a domain. *Either* one that can form the basis for subsequent engineering studies aimed, eventually at requirements development; in this case "wider" boundaries may be sought. *Or* one that experimentally "throws a larger net", that is, seeks a "large" domain so as to explore interfaces between what is thought of as **internal system interfaces**.

Where, then, to start the *domain analysis & description* ? Either one can start "bottom-up", that is, with atomic entities: endurants or perdurants, one-by-one, and work one's way "out", to include composite entities, again endurants or perdurants, to finally reach some satisfaction: *Eureka,* a goal has been reached. Or one can start "top-down", that is, "casting a wide net". The choice is yours. Our presentation, however, is "top down": most general domain aspects first.

Domain science & engineering marks **a new area of computing science**. Just as we are *formalising* the *syntax and semantics of programming languages,* so we are *formalising* the *syntax and semantics of human-assisted domains.*

Just as *physicists* are studying the *natural physical world,* endowing it with *mathematical models,* so we, *computing scientists,* are studying these *domains,* endowing them with *mathematical models.*

A difference between the endeavours of physicists and ours lies in the tools: the physics models are based on *classical mathematics, differential equations* and *integrals,* etc.; our models are based on *mathematical logic, set theory,* and *algebra.*

Where physicists thus classically use a variety of *differential* and *integral calculi* to model the physical world, we shall be using the *analysis & description calculi* presented in this chapter to model primarily artefactual domains. As we shall see, in several examples, there is, however, a need for describing a number of domain aspects both on control theory and computing science grounds – yet the two theories underlying these description tools need be unified. At the time of writing this monograph such a unifying theory has yet to emerge.

---

[49] This "rough" narrative fails to narrate what hubs, links, vehicles, DMVs, bus companies, buses and vehicle associations are. In presenting it here, as we are, we rely on your a priori understanding of these terms. But that is dangerous! The danger, if we do not painstakingly narrate and formalise what we mean by all these terms, then readers (software designers, etc.) may make erroneous assumptions.

4.4 External Qualities

Definition: 29 External Quality: By an **external quality** of an endurant we shall, initially, mean a property that is manifest, one that can be touched or seen, generally, one that "forms" the endurable entities of a domain.

More generally, by an **external quality** of an endurant we shall mean an abstract property about a collection of manifest entities, like a structure of manifest entities, or a structure of abstracted such entities ∎

A Road Transport System, II: Manifest External Qualities
Example 9 Our intention is that the manifest external qualities of a road transport system are those of its roads, their **hub**s[50]i.e., road (or street) intersections, and their **link**s, i.e., the roads (streets) between hubs, and **vehicle**s, i.e., automobiles – that ply the roads – the buses, trucks, private cars, bicycles, etc.   □

A Road Transport System, II: Abstract External Qualities
Example 10 Examples of what could be considered abstract external qualities of a road transport domain are: the aggregate of all hubs and all links, the aggregate of all buses, say into bus companies, the aggregate of all bus companies into public transport, and the aggregate of all vehicles into a department of vehicles. Some of these aggregates may, at first be treated as abstract. Subsequently, in our further analysis & description we may decide to consider some of them as concretely manifested in, for example, actual departments of roads   □

Method Step 2 External Qualities: An important step in the process of unfolding an analysis & description of a domain is to determine which are the external qualities of entities of that domain. Our attempt, in Definition 29, to encircle the *'external quality'* concept may not be fully satisfactory. We shall try "repair" that "failure to be precise" by numerous examples – and otherwise hope that some readers can suggest improved definitions ∎

---

[50] We have **highlighted** certain endurant sort names – as they will re-appear in rather many upcoming examples.

We refer to Fig. 4.1 on the next page where a largest dashed-line "upper left" box indicate, in a way, the concepts entailed by *external qualities*.

4.5 Entities

A core concept of domain modeling is that of an *entity*.

Definition: 30 Entity: By an ***entity*** we shall understand a ***phenomenon***, i.e., something that can be *observed*, i.e., be seen or touched by humans, *or* that can be *conceived* as an *abstraction* of an entity; alternatively, a phenomenon is an entity, *if it exists, it is* **"being"**, *it is that which makes a "thing" what it is: essence, essential nature* [281, Vol. I, pg. 665] ∎

Analysis Predicate Prompt 1 is_entity: The domain analyser analyses "things" (θ) into either entities or non-entities. The method provides the ***domain analysis prompt***:

- is_entity – where is_entity(θ) holds if θ is an entity ∎[51]

is_entity is said to be a *prerequisite prompt* for all other prompts. Prompts, whether analysis, observer or description prompts, are *aide-mémoires*; they are not program constructs; they can not be defined mathematically[52]; think of them as written on the wall of your working place, there to remind you of what you should remember to do.

–––––––––––––––––––––––– On Analysis Prompts ––––––––––––––––––––––––
The is_entity is the first of a number of analysis prompt. They are "applied" by the domain analyser to phenomena of domains. And they yield truth values, true or false, "left" in the mind of the domain analyser.

Method Step 3 "What can be Described": A next step in the development of a *domain analyser & describer* is to decide on what can be described. Both with respect to the universe of discourse and with respect to every subsequently identified entity. The is_entity analysis prompt is the *tool* used to prompt that analysis and decision. The *domain analysers* has great leeway here. They can, perhaps rather arbitrarily, some would say, magisterially, decide on leaving out phenomena for further treatment, phenomena that others would say can be described. An excuse for exclusion could be that the *domain analysers* can claim that the phenomenon is not relevant to their inquiry ∎

To sum up: *An entity is what we can analyse and describe using the analysis & description prompts outlined in this chapter*. Other words for 'entity' are: *'fluid object'* or *'thing'*. Since we shall be needing the term 'fluid' for a specific class of entities, and since the term 'object' is already heavily overloaded, we shall just use the term 'entity'.

The *entities* that we are concerned with are those with which Kai Sørlander's Philosophy is likewise concerned. They are the ones that are *unavoidable* in any description of any

––––––––––––––––––––––
[51] ∎ marks the end of an analysis prompt definition.
[52] See however [65, 68] where we do suggest an underlying mathematical model of domains and give prompts a semantics.

possible world. And then, which are those entities? In both [366] and [369] Kai Sørlander rationally deduces that these entities must be in *space* and *time*, must satisfy laws of physics – like those of Newton and Einstein, but among them are also *living species: plants* and *animals* and hence *humans*. The *living species*, besides still being in *space* and *time*, and satisfying laws of physics, must satisfy further properties.

Figure 4.1 shows an **upper ontology**[53,54] for domains such as we shall focus on in this monograph. We shall briefly review Fig. 4.1 by means of a top-down, left-traversal of the tree (whose root is at the top).

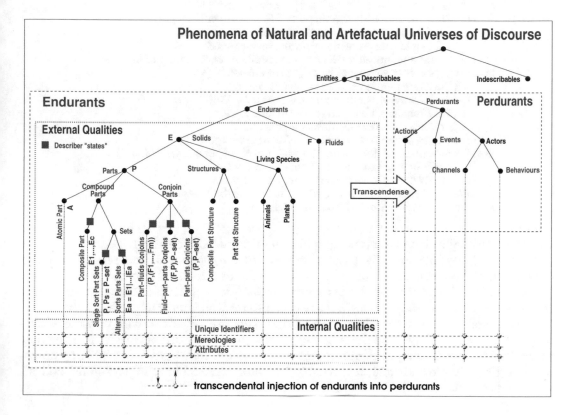

Fig. 4.1 Upper Ontology

4.5.1 A Linnean, Binomial Taxonomy

We shall first present an idealised form of ontology for the domains that we are interested in studying and for whose construction of domain analyses & descriptions we wish to present a method. This idealised form follows that of Carl von Linné (Carl Linneaus, 1707–1778) the Swedish botanist, zoologist, and physician who formalised binomial nomenclature, the modern system of naming organisms. He is known as the "father of modern taxonomy"

---

[53] An **upper ontology** (in the sense used in information science) consists of very general terms that are common across all domains [Wikipedia].

[54] We could organise the ontology differently: entities are either naturals, artefacts or living species, et cetera. If an upper node (•) satisfies a predicate $\mathcal{P}$ then all descendant nodes do likewise.

We refer to the ontology description that now follows, as 'ideal'. It is so, we claim, because it is strictly binomial, and it is, in a sense, and also as a result of being binomial, abstract in that it does not reflect how it should preferably be used. We shall later, on the basis of the following taxonomy, present a workable, we claim, practically useful ontology.

An 'Idealised' Domain Taxonomy ....

[0] Universes of discourse consists of **non-describable phenomena** [1.0] and **describable phenomena** [1.1].

    [1.0] Non-describable phenomena will here be left further un-analysed.

    [1.1] Describable phenomena, are also called **entities** [1.2].

    [1.2] Entities are either **endurants**[55] [2.1] or **perdurants**[56] [2.2].

        [2.1] Endurants are either **physical** [3.1] or **living species**.

            [3.1] Physicals are either **singular**[57] [4.1] or **composites**[58] [4.2].

                [4.1] Singulars are either **atomic parts**[59] [5.1] or are **fluids**[60] [5.2].

                    [5.1] Atomic parts are presently left further un-analysed.

                    [5.2] Liquids are presently left further un-analysed.

                [4.2] Composites are either **definite composites**[61] or **indefinite composites**[62].

            [3.2] Living species are either **plants**[63] [4.3] or **animals**[64] [4.4].

                [4.3] Plants are here left further un-analysed.

                [4.4] Animals are either **humans** [5.3] or **other ...** [5.4].

                    [5.3] Humans are here left further un-analysed.

                    [5.4] Other ... is here left further un-analysed.

        [2.2] Perdurants are either **instantaneous**[65] [3.3] or **prolonged**[66] [3.4].

            [3.3] Instantaneous perdurants are either **actions**[67] [4.5] or **events**[68] [4.6].

                [4.5] We shall here leave actions further un-analysed.

                [4.6] We shall here leave events further un-analysed.

            [3.4] We shall here rename prolonged perdurants into **behaviours**[69]

            [3.4] Behaviours are here left further un-analysed.

....

The above textual listing is rendered graphically in Fig. 4.2 on the next page.

    Figure 4.2 (page 55) shows the basic relational structure of general domain concepts. Figure 4.1 (page 53), in principle, builds on the taxonomy of Fig. 4.2. The ontology of Fig. 4.1 is "massaged" with respect to Fig. 4.2. Some domain analysis & description concepts have been added; some "intermediary" concepts have been inserted, and, most importantly, the 'taxonomy' has evolved into an 'ontology'. Where the taxonomy only dealt with tangible, visible properties[70], the ontology 'adds' intangible, but objectively measurable properties shown by the bottom horizontal *unique identifier, mereology* and *attribute lines* – connected, by downward vertical lines to endurant, respectively "upward" vertical lines to perdurant "nodes". We shall now proceed to justify Fig. 4.1.

---

[55] Cf. Defn. 31 on page 57

[56] Cf. Defn. 32 on page 57

[57] By a singular entity we shall mean a single instance or something to be considered by itself [Merriam Webster].

[58] By a composite we shall mean a grouping of usually two or more endurants.

[59] See Sect. **4.13.1** on page 69

[60] Cf. Defn. 48 on page 67

[61] A definite composite has a given number of endurants.

[62] An indefinite composite has a possibly varying number of endurants.

[63] See Sect. **4.11.1** on page 66

[64] See Sect. **4.11.2** on page 66

[65] An Instantaneous Perdurant occurs at a (or any) single point in time and manifests itself in a similarly instantaneous state change – where a state is the internal qualities value of any assembly of endurants.

[66] A Prolonged Perdurant occurs over time, perdures for either an indefinite or an infinite time interval.

[67] An action is an internally provoked instantaneous state change.

[68] An event is an externally provoked instantaneous state change.

[69] A behaviour is a set of sequences of actions, events and behaviours.

[70] – like those used as the basis for plant determination according to Carl von Linné

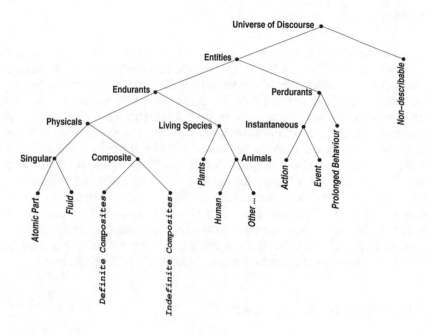

Fig. 4.2 A Binomial Taxonomy. The *[in]definite composites* are defined in terms of *endurants*.

4.5.2 Domain-specific Ontologies

Figures 4.1 and 4.2 illustrate the issue of the domain engineer – having grasped the essence of Chapters 4–7 – and about to develop a domain model for a new, a next, domain, namely that of deciding on an appropriate "ontology–graph"! Two such were shown on page vii. The second of these two will be formally introduced in Sect. **7.13.1** on page 196. We shall return to this issue in due course. For the time being: the ontology–graph of Fig. 4.1 is but one of several possible. Once the domain modelers become familiar with domain modeling they will themselves be able to formulate an ontology graph suited, perhaps *best suited* for their domain modeling endeavour!

4.5.3 A Cursory Overview

There are *describable* phenomena and there are phenomena that we cannot describe. The former we shall call *entities*. The *entities* are either *endurants*, "still" entities – existing in *space*, or are *perdurants*, "alive" entities – existing also in *time*. *Endurants* are either *solid* or *fluid*. *Solid* endurants are *parts*, or *living species*, or are *structures*. *Parts* are either *naturals*, or *artefacts*, i.e. man-made. Natural parts are either *atomic* or *composite* parts. Man-made parts are either *atomic* parts, *composite* parts or are *conjoins*. In this monograph we shall refer to man-made parts as artefacts, and we shall, surprise-surprise, "collapse" our treatment of natural and artefactual parts into just parts. Conjoins are either *part-fluids*, or *fluid-parts*, or *part-parts* conjoins. *Living Species* are either *plants* or *animals*. Among animals we have the *humans*. *Structures* are structures over either a definite number of endurants of usually distinct sorts, or an indefinite number of endurants of the same sort.

4.5.4 Summary

The categorisation into structures, natural parts, artefactual parts, plants, and animals is thus partly based in Sørlander's Philosophy, partly pragmatic. The distinction between endurants and perdurants, are necessitated by Kai Sørlander's Philosophy as entities being in space, respectively entities being in space **and** time. Furthermore: solids and fluids are motivated by arguments of natural sciences; structures are purely pragmatic; plants and animals, including humans, are necessitated by Kai Sørlander's Philosophy. The distinction between natural parts, and artefacts is not necessary in Sørlander's Philosophy, but, we claim, necessary, philosophically, in order to perform the *intentional "pull"*, a transcendental deduction.

The distinction between *part-fluids*, *fluid-parts*, and *part-parts* is pragmatic. We could have chosen another sub-ontology for artefacts. Also, from empirical observation, there seems to be no need for *fluid-fluids* conjoins. In *part-fluids* conjoins the fluids are "contained within" the part; in *fluid-parts* conjoins the fluid, anthropomorphically speaking, "contains the parts"; and in *part-parts* conjoins the parts are monitored and controlled by the part. In a perceived *fluid-fluids* artefact, should the fluid "contain" the fluids? How?

4.5.4.1 Space and Time: Whither Entities?

Are space and time entities? Of course not! They are simply abstract concepts that apply to any entity.

4.6 Endurants and Perdurants

The concepts of endurants and perdurants are not present in, that is, are not essential to Sørlander's Philosophy. Since our departure point is that of *computing science* where, eventually, conventional computing performs operations on, i.e. processes data, we shall, however, introduce these two notions: *endurant* and *perdurant*. The former, in a rough sense, "corresponds" to data; the latter, similarly, to processes.

Philosophers have otherwise spent quite some thoughts on endurants[71] and perdurants[72]. It seems obvious that entities *exists in space*. But how do entities *persist through time*? Two accounts of *persistence*[73] are *endurance theory* (*endurantism*) and *perdurance theory* (*perdurantism*). We shall basically stay clear of these, the footnoted sources, and rely on Kai Sørlander's Philosophy.

Method Step 4   **Initial Focus is on Endurants:** A basic *principle* of the *domain analyser & describer* method is that of **initially focusing on endurants**. Once all we wish to know about domain endurants has been analysed and described, then we shift focus to perdurants ∎

---

[71] en.wikipedia.org/wiki/Formal_ontology#Endurant
[72] https://en.wikipedia.org/wiki/Formal_ontology#Perdurant
[73] plato.stanford.edu/entries/temporal-parts/

4.6.1 Endurants

Definition: 31 Endurant: By an *endurant* we shall understand an entity that can be observed, or conceived and described, as a "complete thing" at no matter which given snapshot of time; alternatively an entity is endurant if it is capable of *enduring*, that is *persist*, *"hold out"* [281, Vol. I, pg. 656]. Were we to "freeze" time we would still be able to observe the entire endurant ∎

Endurants

Example 11 *Geography Endurants: Geography endurants are: fields, meadows, lakes, rivers, forests, hills, mountains, et cetera.* *Railway System Endurants: a railway system, its net, its individual tracks, switch points, trains, their individual locomotives, et cetera.*

A Caveat: Please observe the following: In Example 11 we seemingly rather easily, refer to such things as *fields, meadows, lakes, rivers,* etc., as endurants that can be singled out from one another. It probably took mankind millennia to make this categorisation. Easier, perhaps, with the artefacts: *railway net, track, locomotives,* etc. These endurants were so designated by their designers, and we have kept these designations.

Analysis Predicate Prompt 2 is_endurant: The domain analyser analyses an entity, ϕ, into an endurant as prompted by the ***domain analysis prompt***:

- is_endurant – ϕ is an endurant if **is_endurant**(ϕ) holds.

is_entity is a *prerequisite prompt* for is_endurant ∎

4.6.2 Perdurants

Definition: 32 Perdurant: By a *perdurant* we shall understand an entity for which only a fragment exists if we look at or touch them at any given snapshot in time. Were we to freeze time we would only see or touch a fragment of the perdurant [281, Vol. II, pg. 1552] ∎

Perdurants

Example 12 *Geography Perdurants: the continuous changing of the weather (meteorology); the erosion of coastlines; the rising of some land area and the "sinking" of other land area; volcanic eruptions; earthquakes; et cetera.* *Railway System Perdurants: the ride of a train from one railway station to another; and the stop of a train at a railway station from some arrival time to some departure time* ∎

Analysis Predicate Prompt 3 is_perdurant: The domain analyser analyses an entity e into perdurants as prompted by the ***domain analysis prompt***:

- is_perdurant–e is a perdurant if is_perdurant(e) holds.

is_entity is a *prerequisite prompt* for is_perdurant ∎

Occurrent, accident, continuant and *happening* are synonyms for perdurant.

We shall, in this monograph not develop an analysis calculus for perdurants, but leave such a, to us interesting, research challenge to capable readers.

4.7 Endurants: Solid and Fluid

We decide to facilitate the modeling of two kinds of endurants: solid endurants and fluid endurants. Solid endurants, we allow, may contain fluid endurants.

4.7.1 Solid Endurants

Definition: 33 Solid Endurant: By a **solid endurant** we shall understand an endurant which is separate, individual or distinct in form or concept, or, rephrasing: a body or magnitude of three-dimensional, one having length, breadth and thickness [281, Vol. II, pg. 2046] ∎

Analysis Predicate Prompt 4 is_solid: The domain analyser analyses endurants, e, into solid entities as prompted by the **domain analysis prompt**:

- is_solid–e is solid if is_solid(e) holds ∎

To simplify matters we shall allow separate elements of a solid endurant to be fluid! That is, a solid endurant, i.e., a part, may be conjoined with a fluid endurant, a fluid; we refer to Sect. **4.13.3** on page 72.

Solid Endurants

Example 13 *The individual endurants of the above example of railway system endurants, Example 11 on the previous page, were all solid. Here are examples of solid endurants of pipeline systems. A pipeline and its individual units: wells, pipes, valves, pumps, forks, joins, and sinks.*

Caveat: Be aware of the following problem. Just because you ascribe the type name *valve* to a solid endurant, e, does not "automatically" endow the so-typed entity, e, with all, or at least some of those qualities that *valve values*, such as you and I can agree on as being *valve values*, do possess. No, we have to do much more analysis for "your" naming an entity of type valve, and for that entity to indeed be what others would associate with *valve values*.

That "much more" analysis entails ascribing a sufficient number of *internal qualities* to what we labeled as valves, qualities such as *unique identification, mereology* and *attributes*.

4.7.2 Fluids

Definition: 34 Fluid Endurant: By a **fluid endurant** we shall understand an endurant which is prolonged, without interruption, in an unbroken series or pattern; or, rephrasing: a substance (liquid, gas or plasma) having the property of flowing, consisting of particles that move among themselves [281, Vol. I, pg. 774] ∎

Analysis Predicate Prompt 5 is_fluid: The domain analyser analyses endurants e into fluid entities as prompted by the **domain analysis prompt**:

• is_fluid – e is fluid if is_fluid(e) [is_fluid(e)] holds ∎

Fluids are otherwise liquid, or gaseous, or plasmatic, or granular[74], or plant products, i.e., chopped sugar cane, threshed, or otherwise[75], et cetera.

Fluids

Example 14 *Specific examples of fluids are: water, oil, gas, compressed air, etc. A container, which we consider a solid endurant, may be conjoined with another, a fluid, like a gas pipeline unit may "contain" gas. We refer to Sect.* **4.17.3** *on page 87.*

We cover fluids further in Sect. **4.12** on page 67.

Method Step 5 Solid versus Fluid: One may question the distinction between solid and fluid endurants. For most natural, God-given, and probably all man-made solid endurants the temperature of its surroundings may decide its state of "firmness" or "fluidity"! We decide here to leave this, to some, crucial aspect untreated! ∎

We analyse fluids into liquids, gases and plasmas. Solids have fixed volume and shape. Fluids has fixed volume but variable shape to fit, but not necessarily all of its container. Atoms, ions and molecules of liquids are closely packed together, can vibrate but not move. Gas has both variable volume and shape to fit the entire of its container. Plasma, like gas, has

---

[74] This is a purely pragmatic decision. "Of course" sand, gravel, soil, etc., are not fluids, but for our modeling purposes it is convenient to "compartmentalise" them as fluids!

[75] See footnote 74.

both variable volume and form and contain neutral atoms and electrons and ions that move around freely.

4.8 Parts, Structures and Living Species

We decide to analyse endurants into either of three kinds: *parts*, *structures* and *living species*. The distinction between the first two is pragmatic. The distinction between these and *living species* is motivated in Kai Sørlander's Philosophy.

4.8.1 Compound Endurants, "Roots" and "Siblings"

We need, in the following, to make definitions based on endurants being compounds.

Definition: 35 Compound Endurants: By a **compound endurant** we shall understand an endurant which can be considered as comprising two elements: a *"root"* and one or more, usually more, *"siblings"*. The **"root"** endurant, which is ignored for so-called *endurant structures*, can otherwise be said to "embody", to "host", the *"siblings"* ∎ These, the **"siblings"**, can be said to be sub-ordinate to the *"root"*, also for *endurant structures* ∎ These definitions may seem vague, but are in fact, sufficiently precise ! ∎

Compounds are either *Cartesians* of two or more endurants or *sets* of endurants (of the same sort). We shall model Cartesians, of sort A, not as "products": $A = \times C \times ... \times D$, but by means of *observers* obs_B, obs_C, ..., obs_D, functions, obs_A: $A \rightarrow B$, etc., that apply to a compound "Cartesian" endurant and yields one of its elements. We shall model endurant set sorts conventionally: E = F-**set**.

4.8.2 Parts

Parts are either *natural* parts, or are *artefactual* parts, i.e. man-made. Natural and man-made parts are either *atomic* or *composite*. We additionally analyse artefacts into *conjoins*, i.e., compounds of *a "root" part and a definite number of different sort "sibling" fluids*, or a *"root" fluid and an indefinite number of same-sort "sibling" parts*, or a *"root" part and an indefinite number of same-sort "sibling" parts*. This particular distinction into three kinds of conjoins is pragmatic.

Definition: 38 Parts: By a *part* we shall understand a solid endurant existing in time and subject to laws of physics, including the *causality principle* and *gravitational pull*[76] ∎

Analysis Predicate Prompt 6 is_part: The domain analyser analyses "things" (e) into part. The method provides the ***domain analysis prompt***:

---

[76] This characterisation is the result of our study of relations between philosophy and computing science, notably influenced by Kai Sørlander's Philosophy

- **is_part** – where **is_part(e)** holds if e is a part ∎

Parts are going to be the "workhorse" of our analyses & descriptions of artefactual domains.

A Rough Sketch Domain Description

Example 15 The example is that of the production of rum. From

83 the sowing, watering, and tending to of sugar cane plants;
84 via the "burning" of these prior to harvest;
85 the harvest;
86 the collection of harvest from sugar cane fields to
87 the chopping, crushing, (and sometimes repeated) boiling, cooling and centrifuging of sugar cane when making sugar and molasses (into A, B, and low grade batches);
88 the fermentation, with water and yeast, producing a 'wash';
89 the (pot still or column still) distilling of the wash into rum;
90 the aging of rum in oak barrels;
91 the charcoal filtration of rum;
92 the blending of rum;
93 the bottling of rum;
94 the preparation of cases of rum for sales/export; and
95 the transportation away from the rum distiller of the rum.

Some comments on Example 15: Each of the enumerated items above is phrased in terms of perdurants. Behind each such perdurant lies some endurant. That is, in English, *"every noun can be verbed", and vice-versa*. So we anticipate the transcendence, from endurants to perdurants.

Section **4.13** on page 68 continues our treatment of parts.

4.8.3 Structures

Definition: 39 Endurant Structure: By an ***endurant structure***, or just , we shall understand a solid endurant whose "root" element the domain engineer chooses to ignore, i.e., to **not** endow with ***internal qualities*** such as unique identifiers, mereology and attributes; but whose "siblings" are described as consisting of one or more solid endurants ∎

Analysis Predicate Prompt 7 is_structure: The domain analyser analyses "things" (e) into structures. The method provides the ***domain analysis prompt***:

- **is_structure** – where **is_structure(e)** holds if e is a structure ∎

We refer to Sect. **4.10** for further analysis of structures into *set* and *composite structures*.

4.8.4 Living Species

Living Species are either *plants* or *animals*. Among animals we have the *humans*.

Definition: 40 Living Species, I: By a *living species* we shall understand a solid endurant, subject to laws of physics, and additionally subject to *causality of purpose* ∎[77]

Analysis Predicate Prompt 8 is_living_species: The domain analyser analyses "things" (*e*) into living species. The method provides the **domain analysis prompt**:

- **is_living_species** – where **is_living_species**(*e*) holds if *e* is a living species ∎

We refer to Sect. **4.11** for further treatment of living species.

4.9 Natural Parts and Artefacts

We shall examine two kinds of parts: *natural* and *man-made*, i.e., *artefactual*, parts.

Parts

Example 16 *The geography examples (Example 11 on page 57) are all natural parts. The railway system examples (Example 11 on page 57) are all artefacts*   □

4.9.1 Natural Parts

Definition: 41 Natural Parts: Natural parts are not artefactuals, but are given by nature; are in *space* and *time*; are subject to the *laws of physics*, and also subject to the *principle of causality* and *gravitational pull* ∎ Natural parts are parts which the domain engineer chooses to endow with all three **internal qualities**: unique identification, mereology, and one or more attributes ∎

Analysis Predicate Prompt 9 is_natural_part: The domain analyser analyses "things" (*e*) into natural parts. The method provides the **domain analysis prompt**:

- **is_natural_part** – where **is_natural_part**(*e*) holds if *e* is a natural part ∎

---

[77] See Footnote 76 on page 60 of Definition 38 on page 60.

Natural Parts: River Systems

Example 17 Further examples of natural parts are: a river system – with its short or long stretches of water sources (springs, glaciers, meadows or even lakes) emerging into brooks or streams or rivers; winding or straight brook, stream and river sections; lakes; waterfalls; confluences of brooks, streams and rivers into appropriate ones of these; and divergences of either ones of these into appropriate ones of these ∎

4.9.2 Artefacts – Man-made Parts

Definition: 42 Man-made Parts: Artefacts: Artefacts are man-made either solid or fluid endurants. We shall only consider solid endurants. Man-made fluids are not treated separately but are lumped with natural fluids. Artefacts are subject to the *laws of physics*, and are parts which, like for *natural parts*, the domain engineer chooses to endow with all three *internal qualities*: unique identification, mereology, and one or more attributes ∎

Analysis Predicate Prompt 10 is_artefact: The domain analyser analyses "things" (e) into artefact. The method provides the **domain analysis prompt**:

- **is_artefact** – where **is_artefact**(e) holds if e is an artefact ∎

Artefactual Parts: Financial Service Industry

Example 18 A further example of man-made parts are those of a financial service industry – taken here in a wide sense: (a) customers of any of the below; (b-d) banks: savings & loans, commercial and investment banks; (e) foreign exchange services; (f) insurance; (g-h) stock brokers and exchanges; (i) commodities exchanges, (j) credit card companies; (k) accountancy companies; (l) consumer finance companies; (m) investment funds; and (n-...) government and international overseeing agencies (national banks, the World Bank, the International Monetary Fund (IMF), the European Central Bank (ECB), etc ∎

We shall assume, cf. Sect. **5.4** [*Attributes*], that *artefacts* all come with an *attribute* of kind *intent*, that is, a set of purposes for which the artefact was constructed, and for which it is intended to serve.

4.9.3 A Pragmatic Decision

We now make a rather drastic decision. It is a pragmatic decision, that is, it is not motivated by concerns of syntax, nor is it motivated by concerns of semantics. It is motivated by concerns of usage.

The decision is to henceforth not distinguish between natural and artefactual endurants.

We justify the decision as follows: All of the domains we have researched and engineered, viz. [84], are significantly characterised by their artefacts. All of their domain descriptions focus exclusively on artefacts. We have finally, experimentally, found that a presence of natural parts would not alter the description materially!

4.10 Structures

Structures are conceptual. Endurants are manifest, whether natural or artefactual. The domain modeler may decide to analyse & describe some compound endurants as indeed manifest, that is, in detail, with internal qualities, such that properties can be expressed, "later" in the model, about these endurants. The domain modeler may, however, also decide to analyse & describe some compound endurants as structures, that is, without any internal qualities, and therefore no properties can be expressed, "later" in the model, about these endurants.

4.10.1 General

Structures are "conceptual, composite endurants". A *structure* "gathers" one or more endurants under "one umbrella", often simplifying a presentation of some elements of a domain description. Sometimes, in our domain modeling, we choose to model an endurant as a *structure*, sometimes as a *composite part*; it all depends on what we wish to focus on in our domain model. Thus we choose, when doing so, to model endurants as structures for pragmatic reasons. As such structures are "compounds" where we are interested only in the (external and internal) qualities of the elements, the "siblings", of the compound, but not in the qualities of the structure, i.e., the "root", itself.

Transport System Structures

Example 19 *A transport system is modelled as structured into a road net structure and an automobile structure. The road net structure is then structured as a pair: a structure of hubs and a structure of links. These latter structures are then modelled as set of hubs, respectively links.*

Structures versus Composites

Example 20 *We could have modelled the road net structure as a composite part with unique identity, mereology and attributes which could then serve to model a* road net authority*. We could have modelled the automobile structure as a composite part with unique identity, mereology and attributes which could then serve to model a* department of vehicles   □

Whether to analyse & describe a solid endurant into a structure or a part is a matter of choice. If we choose to analyse a solid endurant into a *part* then it is because we are interested in endowing the part with *internal qualities*, the unique identifiers, mereology and one or more attributes. If we choose to analyse a solid endurant into a *structure* then it is because we are **not** interested in endowing the endurant with *qualities*. When we choose that an endurant sort should be modelled as a part sort with unique identification, mereology and proper attributes, then it is because we eventually shall consider the part sort as being the basis for transcendentally deduced behaviours.

●●●

Part set and composite part structures will not themselves, as parts, be ascribed internal qualities, that is, they are, as parts, considered "invisible", i.e., not manifest. This "invisibility" is not "inherited" by the parts of the part set structure nor the parts of the composite part structure. This "visibility/invisibility" emerges, informally, from the domain part state generator, Sect. **4.19** on page 91.

4.10.2 Composite Structures

Definition: 43 Composite Structure: By a *composite structure* we shall understand a solid endurant which the domain engineer chooses to describe as consisting of a definite number of solid "sibling" endurants of usually distinct sorts but to **not** endow the "root" element with *internal qualities* such as unique identifiers, mereology and attributes ∎

Analysis Predicate Prompt 11 is_composite_structure: The domain analyser analyses "things" (*e*) into composite structures. The method provides the *domain analysis prompt*:

- is_composite_structure – where is_composite structure(*e*) holds if *e* is a composite structure ∎

4.10.3 Set Structures

Definition: 44 Set Structure: By a *set structure* we shall understand a solid endurant which the domain engineer chooses to describe as consisting of an indefinite number of solid "sibling" endurants of the same sort, **and** to **not** endow its "root" element with *internal qualities* such as unique identifiers, mereology and attributes ∎

Analysis Predicate Prompt 12 is_set_structure: The domain analyser analyses "things" (*e*) into set structures. The method provides the *domain analysis prompt*:

- is_set_structure – where is_set_structure(*e*) holds if *e* is a set structure ∎

4.11 Living Species – Plants and Animals

We refer to Sect. **4.8.4** for our first characterisation (Page 62) of the concept of *living species*[78]: an endurant existing in time, subject to laws of physics, and additionally subject to *causality of purpose.*[79]

---

[78] See analysis prompt 8 on page 62.
[79] See Footnote 76 on page 60.

Definition: 45 Living Species, II: Living species must have some *form they can be developed to reach*; a form they must be *causally determined to maintain*. This *development and maintenance* must further engage in *exchanges of matter with an environment*. It must be possible that living species occur in one of two forms: a form which is characterised by *development, form and exchange*; another form which, **additionally**, can be characterised by the *ability of purposeful movement*: **plants**, respectively **animals** ∎

It is appropriate here to mention **Carl Linnaeus** (1707–1778). He was a Swedish botanist, zoologist, and physician who formalised binomial nomenclature, the modern system of naming organisms. He is known as the "father of modern taxonomy". We refer to `www.gutenberg.org/ebooks/20771`.

4.11.1 Plants

Plants

Example 21 *Although we have not yet come across domains for which the need to model the living species of plants were needed, we give some examples anyway: grass, tulip, rhododendron, oak tree.*

Analysis Predicate Prompt 13 `is_plant`: The domain analyser analyses "things" (ℓ) into a plant. The method provides the ***domain analysis prompt***:

• `is_plant` – where `is_plant(`ℓ`)` holds if ℓ is a plant ∎

The predicate `is_living_species(`ℓ`)` is a prerequisite for `is_plant(`ℓ`)`.

4.11.2 Animals

Definition: 46 Animal: We refer to the initial definition of *living species* above – while emphasizing the following traits: (i) a *form that animals can be developed to reach* and (ii) *causally determined to maintain* through (iii) *development and maintenance* in an *exchange of matter with an environment*, and (iv) *ability to purposeful movement* ∎

Analysis Predicate Prompt 14 `is_animal`: The domain analyser analyses "things" (ℓ) into an animal. The method provides the ***domain analysis prompt***:

• `is_animal` – where `is_animal(`ℓ`)` holds if ℓ is an animal ∎

The predicate is_living_species(ℓ) is a prerequisite for is_animal(ℓ).

Animals

Example 22 *Although we have not yet come across domains for which the need to model the living species of animals, in general, were needed, we give some examples anyway: a band of musicians, a swarm of flies, a bunch of crooks, a crew of sailors, a gang of outlaws, a group of people, a herd of cattle, a mob of hair, a pack of dogs, a flock of geese, a pride of lions, and a school of dolphins.*

4.11.2.1 Humans

Definition: 47 Human: A *human* (a *person*) is an *animal*, cf. Definition 46, with the additional properties of having *language*, being *conscious* of *having knowledge* (of its own situation), and *responsibility* ∎

Analysis Predicate Prompt 15 is_human: The domain analyser analyses "things" (ℓ) into a human. The method provides the **domain analysis prompt**:

• **is_human** – where **is_human(ℓ)** holds if ℓ is a human ∎

The predicate is_animal(ℓ) is a prerequisite for is_human(ℓ).

We refer to [75, Sects. 10.4–10.5] for a specific treatment of living species, animals and humans, and to [75] in general for the philosophy background for rationalising the treatment of living species, animals and humans.

We have not, in our many experimental domain modeling efforts had occasion to model humans; or rather: we have modelled, for example, automobiles as possessing human qualities, i.e., "subsuming humans". We have found, in these experimental domain modeling efforts that we often confer anthropomorphic qualities on artefacts, that is, that these artefacts have human characteristics. You, the readers, are reminded that when some programmers try to explain their programs they do so using such phrases as *and here the program does ...* so-and-so!

4.12 Fluids

Definition: 48 Fluids: By a ***fluid*** we shall understand a liquid, or a gas, or a plasma ∎

We shall simplify our treatment of fluids. We model a fluids as potentially consisting of an amalgam of one or more matters of different sorts. So we consider a fluid as a "single" endurant.[80] Composite parts may be conjoined with fluids: natural parts may "contain"

---

[80] Attributes of that "single" fluid may then reveal how it is (chemically or otherwise) composed from distinct matters.

natural and artefactual fluids, artefacts may "contain" natural and artefactual fluids. We leave it to the reader to provide analysis predicates for natural and artefactual fluids.

Natural and Man-made Fluids

Example 23 *A **natural part**, say a land area, may contain glaciers, springs, rivers, lakes, and border seas. An **artefact**, say an automobile, usually contains gasoline, lubrication oil, engine cooler liquid and window screen washer water.*

Fluid matters are either liquid, like water, sewage, or oil; or gaseous, like natural gas; or plasmatic – a combination of granular and liquid forms, like blood. To fluids we, somewhat arbitrarily, but for pragmatic reasons, add these forms of matter: granular, like iron ore, sand, or pebbles (stones, etc.); or agricultural, like sugar cane, chopped wood, grain, etc.

4.13 Atomic, Compound and Conjoin Parts

A distinguishing quality of natural and artefactual parts is whether they are atomic (Sect. **4.13.1**) or compound or conjoins (Sects. **4.13.2**)–**4.13.3**). Please note that we shall, in the following, examine the concept of parts in quite some detail. This is a choice. The choice is based on pragmatics. It is still the domain analyser cum describers' choice whether to consider a solid endurant a compound or a conjoin part or a structure. If the domain engineer wishes to investigate the details of a solid endurant then the domain engineer must choose to model[81] the solid endurant as a part. If not, then as a structure,

Non-atomic Parts: Non-atomic parts are analysed, we suggest, into

- either compound endurants [composites or sets] (Sect. **4.13.2.1** on page 70)
- or conjoins.

Compound sets are further analysed into

- either simple, one part sort sets (Sect. **4.16.1.2** on page 79) or
- several alternative part sort sets (Sect. **4.16.1.2** on page 80).

Conjoins, (Sect. **4.13.3** on page 72), are further analysed and described into:

- part-fluids conjoins (Sect. **4.16.3.1** on page 80 and **4.17.3.1** on page 87),
- fluid-parts-parts conjoins (Sect. **4.16.3.2** on page 81 and **4.17.3.2** on page 88) and
- part-parts conjoins (Sect. **4.16.3.3** on page 81 and **4.17.3.3** on page 89).

We thus distinguish between seven kinds of parts:

- (0) atomic,
- (1) composites,
- (2) single sort part sets,
- (3) alternative sorts parts sets,
- (4) part-fluids,
- (5) fluid-parts-parts and
- (6) part-parts.

Our choice is one of pragmatics. It would sometimes be awkward to model endurants without the facility of concrete sets; and, using the conjoin modeling concept reveals intention! We shall have more to say about this in time.

---

[81] We use the term *'to model'* interchangeably with the phrase *'to analyse & describe'*; similarly *a model* is used interchangeably with *an analysis & description*.

Atomic and Conjoin Parts

Example 24 We shall here hint at some examples. In modeling certain domains, given some further unspecified context, we may choose to model *consumers, retailers, wholesalers* and *consumer product manufacturers* as *atomic*, while *the market* is modelled as a *part-parts conjoins* of *sets* of *consumers, retailers, wholesalers* and *consumer product manufacturers*. In some other context we may choose otherwise! Along another line *wells, pipes, pumps, valves, forks joins* and *sinks* of an oil pipeline system are individually modelled as *part-fluids conjoins* and the oil pipeline system as a *composite* of *sets* of these *part-fluids conjoins* – each *part-fluids conjoin* consisting of the overall *part-fluids conjoin*, an *atomic part* and a definite *set* of *fluids* of different sorts. Similarly for *canal systems, waste management, rum production* and *water management systems* (as in The Netherlands). And finally we may model, as a *fluid-parts conjoin*, air traffic as a single *fluid-parts conjoin* consisting of an *atomic part* (say the *air traffic monitor & advisory authority*) and a *concrete set* of distinct aircraft *parts*. Similarly for *ocean ship monitor & advisory authorities* et cetera.

4.13.1 Atomic Parts

Definition: 49 Atomic Part: *Atomic part*s are those which, in a given context, are deemed to *not* consist of meaningful, separately observable proper *sub-parts*. A ***sub-part*** is a *part*
■

We emphasize the term 'demeed'. The *domain analyser & describer* is the one who is 'deeming'. It is all a choice.

Analysis Predicate Prompt 16 is_atomic: The domain analyser analyses a solid endurant, i.e., a part p into an atomic endurant:

• is_atomic: p is an atomic endurant if is_atomic(p) holds ■

is_solid is a prerequisite prompt of is_atomic.

The is_atomic analysis prompt comes in two variants: is_natural_atomic and is_artefactual_atomic. Similarly for the is_composite analysis prompt: is_natural_composite and is_artefactual_composite. In the following we shall often omit the infix _natural_ or _artefactual_.

Atomic Road Net Parts

Example 25 *From one point of view all of the following can be considered atomic parts: hubs, links[82], and automobiles.*

---

[82] Hub ≡ street intersection; link ≡ street segments with no intervening hubs.

4.13.2 Compound Parts

We, pragmatically, distinguish between compound-, i.e., Cartesian-product-like, and set-oriented, i.e., parts. We shall treat both as concrete type sorts.

Definition: 50 Compound Part: *Compound part*s are those which are either composite parts or are sets of parts ∎

Analysis Predicate Prompt 17 is_compound: The domain analyser analyses a solid endurant, i.e., a part p into a compound:

- is_compound: p is a compound if is_compound(p) holds ∎

4.13.2.1 Composite Parts

Definition: 51 Composite Part: *Composite part*s are those which, in a given context, are deemed to *meaningfully* consist of separately observable a ["root"] part and a definite number of proper ["sibling"] *sub-part*s of distinct sorts ∎

We emphasize the term 'demeed'. The *domain analyser & describer* is the one who is 'deeming'. It is all a choice.

Analysis Predicate Prompt 18 is_composite: The domain analyser analyses a solid endurant, i.e., a part p into a composite endurant:

- is_composite: p is a composite endurant if is_composite(p) holds ∎

is_part is a prerequisite prompt of is_composite.

Composite Automobile Parts

Example 26 *We refer to Example 25 on the previous page. We there viewed automobiles as atomic parts. From another point of view we shall here understand automobiles as composite parts: the engine train, the chassis, the car body, the doors and the wheels. These can again be considered parts.*

4.13.2.2 Set Parts

Whereas compounds consist of a *definite* number of parts of distinct sorts, sets consist of an *indefinite* number of parts of some sort[s].

Definition: 52 Set Part: *Set parts* are those which, in a given context, are deemed to *meaningfully* consist of separately observable a ["root"] part and an indefinite number of proper ["sibling"] *sub-parts* of the same sort ∎

We emphasize the term 'demeed'. The *domain analyser & describer* is the one who is 'deeming'. It is all a choice.

Analysis Predicate Prompt 19 is_set: The domain analyser analyses solid endurant, i.e., a part p into a set endurant:

- is_set: p is a composite endurant if is_set(p) holds ∎

is_part is a prerequisite prompt of is_set.

Set Part Examples

Example 27 *A railway track can be considered a set of railway units – usually themselves considered atomic parts. A library can be considered a set of books – usually themselves considered atomic parts. A container line can be considered a set of container vessels – usually themselves considered non-atomic or conjoin parts.*

We distinguish between two kinds of sets. Sets consisting of elements of the same sort, and set consisting of elements of two or more, alternative sorts.

⋆ **Simple One-Sort Sets**

Definition: 53 Simple One-Sort Sets: Simple one-sort sets are those which, in a given context, are deemed to *meaningfully* consist of separately observable a ["root"] part and an indefinite number of proper ["sibling"] *sub-parts* of the same sort ∎

Analysis Predicate Prompt 20 is_single_sort_set: The domain analyser analyses a solid endurant, i.e., a part p into a set endurant:

- is_single_sort_set: p is a composite endurant if is_single_sort_set(p) holds ∎

is_set(p) is a prerequisite prompt of is_single_sort_set(p).

Simple One-Sort Sets

Example 28 The books of library can be considered a set of same sort books.

⋆ **Alternative Sorts Sets**

Definition: 54 Alternative Sorts Sets: Alternative, several distinct sort sets are those which, in a given context, are deemed to *meaningfully* consist of separately observable a ["root"] part and an indefinite number of proper ["sibling"] *sub-part*s of a definite number of two or more distinct sorts ∎

Analysis Predicate Prompt 21 is_alternative_sorts_set: The domain analyser analyses a solid endurant, i.e., a part p into a set endurant:

- is_alternative_sorts_set: p is a composite endurant if is_alternative_sorts_set(p) holds ∎

is_set(p) is a prerequisite prompt of is_alternative_sorts_set(p).

Alternative Sorts Sets

Example 29 The rail units of a rail track can be considered a set of parts of different sorts: linear rail units, single switch point rail units, double switch point rail units, terminal units, et cetera.

4.13.3 Conjoins

Definition: 55 Conjoin: By a *conjoin* we shall here understand a *part* which can be understood to properly embody two or three further parts ∎

We say that these "further" parts are conjoined.

We suggest three kinds of conjoins: *part-fluids conjoins*, *fluid-parts-parts conjoins* and *part-parts conjoins*. We have decided to include these three endurant categories for the following reason: their use, the fact that the *domain analyser & describer* chooses to model a concept as a conjoin, shall reveal an **intent**. The intents are these. For *part-fluids conjoins* and *part-parts conjoins* the two elements of the conjoin serve two very related, i.e., conjoined, rôles: (a) the *part* as the overall monitor (and potential controller), (b) the *fluids* or *parts* as that which is being monitored and to some extent controlled by the *part*. For *fluid-parts-parts conjoins* the three elements (the fluid (a), respectively the parts (b) and the parts (c)) serve three related, i.e., conjoined, rôles: (a) the *fluid* as the "carrier" of the (b) the *parts* whose *raison d'etre* is that they can "inhabit" the *fluid* and (c) the *parts* whose *raison d'etre* is that they can "service" the former parts, i.e., (b). *We shall think of the fluid (a) as if it was an atomic part but such that it 'embodies' the fluid.*

Analysis Predicate Prompt 22 is_conjoin: The domain analyser analyses endurants e into conjoin entities as prompted by the ***domain analysis prompt***:

- is_conjoin − e is a conjoin if is_conjoin(e) holds ∎

4.13.3.1 Part-Fluids Conjoins

Definition: 56 Part-Fluids Conjoin: By a ***part-fluids conjoin*** we shall understand an endurant which is a composition of a ["root"] part, and one or more (intentionally) distinct ["sibling"] fluids ∎

The *pragmatics* of part-fluids conjoins is that they serve to model such domains as *water & flood management* – as in *The Netherlands State Water Management Authority*[83]; *canal systems*, i.e., artefactual waterways, typically with locks – as in, for example the *Panama Canal Authority*[84]; *water, oil, gas and other pipelines* – as in, for example the (now defunct) *Nabucco West Pipeline Proposal*[85]; *waste management* – as in the *European Union Waste Management Project*[86]; *uni-flow production systems* – as in, for example, the production of spirits, like whiskey, rum, etc., and in industrial manufacturing. Where *road transport nets* typically be modelled as bi-directed, cyclic graphs, the above 'conjoin nets' typically can be modelled as directed, acyclic graphs[87]. A difference between water & flood management and canal systems is that the former primarily manages the water level, by means of pumps, whereas the latter primarily manages the passage of anywhere from [300 tons] barges to [300,000 tons] vessels, by means of locks.

Caveat: We could have stipulated that conjoins consist of one or more ["root"] parts, etc., but it appears, from modeling experience, that to settle on exactly one makes modeling "easier"!

Analysis Predicate Prompt 23 is_part_fluids_conjoin: The domain analyser analyses endurants *e* into part-fluids conjoin entities as prompted by the ***domain analysis prompt***:

• is_part_fluids_conjoin – *e* is a part-fluids conjoin if is_part_fluids_conjoin(*e*) ∎

We emphasize that the *domain analyser & describer* is making a choice. The *domain analyser & describer* is the one who 'chooses'. The context and aims of the domain modeling effort decides which choices to make.

Part-Fluid Conjoins: Pipelines, I
Example 30 A pipeline consists of a number of conjoined pipeline units: The pipeline units (each with their "container" and some fluid). A pipeline unit is either a well (with some, zero, or a maximum of fluid), a pump, pumping or not (with some, zero, or a maximum of fluid), a pipe (with some, zero, or a maximum of fluid), a valve, closed or partially or fully open (with some, zero, or a maximum of fluid), a fork diverting a line into two (with some, zero, or a maximum of fluid) and a join merging two lines into one (with some, zero, or a maximum of fluid), a sink (with some, zero, or a maximum of fluid), Fluid flows in one direction, from wells to sinks. There are no cycles.

---

[83] www.rijkswaterstaat.nl/english/index.aspx
[84] www.pancanal.com/eng
[85] en.wikipedia.org/wiki/Nabucco_pipeline
[86] www.urban-waste.eu/project
[87] – although waste management systems may contain some cyclicity

Part-Fluid Conjoins: Canals with Locks, I

Example 31 A system of canals with locks consists of a number of canal units. A canal unit is a conjoined endurant consisting of a pair: a solid canal unit and a fluid – some ["muddy"] water! Canal units serve to convey canal vessels (pleasure boats, barges) in either direction of the canal system. Solid canal units are either linear (or, for that matter a curved) stretches of a canal; fork/join: diverting/joining one stretch of canal into two, respectively two into one – forks/joins connect linear canal units whose water levels "agree"; or lock sequences of one or more single locks. A lock sequence connects two linear canal units whose water levels "disagree". A single lock allows canal vessels to be lowered/raised in order to be conveyed into next single lock or linear canal units. Single locks may either be open in one or in the opposite direction, for a vessel in the single lock to sail out of the single lock in that direction or into the single lock from the opposite direction, or they may be closed, that is, in the process of lowering or raising its water level. Etc., etc.

Part-Fluids Conjoins: Waste Management, I

Example 32 Waste management [systems] are about the transport and treatment of waste. Waste can, for example, be non-clean water, sewage, chemical side-products, or other. Transport can, for example, be pipes, barrels, conveyor belts, or other. Treatment can, for example, be removing undesired fluids from non-clean water, sewage and chemicals resulting in at least clean water or desired chemical and one or more waste products. A waste treatment system consists, typically, of a number of conjoin units: sources of the waste, waste transport networks, where some segments of these networks converge on treatment plants, from which emerges two or more waste and non-waste networks.

In this monograph we shall exemplify excerpts of many different kinds of (of a category of) domains. A sub-category is that of domains primarily "populated" with conjoins such as those listed in the main opening, the *pragmatics*, paragraph of this section. We refer to Sect. **4.17.3** on page 87, Example 37 on page 88, Sect. **5.3.7** on page 118, Sect. **5.4.9** on page 137 and Sect. **7.10.1** on page 189.

4.13.3.2 Fluid-Parts-Parts Conjoins

Definition: 57 Fluid-Parts-Parts Conjoin: By a *fluid-parts-parts conjoin* we shall understand an endurant which is a composition of (a) the fluid-parts conjoin ["root"] fluid, (b) zero, one or more (intentionally) distinct *fixed* ["sibling"] parts, and (c) zero, one or more (intentionally) distinct *moving* ["sibling"] parts ∎

The *pragmatics* of fluid-parts conjoins is that they serve to model such domains as: *Vessel traffic on the open seas:* the open seas are the fluid (a), i.e., the oceans, seas, great lakes and channels; vessels are the moving parts (c), they ply from harbour to harbour and sometimes on canals (the fixed parts, (b)). *Air traffic in the sky:* (a) the air space is the fluid; (b) airports are the fixed parts; and (c) aircraft of all kinds are the moving parts.

Analysis Predicate Prompt 24 is_fluid_parts_parts_conjoin: The domain analyser analyses endurants e into fluid-parts-parts conjoin entities as prompted by the ***domain analysis prompt***:

- is_fluid_parts_parts_conjoin – e is a fluid-parts conjoin if is_fluid_parts_conjoin(e) holds ■

We again emphasize that the *domain analyser & describer* is making a choice. The *domain analyser & describer* is the one who is 'choose'. The context and aims of the domain modeling effort decides which choices to make.

4.13.3.3 Part-Parts Conjoins

Part-parts conjoins come in two forms: (i) "proper" part-parts which embody a "root" and zero one or more, but a definite number of "siblings; and (ii) a "simplified" part-parts where we ignore the "root". It is up to the domain analyser cum describer to make the choice whether to include the "root" or not. You may think of the latter as representing a structure (the"root") with sets of "siblings".

Analysis Predicate Prompt 25 is_part_parts_conjoin: The domain analyser analyses endurants e into part-parts conjoin entities as prompted by the ***domain analysis prompt***:

- is_part_parts_conjoin – e is a part-parts conjoin if is_part_parts_conjoin(e) holds ■

Part-Parts Conjoin: Container Terminal Ports

Example 33

There is the set of *composite container terminal ports*

There is the *composite part* of the port itself, with its *structures* of *sets* of *container vessels, structures* of *sets* of quay side ship/quay *quay cranes, structures* of *sets* of quay crane to terminal port *bay trucks, structures* of *sets* of *terminal port bays* and *structures* of *sets* of container *land trucks*. The *containers* are embodied in vessel bays, on quay cranes, on bay trucks, in terminal port bays and on land trucks.

There are a set of zero, one or more *container vessels*: each vessel being a *part-parts conjoin* of the "bare" vessel, containing a *part set* of vessel *container bays*.

There is a set quay cranes, each quay crane being a *part-parts conjoin* of the "bare" crane ho[i]sting a *part set* of zero or one container part.

There is a set quay crane to terminal port bay trucks, each bay truck being a *part-parts conjoin* of the "bare" truck ho[i]sting a *part set* of zero, one or two containers.

There is a set of (vessel or terminal port) *container bays*. with each *container bay* being a *structure container rows*, with a *container row* being a *structure container stack*, with a *container stack* being a *sequence containers,*

There is a set of terminal port to and from customer land trucks, each such land truck being a *part-parts conjoin* of the "bare" truck hoisting a *part set* of zero or one container.

We refer to [76, Container Terminals, September 2018], an experimental case study report where we used this, the *atomic, composite* and *concrete set* approach. We refer to [399, 400,

A *Unified Theory of Programming* approach for *rTiMo, BigrTiMo*] an extension of CSP, with real-time and process mobility expressivity as a promising approach.

•••

> **Method Step 6   From Analysis to Description:** We have reached a stage in our unraveling an, or the, *analysis calculus* where it is now possible to "switch" to a, or the, *description calculus*. That is, here is a *step of the method: to conscientiously apply description prompts*. These follow in Sect. **4.17**.

To prepare for the *external qualities description calculi* we must, however, first review how we *discover endurant sorts*, Sect. **4.14**, examine a notion of *states*, Sect. **4.19**, review the unfolding *ontology of endurants*, Sect. **4.15** and introduce some *endurant analysis functions* (not predicates), Sect. **4.16**.

4.14 On Discovering Endurant Sorts

The subject of 'discovery' depends very much on whether the endurant is an artefact or a natural part,

4.14.1 On Discovering Man-made Endurants

Artefacts are man-made. Usually the designers – the engineers, the craftsmen – who make these parts start out by ascribing specific names to them. And these names become our sort names. So the α, β, γ points below are really only relevant for the analysis of natural solid endurants.

4.14.2 On Discovering Natural Endurants

Most of the natural domains that the domain analysers & describers shall encounter are well-known to those persons; that is, they can, "discovery-wise", be treated as man-made. For less well-known natural domains, the domain analysers & describers may be well-advised in following the depth-first "discovery-process" outlined below.

We identify and observe endurants, one-by-one.

> (α) *Our analysis of parts concludes when we have "lifted" our examination of a particular endurant instance to the conclusion that it is of a given sort, that is, reflects a formal concept.*

Thus there is, in this analysis, a "eureka", a step where we shift focus from the concrete to the abstract, from observing specific endurant instances to postulating a sort: from one to the many. If e is an endurant of sort E, then we express that as: $e{:}E$.

In Sect. **4.16** we shall introduce analysis functions for all the endurants of our ontology.

> (β) *The analyser analyses, for each of these endurants, e_i, which formal concept, i.e., sort, it belongs to; let us say that it is of sort E_k; thus the sub-parts of e are of sorts $\{E_1, E_2, \dots, E_n\}$. Some E_k may be natural parts, other artefacts, or structures, or fluids. And parts may be either atomic or composite.*

The domain analyser continues to examine a finite number of other composite parts: $\{p_j, p_\ell, \ldots, p_n\}$. It is then "discovered", that is, decided, that they all consists of the same number of sub-parts $\{e_{i_1}, e_{i_2}, \ldots, e_{i_m}\}$, $\{e_{j_1}, e_{j_2}, \ldots, e_{j_m}\}$, $\{e_{\ell_1}, e_{\ell_2}, \ldots, e_{\ell_m}\}$, ..., $\{e_{n_1}, e_{n_2}, \ldots, e_{n_m}\}$, of the same, respective, endurant sorts.

(γ) It is therefore concluded, that is, decided, that $\{e_i, e_j, e_\ell, \ldots, e_n\}$ *are all of the same endurant sort E with observable part sub-sorts* $\{E_1, E_2, \ldots, E_m\}$.

Above we have *type-font-highlighted* three sentences: (α, β, γ). When you analyse what they "prescribe" you will see that they entail a "depth-first search" for endurant sorts. The β sentence says it rather directly: *"The analyser analyses, for each of these endurants, p_k, which formal concept, i.e., endurant sort it belongs to."* To do this analysis in a proper way, the analyser must ("recursively") analyse structures into sub-structures, parts and fluids, and parts "down" to their atomicity. For the parts (whether natural or man-made) and fluids of structures the analyser cum describer decides on their sort, and work ("recurse") their way "back", through possibly intermediate endurants, to the p_ks. Of course, when the analyser starts by examining atomic parts and fluids, then their endurant structure and part analysis "recursion" is not necessary.

•••

Thus the discovery of natural parts and natural fluids is very much of the kind that the Swedish 18th century botanist, zoologist, and physician Carl von Linné (Carl Linnaeus, 1707–1778) who formulated the so-called binomial nomenclature, the system of naming organisms[88].

4.14.3 An Aside: Taxonomy in Botanics and Zoology

For the discovery of natural parts we must therefore really refer to the *taxonomy* disciplines of botanics https://en.m.wikipedia.org/wiki/Botany and zoology https://en.wikipedia.org/wiki/Zoology. The term systematics, en.m.wikipedia.org/wiki/Systematics, is, more or less, synonymous with taxonomy, en.m.wikipedia.org/wiki/Plant_taxonomy. Typically, for new plant species to be identified botanists make use of a *herbarium*, en.m.wikipedia.org/wiki/Herbarium. Perhaps geographers, for example, should consider establishing digital herbaria, en.wikipedia.org/wiki/Virtual_herbarium, for geographical matters. And, similarly, for each of the more-or-less separately identifiable man-made domains – some of which are listed in [84].

4.15 A Review of the Ontology of Endurants

It is time to review the ontology of endurants. We refer to Figure 4.1 on page 53. Black circles, •, designate a category of entities. There are 21 such endurant categories. Two or three slanted lines connect entity category black circles •. Where no lines emanate from (13 of) these •s, it means that the endurants are either atomic ($p{:}A$), or a composite of endurants ($\{e_1{:}E_1, e_2{:}E_2, \ldots, e_n{:}E_n\}$), or a concrete set of endurants ($\{e_1, e_2, \ldots, e_n\}{:}E$-**set**), or a conjoin, or a fluid ($f{:}F$) – such as so labelled in Figure 4.1 on page 53. In all other cases two or three lines emanates from the other •s. They indicate, for an endurant value of the bullet labelled

---

[88] Linnæus, Systema Naturae, around 1735. Systema naturæ, sive regna tria naturæ systematice proposita per classes, ordines, genera, & species. pp. [112]. Lugduni Batavorum. (Haak), See www.biodiversitylibrary.org/item/15373#page/2/mode/1up

category, that there are two, respectively three choices naming disjoint endurant sorts. In Fig. 4.3 we have, as an example, labelled the two down-ward emanating edges from the **parts** bullet, with the **analysis prompt names** corresponding to the endurant categories upon which they are incident. We represent Fig. 4.1 on page 53 in Fig. 4.3 emphasizing the above points.

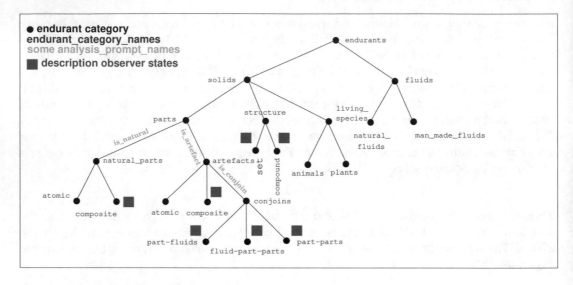

Fig. 4.3 The Endurant Analysis Hierarchy

The table below lists the full ensemble of analysis prompts (several of which will only be covered later).

is_ alternative_ sorts_ set, 72
is_ animal, 66
is_ artefactual_ atomic, 69
is_ artefactual_ composite, 69
is_ artefact, 63
is_ atomic, 69
is_ composite_ structure, 65
is_ composite, 70
is_ compound, 70
is_ conjoin, 72
is_ endurant, 57
is_ entity, 52
is_ fluid_ parts_ parts_ conjoin, 75
is_ fluid, 59
is_ human, 67
is_ living_ species, 62
is_ natural_ atomic, 69

is_ natural_ composite, 69
is_ natural_ part, 62
is_ part_ fluids_ conjoin, 73
is_ part_ parts_ conjoin, 75
is_ part, 60
is_ perdurant, 57
is_ plant, 66
is_ set_ structure, 65
is_ set, 71
is_ single_ sort_ set, 71
is_ solid, 58
is_ structure, 61

has_monitorable_attributes, 160

is_physical_attribute, 224, 135

To connect the presentation of analysis prompts, now, to the presentation of description prompts, we have added seven square magenta-coloured **boxes**, ■, to Figure 4.3. They designate the seven "analysis states" at, or in, which we can apply corresponding *description prompts*. That is, we have built up all the necessary analysis issues and are ready to "take the consequences", that is, to draw the necessary conclusions, given such-and-such an endurant category we can inquire about and describe its sorts and their observer functions.

4.16 Endurant Observer Function Prompts

We need to informally define some observer functions. They are to be used in domain description prompt definitions; one, basically, for each non-atomic endurant sort.

The observer functions "apply" to endurants, e, i.e., to domains, such that if is_category(e) then by observe_category(e) we observe the elements of e: *which are they?* and *of what kind, i.e., sort?*

─────────── On the Non-trivial Nature of Observing ───────────
Observation is at the core of domain analysis. It is far from that straightforward. Many possibilities offer themselves. *Model choices* are abundant. More than one may lead to acceptable, reasonable models. Some may lead to awkward models. This is so since the domain analyser "moves" from the informal, well, in principle, non-formalisable world of "reality" to the formal world of a domain model.

The presentation, below, of the various analysis functions follows the "tree-like" structure of Fig. 4.1 on page 53, in a left-to-right, depth-first traversal – except that we treat structures before conjoins.

─────────── On Observer Prompts ───────────
The observer functions which we are about to introduce, apply to compound and conjoin parts and yield their sub-parts and the sorts of these. *That is, we observe the domain and our observation results in a focus on a subset of that domain and sort information about that subset*

4.16.1 Observe Compound Parts

We start by analysing compound parts, that is, composite (Cartesian-like) parts and set parts, and structures.

4.16.1.1 Observe Composite Parts

Observer Function Prompt 1 observe_composite_parts: The domain analyser analyse parts into a composite part The method provides the ***domain observer prompt***:

- observe_composite_parts directs the domain analyser to observe the definite number of values and corresponding distinct sorts of the part.

  value observe_composite_parts(e) $\equiv$ ((e1,...,en),(" E1,...,En "))

The ordering, ((e1,...,en),(" E1,...,En ")), is arbitrary.

4.16.1.2 Observe Part Sets

★ **Observe Single Sort Part Sets**

Observer Function Prompt 2 `observe_single_sort_part_set`**:** The domain analyser observes parts into single sort part sets. The method provides the **domain observer prompt**:

- `observe_single_sort_part_set` directs the domain analyser to observe the the single sort part set of values and their single sort.

  value observe_single_sort_part_sets(e) ≡ ({p1,p2,...,pn}," P ")

★ **Observe Alternative Sorts Part Sets**

Observer Function Prompt 3 `observe_alternative_sorts_part_set`**:** The domain analyser observes parts into alternative sorts part sets. The method provides the **domain observer prompt**:

- `observe_alternative_sorts_part_set` directs the domain analyser to observe the values and corresponding sorts of the part.

  value observe_alternative_sorts_part_set(e) ≡ ((p1," E1 "),...,(pn," En "))

The set of parts, of different sorts, may have more than one element, $p, p', ..., p''$ being of the same sort Ei.

4.16.2 Observe Structures

Structures are like compounds: they are either composite or are set structures, in which latter case they are either single sort part sets or are alternative sorts part sets. As such we treat them as if they were compounds but shall not later, in Chapter 5, analyse their "root" element for possible internal qualities as they have no "root" element!

4.16.3 Observe Conjoins

4.16.3.1 Observe Part-Fluids Conjoins

Observer Function Prompt 4 `observe_part_fluids`**:** The domain analyser observes a conjoin into a part-fluids conjoin. The method provides the **domain observer prompt**:

- `observe_part_fluids` directs the domain analyser to observe the values and sorts of the part and the fluids:

  value observe_part_fluids(e) ≡ ((p," P "),{(m1," M_1 "),...,(mm," M_m ")})

4.16.3.2 Observe Fluid-Parts-Parts Conjoins

Observer Function Prompt 5 `observe_fluid_parts_parts`: The domain analyser observes a conjoin into a fluid-parts-parts conjoin. The method provides the **domain observer prompt**:

- `observe_fluid_parts_parts` directs the domain analyser to observe the values and sorts of the fluid, the "fixed" parts and the "movable" parts.

  value
      observe_fluid_parts_parts(e)≡((m,{fp1,...fpm},{mp1,...,mpn}),(❝ M,fP,mP ❞))

Elaboration 1 **Type, Values and Type Names:** The endurant analysis functions, this and the below, all illustrate quoting ∎

Fluid and Parts of Transports

Example 34 We exemplify three kinds of transport.

- **Air Transport:** The fluid of air transport is an airspace, an EXTENT.[89] The fixed parts of air transport is a set of two or more airports. The movable parts of air transport is a set of zero, one or more aircraft.
- **Ocean-Shipping:** The fluid of ocean-shipping is the oceans, seen as one, an EXTENT. The fixed parts of ocean-shipping is a set of two or more harbours. The movable parts of ocean-shipping is a set of zero, one or more ships.
- **Rail Transport** The fluid of rail transport is a (possibly bridge- or tunnel-connected) land area, the EXTENT. The fixed parts of rail transport is a connected rail net. The movable parts of ocean-shipping is a set of zero, one or more trains.

4.16.3.3 Observe Part-Parts Conjoins

Observer Function Prompt 6 `observe_part_parts`: The **domain observer prompt**

- `observe_part_parts` directs the domain analyser to observe a "compound" of one or more fluids that the conjoin embodies – together with their fluid sort names.

  value
      observe_part_parts(e) ≡ ((p,(p1,p2,...,pn)),(❝ P ❞,(❝ P1,...,Pn ❞))) ∎

---

[89] For EXTENTs see Item 61 on page 27 of Sect. **3.4** on page 26.

4.17 Calculating Sort Describers

Based on the analyses of Sects. **4.8**, **4.10**, **4.12** and **4.13**, we conclude that there are the following kinds of endurants to sort- (i.e., type) and observer function describe:

- □ *composite parts* (a),
- sets:

  ∞ □ *single sort part sets* (b),
  ∞ □ *alternative sorts part sets* (c),

- conjoins:

∞ □ *part-fluids conjoins,*
∞ □ *fluid-parts-parts conjoins,*
∞ □ *part-parts conjoins,* and

- □□□ *structures*, with their three variants (a-b-c).

Atomic parts are what is left, when compounds, conjoins and structures have no further sub endurants. The general signature of the describer functions are of the form:

    value calculate_...._sorts: E → RSL-Text

─────────────── On Calculation Prompts ───────────────

The calculation prompts, which we are about to introduce, apply to compound and conjoin parts of a domain and yield RSL-**Text**s!

Please note the three "on ... prompts" boxes, pages 52, 79, and above.

- Analysis prompts apply to domain phenomena and yield truth values in the mind of the analyser.
- Observer prompts apply to domain phenomena and yield subsets of domain endurants and [information for the observe about] their sorts.
- Calculation prompts apply to domain phenomena and yield RSL-**Text**s.

4.17.1 Calculating Compound Parts Sorts

Compound parts are either composite parts, with a definite number of elements, or are sets, with an indefinite number of elements. Set parts are either single sort sets or are alternative sorts sets.

4.17.1.1 Calculating Composite Parts Sorts

The above analysis amounts to the analyser first "applying" the *domain analysis* prompt is_composite(e) to a solid endurant, e, where we now assume that the obtained truth value is **true**. Let us assume that endurants e:E consist of sub-endurants of sorts $\{E_1, E_2, \ldots, E_m\}$. Since we cannot automatically guarantee that our domain descriptions secure that E and each E_i ($1 \leq i \leq m$) denotes disjoint sets of entities we must prove it.

Domain Description Prompt 2 calculate_composite_parts_sorts: If is_composite(e) holds, then the analyser "applies" the ***domain description prompt***

- calculate_composite_parts_sorts(e)

resulting in the analyser writing down the *endurant sorts and endurant sort observers* domain
description text according to the following schema:

2. `calculate_composite_parts_sorts(e)` Describer

 let ($\_^{90}$,(" E1,...,En ")) = analyse_composite_parts_sorts(e)^{91} **in**
" **Narration:**
  [s] ... narrative text on sorts ...
  [o] ... narrative text on sort observers ...
  [p] ... narrative text on proof obligations ...
Formalisation:
  type
  [s] E_1, "..." , E_m
  value
  [o] **obs**_E_1: E → E_1, "..." , **obs**_E_m: E → E_m
  proof obligation
  [p] [Disjointness of endurant sorts] "
  end

Elaboration 2 Type, Values and Type Names: Note the use of quotes above. Please observe
that when we write obs_E then obs_E is the name of a function. The E, when juxtaposed to
obs_ is now a name ■

Observer Function Prompt 7 `type_name, type_of, is_`: The definition of **obs**_E_i implicitly implies the definition of

• **obs**_E_i(e)=e_i ⊃ type_name(e_i)≡" E_i "∧ type_of(e_i)≡E_i ∧ is_E_i(e_i)

Modelling Choice 1 *Composites:* For compound endurants and structures the analyser
cum describer chooses some to be modelled as composites.

A Road Transport Domain: Composite

Example 35 ^{92}

96 There is the universe of discourse, UoD.   97 a road net, RN, and

It is composed from   98 a fleet of vehicles, FV.

type   **value**
96 UoD   97 obs_RN: UoD → RN
97 RN   98 obs_FV: UoD → FV □
98 FV

We continue the analysis & description of "our" road transport system:

---

^{90} 90 The use of the underscore, _, shall inform the reader that there is no need, here, for naming a value.
^{91} 91 For `analyse_composite_parts` see Sect. **4.16.1.1** on page 79

99 *The road net consists of*
    a a, as we shall later see, structure, SH, of hubs
      and
    b a, as we shall also later see, structure, SL, of
      links.

100 *The fleet of vehicles consists of*
    a a, as we shall likewise see, structure, SBC, of
      bus companies, and
    b a, as we shall later see, structure, PA, a pool of
      automobiles.

type
99a SH
99b SL
100a SBC
100b PA

value
99a obs_SH: RN → SH
99b obs_SL: RN → SL
100a obs_BC: FV → BC
100b obs_PA: FV → PA

Figure 4.4 graphically depicts [the dotted/dashed lines] Example 35 on the previous page's composition of parts. The fully lined square boxes stand for atomic parts: links, hubs, buses and automobiles. These will be formally introduced in Example 38 on page 90.

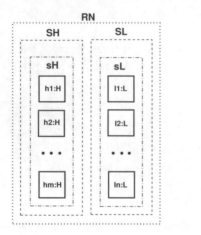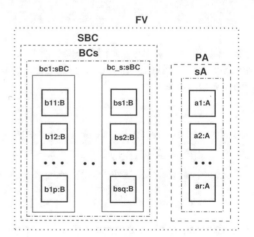

Fig. 4.4 A Road Transport System Compounds and Structures

---

[92] Example 35 on the previous page's **Narration** is not representative of what it should be. Here is a more reasonable narration:

- A road net is a set of hubs (road intersections) and links such that links are connected to adjacent hubs, and such that connected links and hubs form *roads* and where a road is a thoroughfare, route, or way on land between two places that has been paved or otherwise improved to allow travel by foot or some form of conveyance, including a motor vehicle, cart, bicycle, or horse [Wikipedia]

Et cetera for *fleet of vehicles*.

We bring this clarification here, once, and allow ourselves, with the reader's permission, to narrate only very steno-graphically.

4.17.1.2 Calculating Single Sort Part Sets

Domain Description Prompt 3 calculate_single_sort_parts_sort: If is_single_set_-sort_parts(e) holds, then the analyser "applies" the ***domain description prompt***

* calculate_single_sort_parts(e)

resulting in the analyser writing down the *single set sort and sort observers* domain description text according to the following schema:

3. calculate_single_sort_parts_sort(e) Describer

    let (_,❝ P ❞) = analyse_single_sort_part(e)[93] in
❝ **Narration:**
    [s]   ... narrative text on sort ...
    [o]   ... narrative text on sort observer ...
    [p]   ... narrative text on proof obligation ...
Formalisation:
    type
    [s] P
    [s] Ps = P-set
    value
    [o] **obs_**Ps: E → Ps ❞
    end

Elaboration 3 Type, Values and Type Names: Note the use of quotes above. Please observe that when we write obs_Ps then obs_Ps is the name of a function. The Ps, when juxtaposed to obs_ is now a name ∎

Modelling Choice 2 *Single Sort Part Sets:* For compounds and structures the analyser cum describer chooses some to be modelled as sets of endurants of the same sort.

4.17.1.3 Calculating Alternative Sort Part Sets

We leave it to the reader to decipher the calculate_alternative_sort_part_sorts prompt.

Domain Description Prompt 4 calculate_alternative_sort_part_sorts: If is_altern-ative_sort_parts_sorts(e) holds, then the analyser "applies" the ***domain description prompt***

* calculate_alternative_sort_part_sorts(e)

resulting in the analyser writing down the *alternative sort and sort observers* domain description text according to the following schema:

4. calculate_alternative_sort_part_sorts(e) Describer

    let ((p1,❝ E1 ❞),...,(pn,❝ En ❞)) = analyse_alternative_sorts_part_set_sorts(e)[94] in
❝ **Narration:**
    [s]   ... narrative text on alternative sorts ...

---

[93] For analyse_single_sort_part see Sect. **4.16.1.2** on page 79.

[o]   ... narrative text on sort observers ...
[p]   ... narrative text on proof obligations ...
Formalisation:
   type
   [s]   Ea = E_1 | ... | E_n
   [s]   E_1 :: End_1, ..., E_n :: End_n
   value
   [o]   **obs_**Ea: E → Ea
   axiom
   [p]   [disjointness **of** alternative sorts] E_1, ..., E_n
   end

The set of parts, of different sorts, may have more than one element, say $p, p', ..., p''$ being of the same sort E_i. Since parts are not mentioned in the sort description above, cf., ‗, only the distinct alternative sort observers appear in that description.

Alternative Rail Units

Example 36

101 The example is that of a railway system.
102 We focus on railway nets. They can be observed from the railway system.
103 The railway net embodies a set of [railway] net units.
104 A net unit is either a straight or curved **linear** unit, or a simple switch, i.e., a **turnout**, unit[95] or a simple cross-over, i.e., a **rigid** crossing unit, or a single switched cross-over, i.e., a **single** slip unit, or a double switched cross-over, i.e., a **double** slip unit, or a **terminal** unit.
105 As a formal specification language technicality disjointness of the respective rail unit types is afforded by RSL's :: type definition construct.

We refer to Figure 4.5 on the next page.

type
101. RS
102. RN
value
102. obs_RN: RS → RN
type
103. NUs = NU-**set**
104. NU = LU | PU | RU | SU | DU | TU

105. LU :: LinU
105. PU :: PntU
105. SU :: SwiU
105. DU :: DblU
105. TU :: TerU
value
103. obs_NUs: RN → NUs

We continue this example in Example 50 on page 117   □

Modelling Choice 3 *Alternative Sort Part Sets:* For compounds and structures the analyser cum describer chooses some to be modelled as sets of endurants of alternative sorts.

---
[94] For analyse_alternative_sort_part_sorts see Sect. **4.16.1.2** on page 80.
[95] https://en.wikipedia.org/wiki/Railroad_switch

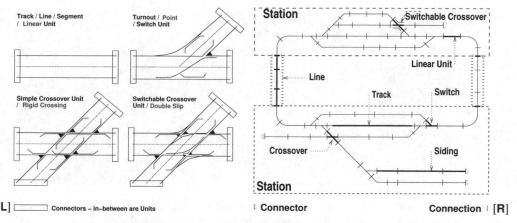

Fig. 4.5 Left: Four net units (LU, PU, SU, DU); Right: A railway net

4.17.2 Calculating Structure Sorts

You will have observed that the *compound parts* and the *structures* endurants have in common that they both analyse into composites, respectively sets. What distinguishes them is that compound parts have internal qualities, but structures have not. Their "siblings" may, and usually will, have. Since this section, i.e., Sect. **4.17**, is about *sort describers* only we can therefore "re-use" the *sort observers* of Sect. **4.17.1** – and need therefore not "repeat" them here.

Modelling Choice 4 Structures: For solid endurants the analyser cum describer chooses some to be modelled as structures, that is, as an endurants with no substance "in-itself", only in it "siblings".

4.17.3 Calculating Conjoin Sorts

We remind the reader of Sect. **4.13.3** on page 72 on *conjoins*.

4.17.3.1 Calculating Part-Fluids Sorts

Domain Description Prompt 5 calculate_part_fluids_sorts: The ***domain description prompt***:

• calculate_part_fluids_sorts(*e*)

yields the *conjoin sorts and conjoin sort observers* domain description text according to the following schema:
5. calculate_part_fluids_sorts(e) Describer
    let ((_,❝ P ❞),((_,❝ M1 ❞),...,(_,❝ Mm ❞))) = analyse_part_fluids_sorts(e)[96] **in**
❝ **Narration:**
    [s] ... narrative text on conjoin sorts ...

[o] ... narrative text on conjoin sort observers ...
Formalisation:
  type
  [s] P
  [s] M1, ..., Mm
  value
  [o] **obs**_P: E → P
  [o] **obs**_M1: E → M1, **"**...**"**, **obs**_Mm: E → Mm **"**
  end

We shall mostly associate more than one fluid with a special kind of conjoins: the so-called *treat*ment conjoins, leaving all other conjoins to embody just one fluid.

Observer Function Prompt 8 `type_name, type_of, is_`: The definitions of **obs**_Mi: E →
Mi implicitly imply the definition of

- 　　　**obs**_Mi(e) = mo ⊃ type_name(mi) ≡ **"** Mi **"**
　　　obs_Mi(e) = mi ⊃ type_of(mi) ≡ Mi

Modelling Choice 5 *Part-Fluids:* For some parts the analyser cum describer chooses for some to be modelled as conjoins, and then in the form of a "master" part of a set of "sibling" fluids.

Pipeline Parts and Fluid
Example 37 We refer to Appendix Sect. **A.1**.

4.17.3.2 Calculating Fluid-Parts-Parts Sorts

Domain Description Prompt 6 `calculate_fluid_parts_parts_sorts`:   The ***domain de-scription prompt***:

- `calculate_fluid_parts_parts_sorts(e)`

yields the *fluid-parts-parts conjoin sorts and conjoin sort observers* domain description text according to the following schema:
6. calculate_fluid_parts_sorts(e) Describer
    let (_,(**"** M,fP,mP **"**)) = analyse_fluid_parts_parts_fluid(e)[97] **in**
"Narration:
    [s] ... narrative text on conjoin sorts ...
    [o] ... narrative text on conjoin sort observers ...
Formalisation:

---
[96] For `analyse_part_fluids_sorts` see Sect. **4.16.3.1** on page 80.

```
type
[s]   M, fP, mP
value
[o]   obs_M: E → M
[o]   obs_fP: E → fP
[o]   obs_mP: E → mP "
end
```

Observer Function Prompt 9 `type_name`, `type_of`, `is_`: The definitions of **obs**_M: E →
M and **obs**_P: E → P implicitly imply the definition of

•   **obs**_M(e)=m ⊃ type_name(m)≡" M "
        obs_fP(e)=fp ⇒ type_name(fp)≡" fP "
        obs_mP(e)=mp ⇒ type_name(mp)≡" mP "
        obs_M(e)=m ⊃ type_of(m)≡M
        obs_fP(e)=fp ⇒ type_of(fp)≡fP
        obs_mP(e)=mp ⇒ type_of(mp)≡mP

Modelling Choice 6 *Fluid-Parts-Parts:* For some parts the analyser cum describer chooses
for some to be modelled as conjoins, and then in the form of a "master" fluid and of a set of
"sibling" fluids.

4.17.3.3 Calculating Part-Parts Sorts

Domain Description Prompt 7 `calculate_part_parts_sorts`: The ***domain description
prompt***:

• calculate_part_parts_sorts(*e*)

yields the *conjoin sorts and conjoin sort observers* domain description text according to the
following schema:
7. `calculate_part_parts_sorts(e)` Describer
     let (_,(" P ",(" P1,...,Pn "))) = analyse_part_parts_sorts(e) **in**
" Narration:
     [s]   ... narrative text on conjoin sorts ...
     [o]   ... narrative text on conjoin sort observers ...
     [p]   ... proof obligation text ...
Formalisation:
     type
     [s]   P, P1, ..., Pn
     value
     [o]   **obs**_P: E → P
     [o]   **obs**_P1: E → P1, ..., **obs**_Pn: E → Pn

---

[97] For analyse_fluid_parts_parts_sorts see Sect. **4.16.3.2** on page 81.

```
axiom
[p]   [ disjointness of P1, ..., Pn ]  ⁹⁹
end
```

Observer Function Prompt 10 `type_name, type_of, is_:` The definitions of **obs_P**: E →
P implicitly imply the definition of

- **obs_P**(e) = p ⊃ type_name(p) ≡ **" P "**
  obs_P(e) = p ⊃ type_of(p) ≡ P
  obs_Pi(e) = pi ⊃ type_name(pi) ≡ **" Pi "**   [i = 1,...,n]
  obs_Pi(e) = pi ⊃ type_of(pi) ≡ Pi   [i = 1,...,n]

Modelling Choice 7 *Part-Parts:* As for composites, structures and, now, in general for conjoins the analyser cum describer chooses for some model of a domain, one subset of the parts forming the conjoin, for another model of supposedly "the same" domain another subset.

A Road Transport Domain: Part-Parts

Example 38

106 The structure of hubs is a set, sH, of atomic hubs, H.
107 The structure of links is a set, sL, of atomic links, L.
108 The structure of buses is a set, sBC, of composite bus companies, BC.
109 The composite bus companies, BC, are sets of buses, sB.
110 The structure of private automobiles is a set, sA, of atomic automobiles, A.

```
106 H, sH = H-set  axiom ∀ h:H • is_atomic(h)
107 L, sL = L-set  axiom ∀ l:L • is_atomic(l)
108 BC, BCs = BC-set  axiom ∀ bc:BC • is_composite(bc)
109 B, Bs = B-set  axiom ∀ b:B • is_atomic(b)
110 A, sA = A-set  axiom ∀ a:A • is_atomic(a)
value
106 obs_sH: SH → sH
107 obs_sL: SL → sL
108 obs_sBC: SBC → BCs
109 obs_Bs: BCs → Bs
110 obs_sA: SA → sA   □
```

4.18 On Endurant Sorts

4.18.1 Derivation Chains

Let E be a composite sort or a structure. Let $E_1, E_2, \ldots, E_m$ be the endurants "discovered" by means of `observe_endurant_sorts(e)` where e:E. We say that $E_1, E_2, \ldots, E_m$ are (immediately) **derived** from E. If E_k is derived from E_j and E_j is derived from E_i, then, by transitivity, E_k is **derived** from E_i.

---

[97] For `analyse_part_parts_sorts` see Sect. **4.16.3.3** on page 81.

4.18.2 No Recursive Derivations

We "mandate" that if E_k is derived from E_j then sort name E_j is different from sort name E_k and there can be no E_k derived from E_j, that is, E_k cannot be derived from E_k. That is, we do not "provide for" recursive domain sorts. It is not a question, actually of allowing recursive domain sorts. It is, we claim to have observed, in very many *analysis & description* experiments, that there are no recursive domain sorts![98]

4.18.3 Names of Part Sorts and Types

The **domain analysis & description** text prompts observe_endurant_sorts, as well as the below-defined observe_part_type, observe_component_sorts and observe_fluid_sorts – as well as the further below defined attribute_names, observe_fluid_sorts, observe_u-nique_identifier, observe_mereology and observe_attributes prompts introduced below – "yield" type names. That is, it is as if there is a reservoir of an indefinite-sized set of such names from which these names are selected, and once obtained are never again selected. There may be domains for which two distinct part sorts may be composed from identical part sorts. *In this case the domain analyser indicates so by prescribing a part sort already introduced.*

4.19 States

In our continued modeling we shall make good use of a concept of states.

Definition: 58 State: By a *state* we shall understand any collection of one or more parts ∎

In Chapter 5 we introduce the notion of *attributes*. Among attributes there are the *dynamic attributes*. They model that internal part quality values may change dynamically. So we may wish, on occasion, to 'refine' our notion of state to be just those parts which have dynamic attributes.

Given any universe of discourse, uod:UoD, we can recursively calculate its "full" state, calc_parts({uod}).

111 Let e be any endurant. Let arg_parts be the parts to be calculated. Let res_parts be the parts calculated. Initialise the calculator with arg_parts={e} and res_parts={}. Calculation stops with arg_parts empty and res_parts the result.
112 If is_composite(e)
113 then we obtain its immediate parts, observe_composite_part(e)
114 add them, as a set, to arg_parts, e removed from arg_parts and added to res_parts calculating the parts from that.

---

[98] Some readers may object, but we insist! If *trees* are brought forward, as an example of a recursively definable domain, then we argue: Yes, trees can be recursively defined. Trees can, as well, be defined as a variant of graphs, and you wouldn't claim, would you, that graphs are recursive? We shall consider the living species of trees (that is, plants), as atomic. Later, in Sect. 5.4, we shall introduce the internal quality of attributes. We may then find that we wish to model certain attributes as 'trees'. Then, by all means, You may do so recursively. But natural trees, having roots and branches cannot be recursively defined, since proper "sub-trees" of trees would then have roots!

115 If is_single_sort_part_set(e)
116 then the parts, ps, of the single sort set are observed,
117 added to arg_parts and e removed from arg_parts and added to res_parts calculating the parts from that.
118 If is_alternative_sorts_part_set(e) then the parts, ((p1,_),(p2,_),...,(pn,_)), of the alternative sorts set are observed, added to arg_parts and e removed from arg_parts and added to res_parts calculating the parts from that.
119 If is_part_parts(e) then we obtain its immediate parts; then suitably *rearrange* argument and result parameters calculating the parts from that.
120 If is_part_fluids(e) then we obtain its immediate parts; then suitably *rearrange* argument and result parameters calculating the parts from that.
121 Etc.
122 If is_structure(e)
123 then it is either a part set structure
124 or a composite part structure
125 and is treated as in lines 113–114 and 116–117, respectively. with the significant difference that the inquired endurant, e, is not "added" to the result argument!

value
111.   calc_parts: E-set → E-set → E-set
111.   calc_parts(arg_parts)(res_parts) ≡
111.   if arg_parts = {} then res_parts else
111.   let e · e ∈ arg_parts in
112.   is_composite(e) →
113.   let ((e1,e2,...,en), _) = observe_composite_part(e) in
114.   calc_parts(arg_parts\{e} ∪ {e1,e2,...,en})(res_parts ∪ {e}) end
115.   is_single_sort_part_set(e) →
116.   let ps = observe_single_sort_part_set(e) in
117.   calc_parts(arg_parts\{e}∪ ps)(res_parts ∪ {e}) end
118.   is_alternative_sort_part_set(e) →
118.   let ((p1,_),(p2,_),...,(pn,_)) = observe_alternative_sorts_part_set(e) in
118.   calc_parts(arg_parts\{e}∪{p1,p2,...,pn})(res_parts ∪ {e}) end
119.   is_part_parts(e) →
119.   calc_parts(arg_parts\{e} ∪ observe_part_parts(e))(res_parts ∪ {e})
120.   is_part_fluids(e) →
120.   calc_parts(arg_parts\{e} ∪ observe_part_fluids(e))(res_parts ∪ {e})
121.   et cetera !
122.   is_structure(e) →
123.   is_part_set_structure(e) →
125.   let ps = observe_single_sort_part_set(e) in
125.   calc_parts(arg_parts\{e} ∪ ps)(res_parts) end
124.   is_composite_part_structure(e) →
125.   let ((p1,_),(p2,_),...,(pn,_)) = observe_alternative_sorts_part_set(e) in
125.   calc_parts(arg_parts\{e} ∪ {p1,p2,...,pn})(res_parts) end
111.   end end

Constants and States

Example 39

126 Let there be given a universe of discourse, rts. It is an example of a state.

From that state we can calculate other states.

127 *The set of all hubs, hs.*
128 *The set of all links, ls.*
129 *The set of all hubs and links, hls.*
130 *The set of all bus companies, bcs.*
131 *The set of all buses, bs.*
132 *The set of all private automobiles, as.*
133 *The set of all parts, ps.*

value
126 *rts*:UoD   [126]
127 *hs*:H-set ≡:H-set ≡ obs_sH(obs_SH(obs_RN(*rts*)))
128 *ls*:L-set ≡:L-set ≡ obs_sL(obs_SL(obs_RN(*rts*)))
129 *hls*:(H|L)-set ≡ *hs*∪*ls*
130 *bcs*:BC-set ≡ obs_BCs(obs_SBC(obs_FV(obs_RN(*rts*))))
131 *bs*:B-set ≡ ∪{obs_Bs(bc)|bc:BC•bc ∈ *bcs*}
132 *as*:A-set ≡ obs_BCs(obs_SBC(obs_FV(obs_RN(*rts*))))
133 *ps*:(UoB|H|L|BC|B|A)-set ≡ *rts*∪*hls*∪*bcs*∪*bs*∪*as*

Method Step 7   Domain State: We have found, once all the state components, i.e., the endurant parts, have had their external qualities analysed, that it is then expedient to define the domain state. It can then be the basis for several concepts of internal qualities.

We refer to Sect. **7.2.1** on page 160 for more on states.

4.20 A Domain Discovery Process, I

In this and some following sections[99] we shall clarify some aspects of the **domain analysis & description** method. A method principle is that of *exhaustively analyse & describe* all external qualities of the domain under scrutiny. A method technique implied here is that sketched in Sect. **5.8** on page 146. The method tools are here all the analysis and description prompts covered so far.

In this initial chapter on **domain analysis & description** we have systematically covered, first, the analysis of external qualities of domain endurants, then the description of these. We have done so in a style which **analysed domains**, as it were, "top-down"; from overall domain universes of discourse; through entities, endurants, solid and fluid endurants; further "across" parts, structures and living species; the natural and artefactual parts of the parts; to finally conclude our external qualities analysis with the atomic, composite and conjoin parts. With the ontology of the external qualities of domain endurants "behind us" we then concluded the main sections of this chapter with the *description* of external domain qualities, that is, *Describer Schemas* 2–6 (pages 83–88). We can now gather all of this together with advice on a systematic process of performing the analysis & description process. Chapters 5 (Sect. **5.8** on page 146) and 7 (Sect. **7.12** on page 193) will likewise systematise the processes of discovering internal endurant qualities and perdurants, respectively.

---

[99] Sects. **5.8** on page 146 and **7.12** on page 193

4.20.1 Two Forms of Ontologies

We can speak of two kinds of ontologies: the general ontologies of domain analysis & description and a specific domain's possible endurant ontologies.

4.20.1.1 Domain Analysis & Description Ontologies

An example of a general domain analysis & description ontology has "permeated" this monograph, namely that of Fig. 4.1 on page 53. It is not the only possible domain analysis & description ontology. The published papers, [73, 81], on which this chapter and its follow-on chapters are built, display "pre-decessor" domain analysis & description ontologies. Section **4.22.5** on page 102 further discusses the issue of varieties of general domain analysis & description ontologies.

4.20.1.2 Specific Domain Ontologies

By an ontology of a specific domain's endurants we mean we mean something that can be displayed as a tree whose root designate a universe of discourse, i.e., the domain, that is, an endurant, and, if composite, whose immediate sub-trees designate the immediate components of the root endurants, et cetera.

Figure 4.4 on page 84 is then the basis for Fig. 4.6 an ontology for the road transport domain so predominantly exemplified in this and the following chapters.

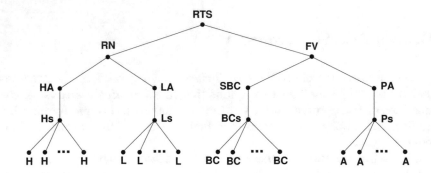

Fig. 4.6 A Road Transport System Ontology

4.20.2 A Domain Discovery Notice Board

Common to all the discovery processes is an idea of a *notice board*. A notice board, at any time in the development of a domain description, is a repository of the analysis and description process. We suggest to model the notice board in terms of three global variables. The new variable holds the parts yet to be described, The ans variable holds the sort name of parts that have so far been described, the gen variable holds the parts that have so far been described, and the txt variable holds the RSL-Text so far generated. We model the txt variable as a map from endurant identifier names to RSL-Text.

```
───────────────  A Domain Discovery Notice Board  ───────────────

variable
    new := {uod} ,
    asn := { " UoD "}
    gen := {} ,
    txt:RSL-Text:= [ uid_UoD(uod) ↦ ⟨" type UoD "⟩ ]
```

4.20.3 An Endurant External Qualities Discovery Process

The discover_sorts pseudo program suggests a systematic way of proceeding through analysis, manifested by the is_··· predicates, to (→) description.

Some comments are in order. The e-set$_a$⊎e-set$_b$ expression yields a set of endurants that are either in e-set$_a$, or in e-set$_a$, or in both, but such that two endurants, e$_x$ and e$_y$ which are of the same endurants type, say E, and are in respective sets is only represented once in the result; that is, if they are type-wise the same, but value-wise different they will only be included once in the result. As this is the first time RSL-Text is put on the notice board we express this as:

• txt := txt ∪ [type_name(v) ↦ ⟨RSL-Text⟩]

Subsequent insertion of RSL-Text for internal quality descriptions and perdurants is then concatenated to the end of previously uploaded RSL-Text.

```
──────  An External Qualities Domain Analysis and Description Process  ──────

value
    discover_sorts: Unit → Unit
    discover_sorts() ≡
        while new ≠ {} do let v • v ∈ new in
            ( new := new \ {v} || gen := gen ∪ {v} || ans := ans \ {type_of(v)} ) ;
            is_atomic(v) → skip ,
            is_compound(v) →
                is_composite(v) →
                    let ((e1,...,en),(" E1,...,En "))=analyse_composite_parts(v) in
                    ( ans := ans ∪ {" E1,...,En "} || new := new ⊎ {e1,...,en}
                    || txt := txt ∪ [type_name(v) ↦ ⟨calculate_composite_part_sorts(v)⟩] ) end,
                is_set(v) →
                    ( is_single_sort_set(v) →
                        let ({p1,...,pn}," P ")=analyse_single_sort_parts_set(v) in
                        ( ans := ans ∪ {" P "} || new := new ⊎ {p1,...,pn} ||
                            txt := txt ∪ [type_name(v) ↦ calculate_single_sort_part_sort(v)] ) end,
                    is_alternative_sorts_set(v) →
                        let ((p1," E1 "),...,(pn," En "))= observe_alternative_sorts_part_set(v) in
                        ( ans := ans ∪ {" E1,...,En "} || new := new ⊎ {p1,...,pn} ||
                            txt := txt ∪ [type_name(v) ↦ calculate_alternative_sorts_part_sort(v)] ) end ),
                is_conjoin(v) →
                    ( is_part_fluids_conjoin(v)  →
                        let ((p," P "),{(m1," M_1 "),...,(mm," M_m ")})=analyse_part_fluids(v) in
                        ( new := new ⊎ {m1,...,mn} || ans := ans ∪ {" P "} ||
                            txt := txt ∪ [type_name(v) ↦ ⟨describe_part_fluids_sorts(v)⟩] ) end,
                    is_fluid_parts_parts_conjoin(v)  →
```

let((m,{fp1,...fpm},{mp1,...,mpn}),(❝ M,fP,mP ❞))=analyse_fluid_parts_parts(v) **in**
(ans := ans ∪ {❝ M,fP,mP ❞} ‖ new := new ⊎ {m,fp1,...fpm}
‖ txt := txt ∪ [type_name(v) ↦ ⟨describe_fluid_parts_parts_sorts(v)⟩]) **end**,
is_part_parts_conjoin(v)   →
　　　let ((p,(p1,p2,...,pn)),(❝ P ❞,(❝ P1,...,Pn ❞)))=analyse_part_parts(v) **in**
　　　(ans := ans ∪ {❝ P,P1,...,Pn ❞} ‖ new := new ⊎ {p,p1,...,pn}
　　　‖ txt := txt ∪ [type_name(v) ↦ ⟨describe_part_parts_sorts(v)⟩]) **end**) **end end**

For structures we remove the structure endurants, here v, from ans as it has no "root" part
to be further analysed and described. This marks – **a major** – difference between composite
endurants and structure endurants.

4.20.4 A Suggested Analysis & Description Approach, I

The discover_sorts process definition is general. Among its many interpretations is one which
we may recommend. We call it *the breadth-first, top-down analysis & description approach.*
The 'breadth-first, top-down' prefix refers to a tree rendition of an ontology for the specific
domain endurants. Figure 4.7 illustrates a breadth-first, top-down traversal of that ontology
– as shown in Fig. 4.6 on page 94: Figure 4.7 does not reveal whether composite bullets,

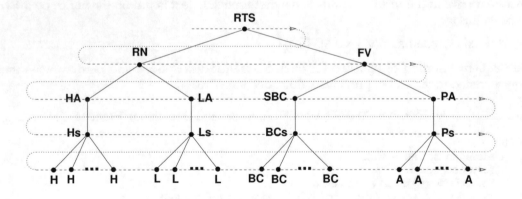

Fig. 4.7 A Breadth-First, Top-Down Traversal

•s, stand for 'real' composites' or for structures. We shall presently leave that to the domain
engineer cum scientist to decide.

We shall follow up on these remarks in Sect. **5.8.2** on page 147.

4.20.5 An Assumption

In the above *External Qualities Domain Analysis and Description Process* Schema we have
conjectured that atomic parts have already had their type and observer function defined.

4.21 Formal Concept Analysis

Domain analysis involves that of concept analysis. As soon as we have identified an entity for analysis we have identified a concept. The entity is usually a spatio-temporal, i.e., a physical thing. Once we speak of it, it becomes a concept. Instead of examining just one entity the domain analyser shall examine many entities. Instead of describing one entity the domain describer shall describe a class of entities. Ganter & Wille's [169] addresses this issue.

4.21.1 A Formalisation

This section is a transcription of Ganter & Wille's [169] *Formal Concept Analysis, Mathematical Foundations*, the 1999 edition, Pages 17–18.

Some Notation: By $\mathcal{E}$ we shall understand the type of entities; by $\mathbb{E}$ we shall understand a phenomenon of type $\mathcal{E}$; by Q we shall understand the type of qualities; by Q we shall understand a quality of type Q; by $\mathcal{E}$-**set** we shall understand the type of sets of entities; by $\mathbb{E}\$$ we shall understand a set of entities of type $\mathcal{E}$-**set**; by Q-**set** we shall understand the type of sets of qualities; and by $Q\$$ we shall understand a a set of qualities of type Q-**set**.

Definition: 59 Formal Context: A *formal context* $\mathbb{K} := (\mathbb{E}\$, \mathbb{I}, Q\$)$ consists of two sets; $\mathbb{E}\$$ of entities and $Q\$$ of qualities, and a relation $\mathbb{I}$ between $\mathbb{E}$ and Q ∎

To express that $\mathbb{E}$ is in relation $\mathbb{I}$ to a Quality Q we write $\mathbb{E} \cdot \mathbb{I} \cdot Q$, which we read as *"entity $\mathbb{E}$ has quality Q"* ∎Example endurant entities are a specific vehicle, another specific vehicle, et cetera; a specific street segment (link), another street segment, et cetera; a specific road intersection (hub), another specific road intersection, et cetera, a monitor. Example endurant entity qualities are (a vehicle) has mobility, (a vehicle) has velocity (≥ 0), (a vehicle) has acceleration, et cetera; (a link) has length (> 0), (a link) has location, (a link) has traffic state, et cetera.

Definition: 60 Qualities Common to a Set of Entities: For any subset, $s\mathbb{E}\$ \subseteq \mathbb{E}\$$, of entities we can define $\mathcal{D}Q$ for "derive[d] set of qualities".

$\mathcal{D}Q : \mathcal{E}\text{-set} \to (\mathcal{E}\text{-set} \times \mathcal{I} \times Q\text{-set}) \to Q\text{-set}$

$\mathcal{D}Q(s\mathbb{E}\$)(\mathbb{E}\$, \mathbb{I}, Q\$) \equiv \{Q \mid Q{:}Q, \mathbb{E}{:}\mathcal{E} \cdot \mathbb{E}{\in}s\mathbb{E}\$ \wedge \mathbb{E} \cdot \mathbb{I} \cdot Q\}$

pre: $s\mathbb{E}\$ \subseteq \mathbb{E}\$$

The above expresses: *"the set of qualities common to entities in $s\mathbb{E}\$$"* ∎

Definition: 61 Entities Common to a Set of Qualities: For any subset, $sQ\$ \subseteq Q\$$, of qualities we can define $\mathcal{D}\mathcal{E}$ for "derive[d] set of entities".

$\mathcal{D}\mathcal{E}: Q\text{-set} \to (\mathcal{E}\text{-set} \times \mathcal{I} \times Q\text{-set}) \to \mathcal{E}\text{-set}$

$\mathcal{D}\mathcal{E}(sQ\$)(\mathbb{E}\$, \mathbb{I}, Q\$) \equiv \{\mathbb{E} \mid \mathbb{E}{:}\mathcal{E}, Q{:}Q \cdot Q{\in}sQ \wedge \mathbb{E} \cdot \mathbb{I} \cdot Q \}$,

pre: $sQ\$ \subseteq Q\$$

The above expresses: *"the set of entities which have all qualities in $sQ\$$"* ∎

Definition: 62 Formal Concept: A *formal concept* of a *context* $\mathbb{K}$ is a pair:

- $(s\mathbb{Q}, s\mathbb{E})$ where
  - ∞ $\mathcal{D}Q(s\mathbb{E})(\mathbb{E}, \mathbb{I}, \mathbb{Q}) = s\mathbb{Q}$ and
  - ∞ $\mathcal{D}\mathcal{E}(s\mathbb{Q})(\mathbb{E}, \mathbb{I}, \mathbb{Q}) = s\mathbb{E}$;
- $s\mathbb{Q}$ is called the ***intent*** of $\mathbb{K}$ and $s\mathbb{E}$ is called the ***extent*** of $\mathbb{K}$ ∎

4.21.2 Types Are Formal Concepts

Now comes the "crunch": *In the* `TripTych` *domain analysis we strive to find formal concepts and, when we think we have found one, we assign a type (or a sort) and qualities to it !*

4.21.3 Practicalities

There is a little problem. To search for all those entities of a domain which each have the same sets of qualities is not feasible. So we do a combination of two things: (i) we identify a small set of entities all having the same qualities and tentatively associate them with a type, and (ii) we identify certain nouns of our national language and if such a noun does indeed designate a set of entities all having the same set of qualities then we tentatively associate the noun with a type. Having thus, tentatively, identified a type we conjecture that type and search for counterexamples, that is, entities which refute the conjecture. This "process" of conjectures and refutations is iterated until some satisfaction is arrived at that the postulated type constitutes a reasonable conjecture.

4.21.4 Formal Concepts: A Wider Implication

The formal concepts of a domain form Galois Connections [169]. We gladly admit that this fact is one of the reasons why we emphasise *formal concept analysis*. At the same time we must admit that this paper does not do justice to this fact. We have experimented with the analysis & description of a number of domains, and have noticed such Galois connections, but it is, for us, too early to report on this. Thus we invite the reader to study this aspect of domain analysis.

4.22 Summary

This chapter's main title was: **DOMAINS – A Taxonomy**. So, the taxonomy of a domain, such as we have studied it and such as we ordain one aspect of ***domain analysis & description***, is about manifestly visible and tangible properties, that is, the *external qualities*. For that study & practice we have suggested a number of analysis & description prompts.

```
———————————— Two Essentials about External Qualities ————————
An essence of 'external quality' is that of an endurant being either solid or fluid. Another
essence of 'external quality' is that of a solid endurant being either atomic or composite.
```

4.22.1 The Description Schemas

We have culminated this chapter with the analysis prompts 1–6 (pages 79–81), and the description prompts 2–7 (pages 83–89).

They all describe the, in our case RSL, domain description text to 'produce' when external quality analysing & describing a given endurant; but what about the description of those endurants *revealed by the analysis & description of that given endurant* ?

The answer is simple. That is up to you! The **domain analysis & description method** primarily gives you the **tools**. But!

- A **principle** of the method could be to secure that all relevant, i.e., implied, endurants are analysed & described.
- A **technique** could be to, somehow, "set aside" all those endurants *revealed by the analysis & description of any given endurant* – with the proviso that no endurant, of **type**, for example, P, is analysed & described more than once.

We refer to Sect. **4.20** on page 93 for a suggested analysis & description technique (cum pseudo program expressed in pseudo RSL).

4.22.2 Modeling Choices

In this chapter we have put forward some advice on **description** choices: We refer to *Modeling Choices* 1–7 (pages 83–90). The **analysis** predicates and functions are merely aids. They do not effect descriptions, but descriptions are based on the result of inquiries based on deployment of these predicates and functions. Real decisions are made when effecting a **description** function. So the rôle of these modeling choice paragraphs is to alert the describer to make judicious choices.

4.22.3 Method Principles, Procedures, Techniques and Tools

Recall that by a method we shall understand a *set of **principles*** for *selecting* and *applying* a *set of **procedures*** which deploy a *set of **techniques*** which *uses* a *set of **tools*** in order to *construct* an *artefact*.

4.22.3.1 Principles of External Qualities

In this chapter we have illustrated the use of the following principles:

Divide and Conquer: We claim that the divide principle is applied in establishing the ontology: in distinguishing between describables and non-describables, in distinguishing between endurants and perdurants, and in otherwise suggesting the taxonomy as illustrated in Fig. 4.1 (page 53). We claim that a guiding principle in this "division" has been Kai Sørlander's Philosophy. And we claim that this "division" has helped and will help "conquer" the complexity of issues as they continue to unfold in the next chapters.

Abstraction: This principle is applied in simply focusing on abstract names for endurant sorts, disregarding any further meaning of these names – meanings that will be "revealed" as we go along in analysing as describing, in the next chapters, first *unique identifiers, mereologies* and *attributes,* then the elements of *perdurants.*

Narration & Formalisation: This principle is applied in developing and presenting the domain endurant descriptions which are always, as shown in both the description schemas and in those examples which do present formalisations, in that they also show narratives.

4.22.3.2 Procedures for Modeling External Qualities

The main procedure for modeling external qualities was presented in Sect. **4.20**.

4.22.3.3 Techniques of External Qualities

In this chapter we have illustrated the use of the following techniques:

Model-oriented Specification: Although we say model-oriented, there really are three aspects to our formal specifications: the use of discrete mathematics[100] – so far logic, sets, Cartesians; the use of RSL's specification/programming-like constructs: *type definitions, function signatures,* etc.; and the use of abstract *sorts* – as "inspired" from algebraic specifications.

Formal Concept Analysis: This technique, whose mathematical foundation was outlined in Sect. **4.21**, involves "top-down" analysis, from most abstract concepts towards less and less abstract concepts, versus "bottom-up" analysis i.e., the "other way around". We refer to Sect. **4.14**.

4.22.3.4 Tools of External Qualities

The main tools are the English language, used in narrative descriptions, the RAISE Specification Language RSL, used in formal descriptions, and the analysis and description prompts – reviewed below – and as used by the domain analyser & describer, but a use that may not necessarily be explicitly recorded, as their "existence" are to mainly serve as *aide-mémoire.*

In this chapter we have introduced a number of external qualities analysis prompts. Let π designate a *phenomena*. The following are some of the external qualities analysis prompts.

- If a phenomenon, ϕ, **is_entity**(ϕ) then it   1 Pg. 52

  - ∞ **is_endurant**(e) or   2 Pg. 57
  - ∞ **is_perdurant**(e).   3 Pg. 57

- If an entity, e, **is_endurant**(e), then it

  - ∞ **is_solid**(e) or   4 Pg. 58
  - ∞ **is_fluid**(e).   5 Pg. 59

- If an endurant, e, **is_solid**(e), then it

---

[100] – thus accounting for our use of the term 'model-oriented'

∞ **is_part**(*e*) or   6 Pg. 60
∞ **is_structure**(*e*) or   7 Pg. 61
∞ **is_living_species**(*e*).   8 Pg. 62

• If a solid endurant, *e*, **is_part**(*e*) then it

∞ **is_natural_part**(*e*) or   9 Pg. 62
∞ **is_artefact**(*e*).   10 Pg. 63

We have "lumped" natural and artefactual parts into just parts. So you will not find this characteristic reflected in Fig. 4.1 on page 53. Still:

• If a solid endurant, *e*, **is_part**(*e*) then it

∞ **is_atomic**(*e*) or   16 Pg. 69
∞ **is_compound**(*e*) or   17 Pg. 70
∞ **is_conjoin**(*e*).   22 Pg. 72

• If a part, *e*, is **is_compound**(*e*) then it

∞ **is_composite**(*e*) or   18 Pg. 70
∞ **is_set**(*e*).   19 Pg. 71

• Analysis of endurants into composites enables

∞ **analyse_composite_parts**(*e*)   1 Pg. 79
   And this, finally, enable
 ∞ **calculate_composite_parts_sorts**(*e*), respectively   2 Pg. 82

• If a compound, *e*, **is_set**(*e*) then it

∞ **is_single_sort_set**(*e*) or   20 Pg. 71
∞ **is_alternative_sorts_set**(*e*).   21 Pg. 72

• Analysis of endurants into sets enables

∞ **analyse_single_sort_part_set**(*e*), respectively   2 Pg. 80
∞ **analyse_alternative_sorts_part_set**(*e*).   3 Pg. 80
   And these, finally, enable
 ∞ **calculate_single_sort_parts_sort**(*e*), respectively   3 Pg. 85
 ∞ **calculate_alternative_sort_part_sorts**(*e*)   4 Pg. 85

• If a compound, *e*, **is_conjoin**(*e*) then it

∞ **is_part_fluids_conjoin**(*e*) or   23 Pg. 73
∞ **is_fluid_parts_conjoin**(*e*) or   24 Pg. 75
∞ **is_part_parts_conjoin**(*e*).   25 Pg. 75

which, respectively enables

∞ **analyse_part_fluids_conjoin**(*e*)   4 Pg. 80
∞ **analyse_fluid_parts_parts_conjoin**(*e*)   5 Pg. 81
∞ **analyse_part_parts_conjoin**(*e*)   6 Pg. 81
   and these, finally enables
 ∞ **calculate_part_fluids_sorts**(*e*),   5 Pg. 87
 ∞ **calculate_fluid_parts_parts_sorts**(*e*),   6 Pg. 88
 ∞ **calculate_part_parts_sorts**(*e*) or   7 Pg. 89

• If a solid endurant, *e*, **is_living_species**(*e*) then it

∞ **is_plant**(*e*) or   13 Pg. 66
∞ **is_animal**(*e*).   14 Pg. 66

- Some animals satisfy

  ∞ is_human(e).   15 Pg. 67

4.22.4 How Much or How Little Do We Analyse and Describe ?

How many of a domain's external qualities do we analyse and describe ? There are two kinds of answers to this question. **An Engineering Answer:** This kind of answer may be relevant for the case of a full scale software development – where a domain engineering phase is followed by a requirements engineering phase which is then followed by a software design phase. We may then try to capture just what we think we need for that subsequent requirements capture, its analysis and prescription. Or, to "guard against unforeseen eventualities", a little more ! Reading engineering domain analysis & description case studies helps. So do experience ! **A Scientific Answer:** Or we try to capture "all" ! Now that is clearly not possible, at least not "in one fell swoop"[101] ! So how do we go about it, as domain scientists cum engineers ? We do it "domain-area-by-domain-area". Sort of, for example like this: First what is thought of as a core domain is analysed & described. Then some additional aspects, i.e., entities, are included in a next analysis & description – leaving out, typically, some initially analysed & described entities. and so on. Just like, for example, physicists, analyse & describe natural world phenomena.

We shall have more to say about what to include and what to exclude in the next chapters.

4.22.5 Varieties of Upper Ontologies

Figure 4.1 on page 53 is referred to as an **upper ontology**. It is not **the** upper ontology. But just one of several possible. We could simplify our analysis and description of endurants by omitting, altogether the notion of conjoins. That would result in an upper ontology as show in Fig. 4.8 on the facing page.

One can certainly make-do with that simpler upper ontology. Other simple upper ontologies can be proposed. Also upper ontologies that are more "complex" than that of Fig. 4.1 on page 53. So what is the "lesson": The lesson here is that the skilled domain analyser cum describer, i.e., the skilled domain scientist cum engineer, in the initial steps of a domain analysis & description, determines the simplicity/complexity of the upper ontology with which the full domain analysis & description is to be pursued. We refer to [73, 81]. These two published papers each have their "simpler" upper ontology.

4.23 Bibliographical Notes

We refer to [73, Sect. 5.3] for a thorough, 2016–2017, five page review of types in formal specification and programming languages.

---

[101] To do something in one fell swoop is to do it suddenly or in a single, swift action.

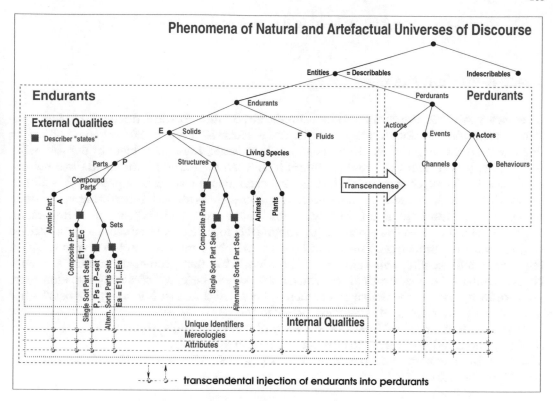

Fig. 4.8 A Simple Upper Ontology

4.24 Exercise Problems

We embark of a series of exercise problems, cf. Sects. **5.13** on page 150, **7.14** on page 201, **8.11** on page 239 and **9.9** on page 297.

4.24.1 Research Problems

Exercise 1 A Research Challenge. Reformulate Composites as Conjoins: In this chapter we have treated artefactual composites apart from conjoins. But, really, are these artefacts not also conjoins ? Reformulate the appropriate text to reflect this "change of ontology" !

Exercise 2 A Research Challenge. Symmetry of Part-Parts Conjoins: Sets versus Composites: In this chapter we have suggested **Fluid-Parts, Part-Fluids** and **Part-Parts** conjoins. The 'plural' **s** in fluid-parts means that we allow a set, more precisely, an indefinite number of parts; the plural **s** in part-fluids means that we expect either a single or a Cartesian of a definite number of fluids, expressed as a Cartesian; and the 'plural' **s** in part-parts means that we allow sets of parts.

[Q1] Consider a **Part-Cartesian-Parts** conjoin, almost like the **Part-Parts** conjoin but with a definite number of parts of possibly distinct sorts. How is that possibility different from the suggestion of research problem 1 above ?

[Q2] Could one contemplate a variant **Part-Fluids** variant where the **s** indicates that we now expect an in definite number of fluids ?

[Q3] Discuss those possibilities, [a–b], and reformulate ontology accordingly.

4.24.2 A Student Exercise

Exercise 3 An MSc Student Exercise. Document System Parts: A document system consists of **person**s and **document**s. To anticipate exercise 32 on page 203 we characterise, so
that the reader can get at what we mean by documents, these as subject to the following
operations: [a] **creation:** before there might have been a number of unrelated documents –
now there is a [new] document, with some *text* created and written by a person; [b] **editing:**
before there was a document – now there is a document with text and editing being done
by a person; [c] **reading:** before there was a document – now there is "the same" document,
only now it has been read by a person; [d] **copying:** before there was a document – now there
is "the same" document, only now it has been copied by a person – and there is a *copy* (of
the former, still existing, separate document) identifying that (former) document and with
all the "contents" of the "original" of which it is a copy – the 'copy' creator is also identified;
[e] **shredding:** before there was a document – now that document no longer "exists" – but
otherwise all other documents remain unchanged !
[Q1] You are to narrate and formalise the parts of the document system.
[Q2] Are shredded documents to be a part of the system ?
This exercise is continued in Exercises 16 on page 151, 17 on page 151, 18 on page 151
and 32 on page 203.

4.24.3 Term Projects

In a textbook as this we cannot primarily rely on simple 10 line problems. It should be clear to
the reader: lecturer and student, that exercise problems must be more-or-less comprehensive;
they must encompass a reasonably well-delineated domain. We now list a number of such
potential problem domains [see [84]]:

- the consumer, retailer, wholesaler, etc., merchandise market;
- financial service industry;
- container line industry – with the (possibly overlapping) subdomain:

  - ∞ container terminal ports,
  - ∞ container stowage, and
  - ∞ container logistics;

- railways systems;
- waste disposal systems,

We suggest that the lecturer, who is using this primer for a dedicated series of lectures on
domain analysis & description,

- "divide" the class students into one or more groups of preferably 4–6 students each.
- that each group be assigned a distinct domain.
- and that, from week-to-week they discuss and write down their analysis and description
  (narratives and formalisations) of that domain, in phases corresponding to this 'Exercise
  Problems' and forthcoming sections: **5.13.3, 7.14.3, 8.11.2** and **9.9.2**.
- For teachers and individual students the publisher provides access to "large scale" examples covering several of the exercise domains that we have listed.

We shall briefly illustrate some external quality aspects of these domains,

- in a first week of study, completely unstructured – since you have not yet learned the full contents of this chapter, "rambling on" — to be followed,
- in a second week of study, once you have learned the "stuff" of this chapter, more structured, and according to the concepts of this chapter.

Exercise 4 An MSc Student Exercise. The Consumer Market, External Qualities: You are to analyse and describe the external qualities of 'the market' domain of artefactual entities including consumers, retailers, wholesalers, possibly importers/exporters, and producers of merchandise aimed at ordinary consumers.

Exercise 5 An MSc Student Exercise. Financial Service Industry, External Qualities: You are to analyse and describe the external qualities of a financial service industry domain of artefactual entities including banks, insurance companies, mortgage institutions, brokers and stock exchanges. Of what solid endurants consists the banks, insurance companies, mortgage institutions, brokers and stock exchanges?

Exercise 6 An MSc Student Exercise. Container Line Industry, External Qualities: You are to analyse and describe the external qualities of a container line industry domain of artefactual entities including containers, container vessels, container terminal ports, trucks (transporting containers between customers and terminal ports), and the container line management. Of what solid endurants consists these and related solid endurants?

Exercise 7 An MSc Student Exercise. Railway Systems, External Qualities: You are to analyse and describe the external qualities of a railway domain of artefactual entities including trains and railway nets. Of what solid endurants consist the trains, and of what solid endurants consist the railway nets?

Exercise 8 A PhD Student Problem. Part-Fluid Conjoins: Canals, External Qualities: We refer to Example 31 on page 74. You are to analyse and describe the external qualities of a canal system of artefactual entities including locks, straight (if curved) stretches of canals, and canal forks and joins (diverting, respectively collecting) water flows.

Exercise 9 A PhD Student Problem. Part-Fluids Conjoins: Rum Production, External Qualities: We refer to Example 15 on page 61. You are to analyse and describe the external qualities of a rum production system of artefactual entities including sugar cane fields, transport links from fields to sugar cane chopping facilities, such facilities, from these to the rum distillery, rum distilleries with their pot- or column stills and other production means, warehouses, and so forth.

Exercise 10 A PhD Student Problem. Part-Fluids Conjoins: Waste Management, External Qualities: We refer to Example 32 on page 74. You are to analyse and describe a waste management systems domain of artefactual entities, say focusing on just the (a) waste conveyors (whether 'belts' or 'pipe') and (b) waste processors: (a) conveyor belts or pipes, their "merging" and "diversion" (joins and forks), their initial sources and ultimate sinks, whether pumps (as for pipe) or no such things (as for mechanically moving belts that either move goods upwards, horizontally, or downwards, etc.); (b) industrial, sewage, agricultural product, leachate[102], or other, biological, etc., treatment. Note that conveyor nets are directional and have no cycles.

---

[102] A leachate is any liquid that, in the course of passing through matter, extracts soluble or suspended solids, or any other component of the fluid through which it has passed.

These exercise problems are continued in Sects. **5.13.3** on page 152, **7.14.3** on page 203, **8.11.2** on page 240 and **9.9.2** on page 297.

Chapter 5
DOMAINS – An Ontology: Internal Qualities

*In this chapter we introduce the concept of internal qualities of endurants, and cover the analysis and description of **unique identifiers**, **mereologies** and **attributes** of endurants. There is yet another, interrelating internal quality: **intentionality**, "something" that expresses intention, design idea, purpose of artefacts – well, some would say, also natural endurants.*

We shall investigate the, as we shall call them, internal qualities of domains. That is the properties of the entities to which we ascribe internal qualities. The outcome of this chapter is that the reader will be able to model the internal qualities of domains. Not just for a particular domain instance, but a possibly infinite set of domain instances[103].

External qualities of endurants of a manifest domain are, in a simplifying sense, those we can see and touch. They, so to speak, take form.

Internal qualities of endurants of a manifest domain are, in a less simplifying sense, those which we may not be able to see or "feel" when touching an endurant, but they can, as we now 'mandate' them, be reasoned about, as for **unique identifiers** and **mereologies**, or be measured by some **physical/chemical** means, or be "spoken of" by **intentional deduction**, and be reasoned about, as we do when we **attribute** properties to endurants.

As it turns out[104], to analyse and describe mereology we need to first analyse and describe unique identifiers; and to analyse and describe attributes we need to first analyse and describe mereologies. Hence:

Method Step 8 Sequential Analysis & Description of Internal Qualities: We advise that the *domain analyser & describer* first analyse & describe unique identification of all endurant sorts; then analyse & describe mereologies of all endurant sorts; finally analyse & describe attributes of all endurant sorts.

In this monograph we shall not suggest the modeling of unique identifiers and mereology of fluids. We shall comment on that in appropriate sections.

5.1 Overview of This Chapter

- Section **5.2** covers the crucial notion of unique identification of endurants;
- Sect. **5.3** the likewise important notion of mereology – relations between parts;
- Sect. **5.4** covers the notion of attributes, which in a sense gives "flesh & blood' to endurants; and

---

[103] By this we mean: You are not just analysing a specific domain, say the one manifested around the corner from where you are, but any instance, anywhere in the world, which satisfies what you have described.

[104] You, the first time reader cannot know this, i.e., the "turns out". Once we have developed and presented the material of this chapter, then you can see it; clearly !

© The Author(s), under exclusive license to Springer Nature Switzerland AG 2021   107
D. Bjørner, *Domain Science and Engineering*, Monographs in Theoretical Computer Science. An EATCS Series,
https://doi.org/10.1007/978-3-030-73484-8_5

- Sect. **5.5** covers the novel notion, in computing, that of "intentional pull".
- Finally Sect. **5.8** follows up on the *domain discovery process* of Sect. **4.20**.

Other sections provide elucidation or summary observations.

5.2 Unique Identifiers

The concept of parts having unique identifiability, that is, that two parts, if they are the same, have the same unique identifier, and if they are not the same, then they have distinct identifiers, that concept is fundamental to our being able to analyse and describe internal qualities of endurants. So we are left with the issue of "sameness"!

5.2.1 On Uniqueness of Endurants

We therefore introduce the notion of unique identification of part endurants. We assume (i) that all part endurants, e, of any domain E, have *unique identifiers*, (ii) that *unique identifiers* (of part endurants e:E) are *abstract values* (of the *unique identifier* sort UI of part endurants e:E), (iii) such that distinct part endurant sorts, E_i and E_j, have distinctly named *unique identifier* sorts, say UI_i and UI_j[105], and (iv) that all $ui_i:UI_i$ and $ui_j:UI_j$ are distinct.

Representation of Unique Identifiers: Unique identifiers are abstractions. When we endow two endurants (say of the same sort) distinct unique identifiers then we are simply saying that these two endurants are distinct. We are not assuming anything about how these identifiers otherwise come about.

Identifiability of Endurants: From a philosophical point of view, and with basis in Kai Sørlander's Philosophy, cf. Paragraph **Identity, Difference and Relations** (Page 15), one can rationally argue that there are many endurants, and that they are unique, and hence uniquely identifiable. From an empirical point of view, and since one may eventually have a software development in mind, we may wonder how unique identifiablity can be accommodated.

Unique identifiability for solid endurants, even though they may be mobile, is straightforward: one can think of many ways of ascribing a unique identifier to any part; solid endurants do not "morph"[106]. Hence one can think of many such unique identification schemas.

Unique identifiability for fluids may seem a bit more tricky. For this monograph we shall not suggest to endow fluids with unique identification. We have simply not experimented with such part-fluids and fluid-parts domains – not enough – to suggest so.

5.2.2 Uniqueness Modeling Tools

The analysis method offers an observer function uid_E which when applied to part endurants, e, yields the unique identifier, *ui*:UI, of e.

Domain Description Prompt 8 `describe_unique_identifier`: We can therefore apply the *domain description prompt*:

---

[105] This restriction is not necessary, but, for the time, we can assume that it is.

[106] – from a state of being solid, but in various "shapes", via states of melting, to states of vapour

- `describe_unique_identifier`

to endurants e:E resulting in the analyser writing down the *unique identifier type and observer domain description text* according to the following schema: **8. describe_unique_identifier Observer**

❝ Narration:
    [s] ... narrative text on unique identifier sort UI ...
    [u] ... narrative text on unique identifier observer uid_E ...
    [a] ... axiom on uniqueness of unique identifiers ...
Formalisation:
    type
    [s] UI
    value
    [u] uid_E: E → UI ❞

is_part(e) is a prerequisite for describe_unique_identifier(e).

    The unique identifier type name, UI above, chosen, of course, by the *domain analyser cum describer*, usually properly embodies the type name, E, of the endurant being analysed and mereology-described. Thus a part of type-name E might be given the mereology type name EI. Generally we shall refer to these names by UI.

Observer Function Prompt 11 type_name, type_of, is_: Given *description schema* 8 we have, so-to-speak, "in-reverse" that
$$\forall \, e{:}F \cdot uid \; F(e){=}ui \Rightarrow type\_of(ui){=}UI \wedge type\_name(ui){=}\text{``}UI\text{''} \wedge is\_UI(ui)$$

Unique Identifiers

Example 40

134 We assign unique identifiers to all parts.
135 By a road identifier we shall mean a link or a hub identifier.
136 By a vehicle identifier we shall mean a bus or an automobile identifier.
137 Unique identifiers uniquely identify all parts.
  a All hubs have distinct [unique] identifiers.

b All links have distinct identifiers.
c All bus companies have distinct identifiers.
d All buses of all bus companies have distinct identifiers.
e All automobiles have distinct identifiers.
f All parts have distinct identifiers.

type
134 H_UI, L_UI, BC_UI, B_UI, A_UI
135 R_UI = H_UI | L_UI
136 V_UI = B_UI | A_UI
value

137a uid_H: H → H_UI
137b uid_L: H → L_UI
137c uid_BC: H → BC_UI
137d uid_B: H → B_UI
137e uid_A: H → A_UI

5.2.3 All Unique Identifiers of a Domain

Given a universe of discourse we can calculate the set of the unique identifiers of all its parts.

```
value
      calculate_all_unique_identifiers: UoD → UI-set
      calculate_all_unique_identifiers(uod) ≡
            let parts = calc_parts({uod})({}) in
            { uid_E(e) | e:E • e ∈ parts } end
```

Road Transport: Unique Identifier Auxiliary Functions
Example 41   Extract Parts from Their Unique Identifiers:

138 From the unique identifier of a part we can retrieve, $\wp$, the part having that identifier.

```
type
138 P = H | L | BC | B | A
value
138 ℘: H_UI→H | L_UI→L | BC_UI→BC | B_UI→B | A_UI→A
138 ℘(ui) ≡ let p:(H|L|BC|B|A)•p∈ps∧uid_P(p)=ui in p end
```

5.2.4 Unique Identifier Constants

Given a domain which do not "grow" or "shrink" in its number of observable endurants we can speak of the constancy of their sets of unique identifiers.

```
value
      all_uniq_ids: Unit → Unit
      all_uniq_ids() ≡
            let ps = calc_parts(uod) in
            { uid_E(p) | p ∈ ps ∧ type_name(p)="E"} end
```

Unique Identifier Constants
Example 42   We can calculate:

139 the set, $h_{ui}s$, of unique hub identifiers;
140 the set, $l_{ui}s$, of unique link identifiers;
141 the map, $hl_{ui}m$, from unique hub identifiers to the set of unique link iidentifiers of the links connected to the zero, one or more identified hubs,
142 the map, $lh_{ui}m$, from unique link identifiers to the set of unique hub iidentifiers of the two hubs connected to the identified link;
143 the set, $r_{ui}s$, of all unique hub and link, i.e., road identifiers;
144 the set, $bc_{ui}s$, of unique bus company identifiers;
145 the set, $b_{ui}s$, of unique bus identifiers;
146 the set, $a_{ui}s$, of unique private automobile identifiers;
147 the set, $v_{ui}s$, of unique bus and automobile, i.e., vehicle identifiers;
148 the map, $bcb_{ui}m$, from unique bus company identifiers to the set of its unique bus identifiers; and
149 the (bijective) map, $bbc_{ui}bm$, from unique bus identifiers to their unique bus company identifiers.

value
139 $h_{ui}s$:H_UI-set ≡ {uid_H(h)|h:H•h ∈ hs}
140 $l_{ui}s$:L_UI-set ≡ {uid_L(l)|l:L•l ∈ ls}
143 $r_{ui}s$:R_UI-set ≡ $h_{ui}s∪l_{ui}s$
141 $hl_{ui}m$:(H_UI $\overrightarrow{m}$ L_UI-set) ≡
141   [h_ui↦luis|h_ui:H_UI,luis:L_UI-set•h_ui∈$h_{ui}s$∧(_,luis,_)=mereo_H($η$(h_ui))] [cf. Item 168]
142 $lh_{ui}m$:(L+UI $\overrightarrow{m}$ H_UI-set) ≡
142   [l_ui↦huis | h_ui:L_UI,huis:H_UI-set • l_ui∈$l_{ui}s$ ∧ (_,huis,_)=mereo_L($η$(l_ui))] [cf. Item 169]
144 $bc_{ui}s$:BC_UI-set ≡ {uid_BC(bc)|bc:BC•bc ∈ bcs}
145 $b_{ui}s$:B_UI-set ≡ ∪{uid_B(b)|b:B•b ∈ bs}
146 $a_{ui}s$:A_UI-set ≡ {uid_A(a)|a:A•a ∈ as}
147 $v_{ui}s$:V_UI-set ≡ $b_{ui}s ∪ a_{ui}s$
148 $bcb_{ui}m$:(BC_UI $\overrightarrow{m}$ B_UI-set) ≡
148   [bc_ui ↦ buis | bc_ui:BC_UI, bc:BC • bc∈bcs ∧ bc_ui=uid_BC(bc) ∧ (_,_,buis)=mereo_BC(bc)]
149 $bbc_{ui}bm$:(B_UI $\overrightarrow{m}$ BC_UI) ≡
149   [b_ui ↦ bc_ui | b_ui:B_UI,bc_ui:BC_ui • bc_ui=**dom**$bcb_{ui}m$∧b_ui∈$bcb_{ui}m$(bc_ui)]

5.2.5 A Domain Law: Uniqueness of Endurant Identifiers

We postulate that the unique identifier observer functions are about the uniqueness of the postulated endurant identifiers, but how is that guaranteed? We know, as *"an indisputable law of domains"*, that they are distinct, but our formulas do not guarantee that! So we must formalise their uniqueness.

_____ **All Parts of a Domain have Unique Identifiers** _____

A Domain Law: 1 All Parts of a Domain have Unique Identifiers:

150 All parts of a described domain have unique identifiers.

axiom
150 **card** calc_parts(uod) = **card** calculate_all_unique_identifiers(uod)

Uniqueness of Road Net Identifiers

Example 43 We must express the following axioms:

151 All hub identifiers are distinct.
152 All link identifiers are distinct.
153 All bus company identifiers are distinct.
154 All bus identifiers are distinct.

155 All private automobile identifiers are distinct.

156 All part identifiers are distinct.

axiom
151 **card** hs = **card** $h_{ui}s$
152 **card** ls = **card** $l_{ui}s$
153 **card** bcs = **card** $bc_{ui}s$
154 **card** bs = **card** $b_{ui}s$
155 **card** as = **card** $a_{ui}s$
156 **card** {$h_{ui}s∪l_{ui}s∪bc_{ui}s∪b_{ui}s∪a_{ui}s$}
156   = **card** $h_{ui}s$+**card** $l_{ui}s$+**card** $bc_{ui}s$+**card** $b_{ui}s$+**card** $a_{ui}s$ □

We ascribe, in principle, unique identifiers to all endurants whether natural or artefactual. We find, from our many experiments, cf. the *Universes of Discourse* example, Page 49, that we really focus on those domain entities which are artefactual endurants and their behavioural "counterparts".

Pipeline Unique Identifiers

Example 44 We refer to Appendix Sect. **A.2**.

Rail Net Unique Identifiers

Example 45

157 With every rail net unit we associate a unique identifier.

158 That is, no two rail net units have the same unique identifier.

159 Trains have unique identifiers.

160 We let *tris* denote the set of all train identifiers.

161 No two distinct trains have the same unique identifier.

162 Train identifiers are distinct from rail net unit identifiers.

type
157. UI
value
157. uid_NU: NU → UI

axiom
158. ∀ ui_i,ui_j:UI •
158.   ui_i = ui_j ≡ uid_NU(ui_i)=uid_NU(ui_j)

5.2.5.1 Unique Identification of Compounds

For structures we do not model their unique identification. But their components, whether the structures are *"Cartesian"* or *"sets"*, may very well be non-structures, hence be uniquely identifiable.

5.3 Mereology

We refer to introductory section Sect. **3.8.2** on mereology as a philosophical–logic subject and Appendix Sect. **B** for closing material on mereology. We shall not endow fluids with mereologies. We shall comment on this in Sect. **5.3.5** on page 116.

Definition: 63 Mereology: Mereology is the study and knowledge of parts and part relations
∎

Mereology, as a logical/philosophical discipline, can perhaps best be attributed to the Polish mathematician/logician Stanisław Leśniewski [122, 64].

5.3.1 Endurant Relations

Which are the relations that can be relevant for "endurant-hood"? There are basically two relations: (i) physical ones, and (ii) conceptual ones.

(i) Physically two or more endurants may be topologically either adjacent to one another, like rails of a line, or within an endurant, like links and hubs of a road net, or an atomic part is conjoined to one or more fluids, or a fluid is conjoined to one or more parts. The latter two could also be considered conceptual "adjacencies".

(ii) Conceptually some parts, like automobiles, "belong" to an embedding endurant, like to an automobile club, or are registered in the local department of vehicles, or are 'intended' to drive on roads.

5.3.2 Mereology Modeling Tools

When the domain analyser decides that some endurants are related in a specifically enunciated mereology, the analyser has to decide on suitable *mereology types* and *mereology observers* (i.e., endurant relations).

163 We may, to illustration, define a **mereology type** of an endurant $e{:}E$ as a triplet type expression over set of unique [endurant] identifiers.

164 There is the identification of all those endurant sorts $E_{i_1}, E_{i_2}, ..., E_{i_m}$ where at least one of whose properties "is_of_interest" to parts $e{:}E$.

165 There is the identification of all those sorts $E_{io_1}, E_{io_2}, ..., E_{io_n}$ where at least one of whose properties "is_of_interest" to endurants $e{:}E$ and vice-versa.

166 There is the identification of all those endurant sorts $E_{o_1}, E_{o_2}, ..., E_{o_o}$ for whom properties of $e{:}E$ "is_of_interest" to endurants of sorts $E_{o_1}, E_{o_2}, ..., E_{o_o}$.

167 The mereology triplet sets of unique identifiers are disjoint and are all unique identifiers of the universe of discourse.

The triplet mereology is just a suggestion. As it is formulated here we mean the three 'sets' to be disjoint. Other forms of expressing a mereology should be considered for the particular domain and for the particular endurants of that domain. We leave out further characterisation of the seemingly vague notion "is_of_interest".

type
164 iEI = iEI1 | iEI2 | ... | iEIm
165 ioEI = ioEI1 | ioEI2 | ... | ioEIn
166 oEI = oEI1 | oEI2 | ... | oEIo
163 MT = iEI-**set** × ioEI-**set** × oEI-**set**
axiom
167 ∀ (iset,ioset,oset):MT •
167   **card** iset + **card** ioset + **card** oset = **card** ∪{iset,ioset,oset}
167   ∪{iset,ioset,oset} ⊆ calc_all_unique_identifiers(uod)

Domain Description Prompt 9 describe_mereology(e): If has_mereology(p) holds for parts p of type P, then the analyser can apply the **domain description prompt**:

- describe_mereology

to parts of that type and write down the *mereology types and observer* domain description text according to the following schema: **9. describe_mereology(e) Observer**

❝ Narration:
  [t]   ... narrative text on mereology type ...
  [m]   ... narrative text on mereology observer ...
  [a]   ... narrative text on mereology type constraints ...
Formalisation:
  type
  [t]   MT = $\mathcal{M}(UI_i, UI_j, ..., UI_k)$
  value
  [m]   mereo_P: P → MT
  axiom [Well–formedness of Domain Mereologies]
  [a] $\mathcal{A}$: $\mathcal{A}(MT)$ ❞

The mereology type name, MT, chosen of course, by the *domain analyser cum describer*, usually properly embodies the type name, E, of the endurant being analysed and mereology-described. The mereology type expression $\mathcal{M}(UI_i, UI_j, ..., UI_k)$ is a type expression over unique identifiers. Thus a part of type-name P might be given the mereology type name MP. $\mathcal{A}(MT)$ is a predicate over possibly all unique identifier types of the domain description. To write down the concrete type definition for MT requires a bit of analysis and thinking
∎

Modelling Choice 8 *Mereology:* As for endurant descriptions the analyser cum describer chooses for some model of a domain, one mereology, for another model of supposedly "the same" domain another mereology.

Mereology of a Road Net
Example 46

168 The mereology of hubs is a pair: (i) the set of all bus and automobile identifiers[107], and (ii) the set of unique identifiers of the links that it is connected to and the set of all unique identifiers of all vehicles (buses and private automobiles).[108]
169 The mereology of links is a pair: (i) the set of all bus and automobile identifiers, and (ii) the set of the two distinct hubs they are connected to.
170 The mereology of a bus company is a set the unique identifiers of the buses operated by that company.
171 The mereology of a bus is a pair: (i) the set of the one single unique identifier of the bus company it is operating for, and (ii) the unique identifiers of all links and hubs[109].
172 The mereology of an automobile is the set of the unique identifiers of all links and hubs[110].

type		**value**	
168	H_Mer = V_UI-set×L_UI-set	168	mereo_H: H → H_Mer
169	L_Mer = V_UI-set×H_UI-set	169	mereo_L: L → L_Mer
170	BC_Mer = B_UI-set	170	mereo_BC: BC → BC_Mer
171	B_Mer = BC_UI×R_UI-set	171	mereo_B: B → B_Mer
172	A_Mer = R_UI-set	172	mereo_A: A → A_Mer

5.3.2.1 Invariance of Mereologies

For mereologies one can usually express some invariants. Such invariants express *"law-like properties"*, facts which are indisputable. We refer to Sect. **5.3.4** on page 116.

---

[107] This is just another way of saying that the meaning of hub mereologies involves the unique identifiers of all the vehicles that might pass through the hub is_of_interest to it.

[108] The link identifiers designate the links, zero, one or more, that a hub is connected to is_of_interest to both the hub and that these links is interested in the hub.

[109] — that the bus might pass through

[110] — that the automobile might pass through

Invariance of Road Nets

Example 47 The observed mereologies must express identifiers of the state of such for road nets:

axiom

168 ∀ (vuis,luis):H_Mer • luis⊆$l_{ui}s$ ∧ vuis=$v_{ui}s$
169 ∀ (vuis,huis):L_Mer • vuis=$v_{ui}s$ ∧ huis⊆$h_{ui}s$ ∧ **card**huis=2
170 ∀ buis:H_Mer • buis = $b_{ui}s$
171 ∀ (bc_ui,ruis):H_Mer•bc_ui∈$bc_{ui}s$∧ruis=$r_{ui}s$
172 ∀ ruis:A_Mer • ruis=$r_{ui}s$

173 For all hubs, h, and links, l, in the same road net,
174 if the hub h connects to link l then link l connects to hub h.

axiom

173 ∀ h:H,l:L • h ∈ hs ∧ l ∈ ls ⇒
173   **let** (_,luis)=mereo_H(h), (_,huis)=mereo_L(l)
174   **in** uid_L(l)∈luis ≡ uid_H(h)∈huis **end**

175 For all links, l, and hubs, h_a,h_b, in the same road net,
176 if the l connects to hubs h_a and h_b, then h_a and h_b both connects to link l.

axiom

175 ∀ h_a,h_b:H,l:L • {h_a,h_b} ⊆ hs ∧ l ∈ ls ⇒
175   **let** (_,luis)=mereo_H(h), (_,huis)=mereo_L(l)
176   **in** uid_L(l)∈luis ≡ uid_H(h)∈huis **end**

5.3.2.2 Deductions made from Mereologies

Once we have settled basic properties of the mereologies of a domain we can, like for unique identifiers, cf. Example 40 on page 109, *"play around"* with that concept: 'the mereology of a domain'.

Possible Consequences of a Road Net Mereology

Example 48

177 are there [isolated] units from which one can not "reach" other units?
178 does the net consist of two or more "disjoint" nets?
179 et cetera.

We leave it to the reader to narrate and formalise the above properly.

5.3.3 Formulation of Mereologies

The **observe_mereology** domain descriptor, Page 114, may give the impression that the mereo type MT can be described "at the point of issue" of the **observe_mereology** prompt. Since the MT type expression may, in general, depend on any part sort the mereo type MT can, for some domains, "first" be described when all part sorts have had their unique identifiers defined.

5.3.4 Fixed and Varying Mereologies

The mereology of parts is not necessarily fixed.

Definition: 64 Fixed Mereology: By a **fixed mereology** we shall understand a mereology of a part which remains fixed over time.

Definition: 65 Varying Mereology: By a **varying mereology** we shall understand a mereology of a part which may vary over time.

Fixed and Varying Mereology

Example 49 Let us consider a road net, cf. Examples 8 on page 49, 35 on page 83, 38 on page 90 Example 46 on page 114 and Example 47 on the previous page. If hubs and links never change "affiliation", that is: hubs are in fixed relation to zero one or more links, and links are in a fixed relation to exactly two hubs then the mereology of Example 46 on page 114 is a *fixed mereology*. If, on the other hand hubs may be inserted into or removed from the net, and/or links may be removed from or inserted between any two existing hubs, then the mereology of Example 46 on page 114 is a *varying mereology*.

5.3.5 No Fluids Mereology

We comment on our decision, for this monograph, to not endow fluids with mereologies. A first reason is that we "restrict" the concept of mereology to part endurants, that is, to solid endurants – those with "more-or-less" *fixed extents*. Fluids can be said to normally not have fixed extents, that is, they can "morph" from small, fixed into spatially extended forms. For domains of part-fluids conjoins this is particularly true. The fluids in such domains flow through and between parts. Some parts, at some times, embodying large, at other times small amounts of fluid. Some proper, but partial amount of fluid flowing from one part to a next. Et cetera. It is for the same reason that we do not endow fluids with identity. So, for this monograph we decide to not suggest the modeling of fluid mereologies.

5.3.6 Some Modeling Observations

It is, in principle, possible to find examples of mereologies of natural parts: rivers: their confluence, lakes and oceans; and geography: mountain ranges, flat lands, etc. But in our experimental case studies, cf. Example on Page 49, we have found no really interesting such cases. All our experimental case studies appears to focus on the mereology of artefacts.

And, finally, in modeling humans, we find that their mereology encompass all other humans and all artefacts! Humans cannot be tamed to refrain from interacting with everyone and everything.

Some domain models may emphasize *physical mereologies* based on spatial relations, others may emphasize *conceptual mereologies* based on logical "connections".

Rail Net Mereology

Example 50 We refer to Example 36 on page 86.

180 A linear rail unit is connected to exactly two distinct other rail net units of any given rail net.
181 A point unit is connected to exactly three distinct other rail net units of any given rail net.
182 A rigid crossing unit is connected to exactly four distinct other rail net units of any given rail net.
183 A single and a double slip unit is connected to exactly four distinct other rail net units of any given rail net.
184 A terminal unit is connected to exactly one distinct other rail net unit of any given rail net.
185 So we model the mereology of a railway net unit as a pair of sets of rail net unit unique identifiers distinct from that of the rail net unit.

value
185.   mereo_NU: NU → (UI-set×UI-set)
axiom
185.   ∀ nu:NU •
185.   **let** (uis_i,uis_o)=mereo_NU(nu) **in**
185.   **case** (**card** uis_i,**card** usi_o) =
180.   (is_LU(nu) → (1,1),
181.   is_PU(nu) → (1,2) ∨ (2,1),
182.   is_RU(nu) → (2,2),
183.   is_SU(nu) → (2,2), is_DU(nu) → (2,2),
184.   is_TU(nu) → (1,0) ∨ (0,1),
185.   _ → **chaos**) **end**
185.   ∧ uis_i∩uis_o={}
185.   ∧ uid_NU(nu) ∉ (uis_i ∪ uis_o)
185.   **end**

Figure 5.1 illustrates the mereology of four rail units.

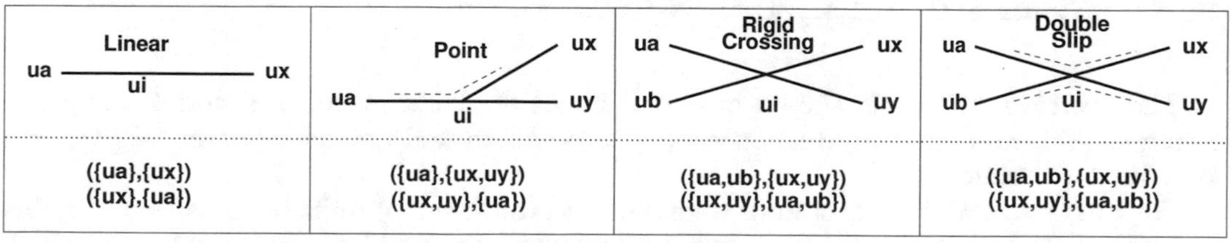

Linear	Point	Rigid Crossing	Double Slip
ua —— ui —— ux	Point, ua ----ui---- uy, ux	ua, ub — ui — ux, uy	ua, ub — ui — ux, uy
({ua},{ux}) ({ux},{ua})	({ua},{ux,uy}) ({ux,uy},{ua})	({ua,ub},{ux,uy}) ({ux,uy},{ua,ub})	({ua,ub},{ux,uy}) ({ux,uy},{ua,ub})

Fig. 5.1 Four Symmetric Rail Unit Mereologies

5.3.7 Conjoin Mereologies

Conjoins, their "roots" and "siblings", enjoy some special mereology relations.[111]

Let us first consider **the pragmatics of conjoins,** e. Part-fluids conjoins, e, are "carriers" or "holders" of fluids. The carrier is p, that is, analyse_conjoin_part(e). The carried or held fluids are $(m_1, m_2, ..., m_m)$, that is, analyse_conjoin_fluids(e). Usually we shall only associate more than one fluid with the so-called *treat*ment conjoin. See below. The carrier or holder, p, somehow provides a "container" for each ℓ_i. We shall, without loss of generality, restrict **supply, pipe, valve, pump** and **dispose** conjoins, see below, to embody just one fluid. Conjoins either serve to transport or to process[112] fluids. Transport is achieved by **moving** fluids between topologically connected conjoins. Processing is achieved by **treating** one or more fluids, of the same conjoin, to interact by being *operated* upon. Conjoins that participate in the transport and treatment of fluids, we conclude, typically form directed, acyclic nets. We shall refer to such nets as *'conjoin nets'*.

Further **pragmatics** are those of the interconnection of conjoins as expressed in their mereologies. First, to transport, they must form, usually directed, acyclic, nets. These nets are sequences of conjoins acting as **pipes**, "interspersed" by conjoins serving to **fork** (divert), from one, a fork conjoin, flow, into two, usually pipe, conjoins, or to **join** (merge) transport from two (or more), usually pipe flow, into one, the join flow, or to **treat**, within a single conjoin, the 'treatment' conjoin, one or more fluids into one or more new and/or replacement fluids. By a **flow net** we shall understand a collection of conjoins formed as an acyclic, directed graph. Figure 5.2 abstracts a possible **conjoin flow net**.

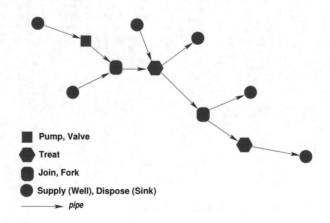

■ Pump, Valve

⬣ Treat

⬢ Join, Fork

● Supply (Well), Dispose (Sink)

────▶ *pipe*

Fig. 5.2 An Abstracted Directed, Acyclic Flow Net of Conjoins

The abstracted flow net shown in Fig. 5.2 is at the basis in domain models for waste management, industrial production supply, production and demand, (water oil gas, etc.) pipe lines, et cetera.

For directed, acyclic nets of fluid transport and treatment of units of connected conjoins we can conclude that there must be units which **supply** [inputs] fluids to the net; units which open or close, by means of **pumps** [empowers] or **valves** [on/off], the flow of fluids; units

---

[111] We remind the reader of the 'pragmatics' paragraph of Sect. **4.13.3** on page 72.

[112] – the **supply, pipe, valve, pump** and **dispose** conjoins transport are restricted to carry just one fluid; the **treat**ment conjoin usually process, hence contain, more than one fluid.

which simply **pipe**s [flows] fluids "along"; units which **fork** [flow] fluids in two [or more][113] ongoing directions; units which **join** two [or more][114] fluid flows into one flow; units which **treat** [process] one or more incoming [in-flowed] and contained fluids[115] into one or more contained and outgoing [out-flowed] fluids[116]; and units which **dispose** [outputs] one [or more][117] fluids[118].

Let us then consider **the technicalities of modeling conjoins** e. The conjoin has a part: observe_conjoin_part(e), p, and it has one or more fluids: observe_conjoin_fluids(e), $(\ell_1, \ell_2, ..., \ell_m)$. The mereology of p includes that of the unique identifier of e.

When we, above, cautiously, write 'includes' it is to say that there may be other topological or conceptual (including intentional) relations.

We can likewise consider fluid-parts conjoins but leave this to the reader.

This section is "conjoined" with Sect. **5.4.9** on page 137.

Pipeline Mereology

Example 51 We refer to Appendix Sect. **A.3**.

5.3.8 Mereologies of Compounds

For structures we do not model their mereologies. But their components, whether the structures are *"Cartesian"* or *"sets"*, may very well be non-structures, hence have mereologies.

5.4 Attributes

To recall: there are three sets of ***internal qualities***: unique identifiers, mereologies and attributes. Unique identifiers and mereologies are rather definite kinds of internal endurant qualities; attributes form more "free-wheeling" sets of ***internal qualities***. Whereas, for this monograph, we suggest to not endow fluids with unique identification and mereologies all endurants, i.e., including fluids, are endowed with attributes.

5.4.1 Inseparability of Attributes from Parts and Fluids

Parts and fluids are typically recognised because of their spatial form and are otherwise characterised by their intangible, but measurable attributes. That is, whereas endurants, whether solid (as are parts) or fluids, are physical, tangible, in the sense of being spatial [or being abstractions, i.e., concepts, of spatial endurants], attributes are intangible: cannot

---

[113] In this monograph we shall just treat the case of two fork outlets.

[114] See footnote 113.

[115] $\ell_{i_1}, \ell_{i_2}, ..., \ell_{i_s}$

[116] $\ell_{o_1}, \ell_{o_2}, ..., \ell_{o_d}$

[117] See footnote 113.

[118] We shall not "speculate" on the possible, general relationships between $\ell_{i_1}, \ell_{i_2}, ..., \ell_{i_s}$ and $\ell_{o_1}, \ell_{o_2}, ..., \ell_{o_d}$.

normally be touched[119], or seen[120], but can be objectively measured[121]. Thus, in our quest for describing domains where humans play an active rôle, we rule out subjective "attributes": feelings, sentiments, moods. Thus we shall abstain, in our domain science also from matters of aesthetics.

We equate all endurants — which have *the same type of unique identifiers the same type of mereologies, and the same types of attributes* — with one sort. Thus removing an internal quality from an endurant makes no sense: the endurant of that type either becomes an endurant of another type or ceases to exist (i.e., becomes a non-entity)!

We can roughly distinguish between two kinds of attributes: those which can be motivated by **physical** (incl. chemical) **concerns**, and those, which, although they embody some form of 'physics measures', appear to reflect on **event histories**: *"if 'something', ϕ, has 'happened' to an endurant, e_a, then some 'commensurate thing', ψ, has 'happened' to another (one or more) endurants, e_b."* where the *'something'* and *'commensurate thing'* usually involve some 'interaction' between the two (or more) endurants. It can take some reflection and analysis to properly identify endurants e_a and e_b and commensurate events ϕ and ψ. Example 65 on page 141 shall illustrate the, as we shall call it, **intentional pull** of event histories.

5.4.2 Attribute Modeling Tools

5.4.2.1 Attribute Quality and Attribute Value

We distinguish between an attribute (as a logical proposition, of a name, i.e.) type, and an attribute value, as a value in some value space.

Observer Function Prompt 12 `analyse_attribute_types`: One can calculate the set of attribute type names of parts and fluids with the following *domain analysis prompt*:

- `analyse_attribute_type_names`

Thus for a part p we may have `analyse_attribute_type_names`$(p) = \{$"A_1","A_2",...,"A_m"$\}$.

5.4.2.2 Attribute Types and Functions

Let us recall that attributes cover qualities other than unique identifiers and mereology. Let us then consider that parts and fluids have one or more attributes. These attributes are qualities which help characterise "what it means" to be a part or a fluid. Note that we expect every part and fluid to have at least one attribute. The question is now, in general, how many and, particularly, which.

---

[119] One can see the red colour of a wall, but one touches the wall.

[120] One cannot see electric current, and one may touch an electric wire, but only if it conducts high voltage can one know that it is indeed an electric wire.

[121] That is, we restrict our domain analysis with respect to attributes to such quantities which are observable, say by mechanical, electrical or chemical instruments. Once objective measurements can be made of human feelings, beauty, and other, we may wish to include these "attributes" in our domain descriptions.

Domain Description Prompt 10 `describe_attributes`**:** The domain analyser experiments, thinks and reflects about endurant, e, attributes. That process is initiated by the **domain description prompt**:

- `describe_attributes(e)`.

The result of that **domain description prompt** is that the domain analyser cum describer writes down the *attribute (sorts or) types and observers* domain description text according to the following schema:
let {" A_1, ..., A_m "} = analyse_attribute_type_names(e) in
" Narration:
        [t]   ... narrative text on attribute sorts ...
        [o]   ... narrative text on attribute sort observers ...
        [p]   ... narrative text on attribute sort proof obligations ...
Formalisation:
        type
        [t] A_1, ..., A_m,
        value
        [o]   attr_A_1: E→A_1, ..., attr_A_m: E→A_m
        proof obligation [Disjointness of Attribute Types]
        [p] $\mathcal{PO}$: **let** P be any part sort **in** [the domain description]
        [p]   **let** a:(A_1|A_2|...|A_m) **in is**_A_i(a) ≠ **is**_A_j(a) [i≠i, i,j:[1..m]] **end end** **"**
end

The **is**_A_j(e) is defined by Ai, i:[1..n].

Modelling Choice 9 *Endurant Attributes:* As for endurant and mereology descriptions the analyser cum describer chooses for some model of a domain, one set of attributes, for another model of supposedly "the same" domain another set of attributes ∎

Let A_1, ..., A_n be the set of all conceivable attributes of endurants $e{:}E$. (Usually n is a rather large natural number, say in the order of a hundred conceivable such.) In any one domain model the domain analyser cum describer selects a modest subset, A_1, ..., A_m, i.e., $m < n$. Across many domain models for *"more-or-less the same"* domain m varies and the attributes, A_1, ..., A_m, selected for one model may differ from those, A'_1, ..., $A'_{m'}$, chosen for another model.

    The **type** definitions: A_1, ..., A_m, inform us that the domain analyser has decided to focus on the distinctly named A_1, ..., A_m attributes.[122] The **value** clauses attr_A_1:P→A_1, ..., attr_A_n:P→A_n are then "automatically" given: if an endurant, e:E, has an attribute A_i then there is postulated, "by definition" [eureka] an attribute observer function attr_A_i:E→A_i et cetera ∎

    We cannot automatically, that is, syntactically, guarantee that our domain descriptions secure that the various attribute types for a endurant sort denote disjoint sets of values. Therefore we must prove it.

5.4.2.3 Attribute Categories

Michael A. Jackson [263] has suggested a hierarchy of attribute categories: from static to dynamic values – and within the dynamic value category: inert values, reactive values, active values – and within the dynamic active value category: autonomous values, biddable values and programmable values. We now review these attribute value types. The review is based on [263, M.A.Jackson]. *Endurant attributes* are either constant or varying, i.e., **static** or **dynamic** attributes.

Attribute Category: 1 By a *static attribute*, a:A, `is_static_attribute`(a), we shall understand an attribute whose values are constants, i.e., cannot change.

---

[122] The attribute type names are chosen by the domain analyser to reflect on domain phenomena.

Static Attributes

Example 52 Let us exemplify road net attributes in this and the next examples. And let us assume the following attributes: year of first link construction and link length at that time. We may consider both to be static attributes: The year first established, seems an obvious static attribute and the length is fixed at the time the road was first built.

Attribute Category: 2 By a **dynamic attribute**, a:A, is_dynamic_attribute(a), we shall understand an attribute whose values are variable, i.e., can change. Dynamic attributes are either *inert, reactive* or *active* attributes.

Attribute Category: 3 By an **inert attribute**, a:A, is_inert_attribute(a), we shall understand a dynamic attribute whose values only change as the result of external stimuli where these stimuli prescribe new values.

Inert Attribute

Example 53 And let us now further assume the following link attribute: link name. We may consider it to be an inert attribute: the name is not "assigned" to the link by the link itself, but probably by some road net authority which we are not modeling.

Attribute Category: 4 By a **reactive attribute**, a:A, is_reactive_attribute(a), we shall understand a dynamic attribute whose values, if they vary, change in response to external stimuli, where these stimuli either come from outside the domain of interest or from other endurants.

Reactive Attributes

Example 54 Let us further assume the following two link attributes: "wear and tear", respectively "icy and slippery". We will consider those attributes to be reactive in that automobiles (another part) travelling the link, an external "force", typically causes the "wear and tear", respectively the weather (outside our domain) causes the "icy and slippery" property.

Attribute Category: 5 By an **active attribute**, a:A, is_active_attribute(a), we shall understand a dynamic attribute whose values change (also) of its own volition. Active attributes are either *autonomous, biddable* or *programmable* attributes.

Attribute Category: 6 By an **autonomous attribute**, a:A, is_autonomous_attribute(a), we shall understand a dynamic active attribute whose values change only "on their own volition". The values of an autonomous attributes are a "law onto themselves and their surroundings".

Autonomous Attributes

Example 55 We enlarge scope of our examples of attribute categories to now also include automobiles (on the road net). In this example we assume that an automobile is driven by a human [behaviour]. These are some automobile attributes: velocity, acceleration, and moving straight, or turning left, or turning right. We shall consider these three attributes to be autonomous. It is the driver, not the automobile, who decides whether the automobile should drive at constant velocity, including 0, or accelerate or decelerate, including stopping. And it is the driver who decides when to turn left or right, or not turn at all.

Attribute Category: 7 By a *biddable attribute*, a:A, is_biddable_attribute(a) we shall understand a dynamic active attribute whose values *are prescribed but may fail to be observed as such*.

Attribute Category: 8 By a *programmable attribute*, a:A, is_programmable_attribute(a), we shall understand a dynamic active attribute whose values can be prescribed.

Programmable Attribute
Example 56 We continue with the automobile on the road net examples. In this example we assume that an automobile includes, as one inseparable entity, "the driver". These are some automobile attributes: position on a link, velocity, acceleration (incl. deceleration), and direction: straight, turning left, turning right. We shall now consider these three attributes to be programmable.

Figure 5.3 captures an attribute value ontology.

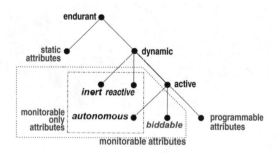

Fig. 5.3 Attribute Value Ontology

Figure 5.3 hints at three categories of dynamic attributes: **monitorable only**, **biddable** and **programmable** attributes.

Attribute Category: 9 By a *monitorable only attribute*, a:A, is_monitorable_only_attribute(a), we shall understand a dynamic active attribute which is either *inert* or *reactive* or *autonomous*.

That is: is_monitorable(e)≡is_inert(e)∨is_reactive(e)∨is_autonomous(e).

Road Net Attributes

Example 57 We treat some attributes of the hubs of a road net.

186 There is a hub state. It is a set of pairs, (l_f, l_t), of link identifiers, where these link identifiers are in the mereology of the hub. The meaning of the hub state in which, e.g., (l_f, l_t) is an element, is that the hub is open, **"green"**, for traffic $from$ link l_f to link l_t. If a hub state is empty then the hub is closed, i.e., **"red"** for traffic from any connected links to any other connected links.

187 There is a hub state space. It is a set of hub states. The current hub state must be in its state space. The meaning of the hub state space is that its states are all those the hub can attain.

188 Since we can think rationally about it, it can be described, hence we can model, as an attribute of hubs, a history of its traffic: the recording, per unique bus and automobile identifier, of the time ordered presence in the hub of these vehicles. Hub history is an *event history*.

```
type                                        188  ∀ ht:H_Traffic,ui:(A_UI|B_UI) •
186  HΣ = (L_UI×L_UI)-set                   188     ui ∈ dom ht ⇒ time_ordered(ht(ui))
axiom                                       value
186  ∀ h:H • obs_HΣ(h) ∈ obs_HΩ(h)          186  attr_HΣ: H → HΣ
type                                        187  attr_HΩ: H → HΩ
187  HΩ = HΣ-set                            188  attr_H_Traffic: H → H_Traffic
188  H_Traffic                              value
188  H_Traffic = (A_UI|B_UI) ⇸ (TIME × VPos)*  188  time_ordered: (TIME × VPos)* → Bool
axiom                                       188  time_ordered(tvpl) ≡ ...
```

In Item 188 we model the time-ordered sequence of traffic as a discrete sampling, i.e., $⇸$, rather than as a continuous function, $→$.

Invariance of Road Net Traffic States

Example 58 We continue Example 57.

189 The link identifiers of hub states must be in the set, $l_{ui}s$, of the road net's link identifiers.

```
axiom
189  ∀ h:H • h ∈ hs ⇒
189     let hσ = attr_HΣ(h) in ∀ (l_{ui}i,l_{ui}i'):(L_UI×L_UI) • (l_{ui}i,l_{ui}i') ∈ hσ ⇒ {l_{ui_i},l'_{ui_i}} ⊆ l_{ui}s end
```

Pipeline Attributes

Example 59 We refer to Appendix Sect. **A.4**.

You may skip Example 60 in a first reading.

Road Transport: Further Attributes

Example 60 Links: We show just a few attributes. . . . .

190 There is a link state. It is a set of pairs, (h_f, h_t), of distinct hub identifiers, where these hub identifiers are in the mereology of the link. The meaning of a link state in which (h_f, h_t) is an element is that the link is open, **"green"**, for traffic $f$rom hub h_f to hub h_t. Link states can have either 0, 1 or 2 elements.

191 There is a link state space. It is a set of link states. The meaning of the link state space is that its states are all those the which the link can attain. The current link state must be in its state space. If a link state space is empty then the link is (permanently) closed. If it has one element then it is a one-way link. If a one-way link, l, is imminent on a hub whose mereology designates that link, then the link is a "trap", i.e., a "blind cul-de-sac".

192 Since we can think rationally about it, it can be described, hence it can model, as an attribute of links a history of its traffic: the recording, per unique bus and automobile identifier, of the time ordered positions along the link (from one hub to the next) of these vehicles.

193 The hub identifiers of link states must be in the set, $h_{ui}s$, of the road net's hub identifiers.

```
type
190 LΣ = H_UI-set                    [programmable, Df.8 Pg.123]
axiom
190 ∀ lσ:LΣ•card lσ=2
190 ∀ l:L • obs_LΣ(l) ∈ obs_LΩ(l)
type
191 LΩ = LΣ-set                      [static, Df.1 Pg.121]
192 L_Traffic                        [programmable, Df.8 Pg.123]
192 L_Traffic = (A_UI|B_UI) ₘ→ (T×(H_UI×Frac×H_UI))*
192 Frac = Real, axiom frac:Fract • 0<frac<1
value
190 attr_LΣ: L → LΣ
191 attr_LΩ: L → LΩ
192 attr_L_Traffic: : → L_Traffic
axiom
192 ∀ lt:L_Traffic,ui:(A_UI|B_UI)•ui ∈ dom ht ⇒ time_ordered(ht(ui))
193 ∀ l:L • l ∈ ls ⇒
193    let lσ = attr_LΣ(l) in ∀ (h_{ui}i,h_{ui}i'):(H_UI×K_UI) •
193    (h_{ui}i,h_{ui}i') ∈ lσ ⇒ {h_{ui_i},h'_{ui_i}} ⊆ h_{ui}s end
```

Bus Companies: ....

Bus companies operate a number of lines that service passenger transport along routes of the road net. Each line being serviced by a number of buses.

194 *Bus companies create, maintain, revise and distribute [to the public (not modeled here), and to buses] bus time tables, not further defined.*

```
type
194 BusTimTbl                        [programmable, Df.8 Pg.123]
value
194 attr_BusTimTbl: BC → BusTimTbl
```

There are two notions of time at play here: the indefinite "real" or "actual" time; and the definite calendar, hour, minute and second time designation occurring in some textual form in, e.g., time tables.

Buses: *We show just a few attributes:* ....

195 *Buses run routes, according to their line number, ln:LN, in the*
196 *bus time table, btt:BusTimTbl obtained from their bus company, and and keep, as inert attributes, their segment of that time table.*
197 *Buses occupy positions on the road net:*
    a *either at a hub identified by some h_ui,*
    b *or on a link, some fraction, f:Fract, down an identified link, l_ui, from one of its identified connecting hubs, fh_ui, in the direction of the other identified hub, th_ui.*
198 *Et cetera.*

```
type
195   LN                              [programmable, Df.8 Pg.123]
196   BusTimTbl                       [inert, Df.3 Pg.122]
197   BPos  == atHub | onLink         [programmable, Df.8 Pg.123]
197a  atHub   :: h_ui:H_UI
197b  onLink  :: fh_ui:H_UI×l_ui:L_UI×frac:Fract×th_ui:H_UI
197b  Fract   = Real, axiom frac:Fract • 0<frac<1
198   ...
value
196   attr_BusTimTbl: B → BusTimTbl
197   attr_BPos: B → BPos
```

Private Automobiles: *We show just a few attributes: . . . .*
We illustrate but a few attributes:

199 *Automobiles have static number plate registration numbers.*
200 *Automobiles have dynamic positions on the road net:*
      [197a] either at a hub identified by some h_ui,
      [197b] or on a link, some fraction, frac:Fract down an identified link, l_ui, from one of its identified
      connecting hubs, fh_ui, in the direction of the other identified hub, th_ui.

```
type
199   RegNo                           [static, Df.1 Pg.121]
200   APos   == atHub | onLink        [programmable, Df.8 Pg.123]
197a  atHub   :: h_ui:H_UI
197b  onLink  :: fh_ui:H_UI × l_ui:L_UI × frac:Fract × th_ui:H_UI
197b  Fract   = Real, axiom frac:Fract • 0<frac<1
value
199   attr_RegNo: A → RegNo
200   attr_APos: A → APos
```

Obvious attributes that are not illustrated are those of velocity and acceleration, forward or backward
movement, turning right, left or going straight, etc. The acceleration, deceleration, even velocity, or turning
right, turning left, moving straight, or forward or backward are seen as command actions. As such they denote
actions by the automobile — such as pressing the accelerator, or lifting accelerator pressure or braking, or
turning the wheel in one direction or another, etc. As actions they have a kind of counterpart in the velocity,
the acceleration, etc. attributes. Observe that bus companies each have their own distinct *bus time table*,
and that these are modeled as *programmable*, Item 194 on the preceding page, page 125. Observe then
that buses each have their own distinct *bus time table*, and that these are model-led as *inert*, Item 196 on
the previous page, page 125. In Items 289–290b Pg. 186 we shall see how the buses communicate with their
respective bus companies in order for the buses to obtain the *programmed* bus time tables "in lieu" of their
inert one ! In Items 188 Pg. 124 and 192 Pg. 125, we illustrated an aspect of domain analysis & description
that may seem, and at least some decades ago would have seemed, strange: namely that if we can think,
hence speak, about it, then we can model it "as a fact" in the domain. The case in point is that we include
among hub and link attributes their histories of the timed whereabouts of buses and automobiles.[123]

Calculating Attributes

201 Given endurant *e* we can *meta-linguistically*[124] calculate names for its static attributes.
202 Given endurant *e* we can *meta-linguistically* calculate name for its monitorable-only at-
     tributes attributes.
203 Given endurant *e* we can *meta-linguistically* calculate names for its controllable attributes.

---

[123] In this day and age of road cameras and satellite surveillance these traffic recordings may not appear so
strange: We now know, at least in principle, of technologies that can record approximations to the hub and
link traffic attributes.

[124] By using the term *meta-linguistically* here we shall indicate that we go outside what is computable – and
thus appeal to the reader's forbearance.

204 These four sets make up all the attributes of endurant *e*.

The type names ST, MA, PT designate mutually disjoint sets, ST, of names of static attributes, sets, MA, of names of monitoriable, i.e., monitorable-only and biddable, attributes, sets, PT, of names of programmable, i.e., fully controllable attributes.

value
201   stat_attr_types: E → ST
202   moni_attr_types: E → MA
203   prgr_attr_types: E → PT

axiom
204   ∀ e:E ·
201   **let** stat_nms = stat_attr_types(e),
202   moni_nms = moni_attr_types(e),
203   prgr_nms = prgr_types(e) **in**
204   **card** stat_nms + **card** moni_nms + **card** prgr_nms
204   = **card**(stat_nms ∪ mon_nms ∪ prgr_nms) **end**

The above formulas are indicative, like mathematical formulas, they are not computable.

205 Given endurant *e* we can *meta-linguistically* calculate its static attribute values, stat_attr_vals;
206 given endurant *e* we can *meta-linguistically* calculate its monitorable-only attribute values, moni_attr_vals; and
207 given endurant *e* we can *meta-linguistically* calculate its programmable attribute values, prgr_attr_vals.

The type names sa1, ..., pap refer to the types denoted by the corresponding types name nsa1, ..., npap.

value
205   stat_attr_vals: E → SA1×SA2×...×SAs
205   stat_attr_vals(e) ≡
205   **let** {nsa1,nsa2,...,nsas} = stat_attr_types(e) **in**
205   (attr_sa1(e),attr_sa2(e),...,attr_sas(e)) **end**

206   moni_attr_vals: E → MA1×MA2×...×MAm
206   moni_attr_vals(e) ≡
206   **let** {nma1,nma2,...,nmam} = moni_attr_types(e) **in**
206   (attr_ma1(e),attr_ma2(e),...,attr_mam(e)) **end**

207   prgr_attr_vals: E → PA1×PA2×...×PAp
207   prgr_attr_vals(e) ≡
207   **let** {npa1,npa2,...,npap} = prgr_attr_types(e) **in**
207   (attr_pa1(e),attr_pa2(e),...,attr_pap(e)) **end**

The "ordering" of type values, (attr_sa1(e),...,attr_sas(e)), (attr_ma1(e),...,attr_mam(e)), et cetera, is arbitrary.

5.4.3 A Discourse on Attribute Kinds

In this, in a sense, discursive, section we shall depart, somewhat, from a more direct presentation of analysis and description prompts. We shall muse, as it were, about the following, perceived kinds of concepts and attributes:

- space, time and substance,
- spatio and temporal attributes,
- natural and artefactual attributes,

- geometric attributes,
- action and event attributes,
- and others!

5.4.3.1 A Discussion of SPACE, TIME and MATTER Attributes

We remind the reader of Chapter 3. Space, SPACE, time, TIME, and substance, MATTER, cannot be sôle attributes of endurants[125]. Endurants exist in space and time. Manifest endurants have substance, i.e., consists of MATTER. These three kinds of properties follow by transcendental deduction from rational reasoning. So it is futile to ascribe attributes sôlely of these kinds to endurants! But, stop here, pause a bit. Somehow we must ascribe what appears to be space, time and substance properties to endurants: length, speed, weight. So what is the problem? The problem is that these latter kinds of properties are artefactual concepts. Mankind have found a need to somehow measure spatial, temporal and substance phenomena.

Spatio-like Attributes: The geographical location of a specific "point"[126] on the surface of earth, represented by its longitude[127] and latitude[128], can be an attribute of an endurant. This is so because the representation are artefactual qualities, not transcendentally deducible facts. POINT are mathematical concepts, created as mathematical abstractions – as are LINEs, CURVEs, SURFACEs and EXTENTs. The respective *Lengths*, *Areas* and *Volumes* of spatial entities are artefactual qualities ascribed by humans and measured in, for example, m, m^2 and m^3, respectively.

Temporal-like Attributes: Other attributes are endowed, as properties of endurants, not by man, but inherently there, given to us. The *Time* at which some action is invoked or some event occurs, is not a TIME; and the *TimeInterval* (time interval or *duration*) between two actions or events is not a TI. Instead humans, after many attempts, have devised ways and means of representing, respectively measuring *Times* and *TimeIntervals*[129]. A DAY is not 24 hours, 0 minute, 0 seconds, and 0 which or whatever fraction of a second you may think of. A SIDERIALYEAR is the TI it takes for the earth to orbit the sun. While doing so, the earth *spins* on its axis. One complete spin takes exactly a DAY. But our concept of a *Day* is that of 24 *Hours*, with each hour "divided" into 60 *Minutes*, and each minute into 60 *Seconds*, and so forth. So *Year, Month, Week, Day, Hour, Minute, Second*, etc., are human constructions devised to represent time intervals. These time interval representations are of some *absolute* kind. They are independent of which endurant, at which POINT in SPACE, e.g., where on earth, they may be related to. The time that an event occurred, or is to occur, or an action was (to be) invoked, are of *absolute* kind. A time, like *"Saturday 16 May, 2020, at 9:27:03 am"* is such an example. Time has, to some physicists, no [absolute] beginning point. There is no *"On the first day and in the first hour of creation"*. So mankind has settled on some, you may say, 'compromise'. We "speak of" time, usually, as if it was an interval: *"Around the year 482 Before Christ*[130]*"*, or *"August 30, 2021: 10:46 am, after Christ*[131]*"*. Time indications must state the, or an approximate *location* on earth, for which they are given, or some other reference frame, e.g., a *time zone*, such as Greenwich Mean Time, GMT or other (CET, EET,

---

[125] But spatial measures, time stamps, time intervals, and substance (matters) may be attributes

[126] By "a specific 'point' " we do not mean a POINT.

[127] Longitude is the angle east or west of a reference meridian to another meridian that passes through that point [Wikipedia].

[128] Latitude is the angle between the equatorial plane and the straight line that passes through that point and through (or close to) the center of the earth [Wikipedia]

[129] To wit: quartz-crystal clocks of the 1930s.

[130] – date of the birth of the Greek philosopher Plato

[131] – time at last editing this text

WET, ET, PST etc.). For early continental continental explorers and ocean seafarers, accurate chronometers became indispensable[132]. As human constructions they have lead to many ingenious means for their measure: *clocks*[133] of many kinds[134]. But clocks do not measure time, only time intervals.

Spatio-temporal-like Attributes: We talk, for example, of speed as distance, i.e., *length*, covered by *time interval*. And we talk, for example, of velocity, i.e., speed with *vectorial direction*. On one hand they are spatio-temporal phenomena, inherent as transcendentally deducible facts. On the other hand we also experience them, and may have need to represent them as attributes. In other words, we must be careful in our analysis.

Action and Event Attributes[135]**:** An important class of attributes record actions and events that occur to endurants. That an action or event occurs or has occurred is immaterial, *but we can talk about it!* As such it may need being recorded in an appropriate attribute. Such recording are, to be meaningful, time-stamped.

Action and Event Attributes

Example 61 From our continuing road transport example we give an example. The occurrence of an automobile at a hub or on a link is an event and can, as such, be recorded in both hub, link and automobile *"history"* attributes. From our likewise continuing pipeline example we give examples. The actions of opening and closing of valves, the actions of starting and ending of pumping, and the events of a pipe unit becoming empty, or overflowing ("choked"), or changing from laminar to turbulent flow[136], can, as such, be recorded in both pipeline unit *"history"* attributes.

Natural and Artefactual Attributes: From the above we can see that in seeking properties of endurants we waver between natural phenomena and artefactual "measures". So we need be clear of the distinction, for an endurant, whether what may seem to be [a kind of] an endurant attribute is really a SPACE, TIME or SUBSTANCE phenomenon; or whether it is one for which we have "invented" measures. The former we refer to as *natural attributes*. They can be expressed using the *physical attribute kinds* detailed in Sect. **5.4.5** next The latter we refer to as *artefactual attributes*. They can be expressed using both *physical attribute kinds* and *domain concepts* such as, for example, *unique identifiers*.

Geometrical Attributes: Manifest endurants reside in space. But we characterise them by such geometric measures as position in some earthly, or relative coordinate system, length, a relative measure, and volume. For intricate geometric objects we may be comprehension-wise better off by presenting them in diagrams, drawings or annotated photos or videos.

---

[132] Christiaan Huygens, following his invention of the pendulum clock in 1656, made the first attempt at a marine chronometer in 1673.

[133] Some references [www.encyclopedia.com]:

- Gibbs, Sharon L. *Greek and Roman Sundials*.
  New Haven, CT: Yale University Press, 1976.
- Landes, David S. *Revolution in Time: Clocks and the Making of the Modern World*.
  Cambridge, MT: The Belknap Press of Harvard University Press, 1983.
- Tannenbaum, Beulah, and Stillman, Myra. *Understanding Time: The Science of Clocks and Calendars*.
  New York: Whittlesey House, McGraw-Hill Book Company, Inc.,1958.

[134] A second is defined as 9,192,631,770 oscillations of the caesium atom, off by only one second after running for 300 million years.

[135] We refer to Defns. 70 on page 161 and 71 on page 162 for definitions of the concepts of *action* and *event*.

[136] Becoming empty, overflowing or transiting between laminar and turbulent flows are fuzzy measures; see Sect. **5.4.10** on page 138.

5.4.3.2 On the Continuity of SPACE and TIME

★ SPACE

Natural and artefactual, that is, mane-made endurants reside in space. We have dealt with space, i.e., SPACE, in Sect. 3.5. Subsidiary spatial concepts are those of VOLUME, AREA, CURVE (or LINE), and POINT. All canal system endurants possess, whether we choose to model them or not, such spatial attributes. We shall not here be bothered by any representation, let alone computational representations, of spatial attributes. They are facts. Any properties that two AREAs, a_i and a_j may have in common – like **bordering**, **overlapping disjoint** or **properly contained** – are facts and should, as such be expressed in terms of **axiom**s. They are not properties that can, hence must, be proven. Once a *domain description*, involving spatial concepts is the base for a *requirements prescription*, then, if these spatial concepts are not *projected* out of the evolving requirements, they must, eventually, be prescribed – or assumed to have – computable representations. In that case axioms concerning spatial quantities are turned into **proof obligations** that must, eventually, be **discharged**.

★ TIME

Natural and artefactual, that is, mane-made endurants reside in time. We have dealt with space in Sect. 3.4. Subsidiary spatial concepts are those of TIME and TIME INTERVALs. All natural endurants possess, whether we choose to model them or not, such temporal attributes. We shall not here be bothered by any representation, let alone computational representations, of temporal attributes. They are facts. Any properties that two TIME INTERVALs, ti_i and ti_j may have in common, like **bordering** or **overlapping**, are facts and should, as such be expressed in terms of **axiom**s[137]. They are not properties that can, hence must, be proven. Once a *domain description*, involving temporal concepts is the base for a *requirements prescription*, then, if these temporal concepts are not *projected* out of the evolving requirements, they must, eventually, be prescribed – or assumed to have – computable representations. In that case axioms concerning temporal quantities are turned into **proof obligations** that must, eventually, be **discharged**.

5.4.3.3 Whither Continuity or Discreteness

The issue of whether to model certain spatial and temporal attributes as continuous or discrete has a philosophical twist [277]. One might argue that some phenomena are of continuous natures, but one might also argue that we, the domain analysers and describers, observe them "at discrete times". You will therefore find that we often choose the latter. That, for example, automobile histories, cf. Examples 57 and 58, are modeled them as discrete phenomena. We could, as well have chosen to model them as continuous phenomena.

5.4.3.4 A Preliminary Conclusion

We could go on finding further varieties of attributes. But we stop here! So why this section? So that you may hopefully be very careful in your assignment of attributes.

---

[137] We refer here to the TIME and TIME INTERVAL operators of Sect. 3.4

5.4.4 Continuous Space- and Time-related Attributes

When analysing & describing attributes of space- and time-related endurants we may decide between either modeling them as continuous functions or as discrete functions, i.e., in the latter case, as if they were "sampled". Examples of what we are referring to are found in Example 57 [Page 124] and Example 60 [Page 124]. Here we model traffic history as discrete samplings rather than, as they "really" are, continuous functions. We have chosen the "simpler" approach of discrete time sampled modeling. A more "correct" modeling would have been that of continuous time modeling. We shall therefore have the following important to say. We are modeling domains. As such there will be many instances of modeling phenomena that are not computable, i.e., not "realisable – inside a computer". But we do not have to worry. Physicists "do that all the time": modeling natural phenomena in terms of continuous functions, so we can, of course, do likewise. When, as in the referenced examples – and others, we we use discrete time (or, elsewhere, continuous space) modeling it is simply for "convenience". We shall, when modeling perdurants, i.e., the behaviours of parts such as automobiles on roads attempt to model their updating of automobile histories, and that is most easily expressible when using discrete time modeling. Continuous time modeling, in the context of our domain analysis & description, has been shown in [41, *Dynamics of Railway Nets: On an Interface between Automatic Control and Software Engineering*]. We leave it at that!

5.4.5 Physics Attributes

In this section we shall muse about the kind of attributes that are typical of natural parts, but which may also be relevant as attributes of artefacts.

Typically, when physicists write computer programs, intended for calculating physics behaviours, they "lump" all of these into the **type Real**, thereby hiding some important physics 'dimensions'. In this section we shall review that which is missing!

The subject of physical dimensions in programming languages is rather decisively treated in David Kennedy's 1996 PhD Thesis [271] — so there really is no point in trying to cast new light on this subject other than to remind the reader of what these physical dimensions are all about.

5.4.5.1 SI: The International System of Quantities

In physics we operate on values of attributes of manifest, i.e., physical phenomena. The type of some of these attributes are recorded in well known tables, cf. Tables 5.1–5.3. Table 5.1 shows the base units of physics.

Base quantity	Name	Type
length	meter	m
mass	kilogram	kg
time	second	s
electric current	ampere	A
thermodynamic temperature	kelvin	K
amount of substance	mole	mol
luminous intensity	candela	cd

Table 5.1 Base SI Units

Table 5.2 shows the units of physics derived from the base units. Table 5.3 shows further units

Name	Type	Derived Quantity	Derived Type
radian	rad	angle	m/m
steradian	sr	solid angle	$m^2 \times m^{-2}$
Hertz	Hz	frequency	s^{-1}
newton	N	force, weight	$kg \times m \times s^{-2}$
pascal	Pa	pressure, stress	N/m^2
joule	J	energy, work, heat	$N \times m$
watt	W	power, radiant flux	J/s
coulomb	C	electric charge	$s \times A$
volt	V	electromotive force	W/A ($kg \times m^2 \times s^{-3} \times A^{-1}$)
farad	F	capacitance	C/V ($kg^{-1} \times m^{-2} \times s^4 \times A^2$)
ohm	Ω	electrical resistance	V/A ($kg \times m^2 \times s^3 \times A^2$)
siemens	S	electrical conductance	A/V ($kg1 \times m^2 \times s^3 \times A^2$)
weber	Wb	magnetic flux	Vxs ($kg \times m^2 \times s^{-2} \times A^{-1}$)
tesla	T	magnetic flux density	Wb/m^2 ($kg \times s^2 \times A^{-1}$)
henry	H	inductance	Wb/A ($kg \times m^2 \times s^{-2} \times A^2$)
degree Celsius	^oC	temp. rel. to 273.15 K	K
lumen	lm	luminous flux	cd×sr (cd)
lux	lx	illuminance	lm/m^2 ($m^2 \times cd$)

Table 5.2 Derived SI Units

of physics derived from the base units. *velocity* is speed with three dimensional direction

Name	Explanation	Derived Type
area	square meter	m^2
volume	cubic meter	m^3
speed	meter per second	m/s
wave number	reciprocal meter	m-1
mass density	kilogram per cubic meter	kg/m^3
specific volume	cubic meter per kilogram	m3/kg
current density	ampere per square meter	A/m^2
magnetic field strength	ampere per meter	A/m
substance concentration	mole per cubic meter	mol/m3
luminance	candela per square meter	cd/m^2
mass fraction	kilogram per kilogram	kg/kg = 1

Table 5.3 Further SI Units

and is, for example, given as

- velocity, meter per second with direction: m/s
- acceleration, meter per second squared and m/s^2
- *(longitude,latitude,azimuth)* measured in radian: (r,r,r)

Table 5.4 shows standard prefixes for SI units of measure and Table 5.5 show fractions of SI units.

Prefix name		deca	hecto	kilo	mega	giga
Prefix symbol		da	h	k	M	G
Factor	10^0	10^1	10^2	10^3	10^6	10^9
Prefix name		tera	peta	exa	zetta	yotta
Prefix symbol		T	P	E	Z	Y
Factor		10^{12}	10^{15}	10^{18}	10^{21}	10^{24}

Table 5.4 Standard Prefixes for SI Units of Measure

Prefix name		deca	hecto	kilo	mega	giga
Prefix symbol		da	h	k	M	G
Factor	10^0	10^1	10^2	10^3	10^6	10^9
Prefix name		tera	peta	exa	zetta	yotta
Prefix symbol		T	P	E	Z	Y
Factor		10^{12}	10^{15}	10^{18}	10^{21}	10^{24}
Prefix name		deci	centi	milli	micro	nano
Prefix symbol		d	c	m	μ	n
Factor	10^0	10^{-1}	10^{-2}	10^{-3}	10^{-6}	10^{-9}
Prefix name		pico	femto	atto	zepto	yocto
Prefix symbol		p	f	a	z	y
Factor		10^{-12}	10^{-15}	10^{-18}	10^{-21}	10^{-24}

Table 5.5 SI Units of Measure and Fractions

The point in bringing this material is that when modeling, i.e., describing domains we must be extremely careful in not falling into the trap of modeling physics types, etc., as we do in programming – by simple **Real**s. We claim, without evidence, that many trivial programming mistakes are due to confusions between especially derived SI units, fractions and prefixes.

5.4.5.2 Units are Indivisible

A volt, kg×m^2×s^{-3}×A^{-1}, see Table 5.2, is "indivisible". It is not a composite structure of mass, length, time, and electric current – in some intricate relationship.

•••

Physical attributes may ascribe mass and volume to endurants. But they do not reveal the substance, i.e., the material from which the endurant is made. That is done by chemical attributes.

5.4.5.3 Chemical Elements

The chemical elements are, to us, what makes up MATTER. The *mole*, mol, substance is about chemical molecules. A mole contains exactly $6.02214076 \times 10^{23}$ (the Avogadro number) constituent particles, usually atoms, molecules, or ions – of the elements, cf. 'The Periodic Table', en.wikipedia.orgwiki/Periodic_table, cf. Fig. 5.4. Any specific molecule is then a compound of two or more elements, for example, calciumphosphat: Ca3(PO4)2.

Moles bring substance to endurants. The physics attributes may ascribe weight and volume to endurants, but they do not explain what it is that gives weight, i.e., fills out the volume.

Road Net

Example 62

Hub attributes:

208 number of lanes,
209 surface,
210 etc.;

type

208. NoL
209. SUR
210. ...
value
208. attr_NoL:H→NoL
209. attr_SUR:H→SUR
210. ...

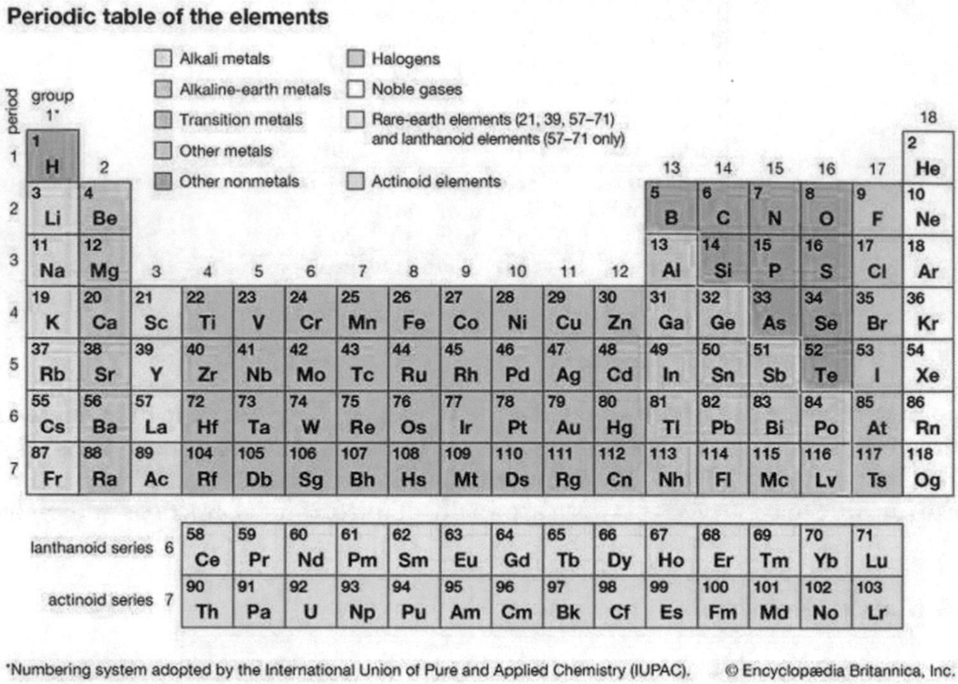

Periodic table of the elements

*Numbering system adopted by the International Union of Pure and Applied Chemistry (IUPAC).   © Encyclopædia Britannica, Inc.

Fig. 5.4 Periodic Table

Link attributes:

211 number of lanes,
212 surface.
213 etc.

value
211. attr_NoL:L→NoL
212. attr_SUR:L→SUR
213. ...

Automobile attributes:

214 Length
215 Width
216 Height

217 Power
218 Fuel (Gasoline, Diesel, Electric,...)
219 Velocity,
220 Acceleration, ...

type
214. Length = Nat:cm
215. Width = Nat:cm
216. Height = Nat:cm
217. BHp = Nat:kg×m^{-2}×s^{-3}
218. Fuel
219. Vel = Real:m×s^{-1}
220. Acc = Real:m×s^{-2}

value
214. attr_Length: A→Length
215. attr_Width: A→Width
216. attr_Height: A→Height
217. attr_BHp: A→BHp
218. attr_Fuel: A→Fuel
219. attr_Vel: A→Vel
220. attr_Acc: A→Acc

5.4.6 Presentation of Physical Attributes

Physical attributes have several dimensions [i] First, as an example, there are the abstract physical units time interval, distance, mass, etc. [ii] Then, to continue with these units, there are the concrete physical units, e.g., s (second), e.g., m (meter) and, e.g., g (gram). [iii] Finally there are the scales 10^n, n a positive natural number, or n a negative such. We suggest that your abstract physical attribute type, A, embodies

221 of what abstract physical units it is, i.e., **obs_phys_unit**,
222 of what concrete physical units it is, i.e., **obs_conr_unit**, and
223 its scale, i.e., **obs_scale**.

type
221 AbsPhysUnit_Attr = "time_interval" | "length" | "mass" | ...
222 ConcPhysUnit_Attr = "second" | "minute" | "hour" | "meter" | "gram" | ...
223 PhysScale_Attr = Intg
value
221 obs_AbsPhysUnit_Attr: E $\overset{\sim}{\to}$ AbsPhysUnit
222 obs_ConcPhysUnit_Attr: E $\overset{\sim}{\to}$ ConcPhysUnit
223 obs_PhysScale_Attr: E $\overset{\sim}{\to}$ PhysScale

These sketched observer functions are partial as they are undefined for non-physical attributes.

5.4.7 The Care and Feeding of Physical Attributes

The above, i.e., Sect. **5.4.6**, suggests that we introduce the following analysis predicates and functions:

224 **is_physical_attribute**: A $\to$ **Bool**,
225 **analyse_abs_phys_attr**: A $\overset{\sim}{\to}$ Abs_Phys_Attr
226 **analyse_conc_phys_attr**: A $\overset{\sim}{\to}$ Conc_Phys_Attr
227 **analyse_phys_attr_scale**: A $\overset{\sim}{\to}$ Phys_Attr_Scale

where the user then defines the concrete Abs_Phys_Attr, Conc_Phys_Attr and Phys_Attr_Scale types as per Sect. **5.4.6**. Then we suggest that the user define a number of "conversion" functions:

- **convert_from_to(from_concrete_unit,to_concrete_unit)**: converts between concrete physical attributes, e.g., pounds and kilograms, meters and yards, meters and kilometers, gram and ounces, etc.,
- **add_concrete_values(v1,v2),subtract_concrete_values(v1,v2),multiply_concrete_-values(v1,v2),etc.** – you see what we mean!

We suggest that the *domain analyser & describer*, when professionally developing domain models for domains that can be characterised by some dominance of physical attribute endurants, be very careful in caring for their physical unit analysis & description. Many aircraft, train and power plant disasters can be referred back to software which handles physical units erroneously. We refer to [8, 77, 192] for more on this issue.

5.4.8 Artefactual Attributes

Despite our pragmatic decision to not distinguish between natural and artefactual parts, cf. Sect. **4.9.3** on page 63, We shall now exemplify classes of attributes sôlely on their parts being man-made. The reason for these exemplifications is that we shall primarily advocate the application of domain analysis & description to domains on the basis of our interest in understanding their artefacts!

5.4.8.1 Examples of Artefactual Attributes

We exemplify some artefactual attributes.

- **Designs.** Artefacts are man-made endurants. Hence "exhibit" a design. My three dimensional villa has floor plans, etc. The artefact attribute: *'design'* can thus be presented by the architect's or the construction engineer's CAD/CAM drawings.
- **States** of an artefact, such as, for example, a road intersection (or railway track) traffic signal; and
- **Currency**, e.g., Kr, \$, £, €, ¥, et cetera, used as an attribute[138], say the cost of a train ticket.
- **Artefactual Dimensions.** Let the domain be that of industrial production whose attributes could then be: production: units produced per year, Units/Year; growth: increase in units produced per year, $Units \times Year^{-2}$; productivity: production per staff, $Units \times Year^{-1} \times Staff^{-1}$ — where the base for units and staff are natural numbers.

Document Artefactual Attributes

Example 63 Let us consider *documents* as artefactual parts. Typical document attributes are: (i) kind of document: book, report, pamphlet, letter and ticket, (ii) publication date, (iii) number of pages, (iv) author/publisher and (v) possible colophon information. *All of these attributes are non-physics quantities.*

Road Net Artefactual Attributes

Example 64   Hub attributes:

228 state: set of pairs of link identifiers from, respectively to which automobiles may traverse the hub;
229 state space: set of all possible hub states.

type
228. $H\Sigma = (LI \times LI)$-set
229. $H\Omega = H\Sigma$-set

value
228. attr_$H\Sigma$:H→HΣ
229. attr_$H\Omega$:H→HΩ

Link attributes:

230 state: set of 0, 1, 2 or 3 pairs of adjacent hub identifiers, the link is closed, open in one direction (closed in the opposite), open in the other direction, or open in both directions; and
231 state space: set of all possible link states.

type
230. $L\Sigma = (LI \times LI)$-set
231. $L\Omega = L\Sigma$-set

value
230. attr_$L\Sigma$:L→LΣ
231. attr_$L\Omega$:L→LΩ

---

[138] One could also consider a [10 €] bank note to be an artefact, i.e., a part.

5.4.9 Conjoin Attributes

This section is "conjoined" with Sect. **5.3.7** on page 118. Part-fluids conjoins, the atomic part and its one or more fluids, enjoy some special attributes relations. We refer to Sect. **5.3.7**'s Fig. 5.2 on page 118. We observe there the following generic flow-net conjoins: **supply**, **pipe**, **pump**, **valve**, **join**, **fork**, **treat** and **dispose**. For these we now suggest some archetypical conjoin part attributes. Indices $_i$ index join inlets: 1, 2 or more, and fork outlet: 1, 2, or more. If index is left out the conjoin unit has at most 1 inlet and at most one outlet.

5.4.9.1 Conjoin Attribute Categories

232 attr_Substance: the substance name of the fluid that can be "carried" by the conjoin part unit.
233 attr_Volume: volume of fluid that the conjoin part can take, measured say in m^3;
234 attr_Max_In_Flow$_i$: typically a volume/sec quantity, measured as $max\_in\_flow_i : m^3/sec;$[139]
235 attr_Max_Out_Flow$_i$: as for in-flow, but now for outlets: $max\_out\_flow_i : m^3/sec;$[140]
236 attr_Curr_In_Flow$_i$: typically a volume/sec quantity, measured as $curr\_in\_flow_i : m^3/sec;$
237 attr_Curr_Out_Flow$_i$: as for in-flow, but now for outlets: $curr\_out\_flow_i : m^3/sec;$
238 Number_of_Flow_Inlets: a natural number n, typically 1 or 2;
239 Number_of_Flow_Outlets: a natural number n, typically 1 or 2;
240 attr_Open_Close: of a valve or pump, e.g., indicated as "open" or "closed";

5.4.9.2 Conjoin Attribute Assignments

supply: We assume a *well* of indefinite capacity.

- attr_Substance[s], attr_Max_Out_Flow_M$_i$, attr_Curr_Out_Flow_M$_i$.
- Possibly other attributes.

pipe: We assume a *pipe* to be as a tube.

- attr_Substance, attr_Volume_Substance, attr_Max_In_Flow, attr_Curr_In_Flow, attr_Max_-Out_Flow, attr_Curr_Out_Flow.
- Possibly other attributes.

pump: We assume a simple positive displacement pump.

- attr_Substance, attr_Volume_Substance, attr_Max_In_Flow, attr_Curr_In_Flow, attr_Max_-Out_Flow, attr_Curr_Out_Flow.
- attr_Pumping_Volume_per_Sec:
- attr_Pumping_Height:
- Possibly other attributes.

valve: We assume a simple butterfly valve.

- attr_Substance, attr_Volume_Substance, attr_Max_In_Flow, attr_Curr_In_Flow, attr_Max_-Out_Flow, attr_Curr_Out_Flow, attr_Open_Close.
- Possibly other attributes.

join: A join has 1 inlet and n outlets, for n usually being two.

---

[139] set by conjoin unit manufacturer to indicate maximum laminar flow
[140] set by conjoin unit manufacturer to indicate maximum laminar flow

- itemize
- attr_Substance, attr_Volume_Substance, attr_Max_In_Flow$_1$, attr_Max_In_Flow$_2$, attr_Curr_-In_Flow$_1$, attr_Curr_In_Flow$_2$, attr_Max_Out_Flow, attr_Curr_Out_Flow.
- Possibly other attributes.

fork: A fork has one inlet and n outlets, for n usually being two.

- itemize
- attr_Substance, attr_Volume_Substance, attr_Max_In_Flow, attr_Curr_In_Flow, attr_Max_-Out_Flow$_1$, attr_Max_Out_Flow$_2$, attr_Curr_Out_Flow$_1$, attr_Curr_Out_Flow$_2$.
- Possibly other attributes.

treat: Besides the attributes of the join and fork units, the **treat**ment units are characterised by the operations that they can perform on their conjoined fluids.

- Operations: Usually a treatment unit can perform one operation on its 'embodied' (conjoined) fluids. But it is always good to generalise, so we say there there are $n \geq 1$ operations. Each operation is characterised by a "recipe scaled" signature. m is the number of distinct fluids, each of substance Substance_i. f_{i_j} is an appropriate fraction, $0 \leq f_{i_j} \leq 1$.
  - ∞ o_1: Operation_1: f_{1_1} Substance_1 $\times f_{1_2}$ Substance_2 $\times \cdots f_{1_m}$ Substance_m
  - ∞ o_2: Operation_2: f_{2_1} Substance_1 $\times f_{2_2}$ Substance_2 $\times \cdots f_{2_m}$ Substance_m
  - ∞ ...
  - ∞ o_m: Operation_n: f_{n_1} Substance_1 $\times f_{n_2}$ Substance_2 $\times \cdots f_{2_m}$ Substance_m
- Possibly other attributes.

dispose: A disposal conjoin usually has indefinite capacity (i.e., volume).

- attr_Substance, attr_Volume_Substance, attr_Max_In_Flow, attr_Curr_In_Flow.
- Possibly other attributes.

We could likewise consider fluid-parts conjoins, but leave that to the reader.

5.4.10 Fuzzy Attributes

Fuzzy sets introduced, notably, by Lotfi Zadeh [403, 1965][141] are somewhat like sets whose elements have degrees of membership. Fuzzy set is a mathematical model of vague qualitative or quantitative data, frequently generated by means of the natural language. We shall thus distinguish between fuzzy attribute values, i.e., vague qualitative values, and fuzzy attributes, i.e., vague quantitative types. Before Klaua and Zadeh fuzziness in logic had been studied as *infinite-valued logic* Łukasiewicz[142] and Alfred Tarski[143].

★ Fuzzy Sets and Fuzzy Logic

We shall informally characterise fuzziness. In classical set theory an element is either a member of some set or it is not, i.e., **true** or **false**. In fuzzy set theory an element has a degree, indicated, for example, by a real number in the interval from and including 0 to and including 1. If membership degree is 0 the element is not in the set. If membership degree is 1 the element is certainly in the set. So when we speak of a fuzzy element, as being either

---

[141] – and, it appears, also, same year, by Dieter Klaua [272, 273].

[142] Hay, L.S., 1963, Axiomatization of the infinite-valued predicate calculus. Journal of Symbolic Logic 28:7786.

[143] Mancosu, Paolo; Zach, Richard; Badesa, Calixto (2004). Many-valued logics. The Development of Mathematical Logic from Russell to Tarski 1900-1935. The Development of Modern Logic. Oxford University Press. pp. 418–420. ISBN 9780199722723.

of an attribute or an attribute value, then we should indicate its *"membership degree"*. For the logic of reasoning over fuzzy attribute values and fuzzy attributes we refer to classical textbooks on fuzzy logic and fuzzy sets, e.g., [266].

★ Fuzzy Attribute Types

So we can think of an attribute A as being fuzzy, **is_fuzzy(A)** to mean that its values are fuzzy, i.e., lie in the open interval from and including 0 to and including 1.

★ Fuzzy Attribute Values

And these values can be represented, in RSL, by **Real**s:

* **type A: fuzzy: Real**

★ Fuzzy Reasoning

A las, we shall not, in this monograph, explore the possibilities of modeling domains using Fuzzy Logic!

★ Fuzziness: A Possible Research Topic ?

Instead we urge readers to do so. The research field of fuzzy sets, logic, systems and engineering is very large. We refer to such peer reviewed journals as

* IEEE Transactions on Fuzzy Systems, IEEE ieeexplore.ieee.org/xpl/RecentIssue.jsp?punumber=91;
* International Journal of Fuzzy Systems, Springer springer.com/journal/40815;
* Fuzzy Sets and Systems, Elsevier journals.elsevier.com/fuzzy-sets-and-systems;
* International Journal of Fuzzy Logic and Intelligent Systems, ijfis.org/main.html;
* Journal of Intelligent & Fuzzy Systems, content.iospress.com/journals/journal-of-intelligent--and-fuzzy-systems/P.

5.4.11 Attributes of Compounds

For structures we do not model their attributes. But their components, whether the structures are *"Cartesian"* or *"sets"*, may very well be non-structures, hence have attributes.

5.4.12 The Inevitability of Space and Time Continuity

Domains "reside" in the real world. Requirements, as we shall see it in Chapter 9, are, in this monograph, for software that is to "reside inside" computers. The real world has of spatial and temporal dimensions but is not bothered by such issues as representation of length and time intervals let alone their precision. So when we ascribe spatial and temporal qualities to, or as, attributes we need not be bothered by their implementation, they simply are, no way of getting around it. So when spatial and temporal aspects are elements of endurant attributes then we shall, of course, model them as do physicists, as, usually, continuous functions.

5.5 Intentionality

The conjoin concept, that of relating some endurants more strongly, in the form of conjoins, reflects one or more intentions. In the next section we shall encircle the 'intention' concept by quoting from Kai Sørlander's Philosophy [366, 367, 368, 369].

5.5.1 Issues Leading Up to Intentionality

Causality of Purpose: If there is to be *the possibility of language and meaning* then there must exist primary entities which are *not entirely encapsulated within the physical conditions*; that they are stable and can influence one another. This is only possible if such primary entities are subject to a *supplementary causality directed at the future*: a *causality of purpose.*

Living Species: These primary entities are here called *living species*. What can be deduced about them ? They are characterised by *causality of purpose*: they *have some form they can be developed to reach;* and which *they must be causally determined to maintain;* this development and maintenance must occur in *an exchange of matter with an environment.* It must be possible that living species occur in one of two forms: one form which is characterised by *development, form* and *exchange,* and another form which, additionally, can be characterised by the ability to *purposeful movements.* The first we call *plants,* the second we call *animals.*

Animate Entities: For an animal to purposefully move around there must be "additional conditions" for such self-movements to be in accordance with the principle of causality: they must have *sensory organs* sensing among others the immediate purpose of its movement; they must have *means of motion* so that it can move; and they must have *instincts, incentives* and *feelings* as causal conditions that what it senses can drive it to movements. And all of this in accordance with the laws of physics.

Animals: To possess these three kinds of "additional conditions", must be built from special units which have an inner relation to their function as a whole; Their *purposefulness* must be built into their physical building units, that is, as we can now say, their *genomes.* That is, animals are built from genomes which give them the *inner determination* to such building blocks for *instincts, incentives* and *feelings.* Similar kinds of deduction can be carried out with respect to plants. Transcendentally one can deduce basic principles of evolution but not its details.

Humans – Consciousness and Learning: The existence of animals is a necessary condition for there being language and meaning in any world. That there can be *language* means that animals are capable of *developing language.* And this must presuppose that animals can *learn from their experience.* To learn implies that animals can *feel* pleasure and distaste and can *learn.* One can therefore deduce that animals must possess such building blocks whose inner determination is a basis for learning and consciousness.

Language: Animals with higher social interaction uses *signs,* eventually developing a *language.* These languages adhere to the same system of defined concepts which are a prerequisite for any description of any world: namely the system that philosophy lays bare from a basis of transcendental deductions and the *principle of contradiction* and its *implicit meaning theory.* A *human* is an animal which has a *language.*

Knowledge: Humans must be *conscious* of having *knowledge* of its concrete situation, and as such that human can have knowledge about what he feels and eventually that human can know whether what he feels is true or false. Consequently *a human can describe his situation correctly.*

Responsibility: In this way one can deduce that humans can thus have *memory* and hence can have *responsibility,* be *responsible.* Further deductions lead us into *ethics.*

●●●

We shall not further develop the theme of *living species: plants and animals,* thus excluding, most notably *humans,* in this chapter. We claim that the present chapter, due to its foundation in Kai Sørlander's Philosophy, provides a firm foundation within which we, or others, can further develop this theme: *analysis & description of living species.*

●●●

Intentionality: *Intentionality* as a philosophical concept is defined by the Stanford Encyclopedia of Philosophy[144] as *"the power of minds to be about, to represent, or to stand for, things, properties and states of affairs."*

Intentional Pull: Two or more artefactual parts of different sorts, but with overlapping sets of intents may excert an *intentional "pull"* on one another. This *intentional "pull"* may take many forms. Let $p_x : X$ and $p_y : Y$ be two parts of *different sorts* (X, Y), and with *common intent,* ι. *Manifestations* of these, their common intent must somehow be *subject to constraints,* and these must be *expressed predicatively.*

When a composite or conjoin artefact models "itself" as put together with a number of other endurants then it does have an intentionality and the components' individual intentionalities does, i.e., shall relate to that. The composite road transport system has intentionality of the road serving the automobile part, and the automobiles have the intent of being served by the roads, across "a divide", and vice versa, the roads of serving the automobiles.

---

[144] Jacob, P. (Aug 31, 2010). *Intentionality.* Stanford Encyclopedia of Philosophy (https://seop.illc.-uva.nl/entries/intentionality/) October 15, 2014, retrieved April 3, 2018.

Natural endurants, for example, rivers, lakes, seas[145] and oceans become, in a way, artefacts with and when mankind using them for transport; natural gas becomes an artefact when drilled for, exploited and piped; and harbours make no sense without artefactual boats sailing on the natural water.

This, perhaps vague, concept of intentionality has yet to be developed into something of a theory. Despite that this is yet to be done, cf. Exercise 12 on page 150, we shall proceed to define an *intentionality analysis function*. First we postulate a set of **intent designators**. An *intent designator* is really a further undefined quantity. But let us, for the moment, think of them as simple character strings, that is, literals, for example "road", "hub", "link", "automobile", "transport", etc.

   type Intent

Observer Function Prompt 13 `analyse_intentionality`: The domain analyser analyses an endurant as to the finite number of intents, zero or more, with which the analyser judges the endurant can be associated. The method provides the ***domain analysis prompt***:

* `analyse_intentionality` directs the domain analyser to observe a set of intents.

   value analyse_intentionality(e) ≡ {i_1,i_2,...,i_n}⊆Intent

---

Intentional Pull: Road Transport

Example 65   *We illustrate the concept of intentional "pull":*

241 automobiles include the intent of `'transport'`,
242 and so do hubs and links.

   241 analyse_intentionality: A → ("transport"|...)-**set**
   242 analyse_intentionality: H → ("transport"|...)-**set**
   242 analyse_intentionality: L → ("transport"|...)-**set**

Manifestations of "transport" is reflected in *automobiles* having the automobile position attribute, APos, Item 200 Pg. 126, *hubs* having the *hub traffic* attribute, H_Traffic, Item 188 Pg. 124, and in *links* having the *link traffic* attribute, L_Traffic, Item 192 Pg. 125.

243 Seen from the point of view of an automobile there is its own traffic history, A_Hist, which is a (time ordered) sequence of timed automobile's positions;
244 seen from the point of view of a hub there is its own traffic history, H_Traffic Item 188 Pg. 124, which is a (time ordered) sequence of timed maps from automobile identities into automobile positions; and
245 seen from the point of view of a link there is its own traffic history, L_Traffic Item 192 Pg. 125, which is a (time ordered) sequence of timed maps from automobile identities into automobile positions.

The *intentional "pull"* of these manifestations is this:

246 The union, i.e. proper merge of all automobile traffic histories, AllATH, must now be identical to the same proper merge of all hub, AllHTH, and all link traffic histories, AllLTH.

type
243 A_Hi = ($\mathbb{T}$ × APos)*
188 H_Trf = A_UI $\overrightarrow{m}$ (TIME × APos)*
192 L_Trf = A_UI $\overrightarrow{m}$ (TIME×APos)*
246 AllATH=TIME $\overrightarrow{m}$ (AUI $\overrightarrow{m}$ APos)
246 AllHTH=TIME $\overrightarrow{m}$ (AUI $\overrightarrow{m}$ APos)
246 AllLTH =TIME $\overrightarrow{m}$ (AUI $\overrightarrow{m}$ APos)
axiom
246   **let** allA=mrg_AllATH({(a,attr_A_Hi(a))|a:A•a ∈ *as*}),
246   allH=mrg_AllHTH({attr_H_Trf(h)|h:H•h ∈ *hs*}),
246   allL =mrg_AllLTH({attr_L_Trf(l)|l:L•h ∈ *ls*}) **in**
246   allA = mrg_HLT(allH,allL) **end**

---

[145] Seas are smaller than oceans and are usually located where the land and ocean meet. Typically, seas are partially enclosed by land. The Sargasso Sea is an exception. It is defined only by ocean currents [oceanservice.noaa.gov/facts/oceanorsea.html].

We leave the definition of the four merge functions to the reader!

Discussion: We endow each automobile with its history of timed positions and each hub and link with their histories of timed automobile positions. These histories are facts! They are not something that is laboriously recorded, where such recordings may be imprecise or cumbersome[146]. The facts are there, so we can (but may not necessarily) talk about these histories as facts. It is in that sense that the purpose ('transport') for which man let automobiles, hubs and link be made with their 'transport' intent are subject to an *intentional "pull"*. *It can be no other way: if automobiles "record" their history, then hubs and links must together "record" identically the same history!*.

Please note, that *intents* are not [thought of as] attributes. We consider *intents* to be a fourth, a comprehensive internal quality of endurants. They, so to speak, govern relations between the three other internal quality of endurants: the unique identifiers, the mereologies and the attributes. That is, they predicate them, "arrange" their comprehensiveness. Much more should be said about intentionality. It is a truly, I believe, worthy research topic of its own. We refer to Exercise 12 on page 150.

An Aspect of Comprehensivess of Internal Qualities
Example 66 Let us illustrate the issues "at play" here.

- Consider a road transport system uod.
  ∞ Applying analyse_intentionality(uod) may yield the set {"transport", ...}.
- Consider a financial service industry, fss.
  ∞ Applying analyse_intentionality(fss) may yield the set {"interest on deposit", ...}.
- Consider a health care system, hcs.
  ∞ Applying analyse_intentionality(hcs) may yield the set {"cure diseases", ...}.

What these analyses of intentionality yields, with respect to expressing intentional pull, is entirely of the discretion of the *domain analyser & describer*   □

We bring the above example, Example 66, to indicate, as the name of the example reveals, "An Aspect of Comprehensivess of Internal Qualities". That the various components of artefactual systems relate in – further to be explored – ways. In this respect, performing domain analysis & description is not only an engineering pursuit, but also one of research. We leave it to the readers to pursue this research aspect of domain analysis & description – while referring to Exercise 12 on page 150.

5.5.2 Artefacts

Humans create artefacts – for a reason, to serve a purpose, that is, with **intent**. Artefacts are like parts. They satisfy the laws of physics – and serve a *purpose*, fulfill an *intent*.

---

[146] or thought technologically in-feasible – at least some decades ago!

5.5.3 Assignment of Attributes

So what can we deduce from the above, a little more than two pages?

The attributes of **natural parts** and **natural fluids** are generally of such concrete types – expressible as some **real** with a dimension[147] of the International System of Units: `https://physics.nist.gov/cuu/Units/units.html`. Attribute values usually enter *differential equations* and *integrals*, that is, classical calculus.

The attributes of **humans**, besides those of parts, significantly includes one of a usually non-empty set of *intents*. In directing the creation of artefacts humans create these with an intent.

Intentional Pull: General Transport

Example 67 *These are examples of human intents: they create roads and automobiles with the intent of transport, they create houses with the intents of living, offices, production, etc., and they create pipelines with the intent of oil or gas transport* ∎

Human attribute values usually enter into *modal logic* expressions.

5.5.3.1 Artefacts, including Man-made Fluids:

Artefacts, besides those of parts, significantly includes a usually singleton set of *intents*.

Intents

Example 68 *Roads and automobiles possess the intent of transport; houses possess either one of the intents of living, offices, production; and pipelines possess the intent of oil or gas transport.*

Artefact attribute values usually enter into *mathematical logic* expressions.

We leave it to the reader to formulate attribute assignment principles for plants and non-human animals.

5.5.4 Galois Connections

Galois Theory was first developed by Évariste Galois [1811-1832] around 1830[148]. Galois theory emphasizes a notion of **Galois connections**. We refer to standard textbooks on Galois Theory, e.g., [372, 2009].

5.5.4.1 Galois Theory: An Ultra-brief Characterisation

To us, an essence of Galois connections can be illustrated as follows:

---

[147] Basic units are *meter*, *kilogram*, *second*, *Ampere*, *Kelvin*, *mole*, and *candela*. Some derived units are: Newton: $kg{\times}m{\times}s^{-2}$, Weber: $kg \times m^2 \times s^{-2} \times A^{-1}$, etc.

[148] en.wikipedia.org/wiki/Galois_theory

- Let us observe[149] properties of a number of endurants, say in the form of attribute types.
- Let the function $\mathcal{F}$ map sets of entities to the set of common attributes.
- Let the function $\mathcal{G}$ map sets of attributes to sets of entities that all have these attributes.
- $(\mathcal{F},\mathcal{G})$ is a Galois connection

  ∞ if, when including more entities, the common attributes remain the same or fewer, and
  ∞ if when including more attributes, the set of entities remain the same or fewer.
  ∞ $(\mathcal{F},\mathcal{G})$ is monotonously decreasing.

LEGO Blocks

Example 69 We[150] have

- There is a collection of LEGO™ blocks.
- From this collection, A, we identify the **red** square blocks, e.
- That is $\mathcal{F}(A)$ is $B = \{$attr_Color(e) = **red**,attr_Form(e)=**square**$\}$.
- We now add all the **blue** square blocks.
- And obtain A'.
- Now the common properties are their **squareness**: $\mathcal{F}(A')$ is $B' = \{$attr_Form(e)=**square**$\}$.
- More blocks as argument to $\mathcal{F}$ yields fewer or the same number of properties.
- The more entities we observe, the fewer common attributes they possess.

Civil Engineering: Consultants and Contractors

Example 70 Less playful, perhaps more seriously, and certainly more relevant to our endeavour, is this next example.

- Let X be the set of civil engineering, i.e., building, consultants, i.e., those who, like architects and structural engineers design buildings – of whatever kind.
- Let Y be the set of building contractors, i.e., those firms who actually implement, i.e., build to, those designs.
- Now a subset, $X_{bridges}$ of X, contain exactly those consultants who specialise in the design of bridges, with a subset, $Y_{bridges}$, of Y capable of building bridges.
- If we change to a subset, $X'' = X_{bridges,tunnels}$ of X, allowing the design of both bridges **and** tunnels, then we obtain a corresponding subset, $Y_{bridges,tunnels}$, of Y.
- So when
  ∞ we enlarge the number of properties from 'bridges' to 'bridges and tunnels',
  ∞ we reduce, most likely, the number of contractors able to fulfill such properties,
  ∞ and vice versa,
- then we have a Galois Connection.

---

[149] The following is an edited version of an explanation kindly provided by Asger Eir, e-mail, June 5, 2020 [151, 152, 86].
[150] The E-mail, June 5, 2020, from Asger Eir

5.5.4.2 Galois Connections and Intentionality

We have a hunch[151] ! Namely that there are some sort of Galois Connections with respect to intentionality.

5.5.4.3 Galois Connections and Intentionality: A Possible Research Topic ?

We leave to the interested reader to pursue this line of inquiry.

5.6 Systems Modeling

5.6.1 General

In Sect. **5.3.7**, as well as in numerous examples we started to reveal some "classes" of domains for the modeling of which it appears that there are some "standard" techniques. For general, usually bi-directed networks of usually atomic parts, we analysed & described these graphs into sets of units whose mereology "revealed" their "interconnection". For less general, usually directed, acyclic networks of usually conjoins, we analysed & described these graphs also into sets of units, now the conjoins, whose mereology now "revealed" their "interconnection". For less topologically, more conceptually and intentionally related aggregations[152] of endurants, we analysed & described as possibly hierarchically organised composite endurants, whose mereology, in their way, "revealed" the "interconnection" of the aggregations.

5.6.2 Passively Mobile Endurants

Some endurants are mobile. Mobile endurants are either actively mobile, i.e., move on their own accord, or passively mobile, i.e., are transported by other endurants. Usually passively mobile endurants are expressed as siblings of part-parts conjoins – where the 'parts' usually consist of a definite number of these: usually zero, one or two.

Credit Card Shopping System

Example 71 A credit card shopping system[153] consists of (i) credit card (user)s, (ii) shops and (iii) credit card honoring banks. The shops offer for sale and users hoard merchandise. We suggest to model, as a fourth element of the system, (iv) the merchandise. And let credit card user and shop attributes reflect their merchandise by their unique identifiers.

Container Terminal Port

---

[151] Hunch: a feeling or guess based on intuition rather than fact.

[152] for lack of a better term

[153] See imm.dtu.dk/~dibj/2016/credit/accs.pdf

Example 72 A container terminal port[154] consists of (i) vessels, (ii) vessel to/from quay cranes, (iii) quay crane to/from stack trucks, (iv) stack or land truck to/from stack cranes, (v) stacks, and (vi) land trucks. Vessels and stacks hold any number of containers over indefinite time intervals. Cranes and trucks hold zero, one or two containers over expectedly short time intervals. We suggest to model, as a seventh element, of a container terminal port (vii) containers; then let vessel, crane, truck and stack attributes reflect their zero or more containers by their unique identifiers.

General Hospital System

Example 73 A general hospital consists of (i) beds, (ii) staff, and (iii) patients. Patients occupy beds are operated upon by medical doctor staff, are otherwise cared for by nurse staff, et cetera. We suggest to model occupants of beds, patients on operating tables, and patients being cared for by nurses by unique patient identifiers.

Thus we suggest the following modeling choices: Actively mobile endurants shall be transcendentally deduced into behaviours. Passively mobile endurants if "embodied" by actively mobile endurants, shall not. If, instead, these passively mobile endurants are modelled as a major set of endurants of their domain they will be modelled as behaviours – with few other actions than responding to *"who, at the moment, transports them"*. All this should be clear after Chapter 7.

5.7 Discussion of Endurants

Domain descriptions are, as we have already shown, formulated, both informally and formally, by means of abstract types, that is, by sorts for which no concrete models are usually given. Sorts are made to denote possibly empty, possibly infinite, rarely singleton, sets of entities on the basis of the qualities defined for these sorts, whether external or internal. By *junk* we shall understand that the domain description unintentionally denotes undesired entities. By **confusion** we shall understand that the domain description unintentionally have two or more identifications of the same entity or type. The question is *can we formulate a [formal] domain description such that it does not denote junk or confusion*? The short answer to this is no! So, since one naturally wishes "no junk, no confusion" what does one do? The answer to that is *one proceeds with great care!*

5.8 A Domain Discovery Process, II

5.8.1 The Process

We shall again emhasize some aspects of the *domain analyser & describer* method. A **method procedures** is that of *exhaustively analyse & describe* all internal qualities of the domain under scrutiny. A **method technique** implied here is that sketched below. The **method tools** are here all the analysis and description prompts covered so far.

---

[154] See imm.dtu.dk/~dibj/2018/yangshan/maersk-pa.pdf

The predecessor of this section is Sect. **4.20** on page 93. Please be reminded of *Discovery Schema 0*'s declaration of *Notice Board* variables (Page 95). In this section we collect (i) the *description of unique identifiers* of all parts of the state; (ii) the *description of mereologies* of all parts of the state; and (iii) the *description of attributes* of all parts of the state. (iii) We finally gather these into the *discover_internal_endurant_qualities* procedures.

```
_____ An Endurant Internal Qualities Domain Analysis and Description Process _____

    discover_uids: Unit → Unit
    discover_uids() ≡
        for ∀ v • v ∈ gen
            do txt := txt † [ type_name(v)↦txt(type_name(v))⌢⟨describe_unique_identifier(v)⟩ ] end
    discover_mereologies: Unit → Unit
    discover_mereologies() ≡
        for ∀ v • v ∈ gen
            do txt := txt † [ type_name(v)↦txt(type_name(v))⌢⟨describe_mereology(v)⟩ ] end
    discover_attributes: Unit → Unit
    discover_attributes() ≡
        for ∀ v • v ∈ gen
            do txt := txt † [ type_name(v)↦txt(type_name(v))⌢⟨describe_attributes(v)⟩ ] end


discover_internal_endurant_qualities: Unit → Unit
    discover_internal_endurant_qualities() ≡
            discover_uids() ;
                axiom [ all parts have unique identifiers ]
            discover_mereologies() ;
                axiom [ all unique identifiers are mentioned in sum total of ]
                     [ all mereologies and no isolated proper sets of parts ]
            discover_attributes() ;
                axiom [ sum total of all attributes span all parts of the state ]

We shall comment on the axioms in the next section.
```

5.8.2 A Suggested Analysis & Description Approach, I

Figure 4.7 on page 96 possibly hints at an analysis & description order in which not only the external qualities of endurants are analysed & described, but also their unique identifiers, mereologies and attributes. In Sect. **4.20.4** on page 96 we were concerned with the analysis & description order of endurants. We now follow up on the remark (in Sect. **4.20.4**) on whether composites are treated as 'real' composites or a structures. Again, it is up to the domain engineer cum scientist to decide, but if endurants are treated as structures then an 'internal qualities' traversal will not have to neither analyse nor describe those qualities for structures.

5.9 Domain Description Laws

The **axiom**s of the immediately above **Discovery Schema** expresses some domain facts: [i] the uniqueness of part identifiers; [ii] that mereologies mention all parts and that the mereologies of no proper subset of parts subset of parts refer only to parts of that subset; and [iii] that part attributes, when they refer, refer only to parts of the state.

5.10 Summary

This chapter's main title was: **DOMAINS – Towards a Statics Ontology**. The term 'statics' pertain to qualities of the 'Domain', not to its 'Ontology'. So, an aspect of the ontology of a domain, such as we have studied it and such as we ordain one aspect of domain analysis & description, is about somehow measurable properties, or about historical actions and events to which endurants of the domain have been subjected, that is, the *internal qualities*. For that study & practice we have suggested a number of analysis & description prompts.

—————————— Three Essentials about Internal Qualities ——————————

There are three essentials about internal qualities of endurants: Unique identifiers are existentially motivated, and are abstract existence markers — cannot be "measured"; mereologies are concerned with parts and "the whole", that is, part relations, and cannot be measured; and attributes are definitely measurable, and enter into property descriptions.

5.10.1 The Description Schemas

We have culminated this chapter with description prompts for **unique identifier** description schema 8 on page 108, **mereology** description schema 9 on page 113 and **attribute** description schema 10 on page 121.

They all describe in, in our case RSL, the domain description text to 'produce' when internal quality analysing & describing a given endurant; but what about the description of those endurants revealed by the analysis & description of that given endurant?

The answer is simple. That is up to you! The **domain analysis & description** method gives you the **tools**, some *techniques* and a few *principles*. But:

- A **principle** of the method could be to secure that all relevant, i.e., implied, endurants are analysed & described.
- A **technique** could be to, somehow, "set aside" all those endurants *revealed by the analysis & description of any given endurant* – with the proviso that no endurant, of **type**, for example, P, is analysed & described more than once.

Same answer that we gave in Sect. **4.22.1** Page 99. A **technique**, such as alluded to above, is show 'formalised' in the pseudo-program of Sect. **5.8** on page 146.

5.10.2 Modeling Choices

In this chapter we have put forward some advice on **description** choices: We refer to **Modeling Choices** 8 on page 114 and 9 on page 121. The **analysis** predicates and functions are merely aids. They do not effect descriptions, but descriptions are based on the result of their inquiry. Real decisions are made when effecting a **description** function. So the rôle of these modeling choice paragraphs is to alert the describer to make judicious choices.

5.10.3 Method Principles, Techniques and Tools

Recall that by a method we shall understand a *set of* **principles** for selecting and applying a *set of* **techniques** using a *set of* **tools** in order to construct an artefact.

5.10.3.1 Principles of Internal Qualities

In this chapter we have illustrated the use of the following techniques:

Divide and Conquer: Application of this principle has in this chapter been quite pronounced: the 'divisions' are those of first (i) the analysis & description of unique identification, then (ii) the analysis & description of mereologies, and then, finally, (iii) the analysis & description of attributes – and in that order. We have found, in numerous case studies [84], that any other "strict" order very often brings confusion![155]

Representational Abstract: Application of this principle has, in this chapter, been to the type definitions of unique identifiers, mereologies and attributes. For unique identifiers in that no representation need be prescribed. For mereologies in that all we are really interested in are which parts "partake" in part-to-part relations. For attributes we have not directed the domain analyser cum describer as how express possible attribute type expressions, and often we just identify an attribute type by its identifier.

5.10.3.2 Procedures for Modeling Internal Qualities

The main procedure for modeling external qualities was presented in Sect. **5.8**.

5.10.3.3 Techniques of Internal Qualities

In this chapter we have illustrated the use of the following principles:

Invariants: We remind the reader of Item 44()v on page 9, and refer to Example 43 on page 111: *Uniqueness of Road Net Identifiers*, Example 47 on page 115: *Invariance of Road Nets* and Example 58 on page 124: *Invariance of Road Net Traffic States*.

Intentional Pull : We remind the reader of Item 44()iv on page 9, and refer to Examples 65 on page 141: *Intentional Pull: Road Transport* and Example 67 on page 143: *Intentional Pull: General Transport*.

5.10.3.4 Tools

⋆ Summary of The Internal Qualities Analysis Calculus

- **analyse_attribute_types** and   Page 120
- **is_physical_attribute**.   Page 135

⋆ Summary of The Internal Qualities Description Calculus

---

[155] "Eager-beaver", inventive "whiz kids" are often caught up in their creativeness and muddle matters up, forget careful and necessary analyses whose absence often shows up late, and much analysis & description work has to be redone!

5.11 Intentional Programming

It seems, to this author, that Charles Simonyi's ideas around *intentional software* is, somehow, related to the concept of *intentional pull*. Not only that, but, as Chapters 7 and 9 will further support, the whole idea of "deriving software" from domain descriptions, also seems somehow "buried" in Simonyi's ideas. We leave it to the reader to study [360, 5, 361, 362, 363, *Simonyi et al., 1995–2006*].

5.12 Bibliographical Notes

We refer to [73, Sect. 5.3] for a thorough, 2016–2017, five page review of types in formal specification and programming languages.

5.13 Exercise Problems

We suggest several classes of exercises, to wit: two or more of *research problems, student exercise* and *term projects.*

5.13.1 Research Problems

Exercise 11 A Research Challenge. Fuzzy Descriptions: Experiment with, present examples, and, possibly, develop analysis & description prompts for Fuzzy attributes.

Exercise 12 A Research Challenge. Intentionality: Suggest possible intentions and possible intentional pulls for domains of artefacts, say as they are mentioned in the *Term Projects* section. Present possible examples. More generally, develop a theory of intentionality.

Exercise 13 A Research Challenge. Galois Connections: Study Galois Connections as, for example presented in [169, Ganter & Wille]. Then search for such connections with respect to internal qualities of pairs of different sort solid endurants. Present examples. Suggest possible [?] analysis & description prompts.

Exercise 14 A PhD Student Problem. Living Species: Humans: Suggest an outline mereology and attribute concepts for humans.

Exercise 15 A PhD Student Problem. Michael Jackson's Categories of Attributes: Suggest a critique of Jackson's categories of attributes, cf. Sect. **5.4.2.3**.

- Is Jackson's categorisation equally applicable to natural parts as well as to artefacts?
- Somehow or other, do artefacts mandate a different categorisation?
- Suggest a categorisation for artefacts.

5.13.2 Student Exercises

Exercise 16 An MSc Student Exercise. Unique Document Identification: We refer to Exercise 3 on page 104.

[Q1] you are to narrate and formalise unique identification for persons and documents. We refer to upcoming Exercises 17, 18 and Exercise 32 on page 203.

Exercise 17 An MSc Student Exercise. Document System Mereologies: We refer to Exercises 3 on page 104 and 16.

We anticipate and elaborate on the **actions** that Exercise 32 on page 203 will be handling.

create: The thus created document shall record (i) the identity of its [person] creator, (ii) time of creation, and (iii) the text it now contains.

edit: The thus edited document shall record (i) the identity of its [person] editor, (ii) the time of edit, and (iii) the *changes* being made to the

- *master document*, whose text is τ_M,
- being edited into the *edited document*, whose text is τ_E,
- such that these changes can be "seen" – for example as follows:
  - ∞ there is a *"forward" editing function, e_F,*
  - ∞ and an *"undo" editing function, e_U,*
  - ∞ such that the text now recorded, in the *edited document*, is $e_F(\tau_M)$,
  - ∞ and such that $e_U(e_F(\tau_M))=\tau_M$.

read: The thus read document shall record (i) the identity of its [person] reader and (ii) the time of read.

copy: As a result of a copy we now have one more document in our system: besides the document, the *original*, we now also have the *copy*.

The original document shall record (i) the identity of its [person] who had copied this document, (ii) the identity of the copy, and (iii) the time of copying.

The copy document shall record (i) the identity of its [person] who made this copy, (ii) the identity of the original document (from which it was made), and (iii) the time of copying.

shred: Let the identity of the document being shredded be d_ι.

Whereas there was a document of that identity, i.e., d_ι, there is, "officially", no longer such a document.

But, since persons can talk about the historical existence of d_ι, we may have to keep track of all shredded documents. See question [Q2] of Exercise 3 on page 104.

Therefore documents in such a *"shredded" document archive* must record (i) the identity of the person who did the shredding and (ii) the time of shredding.

[Q1] you are to narrate and formalise mereologies for persons and documents. We refer to upcoming Exercises 18 and 32 on page 203.

Exercise 18 An MSc Student Exercise. Document System Attributes: We refer to Exercises 3 on page 104 and 16.

In addressing question [Q1] below you will have studied the indented text of Exercise 17. [Q1] you are to narrate and formalise attributes for persons and documents.

We refer to upcoming Exercise 32 on page 203.

Exercise 19 An MSc Student Exercise. A Simple Consumer–Bank–Retailer Credit Card System: The credit card system involves consumers, retailers banks and credit cards. A credit card is an attribute of consumers, one per consumer. Consumers have bank accounts, one per consumer. Retailers stock merchandise for sale, all merchandise are distinct, and have a price tag. Retailers have bank accounts, one per retailer. Banks hold accounts for consumers and retailers. Credit cards identify their [consumer] holder, one per credit card. Now to the problem to be solved. Please note item [g] before you start writing down your solutions.

You are to formulate [a] appropriate sorts for consumers, retailers and banks as parts; [b] appropriate sets of unique identifiers, mereologies and [c] attributes for consumers, retailers and banks; You are to express appropriate well-formedness conditions for [d] all mereologies and [e] all attributes. You are to express an intentional pull [f] relating the bank balances of consumers and retailers. While doing this, you are to [g] spot what might, inadvertently, have been left out in the above, first paragraphs 'presentation' of this, albeit simple consumer-retailer-bank credit card system.

5.13.3 Term Projects

We continue the term projects of Sect. **4.24.3** on page 104.

For the specific domain topic that a group is working on it is to treat, for example, in separate weeks, these topics in the order listed:

- *unique identifiers*, cf. Sect. **5.2**,
- *mereology*, cf. Sect. **5.3**, and
- *attributes*, cf. Sect. **5.4**, the latter possibly over two weeks.

Exercise 20 An MSc Student Exercise. The Consumer Market, Internal Qualities: We refer to Exercise 4 on page 105. You are, in turn, to analyse and describe

- the unique identifiers,
- mereologies,
- a suitable sample of attributes, and
- possible intentional pulls

of consumer markets.

Exercise 21 An MSc Student Exercise. Financial Service Industry, Internal Qualities: We refer to Exercise 5 on page 105. You are, in turn, to analyse and describe

- the unique identifiers,
- mereologies,
- a suitable sample of attributes, and
- possible intentional pulls

of financial service industries.

Exercise 22 An MSc Student Exercise. Container Line Industry, Internal Qualities: We refer to Exercise 6 on page 105. You are, in turn, to analyse and describe

- the unique identifiers,
- mereologies,
- a suitable sample of attributes, and
- possible intentional pulls

of container lines.

Exercise 23 An MSc Student Exercise. Railway Systems, Internal Qualities: We refer to Exercise 7 on page 105. You are, in turn, to analyse and describe

- the unique identifiers,
- mereologies,
- a suitable sample of attributes, and
- possible intentional pulls

of railway systems.

Exercise 24 A PhD Student Problem. Part-Fluid Conjoins: Canals, Internal Qualities: We refer to Example 8 on page 105. You are, in turn, to analyse and describe

- the unique identifiers,
- mereologies,

- a suitable sample of attributes, and
- possible intentional pulls

of canal systems.

Exercise 25 A PhD Student Problem. Part-Fluids Conjoins: Rum Production, Internal Qualities: We refer to Exercise 9 on page 105. You are, in turn, to analyse and describe

- the unique identifiers,
- mereologies,

- a suitable sample of attributes, and
- possible intentional pulls

of rum production.

Exercise 26 A PhD Student Problem. Part-Fluids Conjoins: Waste Management, Internal Qualities: We refer to Exercise 10 on page 105. You are, in turn, to analyse and describe

- the unique identifiers,
- mereologies,

- a suitable sample of attributes, and
- possible intentional pulls

of waste management.

These exercise problems are continued in Sects. **7.14.3** on page 203, **8.11.2** on page 240 and **9.9.2** on page 297.

Chapter 6
TRANSCENDENTAL DEDUCTION

In this chapter we discuss the concept of transcendental deduction.

It should be clear to the reader that in **domain analysis & description** we are reflecting on a number of philosophical issues; first and foremost on those of *ontology*. For this chapter we reflect on a sub-field of epistemology, we reflect on issues of *transcendental* nature. Should you wish to follow-up on the concept of transcendentality, we refer to [203, Immanuel Kant], [253, Oxford Companion to Philosophy, pp 878–880], [14, The Cambridge Dictionary of Philosophy, pp 807–810], [116, The Blackwell Dictionary of Philosophy, pp 54–55 (1998)], [369, Sørlander] and Chapter 2.

6.1 Some Definitions

Definition: 66 Transcendental, A Repeat: By **transcendental** we shall understand the philosophical notion: **the a priori or intuitive basis of knowledge, independent of experience** ∎

A priori knowledge or intuition is central: By *a priori* we mean that it not only precedes, but also determines rational thought.

Definition: 67 Transcendental Deduction, A Repeat: By a **transcendental deduction** we shall understand the philosophical notion: **a transcendental "conversion" of one kind of knowledge into a seemingly different kind of knowledge** ∎

6.2 Some Informal Examples

Some Transcendental Deductions

Example 74 *We give some intuitive examples of transcendental deductions. They are from the "domain" of programming languages. There is the syntax of a programming language, and there are the programs that supposedly adhere to this syntax. Given that, the following are now transcendental deductions.*
The software tool, a syntax checker, that takes a program and checks whether it satisfies the syntax, including the statically decidable context conditions, i.e., the statics semantics – that tool is one of several forms of transcendental deductions.
The software tools, an automatic theorem prover[156] and a model checker, for example SPIN [252], that takes a program and some theorem, respectively a Promela statement, and proves, respectively checks, the program correct with respect the theorem, or the statement.

---

[156] ACL2 [270], Coq [30], Isabelle/HOL [313], STeP [97], PVS [317] and Z3 [98]

© The Author(s), under exclusive license to Springer Nature Switzerland AG 2021
D. Bjørner, *Domain Science and Engineering*, Monographs in Theoretical Computer Science. An EATCS Series,
https://doi.org/10.1007/978-3-030-73484-8_6

A compiler and an interpreter for any programming language.

Yes, indeed, any abstract interpretation [136, 100] reflects a transcendental deduction: firstly, these examples show that there are many transcendental deductions; secondly, they show that there is no single-most preferred transcendental deduction.

A transcendental deduction, crudely speaking, is just any abstraction that can be "linked" to another, not by logical necessity, but by logical (and philosophical) possibility !

Definition: 68 Transcendentality: By **transcendentality** we shall here mean the philosophical notion: the state or condition of being transcendental ∎

─────────────────── **Transcendentality** ───────────────────

Example 75 We can speak of a bus in at least three *senses:*

(i)   The bus as it is being "maintained, serviced, refueled";
(ii) the bus as it "speeds" down its route; and
(iii) the bus as it "appears" (listed) in a bus time table.

The three *senses* are:

(i)   as an **endurant** (here a *part*),
(ii) as a **perdurant** (as we shall see, a *behaviour*), and
(iii) as an **attribute**[157].   □

The above example, we claim, reflects *transcendentality* as follows:

(i)   We have knowledge of an endurant (i.e., a part) being an endurant.
(ii) We are then to assume that the perdurant referred to in (ii) is an aspect of the endurant mentioned in (i) – where perdurants are to be assumed to represent a different kind of knowledge.
(iii) And, finally, we are to further assume that the attribute mentioned in (iii) is somehow related to both (i) and (ii) – where at least this attribute is to be assumed to represent yet a different kind of knowledge.

In other words: two (i–ii) kinds of different knowledge; that they relate *must indeed* be based on *a priori knowledge.* Someone claims that they relate ! The two statements (i–ii) are claimed to relate transcendentally.[158]

6.3 Bibliographical Note

The philosophical concept of *transcendental deduction* is is a subtle one. Arguments of transcendental nature, across the literature of philosophy, does not follow set principles and techniques. We refer to [14, *The Cambridge Dictionary of Philosophy*, pages 807–810] and [116, *The Blackwell Companion to Philosophy*, Chapter 22: Kant (David Bell), pages 589–606, Bunnin and Tsui-James, eds.] for more on 'transcendence'.

───────────────

[157] – in this case rather: as a fragment of a bus time table *attribute*.

[158] – the attribute statement was "thrown" in "for good measure", i.e., to highlight the issue !

6.4 Exercise Problem

Exercise 27 A Research Challenge. An Analysis of Transcendentality: Immanuel Kant uses, it seems, the concept of transcendental deduction, in one way, taking *self-awareness* as a basis. Kai Sørlander uses, it seems, the concept of transcendental deduction, in a rational, logically way, taking *the possibility of truth* as a basis. We shall be using the concept of transcendental deduction, in Chapter 7, it seems, in a more "mechanistic' way, basically taking transcendental deductions to be some form of translation.

It seems, therefore, relevant to subject the concept of transcendental deduction, now understood in a wider sense, that is, one to be clarified, a philosophical analysis, to try understand, as precisely as is philosophically possible, this wider notion, and to possibly uncover some relations between different philosophers' use of transcendentality, among them, and, if worthwhile, in relation to our use.

Chapter 7
DOMAINS – A Dynamics Ontology: Perdurants

In this chapter we transcendentally "morph" **parts** *into* **behaviours.** *We analyse that notion and its constituent notions of* **actors**, **channels** *and* **communication**, **actions** *and* **events**.

We shall investigate the, as we shall call them, perdurants of domains. That is state and time-evolving domain phenomena. The outcome of this chapter is that the reader will be able to model the perdurants of domains. Not just for a particular domain instance, but a possibly infinite set of domain instances[159].

The main transcendental deduction of this chapter is that of associating with each part a behaviour. This section shows the details of that association. Perdurants are understood in terms of a notion of *state* and a notion of *time*.

7.1 Structure of This Chapter

In order to culminate, in Sect. **7.7** we need to treat a number of pre-requisite topics. There are quite a few of these, so a summary-of-what-is-to-come seems reasonable:

- Sect. **7.2** covers primarily the notion of domain states in the form of CSP *variables* – one for each of the parts having monitorable attributes;
- Sect. **7.3** surveys the notions of actors, actions, events and behaviours;
- Sect. **7.4** discuss the modelling of concurrent domain behaviours in terms of CSP processes – with brief subsections on CSP and `Petri nets`;
- Sect. **7.5** then introduces the notions of CSP *channels, output* and *input* – to model interaction between domain behaviours;
- Sect. **7.6** discusses action, event and behaviour signatures in general;
- Sect. **7.7** is now ready to tackle the important issue of defining domain behaviours, including their signatures;
- Sect. **7.8** shows how to express the initialisation of a running domain behaviour;
- Sect. **7.10** loosely discusses the modelling of domain actions; while
- Sect. **7.11** briefly touches upon the modelling of domain events; finally
- Sect. **7.12** follows up on the *domain discovery process* of Sects. **4.20** and **5.8**.

Other sections provide elucidation or summary observations.

7.2 States and Time

We first covered the notions of state in Sects. **2.2.2.7** on page 15 and **4.19** on page 91 and time in Sect. **3.5** on page 29.

---

[159] By this we mean: You are not just analysing a specific domain, say the one manifested around the corner from where you are, but any instance, anywhere in the world, which satisfies what you have described.

D. Bjørner, *Domain Science and Engineering*, Monographs in Theoretical Computer Science. An EATCS Series, https://doi.org/10.1007/978-3-030-73484-8_7

7.2.1 The Issue of States

Example 39 on page 92 illustrated the idea of expressing the values of all parts having dynamic attributes.

We refer to [187] and Appendix Sect. **D.6.2** on page 384.

RSL variables of the form:

variable parts[uid_P(p)]:P := p

are to be declared to model parts that have monitorable attributes; informally:

value
      has_monitorable_attributes: P → **Bool**
      has_monitorable_attributes(p) ≡
            ∃ A · A ∈ analyse_attributes_types(p) · is_monitorable(attr_A(p))

      possible_variable_declaration: P → RSL-Text
      possible_variable_declaration(p) ≡
            if has_monitorable_attributes(p) **then** ❝ **variable** p[uid_P(p)]:P := p ❞ **end**

analyse_attribute_types is defined in domain analysis function prompt 12 on page 120.

—————————————— **declaring_all_monitorable_variables** ——————————————

Translation Schema 1 When we have 'collected' all external endurant descriptions

247 we can, for any given endurant, e, typically a *universe of discourse* domain,
248 calculate_all relevant monitorable_variable declarations;
249 that is, for those parts, p,
250 that have monitorable-only attributes.

248.   declaring_all_monitorable_variables: E → RSL-Text
248.   declaring_all_monitorable_variables(e) ≡
249.   **let** ps = calc_parts(e) **in**
249.   **for** ∀ p · p ∈ ps **do** possible_variable_declaration(p)
248.   **end end**

State Values versus State Variables

Example 76 Item 133 on page 93 expresses the **value** of all parts of a road transport system:

133. ps:(UoB|H|L|BC|B|A)-**set** ≡ $rts∪hls∪bcs∪bs∪as$.

251 We now introduce the set of variables, one for each part value of the domain being modelled.

251. { **variable** vp:(UoB|H|L|BC|B|A) | vp:(UoB|H|L|BC|B|A) · $vp∈ps$ }

7.2.2 Time Considerations

We shall, without loss of generality, assume that actions and events are atomic and that behaviours are composite. Atomic perdurants may "occur" during some time interval, but we omit consideration of and concern for what actually goes on during such an interval. Composite perdurants can be analysed into "constituent" actions, events and "sub-behaviours". We shall also omit consideration of temporal properties of behaviours. Instead we shall refer to two seminal monographs: Specifying Systems [275, Leslie Lamport] and Duration Calculus: A Formal Approach to Real-Time Systems [404, Zhou ChaoChen and Michael Reichhardt Hansen] (and [44, Chapter 15]). For a seminal book on "time in computing" we refer to the eclectic [167, Mandrioli et al., 2012]. And for a seminal book on time at the epistemology level we refer to [374, J. van Benthem, 1991].

7.3 Actors, Actions, Events and Behaviours: A Preview

To us perdurants are further, pragmatically, analysed into *actions*, *events*, and *behaviours*. We shall define these terms below. Common to all of them is that they potentially change a state. Actions and events are here considered atomic perdurants. For behaviours we distinguish between discrete and continuous behaviours.

7.3.1 Actors

Definition: 69 Actor: By an ***actor*** we shall understand something that is capable of **initiating** and **carrying out** actions, events and behaviours ∎

The notion of *"carrying out"* will be made clear in this overall chapter. We shall, in principle, associate an actor with each part[160]. These actors will be described as behaviours. These behaviours evolve around a state. The state is the set of qualities, in particular the dynamic attributes, of the associated parts and/or any possible components or fluids of the parts.

7.3.2 Discrete Actions

Definition: 70 Discrete Action: By a *discrete action* [388, Wilson and Shpall] we shall understand a foreseeable thing which deliberately and potentially changes a well-formed state, in one step, usually into another, still well-formed state, and for which an actor can be made responsible ∎

An action is what happens when a function invocation changes, or potentially changes a state.

7.3.3 Discrete Events

---

[160] This is an example of a *transcendental deduction*.

Definition: 71 Event: By an *event* we shall understand some unforeseen thing, that is, some 'not-planned-for' "action", one which surreptitiously, non-deterministically changes a well-formed state into another, but usually not a well-formed state, and for which no particular domain actor can be made responsible ∎

Events can be characterised by a pair of (before and after) states, a predicate over these and, optionally, a *time* or *time interval*.

We shall use the RSL concepts of *clauses*, i.e., *expressions* and *statements* to model actions. We shall use the CSP concepts of *channels* and *channel communication*, i.e., *message output:* ch[..] ! e and *message input:* ch[..] ? to model events. The notion of event continues to puzzle philosophers [150, 342, 300, 145, 204, 15, 121, 329, 120].

7.3.4 Discrete Behaviours

Definition: 72 Discrete Behaviour: By a ***discrete behaviour*** we shall understand a set of sequences of potentially interacting sets of discrete actions, events and behaviours ∎

Discrete behaviours now become the *focal point* of our investigation. To every part we associate, by transcendental deduction, a behaviour. We shall express these behaviours as CSP *processes* [250]. For those behaviours we must therefore establish their means of *communication* via *channels*; their *signatures*; and their *definitions* – as *translated* from endurant parts.

Behaviours

Example 77 In Fig. 7.5 on page 171 we "symbolically", i.e., the "...", show the following parts: each individual hub, each individual link, each individual bus company, each individual bus, and each individual automobile – and all of these. The idea is that those are the parts for which we shall define behaviours. That figure, however, and in contrast to Fig. 7.5 on page 171, shows the composite parts as not containing their atomic parts, but as if they were "free-standing, atomic" parts. That shall visualize the transcendental interpretation as atomic part behaviours not being somehow embedded in composite behaviours, but operating concurrently, in parallel.   □

7.3.5 Continuous Behaviours

By a ***continuous behaviour*** we shall understand a *continuous time* sequence of *state changes*. We shall not go into what may cause these *state changes*. And we shall not go into continuous behaviours in this monograph.

7.4 Modelling Concurrent Behaviours

We choose to exploit the CSP [250] subset of RSL since CSP is a suitable vehicle for expressing suitably abstract synchronisation and communication between behaviours. (In Sect. **7.4.2** on page 165 we bring, as an informative aside, *The Petri Net Story*.)

The mereology of domain parts induces channel declarations.

CSP channels are loss-free. That is: two CSP processes, of which one offers and the other offers to accept a message do so synchronously and without forgetting that message. To model actual, so-called "real-life" communication via queues or allowing "channels" to forget, then you must model that explicitly in CSP. We refer to [250, 352, 357].

7.4.1 The CSP Story

CSP is a wonderful tool, i.e., a language with which to study and describe *communicating sequential processes*. It is the invention of *Charles Anthony Richard Hoare*. Major publications on CSP are [249, 250, 352, 357].

7.4.1.1 Informal Presentation

CSP processes (models of domain behaviours) $P_i, P_j, ..., P_k$ can proceed in parallel:

P_i ‖ P_j ‖ ... ‖ P_k

Behaviours sometimes synchronise and usually communicate. Synchronisation and communication is abstracted as the sending (ch!m) and receipt (ch?) of messages, m:M, over channels, ch.

type M
channel ch:M

Communication between (unique identifier) indexed behaviours have their channels modelled as similarly indexed channels:

out: ch[idx]!m
in: ch[idx]?
channel {ch[ide]:M|ide:IDE}

where IDE typically is some type expression over unique identifier types.

The expression

P_i ⊓ P_j ⊓ ... ⊓ P_k

can be understood as a choice: either P_i, or P_j, or ... or P_k as *non-deterministically* **internally** chosen with no stipulation as to why!

The expression

P_i ⟦⟧ P_j ⟦⟧ ... ⟦⟧ P_k

can be understood as a choice: either P_i, or P_j, or ... or P_k as *deterministically* **externally** chosen on the basis that the one chosen offers to participate in either an input, ch?, or an output, ch!msg, event. If more than one P_i offers a communication then one is arbitrarily chosen. If no P_i offers a communication the behaviour halts till some P_j offers a communication.

7.4.1.2 A Syntax for CSP

We present the syntax for the CSP used in RSL.

```
P ::= stop
    | skip
    | P ‖ P                        parallel composition (interleave)
    | P ⊓ P                        internal non-deterministic choice
    | P ⫿ P                        external non-deterministic choice
    | P ; P                        sequential composition
    | if B then P else P end       Boolean conditional
    | let v = ch ? in ... end      input value v on channel ch
    | ch ! e ; P                   output value of expression e on channel ch
```

7.4.1.3 Disciplined Uses of CSP

In connection with domain modelling, which uses of CSP appear to be meaningful? To understand our answer let us consider the following. As suggested in Chapters 4–5 the domain of endurants consists of a number of parts, some atomic, some compounded, that is, consisting of a part (a "root") and a number of proper sub-parts (its "siblings"). With Chapter 6 we shall consider each and every part to also represent a behaviour, that is, with sub-parts representing behaviours not "embedded" in "root" part behaviours, but, in a "first approximation" only bound to their roots by mutual mereologies.

    This is a **modelling decision.** We could have chosen a more elaborate one; one that, from the days of Algol 60 [269] was in line with the so-called *'block structure'* concept. But have chosen not to!

Buses and Bus Companies

Example 78 We refer to Example 8 on page 49. A bus company is like a "root" for its fleet of "sibling" buses. But a bus company may cease to exist without the buses therefore necessarily also ceasing to exist. They may continue to operate, probably illegally, without, possibly. a valid bus driving certificate. Or they may be passed on to either private owners or to other bus companies. We use this example as a reason for not endowing a "block structure" concept on behaviours.

So there we are. With a collection of part and sub-part behaviours that need communicate "across" and "within" compounds. To do so they avail themselves of *channels,* ch[i,j], *output,* ch[i,j] ! e and *input,* ch[i,j] ?. The general situation is then that a number of behaviours, P_i and Q_j, wishes to synchronise and communicate. The general, *disciplined* form for doing so can be schematically expressed as follows:

```
P(i,ujs,...)(...) ≡
    ...
    ⊠ { ch[i,j] ! e ; ... | j:UI • j ∈ ... } ;
    ... ;
    P(i,ujs,...)(...)

Q(j,uis,...)(...) ≡
    ...
    ⊠ { let v = ch[i,j] ? in ... end | i:UI • i ∈ uis } ;
    ...
```

Q(j,uis,...)(...)

The ⊠ operator is either ▯, or ⊓, or ∥. We shall abstain from further 'advice' on the use of CSP but refer to either [42, Software Engineering 2, Chapter 21] (*Concurrent Specification Programming*) or standard CSP textbooks [249, 250, 352, 357]. We shall take up this line of inquiry in Sect. **7.7.10** on page 183 –*A Suggested Behaviour Definition* 2 on page 183.

7.4.2 The Petri Net Story

Petri nets[161] are a wonderful concept first invented by *Carl Adam Petri* [328]. It is intended to model a class of *discrete event dynamic systems*. A *Petri net* is a *directed bipartite graph*, in which some *nodes* (traditionally represented by bars) represent **transitions** (i.e. *events*) that may occur, and other nodes represent **places** (i.e. *conditions*, traditionally represented by circles). The **directed arcs** describe which *places* are *pre-* and/or *post-conditions* for which **transitions** (signified by *arrows*). We shall basically recommend the Petri net books by *Wolfgang Reisig*, some of which are [343, 344, 347, 348] – notably [348].

7.4.2.1 Informal Presentation

Figure 7.1 shows a simplest form of *Petri Net*. Let us focus on the left net. The labeled circles designate **places**. The labeled thick, black bar designate a **transition**. The arrows, ⟶s, designate *(flow)* **arcs** and are labeled with a numeral, designating a natural number larger than 0. Inside the places we show 2, 2, respectively 0 **tokens**. Their **constellation** is also called a **marking**. In general, any composition of places, transitions, markings and labels such that arcs emanating from a place are incident upon transitions and such that arcs emanation from transitions are incident upon places, form a syntactically meaningful *Petri net*, also called a **Place-Transition Net**, PTN.

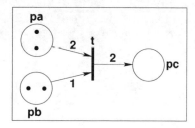 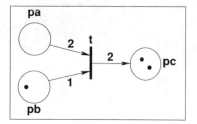

Fig. 7.1 *Two Petri Nets:* Before and after 'firing'

Let us start by focusing on the left *Petri net*. The meaning of the number of tokens in places, the transition input arc labels, and the transition output arc labels are as follows: If the respective

---

[161] The term Petri net stands for the 'language' of *Petri nets*. A *Petri net* is an instance of the language of Petri nets

transition input arc labels can be satisfied by the respective number of tokens in source places then a **firing** can take place. After a firing the Petri net has a new **constellation.**

The following[162] was written (around 2004) by Christian Krogh Madsen[163]

7.4.2.2 An Example – Christian Krogh Madsen

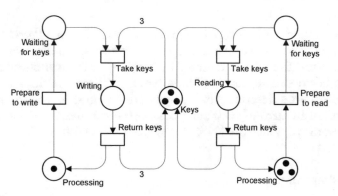

Fig. 7.2 Critical resource sharing

Critical Resource Sharing

Example 79 Figure 7.2 shows an example PTN modelling four processes that access a common critical resource. One process writes to the resource, while the other three processes read from the resource. To ensure data integrity, mutual exclusion must be enforced between the writing process and the reading processes. The protocol for mutual exclusion requires a reading process to claim a key before it may read, while the writing process is required to claim three keys before it may write. A process that cannot get the required number of keys must wait until more keys become available. The place Keys holds a token for each key that is unused. When a process finishes reading or writing it returns the claimed keys to the place Keys and proceeds to do some processing that does not access the critical resource.

7.4.2.3 An RSL Model of Petri nets – Christian Krogh Madsen

★ Syntax of Petri nets

We first formalise a syntax and then a static semantics for Petri nets, as PTN (for place-transition net), with finite capacity places.

- A place transition net consists of a set of places with associated capacities, a set of transitions, a preset, a postset and a marking.

---

[162] – an *An Example* and *An RSL Model of* Petri nets.

[163] Christian Krogh Madsen principally wrote, as part of his MSc. Thesis, Chapters 12–14: Petri Nets, Message and Live Sequence Charts, and Statecharts in [43, Pages 315–508].

- Only well-formed PTNs will be considered.
- Places and transitions are further unspecified entities.
- Presets are a mapping from transitions to sets of pairs of places and weights.
- Postsets are a mapping from transitions to sets of pairs of places and weights.
- A marking is a mapping of places to marks.
- A mark is a non-negative integer.

type
    PTN = {| ptn:PTN′ • wf_PTN(ptn) |}
    PTN′ = (Place $\rightarrow$ **Nat**) × Trans-**set** × Preset × Postset × Marking
    Place
    Trans
    Preset = Trans $\rightarrow$ (Place × **Nat**)-**set**
    Postset = Trans $\rightarrow$ (Place × **Nat**)-**set**
    Marking = Place $\rightarrow$ **Nat**

⋆ A Static Semantics

- A PTN is well-formed if:

    1-2 every transition in the set of transitions is included in the domain of the maps of presets and postsets, and
    3 every place is in the pre- or postset of some transition, and
    4 every transition has a non-empty preset or postset, and
    5 no transition can have a preset or postset that includes the same place more than once with different weights, and
    6 the marking covers all places, and
    7 for every place the number of tokens assigned to it in the marking must be at most equal to the capacity of the place.

value
    wf_PTN : PTN′ → **Bool**
    wf_PTN(ps, ts, pres, posts, mark) ≡
[1] **dom** pres = ts ∧
[2] **dom** posts = ts ∧
[3] {p | p:Place •
            ∃ pns: (Place×**Nat**)-**set**, n:**Nat** •
                (p,n) ∈ pns∧pns ∈ **rng** pres ∪ **rng** posts} = **dom** ps ∧
[4] (∀ t:Trans • t ∈ ts ⇒ pres(t) ∪ posts(t) ≠ {}) ∧
[5] (∀ t:Trans •
            ~(∃ n1, n2 : **Nat**, p : Place •
                n1 ≠ n2 ∧ p ∈ **dom** ps ∧
                ({(p,n1), (p,n2)} ⊆ pres(t) ∨
                {(p,n1), (p,n2)} ⊆ posts(t)))) ∧
[6] **dom** mark = **dom** ps ∧
[7] (∀ p:Place • p ∈ **dom** ps ⇒ mark(p)≤ps(p))

⋆ A Dynamic Semantics

We formalise the dynamic aspects of PTN, namely what it means for a transition to be activated and for a transition to occur.

- A transition is activated:

∞ if for every place in its preset there are at least as many tokens as the weight of the corresponding arrow, and

∞ if for every place in its postset the number of tokens at that place added to the weight of the corresponding arrow is at most equal to the capacity of the place.

- The occurrence of an activated transition produces a new marking

  ∞ in which the number of tokens at each of the places in the preset is reduced by the weight of the corresponding arrow, and

  ∞ in which the number of tokens at each of the places in the postset is increased by the weight of the corresponding arrow.

value

```
activated: Trans×PTN →̃ Bool
activated(t,ptn) ≡
    let (ps,ts,pres,posts,mark) = ptn in
        (∀ p:Place,n:Nat · (p,n) ∈ pres(t) ⇒ mark(p)≥n) ∧
        (∀ p:Place,n:Nat · (p,n) ∈ posts(t) ⇒ mark(p)+n≤ps(p))
    end
    pre let (ps,ts,pres,posts,mark) = ptn in t ∈ ts end


occur: Trans×PTN →̃ PTN
occur(t,ptn) ≡
    let (ps,ts,pres,posts,mark) = ptn in
        (ps,ts,pres,posts,
          mark †
          [p ↦ mark(p)−n | p:Place,n:Nat · (p,n) ∈ pres(t)] †
          [p ↦ mark(p)+n | p:Place,n:Nat · (p,n) ∈ posts(t)])
    end
    pre activated(t,ptn)
```

> End-of-contribution by Christian Krogh Madsen

7.4.2.4 Petri Nets and Domain Science & Engineering – A Research Topic?

We shall not, in this monograph, deal further with Petri nets! So why bring this overall section at all? We bring it because with Petri nets one can model *true concurrency*. With CSP we model only *interleaved concurrency*, that is, no two or more events can be modelled, in CSP, to truly occur simultaneously. With Petri nets they can! We also bring it so that the reader is properly informed. CSP is a textual 'language' where Petri nets is a graphical 'language'. Some people or more gifted with respect to the former, other people more with respect to the latter; few are equally at ease with both 'notations'.

We suggest, as a research topic to study possible combinations of Petri net and RSL specifications, for example with cross-annotations where RSL formula refer to *Petri net* places and transitions, and where *Petri net* places and transitions, refer to RSL formula. Or, whatever springs to mind?

7.5 Channels and Communication

7.5.1 From Mereologies to Channel Declarations

The fact that a part p of sort P with unique identifier p_i, has a mereology, for example the set of unique identifiers $\{q_a, q_b, ..., q_d\}$ identifying parts $\{qa, qb, ..., qd\}$ of sort Q, may mean that parts p and $\{qa, qb, ..., qd\}$ may wish to exchange – for example, attribute – values, one way (from p to the qs) or the other (vice versa) or in both directions.

Figure 7.3 shows two dotted rectangle box diagrams.

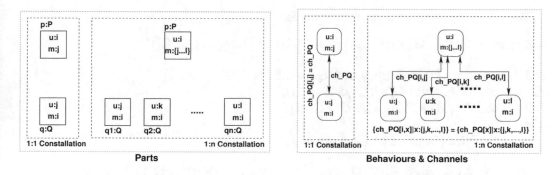

Fig. 7.3 Respective Part and Behaviour/Channel Constellations. u:p unique id. p; m:p mereology p

The left fragment of Fig. 7.3 intends to show a 1:1 Constellation of a single p:P box and a single q:Q part, respectively, indicating, within these parts, their unique identifiers and mereologies. The right fragment of the figure intends to show a 1:n Constellation of a single p:P box and a set of q:Q parts, now with arrowed lines connecting the p part with the q parts. These lines are intended to show channels. We show them with two way arrows. We could instead have chosen one way arrows, in one or the other direction. The directions are intended to show a direction of value transfer. We have given the same channel names to all examples, ch_PQ. We have ascribed channel message types MPQ to all channels.[164] Figure 7.4 shows an arrangement similar to that of Fig. 7.3, but for an m:n Constellation.

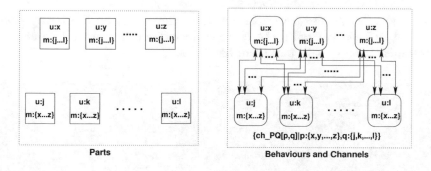

Fig. 7.4 Multiple Part and Channel Arrangements: u:p unique id. p; m:p mereology p

The channel declarations corresponding to Figs. 7.3 and 7.4 are:

---

[164] Of course, these names and types would be distinct for any one domain description.

     channel
[1]   ch_PQ[i,j]:MPQ
[2]   { ch_PQ[i,x]:MPQ | x:{j,k,...,l} }
[3]   { ch_PQ[p,q]:MPQ | p:{x,y,...,z}, q:{j,k,...,l} }

Since there is only one index i and j for channel [1], its declaration can be reduced. Similarly there is only one i for declaration [2]:

     channel
[1]   ch_PQ:MPQ
[2]   { ch_PQ[x]:MPQ | x:{j,k,...,l} }

252 The following description identities holds:

252 { ch_PQ[x]:MPQ | x:{j,k,...,l} } ≡ ch_PQ[j],ch_PQ[k],...,ch_PQ[l],

252 { ch_PQ[p,q]:MPQ | p:{x,y,...,z}, q:{j,k,...,l} } ≡
252   ch_PQ[x,j],ch_PQ[x,k],...,ch_PQ[x,l],
252   ch_PQ[y,j],ch_PQ[y,k],...,ch_PQ[y,l],
252   ...,
252   ch_PQ[z,j],ch_PQ[z,k],...,ch_PQ[z,l]

We can sketch a diagram similar to Figs. 7.3 on the previous page and 7.4 on the preceding page for the case of composite parts.

7.5.2 Channel Declarations

We can simplify the general treatment of channel declarations. Basically all we can say, for any domain, is that any two distinct part behaviours may need to communicate. Therefore we declare a vector of channels indexed by sets of two distinct part identifiers.

     channel { ch[{ij,ik}] | ij,ik:UI • {ij,ik}⊆ all_uniq_ids() ∧ ij≠ik } M

Initially we shall leave the type of messages over channels further undefined. As we, laboriously, work through the definition of behaviours, Sect. 7.7, we shall be able to make M precise. all_uniq_ids was defined in Sect. 5.2.4 on page 110.

In preparation for the next example we show Figure 7.5 on the facing page. In that example we shall however refine the channel declaration indices to two element sets of unique identifiers from specific part identifier types.

Channels

Example 80 *We shall argue for hub-to-link channels based on the mereologies of those parts. Hub parts may be topologically connected to any number, 0 or more, link parts. Only instantiated road nets knows which. Hence there must be channels between any hub behaviour and any link behaviour. Vice versa: link parts will be connected to exactly two hub parts. Hence there must be channels from any link behaviour to two hub behaviours. See the figure above.*
Channel Message Types: . . . .
    We ascribe types to the messages offered on channels.

253 *Hubs and links communicate, both ways, with one another, over channels, hl_ch, whose indexes are determined by their mereologies.*
254 *Hubs send one kind of messages, links another.*

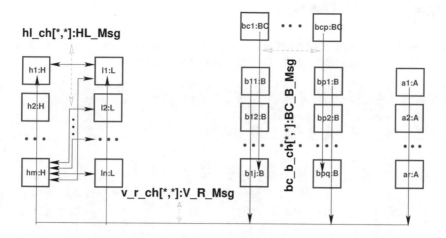

Fig. 7.5 Atomic Behaviours

255 *Bus companies offer timed bus time tables to buses, one way.*
256 *Buses and automobiles offer their current, timed positions to the road element, hub or link they are on,*
one way.

type
254 H_L_Msg, L_H_Msg
253 HL_Msg = H_L_Msg | L_F_Msg
255 BC_B_Msg = T × BusTimTbl
256 V_R_Msg = T × (BPos|APos)

Channel Declarations: ....

257 *This justifies the channel declaration which is calculated to be:*

channel
257 { hl_ch[h_ui,l_ui]:H_L_Msg
257 | h_ui:H_UI,l_ui:L_UI•i ∈ $h_{ui}s$∧j ∈ $lh_{ui}m$(h_ui) }
257 ∪
257 { hl_ch[h_ui,l_ui]:L_H_Msg
257 | h_ui:H_UI,l_ui:L_UI•l_ui ∈ $l_{ui}s$∧i ∈ $lh_{ui}m$(l_ui) }

We shall argue for bus company-to-bus channels based on the mereologies of those parts. Bus companies
need communicate to all its buses, but not the buses of other bus companies. Buses of a bus company need
communicate to their bus company, but not to other bus companies.

258 *This justifies the channel declaration which is calculated to be:*

channel
258 { bc_b_ch[bc_ui,b_ui] | bc_ui:BC_UI, b_ui:B_UI
258 • bc_ui ∈ $bc_{ui}s$ ∧ b_ui ∈ $b_{ui}s$ }: BC_B_Msg

We shall argue for vehicle to road element channels based on the mereologies of those parts. Buses and
automobiles need communicate to all hubs and all links.

259 *This justifies the channel declaration which is calculated to be:*

channel
259 { v_r_ch[v_ui,r_ui] | v_ui:V_UI,r_ui:R_UI
259 • v_ui∈$v_{ui}s$∧r_ui∈$r_{ui}s$ }: V_R_Msg

The channel calculations are described on pages 175–176

□

7.6 Signatures – In General

We shall treat perdurants as function invocations. In our cursory overview of perdurants we shall now focus on one perdurant quality: function signatures.

Definition: 73 Function Signature: By a **function signature** we shall understand a *function name* and a *function type expression* ∎

Definition: 74 Function Type Expression: By a **function type expression** we shall understand a pair of *type expressions*. separated by a *function type constructor* either → (for **total function**) or $\tilde{\to}$ (for **partial function**) ∎

The type expressions are part sort or type, or fluid sort or type, or attribute type names, but may, occasionally be expressions over respective type names involving **-set**, ×, *, $\twoheadrightarrow$ *and* | *type constructors.*

7.6.1 Action Signatures and Definitions

Actors usually provide their initiated actions with arguments, say of type VAL. *Hence the schematic function (action) signature and schematic definition:*

action: VAL → $\Sigma \tilde{\to} \Sigma$
action(v)(σ) **as** σ'
    pre: $\mathcal{P}$(v,σ)
    post: $\mathcal{Q}$(v,σ,σ')

expresses that a selection of the domain state, as designated by the Σ type expression, is acted upon and possibly changed. The partial function type operator $\tilde{\to}$ shall indicate that action(v)(σ) may not be defined for the argument, i.e., initial state σ and/or the argument v:VAL, hence the precondition $\mathcal{P}$(v,σ). The post condition $\mathcal{Q}$(v,σ,σ') characterises the "after" state, σ':Σ, with respect to the "before" state, σ:Σ, and possible arguments (v:VAL). Which could be the argument values, v:VAL, of actions? Well, there can basically be only the following kinds of argument values: parts, components and fluids, respectively unique part identifiers, mereologies and attribute values.

Perdurant (action) analysis thus proceeds as follows: identifying relevant actions, assigning names to these, delineating the "smallest" relevant state[165], ascribing signatures to action functions, and determining action pre-conditions and action post-conditions. Of these, ascribing signatures is the most crucial: In the process of determining the action signature one oftentimes discovers that part or component or fluid attributes have been left ("so far") "undiscovered".

---

[165] By "smallest" we mean: containing the fewest number of parts. Experience shows that the domain analyser cum describer should strive for identifying the smallest state.

7.6.2 Event Signatures and Definitions

Events are usually characterised by the absence of known actors and the absence of explicit "external" arguments. Hence the schematic function (event) signature:

value
    event: $\Sigma \times \Sigma \overset{\sim}{\to}$ **Bool**
    event(σ,σ') **as** tf
        pre: $P(\sigma)$
        post: tf = $Q(\sigma,\sigma')$

The event signature expresses that a selection of the domain as designated by the Σ type expression is "acted" upon, by unknown actors, and possibly changed. The partial function type operator $\overset{\sim}{\to}$ shall indicate that event(σ,σ') may not be defined for some states σ. The resulting state may, or may not, satisfy axioms and well-formedness conditions over Σ – as expressed by the post condition $Q(\sigma,\sigma')$.

    Events may thus cause well-formedness of states to fail. Subsequent actions, once actors discover such "disturbing events", are therefore expected to remedy that situation, that is, to restore well-formedness. We shall not illustrate this point.

7.6.3 Behaviour Signatures

We shall only cover behaviour signatures when expressed in RSL/CSP [187]. The behaviour functions are now called processes. That a behaviour function is a never-ending function, i.e., a process, is "revealed" by the "trailing" **Unit**:

    behaviour: ... → ... **Unit**

That a process takes no argument is "revealed" by a "leading" Unit:

    behaviour: **Unit** → ...

That a process accepts channel, viz.: ch, inputs, is "revealed" as follows:

    behaviour: ... → **in** ch ...

That a process offers channel, viz.: ch, outputs is "revealed" as follows:

    behaviour: ... → **out** ch ...

That a process accepts other arguments is "revealed" as follows:

    behaviour: ARG → ...

where ARG can be any type expression:

    T, T→T, T→T→T, et cetera

where T is any type expression.

7.6.4 Attribute Access, An Interpretation

We shall only be concerned with part attributes. And we shall here consider them in the context of part behaviours. Part behaviour definitions embody part attributes.

- **Static attributes** designate constants. As such they can be "compiled" into behaviour definitions. We choose, thus, to bring static attribute values as explicit behaviour arguments.
- **Monitorable-only attributes** designate time-varying values whose values we choose to access in the following manner:

∞ attr_$A(p)$

where p is a part in the global state, cf. Sect. **4.19** on page 91.
- **Biddable attributes** designate time-varying values whose values we choose to access, respectively biddably **update** in the following manner:

∞ attr_$A(p)$
∞ **update**(attr_A,A,p)

where p is a part in the global state. We shall informally explain the **update** functional below.
- **Programmable attribute** values are calculated by their behaviours. We list them as behaviour arguments. The behaviour definitions may then specify new values. These are provided in the position of the programmable attribute arguments in *tail recursive* invocations of these behaviours.

7.6.4.1 The **update** Functional

The generic **update** function is explained very informally:

[1]   **update**: (P→A) × A × P → P
[2]   **update**(attr_A,a,p) ≡ p′
[3]   **pre** A ∈ analyse_attributes(p) ∧ parts[uid__P(p)] is declared ∧ ...
[4]   **post** attr_A(p′) ≈ a ∧ ...

[1] The first argument is the observe attribute function, the second argument is the attribute value, the third argument is the part, p, being **update**d.
[2] The result of applying the **update** function is a part, $p′$.
[3] The pre-condition is that the attribute type, A, is amongst the attributes of the part, that part p is in the global state, i.e., has been declared as a variable, and more !
[4] The post-condition is that the **update**d attribute of $p′$ approximates the argument attribute value, and "much, much more".

The "much, much more" refers to the following: the unique identifier of $p′$ is that of p; the mereology of $p′$ is that of p; all other attribute values of $p′$ is are those of p; and no other part has changed values.

The above amounts to a "storage model", i.e., a model of domain state variables akin to the storage models put forward first in [28, Bekič and Walk, 1971], see also [24, Bekič, Bjørner, Henhapl, Jones and Lucas, 1974], then in [43, Sect. 8.7.1, Bjørner, 2006].

In the context of domain models we shall (later) introduced an array, parts, of variables global to an entire domain description. For each part, p, with unique identifier, π, there will be a corresponding array element: parts[π]. To obtain a monitorable attribute A value for part p

- is thus expressed as attr_A(parts[π]).

To update a monitorable attribute A to value a:A for part p

- is correspondingly expressed as **update**(attr_A,a,parts[π]).

7.6.4.2 Calculating In/Output Channel Signatures:

260 The function calc_i_o_chn_refs apply to parts and yield RSL-Text.

    a From p we calculate its unique identifier value and its mereology value.
    b If the mereology is not void then a (Currying[166]) right pointing arrow, →, is inserted.[167]
    c If there is an input mereology then the keyword **in** is inserted
      in front of the input mereology;
    d similarly for the **in**put/**out**put mereology;
    e and for the **out**put mereology.

value
260   calc_i_o_chn_refs: P → RSL-Text
260   calc_i_o_chn_refs(p) ≡ ;
260a   let ui = uid_P(p), (ics,iocs,ocs) = **obs_mereo**_(p) **in**
260b   **if** ics ∪ iocs ∪ ocs ∪ atrvs ≠ {} **then** " → " **end** ;
260c   **if** ics ≠{} **then** " **in** " calc_chn_refs(ui,ichs) **end** ;
260d   **if** iocs≠{} **then** " **in,out** " calc_chn_refs(ui,iochs) **end** ;
260e   **if** ocs≠{} **then** " **out** " calc_chn_refs(ui,ochs) **end end**

261 The function calc_chn_refs

    a apply to a pair, (ui,uis) of a unique part identifier type name and a set of unique part identifier type names and yield RSL-Text.
    b If uis is empty no text is generated. Otherwise an array channel declaration is generated.

261a   calc_chn_refs: P_UI × Q_UI-**set** → RSL-Text
261b   calc_chn_refs(pui,quis) ≡
261b   { " (pui,qui)_ch[pui,qui] "| qui:Q_UI•qui ∈ quis }

262 The function calc_all_chn_dcls

    a apply to a pair, (pui,quis) of a unique part identifier and a set of unique part identifiers and yield RSL-Text.
    b If quis is empty no text is generated. Otherwise an array channel declaration
     • { ≪ η(pui,qui)_ch[pui,qui]:η(pui,qui)M ≫| qui:Q_UI•qui ∈ quis }
    is generated.

262a   calc_all_chn_dcls: P_UI × Q_UI-**set** → RSL-Text
262a   calc_all_chn_dcls(pui,quis) ≡
262a   { " (pui,qui)_ch[pui,qui]:M "| qui:Q_UI•qui ∈ quis }

The " (pui,qui) " invocation serves to name both the channel, " (pui,qui)_ch[pui,qui] ", and the channel message type, " M ". That message type has, possibly, to be left open, at this stage of analysis & description. Message types can perhaps best, i.e., easiest be decided upon once all the behaviour body definitions have been completed.

263 The overloaded distributed-fix operator " "[168] is here applied to a pair of unique identifiers. Very informally:

---

[166] https://en.wikipedia.org/wiki/Currying
[167] We refer to the three parts of the mereology value as the input, the input/output and the output mereology (values).
[168] The η operator applies to a type and yields the name of the type.

263   " ... ": $(UI \to \text{RSL-Text})|((X\_UI \times Y\_UI) \to \text{RSL-Text})$
263   " (x_ui, y_ui) " $\equiv$ (" $(x\_ui, y\_ui$ "))

Repeating these channel calculations over distinct parts $p_1, p_2, ..., p_n$ of the same part type P will yield "similar" behaviour signature channel references:

$\{PQ\_ch[p_{1_{ui}}, qui]||p_{1_{ui}}:P\_UI, qui:Q\_UI \cdot qui \in quis\}$
$\{PQ\_ch[p_{2_{ui}}, qui]||p_{2_{ui}}:P\_UI, qui:Q\_UI \cdot qui \in quis\}$
...
$\{PQ\_ch[p_{n_{ui}}, qui]||p_{n_{ui}}:P\_UI, qui:Q\_UI \cdot qui \in quis\}$

These distinct single channel references can be assembled into one:

$\{PQ\_ch[pui, qui] \mid pui:P\_UI, qui:Q\_UI : -pui \in puis, qui \in quis\}$
where $puis = \{p_{1_{ui}}, p_{2_{ui}}, ..., p_{n_{ui}}\}$

As an example we have already calculated the array channels for Fig. 7.4 Pg. 169 – cf. the left, the **Parts**, of that figure – cf. Items [1–3] Pages 169–170. The identities Item 252 Pg. 170 apply.

7.7 Behaviour Signatures and Definitions

In this section we shall finally show the schemas whereby solid endurants, i.e., parts, are transcendentally "morphed" into behaviours.

7.7.1 General on Behaviour Schemas

The general translation schema can be expressed as follows:

```
───────────────────────── is_endurant(e) ─────────────────────────

Translation Schema 2

    value
        TRANSLATE_Endurant: E → RSL-Text
        TRANSLATE_Endurant(e) ≡
            is_part(e)  →
3 Pg. 178              is_atomic(e)                  → TRANSLATE_Atomic(e),
4 Pg. 178              is_composite(e)               → TRANSLATE_Composite(e),
5 Pg. 179              is_single_sort_set(e)         → TRANSLATE_SingleSortSet(e),
6 Pg. 179              is_alternative_sorts_set(e)   → TRANSLATE_AlternativeSortsSet(e),
7 Pg. 179      is_structure(e)                       → TRANSLATE_Structure(e)
8 Pg. 180      is_conjoin(e)                         → TRANSLATE_Conjoin(e),
            is_living_species(e)                     → ..., [ we omit treatment of living species ]
            _                                        → skip
```

We have chosen to not "morph" fluids into behaviours – as expressed by the last clause above.

7.7.1.1 The General Behaviour Signature

We associate with each part, $p{:}P$, a behaviour name $\mathcal{M}_P$. That is, every part p of sort P is associated with the same behaviour name $\mathcal{M}_P$ each individual such behaviour being distinguished by the initial unique identifier constant argument.

Behaviours thus have as their first argument their unique part identifier: uid_P(p). Behaviours evolves around a state, or, rather, a set of values: its possibly changing mereology, mt:MT and the attributes of the part.[169] A behaviour signature is therefore:

$$\mathcal{M}_P\text{: ui:UI}\times\text{me:MT}\times\text{stat\_attr\_types(p)} \rightarrow \text{prgr\_attr\_types(p)} \rightarrow \text{calc\_i\_o\_chn\_refs(p)} \textbf{ Unit}$$

where (i) ui:UI is the unique identifier value and type of part p; (ii) me:MT is the value and type mereology of part p, me = mereo_P(p); (iii) stat_attr_types(p): static attribute types of part $p{:}P$; (iv) prgr_attr_types(p): controllable attribute types of part $p{:}P$; (v) calc_i_o_chn_refs(p) calculates references to the **in**put, the **in**put/**out**put and the **out**put channels serving the attributes shared between part p and the parts designated in its mereology me.

7.7.2 Preamble Definitions

We have, in Chapter 5 and in this chapter, defined a number of analysis predicates, analysis functions, and perdurant calculators. These will be used in the preamble of all the part **Translate** Schemas of this section. We summarise some relevant functions and perdurant calculators.

calc_all_chn_dcls, Item 262a, 175	prgr_attr_types, Item 203, 127
calc_chn_refs, Item 261a, 175	prgr_attr_vals, Item 207, 127
calc_i_o_chn_refs, Item 260, 175	
declaring_ all_ monitorable_ variables, Item 248, 160	stat_attr_types, Item 201, 127
	stat_attr_vals, Item 205, 127
moni_attr_types, Item 202, 127	
moni_attr_vals, Item 205, 127	Translate Endurant, 176

Each **Translate** Schema requires more-or-less all of the below:

264 UI, unique identifier type;

265 MT, mereology type;

266 ST, static attribute types;

267 PT, programmable attribute types;

268 IOR, input/output channel references.

value,

264. UI = type_of(uid_E(e))

265. MT = type_of(mereo_E(e))

266. ST = stat_attr_types(e),

267. PT = prgr_attr_types(e),

268. IOR = calc_i_o_chn_refs(e)

7.7.3 A Behaviour Signature Calculator

For each endurant to be translated we need collect the elements, values and types that are relevant to that endurant's behaviour signature.

---

[169] We presently leave out consideration of possible components and fluids of the part.

collect_signature: E → " UI "×" MT "×" ST "×" PT "×" IOR "
collect_signature(e) ≡
       (type_of(uid_E(e)),type_of(mereo_E(e)),
       stat_attr_types(e),prgr_attr_types(e),
       calc_i_o_chn_refs(e))

So we assume this clause to be part of each *e:E* schema, ..., below:

value
    let (" UI,MT,ST,PT,IOR ") = collect_signature(e) **in** ... **end**

The **TRANSLATE** schemas that now follow make use of `analyse_part_fluids_part` and `analyse_part_fluids_fluids` endurant analysis function prompts defined in Sect. **4.16** on page 79.

7.7.4 Atomic Schema

Let *p:P* be an atomic part. It "translates" into behaviour M_P:

—————————————— **Translate Atomic: is_atomic(e)** ——————————————

Translation Schema 3

  value
      TRANSLATE$_{Atomic}$(e) ≡
         " **value**
             M_P: UI×MT×ST → PT → IOR **Unit**
             M_P(ui,me,sv)(pv) ≡ B_P(ui,me,sv)(pv) "

The signature identifiers UI, MT, ST and PT are taken from the `collect_signature` function. They are always understood syntactically when "occurring" in, e.g., signatures. Expression B_P(ui,me,sv)(pv) stands for the *behaviour definition body* in which the names ui, me, sv, pv are chosen, freely by the domain describer and bound to the *behaviour definition head*, i.e., the left hand side of the ≡. That expression, B_P(ui,me,sv)(pv), may thus stand for quite a complex RSL/CSP clause. We elaborate on that in Sect. **7.7.10**.

7.7.5 Composite Schema

Let P be a composite sort defined in terms of endurant sub-sorts E_1, E_2, ..., E_n. Here we only need be concerned with the *translation* of p:P, translation of "siblings" follows from the sub-sort endurants e_1, e_2, ..., e_n which have been set aside. The behaviour description *translated* from p:P, is thus a behaviour description of the "root", M_P, relying on and handling the unique identifier, mereology and attributes of part *p*

—————————————— **Translate Composite: is_composite(e)** ——————————————

Translation Schema 4

    TRANSLATE$_{Composite}$: E → RSL-Text
    TRANSLATE$_{Composite}$(e) ≡
    " **value**
        M_E: UI × MT × ST → PT → IOR **Unit**

$$\mathcal{M}_E(\text{ui,me,sv})(\text{pv}) \equiv \mathcal{B}_E(\text{ui,me,sv})(\text{pv}) \text{ "}$$

Modelling Choice 10 *Composites:* The above schema mandates that the conjoin behaviour, $\mathcal{M}_E$, be defined. It does not say anything about the subsidiary elements of the composite. They are handled by the analyse_and_describe_perdurant_process, Sect. **7.12** on page 193. Why do we express the above? We do so because the schemas are just suggestions! The *domain analyser & describer* method mandates that all observed parts be described.

7.7.6 Single Sort Set Schema

––––––––––––– **Translate Single Sort Set:** `is_single_sort_set(e)` –––––––––––

Translation Schema 5

$\textsc{Translate}_{SingleSortSet}: \text{E} \rightarrow \text{RSL-Text}$
$\textsc{Translate}_{SingleSortSet}(\text{e}) \equiv$
" value
$\quad\quad \mathcal{M}_E: \text{UI} \times \text{MT} \times \text{ST} \rightarrow \text{PT} \rightarrow \text{IOR} \ \textbf{Unit}$
$\quad\quad \mathcal{M}_E(\text{ui,me,sv})(\text{pv}) \equiv \mathcal{B}_E(\text{ui,me,sv})(\text{pv}) \text{ "}$

7.7.7 Alternative Sorts Set Schema

––––––––––––– **Translate Alternative Sorts Set:** `is_alternative_sorts_set(e)` –––––––

Translation Schema 6

$\textsc{Translate}_{AlternativeSortsSet}: \text{E} \rightarrow \text{RSL-Text}$
$\textsc{Translate}_{AlternativeSortsSet}(\text{e}) \equiv$
" value
$\quad\quad \mathcal{M}_E: \text{UI} \times \text{MT} \times \text{ST} \rightarrow \text{PT} \rightarrow \text{IOR} \ \textbf{Unit}$
$\quad\quad \mathcal{M}_E(\text{ui,me,sv})(\text{pv}) \equiv \mathcal{B}_E(\text{ui,me,sv})(\text{pv}) \text{ "}$

7.7.8 Structure Schema

––––––––––––––––– **Translate Structure:** `is_structure(e)` ––––––––––––

Translation Schema 7

$\textsc{Translate}_{Structure}: \text{E} \rightarrow \text{RSL-Text}$
$\textsc{Translate}_{Structure}(\text{e}) \equiv \text{ " "}$

7.7.9 Conjoin Schemas

---------- **Translate Conjoin:** `is_conjoin(e)` ----------

Translation Schema 8

$\text{TRANSLATE}_{Conjoin}$: E → RSL-Text
$\text{TRANSLATE}_{Conjoin}(e) \equiv$
    is_part_fluids_conjoin(e) → $\text{TRANSLATE}_{Part\ Fluids\ Conjoin}(e)$,
    is_fluid_parts_conjoin(e) → $\text{TRANSLATE}_{Fluid\ Parts\ Conjoin}(e)$,
    is_part_parts_conjoin(e)   → $\text{TRANSLATE}_{Part\ Parts\ Conjoin}(e)$

7.7.9.1 The Part-Fluids Conjoin Schema

The **Part-Fluids Conjoin Schema** reveals more of the "semantics" of conjoins. A part-fluids conjoin gives rise to one behaviour: the conjoin behaviour, $\mathcal{M}_C$, with the additional programmable-like argument of the conjoin fluid. That is, in this monograph, we shall treat fluids as "passive", i.e., not having a behaviour that we define separately from that of $\mathcal{M}_C$.

---------- **Translate Part-Fluids:** `is_part_fluids_conjoin(e)` ----------

Translation Schema 9

let (_,(M1,...,Mm)) = analyse_part_fluids_fluids(e) **in**
value
    $\text{TRANSLATE}_{Part\ Fluids\ Conjoin}(e) \equiv$
      "value
        $\mathcal{M}_C$: UI×MT×ST → PT×(M1×...×Mm) → IOR **Unit**
        $\mathcal{M}_C$(ui,me,sv)(pv,cm) ≡ $\mathcal{B}_P$(ui,me,sv)(pv,cm) **" end**

7.7.9.2 The Fluid-Parts Conjoin Schema

The **Fluid-Parts Conjoin Schema** reveals more of the "semantics" of conjoins. A fluid-parts conjoin gives rise to one behaviour: the conjoin "root" behaviour, $\mathcal{M}_C$. The behaviour of the "sibling" part behaviours is defined separately – as is expressed by the analyse_and_describe_perdurant_process of Sect. **7.12** on page 193. The former, $\mathcal{M}_C$, "keeps track" of the fluid compound, cm, relating the contained fluids to the atomic "root" part. The "sibling" behaviours proceed at their own will.

---------- **Translate Fluid-Parts:** `is_fluid_parts_conjoin(e)` ----------

Translation Schema 10

let (_,CM) = analyse_fluid_parts_fluid(e) **in**
value
    $\text{TRANSLATE}_{Fluid\ Parts\ Conjoin}(e) \equiv$
      "value
        $\mathcal{M}_C$: UI×MT×ST → PT×CM IOR **Unit**
        $\mathcal{M}_C$(ui,me,sv)(pv,cm) ≡ $\mathcal{B}_P$(ui,me,sv)(pv,cm) **" end**

Modelling Choice 11 *Fluid-Parts:* The analyse_and_describe_perdurant_process, cf. Sect. **7.12** on page 193 does prescribe the schema for some arbitrarily chosen part in ps, that is, mandates that all be described – and that is why we are mentioning it here.

A Conjoin Canal Lock

Example 81 Let p be a conjoin canal lock with atom part a and fluid m. Then m is the water, a natural fluid, in the conjoin, housed in the fixed *chamber* of p. and a is the lock mechanics: two *gates* that can open and close, letting water in and out of the lock, a *paddle*, i.e., a valve by means of which water is filled or emptied, a *winding gear*, the mechanism which allows paddles to be lifted (opened) or lowered (closed). et cetera. The M_C behaviour, i.e., the overall behaviour of the canal lock, when it so decides[170]inform the M_A behaviour to operate its mechanics; it does so based on either sampling its container, m, water level, say by means of an dynamic attribute $\mathtt{attr\_Level}(m)$, or receiving appropriate messages from the M_A behaviour. The M_A behaviour, i.e., the lock mechanics, in a sense, is oblivious to the water (and the vessels), and keeps itself occupied by monitoring and controlling its various mechanisms: the *gates, paddles, winding gear,* et cetera.

7.7.9.3 The Part-Parts Conjoin Schema

The **Part-Parts Conjoin Schema** reveals more of the "semantics" of conjoins. A **part-parts** conjoin gives rise to one behaviour: the conjoin's "root" part behaviour, M_C. M_C may be expected to "keep track" of the "sibling" parts, ps – the contained parts to the conjoin part – behaviours.

──────── **Translate Part-Parts: is_part_parts_conjoin(e)** ────────

Translation Schema 11

> **value**
> > $\textsc{Translate}_{Part\ Parts\ Conjoin}(\mathsf{e}) \equiv$
> > > **" value**
> > > > $M_C\colon \mathsf{UI}{\times}\mathsf{MT}{\times}\mathsf{ST} \to \mathsf{PT} \to \mathsf{IOR}$ **Unit**
> > > > $M_C(\mathsf{ui},\mathsf{me},\mathsf{sv})(\mathsf{pv}) \equiv \mathcal{B}_P(\mathsf{ui},\mathsf{me},\mathsf{sv})(\mathsf{pv})$ **"**

The next example focuses only on signatures.

Road Transport Behaviour Signatures

Example 82 *We first decide on names of behaviours. In the translation schemas we gave schematic names to behaviours of the form M_P. We now assign mnemonic names: from part names to names of transcendentally interpreted behaviours and then we assign signatures to these behaviours.*

. . . .

269 $hub_{h_{ui}}$:
> a *there is the usual "triplet" of arguments: unique identifier, mereology and static attributes;*

────────────

[170] We do not model the vessels that travels the canals and enter and leave locks.

b then there are the programmable attributes;

c and finally there are the input/output channel references: first those allowing communication between hub and link behaviours,

d and then those allowing communication between hub and vehicle (bus and automobile) behaviours.

value
269 $\text{hub}_{h_{ui}}$:
269a h_ui:H_UI×(vuis,luis,_):H_Mer×HΩ
269b   → (HΣ×H_Traffic)
269c   → **in,out** { h_l_ch[h_ui,l_ui] | l_ui:L_UI•l_ui ∈ luis }
269d   { ba_r_ch[h_ui,v_ui] | v_ui:V_UI•v_ui∈vuis } **Unit**
269a   **pre:** vuis = $v_{ui}s$ ∧ luis = $l_{ui}s$

....

270 $\text{link}_{l_{ui}}$:
a there is the usual "triplet" of arguments: unique identifier, mereology and static attributes;

b then there are the programmable attributes;

c and finally there are the input/output channel references: first those allowing communication between hub and link behaviours,

d and then those allowing communication between link and vehicle (bus and automobile) behaviours.

value
270 $\text{link}_{l_{ui}}$:
270a l_ui:L_UI×(vuis,huis,_):L_Mer×LΩ
270b   → (LΣ×L_Traffic)
270c   → **in,out** { h_l_ch[h_ui,l_ui] | h_ui:H_UI:h_ui ∈ huis }
270d   { ba_r_ch[l_ui,v_ui] | v_ui:(B_UI|A_UI)•v_ui∈vuis } **Unit**
270a   **pre:** vuis = $v_{ui}s$ ∧ huis = $h_{ui}s$

....

271 $\text{bus\_company}_{bc_{ui}}$:
a there is here just a "doublet" of arguments: unique identifier and mereology;

b then there is the one programmable attribute;

c and finally there are the input/output channel references allowing communication between the bus company and buses.

value
271 $\text{bus\_company}_{bc_{ui}}$:
271a bc_ui:BC_UI×(_,_,buis):BC_Mer
271b   → BusTimTbl
271c   **in,out** {bc_b_ch[bc_ui,b_ui]|b_ui:B_UI•b_ui∈buis} **Unit**
271a   **pre:** buis = $b_{ui}s$ ∧ huis = $h_{ui}s$

....

272 $\text{bus}_{b_{ui}}$:
a there is here just a "doublet" of arguments: unique identifier and mereology;

b then there are the programmable attributes;

c and finally there are the input/output channel references: first the input/output allowing communication between the bus company and buses,

d and the input/output allowing communication between the bus and the hub and link behaviours.

value
272 $\text{bus}_{b_{ui}}$:
272a b_ui:B_UI×(bc_ui,_,ruis):B_Mer
272b   → (LN × BTT × BPOS)
272c   → **out** bc_b_ch[bc_ui,b_ui],
272d   {ba_r_ch[r_ui,b_ui]|r_ui:(H_UI|L_UI)•ui∈$v_{ui}s$} **Unit**
272a   **pre:** ruis = $r_{ui}s$ ∧ bc_ui ∈ $bc_{ui}s$

....

273 automobile$_{a_{ui}}$:

    a there is the usual "triplet" of arguments: unique identifier, mereology and static attributes;

    b then there is the one programmable attribute;

    c and finally there are the input/output channel references allowing communication between the automobile and the hub and link behaviours.

value

273 automobile$_{a_{ui}}$:

273a a_ui:A_UI×(_,_,ruis):A_Mer×rn:RegNo

273b   → apos:APos

273c   **in,out** {ba_r_ch[a_ui,r_ui]|r_ui:(H_UI|L_UI)•r_ui∈ruis} **Unit**

273a   **pre:** ruis = $r_{ui}s$ ∧ a_ui ∈ $a_{ui}s$ □

7.7.10 Core Behaviour

The core processes can be understood as never ending, "tail recursively defined" processes:

──────── **Core Behaviour Part e (I)** ────────

A Suggested Behaviour Definition 1

$\mathcal{B}_P$: UI×MT×ST → PT → IOT **Unit**

$\mathcal{B}_P$(ui,me,sv)(pv) ≡ **let** (me',pv') = $\mathcal{F}_P$(ui,me,sv)(pv) **in** $\mathcal{M}_P$(ui,me',sv)(pa') **end**

$\mathcal{F}_P$: UI×MT×ST → PT→ IOT → MT×PT

We present a rough sketch of $\mathcal{F}_\pi$. The $\mathcal{F}_\pi$ action non-deterministically internal choice chooses between

- either [1,2,3,4]

   ∞ [1] accepting input from

   ∞ [4] a suitable ("offering") part process,

   ∞ [2] optionally offering a reply, and

   ∞ [3] finally delivering an updated state;

- or [5,6,7,8]

   ∞ [5] finding a suitable "order" (val)

   ∞ [8] to a suitable ("inquiring") behaviour (π'),

   ∞ [6] offering that value (on channel ch[π']

   ∞ [7] and then delivering an updated state;

- or [9] doing own work resulting in an updated state.

──────── **Core Behaviour Part e (II)** ────────

A Suggested Behaviour Definition 2

    value

        $\mathcal{F}_P$: UI×MT×ST → PT → IOR → MT×PT

        $\mathcal{F}_P$(ui,me,sv)(pv) ≡

[1]   ⫿ { **let** val = ch[π'] ? **in**

[2]   (ch[π'] ! in_reply(val)(me,sv)(pv) ⊓ **skip**) ;

[3]   in_update(val)(me,sv)(pv) end | π': Π • $\pi' \in$ calc_i_o_chn_refs(p)}
[5] $\sqcap \square$ { let val = await_reply(π')(me,sv)(pv) in
[6]   ch[π'] ! val ;
[7]   out_update(val)(me,sv)(pv) end | π': Π • $\pi' \in$ calc_i_o_chn_refs(p)}
[9] $\sqcap$ (me,own_work(sv)(pv))

in_reply: VAL $\rightarrow$ ST $\rightarrow$ MT×ST $\rightarrow$ $\rightarrow$ PT $\rightarrow$ IOR $\rightarrow$ VAL
in_update: VAL $\rightarrow$ MT×ST $\rightarrow$ PT $\rightarrow$ IOR × (MT×PT)
await_reply: UI $\rightarrow$ MT×ST $\rightarrow$ PT $\rightarrow$ IOR $\rightarrow$ VAL
out_update: VAL $\rightarrow$ MT×ST $\rightarrow$ PT $\rightarrow$ IOR $\rightarrow$ MT×PT
own_work: SA $\rightarrow$ MT×PT $\rightarrow$ IOR $\rightarrow$ MT×PT

We leave these auxiliary functions and VAL undefined.

The in_reply, in_update, await_reply, out_update and own_work functions contain references to static and programmable attributes values by stating their names: sv and pv; and to monitorable attribute, A_m, values by stating attr_A(*part*[*ui*]). Updates. v, to biddable attributes, A_b, are expressed as **update**(A,v,*part*[*ui*]).

Automobile Behaviour

Example 83 We define the behaviours in a different order than the treatment of their signatures. We "split" definition of the automobile behaviour into the behaviour of automobiles when positioned at a hub, and into the behaviour automobiles when positioned at on a link. In both cases the behaviours include the "idling" of the automobile, i.e., its "not moving", standing still.

274 We abstract automobile behaviour at a Hub (hui).
275 The vehicle remains at that hub, "idling",
276 informing the hub behaviour,
277 or, internally non-deterministically,
    a moves onto a link, tli, whose "next" hub, identified by th_ui, is obtained from the mereology of the link identified by tl_ui;
    b informs the hub it is leaving and the link it is entering of its initial link position,
    c whereupon the vehicle resumes the vehicle behaviour positioned at the very beginning (0) of that link,
278 or, again internally non-deterministically,
279 the vehicle "disappears — off the radar" !

```
274  automobile_{a_{ui}}(a_ui,({},(ruis,vuis),{}),rn)
274        (apos:atH(fl_ui,h_ui,tl_ui)) ≡
275   (ba_r_ch[a_ui,h_ui] ! (record_TIME(),atH(fl_ui,h_ui,tl_ui));
276    automobile_{a_{ui}}(a_ui,({},(ruis,vuis),{}),rn)(apos))
277  ⊓
277a  (let ({fh_ui,th_ui},ruis')=mereo_L(℘(tl_ui)) in
277a      assert: fh_ui=h_ui ∧ ruis=ruis'
274   let onl = (tl_ui,h_ui,0,th_ui) in
277b  (ba_r_ch[a_ui,h_ui] ! (record_TIME(),onL(onl)) ||
277b   ba_r_ch[a_ui,tl_ui] ! (record_TIME(),onL(onl))) ;
277c   automobile_{a_{ui}}(a_ui,({},(ruis,vuis),{}),rn)
277c      (onL(onl)) end end)
278  ⊓
279    stop
```

You may skip Example 84 in a first reading.

Further Behaviours of a Road Transport System

Example 84 **Automobile Behaviour (on a link)** ....

280 We abstract automobile behaviour on a Link.
  a Internally non-deterministically, either
      i the automobile remains, "idling", i.e., not moving, on the link,
      ii however, first informing the link of its position,
  b or
      i **if** if the automobile's position on the link *has not yet reached the hub*, **then**
        1 then the automobile moves an arbitrary small, positive **Real**-valued *increment* along the link
        2 informing the hub of this,
        3 while resuming being an automobile ate the new position, or
      ii **else**,
        1 while obtaining a "next link" from the mereology of the hub (where that next link could very well be the same as the link the vehicle is about to leave),
        2 the vehicle informs both the link and the imminent hub that it is now at that hub, identified by th_ui,
        3 whereupon the vehicle resumes the vehicle behaviour positioned at that hub;
  c or
  d the vehicle "disappears — off the radar" !

```
280   automobile_{a_{ui}}(a_ui,(({},ruis,{}),rno)
280                (vp:onL(fh_ui,l_ui,f,th_ui)) ≡
280(a)ii  (ba_r_ch[thui,aui]!atH(lui,thui,nxt_lui) ;
280(a)i   automobile_{a_{ui}}(a_ui,(({},ruis,{}),rno)(vp))
280b   ⊓
280(b)i  (if not_yet_at_hub(f)
280(b)i     then
280(b)i1      (let incr = increment(f) in
274            let onl = (tl_ui,h_ui,incr,th_ui) in
280(b)i2        ba−r_ch[l_ui,a_ui] ! onL(onl) ;
280(b)i3        automobile_{a_{ui}}(a_ui,(({},ruis,{}),rno)
280(b)i3              (onL(onl))
280(b)i      end end)
280(b)ii     else
280(b)ii1     (let nxt_lui:L_UI•nxt_lui ∈ mereo_H(℘(th_ui)) in
280(b)ii2      ba_r_ch[thui,aui]!atH(l_ui,th_ui,nxt_lui) ;
280(b)ii3      automobile_{a_{ui}}(a_ui,(({},ruis,{}),rno)
280(b)ii3            (atH(l_ui,th_ui,nxt_lui)) end)
280(b)i    end)
280c   ⊓
280d     stop
280(b)i1  increment: Fract → Fract
```

Hub Behaviour .... We model the hub behaviour vis-a-vis vehicles: buses and automobiles.

281 The hub behaviour
  a non-deterministically, externally offers
  b to accept timed vehicle positions —
  c which will be at the hub, from some vehicle, v_ui.
  d The timed vehicle hub position is appended to the front of that vehicle's entry in the hub's traffic table;
  e whereupon the hub proceeds as a hub behaviour with the updated hub traffic table.
  f The hub behaviour offers to accept from any vehicle.

g A **post** condition expresses what is really a **proof obligation**: that the hub traffic, ht′ satisfies the **axiom** of the endurant hub traffic attribute Item 188 Pg. 124.

value
281   $\text{hub}_{h_{ui}}$(h_ui,(,(luis,vuis)),hω)(hσ,ht) ≡
281a   ⫴
281b   { **let** m = ba_r_ch[h_ui,v_ui] ? **in**
281c   **assert:** m=(_,atHub(_,h_ui,_))
281d   **let** ht′ = ht † [h_ui ↦ ⟨m⟩⌢ht(h_ui)] **in**
281e $\text{hub}_{h_{ui}}$(h_ui,(,(luis,vuis)),(hω))(hσ,ht′)
281f | v_ui:V_UI•v_ui∈vuis **end end** }
281g   **post:** ∀ v_ui:V_UI•v_ui ∈ **dom** ht′⇒time_ordered(ht′ (v_ui))

Link Behaviour ....

282   The link behaviour non-deterministically, externally offers
283   to accept timed vehicle positions —
284   which will be on the link, from some vehicle, v_ui.
285   The timed vehicle link position is appended to the front of that vehicle's entry in the link's traffic table;
286   whereupon the link proceeds as a link behaviour with the updated link traffic table.
287   The link behaviour offers to accept from any vehicle.
288   A **post** condition expresses what is really a **proof obligation**: that the link traffic, lt′ satisfies the **axiom** of the endurant link traffic attribute Item 192 Pg. 125.

282   $\text{link}_{l_{ui}}$(l_ui,(_,(huis,vuis),_),lω)(lσ,lt) ≡
282   ⫴
283   { **let** m = ba_r_ch[l_ui,v_ui] ? **in**
284   **assert:** m=(_,onLink(_,l_ui,_,_))
285   **let** lt′ = lt † [l_ui ↦ ⟨m⟩⌢lt(l_ui)] **in**
286          $\text{link}_{l_{ui}}$(l_ui,(huis,vuis),hω)(hσ,lt′)
287 | v_ui:V_UI•v_ui∈vuis **end end** }
288   **post:** ∀ v_ui:V_UI•v_ui ∈ **dom** lt′⇒time_ordered(lt′ (v_ui))

Bus Company Behaviour ....
   We model bus companies very rudimentarily. Bus companies keep a fleet of buses. Bus companies create, maintain, distribute bus time tables. Bus companies deploy their buses to honor obligations of their bus time tables. We shall basically only model the distribution of bus time tables to buses. We shall not cover other aspects of bus company management, etc.

289   Bus companies non-deterministically, internally, chooses among
      a updating their bus time tables
      b whereupon they resume being bus companies, albeit with a new bus time table;
290   "interleaved" with
      a offering the current time-stamped bus time table to buses which offer willingness to received them
      b whereupon they resume being bus companies with unchanged bus time table.

271   $\text{bus\_company}_{bc_{ui}}$(bcui,(_,buis,_))(btt) ≡
289a   (**let** btt′ = update(btt,...) **in**
289b $\text{bus\_company}_{bc_{ui}}$(bcui,(_,buis,_))(btt′) **end**)
290   ⨅
290a   (⫴ {bc_b_ch[bc_ui,b_ui] ! btt | b_ui:B_UI•b_ui∈buis
290b $\text{bus\_company}_{bc_{ui}}$(bcui,(_,buis,_))(**record_TIME**(),btt) })

We model the interface between buses and their owning companies — as well as the interface between buses and the road net, the latter by almost "carbon-copying" all elements of the automobile behaviour(s).

291   The bus behaviour chooses to either
      a accept a (latest) time-stamped buss time table from its bus company –
      b where after it resumes being the bus behaviour now with the updated bus time table.
292   or, non-deterministically, internally,
      a based on the bus position
           i if it is at a hub then it behaves as prescribed in the case of automobiles at a hub,
           ii else, it is on a link, and then it behaves as prescribed in the case of automobiles on a link.

```
291   bus_{b_{ui}}(b_ui,(_,(bc_ui,ruis),_))(ln,btt,bpos) ≡
291a     (let btt' = b_bc_ch[b_ui,bc_ui] ? in
291b      bus_{b_{ui}}(b_ui,({},(bc_ui,ruis),{}))(ln,btt',bpos) end)
292   ⊓
292a     (case bpos of
292(a)i      atH(fl_ui,h_ui,tl_ui) →
292(a)i        atH_bus_{b_{ui}}(b_ui,(_,(bc_ui,ruis),_))(ln,btt,bpos),
292(a)ii     aonL(fh_ui,l_ui,f,th_ui) →
292(a)ii       onL_bus_{b_{ui}}(b_ui,(_,(bc_ui,ruis),_))(ln,btt,bpos)
292a     end)
```

Bus Behaviour at a Hub ....

The $atH\_bus_{b_{ui}}$ behaviour definition is a simple transcription of the $automobile_{a_{ui}}$ (atH) behaviour definition: mereology expressions being changed from to , programmed attributes being changed from atH(fl_ui,h_ui,tl_ui) to (ln,btt,atH(fl_ui,h_ui,tl_ui)), channel references a_ui being replaced by b_ui, and behaviour invocations renamed from $automobile_{a_{ui}}$ to $bus_{b_{ui}}$. So formula lines 275–280d below presents "nothing new"!

```
292(a)i  atH_bus_{b_{ui}}(b_ui,(_,(bc_ui,ruis),_))
292(a)i          (ln,btt,atH(fl_ui,h_ui,tl_ui)) ≡
275      (ba_r_ch[b_ui,h_ui] ! (record_TIME(),atH(fl_ui,h_ui,tl_ui));
276      bus_{b_{ui}}(b_ui,({},(bc_ui,ruis),{}))(ln,btt,bpos))
291a     ⊓
277a     (let ({fh_ui,th_ui},ruis')=mereo_L(℘(tl_ui)) in
277a          assert: fh_ui=h_ui ∧ ruis=ruis'
274      let onl = (tl_ui,h_ui,0,th_ui) in
277b      (ba_r_ch[b_ui,h_ui] ! (record_TIME(),onL(onl)) ||
277b       ba_r_ch[b_ui,tl_ui] ! (record_TIME(),onL(onl))) ;
277c     bus_{b_{ui}}(b_ui,({},(bc_ui,ruis),{}))
277c          (ln,btt,onL(onl)) end end )
280c     ⊓
280d     stop
```

Bus Behaviour on a Link ....

The $onL\_bus_{b_{ui}}$ behaviour definition is a similar simple transcription of the $automobile_{a_{ui}}$ (onL) behaviour definition. So formula lines 275–280d below presents "nothing new"!

```
293  – this is the "almost last formula line"!
```

```
292(a)ii  onL_bus_{b_{ui}}(b_ui,(_,(bc_ui,ruis), ))
292(a)ii          (ln,btt,bpos:onL(fh_ui,l_ui,f,th_ui)) ≡
275       (ba_r_ch[b_ui,h_ui] ! (record_TIME(),bpos);
276       bus_{b_{ui}}(b_ui,({},(bc_ui,ruis),{}))(ln,btt,bpos))
291a      ⊓
280(b)i       (if not_yet_at_hub(f)
280(b)i       then
280(b)i1         (let incr = increment(f) in
274             let onl = (tl_ui,h_ui,incr,th_ui) in
280(b)i2        ba_r_ch[l_ui,b_ui] ! onL(onl) ;
280(b)i3        bus_{b_{ui}}(b_ui,({},(bc_ui,ruis),{}))
280(b)i3            (ln,btt,onL(onl))
280(b)i         end end)
280(b)ii      else
280(b)ii1        (let nl_ui:L_UI•nxt_lui∈mereo_H(℘(th_ui)) in
280(b)ii2        ba_r_ch[thui,b_ui]!atH(l_ui,th_ui,nxt_lui) ;
280(b)ii3        bus_{b_{ui}}(b_ui,({},(bc_ui,ruis),{}))
280(b)ii3            (ln,btt,atH(l_ui,h_ui,nxt_lui))
280(b)ii1        end)end)
280c      ⊓
280d          stop
```

7.8 System Initialisation

It is one thing to define the behaviours corresponding to all parts, whether composite or atomic. It is another thing to specify an initial configuration of behaviours, that is, those behaviours which "start" the overall system behaviour. The choice as to which parts, i.e., behaviours, are to represent an initial, i.e., a start system behaviour, cannot be "formalised", it really depends on the "deeper purpose" of the system. In other words: requires careful analysis and is beyond the scope of the present monograph.

We sketch a general system initialisation function. It reflects the decision to transcendentally deduce all parts into behaviours.

value
    initialise_system: $\text{Unit} \rightarrow \text{Unit}$
    initialise_system() $\equiv$
        let ps = calc_parts({uod})({}) **in**
        || { **let** ui = uid_P(p), me = mereo_P(p),
              sv = static_values(p), pv = programmable_values(p) **in**
              $\mathcal{B}_P$(ui,me,sv)(pv) | p:E · p $\in$ ps
              end }
        end

Here index $_P$ has the P be type_name(p).

Initial System

Example 85   **Initial States:** We recall the *hub, link, bus company, bus* and the *automobile states* outlined in Sect. 4.19 on page 91.
value
127   *hs*:H-**set** $\equiv \equiv$ obs_sH(obs_SH(obs_RN(*rts*)))
128   *ls*:L-**set** $\equiv \equiv$ obs_sL(obs_SL(obs_RN(*rts*)))
130   *bcs*:BC-**set** $\equiv$ obs_BCs(obs_SBC(obs_FV(obs_RN(*rts*))))
131   *bs*:B-**set** $\equiv \cup$\{obs_Bs(bc)|bc:BC·bc $\in$ *bcs*\}
132   *as*:A-**set** $\equiv$ obs_BCs(obs_SBC(obs_FV(obs_RN(*rts*))))

Starting Initial Behaviours: We are reaching the end of this domain modelling example. Behind us there are narratives and formalisations Item 96 Pg. 83– Item 279 Pg. 184. Based on these we now express the signature and the body of the definition of a *"system build and execute"* function.

294   The system to be initialised is
    a the parallel compositions (||) of
    b the distributed parallel composition (||{...|...}) of all the hub behaviours,
    c the distributed parallel composition (||{...|...}) of all the link behaviours,
    d the distributed parallel composition (||{...|...}) of all the bus company behaviours,
    e the distributed parallel composition (||{...|...}) of all the bus behaviours, and
    f the distributed parallel composition (||{...|...}) of all the automobile behaviours.

value
294   initial_system: $\text{Unit} \rightarrow \text{Unit}$
294   initial_system() $\equiv$
294b || { hub$_{h_{ui}}$(h_ui,me,hω)(htrf,hσ)
294b | h:H·h $\in$ *hs*, h_ui:H_UI·h_ui=uid_H(h), me:HMetL·me=mereo_H(h),
294b   htrf:H_Traffic·htrf=attr_H_Traffic_H(h),
294b   hω:HΩ·hω=attr_HΩ(h), hσ:HΣ·hσ=attr_HΣ(h)$\wedge$h$\sigma \in$ hω }
294a ||
294c || { link$_{l_{ui}}$(l_ui,me,lω)(ltrf,lσ)
294c   l:L·l $\in$ *ls*, l_ui:L_UI·l_ui=uid_L(l), me:LMet·me=mereo_L(l),
294c   ltrf:L_Traffic·ltrf=attr_L_Traffic_H(l),
294c   lω:LΩ·lω=attr_LΩ(l), lσ:LΣ·lσ=attr_LΣ(l)$\wedge$l$\sigma \in$ lω }
294a ||

```
294d    || { bus_company_{bc_{ui}}(bcui,me)(btt)
294d         bc:BC•bc ∈ bcs, bc_ui:BC_UI•bc_ui=uid_BC(bc), me:BCMet•me=mereo_BC(bc),
294d         btt:BusTimTbl•btt=attr_BusTimTbl(bc) }
294a    ||
294e    || { bus_{b_{ui}}(b_ui,me)(ln,btt,bpos)
294e         b:B•b ∈ bs, b_ui:B_UI•b_ui=uid_B(b), me:BMet•me=mereo_B(b), ln:LN:pln=attr_LN(b),
294e         btt:BusTimTbl•btt=attr_BusTimTbl(b), bpos:BPos•bpos=attr_BPos(b) }
294a    ||
294f    || { automobile_{a_{ui}}(a_ui,me,rn)(apos)
294f         a:A•a ∈ as, a_ui:A_UI•a_ui=uid_A(a), me:AMet•me=mereo_A(a),
294f         rn:RegNo•rno=attr_RegNo(a), apos:APos•apos=attr_APos(a) }    □
```

7.9 Concurrency: Communication and Synchronisation

Translation Schemas 4, 9–11 reveal that two or more parts, which temporally coexist (i.e., at the same time), imply a notion of *concurrency*. Translation Schema 2 on page 183, through the RSL/CSP language expressions ch ! v and ch ?, indicates the notions of *communication* and *synchronisation*. Other than this we shall not cover these crucial notion related to *parallelism*.

7.10 Discrete Actions

In the extensive *Road Transport System* behaviour definitions, that is, in the *Automobile Behaviour at a Hub* Example 83 on page 184, the *Further Behaviours of a Road Transport* (Appendix) Example 84 on page 185 and the *Initial System* example, Example 85 on page 188, we have already "taken the lid off" the subject of *action analysis & description*, that is, unsystematically "revealed" aspects of *action analysis & description*. In this section we shall present a more systematic approach. We cannot do that for the full category of manifest domains such as we have defined domains. But we can single out a a sub-category of *conjoin systems*.

7.10.1 Conjoin Actions

The pragmatics of conjoins include (i) for single fluid conjoins, the transport, along the atomic part of the fluid, in one or both directions; (ii) for multiple, i.e., more than one fluid conjoins, the treatment of one or more of these fluids, mixing, heating, "cleaning", or other; as well as possibly also the transport of one or more of these fluids to or from a conjoin, from or to "an outside", and between conjoins.

Caveat: There is, however, a **problem !** The problem is that the domain phenomena that we really wish to model are not discrete in time, but continuous over time, and that we have no other means of modelling these phenomena that using good old-fashioned mathematical analysis, that is, *partial differential equations* as our analysis & description tool. Why is that a problem? It is a problem because we really have no "integrated" means of mixing the discrete mathematics-based notations – as here expressed in RSL – with that of classical mathematics' partial differential equations, PDE, while making sure that the whole thing, the two notations, RSL and PDE, together makes sense, i.e., have a meaning. Research has gone on for now almost 30 years when this is written, but no real progress has been made. The discrete formal specification language research community, i.e., those of languages like, for example, VDM-SL, Z, RAISE, B, The B Method, et cetera, are naturally "steeped" in proof concerns where were and are not foremost in the minds of the PDE community. We refer to [12] for research papers on so-called *"integrated formal methods"* ∎

So, not choosing a problematic "mixture" of RSL and PDE we settle for just expressing some properties of actions on conjoin net parts. These are actions, to repeat, on parts but they involve fluids and, although they are part actions they have consequences for "their fluids".

To express these operations we associate with conjoins just five simple operations: **supply**, **pump**, **set valve**, **treat** and **dispose**, These operations are operations "performed" by the part element of a conjoin, but they have more-or-less direct influence on the attributes of one or more of the fluid elements of a conjoin. There are no operations on **forks, joins** and **pipes** – what flows into these units flow out: is distributed, is collected and is just plainly forwarded. We shall therefore suggest an algebra of discrete operations. The inspiration for this algebra is derived from *Yuri Gurevitch*'s concept of **evolving algebras**, also now referred to as **abstract state machines**. We refer to [200, 109, 201, 110, 102, 109, 202, 101, 103, 110, 346]. We refer to the operations that we shall suggest as discrete. That is, we shall not here consider these operations as "taking time". We invite the reader to consider a temporal logic for domains while referring to [404, The Duration Calculus] and [275, Temporal Logic of Actions].

The conjoin operation make use of analyse_part_fluids_part and analyse_part_fluids_fluids endurant analysis function prompts defined in Sect. **4.16** on page 79.

7.10.1.1 Discrete Supply of Fluid to Conjoins

A volume or weight amount of an appropriate substance is to be added to fluid m of endurant e.

Conjoin Operation 1

―――――――――――――――― **Supply** ――――――――――

> let p:P = analyse_part_fluids_part(e), (m:M) = analyse_part_fluids_fluids(e) **in**
> ✢ m' := **supply** m **with** $x(m^3|kg)$ **of** attr_Substance(m)
> **end**

The **Supply Schema** is to be understood as follows: A conjoin e, a volume or weight amount, x, and the fluid m of e is indicated. A specified amount, x, of fluid is now added to that of m of e to become the new value, m', for that substance of e. Typically e would be a **supply** unit of the fluid network, cf. Fig. 5.2 on page 118.

7.10.1.2 Discrete Disposal of Fluid from Conjoins

A volume or weight amount, x, of an appropriate substance is to be removed, i.e., disposed, from fluid m_i of endurant e.

Conjoin Operation 2

_____ **Disposal** _____

＋ let p:P = analyse_part_fluids_part(e), (m:M) = analyse_part_fluids_fluids(e) **in**
    m′ := **dispose** $x(m^3|kg)$ **from** m
    end

The **Disposal Schema** is to be understood as follows: A conjoin e, a volume or weight amount, x, of the fluid m of e is indicated. Somehow that amount of fluid is to be removed from that of m of e to become the new value, m′, for that substance of e.

7.10.1.3 Discrete Pumping of Fluid from Conjoins

We shall leave the interpretation of the following schemas, as a challenge, to the reader.

Conjoin Operation 3

_____ **Pump** _____

    let p:P = analyse_part_fluids_part(e),
        (m:M) = analyse_part_fluids_fluids(e) **in**
    let (b,a) = before_after_conjoins(p)(), f = pumping_capacity(p) **in**
    let p_b:PB = analyse_part_fluids_part(b),
        (m_b:MB) = analyse_part_fluids_fluids(b),
        p_a:PA = analyse_part_fluids_part(a),
        (m_a:MA) = analyse_part_fluids_fluids(a) **in**
＋ m_a′ := m_a ⊖ f(m_a); m_b′ := m_b ⊕f(m_a)
    end end end

7.10.1.4 Discrete Opening/Closing of Fluid Transport by Valves

A valve is to be set at a fraction f of "flow-put" where $0 \le f \le 1$.

Conjoin Operation 4

_____ **Valve** _____

    let p:P = analyse_part_fluids_part(e),
        (m:_) = analyse_part_fluids_fluids(e) **in**
＋ m′ := **set valve opening at** f **for fluid** m
    end

7.10.1.5 Discrete Treatment of Fluids of a Conjoin

Conjoin Operation 5

_____ **Treatment** _____

    let p:P = analyse_part_fluids_part(e),

$(m_1, m_2, ... m_m) =$ analyse_part_fluids_fluids(e) **in axiom** $m \geq 1$

✛ $m'_1 :=$ **treat with** a_1/b **of** m_1, c_1/d **of** m_2, ..., e_1/f **of** m_m **with operation** o_1,

✛ $m'_2 :=$ **treat with** a_2/b **of** m_2, c_2/d **of** m_2, ..., e_2/f **of** m_m **with operation** o_2 ,

✛ ...

✛ $m'_m :=$ **treat with** a_m/b **of** m_1, c_m/d **of** m_2, ..., e_m/f **of** m_m **with operation** o_m

axiom $\forall\ i{:}\textbf{Nat} \cdot 1 \leq i \leq m \Rightarrow a_i \leq b \wedge c_i \leq d \wedge ... \wedge e_i \leq f \wedge$
$$\wedge\ \forall\ (x_i, y){:}\{(a_i, b), (c_i, d), ..., (e_i, f)\} \cdot x_1 + x_2 + ... + x_m = y$$

end

If, for some i, m'_i is to have no contribution from some m_j then $x_j/y = 0$, i.e., $x_j = 0$.

The **Treatment Schema** is to be understood as follows: There are up to m 'assignments'. They are to be understood as an equation system. The [to the] right [of :=] m_is all have fixed, initial values. The [to the] left [of :=] m'_i denote a final value. By value we mean that either, for all entries of an 'assignment/equation', we speak **of** Volume, or we speak **of** Weight. Et cetera!

•••

You may think of the above ✛s to single out the actual operations on conjoin parts. The schema text surrounding these ✛ lines serve to identify the quantities involved in the operations. So the conjoin part actions are, in a sense, loosely described. We refer to Exercise 30 on page 202.

•••

This section ends a series of discourses on conjoins. We refer to Sect. **4.17.3** on page 87, Example 37 on page 88, Sect. **5.3.7** on page 118 and Sect. **5.4.9** on page 137. This last "installment" has been but a sketch. We refer to Sect. **8.4** on page 214 on *Rules & Regulations*, Sect. **8.5** on page 217 on *Scripts* and Sect. **8.6** on page 220 on *License Languages*, Pages 214–229, for a continuation of the subject.

7.11 Discrete Events

To clear any possible misunderstanding there are two kinds of events. There are the domain events that we shall analyse & describe; and there are the events of the domain description. The latter are exemplified by CSP's out/input clauses: ch[..]!e (offer value of expression e on channel ch[..]), and ch[..]? (accept value offered on channel ch[..]). We shall use the latter to model the former!

By *domain event* we shall understand a change of domain state for which we do, or cannot, point out a known domain behaviour to be the cause of that event.

Domain Events

Example 86 We informally sketch some domain events. (i) An automobile suddenly skidding off a link or hub, thus, in sense, "disappearing" from the road net, rendering the transport domain in **chaos** – if we are not prepared to model the recovery, as is done in the domain, from such calamities. (ii) A pipeline unit suddenly bursting, i.e., exploding, thus, in a sense, rendering the pipeline in **chaos** – if we are not prepared to model the recovery, as is done in the domain, from such calamities.

We suggest to model domain events as follows. Let

$\mathcal{B}_P$: UI×MT×ST → PT → IOT **Unit**

$\mathcal{B}_P$(ui,me,sv)(pv) ≡ **let** (me′,pv′) = $\mathcal{F}_P$(ui,me,sv)(pv) **in** $\mathcal{M}_P$(ui,me′,sv)(pv′) **end**

be the body of a behaviour definition. Domain events that can be, say approximately, identified as taking place in a resumption of $\mathcal{M}_P$(ui,me′,sv)(pa') can then be expressed in a changed definition of $\mathcal{B}_P$:

value

    $\mathcal{B}_P$: UI×MT×ST → PT → IOT **Unit**

    $\mathcal{B}_P$(ui,me,sv)(pv) ≡

(1.)   **let** (me′,pv′) = $\mathcal{F}_P$(ui,me,sv)(pv) **in**

(2.)   **either:** **chaos**

(3.)   **or:**   **let** (me″,sv′,pv″) = handle_event$_P$(me′,sv,pv′) **in** $\mathcal{M}_P$(ui,me″,sv′)(pv″) **end**

(4.)   ⊓ $\mathcal{M}_P$(ui,me′,sv)(pv′) **end**

    handle_event: MT × ST × PT → MT × ST × PT

We informally explain: (1.) is as for the "un-event" version of $\mathcal{B}_P$. Then modelling the occurrence of possibly not-occurring events means that the behaviour non-deterministically, line (4.), chooses the (2.-3.) model or the (4.) model. (2.) **either** the domain analyser & describer chooses to not handle event handle_event$_P$, and specifies **chaos**; (3.) **or** the domain analyser & describer chooses to model some handling of the event – before resuming $\mathcal{M}_P$. (4.) In this model no event has been "detected" – and life proceeds as normal.

    Similar domain events occurring "during" $\mathcal{F}_P$ can be handled likewise.

7.12 A Domain Discovery Process, III

The predecessors of this section are Sects. **4.20** on page 93 and **5.8** on page 146.

    We shall yet again emphasize some aspects of the *domain analyser & describer* method. A **method principle** is that of *exhaustively analyse & describe* all external qualities of the domain under scrutiny. A **method technique** implied here is that sketched below. The **method tools** are here all the analysis and description prompts covered so far.

7.12.1 Review of the Endurant Analysis and Description Process

The endurant analysis & description process is defined in Sect. **5.8** on page 146.

value

    endurant_analysis_and_description: **Unit** → **Unit**

    endurant_analysis_and_description() ≡

        discover_sorts();

        discover_uids();

        discover_mereologies();

        discover_attributes()

We are now to define a perdurant_analysis_and_description procedure – to follow the above endurant_analysis_and_description procedure.

7.12.2 A Perdurant Analysis and Description Process

We define the perdurant_analysis_and_description procedure in the reverse order of that of Sect. **5.8** on page 146, first the full procedure, then its sub-procedures.

_____ A Domain Endurant Analysis and Description Process _____

```
value
    perdurant_analysis_and_description: Unit → Unit
    perdurant_analysis_and_description() ≡
            discover_state(); axiom [ Note (a) ]
            discover_channels(); axiom [ Note (b) ]
            discover_behaviour_signatures(); axiom [ Note (c) ]
            discover_behaviour_definitions(); axiom [ Note (d) ]
            discover_initial_system() axiom [ Note (e) ]
```

Note **(a) The State:** The state variable parts maps unique identifiers of every part into that part. We might, perhaps should, modify "that part" into a quantity to which monitorable attribute value inquiries, attr_A, apply; and nothing more, that is, "parts" devoid themselves of unique identifiers, mereology, and static and programmable attributes. We refrain from doing so here.

Note **(b) The Channels:** We refer to Sect. **7.5.2** on page 170. Thus we indiscriminately declare a channel for each pair of distinct unique part identifiers whether the corresponding pair of part behaviours, if at all invoked, communicate or not.

Note **(c) Discrete Behaviour Signatures** and **Definitions:** In Sect. **7.7** on page 176 Translation Schemas 3–11 "lump" expression of behaviour *signature* and *definition* into one RSL-Text. Here we separate the two. The reason is one of pragmatics. We find it more productive to first settle on the signatures of all behaviours before tackling the far more time-consuming work on defining the behaviours.

Note **(d) The Running System:** We refer to Sect. **7.8** on page 188.

7.12.2.1 The **discover_state** Procedure

We model the state of all parts as a globally declared **variable** parts, which is modelled as a map from the unique identifiers of parts to their [initial] value, that is, parts(ui). We need basically only model those parts, p, which have monitorable attributes, say A, as their values, attr_A(p), need be read, that is attr_A(parts(ui)).

```
value
    discover_state: Unit → Unit
    discover_state() ≡
            for all v • v ∈ gen do
                    txt := txt † [ type_name(v)↦txt(type_name(v))⌢⟨describe_state(v)⟩ ] end

    describe_state: E → RSL-Text
    describe_state(e) ≡ " variable parts[ uid_E(e) ]:type_name(e) := e "
```

7.12.2.2 The **discover_channels** Procedure

We refer to Sects. **5.2.4** on page 110 and **7.5.2** on page 170.

```
value
```

discover_channels: **Unit** → **Unit**
discover_channels() ≡
      let ch_txt = " **channel** {ch[{ij,ik}]|ij,ik:UI·ij≠ik∧{ij,ik}⊆all_uniq_ids()}:M " **in**
      txt := txt † [type_name(uod)↦⟨ch_txt⟩⌢txt(type_name(uod))]
      end

7.12.2.3 Generate Representative Parts

The domain state, gen, consists of all domain parts. For the discovery of behaviour signatures and definitions it suffices to have exactly one part of each distinct type. Let us refer to the such of such distinct type parts uniq_type_gen:

value
    uniq_type_gen = { p | p ∈ gen, typ_nam(p) ∈ {typ_nam(p)|p ∈ gen} }

7.12.2.4 The **discover_signatures** Procedure

We refer to Sect. **7.7** on page 176.

value
    discover_behaviour_signatures: **Unit** → **Unit**
    discover_behaviour_signatures() ≡
        for all v · v ∈ uniq_type_gen **do**
            let signature =
                is_atomic(v) → ⟨" $\mathcal{M}_P$: UI×MT×ST → PT → IOR **Unit** "⟩,
                is_composite(v) → ⟨" $\mathcal{M}_E$: UI × MT × ST → PT → IOR **Unit** "⟩
                is_structure(v) → ⟨⟩,
                is_part_fluids_conjoin(v) →
                    ⟨" $\mathcal{M}_C$: UI×MT×ST → PT×(M1×M2×...×Mm) → IOR **Unit** "⟩
                is_fluid_parts_conjoin(v) → ⟨" $\mathcal{M}_C$: UI×MT×ST → PT×CM IOR **Unit** "⟩
                is_part_parts_conjoin(v) → ⟨" $\mathcal{M}_C$: UI×MT×ST → PT → IOR **Unit** "⟩ **in**
            txt := txt † [type_name(v)↦txt(type_name(v))⌢ signature]
        end end

7.12.2.5 The **discover_behaviour_definitions** Procedure

We refer to Sect. **7.7** on page 176.

value
    discover_behaviour_definitions: **Unit** → **Unit**
    discover_behaviour_definitions() ≡
        for all v · v ∈ uniq_type_gen **do**
            let definition =
                is_atomic(v) → ⟨" $\mathcal{M}_P$(ui,me,sv)(pv) ≡ $\mathcal{B}_P$(ui,me,sv)(pv) "⟩,
                is_composite(v) → ⟨" $\mathcal{M}_E$(ui,me,sv)(pv) ≡ $\mathcal{B}_E$(ui,me,sv)(pv) "⟩
                is_structure(v) → ⟨⟩,
                is_part_fluids_conjoin(v) → ⟨" $\mathcal{M}_C$(ui,me,sv)(pv,cm) ≡ $\mathcal{B}_P$(ui,me,sv)(pv,cm) "⟩
                is_fluid_parts_conjoin(v) → ⟨" $\mathcal{M}_C$(uic,me,sv)(pv,cm) ≡ $\mathcal{B}_P$(ui,me,sv)(pv,cm) "⟩

$$\text{is\_part\_parts\_conjoin(v)} \rightarrow \langle \text{``} \mathcal{M}_C(\text{ui,me,sv})(\text{pv}) \equiv \mathcal{B}_P(\text{ui,me,sv})(\text{pv}) \text{''} \rangle \text{ in}$$
$$\text{txt} := \text{txt} \dagger [\text{type\_name(v)} \mapsto \text{txt(type\_name(v))} ^\frown \text{definition}]$$

end end

7.12.2.6 The **initialise_system** Procedure

We refer to Sect. **7.8** on page 188 (for initialise_system()).

value
  discover_initial_system: **Unit** → **Unit**
  discover_initial_system() ≡ txt := txt † [UoD ↦ txt(UoD)⌒⟨**``** initialise_system() **''**⟩]

7.13 Summary

This chapter's main title was: **DOMAINS – Towards a Dynamics Ontology**. The term 'Dynamics' pertain to actions, events and behaviours of the 'Domain', not to its 'Ontology'. So, an aspect of the ontology of a domain, such as we have studied it and such as we ordain one aspect of *domain analysis & description*, is also about the time-evolving occurrence, of actions, events and behaviours, that is, the *perdurants*. For that study & practice we have suggested a number of analysis & description prompts.

An Essence about Perdurants

Perdurants "derive", by transcendental deduction, from endurants: parts become behaviours, unique identifiers become behaviour identities, mereologies become directives for behaviour channel interactions, and attributes are elements of behaviour states: static attributes are constants, programmable attributes are [controlled] variables, and monitorable attributes are otherwise accessible, externally set, dynamically changing values.

7.13.1 Solids versus Fluids, Endurants versus Perdurants

In Chapter 4 a distinction was made between solids and fluids. Chapters 5 and 7 focused on the internal qualities of mostly solids and the transcendental deduction of solids, i.e., parts, into behaviours. In this section we "lift" the strict distinction between solids and fluids. From a pragmatic point of view we may suggest that the domain analyser cum describer treat some fluid endurants as solids!

In the referenced chapters a distinction was also made between parts and structures. Th former were then understood, in Chapters 4–5, as leading, in this chapter, to behaviours. From a pragmatic point of view we may suggest that the domain analyser cum describer treat some compound and conjoin parts as structures; that is, not leading to transcendentally deduced behaviours! That is, we may ignore possible internal qualities that we may have ascribed to these parts.

A consequence of the above is that we really only need a domain description ontology as shown in Fig. 7.6 on the facing page.

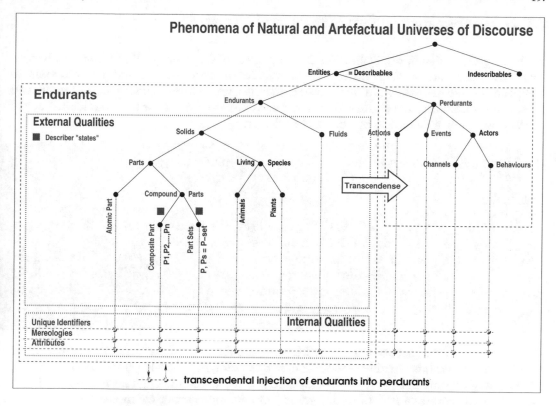

Fig. 7.6 The Essential Upper Ontology

Solid Fluids: A 7 Seas Domain

Example 87 Consider modeling a domain of waterways, vessels, land masses (continents) and harbours. Let the focus of that model be the movement of vessels. In such a model we could model elements of waterways: oceans, seas, rivers, lakes and canals, not as fluids, but a solids. If one were interested in the substance of the waterway parts then one could consider these parts having attributes such as salinity, temperature (ice formations), etc.

7.13.2 Narratives: Too Much or Too Little ?

Narratives on external qualities should be very short. Perhaps it is admissible to just mention sort/part names and their composition, otherwise relying on the readers' goodwill! The real narrative description of endurants comes with their internal qualities: mereology and attributes. And the final narrative description of some endurants comes with the description of their transcendental deduction into behaviours.

7.13.3 Two Separate Issues: Method and Design

We have given a definition, Definition 21 on page 5, of the concept of *method* involving a set of principles for selecting and applying a number of procedures, techniques and tools. In Chapters 4–7 we have shown a number of principles, procedures, techniques and tools; and these were summarised in closing 'Summary' sections, see the one for this chapter just next !.
   We now quote a definition of a concept of design.

Definition: 75 Design: A design is a plan or specification for the construction of an object or system or for the implementation of an activity or process, or the result of that plan or specification in the form of a prototype, product or process. The verb to design expresses the process of developing a design. In some cases, the direct construction of an object without an explicit prior plan (such as in craft-work, some engineering, coding, and graphic design) may also be considered to be a design activity. The design usually has to satisfy certain goals and constraints, may take into account aesthetic, functional, economic, or socio-political considerations, and is expected to interact with a certain environment. Major examples of designs include architectural blueprints, engineering drawings, business processes, circuit diagrams, and sewing patterns `https://en.m.wikipedia.org/wiki/Design` ∎

Design, in the above sense, implies either of a number of various forms of creativity. In that sense, and without further elaboration, at this point, but see Chapter 9, we can say this: domain engineering does **not** involve design, but requirements engineering and software development requires a **full lot** of design. In domain engineering we model a given world. In requirements engineering we seek to model a world as we would like to create it. In this sense domain engineering is akin to physics and requirements engineering to classical forms of engineering.

7.13.4 Method Principles, Procedures, Techniques and Tools

Recall that by a method we shall understand a *set of **principles*** for selecting and applying a *set of **techniques*** using a *set of **tools*** in order to construct an artefact.

7.13.4.1 Principles of Perdurant Analysis & Description

In this chapter we have illustrated the use of the following principles:

- **Divide & Conquer:** That concept is addressed in the sequential treatment of states, channels, behaviour signatures and behaviour definitions.
- **Operational Abstraction:** That concept is addressed in several ways: in the formulation of a notion of domain states and its modelling in terms of RSL variables; in the modelling of domain behaviour interactions in terms of CSP *channels, output* and *input*; in the capturing of one essence of domain behaviours in terms of the signature of CSP process definitions; and in the modelling of domain behaviours in terms of CSP processes.

In this chapter we have put forward some advice on **description** choices: We refer to **Modelling Choices** 10 on page 179 and 11 on page 181. The **analysis** predicates and functions are merely aids. They do not effect descriptions, but descriptions are based on the result of their inquiry. Real decisions are made when effecting a **description** function. So the rôle of these modelling choice paragraphs is to alert the describer to make judicious choices.

7.13.4.2 Procedures for Modeling Perdurants

The main procedure for modeling external qualities was presented in Sect. **7.12**.

7.13.4.3 Techniques of Perdurant Analysis & Description

In this chapter we have illustrated the use of the following techniques:

- **Modelling Behaviours as CSP Processes**: With that choice follows then the "standard" CSP techniques of tail-recursive *specification of concurrent processes/behaviours* [249, 250, 352, 357].
- **Interpretation of Internal Endurant Qualities**: As part of the translation of endurant parts to CSP processes follows the interpretation of *unique part identifiers* as constant process identifiers; part *mereologies* as determinant for CSP communication channel indices; *static* part *attributes* as constant process, "by value" arguments; *programmable* part *attributes* as such process arguments that can be given new values when tail-recursively [re-]invoked; and *monitorable* part *attributes* as "residing" in RSL declared variables, one for each part having monitorable attributes.

7.13.4.4 Tools of Perdurant Analysis & Description

In this chapter we have illustrated the use of the following tools:

⋆ Analysis Functions

• calc_all_chn_dcls	Item 262a on page 175
• calc_chn_refs	Item 261a on page 175
• calc_i_o_chn_refs	Item 260 on page 175
• moni_attr_types	Item 202 on page 126
• moni_attr_vals	Item 205 on page 127
• possible_variable_declaration	Item 249 on page 160
• prgr_attr_types	Item 203 on page 126
• prgr_attr_vals	Item 207 on page 127
• stat_attr_types	Item 201 on page 126
• stat_attr_vals	Item 205 on page 127

⋆ Description Schemas – Translations

7.13.5 The Analysis & Description Calculus Reviewed

We have completed a first, the main task of this monograph: in Chapter 4 the external analysis & description calculus; in Chapter 5 the internal analysis & description calculus;

and in Chapter 7 the transcendental deduction of endurants into perdurants. Appendix **C** summarises the four languages deployed in ***domain analysis & description***.

7.13.6 To Every Mereology a CSP Expression

The title of this final section of this chapter "sounds" like a theorem. Well, in the sense that by 'Mereology' we mean a set of parts, i.e., endurants, each with their mereology; and that by 'CSP Expression' we mean a CSP expression such as achieved by the transcendental deduction of the 'Mereology' into a set of CSP process signatures "et cetera" (!), then the display line is a theorem. This chapter has thus put forward a constructive proof of that theorem!

Whether some form of 'converse', to wit: *to every suitably expressed CSP expression a mereology*, that is, a set of parts, i.e., endurants, each with their mereology, whether that is a theorem, is a challenge we leave to the reader!

7.13.7 Object-Orientedness

Should you, the reader, get some "feeling" of *déjà vu*: *"does this not remind me of some form of object-orientedness"*? then you are not much off the mark! To this author the main works on object-orientedness are Ole-Johan Dahl et al.'s [31, Simula 67] (see also [137, 138, 139]) and Martin Abadi's and Luca Cardelli's [1, *A Theory of Objects*]. Of major object-orientedness influence to the software engineering community were the UML books [265, 108, 107, Unified Modeling Language].

Our treatment is different. First it separates object-orientedness into endurants and perdurants. Then it explains main aspects of perdurants in terms of the transcendental deduction of endurant parts into behaviours. It first focuses on endurants, their analysis into solids and fluids, natural and artefactual, atomic and composite, et cetera. Having done so, it introduces a notion of state, A state then being any set of parts – with these corresponding to objects. But these parts, i.e., objects, are further analysed with respect to: unique identifiers, mereology and attributes. All this before we introduce [object] behaviours.

We claim that our approach, founded with a basis in philosophy, clarifies many issues of UML. It separates issues of identity, mereology and attributes; it systematises issues of well-formedness (invariants, etc.); it combines narratives and formalisations of these; and it provides a "smooth path" from endurants to perdurants — from "static views" to "behavioral views". All these issues are now clearly rooted, and not just postulated.

Definition: 76 Object: So, to us, an **object**, is

- a **part**
- and its **behaviour.**

The part comes with

- its ***unique identifier***,
- a ***mereology***, and
- a variety of ***attributes***.

The ***uniquely identified*** behaviour is defined

- in the context of channels – derived from part *mereologies*,
- with formal parameters reflecting
  - ∞ *static*.
  - ∞ *monitorable* and
  - ∞ *programmable*
    attributes.

We hope the reader will appreciate this firm basis for a notion of object-orientedness!

7.13.8 Specification Structuring

The RAISE [190] Specification Language, RSL [187], as we are using it for specific domain descriptions, has so-called **scheme, class** and **object** structuring constructs. We shall illustrate, ever so briefly, the first two of these in the next chapter, cf. Sect. **8.2.1**'s Example 88 on page 207. The idea of RSL's structuring mechanism is to group related matters, such as a part endurants' external and internal qualities and its transcendentally deduced perdurant description in a suitable one or a few class definitions.

Why have we not used RSL's structuring mechanism throughout? There is one over-riding reason for this. RSL's type, expression, signature and function constructs, the main linguistic "vehicles" for domain descriptions, are all close to common, discrete mathematical notations and are all close to other "standard", formal specification language constructs, i.e., VDM etc.! Not so for RSL's (**scheme, class, object**) structuring constructs. In general, it can be claimed, that the various formal specification languages, if they do, possess rather "diverse" structuring mechanisms. So rather than 'bothering' the reader with such concerns, we do not use any such specification structuring "devices"!

7.13.9 What is Missing?

Whereas Chapters 4 and 5 focused on the analysis & description of external and internal qualities of endurants. This monograph does not contain any analysis & description of perdurants! Surely calculi for behaviours, actions and events can, should and must be developed! We are indeed sorry that we can not include such calculi. Instead we propose, see *Research Problem* 29 on the next page, that you choose that problem for a serious research study.

7.14 Exercise Problems

We suggest several classes of exercises, to wit: two or more of *research problems, student exercise* and *term projects*.

7.14.1 Research Problems

Exercise 28 A Research Challenge. Ontology Graphs: Sections **4.5.2** and **4.22.5** reviewed some ontology graphs. You are to explore this concept of ontology graph. Perhaps establish *A theory of ontology graphs* ! Hint: there is a rich, not always relevant, literature on ontologies. Note: Our ontology graphs are not tree-structured. There are two "trees", one for endurants, one for perdurants. They are held together by the horizontal internal quality "lines": unique identifiers, mereologies, attributes. That is: transcendental deduction must somehow enter a theory of ontology graphs.

Exercise 29 A Research Challenge. Analysis and Description of Behaviours, Actions and Events: We remind the reader of Sect. **7.13.9** on the preceding page. You are to reflect on the kind of thoughts that are going into the construction of the "internals" of the behaviour definitions, say of this chapter, as well as the related actions and events and their interplay. That is, you are to search for analysis and description prompts that may help systematise the "heureka" process of "constructing" the body of behaviour definitions, their actions and events.

Exercise 30 A Research Challenge. PED Specification of Flows in Oil Pipelines: We refer to Example 37 on page 88, Sect. **7.10.1** on page 189, Appendix Sect. **A**, and to Exercise 31 on the next page. This research problem addresses an open problem. You are to assume a domain of oil pipelines. In this monograph many examples and term project exercises show fragments of, respectively are intended to develop, a full domain description of *road transport systems*. Now you have in Appendix **A** a rather complete description of the endurants of an oil pipeline domain[171].

The problem to be studied, and for which we seek partial domain descriptions in some form of classical, and, perhaps, not so classical mathematics: partial differential equations[172], PDE, is the *fluid dynamics*[173] of the flow of oil in pipelines – and, for that matter, in any net of part-fluid-fluid conjoins.

- [Q1] First we ask you to set of the fluid dynamics for each kind of pipeline units: *well, pump, pipe, valve, fork, join* and *sink*.
- [Q2] Then we ask that you, as a "little, preparatory exercise", "glue" the fluid dynamics, i.e., their mathematical equations, of pairs of pipeline units:

  ∞ (*well;pump*), ∞ (*pipe;valve*), ∞ (*fork;(pipe|pipe*))[174] ∞ (*pipe;sink*).
  ∞ (*pump;pipe*), ∞ (*valve;pipe*), ∞ ((*pipe|pipe);join*)[175],
  ∞ (*pipe;pipe*), ∞ (*pipe;fork*), ∞ (*join;pipe*) and

- [Q3] Finally we ask you to consider the fluid dynamics of an entire pipeline system.[176,177] That is, for any pipeline system we seek a definite set of possibly somehow "parameterised" definite sets of Peds, or whatever mathematics it takes, to model the full dynamics of any one such pipeline system !

---

[171] – Examples 13 on page 58 [Solid Endurants], 14 on page 59 [Fluids], 30 on page 73 [Part-Fluid Conjoins: Pipelines, I] and 37 on page 88 [Pipeline Parts and Fluid] addresses this issue.

[172] – for example: Dale R. Durran, Numerical methods for wave equations in geophysical fluid dynamics, Springer Science & Business Media, New York, 1999

[173] www.sciencedirect.com/handbook/handbook-of-mathematical-fluid-dynamics

[174] – the | operator in *(pipe|pipe)* is intended to informally express that two *pipes* "emanate" a *fork*

[175] – the | operator in *(pipe|pipe)* is intended to informally express that two *pipes* "enter" a *join*

[176] Any such pipeline system has its "root" in, say, the formulas of Example 37 on page 88 and Appendix **A** where we present a rather comprehensive description of the endurants of a pipeline system.

[177] Recall that an "entire" road transport system is modelled by Examples 43 on page 111, 46 on page 114, 47 on page 115, 48 on page 115, 57 on page 124, 58 on page 124, 60 on page 124, 62 on page 133, 64 on page 136, 39 on page 92, 76 on page 160, 80 on page 170, 82 on page 181, 83 on page 184, 84 on page 185 and 85 on page 188.

- Make suitable assumptions.[178]
- [Q4] Publish the result!
- [Q5] Then start thinking about how to "blend" the PDEs into an RSL specification. What might we mean by 'blend'?[179]

7.14.2 Student Exercises

Exercise 31 A PhD Student Problem. RSL Specification of Flows in Oil Pipelines: We refer to Sect. **7.10.1** on page 189. It is now suggested that you, in turn, one-by-one, consider the following sub-problems in the context of your domain of conjugate endurants be that of an ocean, canal and harbour (basin) system with cargo liners.

- Define the external qualities of a domain of shipping lines based on the hinted waterways and vessels – and based on there being shipping lines and terminal port that own, keep track of, operate and service (load, unload) the cargo liner vessels.
- Define relevant internal qualities, one-by-one:

  ∞ unique identifiers,   ∞ mereologies and,   ∞ a small set of attributes.

- Now single one or two conjugates and cargo lines and terminal ports out for consideration as behaviours. Suggest, in turn,

  ∞ an overall state,   ∞ signatures of behaviours, and
  ∞ a set of domain model channels,   ∞ definition of behaviours.

Exercise 32 An MSc Student Exercise. Document System Actions: We refer to Exercises 3 on page 104, 16 on page 151, 17 on page 151 and 18 on page 151. We also refer to Sect. **7.10.1** on page 189. [Q1] In line with the **conjoin operation schemas**, shown in Sect. **7.10.1**, you are to provide **document operation schemas** for the operations mentioned in Exercises 3, 16, 17 and 18. We refer to Exercise 33.

Exercise 33 An MSc Student Exercise. Document System Behaviours: We assume and refer to exercise 32. You are to narrate and formalise the full set of document system perdurants: the channels, cf. Sect. **7.5** on page 169 and Example 80 on page 170 the behaviour signatures, cf. Sect. **7.6** on page 172 and Example 82 on page 181, the behaviour definitions, cf. Sect. **7.6** on page 172 and Example 82 on page 181, and the initial, i.e., the 'running' document system, i.e., the "start-up", cf. Sect. **7.8** on page 188 and Example 85 on page 188.

7.14.3 Term Projects

We continue the term projects of Sects. **4.24.3** on page 104 and **5.13.3** on page 152.

For the specific domain topic that a group is working on it is to treat, for example, in separate, typically four, consecutive weeks, these topics in the order listed:

---

[178] Examples of assumptions are that there are defined all the necessary attributes concerning pipeline units' liquid flow properties.

[179] A standard concern is that of being able to carry out either mathematical logic proofs (of properties) or conventional mathematical reasoning over 'blended', say, RSL expressed models and classic mathematical models.

- *Channels,* cf. Sect. **7.5** on page 169 and Example 80 on page 170;
- *Behaviour Signatures,* cf. Sect. **7.6** on page 172 and Example 82 on page 181;
- *Discrete Behaviour Definitions,* cf. Sect. **7.3.4** on page 162, cf. Example 84 on page 185;
- *Running Systems,* cf. Sect. **7.8** on page 188 and Example 85 on page 188.

Exercise 34 An MSc Student Exercise. The Consumer Market, Perdurants: We refer to Exercises 4 on page 105 and 20 on page 152.

Exercise 35 An MSc Student Exercise. Financial Service Industry, Perdurants: We refer to Exercises 5 on page 105 and 21 on page 152.

Exercise 36 An MSc Student Exercise. Container Line Industry, Perdurants: We refer to Exercises 6 on page 105 and 22 on page 152.

Exercise 37 An MSc Student Exercise. Railway Systems, Perdurants: We refer to Exercises 7 on page 105 and 23 on page 152.

Exercise 38 A PhD Student Problem. Part-Fluid Conjoins: Canals, Perdurants: We refer to Exercises 8 on page 105 and 24 on page 152.

Exercise 39 A PhD Student Problem. Part-Fluids Conjoins: Rum Production, Perdurants: We refer to Exercises 9 on page 105 and 25 on page 153.

Exercise 40 A PhD Student Problem. Part-Fluids Conjoins: Waste Management, Perdurants: We refer to Exercises 10 on page 105 and 26 on page 153.

These exercise problems are continued in Sects. **8.11.2** on page 240 and **9.9.2** on page 297.

Chapter 8
DOMAIN FACETS

*In this chapter we introduce the concept of **domain facets**. We cover the following facets: **intrinsics, support technologies, rules and regulations, scripts, license languages, management & organisation** and **human behaviour**.*

In Chapters 4–7 we outlined a *method* for analysing & and describing domains. In this chapter we cover some domain analysis & description principles and techniques not covered in Chapters 4–7. Those chapters focused on *manifest domains*. Here we, on one side, go "outside" the realm of *manifest domains*, and, on the other side, cover what we shall refer to as, *facets* not covered in Chapters 4–7.

8.1 Introduction

We introduce the concept of facets, put it in context and survey the chapter.

8.1.1 Facets of Domains

By a **domain facet** we shall understand *one amongst a finite set of generic ways of analysing a domain: a view of the domain, such that the different facets cover conceptually different views, and such that these views together cover the domain* ▪ Now, the definition of what a *domain facet* is can seem vague. It cannot be otherwise. The definition is sharpened by the definitions of the specific facets. You can say that the definition of *domain facet* is the "sum" of the definitions of these specific facets. The specific facets – so far[180] – are:

- *intrinsics* (Sect. **8.2**),
- *support technology* (Sect. **8.3**),
- *rules & regulations* (Sect. **8.4**),
- *scripts* (Sect. **8.5**),
- *license languages* (Sect. **8.6**),
- *management & organisation* (Sect. **8.7**) and
- *human behaviour* (Sect. **8.8**).

Of these, the *rules & regulations, scripts* and *license languages* are closely related. Vagueness may "pop up", here and there, in the delineation of facets. It is necessarily so. We are not in a domain of computer science, let alone mathematics, where we can just define ourselves precisely out of any vagueness problems. We are in the domain of (usually) really world facts. And these are often hard to encircle.

---

[180] We write: 'so far' in order to "announce", or hint that there may be other specific facets. The one listed are the ones we have been able to "isolate", to identify, in the most recent 10-12 years.

D. Bjørner, *Domain Science and Engineering*, Monographs in Theoretical Computer Science. An EATCS Series, https://doi.org/10.1007/978-3-030-73484-8_8

8.1.2 Relation to Previous Work

The present chapter is a rather complete rewrite of [55]. The reason for the rewriting was the expected publication of [81]. [55] was finalised already in 2006, 10 years ago, before the analysis & description calculus of [81] had emerged. It was time to revise [55] rather substantially.

8.1.3 Structure of Chapter

The structure of this chapter follows the seven specific facets, as listed above. Each section, **8.2.–8.8.**, starts by a definition of that *specific facet*, Then follows an analysis of the abstract concepts involved usually with one or more examples – with these examples making up most of the section. We then "speculate" on derivable requirements thus relating the present chapter to [69]. We close each of the sections, **8.2.–8.8.**, with some comments on how to model the specific facet of that section.

• • •

Examples 88–109 of sections **8.2–8.8** present quite a variety. In that, they reflect the wide spectrum of facets.

• • •

More generally, domains can be characterised by intrinsically being endurant, or function, or event, or behaviour *intensive*. Software support for activities in such domains then typically amount to database systems, computation-bound systems, real-time embedded systems, respectively distributed process monitoring and control systems. Other than this brief discourse we shall not cover the "intensity"-aspect of domains in this chapter.

8.2 Intrinsics

- *By domain* **intrinsics** *we shall understand those phenomena and concepts of a domain which are basic to any of the other facets (listed earlier and treated, in some detail, below), with such domain intrinsics initially covering at least one specific, hence named, stakeholder view* ■

8.2.1 Conceptual Analysis

The principles and techniques of domain analysis & description, as unfolded in Chapters 4–7, focused on and resulted in descriptions of the intrinsics of domains. They did so in focusing the analysis (and hence the description) on the basic endurants and their related perdurants, that is, on those parts that most readily present themselves for observation, analysis & description.

Railway Net Intrinsics

Example 88 We narrate and formalise three railway net intrinsics.

From the view of *potential train passengers* a railway net consists of lines, l:L, with names, ln:Ln, stations, s:S, with names sn:Sn, and trains, tn:TN, with names tnm:Tnm. A line connects exactly two distinct stations.

scheme N0 =
   class
      type
         N, L, S, Sn, Ln, TN, Tnm
      value
         obs_Ls: N → L-set, obs_Ss: N → S-set
         obs_Ln: L → Ln, obs_Sn: S → Sn
         obs_Sns: L → Sn-set, obs_Lns: S → Ln-set
      axiom
         ...
   end

N, L, S, Sn and Ln designate nets, lines, stations, station names and line names. One can observe lines and stations from nets, line and station names from lines and stations, pair sets of station names from lines, and lines names (of lines) into and out from a station from stations. Axioms ensure proper graph properties of these concepts.

From the view of *actual train passengers* a railway net — in addition to the above — allows for several lines between any pair of stations and, within stations, provides for one or more platform tracks, tr:Tr, with names, trn:Trn, from which to embark on or alight from a train.

scheme N1 = extend N0 with
   class
      type
         Tr, Trn
      value
         obs_Trs: S → Tr-set, obs_Trn: Tr → Trn
      axiom
         ...
   end

The only additions are that of track and track name types, related observer functions and axioms.

From the view of *train operating staff* a railway net — in addition to the above — has lines and stations consisting of suitably connected rail units. A rail unit is either a simple (i.e., linear, straight) unit, or is a switch unit, or is a simple crossover unit, or is a switchable crossover unit, etc. Simple units have two connectors. Switch units have three connectors. Simple and switchable crossover units have four connectors. A path, p:P, (through a unit) is a pair of connectors of that unit. A state, $\sigma : \Sigma$, of a unit is the set of paths, in the direction of which a train may travel. A (current) state may be empty: The unit is closed for traffic. A unit can be in any one of a number of states of its state space, $\omega : \Omega$.

scheme N2 = extend N1 with
   class
      type
         U, C
         $P' = U \times (C \times C)$
         $P = \{| \ p{:}P' \cdot \textbf{let} \ (u,(c,c'))=p \ \textbf{in} \ (c,c') \in \ \cup \ obs\_\Omega(u) \ \textbf{end} \ |\}$
         Σ = P-set
         Ω = Σ-set

value
  obs_Us: (N|L|S) → U-set
  obs_Cs: U → C-set
  obs_Σ: U → Σ
  obs_Ω: U → Ω
axiom
    ...
 end

Unit and connector types have been added as have concrete types for paths, unit states, unit state spaces and related observer functions, including unit state and unit state space observers.

Different stakeholder perspectives, not only of intrinsics, as here, but of any facet, lead to a number of different models. The name of a phenomenon of one perspective, that is, of one model, may coincide with the name of a "similar" phenomenon of another perspective, that is, of another model, and so on. If the intention is that the "same" names cover comparable phenomena, then the developer must state the comparison relation.

Intrinsics of Switches

Example 89 The intrinsic attribute of a rail switch is that it can take on a number of states. A simple switch $\left(^{c_|}Y_c^{c_/}\right)$ has three connectors: $\{c, c_|, c_/\}$. c is the connector of the common rail from which one can either "go straight" $c_|$, or "fork" $c_/$ (Fig. 8.1). So we have that a possible state space of such a switch could be ω_{g_s} :
$\{\{\},$
$\{(c,c_|)\}, \{(c_|,c)\}, \{(c,c_|),(c_|,c)\},$
$\{(c,c_/)\}, \{(c_/,c)\}, \{(c,c_/),(c_/,c)\}, \{(c_/,c),(c_|,c)\},$
$\{(c,c_|),(c_|,c),(c_/,c)\}, \{(c,c_/),(c_/,c),(c_|,c)\}, \{(c_/,c),(c,c_|)\}, \{(c,c_/),(c_|,c)\}\}$
The above models a general switch ideally. Any particular switch ω_{p_s} may have $\omega_{p_s} \subset \omega_{g_s}$. Nothing is said about how a state is determined: who sets and resets it, whether determined solely by the physical position of the switch gear, or also by visible or virtual (i.e., invisible, intangible) signals up or down the rail, away from the switch.

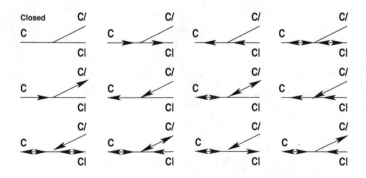

Fig. 8.1 Possible states of a rail switch

An Intrinsics of Documents

Example 90 Think of documents, written, by hand, or typed "onto" a computer text processing system. One way of considering such documents is as follows. First we abstract from the syntax that such a document, or set of more-or-less related documents, or just documents, may have: whether they are letters, with sender and receive addressees, dates written, sent and/or received, opening and closing paragraphs, etc., etc.; or they are books, technical, scientific, novels, or otherwise, or they are application forms, tax returns, patient medical records, or otherwise. Then we focus on the operations that one may perform on documents: their creation, editing, reading, copying, authorisation, "transfer"[181], "freezing"[182], and shredding. Finally we consider documents as manifest parts, cf. Chapter 4, Parts, so documents have unique identifications, in this case, changeable mereology, and a number of attributes. The mereology of a document, d, reflects those other documents upon which a document is based, i.e., refers to, and/or refers to d. Among the attributes of a document we can think of (i) a trace of what has happened to a document, i.e., a trace of all the operations performed on "that" document, since and including creation — with that trace, for example, consisting of time-stamped triples of the essence of the operations, the "actor" of the operation (i.e., the operator), and possibly some abstraction of the locale of the document when operated upon; (ii) a synopsis of what the document text "is all about", (iii) and some "rendition" of the document text. We refer to experimental technical research report [74].

This view of documents, whether "implementable" or "implemented" or not, is at the basis of our view of license languages (for *digital media*, *healthcare* (patient medical record), *documents*, and *transport* (contracts) as that facet is covered in Sect. **8.6**.

8.2.2 Intrinsics Requirements

Chapter 9 illustrates requirements "derived" from the intrinsics of a road transport system – as outlined in Chapters 4–7. So the present chapter has little to add to the subject of requirements "derived" from intrinsics.

8.2.3 On Modeling Intrinsics

Chapters 4–7 outline basic principles, techniques and tools for modeling the intrinsics of manifest domains. Modeling the domain intrinsics can often be expressed in property-oriented specification languages (like CafeOBJ [168]), model-oriented specification languages (like Alloy [262], B [2], VDM-SL [92, 93, 164], RSL [187], or Z [397]), event-based languages (like Petri nets or [347] or CSP [250]), respectively in process-based specification languages (like MSCs [260], LSCs [211], Statecharts [210], or CSP [250]). An area not well-developed is that of modeling continuous domain phenomena like the dynamics of automobile, train and aircraft movements, flow in pipelines, etc. We refer to [316].

---

[181] to other editors, readers, etc.

[182] i.e., prevention of future operations

8.3 Support Technologies

- By a domain **support technology** we shall understand ways and means of implementing certain observed phenomena or certain conceived concepts ∎

The "ways and means" may be in the form of "soft technologies": human manpower, see, however, Sect. **8.8**, or in the form of "hard" technologies: electro-mechanics, etc. The term 'implementing' is crucial. It is here used in the sense that, $\psi\tau$, which is an 'implementation' of a endurant or perdurant, ϕ, is an *extension* of ϕ, with ϕ being an *abstraction* of $\psi\tau$. We strive for the extensions to be *proof theoretic conservative extensions* [289].

8.3.1 Conceptual Analysis

There are [always] basically two approaches the task of analysing & describing the support technology facets of a domain. One either stumbles over it, or one tries to tackle the issue systematically. The "stumbling" approach occurs when one, in the midst of analysing & describing a domain realises that one is tackling something that satisfies the definition of a support technology facet. In the systematic approach to the analysis & description of the support technology facets of a domain one usually starts with a basically intrinsics facet-oriented domain description. We then suggest that the domain engineer "inquires" of every endurant and perdurant whether it is an intrinsic entity or, perhaps a support technology.

Railway Support Technology

Example 91 We give a rough sketch description of possible rail unit switch technologies.

(i) In "ye olde" days, rail switches were "thrown" by manual labour, i.e., by railway staff assigned to and positioned at switches.

(ii) With the advent of reasonably reliable mechanics, pulleys and levers[183] and steel wires, switches were made to change state by means of "throwing" levers in a cabin tower located centrally at the station (with the lever then connected through wires etc., to the actual switch).

(iii) This partial mechanical technology then emerged into electro-mechanics, and cabin tower staff was "reduced" to pushing buttons.

(iv) Today, groups of switches, either from a station arrival point to a station track, or from a station track to a station departure point, are set and reset by means also of electronics, by what is known as interlocking (for example, so that two different routes cannot be open in a station if they cross one another).

It must be stressed that Example 91 is just a rough sketch. In a proper narrative description the software (cum domain) engineer must describe, in detail, the subsystem of electronics, electro-mechanics and the human operator interface (buttons, lights, sounds, etc.). An aspect of supporting technology includes recording the state-behaviour in response to external stimuli. We give an example.

Probabilistic Rail Switch Unit State Transitions

Example 92 Figure 8.2 indicates a way of formalising this aspect of a supporting technology. Figure 8.2 intends to model the probabilistic (erroneous and correct) behaviour of a switch

---

[183] https://en.wikipedia.org/wiki/Pulley and http://en.wikipedia.org/wiki/Lever

when subjected to settings (to switched (s) state) and re-settings (to direct (d) state). A switch may go to the switched state from the direct state when subjected to a switch setting s with probability psd.

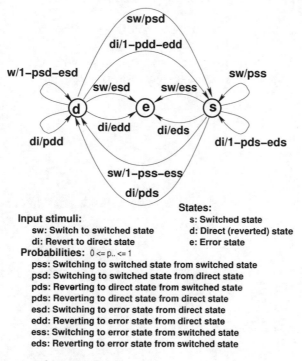

Input stimuli:
    sw: Switch to switched state
    di: Revert to direct state

States:
    s: Switched state
    d: Direct (reverted) state
    e: Error state

Probabilities: $0 <= p.. <= 1$
    pss: Switching to switched state from switched state
    psd: Switching to switched state from direct state
    pds: Reverting to direct state from switched state
    pds: Reverting to direct state from direct state
    esd: Switching to error state from direct state
    edd: Reverting to error state from direct state
    ess: Switching to error state from switched state
    eds: Reverting to error state from switched state

Fig. 8.2 Probabilistic state switching

Traffic Signals

Example 93 A traffic signal represents a technology in support of visualising hub states (transport net road intersection signaling states) and in effecting state changes.

295 A traffic signal, ts:TS, is here[184] considered a part with observable hub states and hub state spaces. Hub states and hub state spaces are programmable, respectively static attributes of traffic signals.

296 A hub state space, $h\omega$, is a set of hub states such that each current hub state is in that hubs' hub state space.

297 A hub state, $h\sigma$, is now modeled as a set of hub triples.

298 Each hub triple has a link identifier l_i ("coming from"), a colour (**red**, yellow or **green**), and another link identifier l_j ("going to").

299 Signaling is now a sequence of one or more pairs of next hub states and time intervals, ti:TI, for example: $<(h\sigma_1, ti_1), (h\sigma_2, ti_2), ..., (h\sigma_{n-1}, ti_{n-1}), (h\sigma_n, ti_n)>$, $n>0$.
    The idea of a signaling is to first change the designated hub to state $h\sigma_1$, then wait ti_1 time units, then set the designated hub to state $h\sigma_2$, then wait ti_2 time units, et cetera,

---

[184] In Chapter 4 a traffic signal was an attribute of a hub.

ending with final state σ_n and a (supposedly) long time interval ti_n before any decisions are to be made as to another signaling. The set of hub states $\{h\sigma_1, h\sigma_2, ..., h\sigma_{n-1}\}$ of $<(h\sigma_1, ti_1), (h\sigma_2, ti_2), ..., (h\sigma_{n-1}, ti_{n-1}), (h\sigma_n, ti_n)>, n>0$, is called the set of intermediate states. Their purpose is to secure an orderly phase out of green via yellow to red and phase in of red via yellow to green in some order for the various directions. We leave it to the reader to devise proper well-formedness conditions for signaling sequences as they depend on the hub topology.

300 A street signal (a semaphore) is now abstracted as a map from pairs of hub states to signaling sequences.

The idea is that given a hub one can observe its semaphore, and given the state, $h\sigma$ (not in the above set), of the hub "to be signaled" and the state $h\sigma_n$ into which that hub is to be signal-led "one looks up" under that pair in the semaphore and obtains the desired signaling.

type
295 TS ≡ H, HΣ, HΩ
value
296 attr_HΣ: H,TS → HΣ
296 attr_HΩ: H,TS → HΩ
type
297 HΣ = Htriple-**set**
297 HΩ = HΣ-**set**
298 Htriple = LI×Colour×LI
axiom
296 ∀ ts:TS · attr_HΣ(ts) ∈ attr_HΩ(ts)
type
298 Colour == **red** | yellow | **green**
299 Signaling = (HΣ×TI)*
299 TI
300 Sempahore = (HΣ×HΣ) $\overrightarrow{m}$ Signalling
value
300 attr_Semaphore:TS → Sempahore

301 We treat hubs as processes with hub state spaces and semaphores as static attributes and hub states as programmable attributes. We ignore other attributes and input/outputs.

302 We can think of the change of hub states as taking place based the result of some internal, non-deterministic choice.

value
301. hub: HI × LI-**set** × (HΩ×Semaphore) → HΣ **in** ... **out** ... **Unit**
301. hub(hi,lis,(hω,sema))(hσ) ≡
301.   ...
302.   ⊓ **let** hσ':HI · ... **in** hub(hi,lis,(hω,sema))(signaling(hσ,hσ')) **end**
301.   ...
301.   **pre**: {hσ,hσ'} ⊆ hω

where we do not bother about the selection of $h\sigma'$.

303 Given two traffic signal, i.e., hub states, $h\sigma_{init}$ and $h\sigma_{end}$, where $h\sigma_{init}$ designates a present hub state and $h\sigma_{end}$ designates a desired next hub state after signaling.

304 Now *signaling* is a sequence of one or more successful hub state changes.

value

303 signaling: $(H\Sigma \times H\Sigma) \times$ Semaphore $\rightarrow H\Sigma \rightarrow H\Sigma$
304 signaling$(h\sigma_{init}, h\sigma_{end}, sema)(h\sigma) \equiv$
304   **let** sg = sema$(h\sigma_{init}, h\sigma_{end})$ **in**
304   signal_sequence(sg)$(h\sigma)$ **end**
304   **pre** $h\sigma_{init} = h\sigma \wedge (h\sigma_{init}, h\sigma_{end}) \in$ **dom** sema

If a desired hub state change fails (i.e., does not meet the **pre**-condition, or for other reasons (e.g., failure of technology)), then we do not define the outcome of signaling.

304 signal_sequence$(\langle\rangle)(h\sigma) \equiv h\sigma$
304 signal_sequence$(\langle(h\sigma', ti)\rangle\frown sg)(h\sigma) \equiv$
304   wait(ti); signal_sequence(sg)$(h\sigma')$

We omit expression of a number of well-formedness conditions, e.g., that the *htriple* link identifiers are those of the corresponding mereology (*lis*), et cetera. The design of the semaphore, for a single hub or for a net of connected hubs has many similarities with the design of interlocking tables for railway tracks [241].

Another example shows another aspect of support technology: Namely that the technology must guarantee certain of its own behaviours, so that software designed to interface with this technology, together with the technology, meets dependability requirements.

Railway Optical Gates

Example 94 Train traffic (itf:iTF), intrinsically, is a total function over some time interval, from time (t:T) to continuously positioned (p:P) trains (tn:TN). Conventional optical gates sample, at regular intervals, the intrinsic train traffic. The result is a sampled traffic (stf:sTF). Hence the collection of all optical gates, for any given railway, is a partial function from intrinsic to sampled train traffics (stf). We need to express quality criteria that any optical gate technology should satisfy — relative to a necessary and sufficient description of a closeness predicate. The following axiom does that:

For all intrinsic traffics, itf, and for all optical gate technologies, og, the following must hold: Let stf be the traffic sampled by the optical gates. For all time points, t, in the sampled traffic, those time points must also be in the intrinsic traffic, and, for all trains, tn, in the intrinsic traffic at that time, the train must be observed by the optical gates, and the actual position of the train and the sampled position must somehow be check-able to be close, or identical to one another.

Since units change state with time, n:N, the railway net, needs to be part of any model of traffic.

type
    T, TN
    $P = U^*$
    NetTraffic == net:N trf:(TN $\xrightarrow{m}$ P)
    iTF = T $\rightarrow$ NetTraffic
    sTF = T $\xrightarrow{m}$ NetTraffic
    oG = iTF $\xrightarrow{\sim}$ sTF
value
    close: NetTraffic $\times$ TN $\times$ NetTraffic $\xrightarrow{\sim}$ **Bool**
axiom
    $\forall$ itt:iTF, og:OG $\cdot$ **let** stt = og(itt) **in**
        $\forall$ t:T $\cdot$ t $\in$ **dom** stt $\Rightarrow$
            $\forall$ Tn:TN $\cdot$ tn $\in$ **dom** trf(itt(t))

$$\Rightarrow \text{tn} \in \textbf{dom } \text{trf}(\text{stt}(t)) \land \text{close}(\text{itt}(t),\text{tn},\text{stt}(t)) \textbf{ end}$$

Check-ability is an issue of testing the optical gates when delivered for conformance to the closeness predicate, i.e., to the axiom.

8.3.2 Support Technologies Requirements

Section 4.4 [Extension] of [69] illustrates a possible toll-gate, whose behaviour exemplifies a support technology. So do pumps of a pipe-line system such as illustrated in Examples 24, 29 and 42–44 in [81]. A pump of a pipe-line system gives rise to several forms of support technologies: from the Egyptian Shadoof [irrigation] pumps, and the Hellenic Archimedian screw pumps, via the 11th century Su Song pumps of China[185], and the hydraulic "technologies" of Moorish Spain[186] to the centrifugal and gear pumps of the early industrial age, et cetera, The techniques – to mention those that have influenced this author – of [404, 268, 315, 241] appear to apply well to the modeling of support technology requirements.

8.3.3 On Modeling Support Technologies

Support technologies in their relation to the domain in which they reside typically reflect real-time embeddedness. As such the techniques and languages for modeling support technologies resemble those for modeling event and process intensity, while temporal notions are brought into focus. Hence typical modeling notations include event-based languages (like Petri nets [347] or CSP) [250]), respectively process-based specification languages (like MSCs, [260], LSCs [211], Statecharts [210], or CSP) [250]), as well as temporal languages (like the Duration Calculus, DC, and [404] and Temporal Logic of Actions, TLA+) [275]).

8.4 Rules & Regulations

- *By a **domain rule** we shall understand some text (in the domain) which prescribes how people or equipment are expected to behave when dispatching their duties, respectively when performing their functions ∎*
- *By a **domain regulation** we shall understand some text (in the domain) which prescribes what remedial actions are to be taken when it is decided that a rule has not been followed according to its intention ∎*

The domain rules & regulations need or may not be explicitly present, i.e., written down. They may be part of the "folklore", i.e., tacitly assumed and understood.

---

[185] https://en.wikipedia.org/wiki/Su_Song
[186] http://www.islamicspain.tv/Arts-and-Science/The-Culture-of-Al-Andalus/Hydraulic-Technology.htm

8.4.1 Conceptual Analysis

Trains at Stations

Example 95

- Rule: In China the arrival and departure of trains at, respectively from, railway stations is subject to the following rule:

  In any three-minute interval at most one train may either arrive to or depart from a railway station.
- Regulation: *If it is discovered that the above rule is not obeyed,* then there is some regulation which prescribes administrative or legal management and/or staff action, as well as some correction to the railway traffic.

Trains Along Lines

Example 96

- Rule: In many countries railway lines (between stations) are segmented into blocks or sectors. The purpose is to stipulate that if two or more trains are moving along the line, then:

  There must be at least one free sector (i.e., without a train) between any two trains along a line.
- Regulation: *If it is discovered that the above rule is not obeyed,* then there is some regulation which prescribes administrative or legal management and/or staff action, as well as some correction to the railway traffic.

At a meta-level, i.e., explaining the general framework for describing the syntax and semantics of the human-oriented domain languages for expressing rules and regulations, we can say the following: There are, abstractly speaking, usually three kinds of languages involved wrt. (i.e., when expressing) rules and regulations (respectively when invoking actions that are subject to rules and regulations). Two languages, Rules and Reg, exist for describing rules, respectively regulations; and one, Stimulus, exists for describing the form of the [always current] domain action stimuli. A syntactic stimulus, sy_sti, denotes a function, se_sti:STI: $\Theta \rightarrow \Theta$, from any configuration to a next configuration, where configurations are those of the system being subjected to stimulations. A syntactic rule, sy_rul:Rule, stands for, i.e., has as its semantics, its meaning, rul:RUL, a predicate over current and next configurations, $(\Theta \times \Theta) \rightarrow$ **Bool**, where these next configurations have been brought about, i.e., caused, by the stimuli. These stimuli express: If the predicate holds then the stimulus will result in a valid next configuration.

type
    Stimulus, Rule, Θ
    STI = $\Theta \rightarrow \Theta$
    RUL = $(\Theta \times \Theta) \rightarrow$ **Bool**
value
    meaning: Stimulus $\rightarrow$ STI
    meaning: Rule $\rightarrow$ RUL
    valid: Stimulus $\times$ Rule $\rightarrow \Theta \rightarrow$ **Bool**

valid(sy_sti,sy_rul)(θ) $\equiv$ meaning(sy_rul)(θ,(meaning(sy_sti))(θ))

A syntactic regulation, sy_reg:Reg (related to a specific rule), stands for, i.e., has as its semantics, its meaning, a semantic regulation, se_reg:REG, which is a pair. This pair consists of a predicate, pre_reg:Pre_REG, where Pre_REG = ($\Theta \times \Theta$) $\rightarrow$ **Bool**, and a domain configuration-changing function, act_reg:Act_REG, where Act_REG = $\Theta \rightarrow \Theta$, that is, both involving current and next domain configurations. The two kinds of functions express: If the predicate holds, then the action can be applied. The predicate is almost the inverse of the rules functions. The action function serves to undo the stimulus function.

type
    Reg
    Rul_and_Reg = Rule $\times$ Reg
    REG = Pre_REG $\times$ Act_REG
    Pre_REG = $\Theta \times \Theta \rightarrow$ **Bool**
    Act_REG = $\Theta \rightarrow \Theta$
value
    interpret: Reg $\rightarrow$ REG

The idea is now the following: Any action (i.e., event) of the system, i.e., the application of any stimulus, may be an action (i.e., event) in accordance with the rules, or it may not. Rules therefore express whether stimuli are valid or not in the current configuration. And regulations therefore express whether they should be applied, and, if so, with what effort. More specifically, there is usually, in any current system configuration, given a set of pairs of rules and regulations. Let (sy_rul,sy_reg) be any such pair. Let sy_sti be any possible stimulus. And let θ be the current configuration. Let the stimulus, sy_sti, applied in that configuration result in a next configuration, θ', where θ' = (meaning(sy_sti))(θ). Let θ' violate the rule, ~valid(sy_sti,sy_rul)(θ), then if predicate part, pre_reg, of the meaning of the regulation, sy_reg, holds in that violating next configuration, pre_reg(θ,(meaning(sy_sti))(θ)), then the action part, act_reg, of the meaning of the regulation, sy_reg, must be applied, act_reg(θ), to remedy the situation.

axiom
    $\forall$ (sy_rul,sy_reg):Rul_and_Reg $\cdot$
        let se_rul = meaning(sy_rul),
            (pre_reg,act_reg) = meaning(sy_reg) **in**
        $\forall$ sy_sti:Stimulus, θ:Θ $\cdot$
            ~valid(sy_sti,se_rul)(θ)
                $\Rightarrow$ pre_reg(θ,(meaning(sy_sti))(θ))
                    $\Rightarrow$ $\exists$ nθ:Θ $\cdot$ act_reg(θ)=nθ $\wedge$ se_rul(θ,nθ)
        end

It may be that the regulation predicate fails to detect applicability of regulations actions. That is, the interpretation of a rule differs, in that respect, from the interpretation of a regulation. Such is life in the domain, i.e., in actual reality.

8.4.2 Rules & Regulations Requirements

Implementation of rules & regulations implies *monitor*ing and partially *control*ling the states symbolised by Θ in Sect. **8.4.1**. Thus some *partial implementation* of Θ must be required; as must some monitoring of states θ:Θ and implementation of the predicates *meaning, valid,* *interpret*, *pre_reg* and action(s) *act_reg*. The emerging requirements follow very much in the line of support technology requirements.

8.4.3 On Modeling Rules and Regulations

Usually rules (as well as regulations) are expressed in terms of domain entities, including those grouped into "the state", functions, events, and behaviours. Thus the full spectrum of model-ling techniques and notations may be needed. Since rules usually express properties one often uses some combination of axioms and wellformedness predicates. Properties sometimes include temporality and hence temporal notations (like Duration Calculus or Temporal Logic of Actions) are used. And since regulations usually express state (restoration) changes one often uses state changing notations (such as found in Allard [262], B and Event-B [2], RSL [187], VDM-SL [92, 93, 164], and Z [397]). In some cases it may be relevant to model using some *constraint satisfaction* notation [11] or some *fuzzy logic* notations [375].

8.5 Scripts

- By a **domain script** we shall understand the structured, almost, if not outright, formally expressed, wording of a procedure on how to proceed, one that has legally binding power, that is, which may be contested in a court of law ∎

8.5.1 Conceptual Analysis

Rules & regulations are usually expressed, even when informally so, as predicates. Scripts, in their procedural form, are like instructions, as for an algorithm.

A Casually Described Bank Script

Example 97 Our formulation amounts to just a (casual) rough sketch. It is followed by a series of four large examples. Each of these elaborate on the theme of (bank) scripts. The problem area is that of how repayments of mortgage loans are to be calculated. At any one time a mortgage loan has a balance, a most recent previous date of repayment, an interest rate and a handling fee. When a repayment occurs, then the following calculations shall take place: (i) the interest on the balance of the loan since the most recent repayment, (ii) the handling fee, normally considered fixed, (iii) the effective repayment — being the difference between the repayment and the sum of the interest and the handling fee — and the new balance, being the difference between the old balance and the effective repayment. We assume repayments to occur from a designated account, say a demand/deposit account. We assume that bank to have designated fee and interest income accounts. (i) The interest is subtracted from the mortgage holder's demand/deposit account and added to the bank's interest (income) account. (ii) The handling fee is subtracted from the mortgage holder's demand/deposit account and added to the bank's fee (income) account. (iii) The effective repayment is subtracted from the mortgage holder's demand/deposit account and also from the mortgage balance. Finally, one must also describe deviations such as overdue repayments, too large, or too small repayments, and so on.

A Formally Described Bank Script

Example 98 First we must informally and formally define the bank state: There are clients (c:C), account numbers (a:A), mortgage numbers (m:M), account yields (ay:AY) and mortgage interest rates (mi:MI). The bank registers, by client, all accounts (ρ:A_Register) and all mortgages (μ:M_Register). To each account number there is a balance (α:Accounts). To each mortgage number there is a loan (ℓ:Loans). To each loan is attached the last date that interest was paid on the loan.

value
    r, r′:**Real axiom** ...
type
    C, A, M, Date
    AY′ = **Real**, AY = {| ay:AY′ · 0<ay≤r |}
    MI′ = **Real**, MI = {| mi:MI′ · 0<mi≤r′ |}
    Bank′ = A_Register × Accounts × M_Register × Loans
    Bank = {| β:Bank′ · wf_Bank(β)|}
    A_Register = C $_{\overrightarrow{m}}$ A-**set**
    Accounts = A $_{\overrightarrow{m}}$ Balance
    M_Register = C $_{\overrightarrow{m}}$ M-**set**
    Loans = M $_{\overrightarrow{m}}$ (Loan × Date)
    Loan,Balance = P
    P = **Nat**

Then we must define well-formedness of the bank state:

value
    ay:AY, mi:MI
    wf_Bank: Bank → **Bool**
    wf_Bank(ρ,α,μ,ℓ) ≡ ∪ **rng** ρ = **dom** α ∧ ∪ **rng** μ = **dom** ℓ
axiom
    ay<mi [∧ ...]

We — perhaps too rigidly — assume that mortgage interest rates are higher than demand/deposit account interest rates: ay<mi. Operations on banks are denoted by the commands of the bank script language. First the syntax:

type
    Cmd = OpA | CloA | Dep | Wdr | OpM | CloM | Pay
    OpA == mkOA(c:C)
    CloA == mkCA(c:C,a:A)
    Dep == mkD(c:C,a:A,p:P)
    Wdr == mkW(c:C,a:A,p:P)
    OpM == mkOM(c:C,p:P)
    Pay == mkPM(c:C,a:A,m:M,p:P,d:Date)
    CloM == mkCM(c:C,m:M,p:P)
    Reply = A | M | P | OkNok
    OkNok == ok | notok
value
    period: Date × Date → Days [for calculating interest]
    before: Date × Date → **Bool** [first date is earlier than last date]

And then the semantics:

```
int_Cmd(mkPM(c,a,m,p,d))(ρ,α,μ,ℓ) ≡
    let (b,d′) = ℓ(m) in
    if α(a)≥p
        then
            let i = interest(mi,b,period(d,d′)),
                ℓ′ = ℓ † [m↦ℓ(m)−(p−i)]
                α′ = α † [a↦α(a)−p,aᵢ↦α(aᵢ)+i] in
            ((ρ,α′,μ,ℓ′),ok) end
        else
            ((ρ,α′,μ,ℓ),nok)
    end end
    pre c ∈ dom μ ∧ a ∈ dom α ∧ m ∈ μ(c)
    post before(d,d′)

    interest: MI × Loan × Days → P
```

The idea about scripts is that they can somehow be objectively enforced: that they can be precisely understood and consistently carried out by all stakeholders, eventually leading to computerisation. But they are, at all times, part of the domain.

8.5.2 Script Requirements

Script requirements call for the possibly interactive computerisation of algorithms, that is, for rather classical computing problems. But sometimes these scripts can be expressed, computably, in the form of programs in a domain specific language. As an example we refer to [131]. [131] illustrates how the design of pension and life insurance products, and their administration, reserve calculations, and audit, can be based on a common formal notation. The notation is human-readable and machine-processable, and specialised to the actuarial domain, achieving great expressive power combined with ease of use and safety. More specifically (a) product definitions based on standard actuarial models, including arbitrary continuous-time Markov and semi-Markov models, with cyclic transitions permitted; (b) calculation descriptions for reserves and other quantities of interest, based on differential equations; and (c) administration rules.

8.5.3 On Modeling Scripts

Scripts (as are licenses) are like programs (respectively like prescriptions program executions). Hence the full variety of techniques and notations for modeling programming (or specification) languages apply [16, 199, 349, 356, 373, 390]. [43, Chaps. 6–9] cover pragmatics, semantics and syntax techniques for defining functional, imperative and concurrent programming languages.

8.6 License Languages

License: a right or permission
granted in accordance with law
by a competent authority
to engage in some business or occupation,
to do some act, or to engage in some transaction
which but for such license would be unlawful ∎

Merriam-Webster Online [301]

8.6.1 Conceptual Analysis

8.6.1.1 The Settings

A special form of scripts are increasingly appearing in some domains, notably the domain of electronic, or digital media. Here *licenses* express that a *licensor*, o, *permits* a *licensee*, u, to *render* (i.e., play) works of proprietary nature CD ROM-like music, DVD-like movies, etc. while obligating the licensee to pay the licensor on behalf of the owners of these, usually artistic works. Classical digital rights license languages, [29, 13, 128, 129, 130, 257, 124, 198, 207, 283, 308, 304, 285, 274, 354, 341, 340, 6, 309], applied to the electronic "downloading", payment and rendering (playing) of artistic works (for example music, literature readings and movies). In this chapter we generalise such applications languages and we extend the concept of licensing to also cover work authorisation (work commitment and promises) in healthcare, public government and schedule transport. The digital works for these new application domains are patient medical records, public government documents and bus/train/aircraft transport contracts. Digital rights licensing for artistic works seeks to safeguard against piracy and to ensure proper payments for the rights to render these works. Healthcare and public government license languages seek to ensure transparent and professional (accurate and timely) healthcare, respectively 'good governance'. Transport contract languages seeks to ensure timely and reliable transport services by an evolving set of transport companies. Proper mathematical definition of licensing languages seeks to ensure smooth and correct computerised management of licenses and contracts.

8.6.1.2 On Licenses

The concepts of licenses and licensing express relations between (i) *actors* (licensors (the authority) and licensees), (ii) *entities* (artistic works, hospital patients, public administration, citizen documents) and bus transport contracts and (iii) *functions* (on entities), and as performed by actors. By issuing a license to a licensee, a licensor wishes to express and enforce certain permissions and obligations: which functions on which entities the licensee is allowed (is licensed, is permitted) to perform. In this chapter we shall consider four kinds of entities: (i) digital recordings of artistic and intellectual nature: music, movies, readings ("audio books"), and the like, (ii) patients in a hospital as represented also by their patient medical records, (iii) documents related to public government, and (iv) transport vehicles, time tables and transport nets (of a buses, trains and aircraft).

8.6.1.3 Permissions and Obligations

The *permissions* and *obligations* issues are, (1) for the owner (agent) of some intellectual property to be paid (an *obligation*) by users when they perform *permitted* operations (rendering, copying, editing, sub-licensing) on their works; (2) for the patient to be professionally treated — by medical staff who are basically *obliged* to try to cure the patient; (3) for public administrators and citizens to enjoy good governance: transparency in law making (national parliaments and local prefectures and city councils), in law enforcement (i.e., the daily administration of laws), and law interpretation (the judiciary) — by agents who are basically *obliged* to produce certain documents while being *permitted* to consult (i.e., read, perhaps copy) other documents; and (4) for bus passengers to enjoy reliable bus schedules — offered by bus transport companies on contract to, say public transport authorities and on sub-contract to other such bus transport companies where these transport companies are *obliged* to honour a contracted schedule.

8.6.2 The Pragmatics

*By **pragmatics** we understand the study and practice of the factors that govern our choice of language in social interaction and the effects of our choice on others.*

In this section we shall rough-sketch-describe pragmatic aspects of the four domains of (1) production, distribution and consumption of artistic works, (2) the hospitalisation of patient, i.e., hospital healthcare, (3) the handling of law-based document in public government and (4) the operational management of schedule transport vehicles. The emphasis is on the pragmatics of the terms, i.e., the language used in these four domains.

8.6.2.1 Digital Media

Digital Media

Example 99 The intrinsic entities of the performing arts are the artistic works: drama or opera performances, music performances, readings of poems, short stories, novels, or jokes, movies, documentaries, newsreels, etc. We shall limit our span to the scope of electronic renditions of these artistic works: videos, CDs or other. In this chapter we shall not touch upon the technical issues of "downloading"(whether "streaming" or copying, or other). That and other issues should be analysed in [398].

★ **Operations on Digital Works:**

For a consumer to be able to enjoy these works that consumer must (normally first) usually "buy a ticket" to their performances. The consumer, i.e., the theatre, opera, concert, etc., "goer" (usually) cannot copy the performance (e.g., "tape it"), let alone edit such copies of performances. In the context of electronic, i.e., digital renditions of these performances the above "cannots" take on a new meaning. The consumer may copy digital recordings, may edit these, and may further pass on such copies or editions to others. To do so, while protecting the rights of the producers (owners, performers), the consumer requests permission to have the digital works transferred ("downloaded") from the owner/producer to the consumer, so that the consumer can render ("play") these works on own rendering devices (CD, DVD, etc., players), possibly can copy all or parts of them, then possibly can edit all or parts of the copies, and, finally, possibly can further license these "edited" versions to other consumers subject to payments to "original" licensor.

⋆ License Agreement and Obligation:

To be able to obtain these permissions the user agrees with the wording of some license and pays for the rights to operate on the digital works.

⋆ Two Assumptions:

Two, related assumptions underlie the pragmatics of the electronics of the artistic works. The first assumption is that the format, the electronic representation of the artistic works is proprietary, that is, that the producer still owns that format. Either the format is publicly known or it is not, that is, it is somehow "secret". In either case we "derive" the second assumption (from the fulfillment of the first). The second assumption is that the consumer is not allowed to, or cannot operate[187] on the works by own means (software, machines). The second assumption implies that acceptance of a license results in the consumer receiving software that supports the consumer in performing all operations on licensed works, their copies and edited versions: rendering, copying, editing and sub-licensing.

⋆ Protection of the Artistic Electronic Works:

The issue now is: how to protect the intellectual property (i.e., artistic) and financial (exploitation) rights of the owners of the possibly rendered, copied and edited works, both when, and when not further distributed.

8.6.2.2 Healthcare

Healthcare

Example 100 Citizens go to hospitals in order to be treated for some calamity (disease or other), and by doing so these citizens become patients. At hospitals patients, in a sense, issue a request to be treated with the aim of full or partial restitution. This request is directed at medical staff, that is, the patient authorises medical staff to perform a set of actions upon the patient. One could claim, as we shall, that the patient issues a license.

⋆ Patients and Patient Medical Records:

So patients and their attendant patient medical records (PMRs) are the main entities, the "works" of this domain. We shall treat them synonymously: PMRs as surrogates for patients. Typical actions on patients — and hence on PMRs — involve admitting patients, interviewing

---

[187] render, copy and edit

patients, analysing patients, diagnosing patients, planning treatment for patients, actually treating patients, and, under normal circumstance, to finally release patients.

⋆ Medical Staff:

Medical staff may request ('refer' to) other medical staff to perform some of these actions. One can conceive of describing action sequences (and 'referrals') in the form of hospitalisation (not treatment) plans. We shall call such scripts for licenses.

⋆ Professional Healthcare:

The issue is now, given that we record these licenses, their being issued and being honoured, whether the handling of patients at hospitals follow, or does not follow properly issued licenses.

8.6.2.3 Government Documents

Documents

Example 101 By public government we shall, following Charles de Secondat, baron de Montesquieu (1689–1755)[188], understand a composition of three powers: the law-making (legislative), the law-enforcing and the law-interpreting parts of public government. Typically national parliament and local (province and city) councils are part of law-making government. Law-enforcing government is called the executive (the administration). And law-interpreting government is called the judiciary [system] (including lawyers etc.).

⋆ Documents:

A crucial means of expressing public administration is through *documents*.[189] We shall therefore provide a brief domain analysis of a concept of documents. (This document domain description also applies to patient medical records and, by some "light" interpretation, also to artistic works — insofar as they also are documents.) Documents are *created*, *edited* and *read*; and documents can be *copied*, *distributed*, the subject of *calculations* (interpretations) and be *shared* and *shredded*.

⋆ Document Attributes:

With documents one can associate, as attributes of documents, the *actors* who created, edited, read, copied, distributed, shared, performed calculations and shredded documents. With these operations on documents, and hence as attributes of documents one can, again conceptually, associate the *location* and *time* of these operations.

⋆ Actor Attributes and Licenses:

With actors (whether agents of public government or citizens) one can associate the *authority* (i.e., the *rights*) these actors have with respect to performing actions on documents. We now intend to express these *authorisations as licenses*.

⋆ Document Tracing:

An issue of public government is whether citizens and agents of public government act in accordance with the laws — with actions and laws reflected in documents such that the action documents enables a trace from the actions to the laws "governing" these actions. We

---

[188] *De l'esprit des lois* (*The Spirit of the Laws*), published 1748

[189] Documents are, for the case of public government to be the "equivalent" of artistic works.

shall therefore assume that every document can be traced back to its law-origin as well as to all the documents any one document-creation or -editing was based on.

8.6.2.4 Transportation

Transportation is one of the prime areas for domain analysis & description: roads and vehicles: private automobiles, buses, trucks, etc., aircraft, shipping, trains.

Passenger and Goods Transport

Example 102

⋆ **A Synopsis:**

Contracts obligate transport companies to deliver bus traffic according to a timetable. The timetable is part of the contract. A contractor may sub-contract (other) transport companies to deliver bus traffic according to timetables that are sub-parts of their own timetable. Contractors are either public transport authorities or contracted transport companies. Contracted transport companies may cancel a subset of bus rides provided the total amount of cancellations per 24 hours for each bus line does not exceed a contracted upper limit The cancellation rights are spelled out in the contract. A sub-contractor cannot increase a contracted upper limit for cancellations above what the sub-contractor was told (in its contract) by its contractor. Et cetera.

⋆ **A Pragmatics and Semantics Analysis:**

The "works" of the bus transport contracts are two: the timetables and, implicitly, the designated (and obligated) bus traffic. A bus timetable appears to define one or more bus lines, with each bus line giving rise to one or more bus rides. Nothing is (otherwise) said about regularity of bus rides. It appears that bus ride cancellations must be reported back to the contractor. And we assume that cancellations by a sub-contractor is further reported back also to the sub-contractor's contractor. Hence eventually that the public transport authority is notified. Nothing is said, in the contracts, such as we shall model them, about passenger fees for bus rides nor of percentages of profits (i.e., royalties) to be paid back from a sub-contractor to the contractor. So we shall not bother, in this example, about transport costs nor transport subsidies. But will leave that necessary aspect as an exercise. The opposite of cancellations appears to be 'insertion' of extra bus rides, that is, bus rides not listed in the time table, but, perhaps, mandated by special events[190]. We assume that such insertions must also be reported back to the contractor. We assume concepts of acceptable and unacceptable bus ride delays. Details of delay acceptability may be given in contracts, but we ignore further descriptions of delay acceptability. but assume that unacceptable bus ride delays are also to be (iteratively) reported back to contractors. We finally assume that sub-contractors cannot (otherwise) change timetables. (A timetable change can only occur after, or at, the expiration of a license.) Thus we find that contracts have definite period of validity. (Expired contracts may be replaced by new contracts, possibly with new timetables.)

⋆ **Contracted Operations, An Overview:**

The actions that may be granted by a contractor according to a contract are: (i) *start:* to commence, i.e., to start, a bus ride (obligated); (ii) *end:* to conclude a bus ride (obligated); (iii) *cancel:* to cancel a bus ride (allowed, with restrictions); (iv) *insert:* to insert a bus ride; and (v) *subcontract:* to sub-contract part or all of a contract.

---

[190] Special events: breakdown (that is, cancellations) of other bus rides, sports event (soccer matches), etc.

8.6.3 Schematic Rendition of License Language Constructs

There are basically two aspects to licensing languages: (i) the [actual] *licensing* [and sub-licensing], in the form of *licenses*, ℓ, by *licensors*, o, of *permissions* and thereby implied *obligations*, and (ii) the carrying-out of these obligations in the form of *licensee*, u, *actions*. We shall treat licensors and licensees on par, that is, some os are also us and vice versa. And we shall think of licenses as not necessarily material entities (e.g., paper documents), but allow licenses to be tacitly established (understood).

8.6.3.1 Licensing

The granting of a license ℓ by a licensor o, to a set of licensees $u_{u_1}, u_{u_2}, ..., u_{u_u}$ in which ℓ expresses that these may perform actions $a_{a_1}, a_{a_2}, ..., a_{a_a}$ on work items $e_{e_1}, e_{e_2}, ..., e_{e_e}$ can be schematised:

> ℓ : **licensor** o **contracts licensees** $\{u_{u_1}, u_{u_2}, ..., u_{u_u}\}$
> **to perform actions** $\{a_{a_1}, a_{a_2}, ..., a_{a_a}\}$ **on work items** $\{e_{e_1}, e_{e_2}, ..., e_{e_e}\}$
> **allowing sub-licensing of actions** $\{a_{a_i}, a_{a_j}, ..., a_{a_k}\}$ **to** $\{u_{u_x}, u_{u_y}, ..., u_{u_z}\}$

The two sets of action designators, *das* :$\{a_{a_1}, a_{a_2}, ..., a_{a_a}\}$ and *sas* :$\{a_{a_x}, a_{a_y}, ..., a_{a_z}\}$ need not relate. **Sub-licensing:** Line 3 of the above schema, ℓ, expresses that licensees $u_{u_1}, u_{u_2}, ..., u_{u_u}$, may act as licensors and (thereby sub-)license ℓ to licensees $us : \{u_{u_x}, u_{u_y}, ..., u_{u_z}\}$, distinct from $sus : \{u_{u_1}, u_{u_2}, ..., u_{u_u}\}$, that is, $us \cap sus = \{\}$. **Variants:** One can easily "cook up" any number of variations of the above license schema. **Revoke Licenses:** We do not show expressions for revoking part or all of a previously granted license.

8.6.3.2 Licensors and Licensees

Licensors and Licensees

Example 103

⋆ **Digital Media:**

For digital media the original licensors are the original producers of music, film, etc. The "original" licensees are you and me! Thereafter some of us may become licensors, etc.

⋆ **Heath-care:**

For healthcare the original licensors are, say in Denmark, the Danish government's *National Board of Health*[191]; and the "original" licensees are the national hospitals. These then sub-license their medical clinics (rheumatology, cancer, urology, gynecology, orthopedics, neurology, etc.) which again sub-licenses their medical staff (doctors, nurses, etc.). A medical

---

[191] In the UK: *The NHS*, etc.

doctor may, as is the case in Denmark for certain actions, not [necessarily] perform these but may sub-license their execution to nurses, etc.

⋆ Documents:

For government documents the original licensor are the (i) heads of parliament, regional and local governments, (ii) government (prime minister) and the heads of respective ministries, respectively the regional and local agencies and administrations. The "original" licensees are (i′) the members of parliament, regional and local councils charged with drafting laws, rules and regulations, (ii′) the ministry, respectively the regional and local agency department heads. These (the ′s) then become licensors when licensing their staff to handle specific documents.

⋆ Transport:

For scheduled passenger (etc.) transportation the original licensors are the state, regional and/or local transport authorities. The "original" licensees are the public and private transport firms. These latter then become licensors licensors licensing drivers to handle specific transport lines and/or vehicles.

8.6.3.3 Actors and Actions

In preparation for Example 104 we show Figure 8.3.

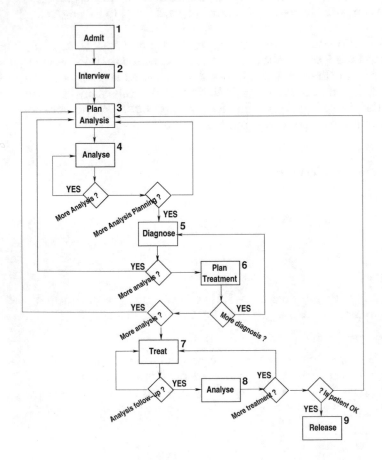

Fig. 8.3 An example single-illness non-fatal hospitalisation plan. States: {1,2,3,4,5,6,7,8,9}

Actors and Actions

Example 104

★ Digital Media:

w refers to a digital "work" with w' designating a newly created one; s_i refers to a sector of some work.

- **render** $w(s_i, s_j, ..., s_k)$:
  - ∞ sectors $s_i, s_j, ..., s_k$ of work w
  - ∞ are rendered (played, visualised) in that order.
- w' **:= copy** $w(s_i, s_j, ..., s_k)$:
  - ∞ sectors $s_i, s_j, ..., s_k$ of work w
  - ∞ are copied and becomes work w'.
- w' **:= edit** w **with** $\mathcal{E}(w_\alpha(s_a, s_b, ..., s_c), ..., w_\gamma(s_p, s_q, ..., s_r))$:
  - ∞ work w is edited
  - ∞ while [also] incorporating references to or excerpts from [other] works
  - ∞ $w_\alpha(s_a, s_b, ..., s_c), ..., w_\gamma(s_p, s_q, ..., s_r)$.
- **read** w:
  - ∞ work w is read, i.e., information about work w is somehow displayed.

- ℓ : **licensor m contracts licensees** $\{\mathbf{u}_{u_1}, \mathbf{u}_{u_2}, ..., \mathbf{u}_{u_u}\}$
  - ∞ **to perform actions** {RENDER, COPY, EDIT, READ}
  - ∞ **on work items** $\{w_{i_1}, w_{i_2}, ..., w_{i_w}\}$.

Et cetera: other forms of actions can be thought of.

★ Heath-care:

- Actors are here limited to the patients and the medical staff.
- We refer to Fig. 8.3 on the preceding page.
- It shows an archetypal hospitalisation plan.
  - ∞ It identifies a number of actions;
  - ∞ π designates patients,
  - ∞ t designates treatment (medication, surgery, ...).
- Actions are performed by medical staff, say h, with h being an implicit argument of the actions.

- **interview** π: a PMR with name, age, family relations, addresses, etc., is established for patient π.
- **admit** π: the PMR records the anamnese (medical history) for patient π.
- **establish analysis plan** π: the PMR records which analyses (blood tests, ECG, blood pressure, etc.) are to be carried out.
- **analyse** π: the PMR records the results of the analyses referred to previously.
- **diagnose** π: medical staff h diagnoses, based on the analyses most recently performed.
- **plan treatment for** π: medical staff h sets up a treatment plan for patient π based on the diagnosis most recently performed.
- **treat** π **wrt.** t: medical staff h performs treatment t on patient π, observes "reaction" and records this in the PMR. Predicate "actions":
- **more analysis** π **?**,
- **more treatment** π **?** and
- **more diagnosis** π **?**.

- **release** π: either the patient dies or is declared ready to be sent 'home'.
- ℓ : **licensor o contracts medical staff** $\{m_{m_1}, m_{m_2}, ..., m_{m_m}\}$
  - ∞ **to perform actions**

∞ {INTERVIEW,	∞ PLAN ANALYSIS,	∞ DIAGNOSE,	∞ TREAT,
∞ ADMIT,	∞ ANALYSE,	∞ PLAN TREATMENT,	∞ RELEASE}

  - ∞ **on patients** $\{\pi_{p_1}, \pi_{p_2}, ..., \pi_{p_p}\}$.

Et cetera: other forms of actions can be thought of.

★ **Documents:**

d refer to documents with d' designating new documents.

- d' := **create based on** $d_x, d_y, ..., d_z$: A new document, named d', is created, with no information "contents", but referring to existing documents $d_x, d_y, ..., d_z$.
- **edit** d **with** $\mathcal{E}$ **based on** $d_{n_\alpha}, d_\beta, ..., d_\gamma$: document d is edited with $\mathcal{E}$ being the editing function and $\mathcal{E}^{-1}$ being its "undo" inverse.
- **read** d: document d is being read.
- d' := **copy** d: document d is copied into a new document named d'.
- **freeze** d: document d can, from now on, only be read.
- **shred** d: document d is shredded. That is, no more actions can be performed on d.
- ℓ : **licensor o contracts civil service staff** $\{c_{c_1}, c_{c_2}, ..., c_{c_c}\}$ **to perform actions** {CREATE, EDIT, READ, COPY, FREEZE, SHRED} **on documents** $\{d_{d_1}, d_{d_2}, ..., d_{d_d}\}$.

Et cetera: other forms of actions can be thought of.

★ **Transport:**

- We restrict, without loss of generality, to bus transport.
  - ∞ There is a timetable, tt.
  - ∞ It records bus lines, l, and specific instances of bus rides, b.
- These are some archetypal operations:
  - ∞ **start bus ride** l, b **at time** t: Bus line l is recorded in tt and its departure in tt is recorded as τ. Starting that bus ride at t means that the start is either on time, i.e., $t=\tau$, or the start is delayed δ_d : τ-t or advanced δ_a : t-τ where δ_d and δ_a are expected to be small intervals. All this is to be reported, in due time, to the contractor.
  - ∞ **end bus ride** l, b **at time** t: Ending bus ride l, b at time t means that it is either ended on time, or earlier, or delayed. This is to be reported, in due time, to the contractor.
  - ∞ **cancel bus ride** l, b **at time** t: t must be earlier than the scheduled departure of bus ride l, b.
  - ∞ **insert an extra bus** l, b' **at time** t: t must be the same time as the scheduled departure of bus ride l, b with b' being a "marked" version of b.
  - ∞ ℓ : **licensor o contracts transport staff** $\{b_{b_1}, b_{b_2}, ..., b_{b_b}\}$ **to perform actions** {START, END, CANCEL, INSERT} **on work items** $\{\mathbf{e}_{e_1}, \mathbf{e}_{e_2}, ..., \mathbf{e}_{e_e}\}$.

Et cetera: other forms of actions can be thought of.

8.6.4 Requirements

Requirements for license language implementation basically amounts to requirements for three aspects. (i) The design of the license language, its abstract and concrete syntax, its interpreter, and its interfaces to distributed licensor and licensee behaviours; (ii) the requirements for a distributed system of licensor and licensee behaviours; and (iii) the monitoring and partial control of the states of licensor and licensee behaviours. The structuring of these distributed licensor and licensee behaviours differ from slightly to somewhat, but not that significant in the four license languages examples. Basically the licensor and licensee behaviours form a set of behaviours. Basically everyone can communicate with everyone. For the case of digital media licensee behaviours communicate back to licensor behaviours whenever a properly licensed action is performed – resulting in the transfer of funds from licensees to licensors. For the case of healthcare some central authority is expected to validate the granting of licenses and appear to be bound by medical training. For the case of documents such checks appear to be bound by predetermined authorisation rules. For the case of transport one can perhaps speak of more rigid management & organisation dependencies as licenses are traditionally transferred between independent authorities and companies.

8.6.5 On Modeling License Languages

Licensors are expected to maintain a state which records all the licenses it has issued. Whenever at licensee "reports back" (the begin and/or the end) of the performance of a granted action, this is recorded in its state. Sometimes these granted actions are subject to fees. The licensor therefore calculates outstanding fees — etc. Licensees are expected to maintain a state which records all the licenses it has accepted. Whenever an action is to be performed the licensee records this and checks that it is permitted to perform this action. In many cases the licensee is expected to "report back", both the beginning and the end of performance of that action, to the licensor. A typical technique of modeling licensors, licensees and patients, i.e., their PMRs, is to model them as (never ending) processes, a la CSP [250]. with input/output, ch ?/ch ! m, communications between licensors, licensees and PMRs. Their states are modeled as programmable attributes.

8.7 Management & Organisation

- *By **domain management** we shall understand such people (such decisions) (i) who (which) determine, formulate and thus set standards (cf. rules and regulations, Sect. 8.4) concerning strategic, tactical and operational decisions; (ii) who ensure that these decisions are passed on to (lower) levels of management and to floor staff; (iii) who make sure that such orders, as they were, are indeed carried out; (iv) who handle undesirable deviations in the carrying out of these orders cum decisions; and (v) who "backstops" complaints from lower management levels and from "floor" staff ∎*

- *By **domain organisation** we shall understand (vi) the structuring of management and non-management staff "oversee-able" into clusters with "tight" and "meaningful" relations; (vii) the allocation of strategic, tactical and operational concerns to within management and non-management staff clusters; and hence (viii) the "lines of command": who does what, and who reports to whom, administratively and functionally ∎*

The '&' is justified from the interrelations of items *(i–viii)*.

8.7.1 Conceptual Analysis

We first bring some examples.

Train Monitoring, I

Example 105 In China, as an example, till the early 1990s, rescheduling of trains occurred at stations and involved telephone negotiations with neighbouring stations ("up and down the lines"). Such rescheduling negotiations, by phone, imply reasonably strict management and organisation (M&O). This kind of M&O reflects the geographical layout of the rail net.

Railway Management and Organisation: Train Monitoring, II

Example 106 We single out a rather special case of railway management and organisation. Certain (lowest-level operational and station-located) supervisors are responsible for the day-to-day timely progress of trains within a station and along its incoming and outgoing lines, and according to given timetables. These supervisors and their immediate (middle-level) managers (see below for regional managers) set guidelines (for local station and incoming and outgoing lines) for the monitoring of train traffic, and for controlling trains that are either ahead of or behind their schedules. By an incoming and an outgoing line we mean part of a line between two stations, the remaining part being handled by neighbouring station management. Once it has been decided, by such a manager, that a train is not following its schedule, based on information monitored by non-management staff, then that manager directs that staff: (i) to suggest a new schedule for the train in question, as well as for possibly affected other trains, (ii) to negotiate the new schedule with appropriate neighbouring stations, until a proper reschedule can be decided upon, by the managers at respective stations, (iii) and to enact that new schedule.[192] A (middle-level operations) manager for regional traffic, i.e., train traffic involving several stations and lines, resolves possible disputes and conflicts.

The above, albeit rough-sketch description, illustrated the following management and organisation issues: (i) There is a set of lowest-level (as here: train traffic scheduling and rescheduling) supervisors and their staff; (ii) they are organised into one such group (as here: per station); (iii) there is a middle-level (as here: regional train traffic scheduling and rescheduling) manager (possibly with some small staff), organised with one such per suitable (as here: railway) region; and (iv) the guidelines issued jointly by local and regional (...) supervisors and managers imply an organisational structuring of lines of information provision and command.

People staff enterprises, the components of infrastructures with which we are concerned, i.e., for which we develop software. The larger these enterprises — these infrastructure components — the more need there is for management and organisation. The role of management is roughly, for our purposes, twofold: first, to perform strategic, tactical and operational work, to set strategic, tactical and operational policies — and to see to it that they are followed. The role of management is, second, to react to adverse conditions, that is, to unforeseen situations, and to decide how they should be handled, i.e., conflict resolution. Policy setting should help non-management staff operate normal situations — those for which no management interference is thus needed. And management "backstops" problems: management takes these

---

[192] That enactment may possibly imply the movement of several trains incident upon several stations: the one at which the manager is located, as well as possibly at neighbouring stations.

problems off the shoulders of non-management staff. To help management and staff know who's in charge wrt. policy setting and problem handling, a clear conception of the overall organisation is needed. Organisation defines lines of communication within management and staff, and between these. Whenever management and staff has to turn to others for assistance they usually, in a reasonably well-functioning enterprise, follow the command line: the paths of organigrams — the usually hierarchical box and arrow/line diagrams.

The *management and organisation* model of a domain is a partial specification; hence all the usual abstraction and modeling principles, techniques and tools apply. More specifically, management is a set of predicate functions, or of observer and generator functions These either parametrise other, the operations functions, that is, determine their behaviour, or yield results that become arguments to these other functions. Organisation is thus a set of constraints on communication behaviours. Hierarchical, rather than linear, and matrix structured organisations can also be modeled as sets (of recursively invoked sets) of equations.

To relate classical organigrams to formal descriptions we first show such an organigram (Fig. 8.4), and then we show schematic processes which — for a rather simple scenario — model managers and the managed!

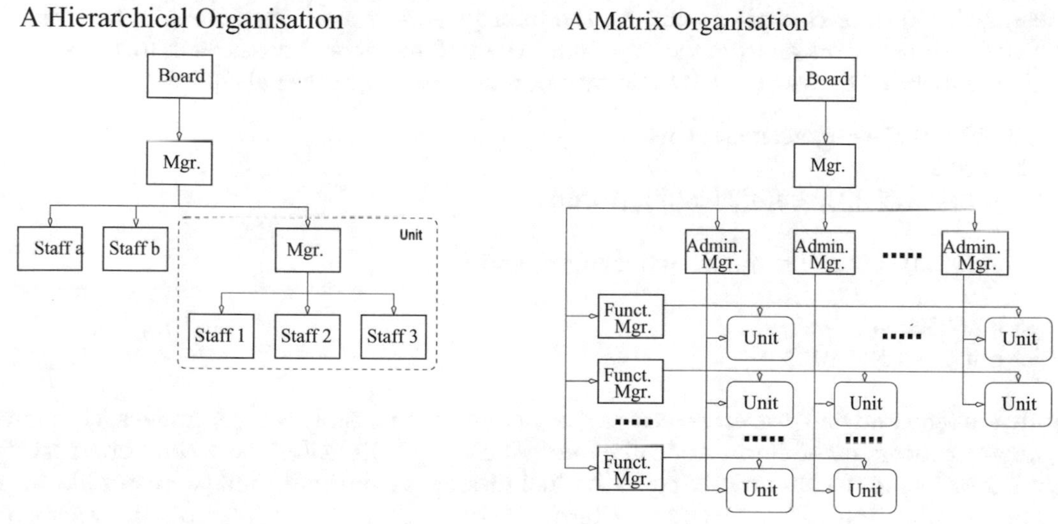

A Hierarchical Organisation   A Matrix Organisation

Fig. 8.4 Organisational Structures

Based on such a diagram, and modeling only one neighbouring group of a manager and the staff working for that manager we get a system in which one manager, mgr, and many staff, stf, coexist or work concurrently, i.e., in parallel. The mgr operates in a context and a state modeled by ψ. Each staff, stf(i) operates in a context and a state modeled by $s\sigma(i)$.

type
   Msg, Ψ, Σ, Sx
   $S\Sigma = Sx \xrightarrow{\sim} \Sigma$
channel
   { ms[i]:Msg | i:Sx }
value
   $s\sigma$:SΣ, ψ:Ψ

   sys: **Unit** $\rightarrow$ **Unit**
   sys() $\equiv$ $\|$ { stf(i)(sσ(i)) | i:Sx } $\|$ mgr(ψ)

In this system the manager, mgr, (1) either broadcasts messages, m, to all staff via message channel ms[i]. The manager's concoction, m_out(ψ), of the message, msg, has changed the manager state. Or (2) is willing to receive messages, msg, from whichever staff i the manager sends a message. Receipt of the message changes, m_in(i,m)(ψ), the manager state. In both cases the manager resumes work as from the new state. The manager chooses — in this model — which of thetwo things (1 or 2) to do by a so-called non-deterministic internal choice ($\sqcap$).

mg: $\Psi \rightarrow$ **in,out** {ms[i]|i:Sx} **Unit**
mgr(ψ) $\equiv$
(1)   **let** (ψ',m)=m_out(ψ) **in** $\parallel$ {ms[i]!m|i:Sx};mgr(ψ') **end**
      $\sqcap$
(2)   **let** $\psi' = \square$ {**let** m=ms[i]? **in** m_in(i,m)(ψ) **end**|i:Sx} **in** mgr(ψ') **end**

m_out: $\Psi \rightarrow \Psi \times$ MSG,
m_in: Sx $\times$ MSG $\rightarrow \Psi \rightarrow \Psi$

And in this system, staff i, stf(i), (1) either is willing to receive a message, msg, from the manager, and then to change, st_in(msg)(σ), state accordingly, or (2) to concoct, st_out(σ), a message, msg (thus changing state) for the manager, and send it ms[i]!msg. In both cases the staff resumes work as from the new state. The staff member chooses — in this model — which of thetwo "things" (1 or 2) to do by a non-deterministic internal choice ($\sqcap$).

stf: i:Sx $\rightarrow \Sigma \rightarrow$ **in,out** ms[i] **Unit**
stf(i)(σ) $\equiv$
(1)   **let** m = ms[i]? **in** stf(i)(st_in(m)(σ)) **end**
      $\sqcap$
(2)   **let** (σ',m) = st_out(σ) **in** ms[i]!m; stf(i)(σ') **end**

st_in: MSG $\rightarrow \Sigma \rightarrow \Sigma$,
st_out: $\Sigma \rightarrow \Sigma \times$ MSG

Both manager and staff processes recurse (i.e., iterate) over possibly changing states. The management process non-deterministically, internal choice, "alternates" between "broadcast"-issuing orders to staff and receiving individual messages from staff. Staff processes likewise non-deterministically, internal choice, alternate between receiving orders from management and issuing individual messages to management. The conceptual example also illustrates modeling stakeholder behaviours as interacting (here CSP-like) processes.

Strategic, Tactical and Operations Management

Example 107 We think of (i) strategic, (ii) tactic, and (iii) operational managers as well as (iv) supervisors, (v) team leaders and the rest of the (vi) staff (i.e., workers) of a domain enterprise as functions. Each category of staff, i.e., each function, works in state and updates that state according to schedules and resource allocations — which are considered part of the state. To make the description simple we do not detail the state other than saying that each category works on an "instantaneous copy" of "the" state. Now think of six staff category activities, strategic managers, tactical managers, operational managers, supervisors, team leaders and workers as six simultaneous sets of actions. Each function defines a step of collective (i.e., group) (strategic, tactical, operational) management, supervisor, team leader and worker work. Each step is considered "atomic". Now think of an enterprise as the "repeated" step-wise simultaneous performance of these category activities. Six "next" states arise. These are, in the reality of the domain, ameliorated, that is reconciled into one state. however with the next iteration, i.e., step, of work having each category apply its work to a reconciled version of the state resulting from that category's previously yielded state and the mediated "global" state. **Caveat:** The below is not a mathematically proper definition. It suggests one !

type

0. $\Sigma, \Sigma_s, \Sigma_t, \Sigma_o, \Sigma_u, \Sigma_e, \Sigma_w$

value

1. str, tac, opr, sup, tea, wrk: $\Sigma_i \rightarrow \Sigma_i$
2. stra, tact, oper, supr, team, work: $\Sigma \rightarrow (\Sigma_{x_1} \times \Sigma_{x_2} \times \Sigma_{x_3} \times \Sigma_{x_4} \times \Sigma_{x_5}) \rightarrow \Sigma$
3. objective: $(\Sigma_s \times \Sigma_t \times \Sigma_o \times \Sigma_u \times \Sigma_e \times \Sigma_w) \rightarrow$ **Bool**
3. enterprise,ameliorate: $(\Sigma_s \times \Sigma_t \times \Sigma_o \times \Sigma_u \times \Sigma_e \times \Sigma_w) \rightarrow \Sigma$
4. enterprise: $(\sigma_s, \sigma_t, \sigma_u, \sigma_e, \sigma_w) \equiv$
6.   **let** $\sigma'_s = \text{stra}(\text{str}(\sigma_s))(\sigma'_t, \sigma'_o, \sigma'_u, \sigma'_e, \sigma'_w),$
7. $\sigma'_t = \text{tact}(\text{tac}(\sigma_t))(\sigma'_s, \sigma'_o, \sigma'_u, \sigma'_e, \sigma'_w),$
8. $\sigma'_o = \text{oper}(\text{opr}(\sigma_o))(\sigma'_s, \sigma'_t, \sigma'_u, \sigma'_e, \sigma'_w),$
9. $\sigma'_u = \text{supr}(\text{sup}(\sigma_u))(\sigma'_s, \sigma'_t, \sigma'_o, \sigma'_e, \sigma'_w),$
10. $\sigma'_e = \text{team}(\text{tea}(\sigma_e))(\sigma'_s, \sigma'_t, \sigma'_o, \sigma'_u, \sigma'_w),$
11. $\sigma'_w = \text{work}(\text{wrk}(\sigma_w))(\sigma'_s, \sigma'_t, \sigma'_o, \sigma'_u, \sigma'_e)$ **in**
12.   **if** objective$(\sigma'_s, \sigma'_t, \sigma'_o, \sigma'_u, \sigma'_e, \sigma'_w)$
13.   **then** ameliorate$(\sigma'_s, \sigma'_t, \sigma'_o, \sigma'_u, \sigma'_e, \sigma'_w)$
14.   **else** enterprise$(\sigma'_s, \sigma'_t, \sigma'_o, \sigma'_u, \sigma'_e, \sigma'_w)$
15.   **end end**

0. Σ is a further undefined and unexplained enterprise state space. The various enterprise players view this state in their own way.
1. Six staff group operations, str, tac, opr, sup, tea and wrk, each act in the enterprise state such as conceived by respective groups to effect a resulting enterprise state such as achieved by respective groups.
2. Six staff group state amelioration functions, ame_s, ame _t, ame_o, ame_u, ame_e and ame_w, each apply to the resulting enterprise states such as achieved by respective groups to yield a result state such as achieved by that group.
3. An overall objective function tests whether a state summary reflects that the objectives of the enterprise has been achieved or not.
4. The enterprise function applies to the tuple of six group-biased (i.e., ameliorated) states. Initially these may all be the same state. The result is an ameliorated state.
5. An iteration, that is, a step of enterprise activities, lines 5.–13. proceeds as follows:
6. strategic management operates
   - in its state space, $\sigma_s : \Sigma$;
   - effects a next (un-ameliorated strategic management) state σ'_s;
   - and ameliorates this latter state in the context of all the other player's ameliorated result states.
7. -11. The same actions take place, simultaneously for the other players: tac, opr, sup, tea and wrk.
12. A test, *has objectives been met*, is made on the six ameliorated states.
13. If test is successful, then the enterprise terminates in an ameliorated state.
14. Otherwise the enterprise recurses, that is, "repeats" itself in new states.

The above "function" definition is suggestive. It suggests that a solution to the fix-point 6-tuple of equations over "intermediate" states, σ'_x, where x is any of s, t, o, u, e, w, is achieveable by iteration over just these 6 equations.

8.7.2 Requirements

Top-level, including strategic management tends to not be amenable to "automation". Increasingly tactical management tends to "divide" time between "bush-fire, stop-gap" actions – hardly automatable and formulating, initiating and monitoring main operations. The initiation and monitoring of tactical actions appear amenable to partial automation. Operational management – with its reliance on rules & regulations, scripts and licenses – is where computer monitoring and partial control has reaped the richest harvests.

8.7.3 On Modeling Management and Organisation

Management and organisation basically spans entity, function, event and behaviour intensities and thus typically require the full spectrum of modeling techniques and notations — summarised in Sect. **8.2.3**.

8.8 Human Behaviour

- *By **domain human behaviour** we shall understand any of a quality spectrum of carrying out assigned work: from (i) careful, diligent and accurate, via (ii) sloppy dispatch, and (iii) delinquent work, to (iv) outright criminal pursuit* ∎

Although we otherwise do not go into any depth with respect to the analysis & description of humans, we shall momentarily depart from this "abstinence".

8.8.1 Conceptual Analysis

To model human behaviour "smacks" of modeling human actors, the psychology of humans, etc.! We shall not attempt to model the psychological side of humans — for the simple reason that we neither know how to do that nor whether it can at all be done. Instead we shall be focusing on the effects on non-human manifest entities of human behaviour.

Banking — or Programming — Staff Behaviour
Example 108 Let us assume a bank clerk, "in ye olde" days, when calculating, say mortgage repayments (cf. Example 97). We would characterise such a clerk as being ***diligent,*** etc., if that person carefully follows the mortgage calculation rules, and checks and double-checks that calculations "tally up", or lets others do so. We would characterise a clerk as being ***sloppy*** if that person occasionally forgets the checks alluded to above. We would characterise a clerk as being ***delinquent*** if that person systematically forgets these checks. And we would call such a person a ***criminal*** if that person intentionally miscalculates in such a way that the bank (and/or the mortgage client) is cheated out of funds which, instead, may be diverted to the cheater. Let us, instead of a bank clerk, assume a software programmer charged with implementing an automatic routine for effecting mortgage repayments (cf. Example 97). We would characterise the programmer as being ***diligent*** if that person carefully follows the mortgage calculation rules, and throughout the development verifies and tests

that the calculations are correct with respect to the rules. We would characterise the programmer as being **sloppy** if that person forgets certain checks and tests when otherwise correcting the computing program under development. We would characterise the programmer as being **delinquent** if that person systematically forgets these checks and tests. And we would characterise the programmer as being a **criminal** if that person intentionally provides a program which miscalculates the mortgage interest, etc., in such a way that the bank (and/or the mortgage client) is cheated out of funds.

A Human Behaviour Mortgage Calculation

Example 109 Example 97 on page 217 gave a semantics to the mortgage calculation request (i.e., command) as would a diligent bank clerk be expected to perform it. To express, that is, to model, how sloppy, delinquent, or outright criminal persons (staff?) could behave we must modify the int_Cmd(mkPM(c,a,m,p,d'))(ρ,α,μ,ℓ) definition.

int_Cmd(mkPM(c,a,m,p,d))$(\rho,\alpha,\mu,\ell) \equiv$
    let $(b,d') = \ell(m)$ **in**
    if $q(\alpha(a),p)$ $[\alpha(a){\le}p\vee\alpha(a){=}p\vee\alpha(a){\le}p\vee...]$
        then
            let $i = f_1(\text{interest}(mi,b,\text{period}(d,d')))$,
            $\ell' = \ell \dagger [m{\mapsto}f_2(\ell(m){-}(p{-}i))]$,
            $\alpha' = \alpha \dagger [a{\mapsto}f_3(\alpha(a){-}p),a_i{\mapsto}f_4(\alpha(a_i){+}i),a_{\text{``staff''}}{\mapsto}f_{\text{``staff''}}(\alpha(a_{\text{``staff''}}){+}i)]$ **in**
            $((\rho,\alpha',\mu,\ell'),\text{ok})$ **end**
        else
            $((\rho,\alpha',\mu,\ell),\text{nok})$
    end end
    pre $c \in \textbf{dom}\ \mu \wedge m \in \mu(c)$

    $q: P \times P \xrightarrow{\sim} \textbf{Bool}$
    $f_1,f_2,f_3,f_4,f_{\text{``staff''}}: P \xrightarrow{\sim} P$ [typically: $f_{\text{``staff''}} = \lambda p.p$]

The predicate q and the functions f_1, f_2, f_3, f_4 and $f_{\text{``staff''}}$ of Example 109 are deliberately left undefined. They are being defined by the "staffer" when performing (incl., programming) the mortgage calculation routine. The point of Example 109 is that one must first define the mortgage calculation script precisely as one would like to see the diligent staff (programmer) to perform (incl., correctly program) it before one can "pinpoint" all the places where lack of diligence may "set in". The invocations of q, f_1, f_2, f_3, f_4 and $f_{\text{``staff''}}$ designate those places. The point of Example 109 is also that we must first domain-define, "to the best of our ability" all the places where human behaviour may play other than a desirable role. If we cannot, then we cannot claim that some requirements aim at countering undesirable human behaviour.

    Commensurate with the above, humans interpret rules and regulations differently, and, for some humans, not always consistently — in the sense of repeatedly applying the same interpretations. Our final specification pattern is therefore:

type
    Action = $\Theta \xrightarrow{\sim} \Theta$-**infset**
value
    hum_int: Rule $\rightarrow \Theta \rightarrow$ RUL-**infset**
    action: Stimulus $\rightarrow \Theta \rightarrow \Theta$
    hum_beha: Stimulus $\times$ Rules $\rightarrow$ Action $\rightarrow \Theta \xrightarrow{\sim} \Theta$-**infset**
    hum_beha(sy_sti,sy_rul)$(\alpha)(\theta)$ **as** θset

post
$$\theta\text{set} = \alpha(\theta) \wedge \text{action(sy\_sti)}(\theta) \in \theta\text{set}$$
$$\wedge\ \forall\ \theta':\Theta\cdot\theta' \in \theta\text{set} \Rightarrow$$
$$\exists\ \text{se\_rul:RUL}\cdot\text{se\_rul} \in \text{hum\_int(sy\_rul)}(\theta)\Rightarrow\text{se\_rul}(\theta,\theta')$$

The above is, necessarily, sketchy: There is a possibly infinite variety of ways of interpreting some rules. A human, in carrying out an action, interprets applicable rules and chooses one which that person believes suits some (professional, sloppy, delinquent or criminal) intent. "Suits" means that it satisfies the intent, i.e., yields **true** on the pre/post-configuration pair, when the action is performed — whether as intended by the ones who issued the rules and regulations or not. We do not cover the case of whether an appropriate regulation is applied or not.

The above-stated axioms express how it is in the domain, not how we would like it to be. For that we have to establish requirements.

8.8.2 Requirements

Requirements in relation to the human behaviour facet is not requirements about software that "replaces" human behaviour. Such requirements were hinted at in Sects. **8.5.2–8.7.2**. Human behaviour facet requirements are about software that checks human behaviour; that its remains diligent; that it does not transgress into sloppy, delinquent, let alone criminal behaviour. When transgressions are discovered, appropriate remedial actions may be prescribed.

8.8.3 On Modeling Human Behaviour

To model human behaviour is, "initially", much like modeling management and organisation. But only 'initially'. The most significant human behaviour modeling aspect is then that of modeling non-determinism and looseness, even ambiguity. So a specification language which allows specifying non-determinism and looseness (like CafeOBJ [168] and RSL [187]) is to be preferred. To prescribe requirements is to prescribe the monitoring of the human input at the computer interface.

8.9 Summary

8.9.1 Method Principles, Techniques and Tools

Recall that by a method we shall understand a *set of* ***principles*** for selecting and applying a *set of* ***techniques*** using a *set of* ***tools*** in order to construct an artefact.

8.9.1.1 Principles of Modelling Domain Facets

We shall just point out one applied principle, that of:

- **Conservative Extension:**[193] This principle of making sure that additional domain descriptions form conservative extensions are applied throughout this chapter:

  ∞ Support Technologies, Sect. **8.3**,
  ∞ Rules & Regulations, Sect. **8.4**,
  ∞ Scripts, Sect. **8.5**,

  ∞ License Languages, Sect. **8.6**,
  ∞ Management & Organisation, Sect. **8.7** and
  ∞ Human Behaviour, Sect. **8.8**.

The concepts of these six additional facets builds upon, i.e., extends, those of Intrinsics, that is, those of Chapters 4–7.

Most of the principles mentioned in earlier chapters have also been applied.

8.9.1.2 Techniques of Modelling Domain Facets

We have already mentioned techniques that have been applied in this chapter's "On Modelling ..." sections: Sects. **8.2.3** on page 209, **8.3.3** on page 214, **8.4.3** on page 217, **8.5.3** on page 219, **8.6.5** on page 229, **8.7.3** on page 234 and **8.8.3** on the facing page. And shall leave it at that.

8.9.1.3 Tools of Modelling Domain Facets

The tools for modelling, i.e., analysing & describing domain facets have already been mentioned in this chapters seven sections on the individual facets.

8.9.2 General Issues

8.9.2.1 Completion

Domain acquisition results in typically up to thousands of units of domain descriptions. Domain analysis subsequently also serves to classify which facet any one of these description units primarily characterises. But some such "compartmentalisations" may be difficult, and may be deferred till the step of "completion". It may then be, "at the end of the day", that is, after all of the above facets have been modeled that some description units are left as not having been described, not deliberately, but "circumstantially". It then behooves the domain engineer to fit these "dangling" description units into suitable parts of the domain description. This "slotting in" may be simple, and all is fine. Or it may be difficult. Such difficulty may be a sign that the chosen model, the chosen description, in its selection of entities, functions, events and behaviours to model — in choosing these over other possible selections of phenomena and concepts is not appropriate. Another attempt must be made. Another selection, another abstraction of entities, functions, etc., may need be chosen. Usually however, after having chosen the abstractions of the intrinsic phenomena and concepts, one can start checking whether "dangling" description units can be fitted in "with ease".

---

[193] We remind the reader of the definition of the concept of 'conservative extension: *An extension of a logical theory is conservative, i.e., conserves, if every theorem expressible in the original theory is also derivable within the original theory [en.wiktionary.org/wiki/conservative_extension]* [[ι 44()ii,π 9]]. See also [358, 153, 104, 22, 254, 172] and en.m.wikipedia.org/wiki/Extension_by_new_constant_and_function_-names

8.9.2.2 Integrating Formal Descriptions

We have seen that to model the full spectrum of domain facets one needs not one, but several specification languages. No single specification language suffices. It seems highly unlikely and it appears not to be desirable to obtain a single, "universal" specification language capable of "equally" elegantly, suitably abstractly modeling all aspects of a domain. Hence one must conclude that the full modeling of domains shall deploy several formal notations – including plain, good old mathematics in all its forms. The issues are then the following which combinations of notations to select, and how to make sure that the combined specification denotes something meaningful. The ongoing series of "Integrating Formal Methods" conferences [12] is a good source for techniques, compositions and meanings.

8.9.2.3 The Impossibility of Describing Any Domain Completely

Domain descriptions are, by necessity, abstractions. One can never hope for any notion of complete domain descriptions. The situation is no better for domains such as we define them than for physics. Physicists strive to understand the manifest world around us – the world that was there before humans started creating "their domains". The physicists describe the physical world "in bits and pieces" such that large collections of these pieces "fit together", that is, are based on some commonly accepted laws and in some commonly agreed mathematics. Similarly for such domains as will be the subject of domain science & engineering such as we cover that subject in [81, 69] and in the present chapter and reports [78, 71]. Individual such domain descriptions will be emphasizing some clusters of facets, others will be emphasizing other aspects.

8.9.2.4 Rôles for Domain Descriptions

We can distinguish between a spectrum of rôles for domain descriptions. Some of the issues brought forward below may have been touched upon in [81, 69].

★ **Alternative Domain Descriptions:**

It may very well be meaningful to avail oneself of a variety of domain models (i.e., descriptions) for any one domain, that is, for what we may consider basically one and the same domain. In control theory (a science) and automation (an engineering) we develop specific descriptions, usually on the form of a set of differential equations, for any one control problem. The basis for the control problem is typically the science of mechanics. This science has many renditions (i.e., interpretations). For the control problem, say that of keeping a missile carried by a train wagon, erect during train movement and/or windy conditions, one may then develop a "self-contained" description of the problem based on some mechanics theory presentation. Similarly for domains. One may refer to an existing domain description. But one may re-develop a textually "smaller" domain description for any one given, i.e., specific problem.

★ **Domain Science:**

A domain description designates a domain theory. That is, a bundle of propositions, lemmas and theorems that are either rather explicit or can be proven from the description. So a domain description is the basis for a theory as well as for the discovery of domain laws, that is, for a domain science. We have sciences of physics (incl. chemistry), biology, etc.

Perhaps it is about time to have proper sciences, to the extent one can have such sciences for human-made domains.

⋆ Business Process Re-engineering:

Some domains manifest serious amounts of human actions and interactions. These may be found to not be efficient to a degree that one might so desire. A given domain description may therefore be a basis for suggesting other *management & organisation* structures, and/or *rules & regulations* than present ones. Yes, even making explicit *scripts* or a *license language* which have hitherto been tacitly understood – without necessarily computerising any support for such a *script* or *license language*. The given and the resulting domain descriptions may then be the basis for *operations research* models that may show desired or acceptable efficiency improvements.

⋆ Software Development:

[69] shows one approach to requirements prescription. Domain analysis & description, i.e., domain engineering, is here seen as an initial phase, with requirements prescription engineering being a second phase, and software design being a third phase. We see domain engineering as indispensable, that is, an absolute must, for software development. [61, *Domains: Their Simulation, Monitoring and Control*] further illustrates how domain engineering is a base for the development of domain simulators, demos, monitors and controllers.

8.9.2.5 Grand Challenges of Informatics[194]

To establish a reasonably trustworthy and believable theory of a domain, say the transportation, or just the railway domain, may take years, possibly 10–15! Similarly for domains such as the financial service industry, the market (of consumers and producers, retailers, wholesaler, distribution cum supply chain), healthcare, and so forth. The current author urges younger scientists to get going! It is about time.

8.10 Bibliographical Notes

To create domain descriptions, or requirements prescriptions, or software designs, properly, at least such as this author sees it, is a joy to behold. The beauty of carefully selected and balanced abstractions, their interplay with other such, the relations between phases, stages and steps, and many more conceptual constructions make software engineering possibly the most challenging intellectual pursuit today. For this and more consult [42, 43, 44].

8.11 Exercise Problems

We suggest several classes of exercises, to wit: two or more of *research problems, student exercise* and *term projects*.

---

[194] In the early-to-mid 2000s there were a rush of research foundations and scientists enumerating *"Grand Challenges of Informatics"*

8.11.1 Research Problems

Exercise 41 A Research Challenge. Mathematical Explanation: The seven facets identified in this chapter are not identified with respect to one another on the basis of some mathematical model. In what [theoretical] computer science sense could one hold them out from one another? If you have a solution please present it.

Exercise 42 A Research Challenge. Other Facets?: In this chapter we have identified six facets beyond the intrinsics. The research challenge here is to identify more facets and to give them a treatment like in this chapter or even as suggested in the above exercise.

8.11.2 Term Projects

We continue the term projects of Sects. **4.24.3** on page 104, **5.13.3** on page 152 and **7.14.3** on page 203.

The students are to identify and analyse & describe at least three distinct facets of their chosen domain, that is:

- variations of intrinsics,
- support technology,
- rules & regulations,
- scripts,
- license language,
- management & organisation, and
- human behaviour.

Exercise 43 An MSc Student Exercise. The Consumer Market, Facets: We refer to Exercises 4 on page 105, 20 on page 152, 34 on page 204 and 43.

Exercise 44 An MSc Student Exercise. Financial Service Industry, Facets: We refer to Exercises 5 on page 105, 21 on page 152 and 35 on page 204.

Exercise 45 An MSc Student Exercise. Container Line Industry, Facets: We refer to Exercises 6 on page 105, 22 on page 152, and 36 on page 204.

Exercise 46 An MSc Student Exercise. Railway Systems, Facets: We refer to Exercises 7 on page 105, 23 on page 152, and 37 on page 204.

Exercise 47 A PhD Student Problem. Part-Fluid Conjoins: Canals, Facets: We refer to Exercises 8 on page 105, 24 on page 152 and 38 on page 204.

Exercise 48 A PhD Student Problem. Part-Fluids Conjoins: Rum Production, Facets: We refer to Exercises 9 on page 105, 25 on page 153 and 39 on page 204.

Exercise 49 A PhD Student Problem. Part-Fluids Conjoins: Waste Management, Facets: We refer to Exercise 10 on page 105, 26 on page 153, and 40 on page 204.

These exercise problems are continued in Sect. **9.9.2** on page 297.

Part III
REQUIREMENTS

Chapter 9
REQUIREMENTS

In this chapter we show one approach to systematically, but, of course, not automatically, "derive" requirements prescriptions from domain descriptions. We shall introduce and treat quite a vocabulary of concepts (i) machine; (ii-iv) domain, interface and machine requirements; (v-ix) projection, instantiation, determination, extension and fitting; and (x) derived requirements.

The approach we show is novel [47]. It does not replace conventional requirements engineering [377]. Merely supplements it. The conventional approach is not founded on domain descriptions, although frequent references are made, more-or-less implicitly, to domains. We therefore find it justified to present the view of this chapter that requirement prescriptions can be rather systematically arrived at from a series of analyses & rewritings of domain descriptions.

A Transcendental Deduction

The "passage" from domain description to requirements prescription marks a transcendental deduction. Domain descriptions designate what is being described[195]. Requirements prescriptions designate what is intended to be implemented by computing[196]. Please note the distinction: At the end of the development of a domain description we have just that: a domain description. At the beginning of the development of a requirements prescription we consider the domain description to be the initial requirements prescription: Thus, seemingly bewildering, in one instance a document is considered a domain description, in the next instance, without that document having been textually changed[197], it is now considered a requirements prescription.

The transition from domain description to requirements prescription also marks a transition from *"no-design mode"* description to *"design-mode"* prescription, We remind the reader of Sect. **7.13.3** on page 198. Please reread that short section carefully while you study this chapter[198].

Thus, in this chapter, we shall be unveiling a number of stages in which an original, perhaps "in-computable", domain description successively becomes an increasingly "more computable" requirements prescription.

---

[195] Yes, but you may be well advised in also taking domain descriptions to denote some mathematical object.

[196] Still, you may be way advised in also taking requirements prescriptions to denote some mathematical object.

[197] Well, it could be said that the only textual change is the heading of the document. Before *domain description*, after *requirements prescription*.

[198] And: when read, be challenged by *Research Problem* 50 on page 297.

© The Author(s), under exclusive license to Springer Nature Switzerland AG 2021
D. Bjørner, *Domain Science and Engineering*, Monographs in Theoretical Computer Science. An EATCS Series,
https://doi.org/10.1007/978-3-030-73484-8_9

9.1 Introduction

We claim that the present chapter contributes to our understanding and practice of *software engineering* as follows: (1) it shows how the new phase of engineering, **domain engineering**, forms a prerequisite for **requirements engineering**; (2) it endows the "classical" form of requirements engineering with a structured set of development stages and steps: (a) first a **domain requirements** stage, (b) to be followed by an **interface requirements** stage, and (c) to be concluded by a **machine requirements** stage; (3) it further structures and gives a reasonably precise contents to the stage of domain requirements: (i) first a **projection** step, (ii) then an **instantiation** step, (iii) then a **determination** step, (iv) then an **extension** step, and (v) finally a **fitting** step — with these five steps possibly being iterated; and (4) it also structures and gives a reasonably precise contents to the stage of interface requirements based on a notion of **shared** entities. Each of the steps (i–v) open for the possibility of *simplifications*. Steps (a–c) and (i-v), we claim, are new. They reflect a serious contribution, we claim, to a logical structuring of the field of requirements engineering and its very many otherwise seemingly diverse concerns.

9.1.1 Some Comments

This chapter is, perhaps, unusual in the following respects: (i) It is a methodology chapter, hence there are no "neat" theories about development, no succinctly expressed propositions, lemmas nor theorems, and hence no proofs[199]. (ii) As a consequence the chapter is borne by many, and by extensive examples. (iii) The examples of this chapter are all focused on a generic road transport net. (iv) To reasonably fully exemplify the requirements approach, illustrating how our method copes with a seeming complexity of interrelated method aspects, the full example of this chapter embodies very many description and prescription elements: hundreds of concepts (types, axioms, functions). (v) This methodology chapter covers a "grand" area of software engineering: Many textbooks and papers are written on *Requirements Engineering*. We postulate, in contrast to all such books (and papers), that *requirements engineering* should be founded on *domain engineering*. Hence we must, somehow, show that our approach relates to major elements of what the *Requirements Engineering* books put forward. (vi) As a result, this chapter is long.

9.1.2 Structure of Chapter

The structure of the chapter is as follows: Section 9.2 provides a fair-sized, hence realistic example. Sections 9.3–9.5 covers our approach to requirements development. Section 9.3 overviews the issue of 'requirements'; relates our approach (i.e., Sects. 9.4–9.5) to *systems, user and external equipment* and *functional requirements*; and Sect. 9.3 also introduces the concepts of the *machine* to be requirements prescribed, the *domain*, the *interface* and the *machine requirements*. Section 9.4 covers the *domain requirements* stages of *projection* (Sect. 9.4.1), *instantiation* (Sect. 9.4.2), *determination* (Sect. 9.4.3), *extension* (Sect. 9.4.4) and *fitting* (Sect. 9.4.5). Section 9.5 covers key features of *interface requirements*: *shared phenomena* (Sect. 9.5.1.1), *shared endurants* (Sect. 9.5.1.2) and *shared actions*, *shared events* and

---

[199] — where these proofs would be about the development theories. The example development of requirements do imply properties, but formulation and proof of these do not constitute new contributions — so are left out.

shared behaviours (Sect. **9.5.1.3**). Section **9.5.1.3** further introduces the notion of *derived requirements*. Section **9.7** concludes the chapter.

9.2 An Example Domain: Transport

Chapters 4–7 brought a version of the "running" *road transport system* example. In order to exemplify the various stages and steps of requirements development we first bring a domain description example. The example follows the steps of an idealised domain description. First we describe the endurants, then we describe the perdurants. Endurant description initially focus on the composite and atomic parts. Then on their "internal" qualities: unique identifications, mereologies, and attributes. The descriptions alternate between enumerated, i.e., labeled narrative sentences and correspondingly "numbered" formalisations. The narrative labels cum formula numbers will be referred to, frequently in the various steps of domain requirements development.

9.2.1 Endurants

Since we have chosen a manifest domain, that is, a domain whose endurants can be pointed at, seen, touched, we shall follow the analysis & description process as outlined in [73] and formalised in [65]. That is, we first identify, analyse and describe (manifest) parts, composite and atomic, abstract (Sect. **9.2.2**) or concrete (Sect. **9.2.2.1**). Then we identify, analyse and describe their unique identifiers (Sect. **9.2.2.2**), mereologies (Sect. **9.2.2.3**), and attributes (Sects. **9.2.2.4–9.2.2.4**).

The example fragments will be presented in a small type-font.

9.2.2 Domain, Net, Fleet and Monitor

The root domain, Δ, is that of a composite traffic system (305a.) with a road net, (305b.) with a fleet of vehicles and (305c.) of whose individual position on the road net we can speak, that is, monitor.[200]

305 We analyse the traffic system into

    a a composite road net,

    b a composite fleet (of vehicles), and

    c an atomic monitor.

type
305   Δ
305a N
305b F
305c M

value
305a obs_N: $\Delta \rightarrow$ N
305b obs_F: $\Delta \rightarrow$ F
305c obs_M: $\Delta \rightarrow$ M

306 The road net consists of two composite parts,

    a an aggregation of hubs and
    b an aggregation of links.

---

[200] The monitor can be thought of, i.e., conceptualised. It is not necessarily a physically manifest phenomenon.

type
306a HA
306b LA

value
306a obs_HA: N → HA
306b obs_LA: N → LA

9.2.2.1 Hubs and Links

307 Hub aggregates are sets of hubs.
308 Link aggregates are sets of links.

309 Fleets are set of vehicles.

type
307 H, HS = H-set
308 L, LS = L-set
309 V, VS = V-set

value
307 obs_HS: HA → HS
308 obs_LS: LA → LS
309 obs_VS: F → VS

310 We introduce some auxiliary functions.

  a links extracts the links of a network.
  b hubs extracts the hubs of a network.

value
310a links: Δ → L-set
310a links(δ) ≡ obs_LS(obs_LA(obs_N(δ)))
310b hubs: Δ → H-set
310b hubs(δ) ≡ obs_HS(obs_HA(obs_N(δ)))

9.2.2.2 Unique Identifiers

Applying `observe_unique_identifier`, the domain description prompt 8 on page 108, to the observed parts yields the following.

311 Nets, hub and link aggregates, hubs and
     links, fleets, vehicles and the monitor all

  a have unique identifiers
  b such that all such are distinct, and
  c with corresponding observers.

type
311a NI, HAI, LAI, HI, LI, FI, VI, MI
value
311c uid_NI: N → NI
311c uid_HAI: HA → HAI
311c uid_LAI: LA → LAI
311c uid_HI: H → HI

311c uid_LI: L → LI
311c uid_FI: F → FI
311c uid_VI: V → VI
311c uid_MI: M → MI
axiom
311b NI∩HAI={}, NI∩LAI={}, NI∩HI={}, etc.

where axiom 311b is expressed semi-formally, in mathematics. We introduce some auxiliary functions:

312 xtr_lis extracts all link identifiers of a traffic
     system.
313 xtr_his extracts all hub identifiers of a traf-
     fic system.

314 Given an appropriate link identifier and a
     net get_link 'retrieves' the designated link.
315 Given an appropriate hub identifier and a
     net get_hub 'retrieves' the designated hub.

value
312 xtr_lis: $\Delta \rightarrow$ LI-set
312 xtr_lis(δ) $\equiv$
312   **let** ls = links(δ) **in** {uid_LI(l)|l:L•l $\in$ ls} **end**
313 xtr_his: $\Delta \rightarrow$ HI-set
313 xtr_his(δ) $\equiv$
313   **let** hs = hubs(δ) **in** {uid_HI(h)|h:H•k $\in$ hs} **end**
314 get_link: LI $\rightarrow \Delta \overset{\sim}{\rightarrow}$ L
314 get_link(li)(δ) $\equiv$
314   **let** ls = links(δ) **in**
314   **let** l:L • l $\in$ ls $\wedge$ li=uid_LI(l) **in** l **end end**
314   **pre:** li $\in$ xtr_lis(δ)
315 get_hub: HI $\rightarrow \Delta \overset{\sim}{\rightarrow}$ H
315 get_hub(hi)(δ) $\equiv$
315   **let** hs = hubs(δ) **in**
315   **let** h:H • h $\in$ hs $\wedge$ hi=uid_HI(h) **in** h **end end**
315   **pre:** hi $\in$ xtr_his(δ)

9.2.2.3 Mereology

We cover the mereologies of all part sorts introduced so far. We decide that nets, hub aggregates, link aggregates and fleets have no mereologies of interest. Applying observe_mereology, the domain description prompt 9 on page 113, to hubs, links, vehicles and the monitor yields the following.

316 Hub mereologies reflect that they are connected to zero, one or more links.
317 Link mereologies reflect that they are connected to exactly two distinct hubs.
318 Vehicle mereologies reflect that they are connected to the monitor.
319 The monitor mereology reflects that it is connected to all vehicles.
320 For all hubs of any net it must be the case that their mereology designates links of that net.
321 For all links of any net it must be the case that their mereologies designates hubs of that net.
322 For all transport domains it must be the case that

    a the mereology of vehicles of that system designates the monitor of that system, and that
    b the mereology of the monitor of that system designates vehicles of that system.

value
316 **obs_mereo_H**: H $\rightarrow$ LI-set
317 **obs_mereo_L**: L $\rightarrow$ HI-set
axiom
317 $\forall$ l:L•**card** mereo_L(l)=2
value
318 **obs_mereo_V**: V $\rightarrow$ MI
319 **obs_mereo_M**: M $\rightarrow$ VI-set
axiom
320 $\forall$ δ:Δ, hs:HS•hs=hubs(δ), ls:LS•ls=links(δ) •
320   $\forall$ h:H•h $\in$ hs•mereo_H(h)$\subseteq$xtr_lis(δ) $\wedge$
321   $\forall$ l:L•l $\in$ ls•mereo_L(l)$\subseteq$xtr_his(δ) $\wedge$
322a **let** f:F•f=obs_F(δ) $\Rightarrow$
322a   **let** m:M•m=obs_M(δ), vs:VS•vs=obs_VS(f) **in**
322a $\forall$ v:V•v $\in$ vs$\Rightarrow$uid_V(v) $\in$ mereo_M(m) $\wedge$ mereo_M(m) = {uid_V(v)|v:V•v $\in$ vs}
322b **end end**

9.2.2.4 Attributes, I

We may not have shown all of the attributes mentioned below — so consider them informally introduced!

- **Hubs:** *locations*[201] are considered static, *hub state*s and *hub state space*s are considered programmable;
- **Links:** *length*s and *location*s are considered static, *link state*s and *link state space*s are considered programmable;
- **Vehicles:** *manufacturer name*, *engine type* (whether diesel, gasoline or electric) and *engine power* (kW/horse power) are considered static; *velocity* and *acceleration* may be considered reactive (i.e., a function of gas pedal position, etc.), *global position* (informed via a GNSS: Global Navigation Satellite System) and *local position* (calculated from a global position) are considered biddable

Applying observe_attributes, the domain description prompt 10 on page 121, to hubs, links, vehicles and the monitor yields the following.

First hubs.

323 Hubs

a have geodetic locations, GeoH,
b have *hub state*s which are sets of pairs of identifiers of links connected to the hub[202],
c and have *hub state space*s which are sets of hub states[203].

324 For every net,

a link identifiers of a hub state must designate links of that net, and
b every hub state of a net must be in the hub state space of that hub.

325 We introduce an auxiliary function: xtr_lis extracts all link identifiers of a hub state.

type
323a   GeoH
323b $H\Sigma = (LI \times LI)$-**set**
323c $H\Omega = H\Sigma$-**set**
value
323a   attr_GeoH: H → GeoH
323b   attr_$H\Sigma$: H → $H\Sigma$
323c   attr_$H\Omega$: H → $H\Omega$
axiom
324   ∀ δ:Δ · **let** hs = hubs(δ) **in**
324   ∀ h:H · h ∈ hs · xtr_lis(h)⊆xtr_lis(δ)
324b   ∧ attr_Σ(h) ∈ attr_Ω(h)
324   **end**
value
325   xtr_lis: H → LI-**set**
325   xtr_lis(h) ≡ {li | li:LI,(li′,li″):LI×LI · (li′,li″) ∈ attr_$H\Sigma$(h) ∧ li ∈ {li′,li″}}

Then links.

326 Links have lengths.
327 Links have geodetic location.
328 Links have states and state spaces:

a States modeled here as pairs, $(hi′,hi″)$, of identifiers the hubs with which the links are connected and indicating directions (from hub $h′$ to hub $h″$.) A link state can thus have 0, 1, 2, 3 or 4 such pairs.

---

[201] By location we mean a geodetic position.
[202] A hub state "signals" which input-to-output link connections are open for traffic.
[203] A hub state space indicates which hub states a hub may attain over time.

b State spaces are the set of all the link states that a link may enjoy.

type
326 LEN
327 GeoL
328a LΣ = (HI×HI)-**set**
328b LΩ = LΣ-**set**
value
326 attr_LEN: L $\rightarrow$ LEN
327 attr_GeoL: L $\rightarrow$ GeoL
328a attr_LΣ: L $\rightarrow$ LΣ
328b attr_LΩ: L $\rightarrow$ LΩ
axiom
328 $\forall$ n:N • **let** ls = xtr–links(n), hs = xtr_hubs(n) **in**
328 $\forall$ l:L•l $\in$ ls $\Rightarrow$
328a **let** lσ = attr_LΣ(l) **in**
328a 0$\leq$**card** l$\sigma\leq$4
328a $\wedge$ $\forall$ (hi′,hi″):(HI×HI)•(hi′,hi″) $\in$ lσ $\Rightarrow$ {hi′,hi″}=mereo_L(l)
328b $\wedge$ attr_LΣ(l) $\in$ attr_LΩ(l)
328 **end end**

Then vehicles.

329 Every vehicle of a traffic system has a position which is either 'on a link' or 'at a hub'.

a An 'on a link' position has four elements: a unique link identifier which must designate a link of that traffic system and a pair of unique hub identifiers which must be those of the mereology of that link.
b The 'on a link' position real is the fraction, thus properly between 0 (zero) and 1 (one) of the length from the first identified hub "down the link" to the second identifier hub.
c An 'at a hub' position has three elements: a unique hub identifier and a pair of unique link identifiers — which must be in the hub state.

type
329 VPos = onL | atH
329a onL :: LI HI HI R
329b R = **Real** **axiom** $\forall$ r:R • 0$\leq$r$\leq$1
329c atH :: HI LI LI
value
329 attr_VPos: V $\rightarrow$ VPos
axiom
329a $\forall$ n:N, onL(li,fhi,thi,r):VPos •
329a $\exists$ l:L•l $\in$obs_LS(obs_N(n)) $\Rightarrow$ li=uid_L(l)$\wedge${fhi,thi}=mereo_L(l),
329c $\forall$ n:N, atH(hi,fli,tli):VPos •
329c $\exists$ h:H•h $\in$obs_HS(obs_N(n)) $\Rightarrow$ hi=uid_H(h)$\wedge$(fli,tli) $\in$ attr_LΣ(h)

330 We introduce an auxiliary function `distribute`.

a `distribute` takes a net and a set of vehicles and
b generates a map from vehicles to distinct vehicle positions on the net.
c We sketch a "formal" `distribute` function, but, for simplicity we omit the technical details that secures distinctness — and leave that to an axiom!

331 We define two auxiliary functions:

a xtr_links extracts all links of a net and
b xtr_hub extracts all hubs of a net.

type
330b   MAP = VI $\overrightarrow{m}$ VPos
axiom
330b   ∀ map:MAP · **card dom** map = **card rng** map
value
330   distribute: VS → N → MAP
330   distribute(vs)(n) ≡
330a   **let** (hs,ls) = (xtr_hubs(n),xtr_links(n)) **in**
330a   **let** vps = {onL(uid_(l),fhi,thi,r) | l:L·l ∈ls∧{fhi,thi} ⊆mereo_L(l)∧0≤r≤1}
330a   ∪ {atH(uid_H(h),fli,tli) | h:H·h ∈hs∧{fli,tli} ⊆mereo_H(h)} **in**
330b   [uid_V(v)↦vp|v:V,vp:VPos·v ∈vs∧vp∈vps] **end**
330   **end**

331a   xtr_links: N → L-**set**
331a   xtr_links(n) ≡ obs_LS(obs_LA(n))
331b   xtr_hubs: N → H-**set**
331a   xtr_hubs(n) ≡ obs_H(obs_HA$_\Delta$(n))

And finally monitors. We consider only one monitor attribute.

332 The monitor has a vehicle traffic attribute.

a For every vehicle of the road transport system the vehicle traffic attribute records a possibly empty list of time marked vehicle positions.
b These vehicle positions are alternate sequences of 'on link' and 'at hub' positions
   i such that any sub-sequence of 'on link' positions record the same link identifier, the same pair of "to' and 'from' hub identifiers and increasing fractions,
   ii such that any sub-segment of 'at hub' positions are identical,
   iii such that vehicle transition from a link to a hub is commensurate with the link and hub mereologies, and
   iv such that vehicle transition from a hub to a link is commensurate with the hub and link mereologies.

type
332 Traffic = VI $\overrightarrow{m}$ (T × VPos)*
value
332 attr_Traffic: M → Traffic
axiom
332b ∀ δ:Δ ·
332b   **let** m = obs_M(δ) **in**
332b   **let** tf = attr_Traffic(m) **in**
332b   **dom** tf ⊆ xtr_vis(δ) ∧
332b   ∀ vi:VI · vi ∈ **dom** tf ·
332b   **let** tr = tf(vi) **in**
332b   ∀ i,i+1:**Nat** · {i,i+1}⊆**dom** tr ·
332b   **let** (t,vp)=tr(i),(t′,vp′)=tr(i+1) **in**
332b   t<t′
332(b)i   ∧ **case** (vp,vp′) **of**
332(b)i   (onL(li,fhi,thi,r),onL(li′,fhi′,thi′,r′))
332(b)i   → li=li′∧fhi=fhi′∧thi=thi′∧r≤r′ ∧ li ∈ xtr_lis(δ) ∧ {fhi,thi} = mereo_L(get_link(li)(δ)),
332(b)ii   (atH(hi,fli,tli),atH(hi′,fli′,tli′))
332(b)ii   → hi=hi′∧fli=fli′∧tli=tli′ ∧ hi ∈ xtr_his(δ) ∧ (fli,tli) ∈ mereo_H(get_hub(hi)(δ)),
332(b)iii   (onL(li,fhi,thi,1),atH(hi,fli,tli))
332(b)iii   → li=fli∧thi=hi ∧ {li,tli} ⊆ xtr_lis(δ) ∧ {fhi,thi}=mereo_L(get_link(li)(δ))

332(b)iii	$\land$ hi $\in$ xtr_his(δ) $\land$ (fli,tli) $\in$ mereo_H(get_hub(hi)(δ)),
332(b)iv	(atH(hi,fli,tli),onL(li$'$,fhi$'$,thi$'$,0))
332(b)iv	$\to$ et cetera,
332b	$\underline{\quad} \to$ **false**
332b	end end end end end

9.2.3 Perdurants

Our presentation of example perdurants is not as systematic as that of example endurants. Give the simple basis of endurants covered above there is now a huge variety of perdurants, so we just select one example from each of the three classes of perdurants (as outline in [73]): a simple hub insertion *action* (Sect. **9.2.3.1**), a simple link disappearance *event* (Sect. **9.2.3.2**) and a not quite so simple *behaviour*, that of road traffic (Sect. **9.2.3.3**).

9.2.3.1 Hub Insertion Action

333 Initially inserted hubs, h, are characterised

    a by their unique identifier which not one of any hub in the net, n, into which the hub is being inserted,

    b by a mereology, {}, of zero link identifiers, and

    c by — whatever — attributes, *attrs*, are needed.

334 The result of such a hub insertion is a net, n',

    a whose links are those of n, and

    b whose hubs are those of n augmented with h.

value

333   insert_hub: H $\to$ N $\to$ N

334   insert_hub(h)(n) **as** n$'$

333a   **pre**: uid_H(h) $\notin$ xtr_his(n)

333b $\land$ **obs_mereo_H**= {}

333c $\land$ ...

334a   **post**: obs_Ls(n) = obs_Ls(n$'$)

334b $\land$ obs_Hs(n) $\cup$ {h} = obs_Hs(n$'$)

9.2.3.2 Link Disappearance Event

We formalise aspects of the link disappearance event:

335 The result net, n$'$:N$'$, is not well-formed.

336 For a link to disappear there must be at least one link in the net;

337 and such a link may disappear such that

338 it together with the resulting net makes up for the "original" net.

value

335   link_diss_event: N $\times$ N$'$ $\times$ **Bool**

335   link_diss_event(n,n$'$) **as** tf

336   **pre**: obs_Ls(obs_LS(n))$\neq${}

337   **post:** $\exists$ l:L•l $\in$ obs_Ls(obs_LS(n)) $\Rightarrow$
338   l $\notin$ obs_Ls(obs_LS(n'))
338                 $\wedge$ n' $\cup$ {l} = obs_Ls(obs_LS(n))

9.2.3.3 Road Traffic

The analysis & description of the road traffic behaviour is composed (i) from the description of the global values of nets, links and hubs, vehicles, monitor, a clock, and an initial distribution, *map*, of vehicles, "across" the net; (ii) from the description of channels between vehicles and the monitor; (iii) from the description of behaviour signatures, that is, those of the overall road traffic system, the vehicles, and the monitor; and (iv) from the description of the individual behaviours, that is, the overall road traffic system, *rts*, the individual vehicles, *veh*, and the monitor, *mon*.

⋆ Global Values:

There is given some globally observable parts.

339 besides the domain, δ:Δ,
340 a net, n:N,
341 a set of vehicles, vs:V-**set**,
342 a monitor, m:M, and
343 a clock, clock, behaviour.
344 From the net and vehicles we generate an initial distribution of positions of vehicles.

The n:N, vs:V-**set** and m:M are observable from any road traffic system domain δ.

value
339 δ:Δ
340 n:N = obs_N(δ),
340 ls:L-**set**=links(δ),hs:H-**set**=hubs(δ),
340 lis:LI-**set**=xtr_lis(δ),his:HI-**set**=xtr_his(δ)
341 va:VS=obs_VS(obs_F(δ)),
341 vs:Vs-**set**=obs_Vs(va),
341 vis:VI-**set** = {uid_VI(v)|v:V•v $\in$ vs},
342 m:obs_M(δ),
342 mi=uid_MI(m),
342 ma:**attributes**(m)
343 clock: $\mathbb{T}$ $\rightarrow$ **out** {clk_ch[vi|vi:VI•vi $\in$ vis]} **Unit**
344 vm:MAP•vpos_map = distribute(vs)(n);

⋆ Channels:

345 We additionally declare a set of vehicle-to-monitor-channels indexed

    a by the unique identifiers of vehicles
    b and the (single) monitor identifier.[204]

    and communicating vehicle positions.

channel
345 {v_m_ch[vi,mi]|vi:VI•vi $\in$ vis}:VPos

---

[204] Technically speaking: we could omit the monitor identifier.

⋆ Behaviour Signatures:

346 The road traffic system behaviour, rts, takes no arguments (hence the first **Unit**)[205]; and "behaves", that is, continues forever (hence the last **Unit**).

347 The vehicle behaviour

    a is indexed by the unique identifier, uid_V(v):VI,

    b the vehicle mereology, in this case the single monitor identifier mi:MI,

    c the vehicle attributes, **obs__attribs**(v)

    d and — factoring out one of the vehicle attributes — the current vehicle position.

    e The vehicle behaviour offers communication to the monitor behaviour (on channel vm_ch[vi]); and behaves "forever".

348 The monitor behaviour takes

    a the monitor identifier,

    b the monitor mereology,

    c the monitor attributes,

    d and — factoring out one of the vehicle attributes — the discrete road traffic, drtf:dRTF, being repeatedly "updated" as the result of **in**put communications from (all) vehicles;

    e the behaviour otherwise behaves forever.

value

346   rts: **Unit** → **Unit**

347   veh$_{vi:VI}$: mi:MI → vp:VPos → **out** vm_ch[vi,mi] **Unit**

348   mon$_{mi:MI}$: vis:VI-**set** → RTF → **in** {v_m_ch[vi,mi]|vi:VI•vi ∈ vis},clk_ch **Unit**

⋆ The Road Traffic System Behaviour:

349 Thus we shall consider our **road traffic system**, rts, as

    a the concurrent behaviour of a number of vehicles and, to "observe", or, as we shall call it, to monitor their movements,

    b the monitor behaviour.

value

349   rts() =

349a   ‖ {veh$_{uid\_VI(v)}$(mi)(vm(uid_VI(v)))|v:V•v ∈ vs}

349b   ‖ mon$_{mi}$(vis)([vi↦⟨⟩|vi:VI•vi ∈ vis])

where, wrt, the monitor, we dispense with the mereology and the attribute state arguments and instead just have a monitor traffic argument which records the discrete road traffic, MAP, initially set to "empty" traces (⟨⟩, of so far "no road traffic"!).

    In order for the monitor behaviour to assess the vehicle positions these vehicles communicate their positions to the monitor via a vehicle to monitor channel. In order for the monitor to time-stamp these positions it must be able to "read" a clock.

350 We describe here an abstraction of the vehicle behaviour **at** a Hub (hi).

    a Either the vehicle remains at that hub informing the monitor of its position,

    b or, internally non-deterministically,

      i moves onto a link, tli, whose "next" hub, identified by thi, is obtained from the mereology of the link identified by tli;

---

[205] The **Unit** designator is an RSL technicality.

    ii informs the monitor, on channel vm[vi,mi], that it is now at the very beginning (0) of the link identified by tli, whereupon the vehicle resumes the vehicle behaviour positioned at the very beginning of that link,

c or, again internally non-deterministically, the vehicle "disappears — off the radar" !

350   veh_{vi}(mi)(vp:atH(hi,fli,tli)) ≡
350a   v_m_ch[vi,mi]!vp ; veh_{vi}(mi)(vp)
350b   ⊓
350(b)i   **let** {hi′,thi}=mereo_L(get_link(tli)(n)) **in**
350(b)i   **assert:** hi′=hi
350(b)ii   v_m_ch[vi,mi]!onL(tli,hi,thi,0) ;
350(b)ii veh_{vi}(mi)(onL(tli,hi,thi,0)) **end**
350c   ⊓ **stop**

351 We describe here an abstraction of the vehicle behaviour **on** a Link (ii). Either

    a the vehicle remains at that link position informing the monitor of its position,
    b or, internally non-deterministically, if the vehicle's position on the link has not yet reached the hub,
      i then the vehicle moves an arbitrary increment ℓ_ϵ (less than or equal to the distance to the hub) along the link informing the monitor of this, or
      ii else,
         1 while obtaining a "next link" from the mereology of the hub (where that next link could very well be the same as the link the vehicle is about to leave),
         2 the vehicle informs the monitor that it is now at the hub identified by thi, whereupon the vehicle resumes the vehicle behaviour positioned at that hub.
    c or, internally non-deterministically, the vehicle "disappears — off the radar" !

351   veh_{vi}(mi)(vp:onL(li,fhi,thi,r)) ≡
351a   v_m_ch[vi,mi]!vp ; veh_{vi}(mi,va)(vp)
351b   ⊓ **if** r + ℓ_ϵ≤1
351(b)i   **then**
351(b)i   v_m_ch[vi,mi]!onL(li,fhi,thi,r+ℓ_ϵ) ;
351(b)i veh_{vi}(mi)(onL(li,fhi,thi,r+ℓ_ϵ))
351(b)ii   **else**
351(b)ii1   **let** li′:LI•li′ ∈ mereo_H(get_hub(thi)(n)) **in**
351(b)ii2   v_m_ch[vi,mi]!atH(li,thi,li′);
351(b)ii2 veh_{vi}(mi)(atH(li,thi,li′)) **end end**
351c   ⊓ **stop**

The Monitor Behaviour

352 The monitor behaviour evolves around

    a the monitor identifier,
    b the monitor mereology,
    c and the attributes, ma:ATTR
    d — where we have factored out as a separate arguments — a table of traces of time-stamped vehicle positions,
    e while accepting messages
      i about time
      ii and about vehicle positions
    f and otherwise progressing "in[de]finitely".

353 Either the monitor "does own work"
354 or, internally non-deterministically accepts messages from vehicles.

    a A vehicle position message, vp, may arrive from the vehicle identified by vi.
    b That message is appended to that vehicle's movement trace – prefixed by time (obtained
      from the time channel),
    c whereupon the monitor resumes its behaviour —
    d where the communicating vehicles range over all identified vehicles.

352 $\mathsf{mon}_{mi}(\mathsf{vis})(\mathsf{trf}) \equiv$
353     $\mathsf{mon}_{mi}(\mathsf{vis})(\mathsf{trf})$
354   ⊓
354a   ⟦⟧{**let** tvp = (clk_ch?,v_m_ch[vi,mi]?) **in**
354b   **let** trf′ = trf † [vi ↦ trf(vi)⌢<tvp>] **in**
354c $\mathsf{mon}_{mi}(\mathsf{vis})(\mathsf{trf}')$
354d   **end end** | vi:VI • vi ∈ vis}

We are about to complete a long, i.e., a 6.3 page example (!). We can now comment on the full example: The domain, $\delta : \Delta$ is a manifest part. The road net, $n : N$ is also a manifest part. The fleet, $f : F$, of vehicles, $vs : VS$, likewise, is a manifest part. But the monitor, $m : M$, is a concept. One does not have to think of it as a manifest "observer". The vehicles are on — or off — the road (i.e., links and hubs). We know that from a few observations and generalise to all vehicles. They either move or stand still. We also, similarly, know that. Vehicles move. Yes, we know that. Based on all these repeated observations and generalisations we introduce the concept of vehicle traffic. Unless positioned high above a road net — and with good binoculars — a single person cannot really observe the traffic. There are simply too many links, hubs, vehicles, vehicle positions and times. Thus we conclude that, even in a richly manifest domain, we can also "speak of", that is, describe concepts over manifest phenomena, including time!

9.2.4 Domain Facets

The example of this section, i.e., Sect. **9.2**, focuses on the *domain facet* [55, 2008] of (i) *intrinsic*. It does not reflect the other *domain facets*: (ii) domain support technologies, (iii) domain rules, regulations & scripts, (iv) organisation & management, and (v) human behaviour. The requirements examples, i.e., the rest of this chapter, thus builds only on the *domain intrinsic*. This means that we shall not be able to cover principles, technique and tools for the prescription of such important requirements that handle failures of support technology or humans. We shall, however point out where we think such, for example, fault tolerance requirements prescriptions "fit in" and refer to relevant publications for their handling.

9.3 Requirements

This and the next three sections, that is, Sects. **9.4–9.5**, are the main sections of this chapter. Section **9.4.** is the most detailed and systematic section. It covers the *domain requirements* operations of *projection*, *instantiation*, *determination*, *extension* and, less detailed, *fitting*. Section **9.5** surveys the *interface requirements* issues of *shared phenomena*: *shared endurants*, *shared actions*, *shared events* and *shared behaviour*, and "completes" the exemplification of the detailed *domain extension* of our requirements into a *road pricing system*. Section **9.5** also covers the notion of *derived requirements*. Sections **9.4.–9.5**. covers *initial requirements*.

By ***initial requirements*** we shall, "operationally" speaking, understand the requirements that are derived from the general principles outlined in these sections ∎

In contrast to these are the further requirements that are typically derived either from the *domain facet descriptions* of *intrinsic*, the *support technology*, the *rules & regulations*, the *organisation & management*, and the *human behaviour facets* [55] — not covered in this chapter, and/or by more conventional means [143, 264, 404, 276, 268, 315, 377].

Definition: 77 Requirements (I): By a ***requirements*** we understand (cf., [256, IEEE Standard 610.12]): *"A condition or capability needed by a user to solve a problem or achieve an objective"* ∎

The objective of requirements engineering is to create a *requirements prescription*: A ***requirements prescription*** specifies observable properties of endurants and perdurants of ***the machine*** such as the requirements stake-holders wish them to be ∎

The ***machine*** is what is required: that is, the *hardware* and *software* that is to be designed and which are to satisfy the requirements ∎

A *requirements prescription* thus (*putatively*) expresses what there should be. A requirements prescription expresses nothing about the design of the possibly desired (required) software. But as the requirements prescription is presented in the form of a model, one can base the design on that model. We shall show how a major part of a requirements prescription can be "derived" from "its" prerequisite domain description.

Rule 1 The "Golden Rule" of Requirements Engineering: Prescribe only those requirements that can be objectively shown to hold for the designed software ∎

"Objectively shown" means that the designed software can either be tested, or be model checked, or be proved (verified), to satisfy the requirements. **Caveat**: Since we do not illustrate formal tests, model checking nor theorem proving, we shall, alas, not illustrate adherence to this rule.

Rule 2 An "Ideal Rule" of Requirements Engineering: When prescribing (including formalising) requirements, also formulate tests and properties for model checking and theorems whose proof should show adherence to the requirements ∎

The rule is labelled "ideal" since such precautions will not be shown in this chapter. The rule is clear. It is a question for proper management to see that it is adhered to. See the "Caveat" above!

Rule 3 Requirements Adequacy: Make sure that requirements cover what users expect ∎

That is, do not express a requirement for which you have no users, but make sure that all users' requirements are represented or somehow accommodated. In other words: the requirements gathering process needs to be like an extremely "fine-meshed net": One must make sure that all possible stake-holders have been involved in the requirements acquisition process, and that possible conflicts and other inconsistencies have been obviated.

Rule 4 Requirements Implementability: Make sure that requirements are implementable ∎

That is, do not express a requirement for which you have no assurance that it can be implemented. In other words, although the requirements phase is not a design phase, one must tacitly assume, perhaps even indicate, somehow, that an implementation is possible. But the requirements in and by themselves, may stay short of expressing such designs. **Caveat**: The domain and requirements specifications are, in our approach, model-oriented. That helps expressing 'implementability'.

Definition: 78 Requirements (II): By *requirements* we shall understand a document which prescribes desired properties of a machine: what endurants the machine shall "maintain", and what the machine shall (must; not should) offer of functions and of behaviours while also expressing which events the machine shall "handle" ∎

By a machine that "maintains" endurants we shall mean: a machine which, "between" users' use of that machine, "keeps" the data that represents these entities. From earlier we repeat:

Definition: 79 Machine: By *machine* we shall understand a, or the, combination of hardware and software that is the target for, or result of the required computing systems development ∎

So this, then, is a main objective of requirements development: to start towards the design of the hardware + software for the computing system.

Definition: 80 Requirements (III): To specify the machine ∎

When we express requirements and wish to "convert" such requirements to a realisation, i.e., an implementation, then we find that some requirements (parts) imply certain properties to hold of the hardware on which the software to be developed is to "run", and, obviously, that remaining — probably the larger parts of the — requirements imply certain properties to hold of that software.

• • •

Whereas domain descriptions may describe phenomena that cannot be computed, requirements prescriptions must describe computable phenomena.

9.3.1 Some Requirements Aspects

We shall unravel requirements in two stages — (i) the first stage is sketchy (and thus informal) (ii) while the last stage is systematic and both informal and formal. The sketchy stage consists of (i.1) a narrative *problem/objective sketch*, (i.2) a narrative *system requirements sketch*, and (i.3) a narrative *user & external equipment requirements sketch*. (ii) The narrative and formal stage consists of *design assumptions* and *design requirements*. It is systematic, and mandates both strict narrative and formal prescriptions. And it is "derivable" from the domain description. In a sense stage (i) is made superfluous once stage (ii) has been completed. The formal, engineering design work is to based on stage (ii). The purpose of the two stages (i–ii) is twofold: to gently lead the requirements engineer and the reader into the requirements problems while leading the requirements engineer and reader to focus on the very requirements essentials.

9.3.1.1 Requirements Sketches

⋆ **Problem, Solution and Objective Sketch**

Definition: 81 Problem, Solution and Objective Sketch: By a problem, solution and objective sketch we understand a narrative which emphasises what the *problem* to be solved is, outlines a possible *solution* and sketches an *objective* of the solution ■

Requirements: Sketch of Objectives

Example 110 The *problem* is that of traffic congestion. The chosen *solution* is to [build and] operate a toll-road system integrated into a road net and charge toll-road users a usage fee. The *objective* is therefore to create a **road-pricing product.** By a road-pricing product we shall understand an information technology-based system containing computers and communications equipment and software that enables the recording of *vehicle* movements within the *toll-road* and thus enables the *owner* of the road net to charge the *owner* of the vehicles *fees* for the usage of that toll-road   □

★ **Systems Requirements**

Definition: 82 System Requirements: By a *system requirements narrative* we understand a narrative which emphasises the overall assumed and/or required hardware and software system equipment ■

Requirements: Road Pricing, A Narrative

Example 111 The requirements are based on the following constellation of system equipment: (i) there is assumed a GNSS: a GLOBAL NAVIGATION SATELLITE SYSTEM; (ii) there are *vehicles* equipped with GNSS receivers; (iii) there is a well-delineated road net called a *toll-road* net with specially equipped *toll-gates* with *vehicle identification sensors*, *exit barriers* which afford (only specially equipped) vehicles to exit[206] from the toll-road net; and (iv) there is a *road-pricing calculator*.

The system to be designed (from the requirements) is the *road-pricing calculator.* These four system elements are required to behave and interact as follows: (a) The GNSS is assumed to continuously offer vehicles information about their global position; (b) *vehicles* shall contain a GNSS receiver which based on the global position information shall regularly calculate their timed local position and offer this to the *calculator* — while otherwise cruising the general road net as well as the toll-road net, the latter while carefully moving through toll-gates; (c) *toll-gates* shall register the identity of vehicles passing the toll-road and offer this information to the calculator; and (d) the *calculator* shall accept all messages from vehicles and gates and use this information to record the movements of vehicles and bill these whenever they exit the toll-road. The requirements are therefore to include **assumptions about** [1] the GNSS satellite and telecommunications equipment, [2] the vehicle GNSS receiver equipment, [3] the vehicle handling of GNSS input and forwarding, to the road pricing system, of its

---

[206] We omit consideration of entry barriers.

interpretation of GNSS input, [4] the toll-gate sensor equipment, [5] the toll-gate barrier equipment, [6] the toll-gate handling of entry, vehicle identification and exit sensors and the forwarding of vehicle identification to the road pricing calculator, and [7] the communications between toll-gates and vehicles, on "one side", and the road pricing calculator, on the "other side". It is in this sense that the requirements are for an information technology-based system of both software and hardware — not just hard computer and communications equipment, but also movement sensors and electro-mechanical "gear" □

⋆ User and External Equipment Requirements

Definition: 83 User and External Equipment Requirements: By a *user and external equipment requirements narrative* we understand a narrative which emphasises assumptions about the human user and external equipment interfaces to the system components ∎

The user and external equipment requirements detail, and thus make explicit, the assumptions listed in Example 111.

Requirements: Road Pricing, User and External Equipment, Narrative

Example 112 The human users of the road-pricing system are: (a) *vehicle drivers,* (b) toll-gate sensor, actuator and barrier *service staff,* and (c) the road-pricing calculator *service staff.* The external equipment are: (1) firstly, the GNSS satellites and the telecommunications equipment which enables *communication* between (i) the GNSS satellites and vehicles, (ii) vehicles and the road-pricing calculator and (iii) toll-gates and the road-pricing calculator. Moreover, the external *equipment* are (2) the toll-gates with their sensors: entry, vehicle identity, and exit, and the barrier actuator. The external *equipment* are, finally, (3), the vehicles! □

That is, although we do indeed exemplify domain and requirements aspects of users and external equipment, we do not expect to machine, i.e., to hardware or software design these elements; *they are assumed already implemented!*

9.3.1.2 The Narrative and Formal Requirements Stage

Definition: 84 Assumption and Design Requirements: By *assumption and design requirements* we understand precise prescriptions of the endurants and perdurants of the (to be designed) system components and the assumptions which that design must rely upon ∎

The specification principles, techniques and tools of expressing *design* and *assumptions*, upon which the design can be relied, will be covered and exemplified, extensively, in Sects. **9.4–9.5**.

9.3.2 The Three Phases of Requirements Engineering

There are, as we see it, three kinds of design assumptions and requirements: (i) *domain requirements*, (ii) *interface requirements* and (iii) *machine requirements*. (i) **Domain requirements** are those requirements which can be expressed sôlely using terms of the domain ∎ (ii) **Interface requirements** are those requirements which can be expressed only using technical terms of both the domain and the machine ∎ (iii) **Machine requirements** are those requirements which, in principle, can be expressed sôlely using terms of the machine ∎

Definition: 85 Verification Paradigm: Some preliminary designations: let $\mathcal{D}$ designate the the domain description; let $\mathcal{R}$ designate the requirements prescription, and let S designate the system design. Now $\mathcal{D}, S \models \mathcal{R}$ shall be read: it must be verified that the System design satisfies the $\mathcal{R}$equirements prescription in the context of the $\mathcal{D}$omain description ∎

The "in the context of $\mathcal{D}$..." term means that proofs of Software design correctness with respect to $\mathcal{R}$equirements will often have to refer to $\mathcal{D}$omain requirements assumptions. We refer to [197, Gunter, Jackson and Zave, 2000] for an analysis of a varieties of forms in which $\models$ relate to variants of $\mathcal{D}, \mathcal{R}$ and S.

9.3.3 Order of Presentation of Requirements Prescriptions

The *domain requirements development* stage — as we shall see — can be sub-staged into: *projection, instantiation, determination, extension* and *fitting*. The *interface requirements development* stage — can be sub-staged into shared: endurant, action, event and behaviour developments, where "sharedness" pertains to phenomena shared between, i.e., "present" in, both the domain (concretely, manifestly) and the machine (abstractly, conceptually). These development stages need not be pursued in the order of the three stages and their sub-stages. We emphasize that one thing is the stages and steps of development, as for example these: projection, instantiation, determination, extension, fitting, shared endurants, shared actions, shared events, shared behaviours, et cetera, another thing is the requirements prescription that results from these development stages and steps. The further software development, after and on the basis of the requirements prescription starts only when all stages and steps of the requirements prescription have been fully developed. The domain engineer is now free to rearrange the final prescription, irrespective of the order in which the various sections were developed, in such a way as to give a most pleasing, pedagogic and cohesive reading (i.e., presentation). From such a requirements prescription one can therefore not necessarily see in which order the various sections of the prescription were developed.

9.3.4 Design Requirements and Design Assumptions

A crucial distinction is between *design requirements* and *design assumptions*. The **design requirements** are those requirements for which the system designer **has to** implement hardware or software in order satisfy system user expectations ∎ The **design assumptions** are those requirements for which the system designer **does not** have to implement hardware or software, but whose properties the designed hardware, respectively software relies on for proper functioning ∎

Requirements: Road Pricing, Design Requirements

Example 113 The design requirements for the road pricing calculator of this chapter are for the design (ii) of that part of the vehicle software which interfaces the GNSS receiver and the road pricing calculator (cf. Items 433–436), (iii) of that part of the toll-gate software which interfaces the toll-gate and the road pricing calculator (cf. Items 441–443) and (i) of the road pricing calculator (cf. Items 472–485) □

Requirements: Road Pricing, Design Assumptions

Example 114 The design assumptions for the road pricing calculator include: (i) that *vehicles* behave as prescribed in Items 432–436, (ii) that the GNSS regularly offers vehicles correct information as to their global position (cf. Item 433), (iii) that *toll-gates* behave as prescribed in Items 438–443, and (iv) that the *road net* is formed and well-formed as defined in Examples 119 – 121 □

Requirements: Road Pricing, Toll-Gate System, Design Requirements

Example 115 The design requirements for the toll-gate system of this chapter are for the design of software for the toll-gate and its interfaces to the road pricing system, i.e., Items 437–438 ∎

Requirements: Road Pricing, Toll-Gate System, Design Assumptions

Example 116 The design assumptions for the toll-gate system include (i) that the vehicles behave as per Items 432–436, and (ii) that the road pricing calculator behave as per Items 472–485 ∎

9.3.5 Derived Requirements

In building up the domain, interface and machine requirements a number of machine concepts are introduced. These machine concepts enable the expression of additional requirements. It is these we refer to as derived requirements. Techniques and tools espoused in such classical publications as [143, 264, 404, 276, 377] can in those cases be used to advantage.

9.4 Domain Requirements

Domain requirements primarily express the assumptions that a design must rely upon in order that that design can be verified. Although domain requirements firstly express assumptions it appears that the software designer is well-advised in also implementing, as data structures and procedures, the endurants, respectively perdurants expressed in the domain requirements prescriptions. Whereas domain endurants are "real-life" phenomena they are now, in domain requirements prescriptions, abstract concepts (to be represented by a machine).

Definition: 86 **Domain Requirements Prescription:** A *domain requirements prescription* is that subset of the requirements prescription whose technical terms are defined in a domain description ∎

To determine a relevant subset all we need is collaboration with requirements, cum domain stake-holders. Experimental evidence, in the form of example developments of requirements prescriptions from domain descriptions, appears to show that one can formulate techniques for such developments around a few domain-description-to-requirements-prescription operations. We suggest these: *projection, instantiation, determination, extension* and *fitting*. In Sect. **9.3.3** we mentioned that the order in which one performs these domain-description-to-domain-requirements-prescription operations is not necessarily the order in which we have listed them here, but, with notable exceptions, one is well-served in starting out requirements development by following this order.

9.4.1 Domain Projection

Definition: 87 **Domain Projection:** By a *domain projection* is meant *a subset of the domain description, one which projects out all those endurants: parts and fluids, as well as perdurants: actions, events and behaviours that the stake-holders do not wish represented or relied upon by the machine* ∎

The resulting document is a *partial domain requirements prescription*. In determining an appropriate subset the requirements engineer must secure that the final "projection prescription" is complete and consistent — that is, that there are no "dangling references", i.e., that all entities and their internal properties that are referred to are all properly defined.

9.4.1.1 Domain Projection — Narrative

We now start on a series of examples that illustrate domain requirements development.

Requirements: Domain Requirements, Projection – A Narrative Sketch

---

[207] By 'relate to ... these' we mean that the required system does not rely on domain phenomena that have been "projected away".

Example 117 We require that the road pricing system shall [at most] relate to the following domain entities – and only to these[207]: the net, its links and hubs, and their properties (unique identifiers, mereologies and some attributes), the vehicles, as endurants, and the general vehicle behaviours, as perdurants. We treat projection together with a concept of *simplification*. The example simplifications are vehicle positions and, related to the simpler vehicle position, vehicle behaviours. To prescribe and formalise this we copy the domain description. From that domain description we remove all mention of the hub insertion action, the link disappearance event, and the monitor   □

As a result we obtain $\Delta_\mathcal{P}$, the projected version of the domain requirements prescription[208].

9.4.1.2 Domain Projection — Formalisation

The requirements prescription hinges, crucially, not only on a systematic narrative of all the projected, instantiated, determined, extended and fitted specifications, but also on their formalisation. In the formal domain projection example we, regretfully, omit the narrative texts. In bringing the formal texts we keep the item numbering from Sect. **9.2**, where you can find the associated narrative texts.

Requirements: Domain Requirements, Projection

Example 118   Main Sorts

type
305    $\Delta_\mathcal{P}$
305a $N_\mathcal{P}$
305b $F_\mathcal{P}$
value
305a   obs_$N_\mathcal{P}$: $\Delta_\mathcal{P} \to N_\mathcal{P}$
305b   obs_$F_\mathcal{P}$: $\Delta_\mathcal{P} \to F_\mathcal{P}$

type
306a $HA_\mathcal{P}$
306b $LA_\mathcal{P}$
value
306a   obs_HA: $N_\mathcal{P} \to HA$
306b   obs_LA: $N_\mathcal{P} \to LA$

Concrete Types

type
307   $H_\mathcal{P}$, $HS_\mathcal{P} = H_\mathcal{P}$-set
308   $L_\mathcal{P}$, $LS_\mathcal{P} = L_\mathcal{P}$-set
309   $V_\mathcal{P}$, $VS_\mathcal{P} = V_\mathcal{P}$-set
value
307   obs_$HS_\mathcal{P}$: $HA_\mathcal{P} \to HS_\mathcal{P}$

308   obs_$LS_\mathcal{P}$: $LA_\mathcal{P} \to LS_\mathcal{P}$
309   obs_$VS_\mathcal{P}$: $F_\mathcal{P} \to VS_\mathcal{P}$
310a   links: $\Delta_\mathcal{P} \to$ L-set
310a   links($\delta_\mathcal{P}$) $\equiv$ obs_$LS_\mathcal{R}$(obs_$LA_\mathcal{R}(\delta_\mathcal{R})$)
310b   hubs: $\Delta_\mathcal{P} \to$ H-set
310b   hubs($\delta_\mathcal{P}$) $\equiv$ obs_$HS_\mathcal{P}$(obs_$HA_\mathcal{P}(\delta_\mathcal{P})$)

Unique Identifiers

type
311a   HI, LI, VI, MI
value
311c   uid_HI: $H_\mathcal{P} \to$ HI
311c   uid_LI: $L_\mathcal{P} \to$ LI

311c   uid_VI: $V_\mathcal{P} \to$ VI
311c   uid_MI: $M_\mathcal{P} \to$ MI
axiom
311b   HI∩LI=∅, HI∩VI=∅, HI∩MI=∅,
311b   LI∩VI=∅, LI∩MI=∅, VI∩MI=∅

Mereology

---

[208] Restrictions of the net to the toll road nets, hinted at earlier, will follow in the next domain requirements steps.

value
316 **obs_mereo**_H$_\mathcal{P}$: H$_\mathcal{P}$ → Ll-set
317 **obs_mereo**_L$_\mathcal{P}$: L$_\mathcal{P}$ → Hl-set
317   **axiom** ∀ l:L$_\mathcal{P}$ • **card** mereo_L$_\mathcal{P}$(l)=2
318 **obs_mereo**_V$_\mathcal{P}$: V$_\mathcal{P}$ → Ml
319 **obs_mereo**_M$_\mathcal{P}$: M$_\mathcal{P}$ → Vl-set
axiom
320 ∀ $\delta_\mathcal{P}$:$\Delta_\mathcal{P}$, hs:HS•hs=hubs(δ), ls:LS•ls=links($\delta_\mathcal{P}$) ⇒
320   ∀ h:H$_\mathcal{P}$•h ∈ hs ⇒ mereo_H$_\mathcal{P}$(h)⊆xtr_his($\delta_\mathcal{P}$) ∧
321   ∀ l:L$_\mathcal{P}$•l ∈ ls • mereo_L$_\mathcal{P}$(l)⊆xtr_lis($\delta_\mathcal{P}$) ∧
322a   **let** f:F$_\mathcal{P}$•f=obs_F$_\mathcal{P}$($\delta_\mathcal{P}$) ⇒ vs:VS$_\mathcal{P}$•vs=obs_VS$_\mathcal{P}$(f) **in**
322a   ∀ v:V$_\mathcal{P}$•v ∈ vs ⇒ uid_V$_\mathcal{P}$(v) ∈ mereo_M$_\mathcal{P}$(m)
322b   ∧ mereo_M$_\mathcal{P}$(m) = {uid_V$_\mathcal{P}$(v)|v:V•v ∈ vs}
322b   **end**

Attributes: We project attributes of hubs, links and vehicles.

First **hubs:**   **axiom**
type   324 ∀ $\delta_\mathcal{P}$:$\Delta_\mathcal{P}$,
323a GeoH   324   **let** hs = hubs($\delta_\mathcal{P}$) **in**
323b H$\Sigma_\mathcal{P}$ = (Ll×Ll)-sett   324   ∀ h:H$_\mathcal{P}$ • h ∈ hs •
323c H$\Omega_\mathcal{P}$ = H$\Sigma_\mathcal{P}$-set   324a   xtr_lis(h)⊆xtr_lis($\delta_\mathcal{P}$)
value   324b   ∧ attr_$\Sigma_\mathcal{P}$(h) ∈ attr_$\Omega_\mathcal{P}$(h)
323b attr_H$\Sigma_\mathcal{P}$: H$_\mathcal{P}$ → H$\Sigma_\mathcal{P}$ 324   **end**
323c attr_H$\Omega_\mathcal{P}$: H$_\mathcal{P}$ → H$\Omega_\mathcal{P}$

Then **links:**

type   327   attr_GeoL: L → GeoL
327 GeoL   328a attr_L$\Sigma_\mathcal{P}$: L$_\mathcal{P}$ → L$\Sigma_\mathcal{P}$
328a L$\Sigma_\mathcal{P}$ = (Hl×Hl)-set   328b attr_L$\Omega_\mathcal{P}$: L$_\mathcal{P}$ → L$\Omega_\mathcal{P}$
328b L$\Omega_\mathcal{P}$ = L$\Sigma_\mathcal{P}$-set   **axiom**
value   328a– 328b on page 249.

Finally **vehicles.** For 'road pricing' we need vehicle positions. But, for "technical reasons", we must abstain from the detailed description given in Items 329–329c.[209] We therefore *simplify* vehicle positions.

355 A simplified vehicle position designates
     a either a link
     b or a hub,

type
355   SVPos = SonL | SatH
355a   SonL :: Ll
355b   SatH :: Hl
axiom
329a' ∀ n:N, SonL(li):SVPos •
329a'   ∃ l:L•l ∈obs_LS(obs_N(n)) ⇒ li=uid_L(l)
329c' ∀ n:N, SatH(hi):SVPos •
329c'   ∃ h:H•h ∈obs_HS(obs_N(n)) ⇒ hi=uid_H(h)

Global Values

value   340 hs:H$_\mathcal{P}$-**set** = hubs($\delta_\mathcal{P}$),
339 $\delta_\mathcal{P}$:$\Delta_\mathcal{P}$,   340 lis:Ll-**set** = xtr_lis($\delta_\mathcal{P}$),
340 n:N$_\mathcal{P}$ = obs_N$_\mathcal{P}$($\delta_\mathcal{P}$),   340 his:Hl-**set** = xtr_his($\delta_\mathcal{P}$)
340 ls:L$_\mathcal{P}$-**set** = links($\delta_\mathcal{P}$),

Behaviour Signatures: We omit the monitor behaviour.

356 We leave the vehicle behaviours' attribute argument undefined.

type

356 ATTR
value
346 trs$_\varphi$: **Unit $\rightarrow$ Unit**
347 veh$_\varphi$: VI$\times$MI$\times$ATTR $\rightarrow$ ... **Unit**

The System Behaviour: We omit the monitor behaviour.
value
349a trs$_\mathcal{P}$()=||{veh$_\varphi$(uid_VI(v),mereo_V(v),_) | v:V$_\mathcal{P}$•v $\in$ vs}

The Vehicle Behaviour: Given the simplification of vehicle positions we *simplify* the vehicle behaviour given in Items 350–351.

350' veh$_{vi}$(mi)(vp:SatH(hi)) $\equiv$
350a'   v_m_ch[vi,mi]!SatH(hi) ; veh$_{vi}$(mi)(SatH(hi))
350(b)i' $\sqcap$ **let** li:LI•li $\in$ mereo_H(get_hub(hi)(n)) **in**
350(b)ii'   v_m_ch[vi,mi]!SonL(li) ; veh$_{vi}$(mi)(SonL(li)) **end**
350c' $\sqcap$ **stop**

351' veh$_{vi}$(mi)(vp:SonL(li)) $\equiv$
351a'   v_m_ch[vi,mi]!SonL(li) ; veh$_{vi}$(mi)(SonL(li))
351(b)ii1' $\sqcap$ **let** hi:HI•hi $\in$ mereo_L(get_link(li)(n)) **in**
351(b)ii2'   v_m_ch[vi,mi]!SatH(hi) ; veh$_{vi}$(mi)(atH(hi)) **end**
351c' $\sqcap$ **stop**

We can simplify Items 350'–351c' further.
357 veh$_{vi}$(mi)(vp) $\equiv$
358   v_m_ch[vi,mi]!vp ; veh$_{vi}$(mi)(vp)
359   $\sqcap$ **case** vp **of**
359   SatH(hi) $\rightarrow$
360   **let** li:LI•li $\in$ mereo_H(get_hub(hi)(n)) **in**
361   v_m_ch[vi,mi]!SonL(li) ; veh$_{vi}$(mi)(SonL(li)) **end**,
359   SonL(li) $\rightarrow$
362   **let** hi:HI•hi $\in$ mereo_L(get_link(li)(n)) **in**
363   v_m_ch[vi,mi]!SatH(hi) ; veh$_{vi}$(mi)(atH(hi)) **end end**
364   $\sqcap$ **stop**

357 This line coalesces Items 350' and 351'.
358 Coalescing Items 350a' and 351'.
359 Captures the distinct parameters of Items 350' and 351'.
360 Item 350(b)i'.
361 Item 350(b)ii'.
362 Item 351(b)ii1'.
363 Item 351(b)ii2'.
364 Coalescing Items 350c' and 351c'.

The above vehicle behaviour definition will be transformed (i.e., further "refined") in Sect. **9.5.1.3**'s Example 127; cf. Items 432– 436 on page 278   □

9.4.1.3 Discussion

Domain projection can also be achieved by developing a "completely new" domain description — typically on the basis of one or more existing domain description(s) — where that "new" description now takes the rôle of being the project domain requirements.

---

[209] The 'technical reasons' are that we assume that the *GNSS* cannot provide us with direction of vehicle movement and therefore we cannot, using only the *GNSS* provide the details of 'offset' along a link (*onL*) nor the "from/to link" at a hub (*atH*).

9.4.2 Domain Instantiation

Definition: 88 Domain Instantiation: By *domain instantiation* we mean a *refinement* of *the partial domain requirements prescription (resulting from the projection step) in which the refinements aim at rendering more concrete, more specific the endurants: parts and fluids, as well as the perdurants: actions, events and behaviours of the domain requirements prescription* ■ Instantiations usually render these concepts less general.

Properties that hold of the projected domain shall also hold of the (therefrom) instantiated domain.

Refinement of endurants can be expressed (i) either in the form of concrete types, (ii) or of further "delineating" axioms over sorts, (iii) or of a combination of concretisation and axioms. We shall exemplify the third possibility. Example 119 express requirements that the road net (on which the road-pricing system is to be based) must satisfy. Refinement of perdurants will not be illustrated (other than the simplification of the *vehicle* projected behaviour).

9.4.2.1 Domain Instantiation

Requirements: Domain Requirements, Instantiation – Road Net 1/2

Example 119 We now require that there is, as before, a road net, $n_I : N_I$, which can be understood as consisting of two, "connected sub-nets". A toll-road net, $trn_I : TRN_I$, cf. Fig. 9.1 on the facing page, and an ordinary road net, $n_{\mathcal{P}'}$. The two are connected as follows: The toll-road net, trn_I, borders some toll-road plazas, in Fig. 9.1 on the next page shown by white filled circles (i.e., hubs). These toll-road plaza hubs are proper hubs of the 'ordinary' road net, $n'_{\mathcal{P}}$.

365 The instantiated domain, $\delta_I : \Delta_I$ has just the net, $n_I : N_I$ being instantiated.
366 The road net consists of two "sub-nets"
   a an "ordinary" road net, $n_o : N_{\mathcal{P}'}$ and
   b a toll-road net proper, $trn : TRN_I$ —
   c "connected" by an interface hil:HIL:
      i That interface consists of a number of toll-road plazas (i.e., hubs), modeled as a list of hub identifiers, hil:HI*.
      ii The toll-road plaza interface to the toll-road net, $trn : TRN_I{}^{210}$, has each plaza, hil[i], connected to a pair of toll-road links: an entry and an exit link: $(l_e : L, l_x : L)$.
      iii The toll-road plaza interface to the 'ordinary' net, $n_o : N_{\mathcal{P}'}$, has each plaza, i.e., the hub designated by the hub identifier hil[i], connected to one or more ordinary net links, $\{l_{i_1}, l_{i_2}, \cdots, l_{i_k}\}$.
366b The toll-road net, $trn : TRN_I$, consists of three collections (modeled as lists) of links and hubs:
      i a list of pairs of toll-road entry/exit links: $\langle (l_{e_1}, l_{x_1}), \cdots, (l_{e_\ell}, l_{x_\ell}) \rangle$,
      ii a list of toll-road intersection hubs: $\langle h_{i_1}, h_{i_2}, \cdots, h_{i_\ell} \rangle$, and
      iii a list of pairs of main toll-road ("*up*" and "*down*") links: $\langle (ml_{i_{1u}}, ml_{i_{1d}}), (m_{i_{2u}}, m_{i_{2d}}), \cdots, (m_{i_{\ell u}}, m_{i_{\ell d}}) \rangle$.
   d The three lists have commensurate lengths (ℓ).

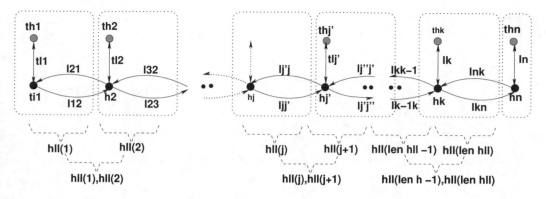

Fig. 9.1 A Toll Road

Requirements: Domain Requirements, Instantiation, Road Net 2/2

Example 119 (Continued) ℓ is the number of toll plazas, hence also the number of toll-road intersection hubs and therefore a number one larger than the number of pairs of main toll-road ("*up*" and "*down*") links

type
365 Δ_I
366 $N_I = N_{\wp'} \times HIL \times TRN$
366a $N_{\wp'}$
366b $TRN_I = (L\times L)^* \times H^* \times (L\times L)^*$
366c $HIL = HI^*$

axiom
366d $\forall\, n_I{:}N_I$.
366d   **let** $(n_\Delta, hil, (exll, hl, lll)) = n_I$ **in**
366d   **len** hil = **len** $exll$ = **len** hl = **len** lll + 1
366d **end**

We have named the "ordinary" net sort (primed) $N_{\wp'}$. It is "almost" like (unprimed) $N_\wp$ — except that the interface hubs are also connected to the toll-road net entry and exit links. The partial concretisation of the net sorts, $N_\wp$, into N_I requires some additional well-formedness conditions to be satisfied.

367 The toll-road intersection hubs all[211] have distinct identifiers.

367 wf_dist_toll_road_isect_hub_ids: $H^* \to$ **Bool**
367 wf_dist_toll_road_isect_hub_ids(hl) $\equiv$ **len** hl = **card** xtr_his(hl)

368 The toll-road links all have distinct identifiers.

368 wf_dist_toll_road_u_d_link_ids: $(L\times L)^* \to$ **Bool**
368 wf_dist_toll_road_u_d_link_ids(lll) $\equiv$ 2 $\times$ **len** lll = **card** xtr_lis(lll)

369 The toll-road entry/exit links all have distinct identifiers.

369 wf_dist_e_x_link_ids: $(L\times L)^* \to$ **Bool**
369 wf_dist_e_x_link_ids(exll) $\equiv$ 2 $\times$ **len** exll = **card** xtr_lis(exll)

---

[210] We (sometimes) omit the subscript $_I$ when it should be clear from the context what we mean.
[211] A 'must' can be inserted in front of all 'all's.

370 Proper net links must not designate toll-road intersection hubs.

370 wf_isoltd_toll_road_isect_hubs: HI*×H*→N$_I$→**Bool**
370 wf_isoltd_toll_road_isect_hubs(hil,hl)(n$_I$) ≡
370   **let** ls=xtr_links(n$_I$) **in**
370   **let** his = ∪ {mereo_L(l)|l:L·l ∈ ls} **in**
370   his ∩ xtr_his(hl) = {} **end end**

371 The plaza hub identifiers must designate hubs of the 'ordinary' net.

371 wf_p_hubs_pt_of_ord_net: HI*→N'$_Δ$→**Bool**
371 wf_p_hubs_pt_of_ord_net(hil)(n'$_Δ$) ≡ **elems** hil ⊆ xtr_his(n'$_Δ$)

372 The plaza hub mereologies must each,
   a besides identifying at least one hub of the ordinary net,
   b also identify the two entry/exit links with which they are supposed to be connected.

372 wf_p_hub_interf: N'$_Δ$→**Bool**
372 wf_p_hub_interf(n$_o$,hil,(exll,_,_)) ≡
372   ∀ i:**Nat** · i ∈ inds exll ⇒
372   **let** h = get_H(hil(i))(n'$_Δ$) **in**
372   **let** lis = mereo_H(h) **in**
372   **let** lis' = lis \ xtr_lis(n') **in**
372   lis' = xtr_lis(exll(i)) **end end end**

373 The mereology of each toll-road intersection hub must identify
   a the entry/exit links
   b and exactly the toll-road 'up' and 'down' links
   c with which they are supposed to be connected.

373 wf_toll_road_isect_hub_iface: N$_I$→**Bool**
373 wf_toll_road_isect_hub_iface(_,_,(exll,hl,lll)) ≡
373   ∀ i:**Nat** · i ∈ inds hl ⇒
373   mereo_H(hl(i)) =
373a   xtr_lis(exll(i)) ∪
373   **case** i **of**
373b   1 → xtr_lis(lll(1)),
373b   len hl → xtr_lis(lll(len hl−1))
373b   _ → xtr_lis(lll(i)) ∪ xtr_lis(lll(i−1))
373   **end**

374 The mereology of the entry/exit links must identify exactly the
   a interface hubs and the
   b toll-road intersection hubs
   c with which they are supposed to be connected.

374 wf_exll: (L×L)*×HI*×H*→**Bool**
374 wf_exll(exll,hil,hl) ≡
374   ∀ i:**Nat** · i ∈ len exll
374   **let** (hi,(el,xl),h) = (hil(i),exll(i),hl(i)) **in**
374   mereo_L(el) = mereo_L(xl)
374   = {hi} ∪ {uid_H(h)} **end**
374   **pre: len** eell = **len** hil = **len** hl

375 The mereology of the toll-road 'up' and 'down' links must
   a identify exactly the toll-road intersection hubs
   b with which they are supposed to be connected.

375 wf_u_d_links: (L×L)*×H*→**Bool**
375 wf_u_d_links(lll,hl) ≡
375   ∀ i:**Nat** · i ∈ inds lll ⇒
375   **let** (ul,dl) = lll(i) **in**
375   mereo_L(ul) = mereo_L(dl) =
375a   uid_H(hl(i)) ∪ uid_H(hl(i+1)) **end**
375   **pre: len** lll = **len** hl+1

We have used some additional auxiliary functions:

xtr_his: $H^* \rightarrow$ HI-set
xtr_his(hl) $\equiv$ {uid_HI(h)|h:H·h $\in$ **elems** hl}
xtr_lis: (L×L)$\rightarrow$LI-set

xtr_lis(l',l'') $\equiv$ {uid_LI(l')}∪{uid_LI(l'')}
xtr_lis: (L×L)*− LI-set
xtr_lis(lll) $\equiv$
∪{xtr_lis(l',l'')|(l',l''):(L×L)·(l',l'')$\in$ **elems** lll}

376 The well-formedness of instantiated nets is now the conjunction of the individual well-formedness predicates above.

376 wf_instantiated_net: $N_I \rightarrow$ **Bool**
376 wf_instantiated_net(n'_Δ,hil,(exll,hl,lll))
367   wf_dist_toll_road_isect_hub_ids(hl)
368    $\wedge$ wf_dist_toll_road_u_d_link_ids(lll)
369    $\wedge$ wf_dist_e_e_link_ids(exll)
370    $\wedge$ wf_isolated_toll_road_isect_hubs(hil,hl)(n')
371    $\wedge$ wf_p_hubs_pt_of_ord_net(hil)(n')
372    $\wedge$ wf_p_hub_interf(n'_Δ,hil,(exll,_,_))
373    $\wedge$ wf_toll_road_isect_hub_iface(_,_,(exll,hl,lll))
374    $\wedge$ wf_exll(exll,hil,hl)
375    $\wedge$ wf_u_d_links(lll,hl)

9.4.2.2 Domain Instantiation — Abstraction

Requirements: Domain Requirements, Instantiation of Road Net, Abstraction

Example 120 Domain instantiation has refined an abstract definition of net sorts, n_P:N_P, into a partially concrete definition of nets, n_I:N_I. We need to show the refinement relation:

- abstraction(n_I) = n_P.

value
377   abstraction: $N_I \rightarrow N_P$
378   abstraction(n'_Δ,hil,(exll,hl,lll)) $\equiv$
379   let n_P:N_P •
379   let hs = obs_HS$_P$(obs_HA$_P$(n'_P)),
379   ls = obs_LS$_P$(obs_LA$_P$(n'_P)),
379   ths = **elems** hl,
379   eells = xtr_links(eell), llls = xtr_links(lll) **in**
380   hs∪ths=obs_HS$_P$(obs_HA$_P$(n_P))
381       $\wedge$ ls∪eells∪llls=obs_LS$_P$(obs_LA$_P$(n_P))
382   n_P **end end**

377 The abstraction function takes a concrete net, n_I:N_I, and yields an abstract net, n_P:N_P.
378 The abstraction function doubly decomposes its argument into constituent lists and sub-lists.
379 There is postulated an abstract net, n_P:N_P, such that
380 the hubs of the concrete net and toll-road equals those of the abstract net, and
381 the links of the concrete net and toll-road equals those of the abstract net.
382 And that abstract net, n_P:N_P, is postulated to be an abstraction of the concrete net.

9.4.2.3 Discussion

Domain descriptions, such as illustrated in [73, *Manifest Domains: Analysis & Description*] and in this chapter, model families of concrete, i.e., specifically occurring domains. Domain instantiation, as exemplified in this section (i.e., Sect. **9.4.2**), "narrow down" these families.

Domain instantiation, such as it is defined, cf. Definition 88 on page 266, allows the requirements engineer to instantiate to a concrete instance of a very specific domain, that, for example, of the toll-road between *Bolzano Nord* and *Trento Sud* in Italy (i.e., $n=7$)[212].

9.4.3 Domain Determination

Definition: 89 Determination: By ***domain determination*** we mean *a refinement of the partial domain requirements prescription, resulting from the instantiation step, in which the refinements aim at rendering less non-determinate, more determinate the endurants: parts and fluids, as well as the perdurants: functions, events and behaviours of the partial domain requirements prescription* ∎

Determinations usually render these concepts less general. That is, the value space of endurants that are made more determinate is "smaller", contains fewer values, as compared to the endurants before determination has been "applied".

9.4.3.1 Domain Determination: Example

We show an example of 'domain determination'. It is expressed sôlely in terms of axioms over the concrete toll-road net type.

Requirements: Domain Requirements, Determination – Toll-roads

Example 121 We focus only on the toll-road net. We single out only two 'determinations':
All Toll-road Links are One-way Links:

383 *The entry/exit and toll-road links*
  a are always all one way links,
  b as indicated by the arrows of Fig. 9.1 on page 267,
  c such that each pair allows traffic in opposite directions.

383 opposite_traffics: $(L \times L)^* \times (L \times L)^* \to$ **Bool**
383 opposite_traffics(exll,lll) $\equiv$
383     $\forall$ (lt,lf):(L×L) • (lt,lf) $\in$ **elems** exll⌢lll $\Rightarrow$
383a   **let** (ltσ,lfσ) = (attr_LΣ(lt),attr_LΣ(lf)) **in**
383a'.   attr_LΩ(lt)={ltσ}$\wedge$attr_LΩ(ft)={ftσ}
383a". $\wedge$ **card** ltσ = 1 = **card** lfσ
383        $\wedge$ **let** ({(hi,hi')},{(hi'',hi''')}) = (ltσ,lfσ) **in**
383c   hi=hi''' $\wedge$ hi'=hi''
383   **end end**

Predicates 383a'. and 383a". express the same property.
All Toll-road Hubs are Free-flow

384 *The hub state spaces are singleton sets of the toll-road hub states which always allow exactly these (and only these) crossings:*
  a from entry links back to the paired exit links,
  b from entry links to emanating toll-road links,

---

[212] Here we disregard the fact that this toll-road does not start/end in neither *Bolzano Nord* nor *Trento Sud*.

    c from incident *toll*-road links to *exit links*, and
    d from incident *toll*-road link to emanating *toll*-road *links*.

384 free_flow_toll_road_hubs: $(L{\times}L)^*{\times}(L{\times}L)^*{\to}$**Bool**
384 free_flow_toll_road_hubs(exl,ll) $\equiv$
384    $\forall$ i:**Nat•**i $\in$ **inds** hl $\Rightarrow$
384   attr_HΣ(hl(i)) =
384a   hσ_ex_ls(exl(i))
384b $\cup$ hσ_et_ls(exl(i),(i,ll))
384c $\cup$ hσ_tx_ls(exl(i),(i,ll))
384d $\cup$ hσ_tt_ls(i,ll)

384a: from *entry* links back to the paired *exit links*:
384a hσ_ex_ls: $(L{\times}L){\to}L\Sigma$
384a hσ_ex_ls(e,x) $\equiv$ {(uid_LI(e),uid_LI(x))}

384b: from *entry* links to emanating *toll*-road *links*:
384b hσ_et_ls: $(L{\times}L){\times}($**Nat**${\times}$(em:L${\times}$in:L)$^*)$${\to}L\Sigma$
384b hσ_et_ls((e,_),(i,ll)) $\equiv$
384b   **case** i **of**
384b   2 $\to$ {(uid_LI(e),uid_LI(em(ll(1))))},
384b   **len** ll+1 $\to$ {(uid_LI(e),uid_LI(em(ll(**len** ll))))},
384b   _ $\to$ {(uid_LI(e),uid_LI(em(ll(i−1)))),
384b   (uid_LI(e),uid_LI(em(ll(i))))}
384b   **end**

The *em* and *in* in the toll-road link list (em:L${\times}$in:L)* designate selectors for *em*anating, respectively *in*cident links. 384c: from incident *toll*-road links to *exit links*:
384c hσ_tx_ls: $(L{\times}L){\times}($**Nat**${\times}$(em:L${\times}$in:L)$^*)$${\to}L\Sigma$
384c hσ_tx_ls((_,x),(i,ll)) $\equiv$
384c   **case** i **of**
384c   2 $\to$ {(uid_LI(in(ll(1))),uid_LI(x))},
384c   **len** ll+1 $\to$ {(uid_LI(in(ll(**len** ll))),uid_LI(x))},
384c   _ $\to$ {(uid_LI(in(ll(i−1))),uid_LI(x)),
384c   (uid_LI(in(ll(i))),uid_LI(x))}
384c   **end**

384d: from incident *toll*-road link to emanating *toll*-road *links*:
384d hσ_tt_ls: **Nat**${\times}$(em:L${\times}$in:L)$^*{\to}L\Sigma$
384d hσ_tt_ls(i,ll) $\equiv$
384d   case i **of**
384d   2 $\to$ {(uid_LI(in(ll(1))),uid_LI(em(ll(1))))},
384d   **len** ll+1 $\to$ {(uid_LI(in(ll(**len** ll))),uid_LI(em(ll(**len** ll))))},
384d   _ $\to$ {(uid_LI(in(ll(i−1))),uid_LI(em(ll(i−1)))),
384d   (uid_LI(in(ll(i))),uid_LI(em(ll(i))))}
384d   **end**

The example above illustrated 'domain determination' with respect to endurants. Typically "endurant determination" is expressed in terms of axioms that limit state spaces — where "endurant instantiation" typically "limited" the mereology of endurants: how parts are related to one another. We shall not exemplify domain determination with respect to perdurants.

9.4.3.2 Discussion

The borderline between instantiation and determination is fuzzy. Whether, as an example, fixing the number of toll-road intersection hubs to a constant value, e.g., $n=7$, is instantiation or determination, is really a matter of choice!

9.4.4 Domain Extension

Definition: 90 Extension: By ***domain extension*** we understand *the introduction of endurants (see Sect. 9.4.4.1) and perdurants (see Sect. 9.5.2) that were not feasible in the original domain, but for which, with computing and communication, and with new, emerging technologies, for example, sensors, actuators and satellites, there is the possibility of feasible implementations, hence the requirements, that what is introduced becomes part of the unfolding requirements prescription* ∎

9.4.4.1 Endurant Extensions

Definition: 91 Endurant Extension: By an ***endurant extension*** we understand the introduction of one or more endurants into the projected, instantiated and determined domain $\mathcal{D_R}$ resulting in domain $\mathcal{D_R}'$, such that these form a *conservative extension* of the theory, $\mathcal{T_{D_R}}$ denoted by the domain requirements $\mathcal{D_R}$ (i.e., "before" the extension), that is: every theorem of $\mathcal{T_{D_R}}$ is still a theorem of $\mathcal{T_{D_R}'}$.

Usually domain extensions involve one or more of the already introduced sorts. In Example 122 we introduce (i.e., "extend") vehicles with GPSS-like sensors, and introduce toll-gates with entry sensors, vehicle identification sensors, gate actuators and exit sensors. Finally road pricing calculators are introduced.

Requirements: Domain Requirements, Endurant Extension 1/2

Example 122   We present the extensions in several steps. Some of them will be developed in this section. Development of the remaining will be deferred to Sect. 9.5.1.3. The reason for this deferment is that those last steps are examples of *interface requirements*. The initial extension-development steps are: [a] vehicle extension, [b] sort and unique identifiers of road price calculators, [c] vehicle to road pricing calculator channel, [d] sorts and dynamic attributes of toll-gates, [e] road pricing calculator attributes, [f] "total" system state, and [g] the overall system behaviour. This decomposition establishes system interfaces in "small, easy steps".

⋆ [a] Vehicle Extension:

385 There is a domain, $\delta_\mathcal{E}:\Delta_\mathcal{E}$, which contains
386 a fleet, $f_\mathcal{E}:F_\mathcal{E}$, that is,
387 a set, $vs_\mathcal{E}:VS_\mathcal{E}$, of
388 extended vehicles, $v_\mathcal{E}:V_\mathcal{E}$ — their extension amounting to
389 a dynamic reactive attribute, whose value, ti-gpos:TiGpos, at any time, reflects that vehicle's *time-stamped global position*.
390 The vehicle's GNSS receiver calculates, *loc_pos*, its local position, lpos:LPos, based on these signals.
391 Vehicles access these *external attributes* via the *external attribute* channel, attr_TiGPos_ch.

type

385 $\Delta_{\mathcal{E}}$
386 $F_{\mathcal{E}}$
387 $VS_{\mathcal{E}} = V_{\mathcal{E}}\text{-set}$
389 $TiGPos = \mathbb{T} \times GPos$
390 GPos, LPos
value
385 $\delta_{\mathcal{E}}:\Delta_{\mathcal{E}}$
386 $obs\_F_{\mathcal{E}}: \Delta_{\mathcal{E}} \rightarrow F_{\mathcal{E}}$,
386 $f = obs\_F_{\mathcal{E}}(\delta_{\mathcal{E}})$
387 $obs\_VS_{\mathcal{E}}: F_{\mathcal{E}} \rightarrow VS_{\mathcal{E}}$,
387 $vs = obs\_VS_{\mathcal{E}}(f)$
387 $vis = xtr\_vis(vs)$
389 $attr\_TiGPos\_ch[vi]?$
390 $loc\_pos: GPos \rightarrow LPos$
channel
391 $\{attr\_TiGPos\_ch[vi]|vi:VI\bullet vi \in vis\}:TiGPos$

We define two auxiliary functions,

392 xtr_vs, which given a domain, or a fleet, extracts its set of vehicles, and
393 xtr_vis which given a set of vehicles generates their unique identifiers.

value
392 $xtr\_vs: (\Delta_{\mathcal{E}}|F_{\mathcal{E}}|VS_{\mathcal{E}}) \rightarrow V_{\mathcal{E}}\text{-set}$
392 $xtr\_vs(arg) \equiv$
392   **is**$\_\Delta_{\mathcal{E}}(arg) \rightarrow$
392       $obs\_VS_{\mathcal{E}}(obs\_F_{\mathcal{E}}(arg))$
392   **is**$\_F_{\mathcal{E}}(arg) \rightarrow$
392       $obs\_VS_{\mathcal{E}}(arg)$,
392   **is**$\_VS_{\mathcal{E}}(arg) \rightarrow arg$
393 $xtr\_vis: (\Delta_{\mathcal{E}}|F_{\mathcal{E}}|VS_{\mathcal{E}}) \rightarrow VI\text{-set}$
393 $xtr\_vis(arg) \equiv \{uid\_VI(v)|v \in xtr\_vs(arg)\}$

⋆ [b] Road Pricing Calculator: Basic Sort and Unique Identifier:

394 The domain $\delta_{\mathcal{E}}:\Delta_{\mathcal{E}}$, also contains a pricing calculator, $c:C_{\delta_{\mathcal{E}}}$, with unique identifier ci:CI.

type
394 C, CI
value
394 $obs\_C: \Delta_{\mathcal{E}} \rightarrow C$
394 $uid\_CI: C \rightarrow CI$
394 $c = obs\_C(\delta_{\mathcal{E}})$
394 $ci = uid\_CI(c)$

⋆ [c] Vehicle to Road Pricing Calculator Channel:

395 Vehicles can, on their own volition, offer the timed local position, viti-lpos:VITiLPos
396 to the pricing calculator, $c:C_{\mathcal{E}}$ along a vehicles-to-calculator channel, v_c_ch.

type
395 $VITiLPos = VI \times (\mathbb{T} \times LPos)$
channel

396   {v_c_ch[vi,ci]|vi:VI,ci:CI•vi∈vis∧ci=uid_C(c)}:VITiLPos

⋆ **[d] Toll-gate Sorts and Dynamic Types:**

We extend the domain with toll-gates for vehicles entering and exiting the toll-road entry and exit links. Figure 9.2 illustrates the idea of gates.

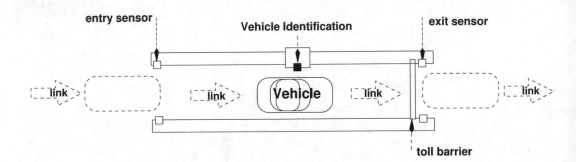

Fig. 9.2 Toll Gate

Requirements: Domain Requirements, Endurant Extension 2/2

Example 122 (Continued) Figure 9.2 is intended to illustrate a vehicle entering (or exiting) a toll-road arrival link. The toll-gate is equipped with three sensors: an arrival sensor, a vehicle identification sensor and an departure sensor. The arrival sensor serves to prepare the vehicle identification sensor. The departure sensor serves to prepare the gate for closing when a vehicle has passed. The vehicle identify sensor identifies the vehicle and "delivers" a pair: the current time and the vehicle identifier. Once the vehicle identification sensor has identified a vehicle the gate opens and a message is sent to the road pricing calculator as to the passing vehicle's identity and the identity of the link associated with the toll-gate (see Items 413- 414 on page 276).

397 The domain contains the extended net, n:$N_\mathcal{E}$,
398 with the net extension amounting to the toll-road net, $TRN_\mathcal{E}$, that is, the instantiated toll-road net, trn:$TRN_\mathcal{I}$, is extended, into trn:$TRN_\mathcal{E}$, with *entry,* eg:EG, and *exit,* xg:XG, toll-gates.

From entry- and exit-gates we can observe

399 their unique identifier and
400 their mereology: pairs of entry-, respectively exit link and calculator unique identifiers; further
401 a pair of gate entry and exit sensors modeled as *external attribute* channels, (ges:ES,gls:XS), and
402 a time-stamped vehicle identity sensor modeled as *external attribute* channels.

type
397    $N_\mathcal{E}$
398    $TRN_\mathcal{E} = (EG×XG)^* × TRN_\mathcal{I}$

399   GI
value
397   obs_N$_\mathcal{E}$: $\Delta_\mathcal{E} \to$ N$_\mathcal{E}$
398   obs_TRN$_\mathcal{E}$: N$_\mathcal{E} \to$ TRN$_\mathcal{E}$
399   uid_G: (EG|XG) $\to$ GI
400   mereo_G: (EG|XG) $\to$ (LI×CI)
398   trn:TRN$_\mathcal{E}$ = obs_TRN$_\mathcal{E}$($\delta_\mathcal{E}$)
channel
401   {attr_entry_ch[gi]|gi:GI•xtr_eGIds(trn)} "enter"
401   {attr_exit_ch[gi]|gi:GI•xtr_xGIds(trn)} "exit"
402   {attr_identity_ch[gi]|gi:GI•xtr_GIds(trn)} TIVI
type
402   TIVI = $\mathbb{T} \times$ VI

We define some **auxiliary functions** over toll-road nets, trn:TRN$_\mathcal{E}$:

403 xtr_eGℓ extracts the ℓist of entry gates,
404 xtr_xGℓ extracts the ℓist of exit gates,
405 xtr_eGIds extracts the set of entry gate identifiers,
406 xtr_xGIds extracts the set of exit gate identifiers,
407 xtr_Gs extracts the set of all gates, and
408 xtr_GIds extracts the set of all gate identifiers.

value
403   xtr_eGℓ: TRN$_\mathcal{E} \to$ EG*
403   xtr_eGℓ(pgl,_) ≡ {eg|(eg,xg):(EG,XG)•(eg,xg)∈ **elems** pgl}
404   xtr_xGℓ: TRN$_\mathcal{E} \to$ XG*
404   xtr_xGℓ(pgl,_) ≡ {xg|(eg,xg):(EG,XG)•(eg,xg)∈ **elems** pgl}
405   xtr_eGIds: TRN$_\mathcal{E} \to$ GI-set
405   xtr_eGIds(pgl,_) ≡ {uid_GI(g)|g:EG•g ∈ xtr_eGs(pgl,_)}
406   xtr_xGIds: TRN$_\mathcal{E} \to$ GI-set
406   xtr_xGIds(pgl,_) ≡ {uid_GI(g)|g:EG•g ∈ xtr_xGs(pgl,_)}
407   xtr_Gs: TRN$_\mathcal{E} \to$ G-set
407   xtr_Gs(pgl,_) ≡ xtr_eGs(pgl,_) ∪ xtr_xGs(pgl,_)
408   xtr_GIds: TRN$_\mathcal{E} \to$ GI-set
408   xtr_GIds(pgl,_) ≡ xtr_eGIds(pgl,_) ∪ xtr_xGIds(pgl,_)
409 A **well-formedness condition** expresses
    a that there are as many entry end exit gate pairs as there are toll-plazas,
    b that all gates are uniquely identified, and
    c that each entry [exit] gate is paired with an entry [exit] link and has that link's unique
       identifier as one element of its mereology, the other elements being the calculator
       identifier and the vehicle identifiers.
    The well-formedness relies on awareness of
410 the unique identifier, ci:CI, of the road pricing calculator, c:C, and
411 the unique identifiers, vis:VI-**set**, of the fleet vehicles.

axiom
409   ∀ n:N$_{\mathcal{R}_3}$, trn:TRN$_{\mathcal{R}_3}$ •
409   **let** (exgl,(exl,hl,lll)) = obs_TRN$_{\mathcal{R}_3}$(n) **in**
409a   **len** exgl = **len** exl = **len** hl = **len** lll + 1
409b   ∧ **card** xtr_GIds(exgl) = 2 * **len** exgl
409c   ∧ ∀ i:**Nat**•i ∈ **inds** exgl•

409c   let ((eg,xg),(el,xl)) = (exgl(i),exl(i)) in
409c   mereo_G(eg) = (uid_U(el),ci,vis)
409c   ∧ mereo_G(xg) = (uid_U(xl),ci,vis)
409   end end

⋆ [e] Toll-gate to Calculator Channels:

412 We distinguish between *entry* and *exit* gates.
413 Toll road entry and exit gates offers the road pricing calculator a pair: whether it is an entry
     or an exit gates, and pair of the passing vehicle's identity and the time-stamped identity
     of the link associated with the toll-gate
414 to the road pricing calculator via a (gate to calculator) channel.

type
412   EE = `entry" | `exit"
413   EEVITiLI = EE×(VI×(𝕋×SonL))
channel
414   {g_c_ch[gi,ci]|gi:GI·gi ∈ gis}:EETiVILI

⋆ [f] Road Pricing Calculator Attributes:

415 The road pricing attributes include a programmable traffic map, trm:TRM, which, for each
     vehicle inside the toll-road net, records a chronologically ordered list of each vehicle's
     timed position, (τ, lpos), and
416 a static (total) road location function, vplf:VPLF. The *vehicle position location function*,
     vplf:VPLF, which, given a local position, lpos:LPos, yields *either* the simple vehicle po-
     sition, svpos:SVPos, designated by the GNSS-provided position, *or* yields the response
     that the provided position is off the toll-road net The vplf:VPLF function is constructed,
     construct_vplf,
417 from awareness, of a geodetic road map, GRM, of the topology of the extended net, $n_\mathcal{E}:N_\mathcal{E}$,
     including the mereology and the geodetic attributes of links and hubs.

type
415   TRM = VI $_{\overrightarrow{m}}$ (𝕋×SVPos)*
416   VPLF = GRM→LPos→(SVPos|`off_N")
417   GRM
value
415   attr_TRM: $C_\mathcal{E}$ → TRM
416   attr_VPLF: $C_\mathcal{E}$ → VPLF

The geodetic road map maps geodetic locations into hub and link identifiers.

327 Geodetic link locations represent the set of point locations of a link.
323a Geodetic hub locations represent the set of point locations of a hub.
418 A geodetic road map maps geodetic link locations into link identifiers and geodetic hub
     locations into hub identifiers.
419 We sketch the construction, *geo_GRM*, of geodetic road maps.

type
418   GRM = (GeoL $_{\overrightarrow{m}}$ LI) ∪ (GeoH $_{\overrightarrow{m}}$ HI)
value
419   geo_GRM: N → GRM
419   geo_GRM(n) ≡

```
419     let ls = xtr_links(n), hs = xtr_hubs(n) in
419     [ attr_GeoL(l)↦uid_LI(l)|l:L•l ∈ ls ]
419     ∪
419     [ attr_GeoH(h)↦uid_HI(h)|h:H•h ∈ hs ] end
```

420 The obtain_SVPos function obtains a simple vehicle position, svpos, from a geodetic road map, grm:GRM, and a local position , lpos:

value

```
420   obtain_SVPos: GRM → LPos → SVPos
420   obtain_SVPos(grm)(lpos) as svpos
420   post: case svpos of
420           SatH(hi)  → within(lpos,grm(hi)),
420           SonL(li)  → within(lpos,grm(li)),
420           "off_N"   → true end
```

where *within* is a predicate which holds if its first argument, a local position calculated from a GNSS-generated global position, falls within the point set representation of the geodetic locations of a link or a hub. The design of the *obtain_SVPos* represents an interesting challenge.

⋆ [g] "Total" System State:

Global values:

421 There is a given domain, $\delta_\mathcal{E}$:$\Delta_\mathcal{E}$;
422 there is the net, $n_\mathcal{E}$:$N_\mathcal{E}$, of that domain;
423 there is toll-road net, $trn_\mathcal{E}$:$TRN_\mathcal{E}$, of that net;
424 there is a set, $egs_\mathcal{E}$:$EG_\mathcal{E}$-**set**, of entry gates;
425 there is a set, $xgs_\mathcal{E}$:$XG_\mathcal{E}$-**set**, of exit gates;
426 there is a set, $gis_\mathcal{E}$:$GI_\mathcal{E}$-**set**, of gate identifiers;
427 there is a set, $vs_\mathcal{E}$:$V_\mathcal{E}$-**set**, of vehicles;
428 there is a set, $vis_\mathcal{E}$:$VI_\mathcal{E}$-**set**, of vehicle identifiers;
429 there is the road-pricing calculator, $c_\mathcal{E}$:$C_\mathcal{E}$ and
430 there is its unique identifier, $ci_\mathcal{E}$:CI.

value

```
421   δ_ℰ:Δ_ℰ
422   n_ℰ:N_ℰ = obs_N_ℰ(δ_ℰ)
423   trn_ℰ:TRN_ℰ = obs_TRN_ℰ(n_ℰ)
424   egs_ℰ:EG-set = xtr_egs(trn_ℰ)
425   xgs_ℰ:XG-set = xtr_xgs(trn_ℰ)
426   gis_ℰ:XG-set = xtr_gis(trn_ℰ)
427   vs_ℰ:V_ℰ-set = obs_VS(obs_F_ℰ(δ_ℰ))
428   vis_ℰ:VI-set = {uid_VI(v_ℰ)|v_ℰ:V_ℰ•v_ℰ ∈ vs_ℰ}
429   c_ℰ:C_ℰ = obs_C_ℰ(δ_ℰ)
430   ci_ℰ:CI_ℰ = uid_CI(c_ℰ)
```

In the following we shall omit the cumbersome $\mathcal{E}$ subscripts.

⋆ [h] "Total" System Behaviour:

The signature and definition of the system behaviour is sketched as are the signatures of the vehicle, toll-gate and road pricing calculator. We shall model the behaviour of the road pricing system as follows: we shall not model behaviours nets, hubs and links; thus we shall model only the behaviour of vehicles, veh, the behaviour of toll-gates, gate, and the behaviour of the road-pricing calculator, calc. The behaviours of vehicles and toll-gates are presented here. But the behaviour of the road-pricing calculator is "deferred" till Sect. **9.5.1.3** since it reflects an interface requirements.

431 The road pricing system behaviour, sys, is expressed as

    a the parallel, ∥, (distributed) composition of the behaviours of all vehicles,

    b with the parallel composition of the parallel (likewise distributed) composition of the behaviours of all entry gates,

    c with the parallel composition of the parallel (likewise distributed) composition of the behaviours of all exit gates,

    d with the parallel composition of the behaviour of the road-pricing calculator,

value
431   sys: **Unit** → **Unit**
431   sys() ≡
431a   ∥ {veh$_{\text{uid\_}V(v)}$(mereo_V(v))|v:V•v ∈ vs}
431b   ∥ ∥ {gate$_{\text{uid\_}EG(eg)}$(mereo_G(eg),"entry")|eg:EG•eg ∈ egs}
431c   ∥ ∥ {gate$_{\text{uid\_}XG(xg)}$(mereo_G(xg),"exit")|xg:XG•xg ∈ xgs}
431d   ∥ calc$_{\text{uid\_}C(c)}$(vis,gis)(rlf)(trm)

432   veh$_{vi}$: (ci:CI×gis:GI-set) → **in** attr_TiGPos[vi] **out** v_c_ch[vi,ci] **Unit**
438   gate$_{gi}$: (ci:CI×VI-set×LI)×ee:EE →
438   **in** attr_entry_ch[gi,ci],attr_id_ch[gi,ci],attr_exit_ch[gi,ci]
438   **out** attr_barrier_ch[gi],g_c_ch[gi,ci] **Unit**
472   calc$_{ci}$: (vis:VI-set×gis:GI-set)×VPLF→TRM→
472   **in** {v_c_ch[vi,ci]|vi:VI•vi ∈ vis},{g_c_ch[gi,ci]|gi:GI•gi ∈ gis} **Unit**

We consider "entry" or "exit" to be a static attribute of toll-gates. The behaviour signatures were determined as per the techniques presented in Chapters 4–7.

Vehicle Behaviour: We refer to the vehicle behaviour, in the domain, described in Sect. **9.2**'s The Road Traffic System Behaviour Items 350 and Items 351, Page 254 and, projected, Page 265.

432 Instead of moving around by explicitly expressed internal non-determinism[213] vehicles move around by unstated internal non-determinism and instead receive their current position from the global positioning subsystem.

433 At each moment the vehicle receives its time-stamped global position, (τ,gpos):TiGPos,

434 from which it calculates the local position, lpos:VPos

435 which it then communicates, with its vehicle identification, (vi,(τ,lpos)), to the road pricing subsystem —

436 whereupon it resumes its vehicle behaviour.

value
432   veh$_{vi}$: (ci:CI×gis:GI-set) →
432   **in** attr_TiGPos_ch[vi] **out** v_c_ch[vi,ci] **Unit**
432   veh$_{vi}$(ci,gis) ≡
433   **let** (τ,gpos) = attr_TiGPos_ch[vi]? **in**
434   **let** lpos = loc_pos(gpos) **in**
435   v_c_ch[vi,ci] ! (vi,(τ,lpos)) ;
436   veh$_{vi}$(ci,gis) **end end**
432   **pre** vi ∈ vis

The *vehicle* signature has *attr_TiGPos_ch*[*vi*] model an external vehicle attribute and *v_c_ch*[*vi,ci*] the *embedded attribute sharing* [73, Sect. 4.1.1 and 4.5.2] between vehicles (their position) and the price calculator's road map. The above behaviour represents an assumption about the behaviour of vehicles. If we were to design software for the monitoring and control of vehicles then the above vehicle behaviour would have to be refined in order to serve as a proper interface requirements. The refinement would include handling concerns about the drivers' behaviour when entering, passing and exiting toll-gates, about the proper function of the GNSS equipment, and about the safe communication with the road price calculator. The above concerns would already have been addressed in a model of *domain facets* such as *human behaviour, technology support*, proper tele-communications *scripts*, et cetera. We refer to Chapter 8.

Gate Behaviour: The entry and the exit gates have "vehicle enter", "vehicle exit" and "timed vehicle identification" sensors. The following assumption can now be made: during the time interval between a gate's vehicle "entry" sensor having first sensed a vehicle entering that gate and that gate's "exit" sensor having last sensed that vehicle leaving that gate that gate's vehicle time and "identify" sensor registers the time when the vehicle is entering the gate and that vehicle's unique identification. We sketch the toll-gate behaviour:

437 We parameterise the toll-gate behaviour as either an entry or an exit gate.

438 Toll-gates operate autonomously and cyclically.

439 The attr_enter_ch event "triggers" the behaviour specified in formula line Item 440–442 starting with a "Raise" barrier action.

440 The time-of-passing and the identity of the passing vehicle is sensed by attr_passing_ch channel events.

441 Then the road pricing calculator is informed of time-of-passing and of the vehicle identity vi and the link li associated with the gate – and with a "Lower" barrier action.

442 And finally, after that vehicle has left the entry or exit gate the barrier is again "Lower"ered and

443 that toll-gate's behaviour is resumed.

type
437   EE = "enter" | "exit"
value
438   gate$_{gi}$: (ci:CI×VI-set×LI)×ee:EE →
438   **in** attr_enter_ch[gi],attr_passing_ch[gi],attr_leave_ch[gi]
438   **out** attr_barrier_ch[gi],g_c_ch[gi,ci] **Unit**
438   gate$_{gi}$((ci,vis,li),ee) ≡
439   attr_enter_ch[gi] ? ; attr_barrier_ch[gi] ! "Lower"
440   **let** (τ,vi) = attr_passing_ch[gi] ? **in assert** vi ∈ vis
441   (attr_barrier_ch[gi] ! "Raise"
441   ‖ g_c_ch[gi,ci] ! (ee,(vi,(τ,SonL(li))))) ;
442   attr_leave_ch[gi] ? ; attr_barrier_ch[gi] ! "Lower"
443   gate$_{gi}$((ci,vis,li),ee)
438   **end**
438   **pre** li ∈ lis

The *gate* signature's *attr_enter_ch*[*gi*], *attr_passing_ch*[*gi*], *attr_barrier_ch*[*gi*] and *attr_leave_ch*[*gi*] model respective *external attributes* [73, Sect. 4.1.1 and 4.5.2] (the *attr_barrier_ch*[*gi*] models reactive (i.e., output) attribute), while *g_c_ch*[*gi,ci*] models the *embedded attribute sharing* between gates (their identification of vehicle positions) and the calculator road map. The above behaviour represents an assumption about the behaviour of toll-gates. If we were to design software for the monitoring and control of toll-gates then the above gate behaviour would have to be refined in order to serve as a proper interface requirements. The refinement would include handling concerns about the drivers' behaviour when entering, passing and exiting toll-gates, about the proper function of the entry, passing and exit sensors, about the proper function of the gate barrier (opening and closing), and about the safe communication with the road price calculator. The above concerns would already have been addressed in a model of *domain facets* such as *human behaviour, technology support*, proper tele-communications *scripts*, et cetera   □

We shall define the *calculator* behaviour in Sect. **9.5.1.3** on page 286. The reason for this deferral is that it exemplifies *interface requirements*.

9.4.4.2 Discussion

The requirements assumptions expressed in the specifications of the vehicle and gate behaviours assume that these behave in an orderly fashion. But they seldom do! The attr_TiGPos_ch sensor may fail. And so may the attr_enter_ch, attr_passing_ch, and attr_leave_ch sensors and the attr_barrier_ch actuator. These attributes represent *support technology* facets. They can fail. To secure fault tolerance one must prescribe very carefully what counter-measures are to be taken and/or the safety assumptions. We refer to [404, 268, 315]. They cover three alternative approaches to the handling of fault tolerance. Either of the approaches can be made to fit with our approach. First one can pursue our approach to where we stand now. Then we join the approaches of either of [404, 268, 315]. [268] likewise decompose the requirements prescription as is suggested here.

9.4.5 Requirements Fitting

Often a domain being described "fits" onto, is "adjacent" to, "interacts" in some areas with, another domain: *transportation* with *logistics, health-care* with *insurance, banking* with *securities trading* and/or *insurance*, and so on. The issue of requirements fitting arises when two or more software development projects are based on what appears to be the same domain. The problem then is to harmonise the two or more software development projects by harmonising, if not too late, their requirements developments.

   We thus assume that there are n domain requirements developments, $d_{r_1}, d_{r_2}, \ldots, d_{r_n}$, being considered, and that these pertain to the same domain — and can hence be assumed covered by a same domain description.

Definition: 92 Requirements Fitting: By ***requirements fitting*** we mean a *harmonisation* of $n > 1$ domain requirements that have overlapping (shared) not always consistent parts and which results in n *partial domain requirements'*, $p_{d_{r_1}}, p_{d_{r_2}}, \ldots, p_{d_{r_n}}$, and m *shared domain requirements*, $s_{d_{r_1}}, s_{d_{r_2}}, \ldots, s_{d_{r_m}}$, that "fit into" two or more of the partial domain requirements ■ The above definition pertains to the result of 'fitting'. The next definition pertains to the act, or process, of 'fitting'.

---

[213] We refer to Items 350b, 350c on page 254 and 351b, 351(b)ii, 351c on page 254

Definition: 93 Requirements Harmonisation: By *requirements harmonisation* we mean a number of alternative and/or co-ordinated prescription actions, one set for each of the domain requirements actions: *Projection, Instantiation, Determination* and *Extension*. They are – we assume n separate software product requirements: *Projection:* If the n product requirements do not have the same projections, then identify a common projection which they all share, and refer to it as the *common projection*. Then develop, for each of the n product requirements, if required, a *specific projection* of the common one. Let there be m such specific projections, $m \leq n$. *Instantiation:* First instantiate the common projection, if any instantiation is needed. Then for each of the m specific projections instantiate these, if required. *Determination:* Likewise, if required, "perform" "determination" of the possibly instantiated common projection, and, similarly, if required, "perform" "determination" of the up to m possibly instantiated projections. *Extension:* Finally "perform extension" likewise: First, if required, of the common projection (etc.), then, if required, on the up m specific projections (etc.). These harmonization developments may possibly interact and may need to be iterated ∎

By a **partial domain requirement**s we mean a domain requirements which is short of (that is, is missing) some prescription parts: text and formula ∎ By a **shared domain requirement**s we mean a domain requirements ∎ By **requirements fitting** m shared domain requirements texts, *sdrs*, into n partial domain requirements we mean that there is for each partial domain requirements, pdr_i, an identified, non-empty subset of *sdrs* (could be all of *sdrs*), $ssdrs_i$, such that textually conjoining $ssdrs_i$ to pdr_i, i.e., $ssdrs_i \oplus pdr_i$ can be claimed to yield the "original" d_{r_i}, that is, $\mathcal{M}(ssdrs_i \oplus pdr_i) \subseteq \mathcal{M}(d_{r_i})$, where $\mathcal{M}$ is a suitable meaning function over prescriptions ∎

9.4.6 Discussion

Facet-oriented Fittings: An altogether different way of looking at domain requirements may be achieved when also considering domain facets — not covered in neither the example of Sect. 9.2 nor in this section (i.e., Sect. 9.4) nor in the following two sections. We refer to [55].

Requirements: Domain Requirements, Fitting

Example 123 Example 122 hints at three possible sets of interface requirements: (i) for a road pricing [sub-]system, as will be illustrated in Sect. 9.5.1.3; (ii) for a vehicle monitoring and control [sub-]system, and (iii) for a toll-gate monitoring and control [sub-]system. The vehicle monitoring and control [sub-]system would focus on implementing the vehicle behaviour, see Items 432- 436 on page 278. The toll-gate monitoring and control [sub-]system would focus on implementing the calculator behaviour, see Items 438- 443 on page 279. The fitting amounts to (a) making precise the narrative and formal texts specific to each of the three (i–iii) separate sub-system requirements are kept separate; (b) ensuring that meaning-wise shared texts that have different names for meaning-wise identical entities have these names renamed appropriately; (c) that these texts are subject to commensurate and ameliorated further requirements development; et cetera □

9.5 Interface and Derived Requirements

We remind the reader that **interface requirements** can be expressed only using terms from both the domain and the machine ∎ Users are not part of the machine. So no reference can be made to users, such as *"the system must be user friendly"*, and the like !²¹⁴ By **interface requirements** we [also] mean *requirements prescriptions which refines and extends the domain requirements by considering those requirements of the domain requirements whose endurants (parts, fluids) and perdurants (actions, events and behaviours) are* **"shared"** *between the domain and the machine (being requirements prescribed)* ∎ The two *interface requirements* definitions above go hand–in–hand, i.e., complement one-another.

By **derived requirements** we mean *requirements prescriptions which are expressed in terms of the machine concepts and facilities introduced by the emerging requirements* ∎

9.5.1 Interface Requirements

9.5.1.1 Shared Phenomena

By **sharing** we mean (a) that *some or all properties* of an **endurant** is represented both in the domain and "inside" the machine, and that their machine representation must at suitable times reflect their state in the domain; and/or (b) that an **action** requires a sequence of several "on-line" interactions between the machine (being requirements prescribed) and the domain, usually a person or another machine; and/or (c) that an **event** arises either in the domain, that is, in the environment of the machine, or in the machine, and need be communicated to the machine, respectively to the environment; and/or (d) that a **behaviour** is manifested both by actions and events of the domain and by actions and events of the machine ∎ So a systematic reading of the domain requirements shall result in an identification of all shared endurants, parts and fluids; and perdurants actions, events and behaviours. Each such shared phenomenon shall then be individually dealt with: **endurant sharing** shall lead to interface requirements for data initialisation and refreshment as well as for access to endurant attributes; **action sharing** shall lead to interface requirements for interactive dialogues between the machine and its environment; **event sharing** shall lead to interface requirements for how such event are communicated between the environment of the machine and the machine; and **behaviour sharing** shall lead to interface requirements for action and event dialogues between the machine and its environment.

⋆ Environment–Machine Interface:

Domain requirements extension, Sect. 9.4.4, usually introduce new endurants into (i.e., 'extend' the) domain. Some of these endurants may become elements of the domain requirements. Others are to be projected "away". Those that are let into the domain requirements either have their endurants represented, somehow, also in the machine, or have (some of) their properties, usually some attributes, accessed by the machine. Similarly for perdurants. Usually the machine representation of shared perdurants access (some of) their properties, usually some attributes. The interface requirements must spell out which domain extensions are shared. Thus domain extensions may necessitate a review of domain projection, instantiations and determination. In general, there may be several of the projection–eliminated parts (etc.) whose dynamic attributes need be accessed in the usual way, i.e., by means of attr_XYZ_ch channel communications (where XYZ is a projection–eliminated part attribute).

---

²¹⁴ So how do we cope with the statement:*"the system must be user friendly"* ? We refer to Sect. **9.5.3.2** on page 291 for a discussion of this issue.

Requirements: Interface Requirements, Projected Extensions

Example 124 We refer to Fig. 9.2 on page 274. We do not represent the GNSS system in the machine: only its "effect": the ability to record global positions by accessing the GNSS attribute (channel):

channel

391   {attr_TiGPos_ch[vi]|vi:VI•vi ∈ xtr_VIs(vs)}: TiGPos

And we do not really represent the gate nor its sensors and actuator in the machine. But we do give an idealised description of the gate behaviour, see Items 438–443 Instead we represent their dynamic gate attributes:

(401) the vehicle entry sensors (leftmost ■s),
(401) the vehicle identity sensor (center■), and
(402) the vehicle exit sensors (rightmost■s)

by channels — we refer to Example 122 (Sect. **9.5.1.3**, Page 275):

channel

401   {attr_entry_ch[gi]|gi:GI•xtr_eGIds(trn)} `enter"
401   {attr_exit_ch[gi]|gi:GI•xtr_xGIds(trn)} `exit"
402   {attr_identity_ch[gi]|gi:GI•xtr_GIds(trn)} TIVI   □

9.5.1.2 Shared Endurants

Requirements: Interface Requirements, Shared Endurants

Example 125 The main shared endurants are the vehicles, the net (hubs, links, toll-gates) and the price calculator. As domain endurants hubs and links undergo changes, all the time, with respect to the values of several attributes: *length, geodetic information, names, wear and tear* (where-ever applicable), *last/next scheduled maintenance* (where-ever applicable), *state* and *state space*, and many others. Similarly for vehicles: their position, velocity and acceleration, and many other attributes. We then come up with something like hubs and links are to be represented as tuples of relations; each net will be represented by a pair of relations a hubs relation and a links relation; each hub and each link may or will be represented by several tuples; et cetera. In this database modeling effort it must be secured that "standard" operations on nets, hubs and links can be supported by the chosen relational database system
□

★ Data Initialisation:

In general, one must prescribe data initialisation, that is provision for an interactive user interface dialogue with a set of proper display screens, one for establishing net, hub or link attributes names and their types, and, for example, two for the input of hub and link attribute values. Interaction prompts may be prescribed: next input, on-line vetting and display of evolving net, etc. These and many other aspects may therefore need prescriptions.

Requirements: Interface Requirements, Shared Endurant Initialisation

Example 126 The domain is that of the road net, n:N. By 'shared road net initialisation' we mean the "ab initio" establishment, "from scratch", of a data base recording the properties of all links, l:L, and hubs, h:H, their unique identifications, uid_L(l) and uid_H(h), their mereologies, mereo_L(l) and mereo_H(h), the initial values of all their static and programmable attributes and the access values, that is, channel designations for all other attribute categories.

444 There are r_l and r_h "recorders" recording link, respectively hub properties – with each recorder having a unique identity.
445 Each recorder is charged with the recording of a set of links or a set of hubs according to some partitioning of all such.
446 The recorders inform a central data base, net_db, of their recordings (ri,hol,(u$_j$,m$_j$,attrs$_j$)) where
447 ri is the identity of the recorder,
448 hol is either a hub or a link literal,
449 u$_j$ = uid_L(l) or uid_H(h) for some link or hub,
450 m$_j$ = mereo_L(l) or mereo_H(h) for that link or hub and
451 attrs$_j$ are *attributes* for that link or hub — where *attributes* is a function which "records" all respective static and dynamic attributes (left undefined).

type
444 RI
value
444 rl,rh:NAT **axiom** rl>0 ∧ rh>0
type
446 M = RI×`link`×LNK | RI×`hub`×HUB
446 LNK = LI × HI-**set** × LATTRS
446 HUB = HI × LI-**set** × HATTRS

value
445 partitioning: L-**set**→**Nat**→(L-**set**)*
445 | H-**set**→**Nat**→(H-**set**)*
445 partitioning(s)(r) **as** sl
445 **post: len** sl = r ∧ ∪ **elems** sl = s
445   ∧ ∀ si,sj:(L-**set**|H-**set**) •
445   si≠{}∧sj≠{}∧{si,sj}⊆**elems** ss⇒si ∩ sj={}

452 The $r_l + r_h$ recorder behaviours interact with the one net_db behaviour

channel
452 r_db: RI×(LNK|HUB)
value
452 link_rec: RI → L-**set** → **out** r_db **Unit**
452 hub_rec: RI → H-**set** → **out** r_db **Unit**
452 net_db: **Unit** → **in** r_db **Unit**

453 The data base behaviour, net_db, offers to receive messages from the link and hub recorders.
454 The data base behaviour, net_db, deposits these messages in respective variables.
455 Initially there is a net, $n : N$,
456 from which is observed its links and hubs.
457 These sets are partitioned into r_l, respectively r_h length lists of non-empty links and hubs.

458 The ab-initio data initialisation behaviour, ab_initio_data, is then the parallel composition of link recorder, hub recorder and data base behaviours with link and hub recorder being allotted appropriate link, respectively hub sets.

459 We construct, for technical reasons, as the reader will soon see, disjoint lists of link, respectively hub recorder identities.

value
453 net_db:
variable
454 lnk_db: (RI×LNK)-**set**
454 hub_db: (RI×HUB)-**set**
value
455 n:N
456 ls:L-**set** = **obs**_Ls(**obs**_LS(n))
456 hs:H-**set** = **obs**_Hs(**obs**_HS(n))
457 lsl:(L-**set**)* = partitioning(ls)(rl)
457 lhl:(H-**set**)* = partitioning(hs)(rh)
459 rill:RI* **axiom len** rill = rl = **card elems** rill
459 rihl:RI* **axiom len** rihl = rh = **card elems** rihl
458 ab_initio_data: **Unit** → **Unit**
458 ab_initio_data() ≡
458 || {lnk_rec(rill[i])(lsl[i])|i:**Nat**·1 ≤i≤rl} ||
458 || {hub_rec(rihl[i])(lhl[i])|i:**Nat**·1 ≤i≤rh}
458 || net_db()

460 The link and the hub recorders are near-identical behaviours.

461 They both revolve around an imperatively stated **for all ... do ... end**. The selected link (or hub) is inspected and the "data" for the data base is prepared from

462 the unique identifier,

463 the mereology, and

464 the attributes.

465 These "data" are sent, as a message, prefixed the senders identity, to the data base behaviour.

466 We presently leave the . . . unexplained.

value
452 link_rec: RI → L-**set** → **Unit**
460 link_rec(ri,ls) ≡
461   **for** ∀ l:L·l ∈ ls **do** uid_L(l)
462   **let** lnk = (uid_L(l),
463   mereo_L(l),
464   attributes(l)) **in**
465   rdb ! (ri,"link",lnk);
466   ... **end**
461   **end**

452 hub_rec: RI × H-**set** → **Unit**
460 hub_rec(ri,hs) ≡
461   **for** ∀ h:H·h ∈ hs **do** uid_H(h)
462   **let** hub = (uid_L(h),
463   mereo_H(h),

```
464                    attributes(h)) in
465        rdb ! (ri,`hub",hub);
466        ... end
461      end
```

467 The net_db data base behaviour revolves around a seemingly "never-ending" cyclic process.
468 Each cycle "starts" with acceptance of some,
469 either link or hub data.
470 If link data then it is deposited in the link data base,
471 if hub data then it is deposited in the hub data base.

```
value
467   net_db() ≡
468      let (ri,hol,data) = r_db ? in
469      case hol of
470        `link" → ... ; lnk_db := lnk_db ∪ (ri,data),
471        `hub" → ... ; hub_db := hub_db ∪ (ri,data)
469      end end ;
467'     ... ;
467      net_db()
```

The above model is an idealisation. It assumes that the link and hub data represent a well-formed net. Included in this well-formedness are the following issues: (a) that all link or hub identifiers are communicated exactly once, (b) that all mereologies refer to defined parts, and (c) that all attribute values lie within an appropriate value range. If we were to cope with possible recording errors then we could, for example, extend the model as follows: (i) when a link or a hub recorder has completed its recording then it increments an initially zero counter (say at formula Item 466); (ii) before the net data base recycles it tests whether all recording sessions has ended and then proceeds to check the data base for well-formedness issues (a–b–c) (say at formula Item 467')   □

The above example illustrates the 'interface' phenomenon: In the formulas, for example, we show both manifest domain entities, viz., n,l,h etc., and abstract (required) software objects, viz., $(ui,me,attrs)$.

★ Data Refreshment:

One must also prescribe data refreshment: an interactive user interface dialogue with a set of proper display screens one for selecting the updating of net, of hub or of link attribute names and their types and, for example, two for the respective update of hub and link attribute values. Interaction-prompts may be prescribed: next update, on-line vetting and display of revised net, etc. These and many other aspects may therefore need prescriptions.

9.5.1.3 Shared Perdurants

We can expect that for every part in the domain that is shared with the machine and for which there is a corresponding behaviour of the domain there might be a corresponding process of the machine. If a projected, instantiated, 'determinated' and possibly extended domain part is dynamic, then it is definitely a candidate for being shared and having an associated machine process.

We now illustrate the concept of shared perdurants via the domain requirements extension example of Sect. **9.4.4**, i.e. Example 122 Pages 272–280.

Requirements: Interface Requirements, Shared Behaviours

Example 127 Road Pricing Calculator Behaviour:

472 The road-pricing calculator alternates between offering to accept communication from
473 either any vehicle
474 or any toll-gate.

472 calc: ci:CI×(vis:VI-set×gis:GI-set)→RLF→TRM→
473   **in** {v_c_ch[ci,vi]|vi:VI•vi ∈ vis},
474   {g_c_ch[ci,gi]|gi:GI•gi ∈ gis} **Unit**
472 calc(ci,(vis,gis))(rlf)(trm) ≡
473   react_to_vehicles(ci,(vis,gis))(rlf)(trm)
472   ⌷
474   react_to_gates(ci,(vis,gis))(rlf)(trm)
472   **pre** ci = ci_ε ∧ vis = vis_ε ∧ gis = gis_ε

The *calculator* signature's v_c_ch[*ci,vi*] and g_c_ch[*ci,gi*] model the *embedded attribute sharing* between vehicles (their position), respectively gates (their vehicle identification) and the calculator road map [73, Sect. 4.1.1 and 4.5.2].

475 If the communication is from a vehicle inside the toll-road net
476 then its toll-road net position, vp, is found from the road location function, rlf,
477 and the calculator resumes its work with the traffic map, trm, suitably updated,
478 otherwise the calculator resumes its work with no changes.

473 react_to_vehicles(ci,(vis,gis),vplf)(trm) ≡
473   **let** (vi,(τ,lpos)) = ⌷{v_c_ch[ci,vi]?|vi:VI•vi∈ vis} **in**
475   **if** vi ∈ **dom** trm
476   **then let** vp = vplf(lpos) **in**
477   calc(ci,(vis,gis),vplf)(trm†[vi↦$\widehat{trm}$⟨(τ,vp)⟩]) **end**
478   **else** calc(ci,(vis,gis),vplf)(trm) **end end**

479 If the communication is from a gate,
480 then that gate is either an entry gate or an exit gate;
481 if it is an entry gate
482 then the calculator resumes its work with the vehicle (that passed the entry gate) now recorded, afresh, in the traffic map, trm.
483 Else it is an exit gate and
484 the calculator concludes that the vehicle has ended its to-be-paid-for journey inside the toll-road net, and hence to be billed;
485 then the calculator resumes its work with the vehicle now removed from the traffic map, trm.

474 react_to_gates(ci,(vis,gis),vplf)(trm) ≡
474   **let** (ee,(τ,(vi,li))) = ⌷ {g_c_ch[ci,gi]?|gi:GI•gi∈ gis} **in**
480   **case** ee **of**
481   "Enter" →
482   calc(ci,(vis,gis),vplf)(trm∪[vi↦⟨(τ,SonL(li))⟩]),
483   "Exit" →

484   billing(vi,trm(vi)⌢⟨(τ,SonL(li))⟩);
485   calc(ci,(vis,gis),vplf)(trm\{vi}) **end end**

The above behaviour is the one for which we are to design software   □

9.5.2 Derived Requirements

Definition: 94 Derived Perdurant: By a **derived perdurant** we shall understand a perdurant which is not shared with the domain, but which focus on exploiting facilities of the software or hardware of the machine ∎

"Exploiting facilities of the software", to us, means that requirements, imply the presence, in the machine, of concepts (i.e., hardware and/or software), and that it is these concepts that the **derived requirements** "rely" on. We illustrate all three forms of perdurant extensions: derived actions, derived events and derived behaviours.

9.5.2.1 Derived Actions

Definition: 95 Derived Action: By a **derived action** we shall understand (a) a conceptual action (b) that calculates a usually non-Boolean valued property from, and possibly changes to (c) a machine behaviour state (d) as instigated by some actor ∎

Requirements: Domain Requirements, Derived Action – Tracing Vehicles

Example 128 The example is based on the *Road Pricing Calculator Behaviour* of Example 127 on the previous page. The "external" actor, i.e., a user of the *Road Pricing Calculator* system wishes to trace specific vehicles "cruising" the toll-road. That user (a *Road Pricing Calculator* staff), issues a command to the *Road Pricing Calculator* system, with the identity of a vehicle not already being traced. As a result the *Road Pricing Calculator* system augments a possibly void trace of the timed toll-road positions of vehicles. We augment the definition of the *calc*ulator definition Items 472–485, Pages 287–288.

486 Traces are modeled by a pair of dynamic attributes:

    a as a programmable attribute, *tra:TRA*, of the set of identifiers of vehicles being traced, and

    b as a reactive attribute, *vdu:VDU* (Visual Display Unit), that maps vehicle identifiers into time-stamped sequences of simple vehicle positions, i.e., as a subset of the *trm:TRM* programmable attribute.

487 The actor-to-calculator *begin* or *end* trace command, *cmd:Cmd*, is modeled as an autonomous dynamic attribute of the *calc*ulator.

488 The *calc*ulator signature is furthermore augmented with the three attributes mentioned above.

489 The occurrence and handling of an actor trace command is modeled as a non-deterministic external choice and a *react_to_trace_cmd* behaviour.

490 The reactive attribute value (attr_vdu_ch?) is that subset of the traffic map (*trm*) which records just the time-stamped sequences of simple vehicle positions being traced (*tra*).

type
486a TRA = VI-**set**
486b VDU = TRM
487   Cmd = BTr | ETr
487   BTr :: VI
487   ETr :: VI

value
488 calc: ci:CI×(vis:VI-**set**×gis:GI-**set**) → RLF → TRM → TRA
473,474   **in** {v_c_ch[ci,vi]|vi:VI•vi ∈ vis},
473,474   {g_c_ch[ci,gi]|gi:GI•gi ∈ gis},
489,490   attr_cmd_ch,attr_vdu_ch **Unit**
472 calc(ci,(vis,gis))(rlf)(trm)(tra) ≡
473   react_to_vehicles(ci,(vis,gis),)(rlf)(trm)(tra)
474   ⏽ react_to_gates(ci,(vis,gis))(rlf)(trm)(tra)
489   ⏽ react_to_trace_cmd(ci,(vis,gis))(rlf)(trm)(tra)
472   **pre** ci = $ci_\mathcal{E}$ ∧ vis = $vis_\mathcal{E}$ ∧ gis = $gis_\mathcal{E}$
490   **axiom** □ attr_vdu_ch[ci]? = trm|tra

The *489,490 attr_cmd_ch,attr_vdu_ch* of the *calculator* signature models the *calculator's* external *command* and *visual display unit* attributes.

491 The *react_to_trace_cmd* alternative behaviour is either a "Begin" or an "End" request which identifies the affected vehicle.
492 If it is a "Begin" request
493 and the identified vehicle is already being traced then we do not prescribe what to do!
494 Else we resume the calculator behaviour, now recording that vehicle as being traced.
495 If it is an "End" request
496 and the identified vehicle is already being traced then we do not prescribe what to do!
497 Else we resume the calculator behaviour, now recording that vehicle as no longer being traced.

491 react_to_trace_cmd(ci,(vis,gis))(vplf)(trm)(tra) ≡
491   **case** attr_cmd_ch[ci]? **of**
                mkBTr(vi) →
492   **if** vi ∈ tra
493   **then chaos**
494   **else** calc(ci,(vis,gis))(vplf)(trm)(tra ∪ {vi}) **end**
                mkETr(vi) →
495   **if** vi ∉ tra
496   **then chaos**
497   **else** calc(ci,(vis,gis))(vplf)(trm)(tra\{vi}) **end**
491   **end**

The above behaviour, Items 472–497, is the one for which we are to design software □

Example 128 exemplifies an action requirement as per definition 95: (a) the action is conceptual, it has no physical counterpart in the domain; (b) it calculates (490) a visual display (vdu); (c) the vdu value is based on a conceptual notion of traffic road maps (trm), an element of the calculator state; (d) the calculation is triggered by an actor (attr_cmd_ch).

9.5.2.2 Derived Events

Definition: 96 Derived Event: By a ***derived event*** we shall understand (a) a conceptual event, (b) that calculates a property or some non-Boolean value (c) from a machine behaviour state change ∎

Requirements: Domain Requirements, Derived Event, Current Maximum Flow

Example 129 The example is based on the *Road Pricing Calculator Behaviour* of Examples 128 and 127 on page 287. By "the current maximum flow" we understand a time-stamped natural number, the number representing the highest number of vehicles which at the time-stamped moment cruised or now cruises around the toll-road net. We augment the definition of the *calc*ulator definition Items 472–497, Pages 287–289.

498 We augment the *calc*ulator signature with
499 a time-stamped natural number valued dynamic programmable attribute, *(t:T,max:Max)*.
500 Whenever a vehicle enters the toll-road net, through one of its [entry] gates,
    a it is checked whether the resulting number of vehicles recorded in the *road traffic map* is higher than the hitherto *max*imum recorded number.
    b If so, that programmable attribute has its number element "upped" by one.
    c Otherwise not.
501 No changes are to be made to the react_to_gates behaviour (Items 474–485 Page 288) when a vehicle exits the toll-road net.

type
499   MAX = $\mathbb{T}$ × NAT
value
488,498 calc: ci:CI×(vis:VI-set×gis:GI-set) → RLF → TRM → TRA → MAX
473,474   in {v_c_ch[ci,vi]|vi:VI•vi ∈ vis}, {g_c_ch[ci,gi]|gi:GI•gi ∈ gis},
473,474   attr_cmd_ch,attr_vdu_ch **Unit**
474   react_to_gates(ci,(vis,gis))(vplf)(trm)(tra)(t,m) ≡
474   **let** (ee,(τ,(vi,li))) = □{g_c_ch[ci,gi]|gi:GI•gi∈ gis} **in**
480   **case** ee **of**
500   "Enter" →
500   calc(ci,(vis,gis))(vplf)(trm∪[vi↦⟨(τ,SonL(li))⟩])
500   (tra)(τ,**if card dom** trm=m **then** m+1 **else** m **end**),
501   "Exit" →
501   billing(vi,trm(vi)⌢⟨(τ,SonL(li))⟩);
501   calc(ci,(vis,gis))(vplf)(trm\{vi})(tra)(t,m) **end**
480   **end**

The above behaviour, Items 472 on page 287 through 500c, is the one for which we are to design software   □

Example 129 exemplifies a derived event requirement as per Definition 96: (a) the event is conceptual, it has no physical counterpart in the domain; (b) it calculates (500b) the max value based on a conceptual notion of traffic road maps (trm), (c) which is an element of the calculator state.

9.5.2.3 No Derived Behaviours

There are no derived behaviours. The reason is as follows. Behaviours are associated with parts. A possibly 'derived behaviour' would entail the introduction of an 'associated' part. And if such a part made sense it should – in all likelihood – already have been either a proper domain part or become a domain extension. If the domain–to–requirements engineer insist on modeling some interface requirements as a process then we consider that a technical matter, a choice of abstraction.

9.5.3 Discussion

9.5.3.1 Derived Requirements

Formulation of derived actions or derived events usually involves technical terms not only from the domain but typically from such conceptual 'domains' as mathematics, economics, engineering or their visualisation. Derived requirements may, for some requirements developments, constitute "sizable" requirements compared to "all the other" requirements. For their analysis and prescription it makes good sense to first having developed "the other" requirements: domain, interface and machine requirements. The treatment of the present chapter does not offer special techniques and tools for the conception, &c., of derived requirements. Instead we refer to the seminal works of [143, 276, 377].

9.5.3.2 Introspective Requirements

Humans, including human users are, in this chapter, considered to never be part of the domain for which a requirements prescription is being developed. If it is necessary to involve humans in the domain description or the requirements prescription then their prescription is to reflect assumptions upon whose behaviour the machine rely. It is therefore that we, above, have stated, in passing, that we cannot accept requirements of the kind: *"the machine must be user friendly"*, because, in reality, it means *"the user must rely upon the machine being 'friendly' "* whatever that may mean. We are not requirements prescribing humans, nor their sentiments !

9.6 Machine Requirements

Other than listing a sizable number of *machine requirement facets* we shall not cover machine requirements in this chapter. The reason for this is as follows. We find, cf. [44, Sect. 19.6], that when the individual machine requirements are expressed then references to domain phenomena are, in fact, abstract references, that is, they do not refer to the semantics of what they name. Hence *machine requirements* "fall" outside the scope of this chapter with that scope being *"derivation" of requirements from domain specifications* with emphasis on derivation techniques that relate to various aspects of the domain.

(A) There are the *technology requirements* of (1) *performance* and (2) *dependability*. Within *dependability requirements* there are (a) *accessibility*, (b) *availability*, (c) *integrity*,

(d) *reliability*, (e) *safety*, (f) *security* and (g) *robustness* requirements. A proper treatment of dependability requirements need a careful definition of such terms as *failure, error, fault,* and, from these *dependability.* (B) And there are the *development requirements* of (i) *process*, (ii) *maintenance*, (iii) *platform*, (iv) *management* and (v) *documentation* requirements. Within *maintenance requirements* there are (ii.1) *adaptive*, (ii.2) *corrective*, (ii.3) *perfective*, (ii.4) *preventive*, and (ii.5) *extensional* requirements. Within *platform requirements* there are (iii.1) *development*, (iii.2) *execution*, (iii.3) *maintenance*, and (iii.4) *demonstration* platform requirements. We refer to [44, Sect. 19.6] for an early treatment of *machine requirements*.

9.7 Summary

9.7.1 A Design Method

In Sect. **7.13.3** on page 198 we introduced, perhaps belatedly, the issue of *design*. We did not characterise the co-issue of *designer*. This we do now.

> **Definition: 97 Designer:** The person who produces a design is called a designer, which is a term generally used for people who work professionally in one of the various design areas – usually specifying which area is being dealt with (such as a fashion designer, product designer, web designer or interior designer), but also others such as architects and engineers. A designer's sequence of activities is called a design process, possibly using design methods. The process of creating a design can be brief (a quick sketch) or lengthy and complicated, involving considerable research, negotiation, reflection, modeling, interactive adjustment and re-design https://en.m.wikipedia.org/wiki/Design ∎

In Sect. **7.13.3** we also stated, and we repeat: *domain engineering does **not** involve design, but requirements engineering and software development requires a **full lot** of design. In domain engineering we model a given world. In requirements engineering we seek to model a world as we would like to create it. In this sense domain engineering is akin to physics and requirements engineering to classical forms of engineering.*

The "room" for design, i.e., for creativity, can now be made precise: We design when we project, instantiate, determinate, extend and fit evolving *domain requirements*; we design when we choose the machine, as in *machine requirements*; and we design when we decide how the machine is to support the software as in *interface requirements*.

In this monograph we shall not advise on either "principles", "procedures", "techniques" nor "tools" for being "creative".

It seems that many of the current software engineering fads – *en vogue* in the past, *in fashion* now, and surely to *inundate* us in the future – are more concerned with design issues than with method issues of understanding the domain and getting the requirements and the therefrom derived software rigorously right.

Some of these "movements" even refer to "method prisons"[215], that is, that following methods from systematically, via rigorously to formally, stands in the way of creativity. We obviously dispute that! But we leave it to papers at conferences to argue the challenge!

We do think, however, that there is much to learn from the various, more-or-less related software engineering movements: Waterfall, Spiral, UML [265, 108, 107], Agile[216], Scrum[217], SEMAT[218], Essence[219], etc. as to issues of design – in the context of methodical domain, requirements and software development.

9.7.2 Method Principles, Techniques and Tools

Recall that by a method we shall understand a *set of **principles*** for selecting and applying a *set of **techniques*** using a *set of **tools*** in order to construct an artefact.

---

[215] http://semat.org/news/-/asset_publisher/eaHEtyeuE9wP/content/escaping-method-prison

[216] [en.wikipedia.org/wiki/Agile_software_development]

[217] [en.wikipedia.org/wiki/Scrum_(software_development)]

[218] [semat.org/]

[219] [essence.ivarjacobson.com/services/what-essence]

9.7.2.1 Principles of Requirements

Some of the principles applied in "deriving" requirements prescriptions from domain descriptions are:
- **Divide & Conquer:** The separation into

  ∞ **domain,**   ∞ **interface** and   ∞ **machine**

  requirements is an example of 'divide & conquer', as is their treatment in the order listed.
- **Refinement:** "By and large" we see the 'transformation' of domain descriptions into requirements pre-scriptions as a refinement though with some exceptional 'deviations'. Instantiation is not a refinement. Determination is. When we say 'by and large' we mean "when everything about a situation is considered together". That is, not all the transformations of this chapter are refinements.
- **Conservative Extension:** The extension(s), in our examples, in this chapter is/are an example of conser-vative extension(s). But there could be other forms of domain extensions which would not be conservative.

9.7.2.2 Techniques of Requirements

The basic technique, in all steps of domain and interface requirements, involve reconsidering the domain sorts and types, then their well-formedness, then their mereologies, et cetera. Further techniques, i.e., sub-techniques derive from that.

9.7.2.3 Tools of Requirements

The tools are the usual ones: informal, but disciplined narratives that are 'fitted' closely to the formalisations.

9.7.3 Concluding Review

We conclude by briefly reviewing what has been achieved, present shortcomings & possible research chal-lenges, and a few words on relations to "classical requirements engineering".

9.7.3.1 What has been Achieved?

We have shown how to systematically "derive" initial aspects of requirements prescriptions from domain descriptions. The stages[220] and steps[221] of this "derivation"[222] are new. We claim that current requirements engineering approaches, although they may refer to a or the 'domain', are not really 'serious' about this: they do not describe the domain, and they do not base their techniques and tools on a reasoned understanding of the domain. In contrast we have identified, we claim, a logically motivated decomposition of requirements into three phases, cf. Footnote 220, of domain requirements into five steps, cf. Footnote 221 (Page 293), and of interface requirements, based on a concept of shared entities, tentatively into (α) shared endurants, (β) shared actions, (γ) shared events, and (δ) shared behaviours (with more research into the $(\alpha$-$\delta)$ techniques needed).

9.7.3.2 Present Shortcomings and Research Challenges

We see three shortcomings: (1) The "derivation" techniques have yet to consider "extracting" requirements from *domain facet descriptions*. Only by including *domain facet descriptions* can we, in "deriving" *require-ments prescriptions*, include failures of, for example, support technologies and humans, in the design of

---

[220] (a) domain, (b) interface and (c) machine requirements

[221] For domain requirements: (i) projection, (ii) instantiation, (iii) determination, (iv) extension and (v) fitting; etc.

[222] We use double quotation marks: "..." to indicate that the derivation is not automatable.

fault-tolerant software. (2) The "derivation" principles, techniques and tools should be given a formal treatment. (3) There is a serious need for relating the approach of the present chapter to that of the seminal text book of [377, Axel van Lamsweerde]. [377] is not being "replaced" by the present work. It tackles a different set of problems. We refer to the penultimate paragraph before the **Acknowledgment** closing.

9.7.3.3 Comparison to "Classical" Requirements Engineering:

Except for a few, represented by two, we are not going to compare the contributions of the present chapter with published journal or conference papers on the subject of requirements engineering. The reason for this is the following. The present chapter, rather completely, we claim, reformulates requirements engineering, giving it a 'foundation', in *domain engineering*, and then developing *requirements engineering* from there, viewing requirements prescriptions as "derived" from domain descriptions. We do not see any of the papers, except those reviewed below [268] and [143], referring in any technical sense to 'domains' such as we understand them.

⋆ **[268, Deriving Specifications for Systems That Are Connected to the Physical World]**

The paper that comes closest to the present chapter in its serious treatment of the [problem] domain as a precursor for requirements development is that of [268, Jones, Hayes & Jackson]. A purpose of [268] (Sect. 1.1, Page 367, last §) is to see "how little can one say" (about the problem domain) when expressing assumptions about requirements. This is seen by [268] (earlier in the same paragraph) as in contrast to our form of domain modeling. [268] reveals assumptions about the domain when expressing *rely guarantee*s in tight conjunction with expressing the *guarantee* (requirements). That is, analysing and expressing requirements, in [268], goes hand-in-hand with analysing and expressing fragments of the domain. The current chapter takes the view that since, as demonstrated in [73], it is possible to model sizable aspects of domains, then it would be interesting to study how one might "derive" — and which — requirements prescriptions from domain descriptions; and having demonstrated that (i.e., the "how much can be derived") it seems of scientific interest to see how that new start (i.e., starting with a priori given domain descriptions or starting with first developing domain descriptions) can be combined with existing approaches, such as [268]. We do appreciate the "tight coupling" of rely–guarantees of [268]. But perhaps one loses understanding the domain due to its fragmented presentation. If the 'relies' are not outright, i.e., textually directly expressed in our domain descriptions, then they obviously must be provable properties of what our domain descriptions express. Our, i.e., the present, chapter — with its background in Chapters 4–7 and [73, Sect. 4.7] — develops — with a background in [263, M.A. Jackson] — a set of principles and techniques for the access of attributes. The "discovery" of the CM and SG channels of [268] and of the type of their messages, seems, compared to our approach, less systematic. Also, it is not clear how the [268] case study "scales" up to a larger domain. The *sluice gate* of [268] is but part of a large ('irrigation') system of reservoirs (water sources), canals, sluice gates and the fields (water sinks) to be irrigated. We obviously would delineate such a larger system and research & develop an appropriate, both informal, a narrative, and formal domain description for such a class of irrigation systems based on assumptions of precipitation and evaporation. Then the users' requirements, in [268], that the sluice gate, over suitable time intervals, is open 20% of the time and otherwise closed, could now be expressed more pertinently, in terms of the fields being appropriately irrigated.

⋆ **[143, Goal-directed Requirements Acquisition]**

Outlines an approach to requirements acquisition that starts with fragments of domain description. The domain description is captured in terms of predicates over *actors, actions, events, entities* and (their) *relations*. Our approach to domain modeling differs from that of [143] as follows: Agents, actions, entities and relations are, in [143], seen as specialisations of a concept of *objects*. The nearest analogy to relations, in [73], as well as in this chapter, is the signatures of perdurants. Our 'agents' relate to solid endurants, i.e., parts, and are the behaviours that evolve around these parts: one agent per part! [143] otherwise include describing parts, relations between parts, actions and events much like [73] and this chapter does. [143] then introduces a notion of *goal*. A **goal**, in [143], is defined as "*a nonoperational objective to be achieved by the desired system. Nonoperational means that the objective is not formulated in terms of objects and actions "available" to some agent of the system* ■[223]" [143] then goes on to exemplify goals. In this, the current chapter, we are not considering *goals*, also a major theme of [377].[224] Typically the expression of goals of [143, 377], are "within" computer & computing science and involve the use of temporal logic.[225] "*Constraints are operational objectives to be achieved by the desired (i.e., required) system, ..., formulated in terms of objects and actions "available" to some agents of the system. ... Goals are made operational through constraints. ... A constraint operationalising a goal amounts to some abstract "implementation" of this goal*" [143]. [143] then goes on to express goals and constraints operationalising these. [143] is a fascinating paper[226] as it shows how to build goals and constraints on domain description fragments.

$$\bullet\ \bullet\ \bullet$$

These papers, [268] and [143], as well as the current chapter, together with such seminal monographs as [404, 315, 377], clearly shows that there are many diverse ways in which to achieve precise requirements prescriptions. The [404, 315] monographs primarily study the $\mathcal{D}, \mathcal{S} \models \mathcal{R}$ specification and proof techniques from the point of view of the specific tools of their specification languages[227]. Physics, as a natural science, and its many engineering 'renditions', are manifested in many separate sub-fields: Electricity, mechanics, statics, fluid dynamics — each with further sub-fields. It seems, to this author, that there is a need to study the [404, 315, 377] approaches and the approach taken in this chapter in the light of identifying sub-fields of requirements engineering. The title of the present chapter suggests one such sub-field.

9.7.4 The Domain Description to Requirements Prescription "Gap"!

Where does a domain description end and a requirements prescription begin ? Well, it's hard to say ! It is hard to say because one can perfectly validly claim that a projected domain description is also a domain description. And likewise when that projection is instantiated ! In fact a domain-requirements prescription could likewise be claimed to be a domain description, but once we "add" references to 'the machine' we no longer have a domain description.

---

[223] We have reservations about this definition: Firstly, it is expressed in terms of some of the "things" it is not ! (To us, not a very useful approach.) Secondly, we can imagine goals that are indeed formulated in terms of objects and actions 'available' to some agent of the system. For example, wrt. the ongoing library examples of [143], *the system shall automate the borrowing of books*, et cetera. Thirdly, we assume that by "'available' to some agent of the system" is meant that these agents, actions, entities, etc., are also required.

[224] An example of a goal — for the road pricing system — could be that of *shortening travel times of motorists, reducing gasoline consumption and air pollution, while recouping investments on toll-road construction*. We consider techniques for ensuring the above kind of goals "outside" the realm of computer & computing science but "inside" the realm of operations research (OR) — while securing that the OR models are commensurate with our domain models.

[225] In this chapter we do not exemplify goals, let alone the use of temporal logic. We cannot exemplify all aspects of domain description and requirements prescription, but, if we were, would then use the temporal logic of [404, The Duration Calculus].

[226] — that might, however, warrant a complete rewrite.

[227] The Duration Calculus [DC], respectively DC, Timed Automata and Z

So what can we then, in general, claim? We can really only claim that as long as there are no considerations expressed, in what is claimed to be a domain description, of machine properties, we have a domain description.

What we strive for in domain descriptions is to capture a sufficiently large fraction of a domain: its endurants and perdurants, their properties and relations, without "being bothered" by possible software implementation concerns.

What we strive for in requirements prescriptions is to capture exactly and all those properties that the desired software should exhibit vis-a-vis its users: satisfy their expectations, fit with their own understanding of their domain. without "being bothered" by possible software efficiency concerns.

The aim of requirements development is to "turn" a domain description into a requirements prescription. In doing so a prime concern is, among others, to "turn" a possibly *in-computable* domain description into a *computable* requirements prescription.

In summary: A requirements prescription "ceases" to be a domain description once reference is made, in the prescription, to the machine, and/or once computability concerns overshadow pleasing abstractions.

9.7.5 Formalisation of Domain-to-Requirements Development

We have shown, informally, the development steps of *projection*: $\mathbb{D} \to \mathbb{R}_P\text{-}\mathbf{set}$[228], *instantiation*: $\mathbb{R}_P \to \mathbb{R}_I\text{-}\mathbf{set}$, *determination*: $\mathbb{R}_I \to \mathbb{R}_D\text{-}\mathbf{set}$, *extension*: $\mathbb{R}_D \to \mathbb{R}_E\text{-}\mathbf{set}$ and *fitting*: $\mathbb{R}_a, \mathbb{R}_b, ..., \mathbb{R}_c \to \mathbb{R}_F\text{-}\mathbf{set}$. We could have formalised these. That is, we could have shown some form of mathematical relations, $\mathbb{R}$: $\mathcal{R}_{DP}(\mathbb{D}, \mathbb{R}_P)$[229], $\mathcal{R}_{PI}(\mathbb{R}_P, \mathbb{R}_I)$, $\mathcal{R}_{ID}(\mathbb{R}_I, \mathbb{R}_D)$, $\mathcal{R}_{DE}(\mathbb{R}_D, \mathbb{R}_E)$, and $\mathcal{R}_{RF}((\mathbb{R}_a, \mathbb{R}_b, ..., \mathbb{R}_c), \mathbb{R}_F)$.

Similarly for the interface requirements steps.

To formalise these development steps one has to bear in minds at least two things: that domain descriptions and initial steps of requirements prescriptions are usually in-computable; and that the step formalisations requires quite some fluency in computer science – familiarity with, for example, [247, *Unifying Theories of Programming*] appears to be a prerequisite.

We refer to research problem 51 on the next page.

9.8 Bibliographical Notes

I have thought about domain engineering for more than 20 years. But serious, focused writing only started to appear since [44, Part IV] — with [40, 37] being exceptions: [46] suggests a number of domain science and engineering research topics; [55] covers the concept of domain facets; [86] explores compositionality and Galois connections. [47, 85] show how to systematically, but, of course, not automatically, "derive" requirements prescriptions from domain descriptions; [59] takes the triptych software development as a basis for outlining principles for believable software management; [51, 64] presents a model for Stanisław Leśniewski's [122] concept of mereology; [56, 60] present an extensive example and are otherwise a precursor for the present chapter; [61] presents, based on the TripTych view of software development as ideally proceeding from domain description via requirements prescription to software design, concepts such as software demos and simulators; [62] anal-

---

[228] $\mathbb{D}, \mathbb{R}$, etc., refer to syntactic specifications, i.e., descriptions and prescriptions. Development, $\to$, is a relation: many possible outcomes are possible.

[229] $\mathcal{R}_{\_}$ refer to mathematical relations.

yses the `TripTych`, especially its domain engineering approach, with respect to [291, 292, Maslow]'s and [327, Peterson's and Seligman's]'s notions of humanity: how can computing relate to notions of humanity; the first part of [65] is a precursor for [73] with the second part of [65] presenting a first formal model of the elicitation process of analysis and description based on the prompts more definitively presented in the current chapter; and with [66] focus on domain safety criticality.

9.9 Exercise Problems

We suggest several classes of exercises, to wit: two or more of *research problems*, *student exercise* and *term projects*.

9.9.1 Research Problems

Exercise 50 A Research Challenge. Design Heurekas: We remind the reader of Sect. **7.13.3** on page 198. You are, we suggest through the actual or experimental development of two–three requirements prescription developments, to discover, if possible, "common" *design heurekas*. We suggest that you experiment with separate domain projection, instantiation, determination and extension sub-projects to search for such possible "common" *design heurekas*. Similarly for interface requirements.

Exercise 51 A Research Challenge. Formalisation of Domain Requirements Operations: We refer to Sect. **9.7.5** on the preceding page. To tackle this problem requires quite some familiarity with for example [247, *Unifying Theories of Programming*].

Exercise 52 A Research Challenge. Bridge to the Hayes-Jackson-Jones Approach: We refer to Pages 294–294. Study [268, Hayes, Jackson and Jones] and related papers. Then suggest ways and means to incorporate their, the HJJ approach, with that of ours. Let either the HJJ be determining the approach sequence or that of ours.

Exercise 53 A Research Challenge. Bridge to the Lamsweerde Approach: We refer to Pages 294–295. Study [143, van Lamsweerde et al.] and related papers. Then suggest ways and means to incorporate their, the KAOS approach, with that of ours. Let either the KAOS be determining the approach sequence or that of ours.

Exercise 54 A Research Challenge. Bridge to Cyber-Physical Computing Systems: Study [315, Olderog and Dierks] and related papers. Then suggest ways and means to incorporate their, the Olderog et al. approach, with that of ours. Let either the Olderog et al. be determining the approach sequence or that of ours.

9.9.2 Term Projects

We continue the term projects of Sects. **4.24.3** on page 104, **5.13.3** on page 152, **7.14.3** on page 203, and **8.11.2** on page 240.

The students are to identify and analyse & describe at least three distinct requirements aspects of their chosen domain:

- domain requirements:
  - ∞ projections,
  - ∞ instantiations,

- ∞ determinations and
- ∞ extension; and

- interface requirements.

Exercise 55 An MSc Student Exercise. The Consumer Market, Requirements: We refer to Exercise 4 on page 105, 20 on page 152, 34 on page 204, and 43 on page 240.

Exercise 56 An MSc Student Exercise. Financial Service Industry, Requirements: We refer to Exercise 5 on page 105, 21 on page 152, 35 on page 204, and 44 on page 240.

Exercise 57 An MSc Student Exercise. Container Line Industry, Requirements: We refer to Exercise 6 on page 105, 22 on page 152, 36 on page 204, and 45 on page 240.

Exercise 58 An MSc Student Exercise. Railway Systems, Requirements: We refer to Exercise 7 on page 105, 23 on page 152, 37 on page 204, and 46 on page 240.

Exercise 59 An MSc Student Exercise. Part-Fluid Conjoins: Pipelines, Requirements: We refer to Appendix **A**.

Exercise 60 A PhD Student Problem. Part-Fluid Conjoins: Canals, Requirements: We refer to Exercise 8 on page 105, 24 on page 152, 38 on page 204, and 47 on page 240.

Exercise 61 A PhD Student Problem. Part-Fluids Conjoins: Rum Production, Requirements: We refer to Exercises 9 on page 105, 25 on page 153, 39 on page 204 and 48 on page 240.

Exercise 62 A PhD Student Problem. Part-Fluids Conjoins: Waste Management, Requirements: We refer to Exercise 10 on page 105, 26 on page 153, 40 on page 204, and 49 on page 240.

Part IV
CLOSING

Chapter 10
DEMOS, SIMULATORS, MONITORS AND CONTROLLERS

*In this chapter we muse, in the sense of 'speculate', over concepts of **demos, simulators, monitors** and **controllers**.*

We sketch some observations of the concepts of domain, requirements and modeling – where abstract interpretations of these models cover both a priori, a posteriori and real-time aspects of the domain as well as 1–1 (i.e., real-time), microscopic and macroscopic simulations, real-time monitoring and real-time monitoring & control of that domain.

10.1 Introduction

The reference frame for these concepts are domain models: carefully narrated and formally described domains. On the basis of a familiarising example[230] of a domain description, we survey more-or-less standard ideas of verifiable software developments and conjecture software product families of demos, simulators, monitors and monitors & controllers – but now these "standard ideas" are recast in the context of core requirements prescriptions being "derived" from domain descriptions. A background setting for this chapter is the concern for (α) professionally developing the right software, i.e., software which satisfies users' expectations, and (ω) software that is right: i.e., software which is correct with respect to user requirements and thus has no "bugs", no "blue screens". The present chapter must be seen in the context of a main line of experimental research around the topics of domain science & engineering and requirements engineering and their relation. We refer to earlier chapters of this monograph.

10.1.1 "Confusing Demos"

This author has had the doubtful honour, on his many visits to computer science and software engineering laboratories around the world, to be presented, by his colleagues' aspiring PhD students, with so-called demos of "systems" that they were investigating. There always was a tacit assumption, namely that the audience, i.e., me, knew, a priori, what the domain "behind" the "system" being "demo'ed" was. Certainly, if there was such an understanding, it was brutally demolished by the "demo" presentation. My questions, such as *"what are you demo'ing"* (et cetera) went unanswered. Instead, while we were waiting to see "something interesting" to be displayed on the computer screen we were witnessing frantic, sometimes failed, input of commands and data, "nervous" attempts with "mouse" clickings, etc. – before something intended was displayed. After a, usually 15 minute, grace period, it was time, luckily, to proceed to the next "demo".

---

[230] – take that of Chapter 4

© The Author(s), under exclusive license to Springer Nature Switzerland AG 2021
D. Bjørner, *Domain Science and Engineering*, Monographs in Theoretical Computer Science. An EATCS Series,
https://doi.org/10.1007/978-3-030-73484-8_10

10.1.2 Aims & Objectives

The aims of this chapter are to present (a) some ideas about software that either "demo", simulate, monitor or monitor & control domains; (b) some ideas about "time scaling": demo and simulation time versus domain time; and (c) how these kinds of software relate. The (undoubtedly very naïve) objectives of the chapter are also to improve the kind of demo-presentations, alluded to above, so as to ensure that the basis for such demos is crystal clear from the very outset of research & development, i.e., that domains be well-described. The chapter, we think, tackles the issue of so-called "model-oriented (or model-based) software development" from altogether different angles than usually promoted.

10.1.3 An Exploratory Chapter

The chapter is exploratory. There will be no theorems and therefore there will be no proofs. We are presenting what might eventually emerge into (α) a theory of domains, i.e., a domain science and (β) a software development theory of domain engineering versus requirements engineering.

The chapter is not a "standard" research chapter: it does not compare its claimed achievements with corresponding or related achievements of other researchers – simply because we do not claim "achievements" which have been reasonably well formalised. But we would suggest that you might find some of the ideas of the chapter (in Sect. **10.2**) worthwhile.

Structure of Chapter: The structure of the chapter is as follows. In Sect. **10.2** we then outline a series of interpretations of domain descriptions. These arise, when developed in an orderly, professional manner, from requirements prescriptions which are themselves orderly developed from the domain description. The essence of Sect. **10.2** is (i) the (albeit informal) presentation of such tightly related notions as *demos* (Sect. **10.2.1**), *simulators* (Sect. **10.2.2** on page 304), *monitors* (Sect. **10.2.3.1** on page 307) and *monitors & controllers* (Sect. **10.2.3.2** on page 307) (these notions can be formalised), and (ii) the conjectures on a product family of domain-based software developments (Sect. **10.2.5** on page 309). A notion of *script-based simulation* extends demos and is the basis for monitor and controller developments and uses. The scripts used in our examples are related to time, but one can define non-temporal scripts – so the "carrying idea" of Sect. **10.2** extends to a widest variety of software. We claim that Sect. **10.2** thus brings these new ideas: a tightly related software engineering concept of *demo-simulator-monitor-controller* machines, and an extended notion of *reference models for requirements and specifications* [197].

10.2 Interpretations

In this main section of the chapter we present a number of interpretations of rôles of domain descriptions.

10.2.1 What Is a Domain-based Demo?

A *domain-based demo* is a software system which *"present"* endurants and perdurants: actions, events and behaviours of a domain. The *"presentation"* abstracts these phenomena and their related concepts in various computer generated forms: visual, acoustic, etc.

10.2.1.1 Examples

There are two main examples. One was given in Chapter 4. The other is summarised below. It is from Chapter 9 on "deriving requirements prescriptions from domain descriptions". The summary follows.

The domain description of Sect. **9.2** outlines an abstract concept of transport nets (of hubs [street intersections, train stations, harbours, airports] and links [road segments, rail tracks, shipping lanes, air-lanes]), their development, traffic [of vehicles, trains, ships and aircraft], etc. We shall assume such a transport domain description below.

Endurants are, for example, presented as follows: (*a*) transport nets by two dimensional (2D) road, railway or air traffic maps, (*b*) hubs and links by highlighting parts of 2D maps and by related photos – and their unique identifiers by labeling hubs and links, (*c*) routes by highlighting sequences of paths (hubs and links) on a 2D map, (*d*) buses by photographs and by dots at hubs or on links of a 2D map, and (*e*) bus timetables by, well, indeed, by showing a 2D bus timetable.

Actions are, for example, presented as follows: (*f*) The insertion or removal of a hub or a link by showing "instantaneous" triplets of "before", "during" and "after" animation sequences. (*g*) The start or end of a bus ride by showing flashing animations of the appearance, respectively the flashing disappearance of a bus (dot) at the origin, respectively the destination bus stops.

Events are, for example, presented as follows: (*h*) A mudslide [or fire in a road tunnel, or collapse of a bridge] along a (road) link by showing an animation of part of a (road) map with an instantaneous sequence of (α) the present link , (β) a gap somewhere on the link, (γ) and the appearance of two ("symbolic") hubs "on either side of the gap". (*i*) The congestion of road traffic "grinding to a halt" at, for example, a hub, by showing an animation of part of a (road) map with an instantaneous sequence of the massive accumulation of vehicle dots moving (instantaneously) from two or more links into a hub.

Behaviours are, for example, presented as follows: (*k*) A bus tour: from its start, on time, or "thereabouts", from its bus stop of origin, via (all) intermediate stops, with or without delays or advances in times of arrivals and departures, to the bus stop of destination (*ℓ*) The composite behaviour of "all bus tours", meeting or missing connection times, with sporadic delays, with cancellation of some bus tours, etc. – by showing the sequence of states of all the buses on the net.

We say that behaviours ((*j*)–(*ℓ*)) are *script-based* in that they (try to) satisfy a bus timetable ((*e*)).

10.2.1.2 Towards a Theory of Visualisation and Acoustic Manifestation

The above examples shall serve to highlight the general problem of visualisation and acoustic manifestation. Just as we need sciences of visualising scientific data and of diagrammatic logics, so *we need more serious studies of visualisation and acoustic manifestation — so amply, but, this author thinks, inconsistently demonstrated by current uses of interactive computing media.*

10.2.2 Simulations

"Simulation is the imitation of some real thing, state of affairs, or process; the act of simulating something generally entails representing certain key characteristics or behaviours of a selected physical or abstract system" [Wikipedia] for the purposes of testing some hypotheses usually stated in terms of the model being simulated <u>and</u> pairs of statistical data and expected outcomes.

10.2.2.1 Explication of Figure 10.1

Figure 10.1 attempts to indicate four things: (i) Left top: the rounded edge rectangle labeled "The Domain" alludes to some specific domain ("out there"). (ii) Left middle: the small rounded rectangle labeled "A Domain Description" alludes to some document which narrates and formalises a description of "the domain". (iii) Left bottom: the medium sized rectangle labeled "A Domain Demo based on the Domain Description" (for short "Demo") alludes to a software system that, in some sense (to be made clear later) "simulates" "The Domain." (iv) Right: the large rectangle (a) shows a horisontal time axis which basically "divides" that large rectangle into two parts: (b) Above the time axis the **"fat"** rounded edge rectangle alludes to the time-wise behaviour, a *domain trace*, of "The Domain" (i.e., the actual, the real, domain). (c) Below the time axis there are eight **"thin"** rectangles. These are labels S1, S2, S3, S4, S5, S6, S7 and S8. (d) Each of these denote a "run", i.e., a time-stamped "execution", a *program trace*, of the "Demo". Their "relationship" to the time axis is this: their execution takes place in the real time as related to that of "The Domain" behaviour.

   A *trace* (whether a domain or a program execution trace) is a time-stamped sequence of states: domain states, respectively demo, simulator, monitor and monitor & control states.

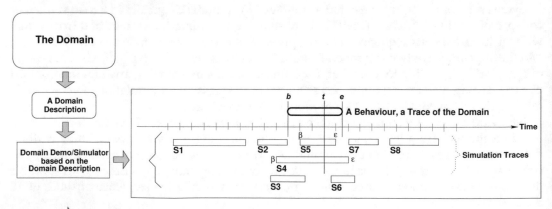

Legend: ⇨ A development; S1, S2, S3, S4, S5, S6, S7, S8: "runs" of the Domain Simulation

Fig. 10.1 Simulations

   From Fig. 10.1 and the above explication we can conclude that "executions" S4 and S5 each share exactly one time point, *t*, at which "The Domain" and "The Simulation" "share" time, that is, the time-stamped execution S4 and S5 reflect a "Simulation" state which at time *t* should reflect (some abstraction of) "The Domain" state.

   Only if the domain behaviour (i.e., trace) fully "surrounds" that of the simulation trace, or, vice-versa (cf. Fig. 10.1[S4,S5]), is there a "shared" time. Only if the 'begin' and 'end' times of the domain behaviour are identical to the 'start' and 'finish' times of the simulation trace, is there an infinity of shared 1–1 times. Only then do we speak of a real-time simulation.

In Fig 10.2 on the next page we show "the same" "Domain Behaviour" (three times) and a (1) simulation, a (2) monitoring and a (3) monitoring & control, all of whose 'begin/start' (b/β) and 'end/finish' (e/ϵ) times coincide. In such cases the "Demo/Simulation" takes place in real-time throughout the 'begin······end' interval.

Let β and ϵ be the 'start' and 'finish' times of either S4 or S5. Then the relationship between t, β, ϵ, b and e is $\frac{t-b}{e-t} = \frac{t-\beta}{\epsilon-t}$ — which leads to a second degree polynomial in t which can then be solved in the usual, high school manner.

10.2.2.2 Script-based Simulation

A script-based simulation is the behaviour, i.e., an execution, of, basically, a demo which, step-by-step, follows a script: that is a prescription for highlighting endurants, actions, events and behaviours.

Script-based simulations where the script embodies a notion of time, like a bus timetable, and unlike a route, can be thought of as the execution of a demos where "chunks" of demo operations take place in accordance with "chunks"[231] of script prescriptions. The latter (i.e., the script prescriptions) can be said to represent simulated (i.e., domain) time in contrast to "actual computer" time. The actual times in which the script-based simulation takes place relate to domain times as shown in Simulations S1 to S8 in Fig. 10.1 and in Fig. 10.2(1–3). Traces Fig. 10.2(1–3) and S8 Fig. 10.1 are said to be *real-time:* there is a one-to-one mapping between computer time and domain time. S1 and S4 Fig. 10.1 are said to be *microscopic:* disjoint computer time intervals map into distinct domain times. S2, S3, S5, S6 and S7 are said to be *macroscopic:* disjoint domain time intervals map into distinct computer times.

In order to concretise the above "vague" statements let us take the example of simulating bus traffic as based on a bus timetable script. A simulation scenario could be as follows. Initially, not relating to any domain time, the simulation "demos" a net, available buses and a bus timetable. The person(s) who are requesting the simulation are asked to decide on the ratio of the domain time interval to simulation time interval. If the ratio is 1 a real-time simulation has been requested. If the ratio is less than 1 a microscopic simulation has been requested. If the ratio is larger than 1 a microscopic simulation has been requested. A chosen ratio of, say 48 to 1 means that a 24 hour bus traffic is to be simulated in 30 minutes of elapsed simulation time. Then the person(s) who are requesting the simulation are asked to decide on the starting domain time, say 6:00am, and the domain time interval of simulation, say 4 hours – in which case the simulation of bus traffic from 6am till 10am is to be shown in 5 minutes (300 seconds) of elapsed simulation time. The person(s) who are requesting the simulation are then asked to decide on the *"sampling times"* or *"time intervals"*: If 'sampling times' 6:00 am, 6:30 am, 7:00 am, 8:00 am, 9:00 am, 9:30 am and 10:00 am are chosen, then the simulation is stopped at corresponding simulation times: 0 sec., 37.5 sec., 75 sec., 150 sec., 225 sec., 262.5 sec. and 300 sec. The simulation then shows the state of selected endurants and actions at these domain times. If *'sampling time interval'* is chosen and is set to every 5 min., then the simulation shows the state of selected endurants and actions at corresponding domain times. The simulation is resumed when the person(s) who are requesting the simulation so indicates, say by a "resume" icon click. The time interval between adjacent simulation stops and resumptions contribute with 0 time to elapsed simulation time – which in this case was set to 5 minutes. Finally the requestor provides some statistical data such as numbers of potential and actual bus passengers, etc.

---

[231] We deliberately leave the notion of chunk vague so as to allow as wide an spectrum of simulations.

Then two clocks are started: a domain time clock and a simulation time clock. The simulation proceeds as driven by, in this case, the bus time table. To include "unforeseen" events, such as the wreckage of a bus (which is then unable to complete a bus tour), we allow any number of such events to be randomly scheduled. Actually scheduled events "interrupts" the "programmed" simulation and leads to thus unscheduled stops (and resumptions) where the unscheduled stop now focuses on showing the event.

10.2.2.3 The Development Arrow

The arrow, ⇨, between a pair of boxes (of Fig. 10.1 on page 304) denote a step of development: (i) from the domain box to the domain description box, ⬇, it denotes the development of a domain description based on studies and analyses of the domain; (ii) from the domain description box to the domain demo box, ⬇, it denotes the development of a software system — where that development assumes an intermediate requirements box which has not been show; (iii) from the domain demo box to either of a simulation traces, ⇨, it denotes the development of a simulator as the related demo software system, again depending on whichever special requirements have been put to the simulator.

10.2.3 Monitoring & Control

Figure 10.2 shows three different kinds of uses of software systems where (2) [Monitoring] and (3) [Monitoring & Control] represent further developments from the demo or simulation software system mentioned in Sect. **10.2.1** and Sect. **10.2.2.2** on the preceding page. We

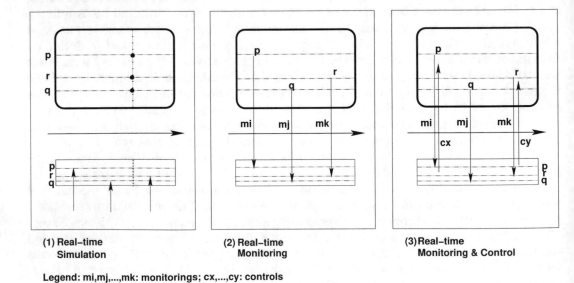

(1) Real–time Simulation   **(2) Real–time Monitoring**   **(3) Real–time Monitoring & Control**

Legend: mi,mj,...,mk: monitorings; cx,...,cy: controls

Fig. 10.2 Simulation, Monitoring and Monitoring & Control

have added some (three) horisontal and labeled (p, q and r) lines to Fig. 10.2 (1,2,3) (with respect to the traces of Fig. 10.1). They each denote a trace of a endurant, an action or an event, that is, they are traces of values of these phenomena or concepts. A (named) endurant value entails a description of the endurant, whither atomic ('hub', 'link', 'bus timetable') or composite ('net', 'set of hubs', etc.): of its unique identity, its mereology and a selection of its attributes. A (named) action value could, for example, be the pair of the before and after states of the action and some description of the function ('insertion of a link', 'start of a bus tour') involved in the action. A (named) event value could, for example, be a pair of the before and after states of the endurants causing, respectively being effected by the event and some description of the predicate ('mudslide', 'break-down of a bus') involved in the event. A cross section, such as designated by the vertical lines (one for the domain trace, one for the "corresponding" program trace) of Fig. 10.2(1) denotes a state: a domain, respectively a program state.

Figure 10.2 (1) attempts to show a real-time demo or simulation for the chosen domain. Figure 10.2 (2) purports to show the deployment of real-time software for monitoring (chosen aspects of) the chosen domain. Figure 10.2 (3) purports to show the deployment of real-time software for monitoring as well as controlling (chosen aspects of) the chosen domain.

10.2.3.1 Monitoring

By *domain monitoring* we mean *"to be aware of the state of a domain"*, its endurants, actions, events and behaviour. Domain monitoring is thus a process, typically within a distributed system for collecting and storing state data. In this process "observation" points — i.e., endurants, actions and where events may occur — are identified in the domain, cf. points p, q and r of Fig. 10.2. Sensors are inserted at these points. The "downward" pointing vertical arrows of Figs. 10.2 (2–3), from "the domain behaviour" to the "monitoring" and the "monitoring & control" traces express communication of what has been sensed (measured, photographed, etc.) [as directed by and] as input data (etc.) to these monitors. The monitor (being "executed") may store these "sensings" for future analysis.

10.2.3.2 Control

By *domain control* we mean *"the ability to change the value"* of endurants and the course of actions and hence behaviours, including prevention of events of the domain. Domain control is thus based on domain monitoring. Actuators are inserted in the domain "at or near" monitoring points or at points related to these, viz. points p and r of Fig. 10.2 (3). The "upward" pointing vertical arrows of Fig. 10.2 (3), from the "monitoring & control" traces to the "domain behaviour" express communication, to the domain, of what has been computed by the controller as a proper control reaction in response to the monitoring.

10.2.4 Machine Development

10.2.4.1 Machines

By a *machine* we shall understand a combination of hardware and software. For demos and simulators the machine is "mostly" software with the hardware typically being graphic display units with tactile instruments. For monitors the "main" machine, besides the hardware and software of demos and simulators, additionally includes *sensors* distributed throughout the domain and the technological machine means of *communicating* monitored signals from the sensors to the "main" machine and the processing of these signals by the main machine. For monitors & controllers the machine, besides the monitor machine, further includes actuators placed in the domain and the machine means of computing and communicating control signals to the actuators.

10.2.4.2 Requirements Development

Essential parts of Requirements to a Machine can be systematically "derived" from a Domain description. These essential parts are the *domain requirements* and the *interface requirements*. Domain requirements are those requirements which can be expressed, say in narrative form, by mentioning technical terms only of the domain. These technical terms cover only phenomena and concepts (endurants, actions, events and behaviours) of the domain. Some domain requirements are *projected, instantiated,* made more *deterministic* and *extended*[232]. We bring examples that are taken from Sect. **9.2**, cf. Sect. **10.2.1.1** on page 303 of the present chapter. (a) By *domain projection* we mean a sub-setting of the domain description: parts are left out which the requirements stake-holders, collaborating with the requirements engineer, decide is of no relevance to the requirements. For our example it could be that our domain description had contained models of road net attributes such as "the wear & tear" of road surfaces, the length of links, states of hubs and links (that is, [dis]allowable directions of traffic through hubs and along links), etc. Projection might then omit these attributes. (b) By *domain instantiation* we mean a specialisation of endurants, actions, events and behaviours, refining them from abstract simple entities to more concrete such, etc. For our example it could be that we only model freeways or only model road-pricing nets – or any one or more other aspects. (c) By *domain determination* we mean that of making the domain description cum domain requirements prescription less non-deterministic, i.e., more deterministic (or even the other way around!). For our example it could be that we had domain-described states of street intersections as not controlled by traffic signals – where the determination is now that of introducing an abstract notion of traffic signals which allow only certain states (of red, yellow and green). (d) By *domain extension* we basically mean that of extending the domain with phenomena and concepts that were not feasible without information technology. For our examples we could extend the domain with bus mounted GPS gadgets that record and communicate (to, say a central bus traffic computer) the more-or-less exact positions of buses – thereby enabling the observation of bus traffic. Interface requirements are those requirements which can be expressed, say in narrative form, by mentioning technical terms both of the domain and of the machine. These technical terms thus cover shared phenomena and concepts, that is, phenomena and concepts of the domain which are, in some sense, also (to be) represented by the machine. Interface requirements represent (i) the initialisation and "on-the-fly" update of machine endurants on the basis of *shared* domain endurants; (ii) the interaction between the machine and the domain while the machine is carrying out a (previous domain) action; (iii) machine responses, if any, to domain events — or domain responses, if any, to machine events cum "outputs"; and (iv) machine monitoring and machine control of domain phenomena. Each of these four (i–iv) interface requirement facets themselves involve projection, instantiation, determination, extension and fitting. Machine requirements are those requirements which can be expressed, say in narrative form, by mentioning technical terms only of the machine. (An example is: visual display units.)

---

[232] We omit consideration of *fitting*.

10.2.5 Verifiable Software Development

10.2.5.1 An Example Set of Conjectures

We illustrate some conjectures.

(A) From a domain, $\mathcal{D}$, one can develop a domain description $\mathbb{D}$. $\mathbb{D}$ cannot be [formally] verified. It can be [informally] validated "against" $\mathcal{D}$. Individual properties, $\mathbb{P}_\mathbb{D}$, of the domain description $\mathbb{D}$ and hence, purportedly, of the domain, $\mathcal{D}$, can be expressed and possibly proved $\mathbb{D} \models \mathbb{P}_\mathbb{D}$ and these may be validated to be properties of $\mathcal{D}$ by observations in (or of) that domain.

(B) From a domain description, $\mathbb{D}$, one can develop requirements, $\mathbb{R}_{DE}$, for, and from $\mathbb{R}_{DE}$ one can develop a domain demo machine specification $\mathbb{M}_{DE}$ such that $\mathbb{D}, \mathbb{M}_{DE} \models \mathbb{R}_{DE}$. The formula $\mathbb{D}, \mathbb{M} \models \mathbb{R}$ can be read as follows: in order to prove that the Machine satisfies the Requirements, assumptions about the Domain must often be made explicit in steps of the proof.

(C) From a domain description, $\mathbb{D}$, and a domain demo machine specification, $\mathbb{S}_{DE}$, one can develop requirements, $\mathbb{R}_{SI}$, for, and from such a $\mathbb{R}_{SI}$ one can develop a domain simulator machine specification $\mathbb{M}_{SI}$ such that $(\mathbb{D}; \mathbb{M}_{DE}), \mathbb{M}_{SI} \models \mathbb{R}_{SI}$. We have "lumped" $(\mathbb{D}; \mathbb{M}_{DE})$ as the two constitute the extended domain for which we, in this case of development, suggest the next stage requirements and machine development to take place.

(D) From a domain description, $\mathbb{D}$, and a domain simulator machine specification, $\mathbb{M}_{SI}$, one can develop requirements, $\mathbb{R}_{MO}$, for, and from such a $\mathbb{R}_{MO}$ one can develop a domain monitor machine specification $\mathbb{M}_{MO}$ such that $(\mathbb{D}; \mathbb{M}_{SI}), \mathbb{M}_{MO} \models \mathbb{R}_{MO}$.

(E) From a domain description, $\mathbb{D}$, and a domain monitor machine specification, $\mathbb{M}_{MO}$, one can develop requirements, $\mathbb{R}_{MC}$, for, and from such a $\mathbb{R}_{MC}$ one can develop a domain monitor & controller machine specification $\mathbb{M}_{MC}$ such that $(\mathbb{D}; \mathbb{M}_{MO}), \mathbb{M}_{MC} \models \mathbb{R}_{MC}$.

10.2.5.2 Chains of Verifiable Developments

The above illustrated just one chain (A–E) of developments. There are others. All are shown in Fig. 10.3.

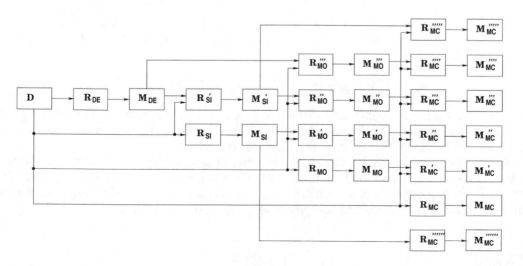

Fig. 10.3 Chains of Verifiable Developments

Figure 10.3 on the previous page can also be interpreted as prescribing a widest possible range of machine cum software products [111, 332] for a given domain. One domain may give rise to many different kinds of DEMO machines, simulators, monitors and monitor & controllers (the unprimed versions of the $\mathbb{M}_T$ machines (where T ranges over DE, SI, MO, MC)). For each of these there are similarly, "exponentially" many variants of successor machines (the primed versions of the $\mathbb{M}_T$ machines). What does it mean that a machine is a primed version? Well, here it means, for example, that $\mathbb{M}'_{SI}$ embodies facets of the demo machine $\mathbb{M}_{DE}$, and that $\mathbb{M}'''_{MC}$ embodies facets of the demo machine $\mathbb{M}_{DE}$, of the simulator $\mathbb{M}'_{SI}$, and the monitor $\mathbb{M}''_{MO}$. Whether such requirements are desirable is left to product customers and their software providers [111, 332] to decide.

10.3 Summary

Our divertimento is almost over. It is time to conclude.

10.3.1 What Have We Achieved

We have characterised a spectrum of strongly domain-related as well as strongly inter-related (cf. Fig. 10.3) software product families: *demos, simulators, monitors* and *monitor & controllers*. We have indicated varieties of these: simulators based on demos, monitors based on simulators, monitor & controllers based on monitors, in fact any of the latter ones in the software product family list as based on any of the earlier ones. We have sketched temporal relations between simulation traces and domain behaviours: *a priori, a posteriori, macroscopic* and *microscopic*, and we have identified the real-time cases which lead on to monitors and monitor & controllers.

10.3.2 What Have We Not Achieved — Some Conjectures

We have not characterised the software product family relations other than by the $\mathbb{D}, \mathbb{M} \models \mathbb{R}$ and $(\mathbb{D}; \mathbb{M}_{xyz}), \mathbb{M} \models \mathbb{R}$ clauses. That is, we should like to prove conjectured type theoretic inclusion relations like:

$$\wp([\![\mathcal{M}_{x_{\underline{mod}\ ext.}}]\!]) \sqsupseteq \wp([\![\mathcal{M}'^{\cdots'}_{x_{\underline{mod}\ ext.}}]\!]), \quad \wp([\![\mathcal{M}'^{\cdots'}_{x_{\underline{mod}\ ext.}}]\!]) \sqsupseteq \wp([\![\mathcal{M}''^{\cdots'}_{x_{\underline{mod}\ ext.}}]\!])$$

where x and y range appropriately, where $[\![\mathcal{M}]\!]$ expresses the meaning of $\mathcal{M}$, where $\wp([\![\mathcal{M}]\!])$ denote the space of all machine meanings and where $\wp([\![\mathcal{M}_{x_{\underline{mod}\ ext.}}]\!])$ is intended to denote that space modulo ("free of") the y facet (here *ext.*, for extension).

That is, it is conjectured that the set of more specialised, i.e., *n* primed, machines of kind *x* is type theoretically "contained" in the set of *m* primed (unprimed) *x* machines ($0 \leq m < n$).

There are undoubtedly many such interesting relations between the DEMO, SIMULATOR, MONITOR and MONITOR & CONTROLLER machines, unprimed and primed.

10.3.3 What Should We Do Next?

This chapter is not a proper theoretical chapter. It tries to throw some light on families and varieties of software, i.e., their relations. It focuses, in particular, on so-called DEMO, SIMULATOR, MONITOR and MONITOR & CONTROLLER software and their relation to the "originating" domain, i.e., that in which such software is to serve, and hence that which is being *extended* by such software, cf. the compounded 'domain' $(\mathbb{D}; \mathbb{M}_i)$ of in $(\mathbb{D}; \mathbb{M}_i), \mathbb{M}_j \models \mathbb{D}$. These notions should be studied formally. All of these notions: requirements projection, instantiation, determination and extension can be formalised. The specification language, in the form used here (without CSP processes, [250]) has a formal semantics and a proof system So the various notions of development, $(\mathbb{D}; \mathbb{M}_i), \mathbb{M}_j \models \mathbb{R}$ and $\wp(\mathbb{M})$ can be formalised.

Chapter 11
WINDING UP

We briefly (i) summarise key concepts of the intrinsics of domain analysis & description, domain facets, requirements engineering; (ii) put forward a number of diverse observations; (iii) and finally quote Tony Hoare's observations on domain engineering.

We are at the end of a major treatise. We have claimed that this monograph introduces a new, initial phase for software engineering as well as a research and engineering topic that is independent of whether we intend a domain analysis & description to be followed by requirements engineering and subsequent software design. We have supported this claim by the material of this monograph. A simple, in a sense "syntactic", summary is in order.

11.1 Programming Languages and Domains

In the quest for precise understanding of programming languages one studies formal syntax and formal semantics for and of these. A programming language is a 'language' "spoken" by and "written in" by programmers. The *domain analysis & description* that we have here pursued has been done so in a quest to understand the language spoken amongst professionals of the domain being modelled. In that sense the two endeavours 'parallel'. The IBM Vienna Labor, from around the mid 1960s to a little beyond the mid 1970s, was a unique center for the study and practice of programming language semantics. One early achievement is reflected in the first conference on *Formal Language Description Languages* [371]. Subsequent achievements were [25, 26, 27, 24]. This author was only there for a short period of two years, 1973–1975. They have determined, to this day, my professional, scientific and engineering focus and direction. I am deeply indebted to colleagues such as the late *Peter Lucas*, to *Kurt Walk*, and to *Cliff Jones*.

11.2 Summary of Chapters 4–7

We refer to the main, the full endurant/perdurant ontology, diagram, Fig. 4.1 on page 53.
Now re-explain what is going on, method-wise, with respect to that diagram, including how the internal qualities glue it all together.

11.2.1 Chapter 4: External Qualities

The left side of the diagram, labeled *external qualities*, takes up a sizable area of the whole. It designates our tackling the analysis of the external qualities of endurants first. The aim of that analysis is to uncover the entire collection of all observable endurants of a domain. One

D. Bjørner, *Domain Science and Engineering*, Monographs in Theoretical Computer Science. An EATCS Series, https://doi.org/10.1007/978-3-030-73484-8_11

does so by asking questions of inspected entities as suggested by the analysis prompts. And when this analysis end up with

- atomic,
- composite,
- part-fluids,

- fluid-parts,
- part-parts conjoins and

- fluid

endurants, one applies a description prompt and starts all over again with analysis and description till all endurants have been external quality-analysed and described, and one is ready to analyse & describe internal qualities.

11.2.2 Chapter 5: Internal Qualities

The bottom side of Fig. 4.1 on page 53, labeled *internal qualities*, takes up a not so visible area of the whole. But it reflects every bit as an important aspect of domain science & engineering. It designates our tackling the analysis of the internal qualities of endurants in the order *unique identifiers*, *mereologies* and *attributes* in the order, "strictly" (!). The internal qualities is what gives "meaning" to endurants.

11.2.3 Chapter 6: Transcendentality

Transcendentality represents a new way of looking at domain description. Before, we claim, there were endurants and perdurants; with no "obvious connection". Now, we claim, perdurants are transcendentally related to endurants; and strongly so.

11.2.4 Chapter 7: Perdurants

The deduction of behaviours from parts marks a major contribution of *domain analysis & description*. The deduction of behaviour signature and definition elements such as *channels* from *mereologies*, *values* from *static attributes*, *state variables* in the form of *"update-able" parameters* from *programmable attributes*, and *part variables* and their access (and possible update) from other *dynamic attributes*, marks another contribution of *domain analysis & description*.

11.3 A Final Summary of Triptych Concepts

The "near exhaustive" summary listings that now follow serve the purpose of reminding the reader of the rather large, perhaps even "exhausting" set of new terms, each to be appropriated thoroughly and now applied!

11.3.1 The Intrinsics of Domain Analysis & Description

This is a summary of the calculi of Chapters 4–7. There are the following issues to be dealt with in an analysis & description of the intrinsics of domain analysis & description, and in the transcendental deduction of parts into behaviours.

11.3.2 Domain Facets

This is a summary of Chapter 8. We have not put forward any kind of calculi for the analysis & description of domain facets; the facets have emerged empirically.

11.3.3 Requirements

This is a summary of Chapter 9. There are the following issues to be dealt with when using this monograph's approach to requirements engineering.

The 10 page example of Sect. **9.2** (pp. 245–255), is "only" a backdrop for the examples of the specific requirements sections; as such it does not reveal any requirements issues.

11.4 Systems Development

We see *computing systems development* as comprising the development of *hardware* and *software*. For software that comprises the development of, or reliance on existing, appropriate *domain descriptions*; the development of *requirements prescriptions* based on these domain models – including but not shown in this monograph, the analysis and prescription of unchanged or changed **business processes** also known as *business process re-engineering* [209, 208, 255, 261]. In the context of formal requirements development we refer to [44, Sect. 19.3: *Business Process Reengineering Requirements*]. There is a whole new dimension, we claim, to *business process engineering and re-engineering* (BPE&BPR) in the light of *domain analysis & description*. Yes, we suggest that someone reviews the possible foundation for BPE&BPR.

11.5 On How to Conduct a Domain Analysis & Description Project

We have established a scientific & engineering discipline of domain analysis & description, part II, and of domain requirements, Chapter 9. We have shown, in the very many examples of this monograph and in quite a collection of experimental studies [84], that that discipline can be applied; but can it be applied just because the reader has now studied that discipline? What is not covered in this monograph is the practical aspects of carrying out the "theory & practice" of constructing domain models. We shall, in itemized form, suggest an approach that we have applied for over 50 years, since the 1973–1975 PL/I compiler project at the IBM Vienna Laboratory; in the CHILL [205] and Ada [95, 96, 134, 314] compiler development projects at The Dansk Datamatik Center, DDC in the 1980s and more.

- It is assumed that you have a team of, for example, 5–7 professional software engineers, persons well-versed[233] in the concepts and methods of this monograph.
- First you set aside a month-long, preliminary **study** of the domain at hand: not a study where you neither analyse nor describe the domain, just a simple literature study, using, for example also the Internet.
- Then you conduct, say over a three month period, an **experimental** domain analysis & description.

  ∞ One purpose of this experiment is to test whether an assumed set of analysis & description prompts "will do the trick", or whether the project must revise the upper ontology for that domain.

  ∞ Another purpose is to structure the project group. During the experiment some first thoughts on major endurants should emerge – and the project group structured accordingly: one project member per major, often composite, part to be responsible for all aspects of the analysis & description of that part – and its composites. On a rotating shift basis other project members shall act as reviewers of each others' work.

- Then the project can enter its **application** stage.[234]

  ∞ The *external qualities* step of the domain analysis & description mainly consists of the Endurant Observers , Sect. **4.17** step. It is the first serious step. It is to be followed by the next steps in strict order.

    ∞ The *unique identifier* step, Sect. **5.2**, in which unique identifiers for all relevant endurant categories are settled.

    ∞ The *mereology* step, Sect. **5.3**, in which the mereology for all relevant endurant categories are settled. This is a crucial step. Care must be taken. This step requires intensive interaction between project members. We advice that each project member "play around" with mereology invariants.

    ∞ The *attributes* step, Sect. **5.4**, in which attributes for all relevant endurant categories are settled. This step is less interaction-intensive – although those attributes which shall later form the basis for work on intentionalities do require some interaction.

    ∞ The *intentionality* step, Sect. **5.5**, has an as yet not fully understood element of engineering research. It completes the first iteration of work on *internal qualities*.

  ∞ The first iteration of work on both *external* and *internal* qualities will usually be followed by several further such iterations – in between the next steps.

  ∞ These next steps are those of *transcendental deductive* work on *perdurants* – also to be pursued in "strict order".

    ∞ In the *states* step, see Sect. **7.2**, we **value** define states of all invariants, ...

    ∞ In the *channels and communication*, see Sect. **7.5**,

    ∞ In the *perdurant signatures*, Sect. **7.6**,

    ∞ In the *discrete behaviour definitions*, see Sect. **7.3.4**,

    ∞ In the *discrete action behaviour definitions*, see Sect. **7.10**,

    ∞ In the *discrete event behaviour definitions*, see Sect. **7.11**,

    ∞ And in a final *channel message type* step we secure that all channel declarations and messages are properly typed.

- Work on the above phases and steps form a major part of domain analysis & description projects.

---

[233] That is: they have a reasonably qualified knowledge of this monograph, can apply this knowledge, have a reasonably qualified knowledge of discrete mathematics, of mathematical logic for computing scientists, formal methods, functional, logic, imperative and parallel programming, and possess both analytic skills and master their mother tongue and English, if it is not their mother tongue.

[234] We refer to this **study, experiment, apply** triplet as **SEA**.

11.6 On Domain Specific Languages

Definition: 98 Domain Specific Language: A **domain specific language** is a language whose semantic domains are analysed & described in a ***domain analysis & description*** ∎

The semantic domains of a formal language are the types of the meaning of that language's combinators, operators, etc.

That is, to define a domain specific language, a DSL, we need first analyse & describe that domain in sufficient generality; then identify such core combinators and operators on which to base a language design. We refer to Sect. **8.6.3** for examples of fragments of DSLs.

The literature on DSL is, to us, large and confused, so we omit bringing references. We did, however, bring an analysis of some of the DSL in [73, Sect. 5.3.1 item 5].

11.7 Some Concluding Observations

We dispense of a few observations.

⋆ Fuzzy Characterisations and Definitions:

The delineations between 'principles' (Item 44 on page 8), 'techniques' (Item 44 on page 8), and 'tools' (Item 44 on page 9) are not fully satisfactory. We have, however, maintained and, as best we could, followed our definition of 'method'. In the various chapters method summary sections we have then, by example, exemplified these three, the *principle*, the *technique* and the *tool* definitions. More generally we distinguish between a definition and a characterisation, and between formal and informal definitions. The definitions of all analysis and description prompts were informal. There is not much else we could have done. The target of the domain analysis & description inquiry is, by necessity, informal in the sense that there are no a priori established domain theories — unlike when computer scientists inquire of their "domain" the computing devices, algorithms, languages for which they have, or do set up precise mathematical models, at their own will.

⋆ Narration versus Formalisation:

The narration and formalisation paradigm exhibits the characterisation, informal and formal definition issue mentioned just above. To make narratives precise seems to be an art. There is an interplay between the processes of narration and formalisation. A good outcome is achieved when a beautiful formalisation helps make the narrative precise and beautiful.

⋆ Modularisation:

By a text module we shall, informally mean a clearly delineated text which denotes a simple complex quantity such as an endurant part with all its external and internal qualities and the corresponding perdurant behaviour. So far our domain specifications have been one big, "flat unstructured" list of **type** and **value definitions**, and **channel** and **variable declarations**. We could have availed ourselves of RSL's **schema**, **class** and **object** text structuring facility. But, except for one example, Example 88 on page 207, we have not!

11.8 A Reflection on Methodologies

This monograph represents a culmination of a lifetime's focus on methodology, specifically *on how to develop software* [42, 43, 44]. In these books, all 4!, I have brought forward a number of *method principles, procedures, techniques* and *tools*. But, surely, other, or alternative such methods could be "touted"! Yes, even the definition of the concept of method could be different[235]. You, will have noticed, for example, that we operate, in Chapter 4, with the *ontology graph* of Fig. 4.1 on page 53, but that page vii shows a simpler, an essential, ontology graph, and that Sects. **4.5.2** and **4.22.5** reviews these ontologies, i.e., ontology graphs.

Common to all "our" methods is their foundation in and use of philosophy and mathematics.

What is the message here?

The message is this: There is no *"cast-in-concrete"*, final, universal method. But it is advisable to work methodically, in order for any individual software engineer to work reasonably efficiently, and for any group of software engineers to work harmoniously. So, as You go along, by yourself, developing software, including their domain descriptions and their requirements prescriptions, settle on a method to follow, possibly modifying a previously used method, or establish new method principles, procedures, techniques and tools. This advice also includes choosing an appropriate ontology graph – perhaps by modifying an "existing" one!

Domain science and software engineering offers an exciting universe!

11.9 Tony Hoare's Reaction to 'Domain Modelling'

We close this monograph as we opened it: As the first item of this monograph Item 1 on page 3, we quoted Tony Hoare. It is likewise fitting to bring as final text also a quote from his hand. In a 2006 e-mail, in response, undoubtedly to my steadfast – perhaps conceived as stubborn – insistence, on domain engineering, Tony Hoare summed up his reaction to domain engineering as follows, and I quote[236]:

*"There are many unique contributions that **can be made by**[237] domain modelling.*

- *The models describe all aspects of the real world that are relevant for any good software design in the area. They describe possible places to define the system boundary for any particular project.*
- *They make explicit the preconditions about the real world that have to be made in any embedded software design, especially one that is going to be formally proved.*
- *They describe the whole range of possible designs for the software, and the whole range of technologies available for its realisation.*
- *They provide a framework for a full analysis of requirements, which is wholly independent of the technology of implementation.*
- *They enumerate and analyse the decisions that must be taken earlier or later in any design project, and identify those that are independent and those that conflict. Late discovery of feature interactions can be avoided."*

Whether they **will be made** — these *contributions* — is up to the reader!

• • •

---

[235] Earlier versions, for example, did not include the concept of *procedure*. [One could reasonably argue that 'procedure' is 'embedded' in the idea of 'method'.]

[236] E-Mail to Dines Bjørner, July 19, 2006

[237] The **emphasis** is mine.

References

1. Martin Abadi and Luca Cardelli. A Theory of Objects. Monographs in Computer Science. Springer, New York, NY, USA, August 1996.
2. Jean-Raymond Abrial. The B Book: Assigning Programs to Meanings and Modeling in Event-B: System and Software Engineering. Cambridge University Press, Cambridge, England, 1996 and 2009.
3. Satyajit Acharya, Chris George, and Hrushikesha Mohanty. Specifying a mobile computing infrastructure and services. In R. K. Ghosh and Hrushikesha Mohanty, editors, Distributed Computing and Internet Technology, First International Conference, ICDCIT 2004, Bhubaneswar, India, December 22-24, 2004, Proceedings, volume 3347 of Lecture Notes in Computer Science, pages 244–254. Springer, 2004.
4. Satyajit Acharya, Chris George, and Hrushikesha Mohanty. Domain consistency in requirements specification. In Fifth International Conference on Quality Software (QSIC 2005), 19-20 September 2005, Melbourne, Australia, pages 231–240. IEEE Computer Society, 2005.
5. W. Aitken, B. Dickens, P. Kwiatkowski, O. de Moor, D. Richter, and Charles Simonyi. Transformation in intentional programming. In Fifth International Conference on Software Reuse, ICSR'98, Victoria, Canada.
6. Open Mobile Alliance. OMA DRM V2.0 Candidate Enabler. http://www.openmobilealliance.org/-release_program/drm_v2_0.html, Sep 2005.
7. Alvis Brāzma. Deductive Synthesis of Dot Expressions. In Baltic Computer Science, volume 502 of Lecture Notes in Computer Science, pages 156–212. Springer, 17–21 May 1991. See [21].
8. Yamine Aït Ameur, J. Paul Gibson, and Dominique Méry. On implicit and explicit semantics: Integration issues in proof-based development of systems. In Leveraging Applications of Formal Methods, Verification and Validation. Specialized Techniques and Applications - 6th International Symposium, ISoLA 2014, Corfu, Greece, October 8–11, 2014, Proceedings, Part II, pages 604–618, 2014.
9. Ian Anderson. A First Course in Discrete Mathematics. Springer, UK, 12 Oct 2000. ISBN 1852332360.
10. Anon. C.C.I.T.T. High Level Language (CHILL), Recommendation Z.200, Red Book Fascicle VI.12. See [206]. ITU (Intl. Telecmm. Union), Geneva, Switzerland, 1980–1985.
11. Krzysztof R. Apt. Principles of Constraint Programming. Cambridge University Press, August 2003. ISBN 0521825830.
12. K. Araki et al., editors. IFM 1999–2018: Integrated Formal Methods, 1st IFM, 1999: e-ISBN-13:978-1-1-4471-851-1, and 2nd IFM, 2000: LNCS 1945, 3rd IFM, 2002: LNCS 2335, 4th IFM, 2004: LNCS 2999, 5th IFM, 2005: LNCS 3771, 6th IFM, 2007: LNCS 4591, 7th IFM, 2009: LNCS 5423, 8th IFM, 2010: LNCS 6396, 9th IFM, 2012: LNCS 7321, 10th IFM, 2013: LNCS 7940, 11th IFM, 2014: LNCS 8739, 12th IFM, 2016: LNCS 9681,13th IFM, 2017: LNCS 10510, 14th IFM, 2018: LNCS 11023, 15th IFM, 2018: LNCS 11918. Springer, Lecture Notes in Computer Science
13. Alapan Arnab and Andrew Hutchison. Fairer Usage Contracts for DRM. In Proceedings of the Fifth ACM Workshop on Digital Rights Management (DRM'05), pages 65–74, Alexandria, Virginia, USA, Nov 2005.
14. Rober Audi. The Cambridge Dictionary of Philosophy. Cambridge University Press, England, 1995 (1996 reprint).
15. Alain Badiou. Being and Event. Continuum, 2005. (L'être et l'événements, Edition du Seuil, 1988).
16. Jaco W. de Bakker. Control Flow Semantics. The MIT Press, Cambridge, Mass., USA, 1995.
17. H. P. Barendregt. The Lambda Caculus — Its Syntax and Semantics. North-Holland Publ.Co., Amsterdam, 1981.
18. H. P. Barendregt. Introduction to Lambda Calculus. Niew Archief Voor Wiskunde, 4:337–372, 1984.
19. H. P. Barendregt. The Lambda Calculus. Number 103 in Studies in Logic and the Foundations of Mathematics. North-Holland, Amsterdam, revised edition, 1991.

© The Author(s), under exclusive license to Springer Nature Switzerland AG 2021
D. Bjørner, *Domain Science and Engineering*, Monographs in Theoretical Computer Science. An EATCS Series, https://doi.org/10.1007/978-3-030-73484-8

20. D.W. Barron, J.N. Buxton, D.F. Hartley, E. Nixon, and C. Strachey. The main features of CPL. Computer Journal, 6:134–143, 1963.
21. J. Barzdin and D. Bjørner, editors. Baltic Computer Science, volume 502 of Lecture Notes in Computer Science. Springer, Heidelberg, Germany, 1991.
22. David Basin and Seán Matthews. A conservative extension of first-order logic and its applications to theorem proving. In FSTTCS 1993: Foundations of Software Technology and Theoretical Computer Science, volume 761 of Lecture Notes in Computer Science, pages 151–160. Springer, 2005.
23. Hans Bekič. An Introduction to ALGOL 68. Annual Review in: 'Automatic Programming', Pergamon Press, 7, 1973.
24. Hans Bekič, Dines Bjørner, Wolfgang Henhapl, Cliff B. Jones, and Peter Lucas. A Formal Definition of a PL/I Subset. Technical Report 25.139, Vienna, Austria, 20 September 1974.
25. Hans Bekič, Peter Lucas, Kurt Walk, and Many Others. Formal Definition of PL/I, ULD Version I. Technical report, IBM Laboratory, Vienna, 1966.
26. Hans Bekič, Peter Lucas, Kurt Walk, and Many Others. Formal Definition of PL/I, ULD Version II. Technical report, IBM Laboratory, Vienna, 1968.
27. Hans Bekič, Peter Lucas, Kurt Walk, and Many Others. Formal Definition of PL/I, ULD Version III. IBM Laboratory, Vienna, 1969.
28. Hans Bekič and Kurt Walk. Formalization of Storage Properties. In Symposium on Semantics of Algorithmic Languages, volume LNM 188. Springer, 1971.
29. Yochai Benkler. Coase's Penguin, or Linux and the Nature of the Firm. The Yale Law Journal, 112, 2002.
30. Yves Bertot and Pierre Castéran. Interactive Theorem Proving and Program Development. Coq'Art: The Calculus of Inductive Constructions. EATCS Series: Texts in Theoretical Computer Science. Springer, 2004.
31. G.M. Birtwistle, O.-J.Dahl, B. Myhrhaug, and K. Nygaard. SIMULA begin. Studentlitteratur, Lund, Sweden, 1974.
32. B.J. Mailloux, J.E.L Peck, C.H.A. Koster and Aad van Wijngaarden. Report on the Algorithmic Language ALGOL 68. Springer, Berlin, Heidelberg, 1969.
33. D. Bjørner and C.B. Jones. The Vienna Development Method: The Meta-Language, volume 61 of LNCS. Springer, 1978.
34. D. Bjørner and O. Oest. Towards a Formal Description of Ada, volume 98 of LNCS. Springer, 1980.
35. Dines Bjørner, editor. Abstract Software Specifications, volume 86 of LNCS. Springer, 1980.
36. Dines Bjørner, editor. Formal Description of Programming Concepts (II). IFIP TC-2 Work.Conf., Garmisch-Partenkirchen, North-Holland Publ.Co., Amsterdam, 1982.
37. Dines Bjørner. Michael Jackson's Problem Frames: Domains, Requirements and Design. In Li ShaoYang and Michael Hinchley, editors, ICFEM'97: International Conference on Formal Engineering Methods, Los Alamitos, November 12–14 1997. IEEE Computer Society.
38. Dines Bjørner. Formal Software Techniques in Railway Systems. In Eckehard Schnieder, editor, 9th IFAC Symposium on Control in Transportation Systems, pages 1-12, Technical University, Braunschweig, Germany, 13-15 June 2000. VDI/VDE-Gesellschaft Mess- und Automatisierungstechnik, VDI-Gesellschaft für Fahrzeug- und Verkehrstechnik. Invited talk.
39. Dines Bjørner. Domain Models of "The Market" – in Preparation for E-Transaction Systems. In Practical Foundations of Business and System Specifications (Eds.: Haim Kilov and Ken Baclawski), The Netherlands, December 2002. Kluwer Academic Press. http://www2.imm.dtu.dk/~dibj/themarket.pdf.
40. Dines Bjørner. Domain Engineering: A "Radical Innovation" for Systems and Software Engineering? In Verification: Theory and Practice, volume 2772 of Lecture Notes in Computer Science, Heidelberg, October 7-11 2003. Springer. The Zohar Manna International Conference, Taormina, Sicily 29 June – 4 July 2003. http://www2.imm.dtu.dk/~dibj/zohar.pdf.
41. Dines Bjørner. Dynamics of Railway Nets: On an Interface between Automatic Control and Software Engineering. In CTS2003: 10th IFAC Symposium on Control in Transportation Systems, Oxford, UK, August 4-6 2003. Elsevier Science Ltd. Symposium held at Tokyo, Japan. Editors: S. Tsugawa and M. Aoki. http://www2.imm.dtu.dk/~dibj/ifac-dynamics.pdf.
42. Dines Bjørner. Software Engineering, Vol. 1: Abstraction and Modelling. Texts in Theoretical Computer Science, the EATCS Series. Springer, 2006. See [48, 52].
43. Dines Bjørner. Software Engineering, Vol. 2: Specification of Systems and Languages. Texts in Theoretical Computer Science, the EATCS Series. Springer, 2006. Chapters 12–14 are primarily authored by Christian Krog Madsen. See [49, 53].
44. Dines Bjørner. Software Engineering, Vol. 3: Domains, Requirements and Software Design. Texts in Theoretical Computer Science, the EATCS Series. Springer, 2006. See [50, 54].
45. Dines Bjørner. A Container Line Industry Domain. Techn. report, Technical University of Denmark, Holte, Denmark, June 2007. imm.dtu.dk/~db/container-paper.pdf.
46. Dines Bjørner. Domain Theory: Practice and Theories, Discussion of Possible Research Topics. In ICTAC 2007, volume 4701 of Lecture Notes in Computer Science (eds. J.C.P. Woodcock et al.), pages 1–17, Heidelberg, September 2007. Springer.

47. Dines Bjørner. From Domains to Requirements. In Montanari Festschrift, volume 5065 of Lecture Notes in Computer Science (eds. Pierpaolo Degano, Rocco De Nicola and José Meseguer), pages 1–30, Heidelberg, May 2008. Springer. imm.dtu.dk/~dibj/montanari.pdf.
48. Dines Bjørner. Software Engineering, Vol. 1: Abstraction and Modelling. Tsinghua University Press, 2008.
49. Dines Bjørner. Software Engineering, Vol. 2: Specification of Systems and Languages. Tsinghua University Press, 2008.
50. Dines Bjørner. Software Engineering, Vol. 3: Domains, Requirements and Software Design. Tsinghua University Press, 2008.
51. Dines Bjørner. On Mereologies in Computing Science. In Festschrift: Reflections on the Work of C.A.R. Hoare, History of Computing (eds. Cliff B. Jones, A.W. Roscoe and Kenneth R. Wood), pages 47–70, London, UK, 2009. Springer. imm.dtu.dk/~dibj/bjorner-hoare75-p.pdf.
52. Dines Bjørner. Chinese: Software Engineering, Vol. 1: Abstraction and Modelling. Tsinghua University Press. Translated by Dr Liu Bo Chao et al., 2010.
53. Dines Bjørner. Chinese: Software Engineering, Vol. 2: Specification of Systems and Languages. Tsinghua University Press. Translated by Dr Liu Bo Chao et al., 2010.
54. Dines Bjørner. Chinese: Software Engineering, Vol. 3: Domains, Requirements and Software Design. Tsinghua University Press. Translated by Dr Liu Bo Chao et al., 2010.
55. Dines Bjørner. Domain Engineering. In Paul Boca and Jonathan Bowen, editors, Formal Methods: State of the Art and New Directions, Eds. Paul Boca and Jonathan Bowen, pages 1–42, London, UK, 2010. Springer.
56. Dines Bjørner. Domain Science & Engineering – From Computer Science to The Sciences of Informatics, Part I of II: The Engineering Part. Kibernetika i sistemny analiz, 2(4):100–116, May 2010.
57. Dines Bjørner. On Development of Web-based Software: A Divertimento of Ideas and Suggestions. Technical Report, Technical University of Vienna, August–October 2010. imm.dtu.dk/~dibj/wfdftp.pdf.
58. Dines Bjørner. The Tokyo Stock Exchange Trading Rules. R&D Experiment, Techn. Univ. of Denmark, Denmark, 2010. imm.dtu.dk/~db/todai/tse-1.pdf, imm.dtu.dk/~db/todai/tse-2.pdf.
59. Dines Bjørner. Believable Software Management. Encyclopedia of Software Engineering, 1(1):1–32, 2011.
60. Dines Bjørner. Domain Science & Engineering – From Computer Science to The Sciences of Informatics, Part II of II: The Science Part. Kibernetika i sistemny analiz, 2(3):100–120, June 2011.
61. Dines Bjørner. Domains: Their Simulation, Monitoring and Control – A Divertimento of Ideas and Suggestions. In Rainbow of Computer Science, Festschrift for Hermann Maurer on the Occasion of His 70th Anniversary. Festschrift (eds. C. Calude, G. Rozenberg and A. Salomaa), pages 167–183. Springer, Heidelberg. Germany, January 2011. imm.dtu.dk/~dibj/maurer-bjorner.pdf.
62. Dines Bjørner. Domain Science and Engineering as a Foundation for Computation for Humanity, chapter 7, pages 159–177. Computational Analysis, Synthesis, and Design of Dynamic Systems. CRC [Taylor & Francis], 2013. (eds.: Justyna Zander and Pieter J. Mosterman).
63. Dines Bjørner. Pipelines – a Domain. Experimental Research Report 2013-2, DTU Compute and Fredsvej 11, DK-2840 Holte, Denmark, Spring 2013. imm.dtu.dk/~dibj/pipe-p.pdf.
64. Dines Bjørner. A Rôle for Mereology in Domain Science and Engineering. Synthese Library (eds. Claudio Calosi and Pierluigi Graziani). Springer, Amsterdam, The Netherlands, October 2014.
65. Dines Bjørner. Domain Analysis: Endurants – An Analysis & Description Process Model. In Shusaku Iida and José Meseguer and Kazuhiro Ogata, editor, Specification, Algebra, and Software: A Festschrift Symposium in Honor of Kokichi Futatsugi. Springer, May 2014. imm.dtu.dk/~dibj/2014/kanazawa/kanazawa-p.pdf.
66. Dines Bjørner. Domain Engineering – A Basis for Safety Critical Software. Invited Keynote, ASSC2014: Australian System Safety Conference, Melbourne, 26–28 May 2014. Technical University of Denmark, Fredsvej 11, DK-2840 Holte, Denmark, December 2014. imm.dtu.dk/~dibj/2014/assc-april-bw.pdf.
67. Dines Bjørner. A Credit Card System: Uppsala Draft. Technical Report: Experimental Research, Technical University of Denmark, Fredsvej 11, DK-2840 Holte, Denmark, November 2016. imm.dtu.dk/~dibj/2016/credit/accs.pdf.
68. Dines Bjørner. Domain Analysis and Description – Formal Models of Processes and Prompts. Technical report, Technical University of Denmark, Fredsvej 11, DK-2840 Holte, Denmark, 2016. Extensive revision of [65]. imm.dtu.dk/~dibj/2016/process/process-p.pdf.
69. Dines Bjørner. From Domain Descriptions to Requirements Prescriptions – A Different Approach to Requirements Engineering. Technical report, Technical University of Denmark, Fredsvej 11, DK-2840 Holte, Denmark, 2016. Extensive revision of [47] compute.dtu.dk/~dibj/2015/faoc-req/faoc-req.pdf.
70. Dines Bjørner. Weather Information Systems: Towards a Domain Description. Technical Report: Experimental Research, Technical University of Denmark, Fredsvej 11, DK-2840 Holte, Denmark, November 2016. imm.dtu.dk/~dibj/2016/wis/wis-p.pdf.
71. Dines Bjørner. Manifest Domains: Analysis & Description – A Philosophical Basis. 2016–2017. imm.dtu.dk/~dibj/2016/apb/daad-apb.pdf.

72. Dines Bjørner. A Space of Swarms of Drones. Research Note, Technical University of Denmark, Fredsvej 11, DK-2840 Holte, Denmark, December 2017. `imm.dtu.dk/~dibj/2017/swarms/swarm-paper.pdf`.

73. Dines Bjørner. Manifest Domains: Analysis & Description. Formal Aspects of Computing, 29(2):175–225, March 2017. Online: 26 July 2016.

74. Dines Bjørner. What are Documents? Research Note, Technical University of Denmark, Fredsvej 11, DK-2840 Holte, Denmark, July 2017. `imm.dtu.dk/~dibj/2017/docs/docs.pdf`.

75. Dines Bjørner. A Philosophy of Domain Science & Engineering – An Interpretation of Kai Sørlander's Philosophy. Research Note, 95 pages, Technical University of Denmark, Fredsvej 11, DK-2840 Holte, Denmark, Spring 2018. `imm.dtu.dk/~dibj/2018/philosophy/filo.pdf`.

76. Dines Bjørner. Container Terminals. Technical report, Technical University of Denmark, Fredsvej 11, DK-2840 Holte, Denmark, September 2018. An incomplete draft report; currently 60+ pages. `imm.dtu.-dk/~dibj/2018/yangshan/maersk-pa.pdf`.

77. Dines Bjørner. Domain analysis & description - the implicit and explicit semantics problem. In Régine Laleau, Dominique Méry, Shin Nakajima, and Elena Troubitsyna, editors, Proceedings Joint Workshop on Handling IMPlicit and EXplicit knowledge in formal system development (IMPEX) and Formal and Model-Driven Techniques for Developing Trustworthy Systems (FM&MDD), Xi'an, China, 16th November 2017, volume 271 of Electronic Proceedings in Theoretical Computer Science, pages 1–23. Open Publishing Association, 2018.

78. Dines Bjørner. Domain Facets: Analysis & Description. Technical report, Technical University of Denmark, Fredsvej 11, DK-2840 Holte, Denmark, May 2018. Extensive revision of [55]. `imm.dtu.dk-/~dibj/2016/facets/faoc-facets.pdf`.

79. Dines Bjørner. To Every Manifest Domain a CSP Expression — A Rôle for Mereology in Computer Science. Journal of Logical and Algebraic Methods in Programming, 1(94):91–108, January 2018. `compute.dtu.dk/~dibj/2016/mereo/mereo.pdf`.

80. Dines Bjørner. Domain Analysis & Description – A Philosophy Basis. Technical report, Technical University of Denmark, Fredsvej 11, DK-2840 Holte, Denmark, November 2019. Submitted for review. `imm.dtu.dk/~dibj/2019/filo/main2.pdf`.

81. Dines Bjørner. Domain Analysis & Description – Principles, Techniques and Modelling Languages. ACM Trans. on Software Engineering and Methodology, 28(2), April 2019. 68 pages. `imm.dtu.-dk/~dibj/2018/tosem/Bjorner-TOSEM.pdf`.

82. Dines Bjørner. A Retailer Market: Domain Analysis & Description. A Comparison Heraklit/DS&E Case Study. Technical Report, Technical University of Denmark, Fredsvej 11, DK-2840 Holte, Denmark, January 2021. http://www.imm.dtu.dk/~dibj/2021/Retailer/BjornerHeraklit2021.pdf.

83. Dines Bjørner. Domain Engineering: Technology Management, Research and Engineering. A JAIST Press Research Monograph # 4, 536 pages, March 2009.

84. Dines Bjørner. Domain Case Studies, Experimental research reports carried out to "discover", try out and refine method principles, techniques and tools: 2021: *The 7 Seas: A Domain of Waterways, Vessels and Harbours* `imm.dtu.dk/~dibj/2021/7seas/The7Seas.pdf`. 2021: *Rivers and Canals – Endurants – A Technical Note*, March 2021. `imm.dtu.dk/~dibj/2021/Graphs/Rivers-and-Canals.pdf`. 2021: *A Retailer Market: Domain Analysis & Description.* `imm.dtu.dk/~dibj/2021/Retailer/BjornerHeraklit-27January2021.pdf` 2019: *Container Terminals*, ECNU, Shanghai, China `imm.dtu.dk/~dibj/2018/-yangshan/maersk-pa.pdf`. 2018: *Documents*, TongJi Univ., Shanghai, China `imm.dtu.dk/~dibj/2017/-docs/docs.pdf`. 2017: *Urban Planning*, TongJi Univ., Shanghai, China `imm.dtu.dk/~dibj/2018/-BjornerUrbanPlanning24Jan2018.pdf`. 2017: *Swarms of Drones*, Inst. of Softw., Chinese Acad. of Sci., Peking, China `imm.dtu.dk/~dibj/2017/swarms/swarm-paper.pdf`. 2013: *Road Transport*, Techn. Univ. of Denmark `imm.dtu.dk/~dibj/road-p.pdf`. 2012: *Credit Cards*, Uppsala, Sweden `imm.dtu.-dk/~dibj/2016/credit/accs.pdf`. 2012: *Weather Information*, Bergen, Norway `imm.dtu.dk/~dibj/-2016/wis/wis-p.pdf`. 2010: *Web-based Transaction Processing*, Techn. Univ. of Vienna, Austria `imm.-dtu.dk/~dibj/wfdftp.pdf`. 2010: *The Tokyo Stock Exchange*, Tokyo Univ., Japan `imm.dtu.dk/~db/-todai/tse-1.pdf`, `imm.dtu.dk/~db/todai/tse-2.pdf`. 2009: *Pipelines*, Techn. Univ. of Graz, Austria `imm.dtu.dk/~dibj/pipe-p.pdf`. 2007: *A Container Line Industry Domain*, Techn. Univ. of Denmark `imm.dtu.dk/~dibj/container-paper.pdf`. 2002: *The Market*, Techn. Univ. of Denmark `imm.dtu.-dk/~dibj/themarket.pdf`. 1995–2004: *Railways*, Techn. Univ. of Denmark - a compendium `imm.dtu.-dk/~dibj/train-book.pdf`. Technical University of Denmark.

85. Dines Bjørner. The Rôle of Domain Engineering in Software Development. Why Current Requirements Engineering Seems Flawed! In Perspectives of Systems Informatics, volume 5947 of Lecture Notes in Computer Science, pages 2–34, Heidelberg, 2010. Springer.

86. Dines Bjørner and Asger Eir. Compositionality: Ontology and Mereology of Domains. Some Clarifying Observations in the Context of Software Engineering in July 2008, eds. Martin Steffen, Dennis Dams and Ulrich Hannemann. In Festschrift for Prof. Willem Paul de Roever. Concurrency, Compositionality, and Correctness, volume 5930 of Lecture Notes in Computer Science, pages 22–59, Heidelberg, July 2010. Springer.

87. Dines Bjørner, Andrei Petrovich Ershov, and Neil Deaton Jones, editors. Partial Evaluation and Mixed Computation. Proceedings of the IFIP TC2 Workshop, Gammel Avernæs, Denmark, October 1987. North-Holland, 1988. 625 pages.

88. Dines Bjørner, Chris W. George, Anne Elisabeth Haxthausen, Christian Krogh Madsen, Steffen Holmslykke, and Martin Penicka. "UML-ising" Formal Techniques. In Proceedings of INT2004 – Integration of Software Specification Techniques for Applications in Engineering, number 3147 in Lecture Notes in Computer Science, pages 423 – 450. Springer, 2004. Invited paper.

89. Dines Bjørner, Chris W. George, and Søren Prehn. Computing Systems for Railways — A Rôle for Domain Engineering. Relations to Requirements Engineering and Software for Control Applications. In Integrated Design and Process Technology. Editors: Bernd Kraemer and John C. Petterson, Texas, USA, 24–28 June 2002. Society for Design and Process Science. http://www2.imm.dtu.dk/~dibj/pasadena-25.pdf.

90. Dines Bjørner, Anne E. Haxthausen, and Klaus Havelund. Formal, Model-oriented Software Development Methods: From VDM to ProCoS and from RAISE to LaCoS. Future Generation Computer Systems, 7, 1992.

91. Dines Bjørner and Martin C. Henson, editors. Logics of Specification Languages. EATCS Series, Monograph in Theoretical Computer Science. Springer, Heidelberg, Germany, 2008.

92. Dines Bjørner and Cliff B. Jones, editors. The Vienna Development Method: The Meta-Language, volume 61 of LNCS. Springer, 1978.

93. Dines Bjørner and Cliff B. Jones, editors. Formal Specification and Software Development. Prentice-Hall, 1982.

94. Dines Bjørner and V. Kotov, editors. Images of Programming: Dedicated to the Memory of Andrei P. Ershov. IFIP TC2. North-Holland Publ. Co., Amsterdam, The Netherlands, 1991.

95. Dines Bjørner and Ole N. Oest. The DDC Ada Compiler Development Project. In Dines Bjørner and Ole N. Oest, editors, Towards a Formal Description of Ada, volume 98 of Lecture Notes in Computer Science, pages 1–19. Springer, 1980.

96. Dines Bjørner and Ole N. Oest, editors. Towards a Formal Description of Ada, volume 98 of LNCS. Springer, 1980.

97. Nikolaj Bjørner, Anca Browne, Michael Colon, Bernd Finkbeiner, Zohar Manna, Henny Sipma, and Tomas Uribe. Verifying Temporal Properties of Reactive Systems: A STeP Tutorial. Formal Methods in System Design, 16:227–270, 2000.

98. Nikolaj Bjørner, Ken McMillan, and Andrey Rybalchenko. Higher-order Program Verification as Satisfiability Modulo Theories with Algebraic Data-types. In Higher-Order Program Analysis, June 2013. http://hopa.cs.rhul.ac.uk/files/proceedings.html.

99. Dines Bjørner. Urban Planning Processes. Research Note, Technical University of Denmark, Fredsvej 11, DK-2840 Holte, Denmark, July 2017. imm.dtu.dk/~dibj/2017/up/urban-planning.pdf.

100. Bruno Blanchet, Patrick Cousot, Radhia Cousot, Laurent Mauborgne, Jerome Feret, Antoine Miné, David Monniaux, and Xavier Rival. A static analyzer for large safety-critical software. In Programming Language Design and Implementation, pages 196–207, 2003.

101. A. Blass. Abstract State Machines and Pure Mathematics. In Y. Gurevich, P. Kutter, M. Odersky and L. Thiele, editor, Abstract State Machines: Theory and Applications, volume 1912 of LNCS, pages 9–21. Springer, 2000.

102. A. Blass and Y. Gurevich. The Linear Time Hierarchy Theorems for Abstract State Machines. Journal of Universal Computer Science, 3(4):247–278, 1997.

103. A. Blass, Y. Gurevich, and J. Van den Bussche. Abstract state machines and computationally complete query languages. In Y. Gurevich, P. Kutter, M. Odersky, L. Thiele, editors, Abstract State Machines: Theory and Applications, volume 1912 of LNCS, pages 22–33. Springer, 2000.

104. Andrzej Blikle and Mikkel Thorup. On conservative extensions of syntax in the process of system development. In Proceedings of VDM'90, VDM and Z—Formal Methods in Software Development, volume 428 of Lecture notes in computer science, page 22. Springer, 1990.

105. Wayne D. Blizard. A Formal Theory of Objects, Space and Time. The Journal of Symbolic Logic, 55(1):74–89, March 1990.

106. C. Böhm. Lambda-Calculus and Computer Science Theory, volume 37 of LNCS. Springer, 1975.

107. Grady Booch, Ivar Jacobson, and James Rumbaugh. The Unified Modeling Language Reference Manual. Object Technology Series. Addison-Wesley, Massachusetts, USA, 1999.

108. Grady Booch, Ivar Jacobson, and James Rumbaugh. The Unified Modeling Language User Guide. Object Technology Series. Addison-Wesley, Massachusetts, USA, 1999.

109. E. Börger, editor. Specification and Validation Methods. Oxford University Press, 1995.

110. E. Börger and R. Stärk. Abstract State Machines. A Method for High-Level System Design and Analysis. Springer, 2003. ISBN 3-540-00702-4.

111. Jan Bosch. Design and Use of Software Architectures: Adopting and Evolving a Product-line Approach. ACM Press/Addison-Wesley, New York, NY, 2000.

112. P. Branquart, J. Lewi, M. Sintzoff, and P.L. Wodon. The composition of semantics in ALGOL 68. Communications of the ACM, 14(11):697–708, 1971.

113. P. Branquart, G. Louis, and P. Wodon. An Analytical Description of CHILL, The CCITT High Level Language, volume 128 of Lecture Notes in Computer Science. Springer, 1982.

114. M. Bunge. Treatise on Basic Philosophy: Ontology I: The Furniture of the World, volume 3. Reidel, Boston, Mass., USA, 1977.

115. M. Bunge. Treatise on Basic Philosophy: Ontology II: A World of Systems, volume 4. Reidel, Boston, Mass., USA, 1979.

116. Nicholas Bunnin and E.P. Tsui-James, editors. The Blackwell Companion to Philosophy. Blackwell Companions to Philosophy, Oxford, (1996) 1998.

117. Dominique Cansell and Dominique Méry. Logical Foundations of the B Method. Computing and Informatics, 22(1–2), 2003.

118. G. Cantor. Über unendliche, linear Punktmannichfaltigkeiten. Gesammelte Abhandlungen, ed. E. Zermelo, Springer, Berlin (Olms, Hildesheim), 1883, 1932 (1962).

119. Rudolf Carnap. Introduction to Semantics. Harvard Univ. Press, Cambridge, Mass., 1942.

120. Roberto Casati and Achille Varzi. Events. In Edward N. Zalta, editor, The Stanford Encyclopedia of Philosophy. Stanford University, 2010.

121. Roberto Casati and Achille C. Varzi, editors. Events. Ashgate Publishing Group, UK, 1996.

122. Roberto Casati and Achille C. Varzi. Parts and Places: the structures of spatial representation. MIT Press, 1999.

123. C.C.I.T.T. The Specification of CHILL. Technical Report Recommendation Z200, International Telegraph and Telephone Consultative Committee, Geneva, Switzerland, 1980.

124. C.E.C. Digital Rights: Background, Systems, Assessment. Commission of the European Communities, Staff Working Paper, 2002. Brussels, 14.02.2002, SEC(2002) 197.

125. D.L. Chalmers, B. Dandanell, J. Gørtz, J. Storbank Pedersen, and E. Zierau. Using RAISE — First Impressions From a LaCoS User Trial. In Proceedings of VDM '91, volume 551 of Lecture Notes in Computer Science. Springer, 1991.

126. Wen Chen, Asif Iqbal, Akbar Abdrakhmanov, Jay Parlar, Chris George, Mark Lawford, T. S. E. Maibaum, and Alan Wassyng. Change impact analysis for large-scale enterprise systems. In Leszek A. Maciaszek, Alfredo Cuzzocrea, and José Cordeiro, editors, ICEIS 2012 - Proceedings of the 14th International Conference on Enterprise Information Systems, Volume 2, Wroclaw, Poland, 28 June - 1 July, 2012, pages 359–368. SciTePress, 2012.

127. Wen Chen, Asif Iqbal, Akbar Abdrakhmanov, Jay Parlar, Chris George, Mark Lawford, Tom Maibaum, and Alan Wassyng. Large-scale enterprise systems: Changes and impacts. In José Cordeiro, Leszek A. Maciaszek, and Joaquim Filipe, editors, Enterprise Information Systems - 14th International Conference, ICEIS 2012, Wroclaw, Poland, June 28 - July 1, 2012, Revised Selected Papers, volume 141 of Lecture Notes in Business Information Processing, pages 274–290. Springer, 2012.

128. C. N. Chong, R. J. Corin, J. M. Doumen, S. Etalle, P. H. Hartel, Y. W. Law, and A. Tokmakoff. LicenseScript: a logical language for digital rights management. Annals of telecommunications special issue on Information systems security, 2006.

129. C. N. Chong, S. Etalle, and P. H. Hartel. Comparing Logic-based and XML-based Rights Expression Languages. In Confederated Int. Workshops: On The Move to Meaningful Internet Systems (OTM), number 2889 in LNCS, pages 779–792, Catania, Sicily, Italy, 2003. Springer.

130. Cheun Ngen Chong, Ricardo Corin, and Sandro Etalle. LicenseScript: A novel digital rights languages and its semantics. In Proc. of the Third International Conference WEB Delivering of Music (WEDEL-MUSIC'03), pages 122–129. IEEE Computer Society Press, 2003.

131. David R. Christiansen, Klaus Grue, Henning Niss, Peter Sestoft, and Kristján S. Sigtryggsson. Actulus Modeling Language - An actuarial programming language for life insurance and pensions. Technical Report, edlund.dk/sites/default/files/Downloads/paper_actulus-modeling-language.pdf, Edlund A/S, Denmark, 2015. This paper illustrates how the design of pension and life insurance products, and their administration, reserve calculations, and audit, can be based on a common formal notation. The notation is human-readable and machine-processable, and specialised to the actuarial domain, achieving great expressive power combined with ease of use and safety.

132. A. Church. The Calculi of Lambda-Conversion, volume 6 of Annals of Mathematical Studies. The Princeton University Press, Princeton, New Jersey, USA, 1941.

133. Manuel Clavel, Francisco Durán, Steven Eker, Patrick Lincoln, Narciso Martí Oliet, José Meseguer, and Carolyn Talcott. Maude 2.6 Manual. Department of Computer Science, University of Illinois and Urbana-Champaign, Urbana-Champaign, Ill., USA, January 2011.

134. G.B. Clemmensen and O. Oest. Formal Specification and Development of an Ada Compiler – A VDM Case Study. In Proc. 7th International Conf. on Software Engineering, 26.-29. March 1984, Orlando, Florida, pages 430–440. IEEE, 1984.

135. CoFI (The Common Framework Initiative). CASL Reference Manual, volume 2960 of Lecture Notes in Computer Science (IFIP Series). Springer, 2004.

136. Patrick Cousot and Rhadia Cousot. Abstract Interpretation: A Unified Lattice Model for Static Analysis of Programs by Construction or Approximation of Fixpoints. In 4th POPL: Principles of Programming and Languages, pages 238–252. ACM Press, 1977.

137. O.-J. Dahl, E.W. Dijkstra, and Charles Anthony Richard Hoare. Structured Programming. Academic Press, 1972.
138. Ole-Johan Dahl. Object Orientation and Formal Techniques. In Charles Anthony Richard Hoare, Dines Bjørner and Hans Langmaack, editors, VDM '90 VDM and Z– Formal Methods in Software Development, pages 1–11. VDM Europe, Springer, April 1990.
139. Ole-Johan Dahl and Olaf Owe. Formal Development with ABEL. In VDM '91: Formal Software Development Methods, pages 320–362. Springer, October 1991. Volume 2.
140. B. Dandanell. Rigorous Development using RAISE. In Proceedings of SIGSOFT '91. ACM, 1991.
141. B. Dandanell. Fast and Rigorous Prototyping in Ada. In Proceedings of Ada in AEROSPACE '91. EUROSPACE, 1992.
142. B. Dandanell, J. Gørtz, J. Storbank Pedersen, and E. Zierau. Experiences from Applications of RAISE. In FME'93: Industrial Strength Formal Methods, volume 670 of Lecture Notes in Computer Science. Springer, 1993.
143. Anne Dardenne, Axel van Lamsweerde, and Stephen Fickas. Goal-directed requirements acquisition. Sci. Comput. Program., 20(1-2):3–50, April 1993.
144. Aristides Dasso and Chris George. Automating software development by cross-utilization of specification tools. In M. H. Hamza, editor, Proceedings of the IASTED Conference on Software Engineering and Applications, November 9-11, 2004, MIT, Cambridge, MA, USA, pages 368–373. IASTED/ACTA Press, 2004.
145. Donald Davidson. Essays on Actions and Events. Oxford University Press, 1980.
146. N. Dean. The Essence of Discrete Mathematics. The Essence of Computing Series. Prentice Hall, 1997.
147. B.T.D. Denvir. Introduction to Discrete Mathematics for Software Engineering. Macmillan, London, 1986.
148. Ražvan Diaconescu, Kokichi Futatsugi, and Kazuhiro Ogata. CafeOBJ: Logical Foundations and Methodology. Computing and Informatics, 22(1–2), 2003.
149. Yihun T. Dile, Prasad Daggupati, Chris George, Raghavan Srinivasan, and Jeffrey G. Arnold. Introducing a new open source GIS user interface for the SWAT model. Environ. Model. Softw., 85:129–138, 2016.
150. F. Dretske. Can Events Move? Mind, 76(479-492), 1967. Reprinted in [121, 1996], pp. 415-428.
151. Asger Eir. Construction Informatics — issues in engineering, computer science, and ontology. PhD thesis, Dept. of Computer Science and Engineering, Technical University of Denmark, February 2004.
152. Asger Eir. Formal Methods and Hybrid Real-Time Systems, chapter Relating Domain Concepts Intensionally by Ordering Connections, pages 188–216. Springer (LNCS Vol. 4700, Festschrift: Essays in Honour of Dines Bjørner and Zhou Chaochen on the Occasion of Their 70th Birthdays), 2007.
153. Ali Enayat. Conservative extensions of models of set theory and generalizations. The Journal of Symbolic Logic, 51(4):1005–1021, December 1986.
154. F. Erasmy and E. Sekerinsky. Stepwise Refinement of Control Software — A Case Study Using RAISE. In FME'94: Industrial Benefits of Formal Methods, volume 873 of Lecture Notes in Computer Science. Springer, 1994.
155. F. Erasmy and E. Sekerinsky. RAISE. In Formal Development of Reactive Systems: Case Study Production Cell, volume 891 of Lecture Notes in Computer Science. Springer, 1995.
156. ESA. Global Navigation Satellite Systems. http://en.wikipedia.org/wiki/Satellite_navigation, European Space Agency. There are several global navigation satellite systems (http://en.wikipedia.org/wiki/Satellite_navigation) either in operation or being developed: (1.) the US developed and operated GPS (NAVSTAR) system, http://en.wikipedia.org/wiki/Global_Positioning_System; (2.) the EU developed and (to be) operated Galileo system, http://en.wikipedia.org/wiki/Galileo_positioning_system; (3.) the Russian developed and (to be) operated GLONASS, http://en.wikipedia.org/wiki/GLONASS; and (4.) the Chinese Compass Navigation System, http://en.wikipedia.org/wiki/Compass_navigation_system.
157. Alessandro Fantechi, Stefania Gnesi, Anne Haxthausen, Jaco van de Pol, Marco Roveri, and Helen Treharne. SaRDIn - A Safe Reconfigurable Distributed Interlocking. In Proceedings of 11th World Congress on Railway Research (WCRR 2016), Milano, 2016. Ferrovie dello Stato Italiane.
158. Alessandro Fantechi and Anne E. Haxthausen. Safety interlocking as a distributed mutual exclusion problem. In Falk Howar and Jiří Barnat, editors, Formal Methods for Industrial Critical Systems, pages 52–66. Springer International Publishing, 2018.
159. Alessandro Fantechi, Anne E. Haxthausen, and Hugo Daniel Macedo. Compositional verification of interlocking systems for large stations. In Alessandro Cimatti and Marjan Sirjani, editors, International Conference on Software Engineering and Formal Methods, volume 10469 of Lecture Notes in Computer Science, pages 236–252. Springer, 2017.
160. Alessandro Fantechi, Anne Elisabeth Haxthausen, and Michel B. R. Nielsen. Model checking geographically distributed interlocking systems using UMC. In 2017 25th Euromicro International Conference on Parallel, Distributed and Network-based Processing (PDP), pages 278–286, 2017.
161. David John Farmer. Being in time: The nature of time in light of McTaggart's paradox. University Press of America, Lanham, Maryland, 1990. 223 pages.

162. Peter Fettke and Wolfgang Reisig. HERAKLIT **case study: retailer**.   Technical report, DFKI and Humboldt University, Saarbrücken University and Berlin, Germany. HERAKLIT working paper v1, http://www.heraklit.org.

163. John Fitzgerald and Peter Gorm Larsen. Developing Software Using VDM-SL. Cambridge University Press, Cambridge, UK, 1997.

164. John Fitzgerald and Peter Gorm Larsen. Modelling Systems – Practical Tools and Techniques in Software Development. Cambridge University Press, UK, 1998. ISBN 0-521-62348-0.

165. Abraham Fraenkel, Yehoshua Bar-Hillel, and Azriel Levy. Foundations of Set Theory. Elsevier Science Publ. Co., Amsterdam, The Netherlands, 2nd revised edition, 1973.

166. Gottlob Frege. Begriffsschrift – Einen der Aritmetischen Nachgebildete Formal Sprache des Reinen Denken. von Luis Nebert, 1879.

167. Carlo A. Furia, Dino Mandrioli, Angelo Morzenti, and Matteo Rossi. Modeling Time in Computing. Monographs in Theoretical Computer Science. Springer, 2012.

168. K. Futatsugi, A.T. Nakagawa, and T. Tamai, editors. CAFE: An Industrial-Strength Algebraic Formal Method, Proceedings from an April 1998 Symposium, Numazu, Japan. Elsevier. 2000.

169. Bernhard Ganter and Rudolf Wille. Formal Concept Analysis — Mathematical Foundations. Springer, January 1999.

170. Signe Geisler and Anne Elisabeth Haxthausen. Stepwise Development and Model Checking of a Distributed Interlocking System - Using RAISE. In Klaus Havelund, Jan Peleska, Bill Roscoe, and Erik de Vink, editors, Formal Methods, Lecture Notes in Computer Science, pages 277–293. Springer International Publishing, 2018.

171. Signe Geisler and Anne Elisabeth Haxthausen. Stepwise development and model checking of a distributed interlocking system using RAISE. Formal Aspects of Computing, 33, 87-125 (2021).

172. Arve Gengelbach and Tjark Weber. Model-theoretic conservative extension for definitional theories. Electronic Notes Theoretical Computer Science, (338):133–145, 2017.

173. Chris George. Heap storage specification and development. In Dines Bjørner, Cliff B. Jones, Mícheál Mac an Airchinnigh, and Erich J. Neuhold, editors, VDM '87, VDM - A Formal Method at Work, VDM-Europe Symposium, Brussels, Belgium, March 23-26, 1987, Proceedings, volume 252 of Lecture Notes in Computer Science, pages 97–105. Springer, 1987.

174. Chris George. The RAISE specification langiage: A tutorial. In Søren Prehn and W. J. Toetenel, editors, VDM '91 - Formal Software Development, 4th International Symposium of VDM Europe, Noordwijkerhout, The Netherlands, October 21-25, 1991, Proceedings, Volume 2: Tutorials, volume 552 of Lecture Notes in Computer Science, pages 238–319. Springer, 1991.

175. Chris George. The NDB database specified in the RAISE specification language. Formal Asp. Comput., 4(1):48–75, 1992.

176. Chris George. A theory of distributing train rescheduling. In Marie-Claude Gaudel and Jim Woodcock, editors, FME '96: Industrial Benefit and Advances in Formal Methods, Third International Symposium of Formal Methods Europe, Co-sponsored by IFIP WG 14.3, Oxford, UK, March 18-22, 1996, Proceedings, volume 1051 of Lecture Notes in Computer Science, pages 499–517. Springer, 1996.

177. Chris George. The development of the RAISE tools. In Bernhard K. Aichernig and T. S. E. Maibaum, editors, Formal Methods at the Crossroads. From Panacea to Foundational Support, 10th Anniversary Colloquium of UNU/IIST, the International Institute for Software Technology of the United Nations University, Lisbon, Portugal, March 18-20, 2002, Revised Papers, volume 2757 of Lecture Notes in Computer Science, pages 49–64. Springer, 2002.

178. Chris George. Tutorial on the RAISE language, method and tools. In Jim Davies, Wolfram Schulte, and Michael Barnett, editors, Formal Methods and Software Engineering, 6th International Conference on Formal Engineering Methods, ICFEM 2004, Seattle, WA, USA, November 8-12, 2004, Proceedings, volume 3308 of Lecture Notes in Computer Science, pages 3–4. Springer, 2004.

179. Chris George. Applicative modelling with RAISE. In Chris George, Zhiming Liu, and Jim Woodcock, editors, Domain Modeling and the Duration Calculus, International Training School, Shanghai, China, September 17-21. 2007, Advanced Lectures, volume 4710 of Lecture Notes in Computer Science, pages 51–118. Springer, 2007.

180. Chris George and Do Tien Dung. Combining and distributing hierarchical systems. In Manfred Broy and Bernhard Rumpe, editors, Requirements Targeting Software and Systems Engineering, International Workshop RTSE '97, Bernried, Germany, October 12-14, 1997, Proceedings, volume 1526 of Lecture Notes in Computer Science, pages 133–153. Springer, 1997.

181. Chris George, Klaus Havelund, Mogens Nielsen, and Kim Ritter Wagner. The RAISE Language, Method and Tools. Formal Aspects of Computing, 1(1), January-March 1989.

182. Chris George and Anne E. Haxthausen. The logic of the RAISE specification language. Comput. Artif. Intell., 22(3-4):323–350, 2003.

183. Chris George and Anne Elisabeth Haxthausen. Logics of Specification Languages, chapter The Logic of the RAISE Specification Language, pages 349–399 in [91]. Springer, 2008.

184. Chris George and Anne Elisabeth Haxthausen. Specification, proof, and model checking of the Mondex electronic purse using RAISE. Formal Aspects of Computing, 20(1):101–116, 2008. Special issue on the Mondex challenge.

185. Chris George, Padmanabhan Krishnan, Percy Antonio Pari Salas, and Jeff W. Sanders. Specification for testing. In Cliff B. Jones, Zhiming Liu, and Jim Woodcock, editors, Formal Methods and Hybrid Real-Time Systems, Essays in Honor of Dines Bjørner and Chaochen Zhou on the Occasion of Their 70th Birthdays, Papers presented at a Symposium held in Macao, China, September 24-25, 2007, volume 4700 of Lecture Notes in Computer Science, pages 280–299. Springer, 2007.

186. Chris George and Huaikou Miao, editors. Formal Methods and Software Engineering, 4th International Conference on Formal Engineering Methods, ICFEM 2002 Shanghai, China, October 21-25, 2002, Proceedings, volume 2495 of Lecture Notes in Computer Science. Springer, 2002.

187. Chris W. George, Peter Haff, Klaus Havelund, Anne Elisabeth Haxthausen, Robert Milne, Claus Bendix Nielsen, Søren Prehn, and Kim Ritter Wagner. The RAISE Specification Language. The BCS Practitioner Series. Prentice-Hall, England, 1992.

188. Chris W. George and Anne Elisabeth Haxthausen. The Logic of the RAISE Specification Language. Computing and Informatics, 22(1–2), 2003.

189. Chris W. George and Anne Elisabeth Haxthausen. Specification and Proof of the Mondex Electronic Purse. In Proceedings of Automated Formal Methods 2006 (AFM 2006), Seattle, 2006.

190. Chris W. George, Anne Elisabeth Haxthausen, Steven Hughes, Robert Milne, Søren Prehn, and Jan Storbank Pedersen. The RAISE Development Method. The BCS Practitioner Series. Prentice-Hall, England, 1995.

191. Chris W. George, Hung Dang Van, Tomasz Janowski, and Richard Moore. Case Studies using The RAISE Method. FACTS (Formal Aspects of Computing: Theory and Software) and FME (Formal Methods Europe). Springer, London, 2002. This book reports on a number of case studies using RAISE (Rigorous Approach to Software Engineering). The case studies were done in the period 1994–2001 at UNU/IIST, the UN University's International Institute for Software Technology, Macau.

192. J Paul Gibson and Dominique Méry. Explicit modelling of physical measures: From Event-B to Java. In Régine Laleau, Dominique Méry, Shin Nakajima, and Elena Troubitsyna, editors, Proceedings Joint Workshop on Handling IMPlicit and EXplicit knowledge in formal system development (IMPEX) and Formal and Model-Driven Techniques for Developing Trustworthy Systems (FM&MDD), Xi'an, China, November 2017, volume 271 of Electronic Proceedings in Theoretical Computer Science, pages 64–79. Open Publishing Association, 2018.

193. Torben Gjaldbæk and Anne Elisabeth Haxthausen. Modelling and Verification of Interlocking Systems for Railway Lines. In Proceedings of the 10th IFAC Symposium on Control in Transportation Systems. Elsevier Science Ltd, Oxford, 2003. ISBN 0-08-044059-2.

194. Mario Gleirscher, Anne Elisabeth Haxthausen, Martin Leucker, and Sven Linker. Analysis of Autonomous Mobile Collectives in Complex Physical Environments (Dagstuhl Seminar 19432). Dagstuhl Reports, 9(10):95–116, 2020.

195. J. Gørtz. Specifying Safety and Progress Properties with RSL. In FME'94: Industrial Benefits of Formal Methods, volume 873 of Lecture Notes in Computer Science. Springer, 1994.

196. James Gosling and Frank Yellin. The Java Language Specification. Addison-Wesley & Sun Microsystems. ACM Press Books, 1996. 864 pp, ISBN 0-10-63451-1.

197. Carl A. Gunter, Elsa L. Gunter, Michael A. Jackson, and Pamela Zave. A Reference Model for Requirements and Specifications. IEEE Software, 17(3):37–43, May–June 2000.

198. Carl A. Gunter, Stephen T. Weeks, and Andrew K. Wright. Models and Languages for Digtial Rights. In Proc. of the 34th Annual Hawaii International Conference on System Sciences (HICSS-34), pages 4034–4038, Maui, Hawaii, USA, January 2001. IEEE Computer Society Press.

199. C.A. Gunther. Semantics of Programming Languages. The MIT Press, Cambridge, Mass., USA, 1992.

200. Y. Gurevich. Evolving Algebras. A Tutorial Introduction. Bulletin of EATCS, 43:264–284, 1991.

201. Y. Gurevich. Evolving Algebras 1993: Lipari Guide. In E. Börger, editor, Specification and Validation Methods, pages 9–36. Oxford University Press, 1995.

202. Y. Gurevich, P. Kutter, M. Odersky, and L. Thiele, editors. Abstract State Machines: Theory and Applications, volume 1912 of LNCS. Springer, 2000.

203. P. Guyer, editor. The Cambridge Companion to Kant. Cambridge University Press, England, 1992.

204. P.M.S. Hacker. Events and Objects in Space and Time. Mind, 91:1–19, 1982. reprinted in [121], pp. 429-447.

205. Peter Haff. A Formal Definition of CHILL. A Supplement to the CCITT Recommendation Z.200. Technical report, Dansk Datamatik Center, 1980.

206. P.L. Haff, editor. The Formal Definition of CHILL. ITU (Intl. Telecmm. Union), Geneva, Switzerland, 1981.

207. Joseph Y. Halpern and Vicky Weissman. A Formal Foundation for XrML. In Proc. of the 17th IEEE Computer Security Foundations Workshop (CSFW'04), 2004.

208. Michael Hammer and James A. Champy. Reengineering the Corporation: A Manifesto for Business Revolution. HarperCollins *Publishers*, London, UK, May 1993. 5 June 2001, Paperback.

209. Michael Hammer and Stephen A. Stanton. The Reengineering Revolutiuon: The Handbook. HarperCollins *Publishers*, London, UK, 1996. Paperback.

210. David Harel. Statecharts: A visual formalism for complex systems. Science of Computer Programming, 8(3):231–274, 1987.

211. David Harel and Rami Marelly. Come, Let's Play – Scenario-Based Programming Using LSCs and the Play-Engine. Springer, 2003.

212. Klaus Havelund. Logics of Specification Languages, chapter RAISE in Perspective. Monographs in Theoretical Computer Science. An EATCS Series. Springer, 2007.

213. A.E. Haxthausen and C.W. George. A Concurrency Case Study Using RAISE. In FME'93: Industrial Strength Formal Methods, volume 670 of Lecture Notes in Computer Science. Springer, 1993.

214. Anne Haxthausen and Xia Yong. A RAISE Specification Framework and Justification Assistant for the Duration Calculus. In Proceedings of ESSLLI-98 Workshop on Duration Calculus, pages 51–58, 1998.

215. Anne E. Haxthausen and Kristian Hede. Formal verification of railway timetables - using the UPPAAL model checker. In Maurice H. ter Beek, Alessandro Fantechi, and Laura Semini, editors, From Software Engineering to Formal Methods and Tools, and Back: Essays Dedicated to Stefania Gnesi on the Occasion of Her 65th Birthday, volume 11865 of Lecture Notes in Computer Science, pages 433–448. Springer, 2019.

216. Anne E. Haxthausen and Jan Peleska. Formal Development and Verification of a Distributed Railway Control System. In Jim Woodcock, Jim Davies, and Jeannette M. Wing, editors, Proceedings of Formal Methods World Congress FM'99, volume 1709 of Lecture Notes in Computer Science, pages 1546–1563. Springer, 1999.

217. Anne E. Haxthausen and Jan Peleska. Formal Development and Verification of a Distributed Railway Control System. IEEE Transaction on Software Engineering, 26(8):687–701, 2000.

218. Anne E. Haxthausen, Jan Peleska, and Ralf Pinger. Applied Bounded Model Checking for Interlocking System Designs. In Steve Counsell and Manuel Núñez, editors, Software Engineering and Formal Methods, volume 8368 of Lecture Notes in Computer Science, pages 205–220. Springer, 2014.

219. Anne Elisabeth Haxthausen. Developing a Translator from C Programs to Data Flow Graphs Using RAISE. In Proceedings of COMPASS'96, pages 89–102. IEEE Computer Society, 1996.

220. Anne Elisabeth Haxthausen. A Domain-specific Framework for Automated Construction and Verification of Railway Control Systems. In B. Buth, G. Rabe, and T. Seyfarth, editors, Proceedings of 28th International Conference on Computer Safety, Reliability, and Security, SAFECOMP 2009, number 5775 in Lecture Notes in Computer Science, pages 1–3. Springer, 2009. Invited paper.

221. Anne Elisabeth Haxthausen. Developing a Domain Model for Relay Circuits. International Journal of Software and Informatics, 3(2–3):241–272, 2009.

222. Anne Elisabeth Haxthausen. Towards a Framework for Modelling and Verification of Relay Interlocking Systems. In 16th Monterey Workshop: Modelling, Development and Verification of Adaptive Systems: the Grand Challenge for Robust Software, 2010. Invited paper.

223. Anne Elisabeth Haxthausen. Towards a Framework for Modelling and Verification of Relay Interlocking Systems. In Radu Calinescu and Ethan Jackson, editors, Foundations of Computer Software. Modeling, Development, and Verification of Adaptive Systems, number 6662 in Lecture Notes in Computer Science, pages 176–192. Springer, 2011. Invited paper. Extended version of [222].

224. Anne Elisabeth Haxthausen. Automated Generation of Safety Requirements from Railway Interlocking Tables. In 5th International Symposium On Leveraging Applications of Formal Methods, Verification and Validation (ISOLA'2012), Part II, number 7610 in Lecture Notes in Computer Science, pages 261–275. Springer, 2012. Invited.

225. Anne Elisabeth Haxthausen. An Institution for Imperative RSL Specifications. In Shusaku Iida, José Meseguer, and Kazuhiro Ogata, editors, Specification, Algebra, and Software. Essays Dedicated to Kokichi Futatsugi, number 8373 in Lecture Notes in Computer Science, pages 441–464. Springer, 2014.

226. Anne Elisabeth Haxthausen. Automated Generation of Formal Safety Conditions from Railway Interlocking Tables. International Journal on Software Tools for Technology Transfer (STTT), Special Issue on Formal Methods for Railway Control Systems, 16(6):713–726, 2014.

227. Anne Elisabeth Haxthausen, Marie Le Bliguet, and Andreas A. Kjær. Modelling and Verification of Relay Interlocking Systems. In 15th Monterey Workshop: Foundations of Computer Software, Future Trends and Techniques for Development, pages 47–55, 2008. Invited paper.

228. Anne Elisabeth Haxthausen, Marie Le Bliguet, and Andreas A. Kjær. Modelling and Verification of Relay Interlocking Systems. In Christine Choppy and Oleg Sokolsky, editors, Foundations of Computer Software, Future Trends and Techniques for Development, number 6028 in Lecture Notes in Computer Science. Springer, 2010. Invited paper. Extended version of [227].

229. Anne Elisabeth Haxthausen and Chris W. George. A Concurrency Case Study Using RAISE. In Proceedings of FME'93: Industrial Strength Formal Methods, volume 670 of Lecture Notes in Computer Science, pages 367–387. Springer, 1993.

230. Anne Elisabeth Haxthausen, Chris W. George, and Marko Schütz-Schmuck. Specification and Proof of the Mondex Electronic Purse. In Proceedings of 1st Asian Working Conference on Verified Software (AWCVS 2006), Macao. UNU-IIST, Report No. 347, 2006.

231. Anne Elisabeth Haxthausen, Andreas A. Kjær, and Marie Le Bliguet. Formal Development of a Tool for Automated Modelling and Verification of Relay Interlocking Systems. In 17th International Symposium on Formal Methods (FM 2011), number 6664 in Lecture Notes in Computer Science, pages 118–132. Springer, 2011.

232. Anne Elisabeth Haxthausen, Hoang Nga Nguyen, and Markus Roggenbach. Comparing Formal Verification Approaches of Interlocking Systems. In Thierry Lecomte, Ralf Pinger, and Alexander Romanovsky, editors, Reliability, Safety, and Security of Railway Systems. Modelling, Analysis, Verification, and Certification: First International Conference, RSSRail Proceedings, pages 160–177. Springer International Publishing, 2016.

233. Anne Elisabeth Haxthausen, Jan Storbank Pedersen, and Søren Prehn. RAISE: a Product Supporting Industrial Use of Formal Methods. Technique et Science Informatiques, 12(3):319–346, 1993.

234. Anne Elisabeth Haxthausen and Jan Peleska. Formal Methods for the Specification and Verification of Distributed Railway Control Systems: From Algebraic Specifications to Distributed Hybrid Real-Time Systems. In Forms '99 - Formale Techniken für die Eisenbahnsicherung Fortschritt-Berichte VDI, Reihe 12, Nr. 436, pages 263–271. VDI-Verlag, Düsseldorf, 2000.

235. Anne Elisabeth Haxthausen and Jan Peleska. A Domain Specific Language for Railway Control Systems. In Proceedings of the Sixth Biennial World Conference on Integrated Design and Process Technology (IDPT-2002), Pasadena, California, pages 23–28, June 23-28 2002.

236. Anne Elisabeth Haxthausen and Jan Peleska. Automatic Verification, Validation and Test for Railway Control Systems based on Domain-Specific Descriptions. In Proceedings of the 10th IFAC Symposium on Control in Transportation Systems. Elsevier Science Ltd, Oxford, 2003. ISBN 0-08-044059-2.

237. Anne Elisabeth Haxthausen and Jan Peleska. Generation of Executable Railway Control Components from Domain-Specific Descriptions. In Proceedings of the Symposium on Formal Methods for Railway Operation and Control Systems (FORMS 2003), pages 83–90. L'Harmattan Hongrie, 2003.

238. Anne Elisabeth Haxthausen and Jan Peleska. A Domain-oriented, Model-based Approach for Construction and Verification of Railway Control Systems. In Cliff B. Jones, Zhiming Liu, and Jim Woodcock, editors, Formal Methods and Hybrid Real-Time Systems: Essays in Honour of Dines Bjørner and Zhou Chaochen on Occasion of their 70th Birthdays, number 4700 in Lecture Notes in Computer Science, pages 320–348. Springer, 2007. Invited paper.

239. Anne Elisabeth Haxthausen and Jan Peleska. Efficient Development and Verification of Safe Railway Control Software. In Cacilie Reinhardt and Klaus Shroeder, editors, Railways: Types, Design and Safety Issues, pages 127–148. Nova Science Publishers, Inc., 2013.

240. Anne Elisabeth Haxthausen and Jan Peleska. Model-checking and Model-based Testing in the Railway Domain. In Formal Modeling and Verification of Cyber-Physical Systems, pages 82–121. Springer Fachmedien Wiesbaden, 2015.

241. Anne Elisabeth Haxthausen, Jan Peleska, and Sebastian Kinder. A formal approach for the construction and and verification of railway control systems. Formal Aspects of Computing, 23:191–219, 2011.

242. Anne Elisabeth Haxthausen, Jan Peleska, and Sebastian Kinder. A Formal Approach for the Construction and Verification of Railway Control Systems. Formal Aspects of Computing, online first 2009. Special issue in Honour of Dines Bjørner and Zhou Chaochen on Occasion of their 70th Birthdays.

243. Anne Elisabeth Haxthausen and Xia Yong. Linking DC together with TRSL. In IFM 2000 2nd Int. Conf. on Integrated Formal Methods, volume 1945 of LNCS, pages 25–44. Springer, 2000.

244. Anders Hejlsberg, Scott Wiltamuth, and Peter Golde. The C# Programming Language. Microsoft .NET Development Series. Addison-Wesley, USA, October 2003. 672 page, ISBN 0321154916.

245. Martin C. Henson, Steve Reeves, and Jonathan P. Bowen. Z Logic and its Consequences. Computing and Informatics, 22(1–2), 2003.

246. Jaakko Hintikka, editor. The Philosophy of Mathematics. Oxford University Press, 1969. Includes essays by E.W. Beth, Leon Henkin, Raymond M. Smullyan, Georg Kreisel, Solomon Feferman, Kurt Gödel, Hartley Rogers Jr., Abraham Robinson and Alfred Tarski.

247. Charles Anthony Richard Hoare and Ji Feng He. Unifying Theories of Programming. Prentice Hall, 1997.

248. Charles Anthony Richard Hoare. Notes on Data Structuring. In [137], pages 83–174, 1972.

249. Charles Anthony Richard Hoare. Communicating Sequential Processes. Communications of the ACM, 21(8), Aug. 1978.

250. Charles Anthony Richard Hoare. Communicating Sequential Processes. C.A.R. Hoare Series in Computer Science. Prentice-Hall International, 1985. Published electronically: usingcsp.com/cspbook.pdf (2004).

251. B.D. Holdt-Jørgensen and S. Prehn. Using Formal Methods for Developing Critical Programs in Ada. In Proceedings of Ada in AEROSPACE '90. EUROSPACE, 1991.

252. Gerard J. Holzmann. The SPIN Model Checker, Primer and Reference Manual. Addison-Wesley, Reading, Massachusetts, 2003.

253. Ted Honderich. The Oxford Companion to Philosophy. Oxford University Press, England, 1995.

254. Lloyd Humberstone. On a conservative extension argument of Dana Scott. Logic Journal of the IGPL, 19(1):241–288, February 2011.

255. V. Daniel Hunt. Process Mapping: How to Reengineer Your Business Processes. John Wiley & Sons, Inc., New York, USA, 1996.

256. IEEE Computer Society. IEEE–STD 610.12-1990: Standard Glossary of Software Engineering Terminology. Technical report, IEEE, Washington, DC 20036-1992, USA. 1990.

257. ContentGuard Inc. XrML: Extensible rights Markup Language. http://www.xrml.org, 2000.

258. D. C. Ince. An Introduction to Discrete Mathematics, Formal System Specification and Z. Oxford Applied Mathematics and Computing Science Series. Oxford University Press, 2nd edition, 1993.

259. Darrell C. Ince. An Introduction to Discrete Mathematics and Formal System Specification. Oxford Applied Mathematics and Computing Science Series. Oxford University Press, UK, 1988.

260. ITU-T. CCITT Recommendation Z.120: Message Sequence Chart (MSC), 1992, 1996, 1999.

261. J. Mike Jacka and Paulette J. Keller. Business Process Mapping: Improving Customer Satisfaction. John Wiley & Sons, Inc., New York, USA, 2002.

262. Daniel Jackson. Software Abstractions: Logic, Language, and Analysis. The MIT Press, Cambridge, Mass., USA, April 2006. ISBN 0-262-10114-9.

263. Michael A. Jackson. Software Requirements & Specifications: a lexicon of practice, principles and prejudices. ACM Press. Addison-Wesley, Reading, England, 1995.

264. Michael A. Jackson. Problem Frames — Analyzing and Structuring Software Development Problems. ACM Press, Addison-Wesley, England, 2001.

265. Ivar Jacobson, Grady Booch, and James Rumbaugh. The Unified Software Development Process. Object Technology Series. Addison-Wesley, Massachusetts, USA, 1999.

266. James J. Buckley and Esfanidar Eslami. An Introduction to Fuzzy Logic and Fuzzy Sets. Springer, 2002.

267. K. Jensen and N. Wirth. Pascal User Manual and Report, volume 18 of LNCS. Springer, 1976.

268. Cliff B. Jones, Ian Hayes, and Michael A. Jackson. Deriving Specfications for Systems That Are Connected to the Physical World. In Cliff Jones, Zhiming Liu, and James Woodcock, editors, Formal Methods and Hybrid Real-Time Systems: Essays in Honour of Dines Bjørner and Zhou Chaochen on the Occasion of Their 70th Birthdays, volume 4700 of Lecture Notes in Computer Science, pages 364–390. Springer, 2007.

269. J.W. Backus, F.L. Bauer, J.Green, C. Katz, J. McCarthy, P. Naur, A.J. Perlis, H. Rutishauser, K. Samelson,B. Vauquois, J.H. Wegstein, A. van Wijngaarden and M. Woodger. Revised Report on the Algorithmic Language Algol 60 – edited by P. Naur. The Computer Journal, 5(4):349367, 1963.

270. Matt Kaufmann, Panagiotis Manolios, and J Strother Moore. Computer-Aided Reasoning: An Approach. Kluwer Academic Publishers, June 2000.

271. Andrew Kennedy. Programming languages and dimensions. PhD thesis, University of Cambridge, Computer Laboratory, April 1996. 149 pages: cl.cam.ac.uk/techreports/UCAM-CL-TR-391.pdf. Technical report UCAM-CL-TR-391, ISSN 1476-298.

272. Dieter Klaua. Über einen Ansatz zur mehrwertigen Mengenlehre. Monatsbreicht, 7:859867, 1965.

273. Dieter Klaus. The Logic of Fuzzy Set Theory: A Historical Approach, page 22 pages. Springer, Heidelberg Germany, 2014. www.researchgate.net/publication/266736510_The_Logic_of_Fuzzy_Set_Theory_A_Historical_Approach.

274. R.H. Koenen, J. Lacy, M. Mackay, and S. Mitchell. The long march to interoperable digital rights management. Proceedings of the IEEE, 92(6):883–897, June 2004.

275. Leslie Lamport. Specifying Systems. Addison-Wesley, Boston, Mass., USA, 2002.

276. Søren Lauesen. Software Requirements - Styles and Techniques. Addison-Wesley, UK, 2002.

277. J.A. Leighton. On Continuity and Discreteness. The Journal of Philosophy, Psychology and Scientific Methods, 7(9):231238, April 1910. doi.org/10.2307/2011222.

278. Shuguang Li, Qing Jiang, and Chris George. Combining case-based and model-based reasoning: a formal specification. In 7th Asia-Pacific Software Engineering Conference (APSEC 2000), 5-8 December 2000, Singapore, pages 416–420. IEEE Computer Society, 2000.

279. Morten P. Lindegaard and Anne Elisabeth Haxthausen. Proof Support for RAISE – by a Reuse Approach based on Institutions. In Proceedings of AMAST'04, number 3116 in Lecture Notes in Computer Science, pages 319–333. Springer, 2004.

280. Morten P. Lindegaard, Peter Viuf, and Anne Elisabeth Haxthausen. Modelling Railway Interlocking Systems. In E. Schnieder and U. Becker, editors, Proceedings of the 9th IFAC Symposium on Control in Transportation Systems 2000, June 13-15, 2000, Braunschweig, Germany, pages 211–217, 2000.

281. W. Little, H.W. Fowler, J. Coulson, and C.T. Onions. The Shorter Oxford English Dictionary on Historical Principles. Clarendon Press, Oxford, England, 1973, 1987. Two vols.

282. Michael J. Loux. Metaphysics, a Contemporary Introduction. Routledge Contemporary Introductions to Philosophy. Routledge, London and New York, 1998 (2nd ed., 2020).

283. IPR Systems Pty Ltd. Open Digital Rights Language (ODRL). http://odrl.net, 2001.

284. E.C. Luschei. The Logical Systems of Leśniewksi. North Holland, Amsterdam, The Netherlands, 1962.

285. Gordon E. Lyon. Information Technology: A Quick-Reference List of Organizations and Standards for Digital Rights Management. NIST Special Publication 500-241, National Institute of Standards and Technology, Technology Administration, U.S. Department of Commerce, Oct 2002.

286. Hugo Daniel Macedo, Alessandro Fantechi, and Anne E. Haxthausen. Compositional model checking of interlocking systems for lines with multiple stations. In Clark Barrett, Misty Davies, and Temesghen Kahsai, editors, NASA Formal Methods: 9th International Symposium, NFM 2017, Proceedings, volume 10227 of Lecture Notes in Computer Science, pages 146–162. Springer International Publishing, 2017.

287. Penelope Maddy. Realism in Mathematics. Oxford University Press, 1990.

288. Penelope Maddy. Naturalism in Mathematics. Oxford University Press, 1997.

289. Tom Maibaum. Conservative Extensions, Interpretations Between Theories and All That. In Michel Bidoit and Max Dauchet, editors, TAPSOFT'97: Theory and Practice of Software Development, volume 1214 of LNCS, pages 40–66, 1997.

290. E. Manero. RAISE and ESA Software Lifecycle. In Proceedings of Ada in AEROSPACE '91. EUROSPACE, 1992.

291. Abraham Maslow. A Theory of Human Motivation. Psychological Review, 50(4):370–96, 1943. http://psychclassics.yorku.ca/Maslow/motivation.htm.

292. Abraham Maslow. Motivation and Personality. Harper and Row Publishers, 3rd ed., 1954.

293. ANSI X3.53-1976. The PL/I programming language. Technical report, American National Standards Institute, Standards on Computers and Information Processing, 1976.

294. John McCarthy. Recursive Functions of Symbolic Expressions and Their Computation by Machines, Part I. Communications of the ACM, 3(4):184–195, 1960.

295. John McCarthy. Towards a Mathematical Science of Computation. In C.M. Popplewell, editor, IFIP World Congress Proceedings, pages 21–28, 1962.

296. John McCarthy. A Basis for a Mathematical Theory of Computation. In Computer Programming and Formal Systems. North-Holland Publ.Co., Amsterdam, 1963.

297. John McCarthy, Paul W. Abrahams, Daniel J. Edwards, Timothy P. Hart, and Michael I. Levin. LISP 1.5 Programmer's Manual. The MIT Press, Cambridge, Mass., 1962.

298. Theodore McCombs. Maude 2,0 Primer. Department of Computer Science, University of Illinois and Urbana-Champaign, Urbana-Champaign, Ill., USA, August 2003.

299. J. M. E. McTaggart. The Unreality of Time. Mind, 18(68):457–84, October 1908. New Series. See also: [333].

300. D.H. Mellor. Things and Causes in Spacetime. British Journal for the Philosophy of Science, 31:282–288, 1980.

301. Merriam Webster Staff. Online Dictionary: http://www.m-w.com/home.htm, 2004. Merriam–Webster, Inc., Springfield, MA 01102, USA.

302. Stephan Merz. On the Logic of TLA+. Computing and Informatics, 22(1–2), 2003.

303. Jacob Mey. Pragmatics: An Introduction. Blackwell Publishers, 13 January, 2001. Paperback.

304. S. Michiels, K. Verslype, W. Joosen, and B. De Decker. Towards a Software Architecture for DRM. In Proceedings of the Fifth ACM Workshop on Digital Rights Management (DRM'05), pages 65–74, Alexandria, Virginia, USA, Nov 2005.

305. R.E. Milne. Transforming Axioms for Data Types into Sequential Programs. In Proceedings of 4th Refinement Workshop. Springer, 1991.

306. R.E. Milne. The Formal Basis for the RAISE Specification Language. In Semantics of Specification Languages, Workshops in Computing. Springer, 1993.

307. Till Mossakowski, Anne Elisabeth Haxthausen, Don Sanella, and Andrzej Tarlecki. CASL — The Common Algebraic Specification Language: Semantics and Proof Theory. Computing and Informatics, 22(1–2), 2003.

308. D. Mulligan and A. Burstein. Implementing copyright limitations in rights expression languages. In Proc. of 2002 ACM Workshop on Digital Rights Management, volume 2696 of Lecture Notes in Computer Science, pages 137–154. Springer, 2002.

309. Deirdre K. Mulligan, John Han, and Aaron J. Burstein. How DRM-Based Content Delivery Systems Disrupt Expectations of "Personal Use". In Proc. of The 3rd International Workshop on Digital Rights Management, pages 77–89, Washington DC, USA, 2003. ACM.

310. Greg Nelson, editor. Systems Programming in Modula 3. Innovative Technologies. Prentice-Hall, Englewood Cliffs, New Jersey, USA, 1991.

311. Mogens Nielsen, Klaus Havelund, Kim Ritter Wagner, and Chris George. The RAISE language, method and tools. In Robin E. Bloomfield, Lynn S. Marshall, and Roger B. Jones, editors, VDM '88, VDM - The Way Ahead, 2nd VDM-Europe Symposium, Dublin, Ireland, September 11-16, 1988, Proceedings, volume 328 of Lecture Notes in Computer Science, pages 376–405. Springer, 1988.

312. Mogens Nielsen, Klaus Havelund, Kim Ritter Wagner, and Chris George. The RAISE language, method and tools. Formal Aspects of Computing, 1(1):85–114, 1989.

313. Tobias Nipkow, Lawrence C. Paulson, and Markus Wenzel. Isabelle/HOL, A Proof Assistant for Higher-Order Logic, volume 2283 of Lecture Notes in Computer Science. Springer, 2002.
314. O. Oest. VDM From Research to Practice. In H.-J. Kugler, editor, Information Processing '86, pages 527–533. IFIP World Congress Proceedings, North-Holland Publ.Co., Amsterdam, 1986.
315. Ernst-Rüdiger Olderog and Henning Dierks. Real-Time Systems: Formal Specification and Automatic Verification. Cambridge University Press, UK, 2008.
316. Ernst Rüdiger Olderog, Anders Peter Ravn, and Rafael Wisniewski. Linking Discrete and Continuous Models, Applied to Traffic Maneuvers. In Jonathan Bowen, Michael Hinchey, and Ernst Rüdiger Olderog, editors, BCS FACS – ProCoS Workshop on Provably Correct Systems, Lecture Notes in Computer Science. Springer, 2016.
317. Sam Owre, Natarajan Shankar, John M. Rushby, and David W. J. Stringer-Calvert. PVS Prover Guide. Computer Science Laboratory, SRI International, Menlo Park, CA, September 1999.
318. Charles Sanders Peirce. Pragmatism as a Principle and Method of right thinking: The 1903 Harvard Lectures on Pragmatism. State University of New York Press, and Cornell Univiversity Press, 14 July 1997.
319. Jan Peleska, Alexander Baer, and Anne E. Haxthausen. Towards Domain-Specific Formal Specification Languages for Railway Control Systems. In E. Schnieder and U. Becker, editors, Proceedings of the 9th IFAC Symposium on Control in Transportation Systems 2000, June 13-15, 2000, Braunschweig, Germany, pages 147–152, 2000.
320. Jan Peleska, Johannes Feuser, and Anne Elisabeth Haxthausen. The Model-Driven openETCS Paradigm for Secure, Safe and Certifiable Train Control Systems. In Francesco Flammini, editor, Railway Safety, Reliability and Security: Technologies and System Engineering, pages 22–52. IGI Global, 2012.
321. Jan Peleska, Daniel Große, Anne Elisabeth Haxthausen, and Rolf Drechsler. Automated Verification for Train Control Systems. In Proceedings of Formal Methods for Automation and Safety in Railway and Automotive Systems (FORMS/FORMAT 2004), Braunschweig, Germany, 2004.
322. Jan Peleska and Anne Elisabeth Haxthausen. Object Code Verification for Safety-Critical Railway Control Systems. In Proceedings of Formal Methods for Automation and Safety in Railway and Automotive Systems (FORMS/FORMAT 2007), Braunschweig, Germany. GZVB e.V., 2007. ISBN 13:978-3-937655-09-3.
323. Jan Peleska, Niklas Krafczyk, Anne Elisabeth Haxthausen, and Ralf Pinger. Efficient data validation for geographical interlocking systems. In Reliability, Safety, and Security of Railway Systems. Modelling, Analysis, Verification, and Certification - Third International Conference, RSSRail 2019, Proceedings, volume 11495 of Lecture Notes in Computer Science, pages 142–158, 2019.
324. R.C. Penner. Discrete Mathematics, Proof Techniques and Mathematical Structures. World Scientific Publishing Co., Singapore, 1 Jan 1999. ISBN 9810240880.
325. Juan Ignacio Perna and Chris George. Model checking RAISE applicative specifications. In Fifth IEEE International Conference on Software Engineering and Formal Methods (SEFM 2007), 10-14 September 2007, London, England, UK, pages 257–268. IEEE Computer Society, 2007.
326. Juan Ignacio Perna and Chris George. Model checking RAISE applicative specifications. Formal Aspects of Computing, 25(3):365–388, 2013.
327. Christopher Peterson and Martin E.P. Seligman. Character strengths and virtues: A handbook and classification. Oxford University Press, 2004.
328. Carl Adam Petri. Kommunikation mit Automaten. Bonn: Institut für Instrumentelle Mathematik, Schriften des IIM Nr. 2, 1962.
329. Chia-Yi Tony Pi. Mereology in Event Semantics. Phd thesis, McGill University, Montreal, Canada, August 1999.
330. Benjamin Pierce. Types and Programming Languages. The MIT Press, 2002.
331. Mike Piff. Discrete Mathematics, An Introduction for Software Engineers. Cambridge University Press, Cambridge, UK, 27 Jun 1991. ISBN 0521386225.
332. K. Pohl, G. Bockle, and F. van der Linden. Software Product Line Engineering. Springer, Berlin, Heidelberg, New York, 2005.
333. Robin Le Poidevin and Murray MacBeath, editors. The Philosophy of Time. Oxford University Press, 1993.
334. Arthur Prior. Changes in Events and Changes in Things, chapter in [333]. Oxford University Press, 1993.
335. Arthur N. Prior. Logic and the Basis of Ethics. Clarendon Press, Oxford, UK, 1949.
336. Arthur N. Prior. Formal Logic. Clarendon Press, Oxford, UK, 1955.
337. Arthur N. Prior. Time and Modality. Oxford University Press, Oxford, UK, 1957.
338. Arthur N. Prior. Past, Present and Future. Clarendon Press, Oxford, UK, 1967.
339. Arthur N. Prior. Papers on Time and Tense. Clarendon Press, Oxford, UK, 1968.
340. Riccardo Pucella and Vicky Weissman. A Logic for Reasoning about Digital Rights. In Proc. of the 15th IEEE Computer Security Foundations Workshop (CSFW'02), pages 282–294. IEEE Computer Society Press, 2002.

341. Riccardo Pucella and Vicky Weissman. A Formal Foundation for ODRL. In Proc. of the Workshop on Issues in the Theory of Security (WIST'04), 2004.
342. A. Quinton. Objects and Events. Mind, 88:197–214, 1979.
343. Wolfgang Reisig. Petri Nets: An Introduction, volume 4 of EATCS Monographs in Theoretical Computer Science. Springer, May 1985.
344. Wolfgang Reisig. A Primer in Petri Net Design. Springer, March 1992. 120 pages.
345. Wolfgang Reisig. The Expressive Power of Abstract State Machines. Computing and Informatics, 22(1–2), 2003.
346. Wolfgang Reisig. The Expressive Power of Abstract State Machines. Computing and Informatics, 22(1–2), 2003. This paper is one of a series: [117, 148, 307, 188, 302, 245] appearing in a double issue of the same journal: Logics of Specification Languages — edited by Dines Bjørner.
347. Wolfgang Reisig. Petrinetze: Modellierungstechnik, Analysemethoden, Fallstudien. Leitfäden der Informatik. Vieweg+Teubner, 1st edition, 15 June 2010. 248 pages; ISBN 978-3-8348-1290-2.
348. Wolfgang Reisig. Understanding Petri Nets Modeling Techniques, Analysis Methods, Case Studies. Springer, 2013. 230+XXVII pages, 145 illus.
349. John C. Reynolds. The Semantics of Programming Languages. Cambridge University Press, 1999.
350. Gerald Rochelle. Behind time: The incoherence of time and McTaggart's atemporal replacement. Avebury series in philosophy. Ashgate, Brookfield, Vt., USA, 1998. vii + 221 pages.
351. Hartley R. Rogers. Theory of Recursive Functions and Effective Computability. McGraw-Hill, 1967.
352. A. W. Roscoe. Theory and Practice of Concurrency. C.A.R. Hoare Series in Computer Science. Prentice-Hall, 1997. http://www.comlab.ox.ac.uk/people/bill.roscoe/publications/68b.pdf.
353. Bertrand Russell. Introduction to Mathematical Philosophy. George Allen and Unwin, London, 1919.
354. Pamela Samuelson. Digital rights management {and, or, vs.} the law. Communications of ACM, 46(4):41–45, Apr 2003.
355. Donald Sannella and Andrzej Tarlecki. Foundations of Algebraic Semantcs and Formal Software Development. Monographs in Theoretical Computer Science. Springer, Heidelberg, 2012.
356. David A. Schmidt. Denotational Semantics: a Methodology for Language Development. Allyn & Bacon, 1986.
357. Steve Schneider. Concurrent and Real-time Systems — The CSP Approach. Worldwide Series in Computer Science. John Wiley & Sons, Chichester, England, January 2000.
358. Joseph R. Schoenfeld. Mathematical Logic. Addison-Wesley Publishing Company, 1967. (On Conservative Extensions, pp 55-56).
359. Peter Sestoft. Java Precisely. The MIT Press, 25 July 2002.
360. Charles Simonyi. The Death of Computer Languages, the Birth of Intentional Programming. In NATO Science Committee Informatics Conference, 1995. scholar.google.com/-url?sa=U&q=www.cs.wpi.edu/~gpollice/cs509-s04/Readings/simonyi95death.pdf.
361. Charles Simonyi. The Future is Intentional. Computer, 32(5):56–57, May 1999.
362. Charles Simonyi. Intentional Programming: Asymptotic Fun? In Position Paper, SDP Workshop, Vanderbilt University, December, 2001. http://scholar.google.com/url?sa=U&q=http://www.nitrd.gov/-subcommittee/sdp/vanderbilt/position_papers/simonyi.pdf.
363. Charles Simonyi, Magnus Christerson, and Shane Clifford. Intentional Software. In Proceedings of the 21st Annual ACM SIGPLAN Conference on Object-oriented Programming Systems, Languages, and Applications. OOPSLA '06, New York, NY, USA: ACM: 451464, 2006.
364. Jens Ulrik Skakkebæk, Anders Peter Ravn, Hans Rischel, and Chao Chen Zhou. Specification of embedded, real-time systems. In Proceedings of 1992 Euromicro Workshop on Real-Time Systems, pages 116–121. IEEE Computer Society Press, 1992.
365. Barry Smith. Mereotopology: A Theory of Parts and Boundaries. Data and Knowledge Engineering, 20:287–303, 1996.
366. Kai Sørlander. Det Uomgængelige – Filosofiske Deduktioner [The Inevitable – Philosophical Deductions, with a foreword by Georg Henrik von Wright]. Munksgaard · Rosinante, 1994. 168 pages.
367. Kai Sørlander. Under Evighedens Synsvinkel [Under the viewpoint of eternity]. Munksgaard · Rosinante, 1997. 200 pages.
368. Kai Sørlander. Den Endegyldige Sandhed [The Final Truth]. Rosinante, 2002. 187 pages.
369. Kai Sørlander. Indføring i Filosofien [Introduction to The Philosophy]. Informations Forlag, 2016. 233 pages.
370. Donald F. Stanat and David F. McAllister. Discrete Mathematics for Computer Science. Prentice-Hall, Inc., 1977.
371. T. B. Steel, editor. Formal Language Description Languages for Computer Programming, IFIP TC-2 Working Conference, 2964, Baden. North-Holland Publ.Co., Amsterdam, 1966.
372. Steven Weintraub. Galois Theory. Springer, 2009.
373. Robert Tennent. The Semantics of Programming Languages. Prentice-Hall Intl., 1997.
374. Johan van Benthem. The Logic of Time, volume 156 of Synthese Library: Studies in Epistemology, Logic, Methhodology, and Philosophy of Science (Editor: Jaakko Hintika). Kluwer Academic Publishers, Dordrecht, The Netherlands, second edition, 1983, 1991.

375. F. Van der Rhee, H.R. Van Nauta Lemke, and J.G. Dukman. Knowledge based fuzzy control of systems. IEEE Trans. Autom. Control, 35(2):148–155, February 1990.
376. J. van Heijenoort. From Frege to Gödel — a Source Book in Mathematical Logic. Harvard University Press, 1967.
377. Axel van Lamsweerde. Requirements Engineering: From System Goals to UML Models to Software Specifications. Wiley, 2009.
378. Abigail Parisaca Vargas, Ana Gabriela Garis, Silvia Lizeth Tapia Tarifa, and Chris George. Model checking LTL formulae in RAISE with FDR. In Michael Leuschel and Heike Wehrheim, editors, Integrated Formal Methods, 7th International Conference, IFM 2009, Düsseldorf, Germany, February 16-19, 2009. Proceedings, volume 5423 of Lecture Notes in Computer Science, pages 231–245. Springer, 2009.
379. Abigail Parisaca Vargas, Silvia Lizeth Tapia Tarifa, and Chris George. A translation from RSL to CSP. In M. Cecilia Bastarrica and Mauricio Solar, editors, XXVII International Conference of the Chilean Computer Science Society (SCCC 2008), 10-14 November 2008, Punta Arenas, Chile, pages 119–126. IEEE Computer Society, 2008.
380. Achille C. Varzi. On the Boundary between Mereology and Topology, pages 419–438. Hölder-Pichler-Tempsky, Vienna, 1994.
381. Achille C. Varzi. Spatial Reasoning in a Holey[238] World, volume 728 of Lecture Notes in Artificial Intelligence, pages 326–336. Springer, 1994.
382. Linh H. Vu, Anne E. Haxthausen, and Jan Peleska. A domain-specific language for generic interlocking models and their properties. In Alessandro Fantechi, Thierry Lecomte, and Alexander Romanovsky, editors, Reliability, Safety, and Security of Railway Systems. Modelling, Analysis, Verification, and Certification: Second International Conference, RSSRail 2017, Pistoia, Italy, November 14-16, 2017, Proceedings, pages 99–115, Cham, 2017. Springer.
383. Linh H. Vu, Anne Elisabeth Haxthausen, and Jan Peleska. A Domain-Specific Language for Railway Interlocking Systems. In Eckehard Schnieder and Géza Tarnai, editors, FORMS/FORMAT 2014 - 10th Symposium on Formal Methods for Automation and Safety in Railway and Automotive Systems, pages 200–209. Institute for Traffic Safety and Automation Engineering, Technische Universität Braunschweig, 2014.
384. Linh H. Vu, Anne Elisabeth Haxthausen, and Jan Peleska. Formal Modeling and Verification of Interlocking Systems Featuring Sequential Release. In Third International Workshop on Formal Techniques for Safety-Critical Systems (FTSCS 2014) Preliminary Proceedings, pages 58–73, 2014.
385. Linh H. Vu, Anne Elisabeth Haxthausen, and Jan Peleska. Formal Verification of the Danish Railway Interlocking Systems. In Marieke Huisman and Jaco van de Pol, editors, Pre-proceedings of 14th International Workshop on Automated Verification of Critical Systems (AVoCS 2014), CTIT Workshop Proceedings Series WP 14-01, pages 257–258. University of Twente, 2014.
386. Linh H. Vu, Anne Elisabeth Haxthausen, and Jan Peleska. Formal Modeling and Verification of Interlocking Systems Featuring Sequential Release. In Formal Techniques for Safety-Critical Systems, volume 476 of Communications in Computer and Information Science, pages 223–238. Springer, 2015. Revised version of [384].
387. Linh H. Vu, Anne Elisabeth Haxthausen, and Jan Peleska. Formal Modeling and Verification of Interlocking Systems Featuring Sequential Release. Science of Computer Programming, 133, Part 2, 2016. http://dx.doi.org/10.1016/j.scico.2016.05.010.
388. George Wilson and Samuel Shpall. Action. In Edward N. Zalta, editor, The Stanford Encyclopedia of Philosophy. Stanford University, summer 2012 edition, 2012.
389. Jeanette M. Wing. Computational thinking. Communications of the ACM, 49(3):33–35, 2006.
390. G. Winskel. The Formal Semantics of Programming Languages. The MIT Press, Cambridge, Mass., USA, 1993.
391. N. Wirth. A Generalization of ALGOL. Communications of the ACM, 6:547–554, 1963.
392. N. Wirth. The Programming Language Pascal. Acta Informatica, 1(1):35–63, 1971.
393. N. Wirth. Programming in Modula-2. Springer, Heidelberg, Germany, 1982.
394. N. Wirth. From Modula to Oberon. Software — Practice and Experience, 18:661–670, 1988.
395. N. Wirth. The Programming Language Oberon. Software — Practice and Experience, 18:671–690, 1988.
396. N. Wirth and J. Gutknecht. The Oberon System. Software — Practice and Experience, 19(9):857–893, 1989.
397. James Charles Paul Woodcock and James Davies. Using Z: Specification, Proof and Refinement. Prentice Hall International Series in Computer Science, 1996.
398. JianWen Xiang and Dines Bjørner. The Electronic Media Industry: A Domain Analysis and a License Language. Technical note, JAIST, School of Information Science, 1-1, Asahidai, Tatsunokuchi, Nomi, Ishikawa, Japan 923-1292, Summer 2006.
399. WanLing Xie, ShuangQing Xiang, and HuiBiao Zhu. A UTP approach for rTiMo. Formal Aspects of Computing, 30(6):713–738, 2018.

---

[238] holey: something full of holes

400. Xie WanLing, Zhu HuiBiao, and Xu QiWen. A process calculus BigrTiMo of mobile systems and its formal semantics. Formal Aspects of Computing, 33(2):207–249, 2021.
401. Wang Yi. A Calculus of Real Time Systems. PhD thesis, Department of Computer Sciences, Chalmers University of Technology, Göteborg, Sweden, 1991.
402. Xia Yong and Chris George. An operational semantics for timed RAISE. In Jim Woodcock, Jim Davies, and Jeannette M. Wing, editors, Proceedings of Formal Methods World Congress FM'99, volume 1709 of Lecture Notes in Computer Science, pages 1008–1027. Springer, 1999.
403. Lotfi A. Zadeh. Fuzzy sets. Information and Control, 8(3):338–353, 1965. cs.berkeley.edu/ zadeh/papers/Fuzzy Sets-Information and Control-1965.pdf Archived 2015-08-13 at the Wayback Machine.
404. Chao Chen Zhou and Michael R. Hansen. Duration Calculus: A Formal Approach to Real-time Systems. Monographs in Theoretical Computer Science. An EATCS Series. Springer, 2004.
405. E. Zierau. Use of the Formal Method RAISE in Practice. In Proceedings of SAFECOMP '94, 1994.

Appendix A
A PIPELINES DOMAIN – ENDURANTS

*In this appendix we present an example description of the endurants of a domain of pipelines. Thus the example illustrates major aspects of a domain of conjoins. The various sections slavishly follow the steps of domain analyser & describer: endurants, Sect. **A.1**, unique identifiers, Sect. **A.2**, mereologies, Sect. **A.3**, and attributes. Sect. **A.4**.*

A.1 Solids and Fluids

A.1.1 Flow Net Parts

The concept of a flow net[1] is illustrated in, for example, oil *pipelines*. See Figure **A**.1.

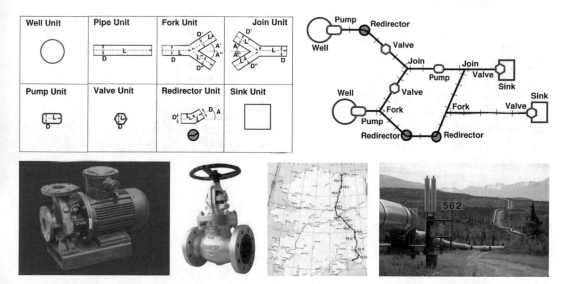

Fig. A.1 Miscellaneous Pipeline Pictures

Top row: oil unit graphics; diagram of a simple oil pipeline. Bottom row: a pump; a valve; map of the Trans-Alaska Pipeline System (TAPS); photo of TAPS.

---

[1] – of conjoined parts and fluids

© The Author(s), under exclusive license to Springer Nature Switzerland AG 2021
D. Bjørner, *Domain Science and Engineering*, Monographs in Theoretical Computer Science. An EATCS Series,
https://doi.org/10.1007/978-3-030-73484-8

A.1.1.1 Narrative

502 There is the pipeline system pl:PL.
503 From a pipeline system we choose to observe a pipeline aggregate of conjoined pipe elements, pla:PLA.
504 The pipeline aggregate of conjoined pipe elements is modelled here as a set of conjoined pipe elements, cps:CPs.

By a conjoined pipe element, pe:PE, we here mean

505 the conjoined pipe element, i.e., pe:PE,
from which we choose to observe
506 one fluid, m:M, here the oil.

A conjoined pipe element[2], 505, is either a

507 a well (a volume from which fluid is pumped),
508 a pump (which moves the fluids, (m:M), by mechanical action),
509 a pipe (along which fluid can move),
510 a valve (which is either fully open, or fully closed, or at some position in-between thus facilitating to a full degree or some partial degree, or hinder the flow of, in this case, oil),
511 a fork (which "diverts" [in this example] a single flow into two flows),
512 a join (which "merges" [in this example] two flows into a single flow), or
513 a sink (a volume into which fluid is "spilled".).

A.1.1.2 Formalisation

type
502. PL
503. PLA
504. cPEs = PE-set
505. PE == We|Pu|Pi|Va|Fo|Jo|Si
506. M
507. We :: Well
508. Pu :: Pump
509. Pi :: Pipe
510. Va :: Valve
511. Fo :: Fork
512. Jo :: Join
513. Si :: Sink
type
503. obs_PLA: PL → PLA
504. obs_cPEs: PLA → cPEs
506. obs_M: PE → M

A.1.2 Pipeline States

A.1.2.1 Narrative

514 Given a pipeline, pl:PL, we can calculate the set of all its pipe elements.

A.1.2.2 Formalisation

value
514. all_pipeline_units: PL → PE-set
514. all_pipeline_units(pl) ≡ obs_cPEs(obs_PLS(pl))

---

[2] We ignore *join-fork* and *redirect* units.

A.2 Unique Identifiers

515 There is a set of identifiers, UI.
516 Each pipe unit is endowed with such an identifier.
517 All such identifiers of pipe elements of a pipeline are distinct, i.e., unique: no two pipe elements are endowed with identical such identifiers.

type
515. UI
value
516. uid_PE: PE → UI
axiom
517. ∀ pl:PL ·
517.   ∀ pe_i,pe_j:PE ·
517.   {pe_i,pe_j}∈ all_pipeline_units(pl)
517.   ⇒ pe_i≠pe_i ≡ uid_PE(pe_i)≠uid_PE(pe_j)

A.3 Mereologies

A.3.1 The Pipeline Unit Mereology

Pipeline units serve to conduct fluids. The flow of these occur in only one direction: from so-called input to so-called output.

518 Wells have exactly one connection to an output unit.
519 Pipes, pumps, valves and redirectors have exactly one connection from an input unit and one connection to an output unit.
520 Forks have exactly one connection from an input unit and exactly two connections to distinct output units.
521 Joins have exactly two connections from distinct input units and one connection to an output unit.
522 Sinks have exactly one connection from an input unit.
523 Thus we model the mereology of a pipeline unit as a pair of disjoint sets of unique pipeline unit identifiers.

type
523 PM′=(UI-set×UI-set), PM={|(iuis,ouis):PM′·iuis ∩ ouis={}|}
value
523 mereo_PE: PE → PM

A.3.2 Partial Wellformedness of Pipelines, 0

The well-formedness inherent in narrative lines 518–522 are formalised:

axiom [Well–formedness of Pipeline Systems, PL (0)]
    ∀ pl:PL,pe:PE · pe ∈ all_pipeline_uits(pl) ⇒
        let (iuis,ouis)=mereo_PE(pe) **in**

```
                case (card iuis,card ouis) of
518                   (0,1) → is_We(pe),
519                   (1,1) → is_Pi(pe)∨is_Pu(pe)∨is_Va(pe),
520                   (1,2) → is_Fo(pe),
521                   (2,1) → is_Jo(pe),
522                   (1,0) → is_Si(pe), _ → false
                end end
```

A.3.3 Partial Well-formedness of Pipelines, 1

To express full well-formedness we need express that pipeline nets are acyclic. To do so we first define a function which calculates all routes in a net.

A.3.3.1 Shared Connectors

Two pipeline units, pe_i with unique identifier π_i, and pe_j with unique identifier π_j, that are connected, such that an outlet marked π_j of p_i "feeds into" inlet marked π_i of p_j, are said to **share** the connection (modeled by, e.g., $\{(\pi_i, \pi_j)\}$)

A.3.3.2 Routes

524 The observed pipeline units of a pipeline system define a number of routes (or pipelines):
Basis Clauses:
525 The null sequence, $\langle\rangle$, of no units is a route.
526 Any one pipeline unit, pe, of a pipeline system forms a route, $\langle pe\rangle$, of length one.
Inductive Clauses:
527 Let $r_i^\frown\langle pe_i\rangle$ and $\langle pe_j\rangle^\frown r_j$ be two routes of a pipeline system.
528 Let $pe_{i_{ui}}$ and $pe_{j_{ui}}$ be the unique identifiers pe_i, respectively pe_j.
529 If one of the output connectors of pe_i is $pe_{i_{ui}}$
530 and one of the input connectors of pe_j is $pe_{j_{ui}}$,
531 then $r_i^\frown\langle pe_i, pe_j\rangle^\frown r_j$ is a route of the pipeline system.
Extremal Clause:
532 Only such routes which can be formed by a finite number of applications of the clauses form a route.

```
type
524.  R = PE^ω
value
524   routes: PL →̃ R-infset
524   routes(ps) ≡
524      let cpes = pipeline_units(pl) in
525      let rs = {⟨⟩}
526          ∪ {⟨pe⟩|pe:PE•pe ∈ cpes} ∪
531          ∪ {ri⁀⟨pe_i⟩⁀⟨pe_j⟩⁀rj | pei,pej:PE • {pe_i,pe_j}⊆cpes
527              ∧ ri⁀⟨pe_i⟩,⟨pe_j⟩⁀rj:R • {ri⁀⟨pe_i⟩,⟨pe_j⟩⁀rj}⊆rs
528,529            ∧ pe_i_ui = uid_PE(pe_i) ∧ pe_i_ui ∈ xtr_oUOs(pe_i)
528,530            ∧ pe_j_ui = uid_PE(pe_j) ∧ pe_j_ui ∈ xtr_iUIs(pe_j)} in
```

532   rs **end end**

xtr_iUIs: PE → UI-set, xtr_iUIs(u) ≡ **let** (iuis,_)=mereo_PE(pe) **in** iuis **end**
xtr_oUIs: PE → UI-set, xtr_oUIs(u) ≡ **let** (_,ouis)=mereo_PE(pe) **in** ouis **end**

A.3.3.3 Wellformed Routes

533 The observed pipeline units of a pipeline system forms a net subject to the following constraints:

  a unit output connectors, if any, are connected to unit input connectors;
  b unit input connectors, if any, are connected to unit output connectors;
  c there are no cyclic routes;
  d nets has all their connectors connected, that is, "starts" with wells
  e and "ends" with sinks.

value
533. wf_Net: PL → **Bool**
533. wf_Net(pl) ≡
533.   **let** cpes = all_pipeline_units{pl} **in**
533.   ∀ pe:PE · pe ∈ cpes ⇒ **let** (iuis,ouis) = mereo_PE(pe) **in**
533.   **axiom** 518.–522.
533a.   ∧ ∀ pe_:UI·pe_ui ∈ iuis ⇒
533a.   ∃ pe′:PE·pe′≠pe∧pe′isin cpes∧uid_PE(pe′)=pe_ui∧pe_ui∈xtr_iUIs(pe′)
533b.   ∧ ∀ pe_ul:UI·pe_ui ∈ ouis ⇒
533b.   ∃ pe′:PE·pe′≠pe∧pe′isin cpes∧uid_PE(pe′)=pe_ui∧pe_ui∈xtr_oUIs(pe′)
533c.   ∧ ∀ r:R·r ∈ routes(pl) ⇒
533c.   ~∃ i,j:Nat·i≠j∧{i,j}∈ **inds** r∧r(i)=r(j)
533d.   ∧ ∃ we:We · we ∈ us ∧ r(1) = mkWe(we)
533e.   ∧ ∃ si:Si · si ∈ us ∧ r(**len** r) = mkSi(si)
524.   **end end**

A.4 Attributes

We speak of four kinds of attributes: **Geometric Unit Attributes**, **Spatial Unit Attributes**, **Unit Action Attributes** and **Flow Attributes**.

A.4.1 Geometric Unit Attributes

534 Common static unit attributes are Diameters and Lengths.
535 Well units have one output "Diameter"; pipe, Valve, Pump and Redirector units have Diameter; and Sink units have one input "Diameter".
536 Pipe, valve and pumps units have Length.
537 Fork units have one input Diameter, two output Diameters: iD, oD_1, oD_2, and Lengths from input to a fork center, and from that to the two outputs: iL, oL_1, oL_2.

538 Join units have the "reverse": one output Diameter, two input Diameters: oD, iD$_1$, iD$_2$, and Lengths from the two inputs to a join center, and from that to the single output: iL$_1$, iL$_2$, oL.

539 Redirector units have Lengths from the input to a "center" (where the unit redirection can be said to be "centered"), and from that center to the output: iL, oL.

type
534.   D, L
value
535.   attr_D: (We|Pi|Va|Pu|Rd|Si) → D
536.   attr_L: (Pi|Va|Pu) → L
537.   attr_Ds: Fo → (D×(D×D))
537.   attr_Ls: Fo → (L×(L×L))
538.   attr_Ds: Jo → ((D×D)×D)
538.   attr_Ls: Jo → ((L×L)×L)
539.   attr_Ls: Rd → L×L

We omit detailing the angles with which the two segments emanate from the input segment of fork, the two segments are incident upon the put segment of a join, and a redirector deviates the output segment from its input segment. The oil unit graphics of Fig. **A**.1 hints at these angles.

A.4.2 Spatial Unit Attributes

Pipelines are laid down in flat and hilly, even mountainous terrains. Any one pipeline unit has spatial locations. We shall refrain from detailing (let alone formalising) the spatial attributes of units. But we can suggest the following: Every unit has some *spatial* attributes: As fluid flow in units is one-directional we can associate with any unit a unique **point**. With pumps, valves, forks and joins we may associate that point with "the middle, center" of the unit. With wells and sinks we may associate that point with the point of the well, respectively the sink, where oil is delivered, respectively accepted from the pipeline. With pipes we suggest to associate that point with the mid-point, "halfway along the pipe". Similarly we can associate a **length** with some units. Pumps, valves, forks and joins we suggest to have length 0. So only pipes have lengths. We suggest that the length of a pipe is the actual, perhaps, curved, length between its two end-points. We bring this example as an illustration of the use of analysis and description prompts, and not as an example of a full-fledged pipeline domain description, we shall refrain from systematically narrating and formalising these spatial unit attributes and the consequences of doing so[3].

A.4.3 Unit Action Attributes

540 Valve units are either 100% open, or 100% closed. [4]
541 Pump units are either pumping, or not_pumping.[5]

type

---

[3] The 'consequences' alluded to are those of the spatial well-formedness of pipelines.

[4] Without loss of generality we do not model fractional open/closed status.

[5] Without loss of generality we do not model fractional pumping status.

540. OC == "open" | "closed"
541. PS == "pumping" | "not_pumping"
value
540. attr_OC: Va → OC
541. attr_PS: Pu → PS

A.4.4 Flow Attributes

A.4.4.1 Flows and Leaks

We now wish to examine the flow of fluid in pipeline units. So we postulate a unit attribute Flow. We use two types

542 **type** Flow, Leak = Flow.

Productive flow, Flow, and wasteful leak, Leak, is measured, for example, in terms of volume of fluid per second. We then postulate the following unit attributes "measured" at the point of in- or out-flow or in the interior of a unit.

543 current flow of fluid into a unit input connector,
544 maximum flow of fluid into a unit input connector while maintaining laminar flow,
545 current flow of fluid out of a unit output connector,
546 maximum flow of fluid out of a unit output connector while maintaining laminar flow,
547 current leak of fluid at a unit input connector,
548 maximum guaranteed leak of fluid at a unit input connector,
549 current leak of fluid at a unit input connector,
550 maximum guaranteed leak of fluid at a unit input connector,
551 current leak of fluid from "within" a unit, and
552 maximum guaranteed leak of fluid from "within" a unit.

type
542 Flow, Leak = Flow
value
543 attr_cur_iFlow: PE → UI → Flow
544 attr_max_iFlow: PE → UI → Flow
545 attr_cur_oFlow: PE → UI → Flow
546 attr_max_oFlow: PE → UI → Flow
547 attr_cur_iLeak: PE → UI → Leak
548 attr_max_iLeak: PE → UI → Leak
549 attr_cur_oLeak: PE → UI → Leak
550 attr_max_oLeak: PE → UI → Leak
551 attr_cur_Leak: PE → Leak
552 attr_max_Leak: PE → Leak

The maximum flow attributes are static attributes and are typically provided by the manufacturer as indicators of flows below which laminar flow can be expected. The current flow attributes may be considered either reactive or biddable attributes.

It may be difficult or costly, or both, to ascertain flows and leaks in fluid-based domains. But one can certainly speak of these concepts. This casts new light on *domain modeling*. That is in contrast to incorporating such notions of flows and leaks in *requirements modeling* where one has to show implement-ability. Modeling flows and leaks is important to the modeling of fluid-based domains.

553 For every unit of a pipeline system, except the well and the sink units, the following law
    apply.
554 The flows into a unit equal

   a the leak at the inputs
   b plus the leak within the unit
   c plus the flows out of the unit
   d plus the leaks at the outputs.

axiom [Well–formedness of Pipeline Systems, PL (2)]
553 ∀ pl:PL,b:B\We\Si,pe:PE ·
553   b ∈ mereo_Bs(pl)∧u=mereo_(b)⇒
553   **let** (iuis,ouis) = mereo_PE(pe) **in**
554   sum_cur_iF(u)(iuis) =
554a   sum_cur_iL(u)(iuis)
554b   ⊕ attr_cur_Leak(pe)
554c   ⊕ sum_cur_oFlow(pe)(ouis)
554d   ⊕ sum_cur_oLeak(pe)(ouis)
553   **end**

A.4.4.2 Intra Unit Flow and Leak Law

555 The sum_cur_iFlow (cf. Item 554) sums current input flows over all input connectors.
556 The sum_cur_iLeak (cf. Item 554a) sums current input leaks over all input connectors.
557 The sum_cur_oFlow (cf. Item 554c) sums current output flows over all output connectors.
558 The sum_cur_oLeak (cf. Item 554d) sums current output leaks over all output connectors.

555   sum_cur_iFlow: PE → UI-**set** → Flow
555   sum_cur_iFlow(u)(iuis) ≡ ⊕ {attr_cur_iFlow(u)(ui)|ui:UI·ui ∈ iuis}
556   sum_cur_iLeak: PE → UI-**set** → Leak
556   sum_cur_iLeak(u)(iuis) ≡ ⊕ {attr_cur_iLeak(u)(ui)|ui:UI·ui ∈ iuis}
557   sum_cur_oFlow: PE → UI-**set** → Flow
557   sum_cur_oFlow(u)(ouis) ≡ ⊕ {attr_cur_iFlow(u)(ui)|ui:UI·ui ∈ ouis}
558   sum_cur_oLeak: PE → UI-**set** → Leak
558   sum_cur_oLeak(u)(ouis) ≡ ⊕ {attr_cur_iLeak(u)(ui)|ui:UI·ui ∈ ouis}
    ⊕: (Flow|Leak) × (Flow|Leak) → Flow

where ⊕ is both an infix and a distributed-fix function which adds flows and or leaks   □

A.4.4.3 Inter Unit Flow and Leak Law

559 For every pair of connected units of a pipeline system the following law apply:

   a the flow out of a unit directed at another unit minus the leak at that output connector
   b equals the flow into that other unit at the connector from the given unit plus the leak at
     that connector.

axiom [Well–formedness of Pipelines, PL (3)]
559   ∀ pl:PL, pe,pe':PE ·
559   {pe,pe'}⊆all_pipeline_units(pl)
559   ∧pe≠pe'

```
559        ∧ let (iuis,ouis)=mereo_PE(pe), (iuis′,ouis′)=mereo_PE(pe′),
559              ui=uid_PE(pe), ui′=mereo_PE(pe′) in
559          ui ∈ iuis ∧ ui′ ∈ ouis′ ⇒
559a            attr_cur_oFlow(pe′)(ui′) − attr_leak_oFlow(pe′)(ui′)
559b            = attr_cur_iFlow(pe)(ui) + attr_leak_iFlow(pe)(ui)
559            end
559    comment: b′ precedes b
```

From the above two laws one can prove the **theorem:** *"what is pumped from the wells equals what is leaked from the systems plus what is output to the sinks."*

Appendix B
MEREOLOGY, A MODEL

We first present informal examples of mereologies. Then an axiom system for mereology. Then a model of mereology. And finally we sketch a proof that the model satisfies the axioms.

B.1 Examples of Illustrating Aspects of Mereology

We present six examples of systems illustrating the concept of mereology.

B.1.1 Air Traffic

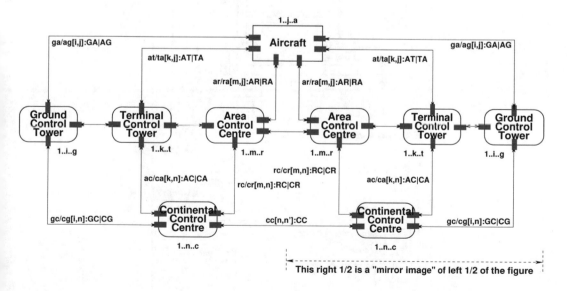

Fig. B.1 A schematic air traffic system

Figure **B**.1 shows nine adjacent (9) boxes and eighteen adjacent (18) lines. Boxes and lines are parts. The line parts "neighbours" the box parts they "connect". Individually boxes and

© The Author(s), under exclusive license to Springer Nature Switzerland AG 2021
D. Bjørner, *Domain Science and Engineering*, Monographs in Theoretical Computer Science. An EATCS Series,
https://doi.org/10.1007/978-3-030-73484-8

lines represent adjacent parts of the composite air traffic "whole". The rounded corner boxes denote buildings. The sharp corner box denote aircraft. Lines denote radio telecommunication. The "overlap" between neigbouring line and box parts are indicated by "connectors". Connectors are shown as small filled, narrow, either horisontal or vertical "filled" rectangle[6] at both ends of the double-headed-arrows lines, overlapping both the line arrows and the boxes. The index ranges shown attached to, i.e., labeling each unit, shall indicate that there are a multiple of the "single" (thus representative) box or line unit shown. These index annotations are what makes the diagram of Fig. **B**.1 schematic. Notice that the 'box' parts are fixed installations and that the double-headed arrows designate the ether where radio waves may propagate. We could, for example, assume that each such line is characterised by a combination of location and (possibly encrypted) radio communication frequency. That would allow us to consider all lines for not overlapping. And if they were overlapping, then that must have been a decision of the air traffic system.

B.1.2 Buildings

Figure **B**.2 shows a building plan — as a composite part.

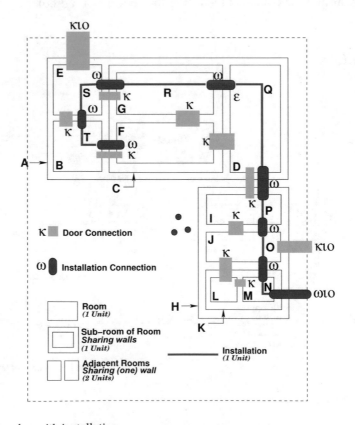

Fig. B.2 A building plan with installation

The building consists of two buildings, A and H. The buildings A and H are neighbours, i.e., shares a common wall. Building A has rooms B, C, D and E, Building H has roomsl, J and

---

[6] There are 36 such rectangles in Fig. **B**.1 on the preceding page.

K; Rooms L and M are within K. Rooms F and G are within C. The thick lines labeled N, O, P, Q, R, S, and T models either electric cabling, water supply, air conditioning, or some such "flow" of gases or liquids. Connection $\kappa\iota o$ provides means of a connection between an environment, shown by dashed lines, and B or J, i.e. "models", for example, a door. Connections κ provides "access" between neighbouring rooms. Note that 'neighbouring' is a transitive relation. Connection $\omega\iota o$ allows electricity (or water, or oil) to be conducted between an environment and a room. Connection ω allows electricity (or water, or oil) to be conducted through a wall. Et cetera. Thus "the whole" consists of A and H. Immediate sub-parts of A are B, C, D and E. Immediate sub parts of C are G and F. Et cetera.

B.1.3 A Financial Service Industry

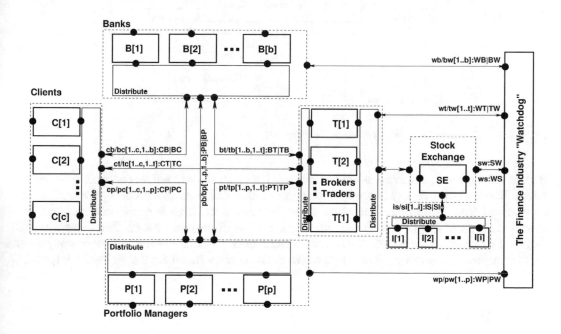

Fig. B.3 A Financial Service Industry

Figure **B**.3 is rather rough-sketchy! It shows seven (7) larger boxes [6 of which are shown by dashed lines], six [6] thin lined "distribution" boxes, and twelve (12) double-arrowed lines. Boxes and lines are parts. (We do not described what is meant by "distribution".) Where double-arrowed lines touch upon (dashed) boxes we have connections. Six (6) of the boxes, the dashed line boxes, are composite parts, five (5) of them consisting of a variable number of atomic parts; five (5) are here shown as having three atomic parts each with bullets "between" them to designate "variability". Clients, not shown, access the outermost (and hence the "innermost" boxes, but the latter is not shown) through connections, shown by bullets, •.

B.1.4 Machine Assemblies

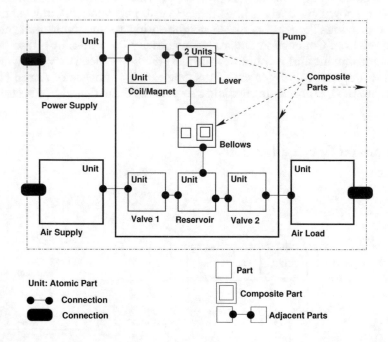

Fig. B.4 An air pump, i.e., a physical mechanical system

Figure **B**.4 shows a machine assembly. Square boxes designate either composite or atomic parts. Black circles or ovals show connections. The full, i.e., the level 0, composite part consists of four immediate parts and three internal and three external connections. The Pump is an assembly of six (6) immediate parts, five (5) internal connections and three (3) external connectors. Et cetera. Some connections afford "transmission" of electrical power. Other connections convey torque. Two connections convey input air, respectively output air.

B.1.5 Oil Industry

B.1.5.1 "The" Overall Assembly

Figure **B**.5 on the next page shows a composite part consisting of fourteen (14) composite parts, left-to-right: one oil field, a crude oil pipeline system, two refineries and one, say, gasoline distribution network, two seaports, an ocean (with oil and ethanol tankers and their sea lanes), three (more) seaports, and three, say gasoline and ethanol distribution networks. Between all of the neighbouring composite parts there are connections, and from some of these composite parts there are connections (to an external environment). The crude oil pipeline system composite part will be concretised next.

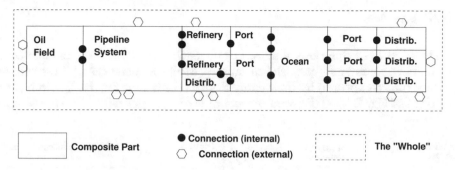

Fig. B.5 A Schematic of an Oil Industry

B.1.5.2 A Concretised Composite Pipeline

Figure **B**.6 shows a pipeline system. It consists of 32 atomic parts: fifteen (15) pipe units (shown as directed arrows and labeled p1–p15), four (4) input node units (shown as small circles, ○, and labeled in$i$–inℓ), four (4) flow pump units (shown as small circles, ○, and labeled fp$a$–fp$d$), five (5) valve units (shown as small circles, ○, and labeled vx–vw), three (3) join units (shown as small circles, ○, and labeled jb–jc), two (2) fork units (shown as small circles, ○, and labeled fb–fc), one (1) combined join & fork unit (shown as small circles, ○, and labeled jafa), and four (4) output node units (shown as small circles, ○, and labeled on$p$–on$s$).

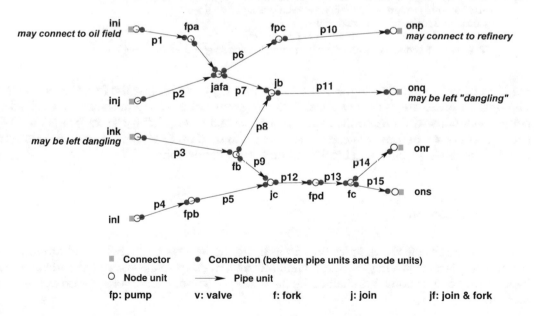

Fig. B.6 A Pipeline System

In this example the routes through the pipeline system start with node units and end with node units, alternates between node units and pipe units, and are connected as shown by fully filled-out dark coloured disc connections. Input and output nodes have input, respectively output connections, one each, and shown as lighter coloured connections. In [63] we present a description of a class of abstracted pipeline systems.

B.1.6 Railway Nets

The left of Fig. **B**.7 [L] diagrams four rail units, each with two, three or four connectors shown as narrow, somewhat "longish" rectangles. Multiple instances of these rail units can be assembled (i.e., composed) by their connectors as shown on Fig. **B**.7 [L] into proper rail nets. The right of Fig. **B**.7 [R] diagrams an example of a proper rail net. It is assembled from

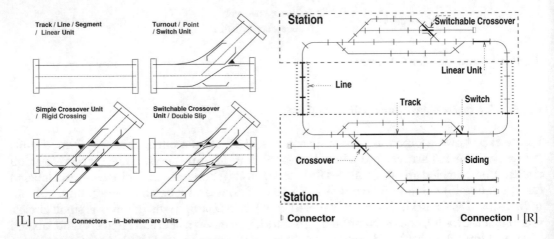

Fig. B.7 Railway Concepts. To the left: Four rail units.To the right: A "model" railway net:
An Assembly of four Assemblies: two stations and two lines.
Lines here consist of linear rail units.
Stations of all the kinds of units shown to the left.
There are 66 connections and four "dangling" connectors

the kind of units shown in Fig. **B**.7 [L]. In Fig. **B**.7 [R] consider just the four dashed boxes: The dashed boxes are assembly units. Two designate stations, two designate lines (tracks) between stations. We refer to the caption four line text of Fig. **B**.7 for more "statistics". We could have chosen to show, instead, for each of the four "dangling' connectors, a composition of a connection, a special "end block" rail unit and a connector.

B.1.7 Discussion

We have brought these examples only to indicate the issues of a "whole" and atomic and composite parts, adjacency, within, neighbour and overlap relations, and the ideas of attributes and connections. We shall make the notion of 'connection' more precise in the next section.

B.2 An Axiom System for Mereology

Classical axiom systems for mereology focus on just one sort of "things", namely $\mathcal{P}$arts. Leśniewski had in mind, when setting up his mereology to have it supplant set theory. So parts could be composite and consisting of other, the sub-parts — some of which would be atomic; just as sets could consist of elements which were sets — some of which would be empty.

B.2.1 Parts and Attributes

In our axiom system for mereology we shall avail ourselves of one sort: $\mathcal{P}$arts.

- **type** $\mathcal{P}$.

Do not think of "parts" $\mathcal{P}$ being "robust" in the sense of being rigid bodies. Think, more of them as point space sets. Of course, parts $\mathcal{P}$ are really what the below axioms expresses. Allow two or more of these parts to share points, i.e., to "protrude" into one-another; then the axioms are easier, we find, to comprehend.

B.2.2 The Axioms

The axiom system to be developed in this section is a variant of that in [122]. We introduce the following relations between parts:

part_of:	$\mathbb{P} : \mathcal{P} \times \mathcal{P} \to$ **Bool**	Page 355
proper_part_of:	$\mathbb{PP} : \mathcal{P} \times \mathcal{P} \to$ **Bool**	Page 355
overlap:	$\mathbb{O} : \mathcal{P} \times \mathcal{P} \to$ **Bool**	Page 355
underlap:	$\mathbb{U} : \mathcal{P} \times \mathcal{P} \to$ **Bool**	Page 356
over_crossing:	$\mathbb{OX} : \mathcal{P} \times \mathcal{P} \to$ **Bool**	Page 356
under_crossing:	$\mathbb{UX} : \mathcal{P} \times \mathcal{P} \to$ **Bool**	Page 356
proper_overlap:	$\mathbb{PO} : \mathcal{P} \times \mathcal{P} \to$ **Bool**	Page 356
proper_underlap:	$\mathbb{PU} : \mathcal{P} \times \mathcal{P} \to$ **Bool**	Page 356

Part-hood, $\mathbb{P}$, expresses that p_x is part of p_y as $\mathbb{P}(p_x,p_y)$.[7]
Part p_x is part of itself (reflexivity) (**B**.1).
If a part p_x is part p_y and, vice versa, part p_y is part of p_x, then $p_x = p_y$ (anti-symmetry) (**B**.2).
If a part p_x is part of p_y and part p_y is part of p_z, then p_x is part of p_z (transitivity) (**B**.3).

$$\forall p_x : \mathcal{P} \bullet \mathbb{P}(p_x,p_x) \tag{B.1}$$
$$\forall p_x,p_y : \mathcal{P} \bullet (\mathbb{P}(p_x,p_y) \wedge \mathbb{P}(p_y,p_x)) \Rightarrow p_x = p_y \tag{B.2}$$
$$\forall p_x,p_y,p_z : \mathcal{P} \bullet (\mathbb{P}(p_x,p_y) \wedge \mathbb{P}(p_y,p_z)) \Rightarrow \mathbb{P}(p_x,p_z) \tag{B.3}$$

Proper Part-hood, $\mathbb{PP}$, expresses p_x is a proper part of p_y as $\mathbb{PP}(p_x,p_y)$.
$\mathbb{PP}$ can be defined in terms of $\mathbb{P}$.
$\mathbb{PP}(p_x,p_y)$ holds if p_x is part of p_y, but p_y is not part of p_x.

$$\mathbb{PP}(p_x,p_y) \triangleq \mathbb{P}(p_x,p_y) \wedge \neg\mathbb{P}(p_y,p_x) \tag{B.4}$$

Overlap, $\mathbb{O}$, expresses a relation between parts.
Two parts are said to overlap if they have some part in common.

$$\mathbb{O}(p_x,p_y) \triangleq \exists p : \mathcal{P} \bullet \mathbb{PP}(p,p_x) \wedge \mathbb{PP}(p,p_y) \tag{B.5}$$

Underlap, $\mathbb{U}$, expresses a relation between parts.

---

[7] Our notation now is not RSL but a conventional first-order predicate logic notation.

Two parts are said to underlap if there exists a part p_z of which p_x is a part and of which p_y is a part.

$$\mathbb{U}(p_x,p_y) \stackrel{\triangle}{=} \exists p_z : \mathcal{P} \bullet \mathbb{P}(p_x,p_z) \wedge \mathbb{P}(p_y,p_z) \qquad \text{(B.6)}$$

Think of the underlap p_z as an "umbrella" which both p_x and p_y are "under".
Over-cross, $\mathbb{OX}$, p_x and p_y are said to over-cross if p_x and p_y overlap and p_x is not part of p_y.

$$\mathbb{OX}(p_x,p_y) \stackrel{\triangle}{=} \mathbb{O}(p_x,p_y) \wedge \neg\mathbb{P}(p_x,p_y) \qquad \text{(B.7)}$$

Under-cross, $\mathbb{UX}$, p_x and p_y are said to under cross if p_x and p_y underlap and p_y is not part of p_x.

$$\mathbb{UX}(p_x,p_y) \stackrel{\triangle}{=} \mathbb{U}(p_x,p_z) \wedge \neg\mathbb{P}(p_y,p_x) \qquad \text{(B.8)}$$

Proper Overlap, $\mathbb{PO}$, expresses a relation between parts.
p_x and p_y are said to properly overlap if p_x and p_y over-cross and if p_y and p_x over-cross.

$$\mathbb{PO}(p_x,p_y) \stackrel{\triangle}{=} \mathbb{OX}(p_x,p_y) \wedge \mathbb{OX}(p_y,p_x) \qquad \text{(B.9)}$$

Proper Underlap, $\mathbb{PU}$, p_x and p_y are said to properly underlap if p_x and p_y under-cross and p_y and p_x under-cross.

$$\mathbb{PU}(p_x,p_y) \stackrel{\triangle}{=} \mathbb{UX}(p_x,p_y) \wedge \mathbb{UX}(p_y,p_x) \qquad \text{(B.10)}$$

B.3 An Abstract Model of Mereologies

B.3.1 Parts and Sub-parts

560 We distinguish between **atomic** and **composite parts.**
561 Atomic parts do not contain separately distinguishable parts.
562 Composite parts contain at least one separately distinguishable part.

type
560. P == AP | CP[8]
561. AP :: mkAP(...)[9]
562. CP :: mkCP(...,s_sps:P-set)[10] **axiom** $\forall$ mkCP(_,ps):CP $\bullet$ ps$\neq$\{\}

It is the domain analyser who decides what constitutes "the whole", that is, how parts relate to one another, what constitutes parts, and whether a part is atomic or composite. We refer

---

[8] In the RAISE [190] Specification Languge, RSL [187], writing type definitions X == Y|Z means that Y and Z are to be disjoint types. In Items 561.–562. the identifiers mkAP and mkCP are distinct, hence their types are disjoint.

[9] Y :: mkY(...): y values (...) are marked with the "make constructor" mkY, cf. [294, 295].

[10] In Y :: mkY(s_w:W,...) s_w is a "selector function" which when applied to an y, i.e., s_w(y) identifies the W element, cf. [294, 295].

to the proper parts of a composite part as sub-parts. Figure **B**.8 illustrates composite and atomic parts. The *slanted sans serif* uppercase identifiers of Fig. **B**.8 *A1, A2, A3, A4, A5, A6* and *C1, C2, C3* are meta-linguistic, that is. they stand for the parts they "decorate"; they are not identifiers of "our system".

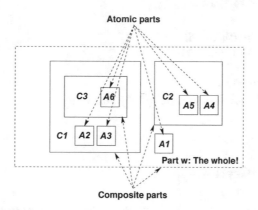

Fig. B.8 Atomic and Composite Parts

B.3.2 No "Infinitely" Embedded Parts

The above syntax, Items 560–562, does not prevent composite parts, p, to contain composite parts, p', "ad-infinitum"! But we do not wish such "recursively" contained parts!

563 To express the property that parts are finite we introduce a notion of *part derivation*.
564 The part derivation of an atomic part is the empty set.
565 The part derivation of a composite part, p, mkC(...,ps) where ... is left undefined, is the set ps of sub-parts of p.

value
563. pt_der: P → **P-set**
564. pt_der(mkAP(...)) ≡ {}
565. pt_der(mkCP(...,ps)) ≡ ps

566 We can also express the part derivation, pt_der(ps) of a set, ps, of parts.
567 If the set is empty then pt_der({}) is the empty set, {}.
568 Let mkA(pq) be an element of ps, then pt_der({mkA(pq)}∪ps') is ps'.
569 Let mkC(pq,ps') be an element of ps, then pt_der(ps'∪ps) is ps'.

566. pt_der: **P-set** → **P-set**
567. pt_der({}) ≡ {}
568. pt_der({mkA(..)}∪ps) ≡ ps
569. pt_der({mkC(..,ps')}∪ps) ≡ ps'∪ps

570 Therefore, to express that a part is finite we postulate
571 a natural number, n, such that a notion of iterated part set derivations lead to an empty set.

572 An iterated part set derivation takes a set of parts and part set derive that set repeatedly, *n* times.

573 If the result is an empty set, then part *p* was finite.

value
570. no_infinite_parts: P → **Bool**
571. no_infinite_parts(p) ≡
571.   ∃ n:**Nat** · it_pt_der({p})(n)={}
572. it_pt_der: P-set → **Nat** → P-set
573. it_pt_der(ps)(n) ≡
573.   **let** ps' = pt_der(ps) **in**
573.   **if** n=1 **then** ps' **else** it_pt_der(ps')(n−1) **end end**

B.3.3 Unique Identifications

Each part can be uniquely distinguished for example by an abstraction of its properties at a time of origin. In consequence we also endow conceptual parts with unique identifications.

574 In order to refer to specific parts we endow all parts, whether atomic or composite, with **unique id**entifications.

575 We postulate functions which observe these **unique id**entifications, whether as parts in general or as atomic or composite parts in particular.

576 such that any to parts which are distinct have **unique id**entifications.

type
574. UI
value
575. uid_UI: P → UI
axiom
576. ∀ p,p':P · p≠p' ⇒ uid_UI(p)≠uid_UI(p')

A model for uid_UI can be given. Presupposing subsequent material (on attributes and mereology) — "lumped" into part qualities, pq:PQ, we augment definitions of atomic and composite parts:

type
561. AP :: mkA(s_pq:(s_uid:UI,...))
562. CP :: mkC(s_pq:(s_uid:UI,...),s_sps:P-set)
value
575. uid_UI(mkA((ui,...))) ≡ ui
575. uid_UI(mkC((ui,...)),...) ≡ ui

Figure **B**.9 illustrates the unique identifications of composite and atomic parts. No two parts have the same unique identifier.

577 We define an auxiliary function, no_prts_uis, which applies to a[ny] part, *p*, and yields a pair: the number of sub-parts of the part argument, and the set of unique identifiers of parts within *p*.

578 no_prts_uis is defined in terms of yet an auxiliary function, sum_no_pts_uis.

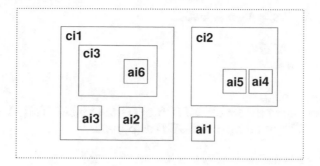

Fig. B.9 ai_j: atomic part identifiers, ci_k: composite part identifiers

value

577.   no_prts_uis: P → (**Nat** × UI-**set**) → (**Nat** × UI-**set**)
577.   no_pts_uis(mkA(ui,...))(n,uis) ≡ (n+1,uis∪{ui})
577.   no_pts_uis(mkC((ui,...),ps))(n,uis) ≡
577.   **let** (n′,uis′) = sum_no_pts_uis(ps) **in**
577.   (n+n′,uis∪uis′) **end**
577.   **pre**: no_infinite_parts(p)
578.   sum_no_pts_uis: P-**set** → (**Nat** × UI-**set**) → (**Nat** × UI-**set**)
578.   sum_no_pts_uis(ps)(n,uis) ≡
578.   **case** ps **of**
578.   {}→(n,uis),
578.   {mkA(ui,...)}∪ps'→sum_no_pts_uis(ps′)(n+1,uis∪{ui}),
578.   {mkC((ui,...),ps')}∪ps" →
578.   **let** (n″,uis″)=sum_no_pts_uis(ps′)(1,{ui}) **in**
578.   sum_no_pts_uis(ps″)(n+n″,uis∪uis") **end**
578.   **end**
578.   **pre**: ∀ p:P•p ∈ ps ⇒ no_infinite_parts(p)

579 That no two parts have the same unique identifier can now be expressed by demanding that the number of parts equals the number of unique identifiers.

axiom

579.   ∀ p:P • **let** (n,uis)=no_prts_uis(0,{}) **in** n=**card** uis **end**

B.3.4 Attributes

B.3.4.1 Attribute Names and Values

580 Parts have sets of named attribute values, attrs:ATTRS.
581 One can observe attributes from parts.
582 Two distinct parts may share attributes:

   a For some (one or more) attribute name that is among the attribute names of both parts,
   b it is always the case that the corresponding attribute values are identical.

type

580. ANm, AVAL, ATTRS = ANm $_{\overrightarrow{m}}$ AVAL

value
581. attr_ATTRS: P $\rightarrow$ ATTRS
582. share: P$\times$P $\rightarrow$ **Bool**
582. share(p,p') $\equiv$
582.   p$\neq$p' $\wedge$ ~trans_adj(p,p') $\wedge$
582a. $\exists$ anm:ANm $\cdot$ anm $\in$ **dom** attr_ATTRS(p) $\cap$ **dom** attr_ATTRS(p') $\Rightarrow$
582b. $\square$ (attr_ATTRS(p))(anm) = (attr_ATTRS(p'))(anm)

The function trans_adj is defined in Sect. **B.4.4** on page 362.

B.3.4.2 Attribute Categories

We define some auxiliary functions:

583 $\mathcal{S}_{\mathcal{A}}$ applies to attrs:ATTRS and yields a grouping $(sa_1,sa_2,...,sa_{n_s})$[11], of **static** attribute values.

584 $\mathcal{C}_{\mathcal{A}}$ applies to attrs:ATTRS and yields a grouping $(ca_1,ca_2,...,ca_{n_c})$[12] of **controllable** attribute values.

585 $\mathcal{E}_{\mathcal{A}}$ applies to attrs:ATTRS and yields a set, $\{eA_1,eA_2,...,eA_{n_e}\}$[13] of **external** attribute names.

type
    SA,CA = AVAL*
    EA = ANm−st
value

583. $\mathcal{S}_{\mathcal{A}}$: ATTRS $\rightarrow$ SA
584. $\mathcal{C}_{\mathcal{A}}$: ATTRS $\rightarrow$ CA
585. $\mathcal{E}_{\mathcal{A}}$: ATTRS $\rightarrow$ EA

The attribute names of static, controllable and external attributes do not overlap and together make up the attribute names of attrs.

B.3.5 Mereology

In order to illustrate other than the within and adjacency part relations we introduce the notion of mereology. Figure **B**.10 on the facing page illustrates a mereology between parts. A specific mereology-relation is, visually, a •—• line that connects two distinct parts.

586 The mereology of a part is a set of unique identifiers of other parts.

type
586. ME = UI-set

We may refer to the connectors by the two element sets of the unique identifiers of the parts they connect. For **example** with respect to Fig. **B**.10 on the next page:

- $\{ci_1,ci_3\}$,
- $\{ai_2,ai_3\}$,
- $\{ai_6,ci_1\}$,
- $\{ai_3,ci_1\}$,
- $\{ai_6,ai_5\}$ and
- $\{ai_1,ci_1\}$.

---

[11] – where $\{sa_1,sa_2,...,sa_{n_s}\}\subseteq$**rng** attrs
[12] – where $\{ca_1,ca_2,...,ca_{n_s}\}\subseteq$**rng** attrs
[13] – where $\{eA_1,eA_2,...,eA_{n_e}\}\subseteq$**dom** attrs

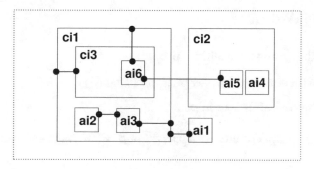

Fig. B.10 Mereology: Relations between Parts

B.3.6 The Model

587 The "whole" is a part.
588 A part value has a part sort name and is either the value of an atomic part or of an abstract composite part.
589 An atomic part value has a part quality value.
590 An abstract composite part value has a part quality value and a set of at least of one or more part values.
591 A part quality value consists of a unique identifier, a mereology, and a set of one or more attribute named attribute values.

```
587    W = P
588     P = AP | CP
589    AP :: mkA(s_pq:PQ)
590    CP :: mkC(s_pq:PQ,s_ps:P-set)
591    PQ = UI×ME×(ANm ⇻ AVAL)
```

We now assume that parts are not "recursively infinite", and that all parts have unique identifiers

B.4 Some Part Relations

B.4.1 'Immediately Within'

592 One part, p, is said to be *immediately within*, imm_within(p,p'), another part, if p' is a composite part and p is observable in p'.

value
```
592.   imm_within: P × P → Bool
592.   imm_within(p,p') ≡
592.      case p' of
592.         (_,mkA(_,ps)) → p ∈ ps,
592.         (_,mkC(_,ps)) → p ∈ ps,
592.         _ → false
592.      end
```

B.4.2 'Transitive Within'

We can generalise the 'immediate within' property.

593 A part, p, is transitively within a part p', trans_within(p,p'),

    a either if p, is immediately within p'
    b or
    c if there exists a (proper) composite part p'' of p' such that trans_within(p'',p).

value
593.   trans_within: P × P → **Bool**
593.   trans_within(p,p') ≡
593a.   imm_within(p,p')
593b.   ∨
593c.   **case** p' **of**
593c.   (_,mkC(_,ps)) → p ∈ ps ∧
593c.   ∃ p'':P· p'' ∈ ps ∧ trans_within(p'',p),
593c.   _ → **false**
593.   **end**

B.4.3 'Adjacency'

594 Two parts, p,p', are said to be *immediately adjacent*, imm_adj(p,p')(c), to one another, in a composite part c, such that p and p' are distinct and observable in c.

value
594.   imm_adj: P × P → P → **Bool**
594.   imm_adj(p,p')(mkA(_,ps)) ≡ p≠p' ∧ {p,p'}⊆ps
594.   imm_adj(p,p')(mkC(_,ps)) ≡ p≠p' ∧ {p,p'}⊆ps
594.   imm_adj(p,p')(mkA(_)) ≡ **false**

B.4.4 Transitive 'Adjacency'

We can generalise the immediate 'adjacent' property.

595 Two parts, p',p'', of a composite part, p, are trans_adj(p', p'') in p

    a either if imm_adj(p',p'')(p),
    b or if there are two p''' and p'''' such that
      i p''' and p'''' are immediately adjacent parts of p and
      ii p is equal to p''' or p''' is properly within p and p' is equal to p'''' or p'''' is properly within p'

We leave the formalisation to the reader.

B.5 Satisfaction

We shall sketch a proof that the *model* of Sect. **B.3**, *satisfies*, i.e., is a model of, the *axioms* of Sect. **B.2**.

B.5.1 A Proof Sketch

We assign

596 P as the meaning of $\mathcal{P}$
597 ATR as the meaning of $\mathcal{A}$,
598 imm_within as the meaning of $\mathbb{P}$,
599 trans_within as the meaning of $\mathbb{PP}$,
600 $\in$: ATR×ATTRS-set→**Bool** as the meaning of $\in$: $\mathcal{A} \times \mathcal{P} \rightarrow$**Bool** and
601 sharing as the meaning of $\mathcal{O}$.

With the above assignments it is now easy to prove that the other axiom-operators $\mathbb{U}$, $\mathbb{PO}$, $\mathbb{PU}$, $\mathcal{OX}$ and $\mathbb{UX}$ can be modeled by means of imm_within, within, ATTR×ATTRS-set→**Bool** and sharing.

Appendix C
FOUR LANGUAGES

*In this appendix we recall the four language tools of the **domain analysis & description**: (i) the calculi of analysis and description prompts; (ii) the 'language' of explaining domain analysis & description; (iii) the RSL: Raise Specification Language, and (iv) the 'language' of domains.*

Usually mathematics, in many of its shades and forms, is deployed in *describing* properties of nature, as when pursuing physics. Usually the formal specification languages of *computer & computing science* have a precise semantics and a consistent proof system. To have these properties those languages must deal with *computable objects*. *Domains are not computable.*

C.1 The Domain Analysis & Description Calculi

We separate the calculi into two: the analysis functions, and the description functions. None of these are computable functions as they have no formal basis. They are tools in helping us to achieve a formal, computable basis on which to understand the analysed & described domains.

C.1.1 The Analysis Calculus

Use of the *analysis language* is not written down. It consists of a number of single, usually is_ or has_, prefixed *domain analysis prompt* and *domain description prompt* names. The **domain analysis prompts** are:

⋆ The Analysis Predicate Prompts

is_ alternative_ sorts_ set, 72
is_ animal, 66
is_ artefactual_ atomic, 69
is_ artefactual_ composite, 69
is_ artefact, 63
is_ atomic, 69
is_ composite_ structure, 65
is_ composite, 70
is_ compound, 70
is_ conjoin, 72
is_ endurant, 57
is_ entity, 52
is_ fluid_ parts_ parts_ conjoin, 75
is_ fluid, 59
is_ human, 67
is_ living_ species, 62
is_ natural_ atomic, 69

is_ natural_ composite, 69
is_ natural_ part, 62
is_ part_ fluids_ conjoin, 73
is_ part_ parts_ conjoin, 75
is_ part, 60
is_ perdurant, 57
is_ plant, 66
is_ set_ structure, 65
is_ set, 71
is_ single_ sort_ set, 71
is_ solid, 58
is_ structure, 61

has_monitorable_attributes, 160

is_physical_attribute, 224, 135

D. Bjørner, *Domain Science and Engineering*, Monographs in Theoretical Computer Science. An EATCS Series, https://doi.org/10.1007/978-3-030-73484-8

★ The Analysis Function Prompts

They apply to phenomena in the domain, that is, to "the world out there"! Except for the analyse_$\cdots$ and attribute types functions, these queries result in truth values; the analyse_$\cdots$ result in the domain scientist cum engineer noting down, in memory or in typed form, suggestive names [of endurant sorts]; and attribute_types results in suggestive names [of attribute types]. The truth-valued queries directs, as we shall see, the domain scientist cum engineer to either further analysis or to "issue" some domain description prompts.

C.1.2 The Description Calculus

The 'name'-valued queries help the human analyser to formulate the result of **domain description prompts**:

★ The Description Prompts

Again they apply to phenomena in the domain, that is, to "the world out there"! In this case they result in RSL-Text!

The **description language** is RSL$^+$. It is a basically applicative subset of RSL [187], that is: no assignable variables. Also we omit RSL's elaborate scheme, class, object notions.

★ The Description Language Primitives

- **Endurants:**

    ∞ **obs**_E$_i$, dfn. 2, [o] pg. 83, dfn. 2, [s] pg. 83

- **Unique Identifiers:**

    ∞ uid_P, dfn. 8, [u] pg. 109

- **Mereologies:**

    ∞ mereo_P, dfn. 9, [m] pg. 114

- **Attributes:**

    ∞ attr_A$_i$, dfn. 10, [a] pg. 121

We refer, generally, to all these functions as observer functions. They are defined by the analyser cum describer when "applying" description prompts. That is, they should be considered user-defined. In our examples we use the non-bold-faced observer function names.

C.2 The Language of Explaining Domain Analysis & Description

English, Philosophy and Discrete Mathematics Notation

In explaining the *analysis & description prompts* we use a natural language which contains terms and phrases typical of (i) the technical language of *computer & computing science*, and (ii) the language of *philosophy*, more specifically *ontology*, and discrete mathematics notation. The reason for the former should be obvious. The reason for the latter is given as follows: We are, on one hand, dealing with real, actual segments of domains characterised by their basis in nature, in economics, in technologies, etc., that is, in informal "worlds", and, on the other hand, we aim at a formal understanding of those "worlds". There is, in other words, the task of explaining how we observe those "worlds", and that is what brings us close to some issues well-discussed in *philosophy*.

C.3 The RSL: Raise Specification Language

RSL is the target language into which the domain description prompts express their results.

The author has been involved in both the development, research into and extensive use of both VDM and RAISE/RSL. He instigated the mainly UK/Danish project that led to RAISE/RSL. From around 1993 he has used RSL on an almost daily basis.

The RAISE Specification Language is basically a model-oriented specification language. Bases for RSL are VDM [92, 93, 164], discrete mathematics, and CSP [250]. For initial specifications, like, e.g., domain descriptions, we advice to focus on the functional, i.e., the applicative aspects of RSL.

The prime references to the RAISE Method and the RSL, Raise Specification Language, are [190, 187]. Short introductions to RAISE and RSL are [188, 179, 183, George et al.].

Early publications: [125, 140, 251, 141, 290, 142, 154, 195, 405, 155, Dandanell et al.]; theoretical investigations [305, 306, Milner]; case studies [191, 2001]; and by the current author [42, 43, 44, Bjørner].

Chris W. George is one of the masterminds, since the mid-to-late 1980s, of RAISE, focusing very much on correctness issues, is the prime author of most of these papers: [173, 311, 312, 174, 175, 213, 176, 180, 402, 278, 186, 177, 182, 178, 3, 144, 88, 4, 325, 179, 185, 179, 379, 184, 378, 126, 127, 127, 326, 149, Chris W. George et al.].

Klaus Havelund, who was with the RAISE project at the Danish industrial partner, CR, in its early days, besides co-authoring [187, 190], was a prime author of many of the RAISE project technical reports – as well of these early publications: [311, 181, 90, 212].

Anne Elisabeth Haxthausen, who was with the RAISE project at the Danish industrial partner, CR, in its early days, besides co-authoring [187, 190], is a prime author of several very relevant RAISE/RSL (etc.) papers: [233, 229, 219, 214, 216, 319, 243, 280, 217, 243, 234, 235, 237, 236, 193, 88, 279, 321, 189, 230, 322, 238, 184, 227, 221, 220, 242, 228, 222, 223, 231, 320, 224, 239, 218, 226, 225, 385, 383, 384, 386, 240, 387, 157, 232, 387, 160, 286, 159, 382, 170, 158, 323, 215, 171, 194].

There is a RAISE Web page: RAISE Tools: https://raisetools.github.io/. From here one should be able to download the RAISE Tools.

C.4 The Language of Domains

We consider a domain through the *semiotic looking glass* of its *syntax* and its *semantics*; we shall not consider here its possible *pragmatics*. By *"its syntax"* we shall mean the form and "contents", i.e., the *external* and *internal qualities* of the *endurants* of the domain, i.e., those *entities* that endure. By *"its semantics"* we shall, by a *transcendental deduction*, mean the *perdurants*: the *actions*, the *events*, and the *behaviours* that center on the the endurants and that otherwise characterise the domain.

Appendix D
AN RSL PRIMER

This is an ultra-short introduction to the RAISE Specification Language, RSL.

D.1 Types

The reader is kindly asked to study first the decomposition of this section into its sub-parts and sub-sub-parts.

D.1.1 Type Expressions

Type expressions are expressions whose value are type, that is, possibly infinite sets of values (of "that" type).

D.1.1.1 Atomic Types

Atomic types have (atomic) values. That is, values which we consider to have no proper constituent (sub-)values, i.e., cannot, to us, be meaningfully "taken apart".

RSL has a number of built-in atomic types. There are the Booleans, integers, natural numbers, reals, characters, and texts.

type
    [1] **Bool**
    [2] **Int**
    [3] **Nat**
    [4] **Real**
    [5] **Char**
    [6] **Text**

D.1.1.2 Composite Types

Composite types have composite values. That is, values which we consider to have proper constituent (sub-)values, i.e., can, to us, be meaningfully "taken apart".

© The Author(s), under exclusive license to Springer Nature Switzerland AG 2021
D. Bjørner, *Domain Science and Engineering*, Monographs in Theoretical Computer Science. An EATCS Series,
https://doi.org/10.1007/978-3-030-73484-8

From these one can form type expressions: finite sets, infinite sets, Cartesian products, lists, maps, etc.

Let A, B and C be any type names or type expressions, then:

[7] A-**set**
[8] A-**infset**
[9] A × B × ... × C
[10] A*
[11] A$^{\omega}$
[12] A $\overrightarrow{m}$ B
[13] A → B
[14] A $\overset{\sim}{\rightarrow}$ B
[15] A | B | ... | C
[16] mk_id(sel_a:A,...,sel_b:B)
[17] sel_a:A ... sel_b:B

The following are generic type expressions:

1 The Boolean type of truth values **false** and **true**.
2 The integer type on integers ..., −2, −1, 0, 1, 2, ...
3 The natural number type of positive integer values 0, 1, 2, ...
4 The real number type of real values, i.e., values whose numerals can be written as an integer, followed by a period ("."), followed by a natural number (the fraction).
5 The character type of character values "a", "bb", ...
6 The text type of character string values "aa", "aaa", ..., "abc", ...
7 The set type of finite cardinality set values.
8 The set type of infinite and finite cardinality set values.
9 The Cartesian type of Cartesian values.
10 The list type of finite length list values.
11 The list type of infinite and finite length list values.
12 The map type of finite definition set map values.
13 The function type of total function values.
14 The function type of partial function values.
15 The postulated disjoint union of types A, B, . . . , and C.
16 The record type of mk_id-named record values mk_id(av,...,bv), where av, . . . , bv, are values of respective types. The distinct identifiers sel_a, etc., designate selector functions.
17 The record type of unnamed record values (av,...,bv), where av, . . . , bv, are values of respective types. The distinct identifiers sel_a, etc., designate selector functions.

D.1.2 Type Definitions

D.1.2.1 Concrete Types

Types can be concrete in which case the structure of the type is specified by type expressions:

type
    A = Type_expr

Some schematic type definitions are:

[1] Type_name = Type_expr /* without | s or subtypes */
[2] Type_name = Type_expr_1 | Type_expr_2 | ... | Type_expr_n
[3] Type_name ==
            mk_id_1(s_a1:Type_name_a1,...,s_ai:Type_name_ai) |
            ... |
            mk_id_n(s_z1:Type_name_z1,...,s_zk:Type_name_zk)
[4] Type_name :: sel_a:Type_name_a ... sel_z:Type_name_z
[5] Type_name = {| v:Type_name' $\cdot$ $\mathcal{P}$(v) |}

where a form of [2–3] is provided by combining the types:

    Type_name = A | B | ... | Z
    A == mk_id_1(s_a1:A_1,...,s_ai:A_i)
    B == mk_id_2(s_b1:B_1,...,s_bj:B_j)
    ...
    Z == mk_id_n(s_z1:Z_1,...,s_zk:Z_k)

Types A, B, ..., Z are disjoint, i.e., shares no values, provided all mk_id_k are distinct and due to the use of the disjoint record type constructor ==.

axiom
    $\forall$ a1:A_1, a2:A_2, ..., ai:Ai $\cdot$
        s_a1(mk_id_1(a1,a2,...,ai))=a1 $\wedge$ s_a2(mk_id_1(a1,a2,...,ai))=a2 $\wedge$
        ... $\wedge$ s_ai(mk_id_1(a1,a2,...,ai))=ai $\wedge$
    $\forall$ a:A $\cdot$ **let** mk_id_1(a1',a2',...,ai') = a **in**
        a1' = s_a1(a) $\wedge$ a2' = s_a2(a) $\wedge$ ... $\wedge$ ai' = s_ai(a) **end**

Note: Values of type A, where that type is defined by A::B×C×D, can be expressed A(b,c,d) for b:B, c:D, d:D.

D.1.2.2 Subtypes

In RSL, each type represents a set of values. Such a set can be delimited by means of predicates. The set of values b which have type B and which satisfy the predicate $\mathcal{P}$, constitute the subtype A:

type
    A = {| b:B $\cdot$ $\mathcal{P}$(b) |}

D.1.2.3 Sorts — Abstract Types

Types can be (abstract) sorts in which case their structure is not specified:

type
    A, B, ..., C

D.2 The RSL Predicate Calculus

D.2.1 Propositional Expressions

Let identifiers (or propositional expressions) a, b, ..., c designate Boolean values (**true** or **false** [or **chaos**]). Then:

> **false, true**
> a, b, ..., c ~a, a∧b, a∨b, a⇒b, a=b, a≠b

are propositional expressions having Boolean values. ~, ∧, ∨, ⇒, =, ≠ and □ are Boolean connectives (i.e., operators). They can be read as: not, and, or, if then (or implies), equal and not equal.

D.2.2 Simple Predicate Expressions

Let identifiers (or propositional expressions) a, b, ..., c designate Boolean values, let x, y, ..., z (or term expressions) designate non-Boolean values and let i, j, ..., k designate number values, then:

> ∀ x:X • $\mathcal{P}(x)$
> ∃ y:Y • $\mathcal{Q}(y)$
> ∃ ! z:Z • $\mathcal{R}(z)$

are quantified expressions — also being predicate expressions.

They are "read" as: For all x (values in type X) the predicate $\mathcal{P}(x)$ holds; there exists (at least) one y (value in type Y) such that the predicate $\mathcal{Q}(y)$ holds; and there exists a unique z (value in type Z) such that the predicate $\mathcal{R}(z)$ holds.

D.3 Concrete RSL Types: Values and Operations

D.3.1 Arithmetic

type
    Nat, Int, Real
value
    +,−,∗: **Nat×Nat→Nat** | **Int×Int→Int** | **Real×Real→Real**
    /: **Nat×Nat$\tilde{\rightarrow}$Nat** | **Int×Int$\tilde{\rightarrow}$Int** | **Real×Real$\tilde{\rightarrow}$Real**
    <,≤,=,≠,≥,> (**Nat|Int|Real**) → (**Nat|Int|Real**)

D.3.2 Set Expressions

D.3.2.1 Set Enumerations

Let the below a's denote values of type A, then the below designate simple set enumerations:

$\{\{\}, \{a\}, \{e_1,e_2,...,e_n\}, ...\} \in$ **A-set**
$\{\{\}, \{a\}, \{e_1,e_2,...,e_n\}, ..., \{e_1,e_2,...\}\} \in$ **A-infset**

D.3.2.2 Set Comprehension

The expression, last line below, to the right of the ≡, expresses set comprehension. The expression "builds" the set of values satisfying the given predicate. It is abstract in the sense that it does not do so by following a concrete algorithm.

type
    A, B
    P = A → **Bool**
    Q = A $\overset{\sim}{\rightarrow}$ B
value
    comprehend: A-**infset** × P × Q → B-**infset**
    comprehend(s,P,Q) ≡ { Q(a) | a:A • a ∈ s ∧ P(a)}

D.3.3 Cartesian Expressions

D.3.3.1 Cartesian Enumerations

Let *e* range over values of Cartesian types involving *A, B, ..., C*, then the below expressions are simple Cartesian enumerations:

type
    A, B, ..., C
    A × B × ... × C
value
    (e1,e2,...,en)

D.3.4 List Expressions

D.3.4.1 List Enumerations

Let *a* range over values of type *A*, then the below expressions are simple list enumerations:

$\{\langle\rangle, \langle e\rangle, ..., \langle e1,e2,...,en\rangle, ...\} \in A^*$
$\{\langle\rangle, \langle e\rangle, ..., \langle e1,e2,...,en\rangle, ..., \langle e1,e2,...,en,... \rangle, ...\} \in A^\omega$

$\langle$ a_*i* .. a_*j* $\rangle$

The last line above assumes a_i and a_j to be integer-valued expressions. It then expresses the set of integers from the value of e_i to and including the value of e_j. If the latter is smaller than the former, then the list is empty.

D.3.4.2 List Comprehension

The last line below expresses list comprehension.

type
    A, B, P = A → **Bool**, Q = A $\xrightarrow{\sim}$ B
value
    comprehend: A^ω × P × Q $\xrightarrow{\sim}$ B^ω
    comprehend(l,P,Q) ≡
        ⟨ Q(l(i)) | i **in** ⟨1..**len** l⟩ • P(l(i))⟩

D.3.5 Map Expressions

D.3.5.1 Map Enumerations

Let (possibly indexed) u and v range over values of type $T1$ and $T2$, respectively, then the below expressions are simple map enumerations:

type
    T1, T2
    M = T1 $\overrightarrow{m}$ T2
value
    u,u1,u2,...,un:T1, v,v1,v2,...,vn:T2
    [], [u↦v], ..., [u1↦v1,u2↦v2,...,un↦vn] ∀ ∈ M

D.3.5.2 Map Comprehension

The last line below expresses map comprehension:

type
    U, V, X, Y
    M = U $\overrightarrow{m}$ V
    F = U $\xrightarrow{\sim}$ X
    G = V $\xrightarrow{\sim}$ Y
    P = U → **Bool**
value
    comprehend: M×F×G×P → (X $\overrightarrow{m}$ Y)
    comprehend(m,F,G,P) ≡
        [F(u) ↦ G(m(u)) | u:U • u ∈ **dom** m ∧ P(u)]

D.3.6 Set Operations

D.3.6.1 Set Operator Signatures

value

18 ∈: A × A-infset → **Bool**
19 ∉: A × A-infset → **Bool**
20 ∪: A-infset × A-infset → **A-infset**
21 ∪: (A-infset)-infset → **A-infset**
22 ∩: A-infset × A-infset → **A-infset**
23 ∩: (A-infset)-infset → **A-infset**
24 \: A-infset × A-infset → **A-infset**
25 ⊂: A-infset × A-infset → **Bool**
26 ⊆: A-infset × A-infset → **Bool**
27 =: A-infset × A-infset → **Bool**
28 ≠: A-infset × A-infset → **Bool**
29 **card**: A-infset $\overset{\sim}{\rightarrow}$ **Nat**

D.3.6.2 Set Examples

examples
   a ∈ {a,b,c}
   a ∉ {}, a ∉ {b,c}
   {a,b,c} ∪ {a,b,d,e} = {a,b,c,d,e}
   ∪{{a},{a,b},{a,d}} = {a,b,d}
   {a,b,c} ∩ {c,d,e} = {c}
   ∩{{a},{a,b},{a,d}} = {a}
   {a,b,c} \ {c,d} = {a,b}
   {a,b} ⊂ {a,b,c}
   {a,b,c} ⊆ {a,b,c}
   {a,b,c} = {a,b,c}
   {a,b,c} ≠ {a,b}
   card {} = 0, **card** {a,b,c} = 3

D.3.6.3 Informal Explication

18 ∈: The membership operator expresses that an element is a member of a set.
19 ∉: The nonmembership operator expresses that an element is not a member of a set.
20 ∪: The infix union operator. When applied to two sets, the operator gives the set whose members are in either or both of the two operand sets.
21 ∪: The distributed prefix union operator. When applied to a set of sets, the operator gives the set whose members are in some of the operand sets.
22 ∩: The infix intersection operator. When applied to two sets, the operator gives the set whose members are in both of the two operand sets.
23 ∩: The prefix distributed intersection operator. When applied to a set of sets, the operator gives the set whose members are in some of the operand sets.
24 \: The set complement (or set subtraction) operator. When applied to two sets, the operator gives the set whose members are those of the left operand set which are not in the right operand set.
25 ⊆: The proper subset operator expresses that all members of the left operand set are also in the right operand set.
26 ⊂: The proper subset operator expresses that all members of the left operand set are also in the right operand set, and that the two sets are not identical.

27 =: The equal operator expresses that the two operand sets are identical.
28 ≠: The nonequal operator expresses that the two operand sets are not identical.
29 **card**: The cardinality operator gives the number of elements in a finite set.

D.3.6.4 Set Operator Definitions

The operations can be defined as follows (≡ is the definition symbol):

value
$s' \cup s'' \equiv \{ a \mid a{:}A \cdot a \in s' \vee a \in s'' \}$
$s' \cap s'' \equiv \{ a \mid a{:}A \cdot a \in s' \wedge a \in s'' \}$
$s' \setminus s'' \equiv \{ a \mid a{:}A \cdot a \in s' \wedge a \notin s'' \}$
$s' \subseteq s'' \equiv \forall a{:}A \cdot a \in s' \Rightarrow a \in s''$
$s' \subset s'' \equiv s' \subseteq s'' \wedge \exists a{:}A \cdot a \in s'' \wedge a \notin s'$
$s' = s'' \equiv \forall a{:}A \cdot a \in s' \equiv a \in s'' \equiv s \subseteq s' \wedge s' \subseteq s$
$s' \neq s'' \equiv s' \cap s'' \neq \{\}$
card s ≡
    if s = {} **then** 0 **else**
    let a:A · a ∈ s **in** 1 + **card** (s \ {a}) **end end**
    pre s /∗ is a finite set ∗/
card s ≡ **chaos** /∗ tests for infinity of s ∗/

D.3.7 Cartesian Operations

type
    A, B, C
    g0: G0 = A × B × C
    g1: G1 = (A × B × C)
    g2: G2 = (A × B) × C
    g3: G3 = A × (B × C)

value
    va:A, vb:B, vc:C, vd:D
    (va,vb,vc):G0,

(va,vb,vc):G1
((va,vb),vc):G2
(va3,(vb3,vc3)):G3

decomposition expressions
    let (a1,b1,c1) = g0,
        (a1′,b1′,c1′) = g1 **in** .. **end**
    let ((a2,b2),c2) = g2 **in** .. **end**
    let (a3,(b3,c3)) = g3 **in** .. **end**

D.3.8 List Operations

D.3.8.1 List Operator Signatures

value
    hd: $A^\omega \xrightarrow{\sim} A$
    tl: $A^\omega \xrightarrow{\sim} A^\omega$
    len: $A^\omega \xrightarrow{\sim}$ **Nat**
    inds: $A^\omega \rightarrow$ **Nat-infset**

    elems: $A^{\omega} \rightarrow$ **A-infset**
    .(.): $A^{\omega} \times$ **Nat** $\overset{\sim}{\rightarrow}$ A
    $\widehat{}$: $A^{*} \times A^{\omega} \rightarrow A^{\omega}$
    =: $A^{\omega} \times A^{\omega} \rightarrow$ **Bool**
    $\neq$: $A^{\omega} \times A^{\omega} \rightarrow$ **Bool**

D.3.8.2 List Operation Examples

examples
    hd⟨a1,a2,...,am⟩=a1
    tl⟨a1,a2,...,am⟩=⟨a2,...,am⟩
    len⟨a1,a2,...,am⟩=m
    inds⟨a1,a2,...,am⟩={1,2,...,m}
    elems⟨a1,a2,...,am⟩={a1,a2,...,am}
    ⟨a1,a2,...,am⟩(i)=ai
    ⟨a,b,c⟩$\widehat{}$⟨a,b,d⟩ = ⟨a,b,c,a,b,d⟩
    ⟨a,b,c⟩=⟨a,b,c⟩
    ⟨a,b,c⟩ $\neq$ ⟨a,b,d⟩

D.3.8.3 Informal Explication

- **hd**: Head gives the first element in a nonempty list.
- **tl**: Tail gives the remaining list of a nonempty list when Head is removed.
- **len**: Length gives the number of elements in a finite list.
- **inds**: Indices give the set of indices from 1 to the length of a nonempty list. For empty lists, this set is the empty set as well.
- **elems**: Elements gives the possibly infinite set of all distinct elements in a list.
- $\ell(i)$: Indexing with a natural number, i larger than 0, into a list ℓ having a number of elements larger than or equal to i, gives the ith element of the list.
- $\widehat{}$: Concatenates two operand lists into one. The elements of the left operand list are followed by the elements of the right. The order with respect to each list is maintained.
- =: The equal operator expresses that the two operand lists are identical.
- $\neq$: The nonequal operator expresses that the two operand lists are not identical.

The operations can also be defined as follows:

D.3.8.4 List Operator Definitions

value
    is_finite_list: $A^{\omega} \rightarrow$ **Bool**

    len q $\equiv$
        case is_finite_list(q) **of**
            true $\rightarrow$ **if** q = ⟨⟩ **then** 0 **else** 1 + **len tl** q **end**,
            false $\rightarrow$ **chaos end**

    inds q $\equiv$
        case is_finite_list(q) **of**

$$\text{true} \rightarrow \{\, i \mid i\text{:Nat} \cdot 1 \le i \le \text{len } q \,\},$$
$$\text{false} \rightarrow \{\, i \mid i\text{:Nat} \cdot i \ne 0 \,\} \text{ end}$$

$$\text{elems } q \equiv \{\, q(i) \mid i\text{:Nat} \cdot i \in \text{inds } q \,\}$$

q(i) ≡
  if i=1
    then
      if q≠⟨⟩
        then let a:A,q′:Q · q=⟨a⟩⌢q′ **in** a **end**
        else chaos end
      else q(i−1) **end**

fq⌢iq ≡
   ⟨ **if** 1 ≤ i ≤ **len** fq **then** fq(i) **else** iq(i − **len** fq) **end**
    | i:Nat · **if len** iq≠**chaos then** i ≤ **len** fq+**len end** ⟩
   pre is_finite_list(fq)

iq′ = iq″ ≡
   inds iq′ = **inds** iq″ ∧ ∀ i:Nat · i ∈ **inds** iq′ ⇒ iq′(i) = iq″(i)

iq′ ≠ iq″ ≡ ~(iq′ = iq″)

D.3.9 Map Operations

D.3.9.1 Map Operator Signatures and Map Operation Examples

value
  m(a): M → A $\overset{\sim}{\rightarrow}$ B, m(a) = b

  dom: M → A-**infset** [domain of map]
    dom [a1↦b1,a2↦b2,...,an↦bn] = {a1,a2,...,an}

  rng: M → B-**infset** [range of map]
    rng [a1↦b1,a2↦b2,...,an↦bn] = {b1,b2,...,bn}

  †: M × M → M [override extension]
    [a↦b,a′↦b′,a″↦b″] † [a′↦b″,a″↦b′] = [a↦b,a′↦b″,a″↦b′]

  ∪: M × M → M [merge ∪]
    [a↦b,a′↦b′,a″↦b″] ∪ [a‴↦b‴] = [a↦b,a′↦b′,a″↦b″,a‴↦b‴]

  \: M × A-**infset** → M [restriction by]
    [a↦b,a′↦b′,a″↦b″]\{a} = [a′↦b′,a″↦b″]

  /: M × A-**infset** → M [restriction to]
    [a↦b,a′↦b′,a″↦b″]/{a′,a″} = [a′↦b′,a″↦b″]

  =,≠: M × M → **Bool**

$\circ$: $(A \xrightarrow{\sim} B) \times (B \xrightarrow{\sim} C) \to (A \xrightarrow{\sim} C)$ [composition]
$\quad [a\mapsto b, a'\mapsto b'] \circ [b\mapsto c, b'\mapsto c', b''\mapsto c''] = [a\mapsto c, a'\mapsto c']$

D.3.9.2 Map Operation Explication

- $m(a)$: Application gives the element that a maps to in the map m.
- **dom**: Domain/Definition Set gives the set of values which maps to in a map.
- **rng**: Range/Image Set gives the set of values which are mapped to in a map.
- †: Override/Extend. When applied to two operand maps, it gives the map which is like an override of the left operand map by all or some "pairings" of the right operand map.
- ∪: Merge. When applied to two operand maps, it gives a merge of these maps.
- \: Restriction. When applied to two operand maps, it gives the map which is a restriction of the left operand map to the elements that are not in the right operand set.
- /: Restriction. When applied to two operand maps, it gives the map which is a restriction of the left operand map to the elements of the right operand set.
- =: The equal operator expresses that the two operand maps are identical.
- ≠: The nonequal operator expresses that the two operand maps are not identical.
- $\circ$: Composition. When applied to two operand maps, it gives the map from definition set elements of the left operand map, m_1, to the range elements of the right operand map, m_2, such that if a is in the definition set of m_1 and maps into b, and if b is in the definition set of m_2 and maps into c, then a, in the composition, maps into c.

D.3.9.3 Map Operation Redefinitions

The map operations can also be defined as follows:

value
$\quad$ **rng** m ≡ { m(a) | a:A • a ∈ **dom** m }

$\quad$ m1 † m2 ≡
$\quad\quad$ [a↦b | a:A,b:B •
$\quad\quad\quad$ a ∈ **dom** m1 \ **dom** m2 ∧ b=m1(a) ∨ a ∈ **dom** m2 ∧ b=m2(a)]

$\quad$ m1 ∪ m2 ≡ [a↦b | a:A,b:B •
$\quad\quad\quad\quad\quad$ a ∈ **dom** m1 ∧ b=m1(a) ∨ a ∈ **dom** m2 ∧ b=m2(a)]

$\quad$ m \ s ≡ [a↦m(a) | a:A • a ∈ **dom** m \ s]
$\quad$ m / s ≡ [a↦m(a) | a:A • a ∈ **dom** m ∩ s]

$\quad$ m1 = m2 ≡
$\quad\quad$ **dom** m1 = **dom** m2 ∧ ∀ a:A • a ∈ **dom** m1 ⇒ m1(a) = m2(a)
$\quad$ m1 ≠ m2 ≡ ~(m1 = m2)

$\quad$ m$\circ$n ≡
$\quad\quad$ [a↦c | a:A,c:C • a ∈ **dom** m ∧ c = n(m(a))]
$\quad\quad$ **pre rng** m ⊆ **dom** n

D.4 λ-Calculus + Functions

D.4.1 The λ-Calculus Syntax

type /* A BNF Syntax: */
    $\langle L \rangle$ ::= $\langle V \rangle \mid \langle F \rangle \mid \langle A \rangle \mid (\langle A \rangle)$
    $\langle V \rangle$ ::= /* variables, i.e. identifiers */
    $\langle F \rangle$ ::= $\lambda \langle V \rangle \cdot \langle L \rangle$
    $\langle A \rangle$ ::= ($\langle L \rangle \langle L \rangle$)
value /* Examples */
    $\langle L \rangle$: e, f, a, ...
    $\langle V \rangle$: x, ...
    $\langle F \rangle$: λ x • e, ...
    $\langle A \rangle$: f a, (f a), f(a), (f)(a), ...

D.4.2 Free and Bound Variables

Let x, y be variable names and e, f be λ-expressions.

- $\langle V \rangle$: Variable x is free in x.
- $\langle F \rangle$: x is free in $\lambda y \cdot e$ if $x \neq y$ and x is free in e.
- $\langle A \rangle$: x is free in $f(e)$ if it is free in either f or e (i.e., also in both).

D.4.3 Substitution

In RSL, the following rules for substitution apply:

- **subst**($[N/x]x$) $\equiv$ N;
- **subst**($[N/x]a$) $\equiv$ a,

    for all variables a$\neq$ x;

- **subst**($[N/x](P\ Q)$) $\equiv$ (**subst**($[N/x]P$) **subst**($[N/x]Q$));
- **subst**($[N/x](\lambda x \cdot P)$) $\equiv \lambda$ y•P;
- **subst**($[N/x](\lambda$ y•P)) $\equiv \lambda y \cdot$ **subst**($[N/x]P$),

    if x$\neq$y and y is not free in N or x is not free in P;

- **subst**($[N/x](\lambda y \cdot P)$) $\equiv \lambda z \cdot$**subst**($[N/z]$**subst**($[z/y]P$)),

    if y$\neq$x and y is free in N and x is free in P
    (where z is not free in (N P)).

D.4.4 α-Renaming and β-Reduction

- α-renaming: λx•M

If x, y are distinct variables then replacing x by y in λx·M results in λy·**subst**([y/x]M). We can rename the formal parameter of a λ-function expression provided that no free variables of its body M thereby become bound.

- β-reduction: $(\lambda$x·M)(N)
  All free occurrences of x in M are replaced by the expression N provided that no free variables of N thereby become bound in the result. $(\lambda$x·M)(N) $\equiv$ **subst**([N/x]M)

D.4.5 Function Signatures

For sorts we may want to postulate some functions:

type
    A, B, C
value
    obs_B: A $\rightarrow$ B,
    obs_C: A $\rightarrow$ C,
    gen_A: B×C $\rightarrow$ A

D.4.6 Function Definitions

Functions can be defined explicitly:

value
    f: Arguments $\rightarrow$ Result
    f(args) $\equiv$ DValueExpr

    g: Arguments $\overset{\sim}{\rightarrow}$ Result
    g(args) $\equiv$ ValueAndStateChangeClause
    pre P(args)

Or functions can be defined implicitly:

value
    f: Arguments $\rightarrow$ Result
    f(args) **as** result
    post P1(args,result)

    g: Arguments $\overset{\sim}{\rightarrow}$ Result
    g(args) **as** result
    pre P2(args)
    post P3(args,result)

The symbol $\overset{\sim}{\rightarrow}$ indicates that the function is partial and thus not defined for all arguments. Partial functions should be assisted by preconditions stating the criteria for arguments to be meaningful to the function.

D.5 Other Applicative Expressions

D.5.1 Simple let Expressions

Simple (i.e., nonrecursive) **let** expressions:

   let a = $\mathcal{E}_d$ **in** $\mathcal{E}_b$(a) **end**

is an "expanded" form of:

   $(\lambda a.\mathcal{E}_b(a))(\mathcal{E}_d)$

D.5.2 Recursive let Expressions

Recursive **let** expressions are written as:

   let f = λa:A $\cdot$ E(f) **in** B(f,a) **end**

is "the same" as:

   let f = YF **in** B(f,a) **end**

where:

   F $\equiv$ λg$\cdot\lambda$a$\cdot$(E(g)) and YF = F(YF)

D.5.3 Predicative let Expressions

Predicative **let** expressions:

   let a:A $\cdot$ $\mathcal{P}$(a) **in** $\mathcal{B}$(a) **end**

express the selection of a value a of type A which satisfies a predicate $\mathcal{P}$(a) for evaluation in the body $\mathcal{B}$(a).

D.5.4 Pattern and "Wild Card" let Expressions

Patterns and wild cards can be used:

   let {a} $\cup$ s = set **in** ... **end**
   let {a,_} $\cup$ s = set **in** ... **end**

   let (a,b,...,c) = cart **in** ... **end**
   let (a,_,...,c) = cart **in** ... **end**

let ⟨a⟩⁀ℓ = list **in** ... **end**
let ⟨a,_,b⟩⁀ℓ = list **in** ... **end**

let [a↦b] ∪ m = map **in** ... **end**
let [a↦b,_] ∪ m = map **in** ... **end**

D.5.5 Conditionals

Various kinds of conditional expressions are offered by RSL:

if b_expr **then** c_expr **else** a_expr
end

if b_expr **then** c_expr **end** ≡ /∗ same as: ∗/
    if b_expr **then** c_expr **else skip end**

if b_expr_1 **then** c_expr_1
elsif b_expr_2 **then** c_expr_2
elsif b_expr_3 **then** c_expr_3
...
elsif b_expr_n **then** c_expr_n **end**

case expr **of**
    choice_pattern_1 → expr_1,
    choice_pattern_2 → expr_2,
    ...
    choice_pattern_n_or_wild_card → expr_n
end

D.5.6 Operator/Operand Expressions

⟨Expr⟩ ::=
        ⟨Prefix_Op⟩ ⟨Expr⟩
        | ⟨Expr⟩ ⟨Infix_Op⟩ ⟨Expr⟩
        | ⟨Expr⟩ ⟨Suffix_Op⟩
        | ...
⟨Prefix_Op⟩ ::=
        − | ∼ | ∪ | ∩ | **card** | **len** | **inds** | **elems** | **hd** | **tl** | **dom** | **rng**
⟨Infix_Op⟩ ::=
        = | ≠ | ≡ | + | − | ∗ | ↑ | / | < | ≤ | ≥ | > | ∧ | ∨ | ⇒
        | ∈ | ∉ | ∪ | ∩ | \ | ⊂ | ⊆ | ⊇ | ⊃ | ⁀ | † | °
⟨Suffix_Op⟩ ::= !

D.6 Imperative Constructs

D.6.1 Statements and State Changes

Often, following the RAISE method, software development starts with highly abstract-applicative constructs which, through stages of refinements, are turned into concrete and imperative constructs. Imperative constructs are thus inevitable in RSL.

Unit
value
    stmt: **Unit** → **Unit**
    stmt()

- Statements accept no arguments.
- Statement execution changes the state (of declared variables).
- **Unit** → **Unit** designates a function from states to states.
- Statements, stmt, denote state-to-state changing functions.
- Writing () as "only" arguments to a function "means" that () is an argument of type **Unit**.

D.6.2 Variables and Assignment

    0. **variable** v:Type := expression
    1. v := expr

D.6.3 Statement Sequences and skip

Sequencing is expressed using the ';' operator. **skip** is the empty statement having no value or side-effect.

    2. **skip**
    3. stm_1;stm_2;...;stm_n

D.6.4 Imperative Conditionals

    4. **if** expr **then** stm_c **else** stm_a **end**
    5. **case** e **of**: p_1→S_1(p_1),...,p_n→S_n(p_n) **end**

D.6.5 Iterative Conditionals

    6. **while** expr **do** stm **end**
    7. **do** stmt **until** expr **end**

D.6.6 Iterative Sequencing

8. **for** e **in** list_expr • P(b) **do** S(b) **end**

D.7 Process Constructs

D.7.1 Process Channels

Let A and B stand for two types of (channel) messages and i:KIdx for channel array indexes, then:

channel c:A
channel { k[i]:B • i:Idx }
channel { k[i,j,...,k]:B • i:Idx,j:Jdx,...,k:Kdx }

declare a channel, c, and a set (an array) of channels, k[i], capable of communicating values of the designated types (A and B).

D.7.2 Process Composition

Let P and Q stand for names of process functions, i.e., of functions which express willingness to engage in input and/or output events, thereby communicating over declared channels. Let P() and Q stand for process expressions, then:

P ‖ Q   Parallel composition
P ⫿ Q   Nondeterministic external choice (either/or)
P ⊓ Q   Nondeterministic internal choice (either/or)
P ⫤ Q   Interlock parallel composition

express the parallel (‖) of two processes, or the nondeterministic choice between two processes: either external (⫿) or internal (⊓). The interlock (⫤) composition expresses that the two processes are forced to communicate only with one another, until one of them terminates.

D.7.3 Input/Output Events

Let c, k[i] and e designate channels of type A and B, then:

c ?, k[i] ?   Input
c ! e, k[i] ! e Output

expresses the willingness of a process to engage in an event that "reads" an input, respectively "writes" an output.

D.7.4 Process Definitions

The below signatures are just examples. They emphasise that process functions must somehow express, in their signature, via which channels they wish to engage in input and output events.

value
    P: **Unit** → **in** c **out** k[i]
    Unit
    Q: i:KIdx → **out** c **in** k[i] **Unit**

    P() ≡ ... c ? ... k[i] ! e ...
    Q(i) ≡ ... k[i] ? ... c ! e ...

The process function definitions (i.e., their bodies) express possible events.

D.8 Simple RSL Specifications

Often, we do not want to encapsulate small specifications in schemas, classes, and objects, as is often done in RSL. An RSL specification is simply a sequence of one or more types, values (including functions), variables, channels and axioms:

    type
      ...
    variable
      ...
    channel
      ...
    value
      ...
    axiom
      ...

D.9 RSL Module Specifications

D.9.1 Modules

Modules are clusters of one or more declarations:

Id =
    class
        declaration_1
        declaration_2
        ...
        declaration_n
    end

where declarations are either

- types
- values
- axioms
- variables
- channels
- modules

By a **class** we mean a possibly infinite set of one or more mathematical entities satisfying the declarations.

D.9.2 Schemes

scheme Id =
    class
        declaration_1
        declaration_2
        ...
        declaration_n
    end

By a **scheme** we mean a named possibly infinite set of one or more mathematical entities satisfying the declarations.

D.9.3 Module Extension

Id = **extend** Id_1,Id_2,...,Id_m **with**
    class
        declaration_1
        declaration_2
        ...
        declaration_n
    end

Usually we make sure that the extensions are conservative [358, 153, 104, 22, 254, 172].
    Etcetera !

Appendix E
INDEXES

E.1 Definitions

Chapter 1 introduces 50 concepts and Chapters 2–10 introduce 98 definitions.

Chapter 1 Concepts

Abstraction, 3, 9
   Divide and Conquer, 9
   Operational, 9
   Representational, 9
Algebraic Semantics, 7
Axiomatic Semantics, 7
Calculation, 3
Computation, 3
Computer, 4
Computer Science, 4
Computing Science, 4
Conservative Extension, 9
Denotational Semantics, 7
Divide and Conquer, Abstraction, 9
Domain Engineering, 4
Domain Requirements, 4
Domain/ Machine Interface, 5
Engineering, 4
   of Domain, 4
   of Requirements, 6
   of Software, 7
Epistemology, 4
Formal Method:, 4

Formalisation, Narration, 9
Hardware, 5
Informatics, 10
Informatics Thinking, 10
Information Technology, 10
Intentional Pull, 9
Interface of Domain/ Machine, 5
Invariant, 9
Language, 5
Linguistics, 5
Machine, 5
Machine Requirements, 5
Mathematics, 5
Mereology, 5
Metaphysics, 5
Method, 5, 8
   Principle, 8
   Procedure, 8
   Technique, 8
   Tool, 9
Methodology, 5
Model, 5
Modelling, 6
Narration Formalisation, 9
Nondeterminism, 9

Chapters 2–10 Definitions

E.2 Concepts

E.3 Examples

There are 129 examples.

E.4 Method Hints

We have made 8 explicit method hints.

1 Select Domain of Interest, 49
2 External Qualities, 51
3 ''What can be Described'', 52
4 Initial Focus is on Endurants, 56
5 Solid versus Fluid, 59

6 From Analysis to Description, 76

7 Domain State, 93

8 Sequential Analysis & Description of
        Internal Qualities, 107

E.5 Analysis Predicate Prompts

There are 25 analysis predicates.

E.6 Analysis Function Prompts

There are 13 analysis functions.

E.7 Attribute Categories

There are 9 attribute categories.

E.8 Perdurant Calculations

E.9 Description Prompts

There are 10 description prompts.

E.10 Endurant to Perdurant Translation Schemas

There are 11 perdurant schemas.

E.11 RSL Symbols

List of Figures

© The Author(s), under exclusive license to Springer Nature Switzerland AG 2021   401
D. Bjørner, *Domain Science and Engineering*, Monographs in Theoretical Computer Science. An EATCS Series,
https://doi.org/10.1007/978-3-030-73484-8